AMERICAN VOICES,
AMERICAN LIVES

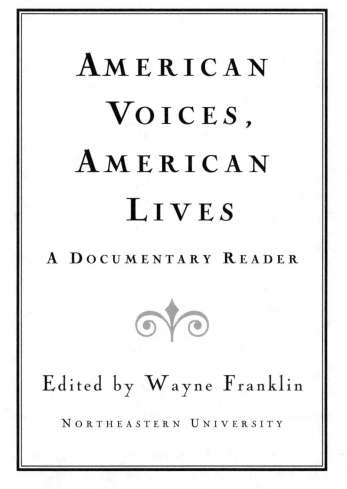

AMERICAN VOICES, AMERICAN LIVES

A DOCUMENTARY READER

Edited by Wayne Franklin

NORTHEASTERN UNIVERSITY

W.W. NORTON & COMPANY / NEW YORK / LONDON

Copyright © 1997 by W. W. Norton & Company, Inc.

All rights reserved.
Printed in the United States of America.
First Edition.

The text of this book is composed in 10.5/12.5 Electra
with the display set in Nicholas Cochin.
Composition & manufacturing by the Maple-Vail Book Manufacturing Group.
Book design by JAM Design.

Library of Congress Cataloging-in-Publication Data

American voices, American lives : a documentary reader / edited by
Wayne Franklin.
p.   cm.
Includes bibliographical references (p.   ) and index.
ISBN 0-393-97094-9 (pbk.)
1. United States—History—Sources.   I. Franklin, Wayne.
E173.A7594   1997
973—dc20   96-28798

W. W. Norton & Company, Inc., 500 Fifth Avenue, New York, N.Y. 10110
http://www.wwnorton.com
W. W. Norton & Company Ltd., 10 Coptic Street, London WC1A 1PU

1 2 3 4 5 6 7 8 9 0

CONTENTS

INTRODUCTION

To be human is to have a story and the desire to tell it. In all places and times, humans have relied on narrative to link events in causal and temporal chains, binding speaker and listener, writer and reader, in a community of assumptions, values, and judgments. By telling stories, we convert what separates us into a means of renewing and deepening our ties with others. To this extent, *American Voices, American Lives* provides local instances of a universal pattern by which people have negotiated difference and created community. Always evident in these "stories" are their healing effect as they allow the teller to overcome events by substituting a story for the felt burden of experience, shifting some of the burden's weight onto the listener.

SCOPE AND USES

By gathering American personal narratives from the time of Columbus to the end of the nineteenth century, *American Voices, American Lives* explores how Americans have shaped and shared their experience across many periods. Interdisciplinary by design, it is intended to serve as a reader for courses in American studies, American history, and American literature by offering a wide variety of documents from differing perspectives. There are letters, diaries, travel accounts, autobiographies, slave narratives, interrogations, historical tales, crime narratives, biographies, depositions, immigrant tales, oral histories, speeches, captivity narratives, legal documents, confessions, newspaper accounts, Indian autobiographies, and many other kinds of writing documenting public events and private life. More than eighty figures are represented with generous selections (in many cases complete texts, as with the 1831 *Confessions of Nat Turner*), carefully modernized for ease of study and accompanied by explanatory notes and introductions that set the context for each selection. In a number of cases, groups of related texts are arranged into larger units to encourage comparison. One such section is concerned with Hannah Dustan, a New Englander who escaped captivity in 1697 by killing and scalping the Native

xi

American family holding her prisoner, but who left no personal version of her story. This section includes an array of accounts running from contemporary diary entries up to nineteenth-century poems and short stories displaying the ways in which such a figure was continually refashioned as her story was told and retold.

Among the people given voice here, relatively few are household names. Personal writings long famous in their own right, such as the autobiographies of Benjamin Franklin or Henry Adams, not only are readily available in many separate editions but also have long occupied prominent places in anthologies, and hence are generally excluded from the present collection. Instead, *American Voices, American Lives* seeks to broaden the array of figures available for study by emphasizing those less accessible in the past. The section featuring Hannah Dustan represents the first time a collection of so many versions of her intriguing story has been made available for modern study. Most other selections feature the direct first-person statements — the self-fashionings — of individuals whose often obscure lives can offer a variety of fresh insights into four centuries of American experience. Instructive here is the study of the English sailor Job Hortop, abandoned on the Mexican coast by the slave-trader Sir John Hawkins in 1568. When poor Hortop at last returned to England twenty-three years later, he must have been moved to tell his tale because his life seemed to matter so little to those in power; he clung to the details of his suffering as if they were the only proof he could muster that he in fact had lived. This characteristic of Hortop's story — his drive to be heard and counted — is an enduring pattern throughout the selections. Even figures from elevated social positions (such as the Civil War diarist Mary Boykin Chesnut, who was genuinely privileged) shape this impulse to rescue their lives by pouring their experience into words.

The uses of these tales are many. For survey courses in American literature, the book offers an enriching addition to existing anthologies by virtue of the range of voices and forms included. Because the great majority of these figures were not primarily writers, but turned to writing (or in some instances oral tales) as a means of dealing with powerful experiences, they add perspectives otherwise lacking in survey anthologies, especially since by design the selections here do not duplicate the great majority of "canon-expanding" items recently added to those anthologies. (For example, the narratives of Olaudah Equiano and Harriet Jacobs, now regularly included in literature anthologies, are bypassed here in favor of several other items of equivalent interest that do not appear in those collections — such as two 1730s narratives concerning the Maryland slave Ayuba Suleiman Diallo, or a trio of 1930s oral histories concerning former slave women.) Similarly, because the writers in *American Voices, American Lives* made use of more varied forms of expression than are included in most anthologies, their narratives enrich our sense of American literary expression. In any instance, whatever a writer's nominal subject or origin, the editor has sought vivid texts that most of all encourage readers to explore the links between language and experience for the individual writer and the culture at large.

For literature courses other than surveys, such as those focused on autobiography, the present collection likewise extends the range of figures and forms beyond those ordinarily studied. In the process, it urges students to probe the very nature of personal writing and the complex array of conditions that surround it. Particularly important in this last regard is its concern with the role of memory in the construction of personal narrative, a theme stressed in many groups of retrospective texts focused on key events such as the Revolution or the Civil War but dating from long after the periods in question. Rather than presenting such events simply through contemporary journals, *American Voices, American Lives* stresses how various figures came to reflect on and interpret them, often many years or decades later.

Many of these considerations should help make this book appropriate for courses in American history and American studies as well. The broad base of ordinary writings—documents often written "from the bottom up," as with the many women's texts and items documenting slavery from the viewpoint and in the voice of slaves—helps the book emphasize the close connections between social experience and personal narrative. Every major phase in American historical experience to 1900 is engaged by the writings. Texts written in various places and from different perspectives cover the "first encounters" between Europeans and Native Americans and the wars and accommodations that ensued between them, as well as the encounters between the different colonial powers in the first century of North American settlement. A Lenni-Lenape oral tale about Henry Hudson's 1609 voyage, first written down around 1800 in Ohio, focuses attention not only on that moment of encounter but also on how both parties perceived and remembered it. Five letters written by the Dutch widow Maria van Cortlandt van Rensselaer as she sought to oversee the affairs of a vast estate in New York in the 1670s and 1680s give insight not only into the workings of the colonial system at a time of transition from Dutch to English authority, but also into gender relations. The collection is designed so that texts across the book may be fruitfully brought into play with each other to shed light on key phases and themes in American history. No text plays only one note. An official French interrogation of two boys who survived La Salle's ill-fated Texas colony may at first seem to be a straightforward "encounter" document, but it also is one of several texts in the collection that bring childhood into focus across American history. In these cases and others, the book's engagement with multiple historical contexts both in the choice of selections and in the editorial apparatus ought to make it an especially useful adjunct to the U.S. history survey as well as courses in American social history.

Finally, the continuing stress here on cultural issues and values gives *American Voices, American Lives* real usefulness for introductory courses in American studies. Because it emphasizes the experience of ordinary Americans, conveys it largely in their own words, and is attentive to the material, social, and intellectual frameworks within which they lived their lives, it can provide students with a firsthand reader that allows them to explore a wide variety of issues. Its historical grounding makes it an ideal supplement to modern readers aimed at the understanding of contemporary society. Its chronological organization, on the other hand, does not work against synchronic analysis, since as noted above key constellations of questions recur throughout. Those interested in questions of identity, ethnicity, race, gender, and class will find many texts that promote, and indeed demand, fruitful consideration of these issues across a variety of situations. Because certain standard texts are purposefully excluded (for instance, Crèvecoeur's "What Is an American?"), but the questions they concern are not, the fresh materials here will provoke new discussions of older issues as well. Introductions to the various texts, providing essential information about the writers and their lives, aim to stimulate further study of the means by which individual experience acquires cultural shape and meaning.

PERSONAL NARRATIVE, AUTOBIOGRAPHY, AND SOCIAL MEANING

BECAUSE AUTOBIOGRAPHY HAS ATTRACTED CONSIDERABLE ATTENTION IN AMERIcan cultural studies over the past several decades, any serious consideration of personal writing must engage autobiography as both a practice and a critical term. It is worth reminding ourselves at the outset that the term "autobiography" is of relatively recent coinage, and that it has been cast back over earlier examples of personal writing that did not originally bear the label, such as Benjamin Franklin's "Memoirs." Such anachronisms are common in cultural studies and historical scholarship, as the descriptive names used for events or movements always reflect later understanding and inevitably simplify what they name. When such names distort our sense of what is under study, however, they need to be approached with caution.

In the case of the term "autobiography," modern understanding is complex. A looser sense has tended to give way to a more strict one in twentieth-century usage, although both still survive. Under the former, a wide range of personal writing is included, in keeping with a pragmatic understanding of the original Greek components of the term autobiography *(self-written-life)*; under the more strict sense of the term, it is argued that autobiography must display aesthetic coherence and a concern with the significance of a life as a whole, not just an episode or two. If a work is episodic, unconcerned with the overall shape of experience, and driven by events rather than consciousness, it may be personal but it is not an autobiography. The looser sense of the term seems especially implied when the adjective "autobiographical" is used, whereas the noun tends to be more restrictive: many pieces of writing may be autobiographical (including, say, most private letters), but to be an autobiography, it often is presumed that a text must be substantial, serious, and complex. These are useful and real distinctions between differing intentions and characteristics, but they also may be employed in counterproductive ways. In particular, the discrimination of the two types may mask social distinctions that have little to do with writing per se. That is, the kind of coherent selfhood expected of genuine autobiography is a social product, the result of countless factors such as wealth, education, class, race, and gender. Its presence or absence in a personal text may reflect the artistic intentions of the writer, but is more likely to register his or her social location and general opportunity. In practice, then, strict interpretation of the term autobiography winds up drawing the distinction between genuine autobiography and everything else in a way that pretty well copies the lines between dominant and subordinate groups in society: children, for instance, seem almost automatically incapable of writing autobiographies because of their youth, relative lack of integration as selves, and minimal access to the kind of language deemed appropriate to the endeavor.

It is worth keeping such distinctions in mind as one reads the variety of texts in *American Voices, American Lives*. It also is worth pondering the roles such personal writing has played in American experience. Although autobiographical writing obviously did not originate here, it has occupied an important place in American culture from a very early point. The spatial and political structure of the colonial world may have given it special significance. European travelers seeking to explain their experiences, either to themselves or to their sponsors and rulers, frequently composed personal narratives concerned with New World events, places, and peoples but addressed to Old World audiences. In these texts, the writer assumed a position of prominence in between the world described and the world addressed. Because very few people back home had access to what happened across the sea except through travelers' narratives — it could be difficult even for a monarch to check such tales against actual conditions — those narratives took on crucial political and cultural importance. In effect, they served as verbal substitutes for the New World, much as a map of a foreign country *becomes* that country for people elsewhere seeking to learn about it. Hernán Cortés, realizing the dynamics involved in transatlantic narrative, wrote letters that sought to placate the Emperor Charles V and explain the invasion of Mexico, which he had accomplished by disobeying superiors who now had the emperor's ear. Everything he said about the landscape of Mexico, its people and their extraordinary cities, and his own deeds and motives was said in part to direct the emperor's attention toward certain "inescapable" conclusions.

Extenuating narratives can be found in historical contexts worldwide, particularly when imperial powers control large expanses of space, but in the New World the very speed and scope of European expansion gave personal narrative a new prominence and power. Never before in human history had so many groups of people responsible to distant authorities, be they rulers or investors or simply communities and families back home, spread themselves so far so quickly, attenuating the lines of control and creating the need to restore in language what may have been weakened or lost in fact. Nor was this pattern of narrative confined to the Europeans. For the Native Americans, sudden contact with unexpected peoples from beyond the sea gave rise to a whole new range of stories charged with poignant meaning, as with the Sac leader Black Hawk's account, included herein, of his forced tour of eastern cities following his military defeat in 1832. In oral tales and texts recorded in native hieroglyphs or the European alphabet, Native Americans sought to relay their own first impressions—full of wonder or distress—across space and time. The importance of personal narrative in American culture arose from a need, felt on both sides of such divides, to register what was happening as old assumptions were tested against troubling new conditions.

Personal accounts of events capture the essence of a particular moment in a way that the inventions of literature cannot. In an intriguing study conducted in the 1950s, two psycholinguists were able to distinguish the verbal patterns in notes left by actual suicide victims from those in notes written by what they called "pseudocides"—individuals who were instructed to write the kind of note they thought they might write if they themselves were on the verge of suicide. Although the control group was able to intuit a good deal about the kinds of things a suicide note might say, and even how it might say them, the researchers found that the conflicted emotional tone, the level of errors and disorganization, and other key traces in the genuine notes were generally missed by the pseudocides. Although both groups in one sense were writing from a similar perspective, the fact that the actual suicides experienced something that the other group only imagined was sufficient to separate their notes. One might speculate that the English sailor Job Hortop's tale of actual abandonment would exhibit similar differences when compared with a literary text such as *Robinson Crusoe*, which sought to imagine the same extreme conditions. The world of Daniel Defoe's hero would seem more coherent and self-contained, Crusoe himself more in control of events, as judged against the way in which Hortop, stripped of agency, became the victim of circumstances he could barely endure.

Are suicide notes, with all their finality, condensed autobiographies? They certainly are autobiographical, and so are many other kinds of writing we may not associate with the idea. In 1809, the American Revolutionary Thomas Paine started to dictate his will, but before directing the distribution of his property he began to tell of what he had accomplished in life: "I, Thomas Paine, of the State of New York, author of the work entitled *Common Sense*, written in Philadelphia, in 1775, and published in that city the beginning of January, 1776, which awaked America to a declaration of Independence on the fourth of July following, which was as fast as the work could spread through such an extensive country. . . ." Paine went on to list other publications through another dozen lines, even noting that he had a third part of the *Age of Reason* by him in manuscript, before returning to the ostensible purpose of the document: distributing his more mundane property. He could not resist telling his story in his own way and at his own time, emphasizing what he thought really mattered, connecting his own deeds to the important patterns of his age, even apologizing for the apparent slowness with which his call for independence had spread through the colonies by reminding his audience—technically in this case his heirs and the probate officials, though in another sense all posterity, his intellectual heirs—that the conditions in America at the time had slowed the pamphlet's way.

At the time Paine wrote, personal narrative had long been important in New World culture, as suggested earlier, but a variety of new circumstances were giving it even more prominence. The weakness of actual community in the country made its assertion in language of critical importance. Americans, long adept at fashioning social consensus out of discrete personal narratives, infused the old habit with new significance as they set about consciously building national institutions. At the same time, the new values of self-reliance and relatively unrestrained action in a "free" marketplace (for those whom society considered free) made tales of individual struggle especially appealing as well. The rise of the nation and the rise of this form of expression at the same time were more than coincidental. Benjamin Franklin's "Memoirs," begun prior to the Revolution as a private letter addressed to his son, emerged after peace was achieved in 1783 as an attempt at telling—for publication—a consciously *American* tale. Hence Franklin included in his text a letter from merchant Benjamin Vaughan, who had read the earlier parts in manuscript, noting the need of the country for guidance. Vaughan urged Franklin to finish the work as "a table of the internal circumstances of [the] country," which Franklin did, changing his intended audience and his sense of the story's contexts. Benjamin Franklin was moving away from "pure" autobiography in the later sense of that term, and choosing instead to embed his own story in that of his culture. That change hardly marked him as an original, however, for many other Americans have linked themselves to a wider community through the tales borne on their voices or caught in their journals, letters, and humble memoirs. If to be human is to have a story to tell, in American experience that general principle has been enshrined as a cultural institution. We can learn a great deal about the culture at large by listening to ordinary Americans tell where they come from, who they are, and what they have endured and accomplished. *American Voices, American Lives* provides a rich opportunity for doing just that.

A WORD ON THE TEXTS

IN ORDER TO MAKE THESE DOCUMENTS OF AMERICAN EXPERIENCE AS ACCESSIble as possible, they have been edited so as to remove needless uncertainties due to antique spelling, haphazard punctuation, and local peculiarities of expression that do not substantially contribute to meaning. Many of the older documents in fact seem refreshingly close to us in language once such accidental remnants of old practices—important as they are for other purposes—are removed. Since we customarily find Shakespeare available in modernized texts, and read even, say, William Bradford's history of Plymouth colony in a form closer to our practice than his manuscript embodies, it does seem right to make these other, less-often-heard voices come across as directly as good scholarship allows.

A few words might be added here specifying the kinds of changes the editor has introduced. Personal texts of the sort included in this collection often followed torturous paths toward first publication, especially in the older periods covered by *American Voices, American Lives*. In some instances in which a text was published during the author's life, the author did not intend publication, did not arrange for publication, and had little or no control over the form in which the text first appeared. In such cases, copying the original text in all details, especially when haphazard spelling and punctuation severely interfere with comprehension, seems misguided. Similar points may be made regarding non-English texts first translated prior to this century, or any texts first published long after the author's life. *American Voices, American Lives* presents such texts in a conservatively modernized form. In a few instances (as with John Easton's 1675 letter on "King Philip's War," not published until this century), the originals are marred by redundancies that have been silently removed to insure that the original meaning emerges with as little hindrance as possible. Such changes are few, however, as are those that silently substitute a more correct form of a word for a confusing original.

Paragraphing and indeed the formation of sentences as we are accustomed to them in modern prose have resulted in part from the slow development of printing practice. A fair number of the personal texts included here were written by individuals almost completely unfamiliar with the terms of that practice, and hence were not originally paragraphed, or were inconsistently broken into paragraphs and sentences. In these instances, and in a few cases where more-recent items fall into similar confusion (as with the *Confessions of Nat Turner*), originals have been carefully reformatted by the editor. The aim has been to keep the flavor of the original while making the new version more palatable to readers accustomed to rationalized modern texts. An allied point is that many of the older texts emerged from oral practice, so that the headlong rhythms of spoken English sometimes can be heard in the printed originals. For instance, strings of coordinating conjunctions (particularly *and* and *but*) will run like children at recess through the body of a text, much as they do in the bulk of informal conversation today. Where such rudimentary structures do not confuse the modern reader they are left intact; where, however, they weary attention or seem to send the narrative into endless cartwheels of logic, they have been reined in. In instances in which more than a single chapter of a text is included in this book (as with John Muir's *The Story of My Boyhood and Youth*), chapter titles have been silently dropped, since they often make sense only in the context of the book as a whole.

It is important to stress that in no instance has a text been "rewritten" or profoundly altered. Some very brief additions have been made in the interest of sense, but (except when they replace parallel but confusing words removed from the original) these are clearly placed within square brackets. Any other omissions from the originals are indicated by ellipses, with the exception of texts organized by dated entries (as with a diary): in such cases, each entry bears its original date or a date assigned in brackets by the editor, so that the omission of intervening entries can be readily inferred. (It should be added that in a very few instances, as with Maria van Cortlandt's letters, there may be losses in the original manuscripts, to which attention is drawn at the proper points.) Capitalization is generally handled in accord with conservative modern practice; eighteenth-century texts in particular seem strewn with uppercase abstractions, which in *American Voices, American Lives* reassume their more modest role as lowercase concretions. Names of people (and of ships) are generally left in their original forms, though for persons the editor's notes give the correct forms when the individual has been identified (as, for instance, when U. S. Grant gives the Confederate general Hébert's name as Hebért); place names, however, are generally modernized so that a reader may follow the action of a given narrative on a map with as few trips to historical gazetteers as possible. Routine abbreviations (including "&" for "and" and "&c" for "etc.") are spelled out or converted to modern form, and contractions are generally brought into conformity with modern practice, while references to dates, times, and monetary units are made consistent within individual selections. Finally, English words that occur in texts originally written in other languages are retained in their original (often interesting) forms except in a few cases where those forms are confusingly obscure.

For those wishing to check the originals, or to explore further the tales they contain, an appendix gives reference to the exact sources from which all texts derive.

ACKNOWLEDGMENTS

AS THIS BOOK SUGGESTS, ANY ONE STORY EXISTS IN A WEB OF OTHERS. IN MY own case, the story behind the book touches at many points on long-term and short-term relationships, personal and institutional. I am grateful for my former colleagues in American Studies and English at the University of Iowa, where this book was conceived, for their general aid and particular encouragements. That my own interest in American travel writing was extended into other kinds of personal narrative during my years at Iowa surely is owing to the examples of Bob Sayre and Al Stone, not to mention many other faculty members and students, including among the latter especially Wayne Prophet. Carl Klaus first got me thinking about textbooks as venues for various kinds of inquiry. Lyell Henry of Iowa City, officially a political scientist but in actuality a student of the uncanny in American popular culture, provided dry wit and comradery on many occasions. Since moving to Northeastern University in 1994, I have been happy to find excellent support for my work here as well. My colleagues in American literature, including Earl Harbert and Guy Rotella, have helped make me feel at home and have shared their enthusiasms—and mine—with genuine grace. Students at Northeastern likewise have responded to my interests in American personal writing with interest of their own. The Davis Foundation, through its support of my appointment, has provided much appreciated time and resources to help bring this effort to its conclusion. Also in Massachusetts, the American Antiquarian Society has opened its collections to my research, not only on this topic but many others, and I am grateful to president Ellen Dunlap, librarian Nancy Burkett, and director of research and publications John Hench, as well as many members of the staff, for their spacious and generous support. The editors at W. W. Norton, especially Anna Karvellas and Julia Reidhead, have prodded me along on this project, on which I hope they now can pride themselves. No one who has not had such editors can imagine how consistently they add to a project. The scholars who were consulted by Norton on the project, including Nina Baym, Jeffrey Rubin-Dorsky, Lucy Rinehart, and Michael C. Steiner, added a great deal to the final version through their critiques of the original one. Finally, I remain thankful for and to my wife, Nan: without her, my own story would be so very different!

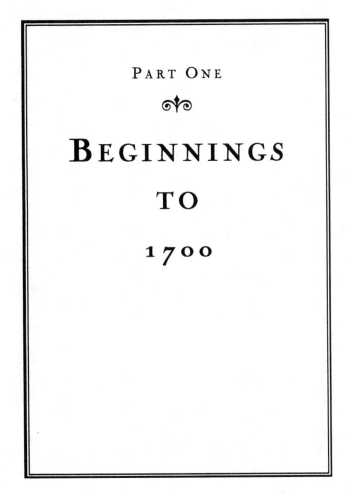

PART ONE

❧

BEGINNINGS
TO
1700

1

THE GREAT CANOE RIDE
OF DIEGO MÉNDEZ

DIEGO MÉNDEZ, BORN AROUND 1472 IN THE SPANISH REGION OF SEGURA, recalled in his 1536 "last will" how he had served Christopher Columbus during the latter's disastrous fourth voyage to the New World (1502–4). The recollection served a purpose: for the many heroic services Méndez rendered during the voyage, Columbus had promised him appointment to the post of chief magistrate in the Santo Domingo settlement on the West Indian island of Hispaniola, a position that might have proved very lucrative. The heirs of Columbus, however, kept the position to themselves, and Méndez, without whom the fourth voyage might have been a complete disaster and on whom they themselves had relied for many years after the death of Columbus in 1506, received only the gift of their injustice. In his will, Méndez told of his experience on Columbus's final voyage as a way of emphasizing the heirs' greedy indifference to him and perhaps exacting some inheritance for his family.

The voyage had led Columbus's four ships first to several ports in Hispaniola (now the Dominican Republic and Haiti), after which they searched for gold along the north shore of "Veragua" (Panama), where they became trapped behind a large sand bar in the mouth of Rio Belén in the vicinity of the Guaymi Indians. Later, Columbus made his way to the island of Jamaica, where his two remaining ships ran aground and, useless for sailing, were converted into temporary shelters on the beach. There the more than one hundred men left in the party endured a year of prolonged suffering, apparently abandoned and racked by mutiny and mutual self-destruction. They were at last rescued by Méndez, who had led a small party in native canoes across the sea to Hispaniola, where the enemies of Columbus detained him before he managed to return with aid. "Hitherto I have wept for others," Columbus was to write during this torturous period; "now, Heaven have mercy on me, and may the earth weep for me."

Columbus was fortunate to have such a man in the party, for brutal fearlessness and courtly diplomacy apparently vied for the upper hand in his character. Méndez could fight when he had to, but he also could charm and mystify his opponents. These traits allowed him to bluff his way into the center of a village of the Guaymi Indians by claiming he had come to heal their ailing chief, and to use a simple haircut as a means of fascinating and pacifying them. (Later, he was to urge and lead a preemptive attack on them.) The aplomb with which Méndez narrates this encounter is typical of his prose throughout the will, which, written as it was long after the events narrated, shows a sense of anecdotal clarity that documents written on the spot (such as Columbus's own letter, carried by Méndez on the canoe ride back to Hispaniola) did not. Columbus dissolved into a lament over his misfortunes, whereas Méndez ended his will by calling on his heirs to erect a stone over his grave on which was to be carved "a canoe, which is a hollowed tree in which the Indians navigate, for in such a one I navigated three hundred leagues, and above [this image] let them set just the letters which read, 'Canoa.' "

In this adventure story recollected in the tranquility of a man's last days, a modern reader may locate what is lacking in most of the earlier documents of the Columbian voyages: namely, a sense of the complex political context within which these peoples from such different worlds were first encountering each other and a sense of how to keep afloat regardless of how high the tide of events might rise.

DIEGO MÉNDEZ DE SEGURA

from his "Last Will" (1536)

DIEGO MÉNDEZ, INHABITANT OF THE CITY OF SANTO DOMINGO, IN THE ISLAND of Española, being in the town of Valladolid, where at the time was the court of their majesties, made his testament on the sixth day of the month of June in the year one thousand five hundred and thirty-six, before Fernan Perez, clerk of their majesties and their notary public in their court and in all their kingdoms and lordships, there being witness, Diego de Arana, Juan Diez Miranda de la Cuadra, Martin de Orduña, Lucas Fernandez, Alonso de Angulo, Francisco de Hinojosa, and Diego de Aguilar, all servants of the lady vicereine of the Indies.[1] And among other clauses of the said will, there is one which runs literally as follows.

Clause of the will. Item: The very illustrious lords, the admiral Don Christopher Columbus, of glorious memory, and his son, the admiral Don Diego Columbus, and his grandson, the admiral Don Luis, whom may God long preserve, and through them, the vicereine, my lady, as his tutor and guardian, are in debt to me on the ground of the many and great services which I have rendered to them, in which I have consumed and spent the greater part of my life, even to its close, in their service.

[1] The last named was María de Toledo y Rojas, the widow of Diego Columbus, son of Christopher. Don Luis, mentioned below, was their son.

Especially did I serve the great admiral, Don Christopher, going with his lordship to the discovery of islands and Tierra Firme,[2] in which service I many times put myself in danger of death in order to save his life and the lives of those who went and were with him. More particularly did I so, when we were shut up in the harbour of the Rio Belén or Yebra, where we were owing to the force of the violent seas and winds which drove up and raised the sand in such quantities that they closed the entrance of the harbor.

His lordship being there in great affliction, there assembled a vast multitude of the Indians of the country, in order to come to burn our ships and to kill us all, under pretence, as they said, that they were going to attack other Indians, of the provinces of Cobrava and Aurira,[3] with whom they were at war. And although many of them passed by that harbor in which our ships were, no one in the fleet took notice of the matter, but I only. And I went to the admiral and said to him: "My lord, these people who had passed by here say that they are going to join with those of Veragua to make war on those of Cobrava and Aurira. I do not believe it, but, on the contrary, I think that it is in order to burn the ships and to kill us all that they are joined together." And such was the fact.

And when the admiral asked me how the danger might be prevented, I told his lordship that I would go with a boat and proceed along the coast towards Veragua, in order to see where they pitched their camp. I had not gone half a league when I found a thousand men of war with many provisions and stores, and I landed alone among them, leaving my boat afloat. And I spoke to them as well as I knew how, and offered to do battle with them with that armed boat. But they strongly refused this offer, saying that they had no need of it. And so I returned to the boat and was there all night in view of them, so that they saw that they could not go to the ships to burn and destroy them, as they had intended, without my seeing them. And they changed their purpose and that night they all went to Veragua, and I returned to the ships and gave an account of all to his lordship, and he did not think it a small matter.

And when he talked over this matter with me and discussed how the intention of these people might be more clearly known, I offered to go there with a single companion, and I undertook this task, being more certain of death than of life. And having journeyed along the beach as far as the river of Veragua, I found two canoes of strange Indians who related to me in great detail how those people were gone to burn the ships and to kill us all, and that they had abandoned their intention owing to a boat which came upon them there, and that they still designed to return to do this after two days. And I asked them to take me in their canoes up the river and offered payment to them for this, and they refused, warning me that on no account should I go, since it was certain that if we went, they would kill both me and the companion whom I had with me.

And despite their advice, I brought it about that they should take me in

---

[2] The South American landmass; Rio Belén or Yebra: a river in the isthmus of Panama, named after Bethlehem by Columbus because his ships arrived there on the feast of the Epiphany, January 6, when the three wise men came to visit the infant Jesus in that town.
[3] Two areas in the interior of Panama ("Veragua").

their canoes up the river as far as the villages of the Indians, who were all drawn up in battle array and who did not wish me to go to the chief residence of their cacique.[4] I pretended that I was going to him as a surgeon to cure him of a wound which he had in one leg, and in return for the gifts which I made to them, they allowed me to go to the royal residence. It was on the top of a level hill, with a large open space about it, surrounded by the heads of three hundred dead whom they had killed in a battle.

As I crossed the whole open space and approached the royal house, there was a great uproar among the women and children who were at the gate, and they went screaming into the palace. Out of it came a son of the chief, very enraged, uttering angry words in his own language, and laying hands on me, he sent me with one push far from him. When, in order to appease him, I said that I was come to cure his father's leg and showed an ointment which I carried for this purpose, he replied that on no account was I to go in where his father was. And seeing that in that way I could not soothe him, I brought out a comb and a pair of scissors and a mirror, and caused my companion, Escobar,[5] to comb my hair and cut it. When he and those who were there saw this, they were amazed, and then I caused Escobar to comb his hair and cut it with the scissors, and I gave him the scissors and the comb and the mirror, and at that he was appeased. And I asked them to bring something to eat, and they brought it at once, and we ate and drank in love and good-fellowship, and became friends. I took my leave of him and came to the ships, and gave an account of all this to my lord admiral, who was no little pleased to learn all these facts and to know what had befallen me. And he commanded strict watch to be kept in the ships and in certain straw huts which we had built there on the shore with the intention that I should remain there with some people to examine and discover the secrets of the country.

On the morning of the next day, his lordship called me to take counsel with him as to what had best be done, and my opinion was that we should take that lord and all his captains, since when they were made prisoner, the common people would be subdued. And his lordship was of the same opinion, and I suggested the stratagem and plan by which this might be achieved, and his lordship ordered that the lord adelantado, his brother, and I with him should go with eighty men to carry the said plan into effect. And we went and the Lord gave us such good fortune that we took the cacique and most of his captains and wives and sons and grandsons, with all the chief men of his family. We sent them prisoners to the ships, but the cacique escaped from the man to whom he had been entrusted owing to his careless watch, a circumstance which afterwards did us much damage.

At that moment, it pleased God that it should rain heavily, and owing to the flood which followed, the harbor was opened for us, and the admiral brought the ships out to sea in order to go to Castile,[6] I remaining on land in

[4] Leader (Arawak).
[5] Rodrigo de Escobar was a common sailor on the ship *Vizcaya*.
[6] Spanish kingdom ruled by Isabella, the patron of Columbus.

order to stay there as purser of his highness, with seventy men, and there was left with me there the greater part of the supplies of biscuit and wine and oil and vinegar. Just as the admiral had got out to sea, and while I remained on land with some twenty men, for the rest had gone with the admiral to take leave of him, suddenly there came upon me many natives, so that there were more than four hundred men armed with bows and arrows and slings. They spread across the mountain opposite, and they gave a shriek and then another and again another, and, thanks be to God, they thus gave me time to prepare for the battle and to make ready a defence against them. While I was on shore among the huts which had been built, and they were on the mountain at an arrow's flight's distance, they began to shoot their arrows and to hurl their darts as if they were attacking a bull, and the arrows and missiles were as thick as hailstones and continuous. Some of them separated from the rest to come to attack us with clubs, but none of them got back, for they were left there, with their arms and legs cut off with swords and dead. At this the rest took such fright that they fled, we having lost in the fight seven out of the twenty that we were, and of them there fell ten or nine of those who came most boldly against us. This fight lasted three full hours, and Our Lord gave us a miraculous victory, we being so few and they so very numerous.

When this fight was over, there came from the ships captain Diego Tristan with the boats to go up the river in order to fetch water for their voyage. And although I advised him and warned him that he should not go up the river, he would not believe me, and against my will, he went up it with the two boats and twelve men. There those people came upon him and fought with him and slew him and all whom he had with him, so that one alone escaped by swimming and brought the news. And they took the boats and broke them to pieces, as a result of which we were left in a great difficulty, for the admiral was at sea with his ships without boats while we were on land without means by which we could go to him. In addition to all this, the Indians did not cease to come to attack us, every moment sounding trumpets and small drums and making loud cries, believing that they had us at their mercy. The defence which we had against these people consisted in two very good brass falconets and much powder and ball, with which we so terrified them that they did not dare to come up to us.

This lasted for the space of four days, during which time I caused many bags to be made from the sails of the one ship which remained to us, and in them I placed all the biscuit which we had. I then took two canoes and secured the one to the other with sticks fastened across the tops, and in these I loaded all the biscuit and the pipes of wine and oil and vinegar fastened with a rope, and towing them over the sea, when it was calm, in seven journeys which they made, they brought all to the ships, and the people who were with me they also carried little by little. I remained with five men to the last, when it was night, and in the last boatful I embarked. The admiral thought highly of this, and was not content with embracing me and kissing me on the cheeks, for having performed so great a service as I had done, but also asked that I would take the command of the flagship and the control of all the people and of the voyage, and this I accepted in order to do service to him, it being, as it was, a matter of great labor.

On the last day of April, in the year one thousand five hundred and three, we left Veragua with three ships, intending to make our way back to Castile. And as the ships were all pierced and eaten by worms, we could not keep them above water. Having gone twenty leagues, we abandoned one, the other two remaining to us being in a worse state than she was, so that all the crews with the pumps and kettles and vessels were not sufficient to draw off the water which came through the worm holes. In this way, not without very great toil and danger, intending to come to Castile, we navigated for thirty-five days, and at the end of that time we reached the island of Cuba at its lowest point, in the province of Homo, there where now is the town of la Trinidad. Thus we were three hundred leagues further from Castile than when we left Veragua to go there, and, as I have said, the ships were in a bad state, and could not be sailed, and our provisions almost exhausted. It pleased our Lord God that we should be able to reach the island of Jamaica, where we ran the two ships aground, and made of them two houses, roofed with straw, in which we remained, not without great danger from the people of that island, who were not subdued or conquered, and who might set fire to our dwellings in the night, which they would have been easily able to do despite our greatest watchfulness.

There I had to give out the last ration of biscuit and wine. I took a sword in my hand and three men with me, and went inland into this island, because no one dared to go to seek food for the admiral and those who were with him. And it pleased God that I found people so gentle that they did me no ill, but were friendly to me and gave me food with good will. And in a village which is called Aguacadiba, I agreed with the Indians and their cacique that they should make cassava[7] bread, and that they should hunt and fish and that of all the provisions they should give to the admiral a certain amount every day and that they should bring it to the ships, where there should be someone who would pay them in blue beads and combs and knives and hawks' bells and fish-hooks and other articles which we had brought for this purpose. And with this understanding, I sent one of the Christians whom I had with me to the admiral, in order that he might send someone who should have the charge of paying for those provisions and of seeing that they were supplied.

And thence I went to another village which was three leagues from the first and I made the same agreement with the cacique and the Indians of that village, and I sent another Christian to the admiral in order that he might send there another person on the same mission. And from there I went on further and reached a great cacique who was called Huareo, in the place that is now called Melilla, which was thirteen leagues from the ships. By him I was very well received, for he gave me abundance to eat, and commanded that all his vassals should in three days bring many provisions, which they laid before him,

---

[7]A plant whose root also serves as the source of tapioca.

and I paid him for them in such manner that they were content. And I agreed with him that they should bring them regularly, and that there should be someone who would there pay for them, and with this agreement I sent another Christian to the admiral. And I asked the cacique to give me two Indians who should go with me to the end of the island, in order that one might carry the hammock in which I slept and the other the food.

In this manner I journeyed as far as the eastern end of the island and I came to a cacique who was called Ameyro, with whom I entered into close friendship, giving him my name and taking his, which among them is regarded as a sign of great brotherhood. From him I bought a very good canoe which he had, and for it I gave him a very good brass helmet which I carried in a bag and a cloak and one of the two shirts which I had. In that canoe, with six Indians whom the cacique had given to me to aid in navigating, I embarked and went by sea, looking for the place which I had left.

When I reached the places whence I had sent the provisions, I found in them the Christians whom the admiral had sent, and I gave them charge of all the provisions which I had found for them, and I went myself to the admiral. By him I was very well received. He was not content with seeing me and embracing me, but asked concerning all that had occurred on the expedition, giving thanks to God Who had brought me back and Who had delivered me in safety from so savage a people. And as at the time when I reached the ships, there was not in them a crust to eat, all were very glad with my coming, for hunger was killing them in a time of so great need. And after that time henceforth every day came the Indians, laden with provisions, to the ships, from those places where I had made agreement, and there was enough for the two hundred and thirty persons who were with the admiral.

Ten days after this, the admiral called me aside and declared to me the great danger in which he was, speaking thus to me: "Diego Méndez, my son; no one of all those whom I have here realizes the great peril in which we are, save only I and you. For we are very few and these savage Indians are many and very fickle and capricious, and at the moment when they have the fancy to come and burn us here where we are in these two ships, converted into houses with straw roofs, they will easily be able to set fire to them from the land and consume us all here. And the agreement which you have made with them for bringing provisions, which they bring with such good will, may appear tomorrow to them to be disagreeable, and they may bring us nothing, and we are not in a position to take it from them by force, if it be not that which they wish. I have devised a remedy if you think it fitting, that in this canoe which you have bought, some one adventure to cross to the island of Española, to buy a ship in which it may be possible to escape from the very great danger in which we are. Tell me your opinion."

I answered him: "My Lord, I well see the danger in which we are, which is much greater than that which might be thought. The passage from this island to the island of Española in so small a vessel as the canoe, I regard not only as dangerous, but as impossible, for I know of no one who would dare to venture into so very obvious a danger as to attempt to cross a gulf of forty leagues of sea and among islands where the sea is very rough and rarely calm."

His lordship did not agree with me, earnestly persuading me that I was the one who should do this, and to this I replied: "My lord, I have many times put my life in danger to save yours and the lives of all those who are here, and Our Lord has miraculously preserved my life. Nevertheless there have not been wanting murmurers who have said that your lordship entrusts to me all honorable undertakings, there being in the company others who would perform them as well as I. And accordingly it seems to me that your lordship should call them all together and propound this business to them, in order to see if among them all there is any one who is willing to undertake it, which I doubt. And when they all hold back, I will expose my life to death for your service, as I have many times done."

Immediately on the following day his lordship caused all to assemble before him and proposed the matter to them as he had done to me. And when they heard it, they were all silent, and some said that it was out of the question to discuss such a thing, since it was impossible in so small a vessel to cross so rough and dangerous a gulf of forty leagues, such as this, between two islands where very strong ships had been lost in going to make discoveries, without being able to break or to resist the force and fury of the currents.

Then I rose and said: "My lord, I have no more than one life. I am ready to adventure it for the service of your lordship and for the good of all those who are here, since I have hope in our Lord God that, being witness of the motive from which I act, He will deliver me, as He has many times delivered me." When the admiral heard my resolution, he rose and embraced me and kissed me on the cheek, saying: "Well did I know that there was here no one save yourself who would dare to undertake this enterprise. I have hope in our Lord God that you will issue from it victoriously, as you have issued from the other enterprises which you have undertaken."

On the following day I drew my canoe on shore, and fixed a false keel to it, and pitched and greased it, and I nailed some boards on the stern and bow as defence against the sea that it might not come in as it might come owing to the low freeboard.[8] And I put up a mast and sail, and laid in the supplies necessary for me and for one Christian and for six Indians, for we were eight persons, and the canoe would not carry more. And I took my leave of his lordship and of them all, and went up the coast of the island of Jamaica where we were, there being from the place where the ships were to the end of the island thirty-five leagues. This distance I navigated with great danger and toil, for on the journey I was made prisoner by Indians, sea raiders, from whom God miraculously delivered me.

Having reached the end of the island, while waiting there for the sea to grow calm in order to continue my voyage, many Indians gathered together and resolved to kill me and to take the canoe and that which was in it, and

---

[8]The line determining a ship's height above the water; in this case, the top edge of the canoe's hull.

being so gathered together, they cast lots for my life, to see to which of them would fall the execution of their design. When I became aware of this, I went secretly to my canoe which I had three leagues from there, and set sail and came to where the admiral was, it being fifteen days since I had left there. I told him all that had happened, how God had miraculously delivered me out of the hands of those savages.

His lordship was very joyful at my arrival and asked me if I would again set out on my voyage. I said that I would if I might take some men who should remain with me at the end of the island until I put out to sea to prosecute my voyage. His lordship gave me seventy men and with them his brother, the adelantado, who were to go and to remain with me until I embarked and to wait for three days afterwards. And in this way I went back to the end of the island where I remained four days.

Finding that the sea became calm, I took my leave of them and they of me, with many tears, and I commended myself to God and to Our Lady of Antigua, and I navigated for five days and four nights without leaving hold of the oar, steering the canoe, while my companions rowed. It pleased Our Lord God that at the end of five days, I should reach the island of Española at cape San Miguel, there having been two days during which we had neither eaten nor drunk, our provisions being exhausted.

I beached my canoe on a very beautiful part of the coast, where there came at once many people of the land and they brought with them many eatables, and there I remained for two days resting. I took six Indians from there, leaving those whom I had brought, and began to navigate along the coast of the island of Española. It was a hundred and thirty leagues from there to the city of Santo Domingo, to which place I had to go, since the governor who was the comendador de Lares[9] was there.

Having gone for eighty leagues along the coast of the island, not without great dangers and labor, because the island was not conquered or pacified, I reached the province of Azoa, which is twenty-four leagues from Santo Domingo. There I learned from the comendador Gallego that the governor had gone to the province of Xaragua to pacify it; that province was fifty leagues from there. When I heard this, I left my canoe and made my way by land to Xaragua, where I found the governor.

He detained me there for seven months, until he had burned and hanged eighty-four caciques, lords of vassals, and with them Nacaona, the greatest lady of the island, whom all those obeyed and served.[1] And when this had been

[9]Don Nicolás de Ovando was appointed governor of Spain's colonies in America in 1502; he held the title of "Commander of Lares" with the Knights of St. Julian, an order of crusaders headquartered in the Spanish town of Alcantara. When Méndez arrived on the island of Hispaniola, Commander Gallego informed him that Ovando was waging a brutal war against the natives in the western province of Xaragua.

[1]Or Anacaona (sister of the former cacique of Xaragua, Behechio, and widow of Caonabo, a cacique in the same area who staunchly opposed Columbus during the second voyage). Well-liked by many Spaniards, she ruled Xaragua at the time of Ovando's offensive, and her execution was reported to have greatly angered Queen Isabella.

accomplished, I went on foot to the district of Santo Domingo, which was seventy leagues from there, and I remained there expecting ships to come from Castile, since it was more than a year since any had come. And in this interval, it pleased God that three ships should come, of which I bought one and loaded her with provisions, with bread and wine and flesh and pigs and sheep and fruits, and sent her to where the admiral was in order that he might come in her with all the people, so that they might reach Santo Domingo from there and thence go to Castile. And I myself went forward in the other two ships to give an account to the king and queen of all that had occurred on that voyage.

It appears to me that it will be well that I should say something of that which befell the admiral and his company during the year that they remained lost in that island. A few days after I had departed, the Indians became disaffected and would not bring food as before. He caused all the caciques to be summoned and told them that he marvelled that they should not bring food as they had been accustomed to do, knowing that, as he had told them, he had come there by the command of God and that God was offended with them and that on that very night He would show this to them by signs which He would cause to appear in the heavens. And as on that night there was an almost total eclipse of the moon, he told them that God did this from anger with them because they did not bring food. They believed him and were very terrified, and they promised that they would always bring him food. And in fact they did so, until the ship arrived with the supplies which I sent, at which the admiral and all those who were with him felt no small joy. For afterwards in Castile his lordship told me that in all his life he had never seen so joyful a day, and that he had never thought that he would leave that place alive. And in this ship he embarked and came to Santo Domingo and thence to Castile.

I have wished to set forth here this brief summary of my labors and of my great and distinguished services. And they are such as never man did to a lord, nor will such be done henceforth in the world. And I do this to the end that my children may know it and that they may be animated to service, and that her ladyship[2] may know that she is obliged to give to them many rewards.

When his lordship came to the court, and was in Salamanca,[3] confined to his bed by gout, and I alone was in charge of his affairs, and endeavoring to secure the restitution of his estate and of his government for his son, Don Diego, I spoke thus to him: "My lord, your lordship already knows how greatly I have served you and how much I have toiled night and day in your interest. I beseech your lordship to grant me some recompense for that which I have done." And he answered me joyfully that I should ask and he would do it, since that was very reasonable. And then I told him my wish and asked that his lordship would grant me the office of chief constable of the island of Española for my life. And his lordship answered that he did so with great good will, and

[2] The vicereine, María de Toledo.
[3] Columbus finally escaped Jamaica for Hispaniola at the end of June 1504, arrived in Spain that November, shortly before the death of Queen Isabella, and was in Salamanca, in the western part of Spain, from late October 1505 until the following spring.

that it was little in return for all the service that I had rendered to him. And he commanded me that I should tell this to the lord Don Diego, his son, and he was very glad that the grant of the said office had been made to me, and he said that if his father gave it to me with one hand, he gave it with both hands. And this promise holds good as much now as it did then.

When I had succeeded, not without great labor on my part, in bringing about the restitution of the government of the Indies to the admiral, Don Diego, my lord, his father being dead, I asked for the appointment to the said office. His lordship answered me that he had given it to the adelantado, his uncle, but that he would give me something else equivalent to it. I said that he should give that to his uncle, and that he should give to me that which his father and he had promised to me, the which he did not do. And I was left burdened with services without any reward, and the lord adelantado, without having done service, was left with my office and with the reward of all my exertions.

When his lordship arrived at the city of Santo Domingo and assumed the reins as governor, he gave this office to Francisco de Garay,[4] a servant of the lord adelantado, on whose behalf it was to be held. This was on the tenth of July in the year one thousand five hundred and ten. The office was then worth at the least a conto[5] a year, and for this my lady, the vicereine, as tutor and guardian of my lord, the viceroy, and he are truly chargeable to me and they owe it to me in justice and on the score of conscience. For the grant of the post was made to me, and nothing has been done to compensate me from the day on which it was given to the adelantado down to the last day of my life, for if it had been given to me, I should have been the richest man in the island and the most honored, and because it was not given to me, I am the poorest in it, so much so that I have no house in which I may live without rent.

And as it would be very difficult to pay me that which the office has produced in revenue, I wish to put forward a compromise and it is this, that her ladyship grant the office of chief constable of the city of Santo Domingo to one of my sons for life, and to the other grant the office of lieutenant of the admiral in the said city. By the grant of these two offices to my sons in the manner that I have said, and by placing them in charge of someone who may hold them on their behalf until they come of age, her ladyship will discharge the conscience of the admiral, her father, and I shall regard myself as satisfied in respect of the pay due to me for my services. And on this I will not say more than that I leave it to the consciences of their lordships, and let them do in the matter that which they think best.

Item:[6] I leave as my trustees and as executors of this my testament, here in the court, the bachelor Estrada and Diego de Arana, jointly with the vice-

---

[4] A Spanish nobleman (and thus no ordinary "servant"), Garay had come to the Indies with Columbus on the second voyage of 1493. Later, on Hispaniola, he became very wealthy by exploiting the native population.

[5] A Portuguese coin worth 1,000 escudos.

[6] I.e., the next clause in Méndez's will.

reine, my lady, and I ask her ladyship to accept this charge and I command them that they do likewise.

Another clause. Item: I command that my trustees buy a great stone, the best that they can find, and set it above my tomb, and that around the edge of it there be written these words: "Here lies the honorable gentleman, Diego Méndez, who greatly served the royal crown of Spain in the discovery and conquest of the Indies with the admiral, Don Christopher Columbus, of glorious memory, who discovered them, and afterwards by himself with his own ships at his own cost. He died, etc. I beg of your charity an Our Father and a Hail Mary."

Item: In the middle of the said stone, let there be carved a canoe, which is a hollowed tree in which the Indians navigate, for in such a one I navigated three hundred leagues, and above it let them set just the letters which read, "Canoa."

My dear and beloved sons, born of my very dear and beloved wife, Doña Francisca de Ribera, the blessing of God Almighty, the Father, the Son, and the Holy Ghost, and my blessing, descend upon you and encompass you, and make you Catholic Christians and give you grace that you may ever love and fear Him. Sons; I earnestly desire you to keep peace and concord and that you be very obliging and not proud, but very humble and courteous towards all with whom you have to do, that all may feel love towards you. Serve loyally the admiral, my lord, and may his lordship make you great rewards, being that which he is, and because my great services merit it. And above all, I command you, my sons, that you be very devout and hear very devoutly the divine offices, and so doing, may Our Lord God grant you long life. May it please Him, of His infinite goodness, to make you as good men as I desire that you may be and may He guide you always with His hand. Amen.

The books which I send you from here are the following:

The Art of Well-Dying of Erasmus.
A sermon of Erasmus in Castilian.
Josephus, *De Bello Judiaco.*
The Moral Philosophy of Aristotle.
The books which are called *Lingua Erasmi.*
The Book of the Holy Land.
The Colloquies of Erasmus.
A *Treatise on the Complaints of Peace.*
A *Book of Contemplations on the Passion of our Redeemer.*
A treatise on the *Avenging of the Death of Agamemnon.*
And other small tracts.

My sons, I have already told you that these books I leave to you as heirlooms, under the conditions stated above in my testament, and I desire that they be placed with certain writings of mine, which will be found in the chest which is at Seville, which is of cedar, as has already been said. Let them also place in it the marble mortar which is in the possession of the lord Don Fernando or of his majordomo.

I, Diego Méndez, declare that this document, contained in thirteen sheets, is my testament and last will, for I have ordained it and caused it to be written down, and I have signed it with my name, and by it I revoke and annul any other wills whatsoever made by me at whatsoever time and place, and I wish that this only be valid, which is made in the town of Valladolid on the nineteenth day of the month of June, in the year of Our Redeemer one thousand five hundred and thirty-six. Diego Méndez.

And I, the said Garcia de Vera, clerk and notary public, was present at all which has been herein said, wherein I am mentioned, and by order of the said lord, the lieutenant, and by request of the said bachelor Estrada, this testament in these twenty-six leaves of paper, a complete document, as here appears, I have caused to be copied as it was presented and laid before me, and as it originally was left in my possession. And accordingly I here affix this my seal *(here it was sealed)* in witness of the truth. Garcia de Vera. *(Signed.)*

2

AN ENGLISH FUGITIVE IN
MEXICO AND SPAIN

JOB HORTOP WAS A GUNPOWDER MAKER FROM THE LONDON SUBURB OF Redriffe who shipped as a gunner in 1567 on the last of Sir John Hawkins's several slaving voyages to the West African coast. Hortop did not return to England for twenty-three years, during which time his active mind caught and retained details of the horrific events he witnessed at sea, in Mexico, and during his long imprisonment in Spain.

Sir John Hawkins had the dubious distinction of first involving the English in the bloody slave trade, raiding African villages as early as 1562 and selling his surviving prisoners in the heretofore "closed" markets of Spanish America. On the 1567 voyage, Hawkins touched at the Caribbean island of Dominica before passing to the Venezuelan coast, then worked his way west and north to Mexico. Hawkins's bold strategy of breaking into the world of Spanish commerce, like that of Sir Francis Drake, his subordinate on the 1567 voyage and later his commander, violated Spanish policy and contributed to the worsening of Anglo-Spanish relations during the reign (1558–1603) of the protestant English queen Elizabeth I. Such interloping behavior was one cause of Spain's ultimate attempt to invade and conquer England with the great Armada of 1588, but even in the 1560s Hawkins's actions triggered serious military clashes. In 1568 at the port of San Juan de Ulúa, near Vera Cruz on Mexico's Caribbean coast, Hawkins encountered the powerful fleet of the viceroy Don Martín Enríquez de Almanza, who had just been dispatched by Spanish king Philip II as his personal substitute in the Indies. The fierce battle that ensued cost many lives on both sides, and left Hawkins with only two ships. His supplies eventually ran so low that his men, struggling to survive on a diet of "hides, cats, rats, parrots, monkeys, and dogs," had to be divided into two parts, one of them made up of volunteers (including Hortop) to be put ashore.

Thus began Hortop's peculiar part of the story. From the tense dealings with the local Native Americans—so taken with the Englishmen's strange garb that they attacked and stripped even those who went off into the brush to urinate—to their capture by the Spaniards and their transfer to Mexico City and eventually to Spain, the story offers a fascinating glimpse of the rivalry between cultures—European and Native American, Spanish and English, Catholic and Protestant—that constituted much of the larger story of Europe's early expansion into the New World. Hortop's trials: the naked wandering in Mexico and the grim hospital there; the long voyage back across the Atlantic as a prisoner; his confinement in the "Contractation House" in Seville; his desperate escape attempt ending in worse confinement in the Inquisitorial prison across the river in Triana; the auto-da-fé in which two of his companions were executed as the crowds shouted "Burn those heretics!"; his twelve years of hard labor in the galleys; his four additional years of confinement; the difficult negotiation that allowed him to buy his freedom in 1588; and his three more years of hard labor for the man who loaned him the necessary money—all these experiences read as if scratched into Hortop's memory with a sharp instrument. The details have a stark clarity and the overall tale possesses a rare compression and sense of understated suffering, as if it was ready to spill from him when he at last arrived in England in 1590. As he assumes the mantle of the biblical Job, Hortop neither draws out the pain nor passes over it. Hawkins, who had made it back from what he called "this sorrowful voyage" in 1569, had lost so many of his men on the return voyage that he thought it would take "a painful man with his pen" to write the whole history of the venture, and writing the tale would consume as much "time as he had that wrote the lives and deaths of the martyrs." Although Hortop had not gone back with Hawkins, it was Hortop more than Hawkins who knew what martyrdom was like, and Hortop who painfully penned this narrative so many years later.

JOB HORTOP

The Travails of an Englishman (1591)

NOT UNTRULY NOR WITHOUT CAUSE SAID JOB THE FAITHFUL SERVANT OF God (whom the sacred Scriptures tell us, to have dwelt in the land of Hus)[1] that man being born of a woman, living a short time, is replenished with many miseries: which some know by reading of histories, many by the view of others' calamities, and I by experience in myself, as this present treatise ensuing shall show.

It is not unknown unto many, that I Job Hortop powder-maker[2] was born at Bourne, a town in Lincolnshire, from my age of twelve years brought up in Redriffe near London, with Mr. Francis Lee, who was the Queen's Majesty's

---

[1] "There was a man in the land of Uz [or Hus], whose name was Job; and that man was perfect and upright, and one that feared God, and eschewed evil" (Job 1:1). His faithfulness tested by Satan through a series of disasters, with the connivance of God, in the end Job is restored to his prior good fortune, but not before he despairs, "Man that is born of a woman is of few days, and full of trouble" (14:1).

[2] A manufacturer of gunpowder; hence Hortop's service as a gunner on the *Jesus of Lubeck*.

powder-maker, whom I served, until I was pressed to go on the third voyage to the West Indies, with the right worshipful Sir John Hawkins, who appointed me to be one of the gunners in her Majesty's ship called the *Jesus of Lubeck,* who set sail from Plymouth in the month of October 1567, having with him another ship of her Majesty's, called the *Minion,* and four ships of his own, namely the *Angel,* the *Swallow,* the *Judith,* and the *William and John.* He directed his vice-admiral, that if foul weather did separate them, to meet at the island of Tenerife.[3] After which by the space of seven days and seven nights, we had such storms at sea, that we lost our long boats and a pinnace,[4] with some men: coming to the isle of Tenerife, there our general heard that his vice-admiral with the *Swallow,* and the *William and John* were at the island called Gomera, where finding his vice-admiral, he anchored, took in fresh water, and set sail for Cape Blanc,[5] where in the way we took a Portuguese caravel,[6] laden with fish called mullets: from thence we sailed to Cape Verde. In our course thither we met a Frenchman of Rochelle called Captain Bland, who had taken a Portuguese caravel, whom our vice admiral chased and took. Captain Drake, now Sir Francis Drake, was made master and captain of the caravel, and so we kept our way till we came to Cape Verde, and there we anchored, took our boats, and set soldiers on shore. Our general was the first that leapt on land, and with him Captain Dudley: there we took certain Negroes, but not without damage to ourselves. For our general, Captain Dudley, and eight other of our company were hurt with poisoned arrows: about nine days after, the eight that were wounded died. Our general was taught by a Negro, to draw the poison out of his wound with a clove of garlic, whereby he was cured. From thence we went to Sierra Leone,[7] where be monstrous fishes called sharks, which will devour men. I amongst others was sent in the *Angel* with two Pinnaces into the river called Calousa, to seek two Caravels that were there trading with the Negroes: we took one of them with the Negroes, and brought them away.

In this river in the night time we had one of our pinnaces bulged[8] by a sea-horse, so that our men swimming about the river, were all taken into the other pinnaces, except two that took hold one of another, and were carried away by the sea-horse. This monster hath the just proportion of a horse, saving that his legs be short, his teeth very great, and a span[9] in length: he useth[1] in

---

[3] Like Gomera, one of the Canary Islands, sixty miles off the Atlantic coast of Africa. The term "vice-admiral" (like "general" and "viceroy" later on) is used both for the person holding the position and for his vessel.

[4] A small vessel often used for coastal explorations.

[5] A headland on the West African coast of Mauritania. Cape Verde: the westernmost point of Africa, in Senegal, some five hundred miles farther south.

[6] A small ship of three or four masts.

[7] A country some five hundred miles farther south on the West African coast.

[8] Smashed in; the "sea-horse," from Hortop's description, probably was a "river-horse," or hippopotamus.

[9] The spread of a human hand.

[1] I.e., is accustomed.

the night to go on land into the woods, seeking at unawares to devour the Negroes in their cabins, whom they by their vigilancy prevent,[2] and kill him in this manner. The Negroes keep watch, and diligently attend their coming, and when they are gone into the woods, they forthwith lay a great tree overthwart the way, so that at their return, for that their legs be so short, they cannot go over it: then the Negroes set upon them with their bows, arrows and darts, and so destroy them.

From thence we entered the river called the Casserroes, where there were other caravels trading with the Negroes, and them we took. In this island betwixt the river and the main, trees grow with oysters upon them. There grow palmetto trees, which be as high as a ship's mainmast, and on their tops grow nuts, wine and oil, which they call palmetto wine and palmetto oil. The plantain tree also groweth in that country; the tree is as big as a man's thigh, and as high as a fir pole, the leaves thereof be long and broad, and on the top grow the fruit which are called plantanos: they are crooked, and a cubit long, and as big as a man's wrist, they grow on clusters: when they be ripe they be very good and dainty to eat: sugar is not more delicate in taste then they be.[3]

From thence with the *Angel*, the *Judith*, and the two pinnaces, we sailed to Sierra Leone, where our general at that time was, who with the captains and soldiers went up into the river called Taggarin, to take a town of the Negroes, where he found three kings of that country with fifty thousand Negroes besieging the same town, which they could not take in many years before, when they had warred with it. Our general made a breech, entered and valiantly took the town, wherein were found five Portuguese which yielded themselves to his mercy, and he saved their lives: we took and carried thence for traffic to the West Indies five hundred Negroes. The three kings drove seven thousand Negroes into the sea at low water, at the point of the land, where they were all drowned in the ooze, for that they could not take their canoes to save themselves. We returned back again in our pinnaces to the ships, and there took in fresh water, and made ready sail towards Rio Grande.[4] At our coming thither we entered with the *Angel*, the *Judith*, and the two pinnaces, and found there seven Portuguese caravels, which made great fight with us. In the end by God's help we won the victory, and drove them to the shore, from whence with the Negroes they fled, and we fetched the caravels from the shore into the river. The next morning Mr. Francis Drake with his caravel, the *Swallow*, and the *William and John* came into the river, with Captain Dudley and his soldiers, who landed, being but a hundred soldiers, and fought with seven thousand Negroes, burned the town, and returned to our general with the loss of one man.

[2] I.e., get ahead of.
[3] The plants referred to here are the mangrove, a maritime tree also known as the oyster tree because oysters attach themselves to its roots; the palm (palmetto), from which oil is derived (wine is produced from the sap); and the plantain, a relative of the banana, whose high trunk resembles that of the fir.
[4] This Rio Grande flows into the Atlantic from the West African country of Guinea-Bissau, halfway between Cape Blanc and Cape Verde.

In that place there be many musk-cats,[5] which breed in hollow trees: the Negroes take them in a net, and put them in a cage, and nourish them very daintily, and take the musk from them with a spoon.

Now we directed our course from Guinea towards the West Indies.

And by the way died Captain Dudley.

In sailing towards the Indies, the first land that we escried,[6] was the island called Dominica,[7] where at our coming we anchored, and took in fresh water and wood for our provision: which done, we sailed towards the island called Margarita, where our general in despite of the Spaniards anchored landed, and took in fresh victuals. A mile off the island there is a rock in the sea, wherein do breed many fowls like unto barnacles:[8] in the night we went out in our boats, and with cudgels we killed many of them, and brought them with many of their eggs aboard with us: their eggs be as big as turkeys' eggs, and speckled like them. We did eat them, and found them very good meat.[9]

From thence we sailed to Burboroata,[1] which is in the mainland of the West Indies: there we came in, moored our ships, and tarried two months trimming and dressing our ships, and in the meantime traded with certain Spaniards of that country. There our general sent us unto a town called Placencia, (which stood on a high hill) to have entreated a bishop that dwelt there for his favor and friendship in their laws, who hearing of our coming, for fear forsook town.

In our way up the hill to Placencia, we found a monstrous venemous worm[2] with two heads: his body was as big as a man's arm, and a yard long: our master Robert Barret did cut him in sunder with his sword, and it made it as black as if it were colored with ink.

Here be many tigers, monstrous and furious beasts, which by subtlety devour and destroy many men: they use the traded ways,[3] and will show themselves twice or thrice to the travellers, and so depart secretly, lurking till they be past, then suddenly and at unawares they leap upon them and devour them: they had[4] so used two of our company, had not one of them looked behind. Our general sent three ships unto the island called Curaçao,[5] to make provision for the rest, where they remained until his coming. He sent from thence the *Angel* and the *Judith* to Rio de Hacha, where we anchored before the town.

---

[5] An animal like the civet cat, from which a strong-scented glandular secretion is derived.

[6] Descried, i.e., perceived.

[7] An island in the Lesser Antilles, southeast of Puerto Rico and northeast of Margarita, an island off the coast of Venezuela.

[8] A breed of European goose.

[9] I.e., food.

[1] On the Golfo Triste along the coast of Venezuela, west of Margarita Island; Placencia: a town inland from Burboroata.

[2] I.e., snake; perhaps a boa.

[3] I.e., routes commonly traveled by humans.

[4] Would have.

[5] Off the coast of Venezuela; the men who went there were to prepare food ("make provision") for the others.

The Spaniards shot three pieces at us from the shore, whom we requited with two of ours, and shot through the governor's house: we weighed anchor, and anchored again without shot[6] of the town, where we rode five days in despite of the Spaniards and their shot. In the mean space there came a caravel of advice[7] from Santo Domingo, whom with the *Angel*, and the *Judith* we chased and drove to the shore: we fetched him from thence in spite of two hundred Spaniards' arquebus[8] shot, and anchored again before the town, and rode there with them, till our general's coming, who anchored, landed his men, and valiantly took the town, with the loss of one man, whose name was Thomas Surgeon: we landed and planted on the shore for our safeties, our field ordinance: we drove the Spaniards up into the country above two leagues, whereby they were forced to trade with our general, to whom he sold most part of his Negroes.

In this river we killed a monstrous lagarto or crocodile in this port at sunset: seven of us went in the pinnace up into the river, carrying with us a dog, unto whom with ropeyarn[9] we bound a great hook of steel, with a chain that had a swivel, which we put under the dog's belly, the point of the hook coming over his back fast bound, as aforesaid: we put him over board, and veered out[1] our rope by little and little, rowing away with our boat: the lagarto came and presently swallowed up the dog, then did we row hard, till we had choked him: he plunged and made a wonderful stir in the water: we leapt on shore, and hauled him on land: he was twenty-three foot by the rule, headed like a hog, in body like a serpent, full of scales as broad as a saucer: his tail long and full of knots as big as a falcon[2] shot: he hath four legs, his feet have long nails like unto a dragon: we opened him, took out his guts, flayed him, dried his skin, and stuffed it with straw, meaning to have brought it home, had not the ship been cast away. This monster will carry away and devour both man and horse.

From hence we shaped our course to Santa Martha,[3] where we landed, traded, and sold certain Negroes: there two of our company killed a monstrous adder, going towards his cave with a coney[4] in his mouth: his body was as big as any man's thigh, and seven foot long: upon his tail he had sixteen knots, every one as big as a great walnut, which they say, do show his age: his color was green and yellow: they opened him, and found two conies in his belly.

From thence we sailed to Cartagena,[5] where we went in, moored our ships, and would have traded with them, but they durst not for fear of the king:

---

[6] Beyond the range.
[7] A ship bearing news.
[8] A heavy but portable matchlock gun.
[9] The material from which rope is made.
[1] Let run out.
[2] A small cannon, whose shot are about the size of the "knots" or bumps on the tail of the alligator (not crocodile).
[3] A coastal town west of the Golfo Triste, in modern Colombia.
[4] Rabbit.
[5] Farther along the Colombian coast; botijos: earthen jars.

we brought up the *Minion* against the castle, and shot at the castle and town: then we landed in an island, where were many gardens: there in a cave we found certain botijos of wine, which we brought away with us, in recompence whereof, our general commanded to be set on shore woollen and linen cloth, to the value thereof. From hence by foul weather we were forced to seek the port of St. John de Ulua.[6] In our way thwart of Campeche we met with a Spaniard, a small ship, who was bound for Santo Domingo: he had in him a Spaniard called Augustin de Villa Nueva, who was the man that betrayed all the noblemen in the Indies, and caused them to be beheaded, wherefore he with two friars fled to Santo Domingo:[7] them we took and brought with us into the Port of St. John de Ulua. Our general made great account of him, and used him like a nobleman: howbeit in the end he was one of them that betrayed us. When we had moored our ships, and landed, we mounted the ordinance that we found there in the island, and for our safeties kept watch and ward. The next day after we discovered the Spanish fleet, whereof Luçon a Spaniard was general: with him came a Spaniard called Don Martin Henriquez, whom the king of Spain sent to be his viceroy of the Indies. He sent a pinnace with a flag of truce unto our general, to know of what country those ships were that rode there in the King of Spain's port; who said, they were the Queen of England's ships, which came in there for victuals for their money: wherefore if your general will come in here, he shall give me victuals and all other necessaries, and I will go out on the one side of the port, and he shall come in on the other side. The Spaniard returned for answer, that he was a viceroy, and had a thousand men, and therefore he would come in. Our general said, "If he be a viceroy, I represent my Queen's person, and I am a viceroy as well as he: and if he have a thousand men, my powder and shot will take the better place." Then the viceroy after counsel among themselves, yielded to our general's demand, swearing by his King and his Crown, by his commission and authority that he had from his King, that he would perform it, and thereupon pledges were given on both parts. Our general bearing a godly and Christian mind, void of fraud and deceit, judged the Spaniards to have done the like, delivered to them six gentlemen, not doubting to have received the like from them: but the faithless Spaniards, in costly apparel gave of the basest of their company, as afterwards it was well known.[8] These things finished, proclamation was made on both sides, that on pain of death no occasion should be given, whereby any quarrel should grow to the breach of the league, and then they peaceably entered the port, with great triumph on both sides.

---

[6] San Juan de Ulúa, an island defending the harbor at Vera Cruz, Mexico; on their way there, the ships would have passed Campeche, on the western coast of the Yucatán Peninsula.

[7] Hortop's exaggerated comment about the executions of "all the noblemen in the Indies" refers in a confused manner to the alleged conspiracy of Martín Cortés, son of the conqueror of Mexico, to wrest control of that country from the Spanish crown in the mid-1560s. Agustín de Villaneuva was one of the royalists who opposed the rebels, some of whom were executed.

[8] That is, the Spanish leader dressed the "lowest" members of his company in fine apparel, so that Hawkins would think he was receiving "gentlemen" as hostages.

The Spaniards presently brought a great hulk, a ship of six hundred [tons], and moored her by the side of the *Minion*, and they cut out ports in their other ships, planting their ordinance towards us, in the night they filled the hulk with men, to lay the *Minion* aboard,[9] as the sequel did show, which made our general doubtful of their dealings: wherefore, for that he could speak the Spanish tongue, he sent Robert Barret aboard the viceroy, to know his meaning in those dealings, who willed him with his company to come in to him, whom he commanded presently to be set in the bilbows, and forthwith a cornet (for a watchword among the false Spaniards) was sounded for the enterprising of their pretended treason against our general, whom Augustine de Villa Nueva sitting at dinner with him, should then presently have killed with a poniard[1] which he had privily[2] in his sleeve, which was espyed and prevented by one John Chamberlayne, who took the poniard out of his sleeve. Our general hastily rose up, and commanded him to be put prisoner in the steward's room, and to be kept with[3] two men. The faithless Spaniards, thinking all things to their desire had been finished, suddenly sounded a trumpet, and therewith three hundred Spaniards entered the *Minion*, whereat our general with a loud and fierce voice called unto us, saying, "God and Saint George, upon those traitorous villains, and rescue the *Minion*, I trust in God the day shall be ours": and with that the mariners and soldiers leapt out of the *Jesus of Lubeck* into the *Minion*, and beat out the Spaniards, and with a shot out of her fired the Spaniards' vice admiral, where the most part of three hundred Spaniards were spoiled, and blown overboard with powder. Their admiral also was on fire half an hour: we cut our cables, wound off our ships, and presently fought with them: they came upon us on every side, and continued the fight from ten of the clock until it was night: they killed all our men that were on shore in the island, saving three, which by swimming got aboard the *Jesus of Lubeck*. They sunk the general's ship called the *Angel*, and took the *Swallow*: the Spaniard's admiral had above threescore shot through her: many of his men were spoiled: four other of their ships were sunk. There were in that fleet, and that came from the shore to rescue them, fifteen hundred: we slew of them five hundred and forty, as we were credibly informed by a note that came to Mexico. In this fight the *Jesus of Lubeck* had five shot through her mainmast: her foremast was struck in sunder under the hounds[4] with a chain shot, and her hull was wonderfully pierced with shot, therefore it was impossible to bring her away. They set two of their own ships on fire, intending therewith to have burnt the *Jesus of Lubeck*, which we prevented by cutting our cables in the hawse, and winding off by our stern fast.[5]

[9] I.e., as later stated, to rush the English ship with the men.
[1] A dagger with a slender triangular or square blade.
[2] Secretly.
[3] Watched by.
[4] Framing at the masthead (top of the first stage of a compound mast) to support the topmast.
[5] I.e., they cut their main anchor lines where they came in through the hawse hole at the bow, and then backed off by pulling the ship toward a rear anchor, attached to a line (the "stern fast") at the stern.

The *Minion* was forced to set sail and stand off from us, and come to an anchor without shot of the island. Our general courageously cheered up his soldiers and gunners, and called to Samuel his page for a cup of beer, who brought it him in a silver cup, and he drinking to all men willed the gunners to stand by their ordinance lustily like men. He had no sooner set the cup out of his hand, but a demi-culverin[6] shot struck away the cup and a cooper's plane that stood by the mainmast, and ran out on the other side of the ship: which nothing dismayed our general, for he ceased not to encourage us, saying, "Fear nothing, for God, who hath preserved me from this shot, will also deliver us from these traitors and villains." Then Captain Bland meaning to have turned out of the port, had his mainmast struck overboard with a chain shot that came from the shore, wherefore he anchored, fired[7] his ship, took his pinnace with all his men, and came aboard the *Jesus of Lubek* to our general, who said unto him, that he thought he would not have run away from him: he answered, that he was not minded[8] to have run away from him, but his intent was to have turned up, and to have laid the weathermost ship of the Spanish fleet aboard,[9] and fired his ship in hope therewith to have set on fire the Spanish fleet, he said if he had done so he had done well. With this, night came on. Our general commanded the *Minion*, for safeguard of her masts to be brought under the *Jesus of Lubeck*'s lee[1]: he willed Mr. Francis Drake to come in with the *Judith*, and to lay the *Minion* aboard, to take in men and other things needful, and to go out, and so he did.

At night when the wind came off the shore, we set sail, and went out in despite of the Spaniards and their shot, where we anchored, with two anchors under the island, the wind being northerly, which was wonderful dangerous, and we feared every hour to be driven with the lee shore.[2] In the end when the wind came larger, we weighed anchor, and set sail, seeking the river of Panuco[3] for water, whereof we had very little, and victuals were so scarce, that we were driven to eat hides, cats, rats, parrots, monkeys, and dogs: wherefore our general was forced to divide his company into two parts, for there was a mutiny among them for want of victuals: and some said that they had rather be on the shore to shift for themselves amongst the enemies, than to starve on shipboard. He asked them who would go on shore, and who would tarry on shipboard, those that would go on shore, he willed to go on foremast, and those that would tarry, on baft mast[4]: fourscore and sixteen of us were willing to depart. Our general

[6] A long cannon firing a smallish ball.
[7] Set fire to.
[8] Of a mind to.
[9] Bland intended to come alongside the outermost ship in the Spanish fleet.
[1] To be moored in such a way that the other ship would shield it from the wind.
[2] A lee shore has the wind blowing toward it from the sea; a ship facing a lee shore runs the risk of being blown aground or wrecked.
[3] The Panuco enters the Caribbean farther north on the Mexican coast, at present Tampico; a town named for the river lies slightly inland.
[4] Hawkins tells the leavers to gather by the foremast, the stayers to gather by the sternmast.

gave unto every one of us six yards of roan cloth,[5] and money to them that demanded it. When we were landed, he came unto us, where friendly embracing every one of us, he was greatly grieved that he was forced to leave us behind him, he counselled us to serve God, and to love one another, and thus courteously he gave us a sorrowful farewell, and promised if God sent him safe home, he would do what he could, that so many of us as lived should by some means be brought into England, and so he did.

Since my return into England I have heard that many misliked that he left us so behind him, and brought away Negroes: but the reason is this, for them he might have had victuals, or any other thing needful, if by foul weather he had been driven upon the islands, which for gold nor silver he could not have had.

And thus our general departed to his ship, and we remained on land, where for our safeties, fearing the wild Indians that were about us, we kept watch all night, and at sunrising we marched on our way, three and three in a rank, until that we came into a field under a grove, where the Indians came upon us, asking us what people we were, and how we came there. Two of our company, namely Anthony Goddard and John Cornish, for that they could speak the Spanish tongue, went to them, and said we were Englishmen, that never came in that country before, and that we had fought with the Spaniards, and for that we lacked victuals, our general set us on shore: they asked us whither we intended to go, we said to Panuco. The captain of the Indians willed us to give unto them some of our clothes and shirts, which we did: then he bade us give them all, but we would not so do, whereupon John Cornish was then slain with an arrow, which an Indian boy that stood by the captain shot at him, wherefore he struck the boy on the neck with his bow, that he lay for dead, and willed us to follow him, who brought us into a great field, where we found fresh water: he bade us sit down about the pond and drink, and he with his company would go in the mean space to kill five or six deer, and bring them to us. We tarried there til three of the clock, but they came not: there one of our company whose name was John Cooke, with four other departed from us into a grove to seek relief,[6] where presently they were taken by the Indians, and stripped as naked as ever they were born, and so returned to us.

Then we divided ourselves into two parts, half to Anthony Goddard, and the rest to James Collier, and thus severally[7] we sought for Panuco. Anthony Goddard with his company, bid us farewell, they passed a river, where the Indians robbed many of them of their clothes, and so passing on their way, came to a stony hill, where they stayed. James Collier with his company that day passed the same river, and were also robbed, and one of them slain by chance: we came that night unto the hill, where Anthony Goddard and his

---

[5] Roan is a reddish color, but the term also referred to a cheap grade of sheepskin.
[6] To "relieve" themselves.
[7] Each group by itself.

company rested, there we remained til morning, and then we marched altogether from thence, entering between two groves, where the Indians robbed us of all our clothes, and left us naked, they hurt many, and killed eight of us. Three days after we came to another river, there the Indians showed us the way to Panuco, and so left us: we passed the river into the wilderness, where we made wreaths of green grass, which we wound about our bodies, to keep us from the sun, and gnats of that country. We travelled there seven days, and seven nights, before we came to Panuco, feeding on nothing but roots, and guavas, a fruit like figs. At our coming to the river of Panuco two Spanish horsemen came over unto us in a canoe: they asked us how long we had been in the wilderness, and where our general was, for they knew us to be of the company that had fought with their countrymen: we told them seven days and seven nights, and for lack of victuals our general set us on shore, and he was gone away with his ships. They returned to their governor, who sent them with five canoes to bring us all over, which done, they set us in array, where a hundred horsemen with their lances, came forcibly upon us, but did not hurt us, they carried us prisoners to Panuco, where we remained one night. In the river of Panuco there is a fish like a calf, the Spaniards call it a mallatin,[8] he hath a stone in his head, which the Indians use for the disease of the colic, in the night he cometh on land, and eateth grass. I have eaten of it, and it eateth not much unlike to bacon. From thence we were sent to Mexico [City], which is ninety leagues from Panuco. In our way thither, twenty leagues from the seaside, I did see white crabs running up and down the sands, I have eaten of them, and they be very good meat. There groweth a fruit which the Spaniards call avocottes,[9] it is proportioned like an egg, and as black as a coal, having a stone in it, and it is an excellent good fruit. There also groweth a strange tree which they call maguey,[1] it serveth them to many uses, below by the root they make a hole, wherat they do take out of it twice every day a certain kind of liquor, which they seethe[2] in a great kettle, till the third part be consumed, and that it wax thick, it is as sweet as any honey, and they do eat it. Within twenty days after that they have taken all the liquor from it, it withereth, and they cut it down, and use it as we use our hemp here in England, which done, they convert it to many uses: of some part they make mantles, ropes, and thread: of the ends they make needles to sew their saddles, panels, and other furniture[3] for their horses: of the rest they make tiles to cover their houses, and they put it to many other purposes.

And thus we came to Mexico [City], which is seven or eight miles about, seated in a great fen, environed with four hills, it hath but two ways of entrance,

---

[8] Here, as elsewhere, Hortop's natural history seems to verge on the fantastic.
[9] The avocado.
[1] The agave, a succulent shrub composed of cupped, bladelike leaves, from which the alcoholic pulque and ultimately mescal are derived, and the fibers of which are used to produce sisal, which resembles hemp.
[2] Poach or simmer in water.
[3] Furnishings or equipment; panel: a saddle cloth.

and it is full of creeks, in the which in their canoes they pass from place to place, and to the islands there within. In the Indies ordinarily three times a year be wonderful earthquakes, which put the people in great fear and danger: during the time of two years that I was in Mexico, I saw them six times: when they come they throw down trees, houses, and churches. There is a city twenty-five leagues from Mexico, called Tlaxcala, which is inhabited with a hundred thousand Indians, they go in white shirts, linen breeches, and long mantles, and the women wear about them a garment much like unto a flannel petticoat. The king's palace was the first place we were brought unto in Mexico, where without[4] we were willed to sit down. Much people, men, women, and children came wondering about us, many lamented our misery, and some of their clergy asked us if we were Christians, we said, we praised God, we were as good Christians as they: they asked how they might know that, we said, "By our confessions." From thence we were carried in a canoe to a tanner's house, which standeth a little from the city: the next morning two friars and two priests came thither to us, and willed us to bless ourselves, and say our prayers in the Latin tongue, that they might understand us, many of our company did so, whereupon they returned to the viceroy, and told him that we were good Christians, and that they liked us well, and then they brought us much relief, with clothes, our sick men were sent to their hospitals, where many were cured, and many died. From the tanner's house we were led to a gentleman's place, where upon pain of death we were charged to abide, and not to come into the city, thither we had all things necessary brought us: on Sundays and holy days much people came, and brought us great relief.

The viceroy practised[5] to hang us, and caused a pair of new gallows to be set up, to have executed us, wherunto the noblemen of that country would not consent, but prayed him to stay until the ship of advice brought news from the King of Spain, what should be done with us, for they said they could not find anything by us,[6] whereby they might lawfully put us to death.

The viceroy then commanded us to be sent to an island thereby, and he sent for the Bishop of Mexico, who sent four priests to the island, to examine and confess us, who said, that the viceroy would burn us, when we were examined and confessed according to the laws of the country. They returned to the bishop, and told him that we were very good Christians. The bishop certified the viceroy of our examinations and confessions, and said that we were good Christians, therefore he would not meddle with us. Then the viceroy sent for our master, R. Barret, whom he kept prisoner in his palace, until the fleet was departed for Spain. The rest of us he sent to a town seven leagues from Mexico called Texcoco, to card wool among the Indian slaves, which drudgery we disdained, and concluded to beat our masters, and so we did: wherefore they sent to the viceroy, desiring him for God's sake and our lady's, to send for us, for

---

[4] I.e., outside which.
[5] Made preparations.
[6] Any cause.

they would not keep us any longer, they said that we were devils and no men.

The viceroy sent for us, and imprisoned us in a house in Mexico, from thence he sent Anthony Goddard, and some other of our company with him into Spain, with Luçon, the general that took us: the rest of us stayed in Mexico two years after, and then were sent prisoners into Spain, with Don Juan de Velasco de Varre, admiral and general of the Spanish fleet, who carried with him in his ship, to be presented to the King of Spain, the anatomy[7] of a giant, which was sent from China to Mexico, to the viceroy Don Martin Henriquez, to be sent to the King of Spain for a great wonder. It did appear by the anatomy, that he was of a monstrous size, the skull of his head was near as big as half a bushel, his neckbones, shoulderplates, armbones, and all other lineaments of his other parts, were huge and monstrous to behold, the shank of his leg from the ankle to the knee was as long as from any man's ankle up to his waist, and of bigness accordingly.

At this time, and in this ship, were also sent to be presented to the King of Spain, two chests full of earth with ginger growing in them, which were also sent from China, to be sent to the King of Spain. The ginger runneth in the ground like to licorice, the blades grow out of it in length and proportion like unto the blades of wild garlic, which they cut every fifteen days, they use to[8] water them twice a day, as we do our herbs here in England, they put the blades in their pottage, and use them in their other meats, whose excellent savor and taste is very delightful, and procureth a good appetite.

When we were shipped in the port of St. John de Ulua, the general called our master Robert Barret and us with him into his cabin, and asked us if we would fight against Englishmen if we met them at the sea, we said that we would not fight against our Crown, but if we met with any other, we would do what we were able. He said if we had said otherwise he would not have believed us, and for that we should be the better used, and have allowance as other men had: and he gave a charge[9] to every one of us, according unto our knowledge. Robert Barret was placed with the pilot, I was put in the gunner's room, William Cawse with the boatswain, John Beare with the quartermasters, Edward Rider, and Geffrey Giles, with the ordinary mariners, Richard the master's boy attended on him and the pilot: shortly after we departed from the port of St. John de Ulua with all the fleet of Spain, for the port called Havana: we were twenty-six days sailing thither. There we came in, anchored, took in fresh water, and stayed sixteen days for the fleet of Nombre de Dios, which is the fleet that brings the treasure from Peru.[1]

The general of that fleet was called Diego Flores de Valdes. After his coming, when he had watered his ships, both the fleets joined in one, and Don Juan de Velasco de Varre was the first fifteen days general of both the fleets,

[7] Skeleton.
[8] Tend to.
[9] Job.
[1] A port on the northern coast of Panama.

who turning through the channel of Bahama, his pilot had like to have cast away all the fleet upon the cape called Canaveral,[2] which was prevented by me Job Hortop, and our master Robert Barret: for I being in the second watch descried land, and called to Robert Barret, bidding him look overboard, for I saw land under the lee-bow of the ship: he called to the boatswain, and bid him let fly the foresail sheet, and lay the helm upon the lee, and cast the ship about.[3] When we were cast about, we were but in seven fathom water: we shot off a piece, giving advice to the fleet to cast about, and so they did. For this we were beloved of the general, and all the fleet. The general was in a great rage, and swore by the king, that he would hang his pilot: for he said, that twice before he had almost cast away the admiral. When it was day, he commanded a piece to be shot off, to call to council: the other admiral in his ship came up to him, and asked what the matter was, he said, that his pilot had cast away his ship and all the fleet, had it not been for two of the Englishmen, and therefore he would hang him. The other admiral with many fair words persuaded him to the contrary.

When we came in the height of Bermuda, we discovered a monster in the sea, who showed himself three times unto us from the middle upwards, in which parts he was proportioned like a man, of the complexion of a mulatto, or tawny Indian. The general did command one of his clerks to put it in writing, and he certified[4] the king and his nobles thereof. Presently after this, for the space of sixteen days we had wonderful foul weather, and then God sent us a fair wind, until such time as we discovered the island called Fayal.[5]

On St. James day we made rockets, wheels, and other fireworks, to make pastime that night, as it is the order of the Spaniards. When we came near the land, our master R. Barret conferred with us, to take the pinnace one night, when we came on the island called Terceira, to free ourselves from the danger and bondage that we were going into, whereunto we agreed; none had any pinnace astern then but our ship, which gave great courage to our enterprise: we prepared a bag of bread, and a botijo of water, which would have served us nine days, and provided ourselves to go: our master borrowed a small compass of the master gunner of the ship, who lent it him, but suspected his intent, and closely[6] made the general privy to it, who for a time dissembled the matter. In the end seeing our pretense, he called R. Barret, commanding his head to be put in the stocks, and a great pair of iron bolts on his legs, and the rest of us to be set in the stocks by the legs. Then he willed a piece to be shot off, and he

[2] From Havana, the fleet has sailed around the western end of Cuba, turned northeast, and then gone up through the narrow passage between the Bahama Islands and Florida, whose Cape Canaveral jutted dangerously into the sea.

[3] The orders called for the boatswain, who would be in charge of the crew on deck, to let the air out of the mainsail on the foremast so as to slow the vessel, turn the rudder hard away from the wind, and try to reverse the direction of the vessel.

[4] Formally assured, via the "writing."

[5] In the Azores, like Terceira, due west of Spain in the North Atlantic.

[6] Secretly.

sent the pinnace for the other admiral, and all the captains, masters and pilots of both fleets to come aboard of him. He commanded the main yard[7] to be struck down, and to put two pulleys, on every yardarm one; the hangman was called, and we were willed to confess ourselves, for he swore by the king that he would hang us.

When the other admiral, and the rest were come aboard, he called them into his council chamber, and told them that he would hang the master of the Englishmen, and all his company. The admiral, whose name was Diego Flores de Valdes, asked him wherefore: he said, that we had determined to rise in the night with the pinnace, and with a ball of fireworks to set the ship on fire, and go our way: therefore, said he, "I will have you the captains, masters, and pilots, to set your hands unto that, for I swear by the king that I will hang them," Diego Flores de Valdes answered, "I nor the captains, masters, and pilots will not set our hands to that," for he said, if he had been prisoner as we were, he would have done the like himself. He counselled him to keep us fast in prison, till he came into Spain, and then send us to the Contratation House[8] in Seville, where, if we had deserved death the law would pass on us, for he would not have it said that in such a fleet as that was, six men and a boy should take the pinnace, and go away, and so he returned to his ship again.

When he was gone, the general came to the mainmast to us, and swore by the king, that we should not come out of the stocks til we came into Spain: within sixteen days after we came over the bar of San Lucar,[9] and came up to the Hurcados, then he put us into a pinnace in the stocks, and sent us prisoners to the Contratation House in Seville. From thence after one year we broke prison, on St. Steven's day at night, seven of our company escaped. Robert Barret; I, Job Hortop; John Emerie; Humphrey Roberts; and John Gilbert were taken, and brought back to the Contratation House, where we remained in the stocks til twelve tide[1] was past. Then our keeper put up a petition to the judge of the Contratation House, that we might be sent to the great prison house in Seville, for that we broke prison, whereupon we were presently led thither, where we remained one month, and then from thence, to the castle of the Inquisition House in Triana,[2] where we continued one year: which expired, they brought us out in procession, every one of us having a candle in his hand, and the coat with St. Andrew's cross[3] on our backs: they brought us up on an

---

[7] The crosspiece on the mainmast to which the mainsail is attached.

[8] The Casa de la Contratación in the Spanish city of Seville, on the Guadalquivir River, where contracts for the West Indies trade were made.

[9] Sanlúcar de Barrameda lies at the mouth of the Guadalquivir River seventy miles below Seville; Hurcados: Los Horcades, a shipbuilding town upstream from Sanlúcar.

[1] Epiphany, January 6, is the ending of the twelfthtide following Christmas; the escapees had made their break on St. Stephen's Day, December 26.

[2] Triana lies across the river from Seville. The Spanish Inquisition was established in 1232, but assumed its most feared form in the late fifteenth century; it targeted Moors, Jews, heretics (including Protestant Englishmen), freemasons, humanists, homosexuals, and others in disfavor with the state.

[3] An X-shaped cross, named after the apostle Andrew, who is said to have been crucified on one.

high scaffold, that was set up in the place of St. Francis, which is in the chief street of Seville: there they set us down upon benches, every one in his degree, and against us on another scaffold sat all the judges, and the clergy on their benches: the people wondered, and gazed on us, some pitying our cases, others said, "Burn those heretics." When we had sat there two hours, we had a sermon made to us: after which one called Bresinia, secretary to the Inquisition, went up into the pulpit with the process, and called Robert Barret and John Gilbert, whom two familiars of the Inquisition brought from the scaffold before the judges, where the secretary read the sentence, which was that they should be burnt, and so they returned to the scaffold, and were burnt.

Then I, Job Hortop, and John Bone were called, and brought to the place, as before, where we heard our sentence, which was, that we should go to the galleys, and there row at the oars' end ten years, and then to be brought back to the Inquisition House, to have the coat with St. Andrew's cross put on our backs, and from thence to go to the everlasting prison remediless,[4] and so we were returned from the scaffold from whence we came. Thomas Marks and Thomas Ellis were called, and had sentence to serve in the galleys eight years, and Humphrey Roberts, and John Emery to serve five years, and so were returned to the benches on the scaffold, where we sat til four of clock in the afternoon. Then we were led again to the Inquisition House, from whence we were brought. The next day in the morning Bresinia the treasurer came thither to us, and delivered to every one of us his sentence in writing. I with the rest were sent to the galleys, where we were chained four and four together: every man's daily allowance was twenty-six ounces of coarse black bisquit and water, our clothing for the whole year two shirts, two pair of breeches of coarse canvas, a red coat of coarse cloth, soon on, and soon off, and a gown of hair with a friar's hood: our lodging was on the bare boards, and banks of the galleys, our heads and beards were shaven every month, hunger, thirst, cold, and stripes we lacked none, til our several[5] times expired. And after the time of twelve years, for I served two years above my sentence, I was sent back to the Inquisition House in Seville, and there having put on the coat with St. Andrew's cross, I was sent to the everlasting prison remediless, where I wore the coat four years, and then upon great suit,[6] I had it taken off for fifty ducats, which Hernando de Soria treasurer of the king's mint lent me, whom I served for it as a drudge seven years, and until the month of October last, 1590, and then I came from Seville to San Lucar, where I made means to come away in a fly-boat,[7] that was laden with wines and salt, which were Flemings' goods, the King of Spain's subjects, dwelling in Seville, married to Spanish women, and sworn to their king.[8] In this month of October last, departing from San Lucar, at sea, off the

---

[4] A prison from which there was no hope of release or legal remedy.

[5] Individual.

[6] I.e., much petitioning.

[7] A fast, often flat-bottomed, coastal boat.

[8] The Flemings were natives of Flanders, then under the rule of the Spanish crown; the "Fleming" later on is the flyboat on which Hortop has escaped.

southernmost cape, we met an English ship, called the galleon *Dudley*, who took the Fleming, and me out of him, and brought me to Portsmouth,[9] where they set me on land, the second day of December last past, 1590. From thence I was sent by Mr. Muns the lieutenant of Portsmouth, with letters to the right honorable the Earl of Sussex, who commanded his secretary to take my name and examination, how long I had been out of England, and with whom I went, which he did. And on Christmas even I took my leave of his honor, and came to Redriffe.

The computation of my imprisonment:

I suffered imprisonment in Mexico two years.

In the Contratation House in Seville one year.

In the Inquisition House in Triana one year.

I was in the galleys twelve years.

In the everlasting prison remediless, with the coat with St. Andrew's cross on my back four years.

And at liberty I served as a drudge Hernando de Soria three years, which is the full complement of twenty-three years.

Since my departure from England, until this time of my return, I was five times in great danger of death, besides the many perils I was in, in the galleys.

First in the port of St. John de Ulua, where being on shore, with many other of our company, which were all slain saving I, and two other that by swimming got aboard the *Jesus of Lubeck*.

Secondly, when we were robbed by the wild Indians.

Thirdly, after we came to Mexico, the viceroy would have hanged us.

Fourthly, because he could not have his mind to hang us, he would have burnt us.

Fifthly, the general that brought us into Spain, would have hanged us at sea.

Thus having truly set down unto you my travels, misery and dangers, endured the space of twenty-three years, I end.

---

[9] An English port and naval base (hence the lieutenant stationed there) on the southern coast.

3

UP THE JAMES RIVER
IN THE SPRING OF 1607

THE ENGLISH NAMED A WIDE STRETCH OF THE NORTH AMERICAN COAST "VIR-ginia" after their "Virgin Queen" Elizabeth I as early as 1584, when Sir Walter Ralegh was focusing his attention on the Albemarle and Pamlico sounds of what is now North Carolina. The settlements attempted there at the time failed miserably, and it was another quarter century before England successfully planted any American colony. The focus by then had shifted farther north, to the area now known by Ralegh's more general term, but so frail was this new Virginia that two more decades passed before its success was assured.

When the colonists of this venture first left England in January 1607, Queen Elizabeth had been dead for four years, so their own naming of the American scene honored her successor and cousin, James I: the Powhatan River thus became the "James," and the vulnerable camp they established on a swampy island along its northern shore was called "James Towne" or, after it was fortified, "James Fort." Almost as soon as the bickering gentlemen and workers stepped onto the Virginia shore that spring and began to clear ground and build their first structures, a party of some two dozen set off, under the command of the one-armed seaman and privateer Captain Christopher Newport, to explore the upper reaches of the James. Among the personnel of this venture were several well-remembered figures besides Newport, including George Percy, the younger brother of the earl of Northumberland and an Oxford graduate who was to prove himself capable of infinite sympathy with his own coming misfortunes; Captain John Smith, who as an experienced soldier was no stranger to misfortune, and hence did not like Percy or most of the other "soft" gentlemen of the colony—although Smith himself was to miss much of the suffering that buffeted the others; and Gabriel Archer, a graduate of Cambridge who soon became a staunch enemy of Smith, and who was to perish in the disastrous "starving time" that almost wiped out the whole colony in the winter of 1609–10. (Smith, who had been wounded in a gunpowder explosion as he slept on his ship during another reconnaissance the summer before, by that time had gone back to England to recover, and never returned to the colony.)

Although John Smith might have been looked to for an account of the 1607 river voyage, apparently it was Archer who wrote the "Relation of the Discovery of Our River" printed here. The narrative expresses from this early moment of the English effort an exuberant, even giddy delight in all the places to be visited—and humorously named. It also expresses an innocence about the local Native Americans that consistently underestimates their memory of what had occurred in the first Virginia colonies of the Roanoke period, and overlooks the capacity of these new English settlers to repeat the old mistakes and old outrages. Newport went upriver as far as the future site of Richmond, home of Powhatan, the great leader of a league of Virginia natives, but despite Archer's assumptions to the contrary, Newport never actually encountered Powhatan— only that man's son. The message of Powhatan himself got through, nonetheless; about to push farther inland toward the domain of one of Powhatan's enemies, the English were warned to turn back and, for once reining themselves in, did so. They dawdled on the downriver voyage as if they were on a pleasure cruise, however, encountering and being entertained by, among others, the native Queen Apumatec. By the time they arrived in Jamestown, a party of some two hundred Paspahegh Indians was attacking the stunned colonists. The voyagers might have known better, as this was not the first violent encounter between the two. The English had settled, after all, smack in the middle of Paspahegh hunting territory, and the wider region was full of Indians and full of complex political animosities and conflicts for which not even the tangled rivalries and bloody wars of Europe seem to have prepared the settlers. Newport and Archer's return to Jamestown thus began a period of intensive fortification (hence the term "James Fort") while, as the narrative goes on to report, straggling fights between the English and the local population dropped man after man among the settlers. Soon after his account ends, the English who escaped death in warfare started to die of disease, so that the history of the next few months came to resemble one long obituary. From the perspective of that sober period, the little voyage up the James in May 1607 may well have seemed to mark, beyond its own more worrisome suggestions, a moment of gentle delight.

[GABRIEL ARCHER?]

"A Relation of the Discovery of Our River, from James Fort into the Main"[1], (1607)

THURSDAY THE 21ST OF MAY, CAPTAIN NEWPORT (HAVING FITTED OUR SHALLOP with provision and all necessaries[2] belonging to a discovery) took five gentlemen, four mariners, and fourteen sailors, with whom he proceeded with a

[1] The main part of Virginia, or the Virginia mainland; James Fort: Jamestown, laid out as a fort located on low, swampy ground (now underwater) along the northern shore of the James River, about thirty miles above its junction with Chesapeake Bay.
[2] Needed supplies; shallop: a small vessel used in coastal exploration.

perfect resolution not to return, but either to find the head of this river, the lake mentioned by others heretofore, the sea again, the mountains Apalatsi, or some issue.[3]

The names of the discoverers are these   } Captain Christopher Newport

George Percy, Esq.
Captain Gabriell Archer
Captain John Smith
Master John Brookes
Master Thomas Wotton

Francis Nellson
John Collson
Robert Tyndall
Mathew Fitch
} mariners

1 Jonas Poole
2 Robert Markham
3 John Crookdeck
4 Oliver Browne
5 Benjamin White
6 Rychard Genoway
7 Thomas Turnbrydg
8 Thomas Godword
9 Robert Jackson
10 Charles Clarke
11 Stephen
12 Thomas Skynner
13 Jeremy Deale
14 Danyell

Thus from James Fort we took our leave about noon, and by night we were up the river eighteen miles at a low meadow point, which I call Wynauk. Here came the people, and entertained us with dances and much rejoicing. This kingdom Wynauk is full of pearl mussels.[4] The King of Paspahegh[5] and this king is at odds, as the Paspaheghans told me, and demonstrated by their hurts: here we anchored all night. Friday, omitting[6] no time, we passed up some sixteen miles further, where we found an islet, on which were many turkeys, and great store of young birds like blackbirds, whereof we took divers, which we brake our fast withal.[7] Now spying eight savages in a canoe, we hailed them by our word of kindness, "Wingapoh,"[8] and they came to us. In conference by signs with them, one seemed to understand our intention, and offered with his foot to describe the river to us.[9] So I gave him a pen and paper (showing first

---

[3] Something worthy of the effort; Apalatsi: the Appalachians.
[4] I.e., oysters; Wynauk: a point along the James now called Weyanoke.
[5] A point on the James about halfway between Jamestown and Weyanoke, and the center of the territory of this other native group, who figure later in the narrative as the attackers of Jamestown.
[6] Losing.
[7] I.e., which we had for breakfast; divers: various.
[8] "Good man" (Algonkian).
[9] I.e., offered to draw the river's course with his foot.

the use) and he laid out the whole river from the Chesapeake Bay to the end of it so far as passage was for boats.[1] He told us of two islets in the river we should pass by, meaning that one whereon we were, and then come to an overfall[2] of water, beyond that [he told us] of two kingdoms which the river runs by, then, a great distance off, the mountains "Quirank," as he named them, beyond which by his relation is that which we expected.[3] This fellow parting from us promised to procure us wheat if we would stay a little before,[4] and for that intent went back again to provide it: but we coming by the place where he was, with many more very desirous of our company, stayed not, as being eager of our good tidings.[5] He notwithstanding with two women and another fellow of his own consort, followed us some six miles with baskets full of dried oysters, and met us at a point, where calling to us, we went ashore and bartered with them for most of their victuals. Here the shore began to be full of great cobblestones, and higher land. The river scants of his breadth two mile before we come to the islet mentioned, which I call "Turkey Isle," yet keeps it a quarter of a mile broad most commonly, and deep water for shipping.[6] This fellow with the rest overtook us again upon the doubling of another point. Now they had gotten mulberries, little sweet nuts like acorns (a very good fruit), wheat, beans and mulberries sodden together[7] and gave us. Some of them desired to be set over the river, which we did, and they parted. Now we passed a reach of three miles [and a] half in length, high stony ground on Popham Side five or six fathom eight oar's length from the shore. This day we went about thirty-eight miles and came to an anchor at a place I call "Poor Cottage," where we went ashore, and were used kindly by the people.[8] We sod our kettle by the water side within night, and rested aboard.[9]

Saturday we passed a few short reaches; and [within] five miles of Poor Cottage we went ashore. Here we found our kind comrades again, who had given notice all along as they came [in sight] of us: by which we were enter-

[1] As far as boats could go.
[2] Falls.
[3] I.e., his account was pretty much what we expected to hear; Quirank: this particular name for the mountains mentioned by the Wynauk mapmaker is obscure, but he presumably was referring to the Blue Ridge Mountains, inland about 150 miles from his village.
[4] I.e., delay a bit.
[5] More of the Wynauks very much wanted to meet the English, but Newport pushed on in order to keep the good "tidings," or news of discoveries, coming in.
[6] I.e., the river narrows about two miles downstream of Turkey Island (still so called, about forty miles upstream from the mouth of the James), but after that point is usually at least a quarter mile wide, and deep enough for ships to pass.
[7] Boiled together.
[8] Because the channel of the modern James has been shortened in this area, the precise location of the stretch of river along "Popham Side" where the bank was high and rocky and the water was thirty or thirty-five feet deep some fifty feet from shore is hard to establish, as is the place the author calls "Poor Cottage." Sir John Popham (1531–1607) was an influential English jurist and a strong backer of English settlement in Virginia; the author named the south bank or "side" of the James after him and called the north "Salisbury Side," after another important backer of the enterprise, Sir Robert Cecil, earl of Salisbury (1563?–1612).
[9] I.e., they boiled their food over fires on shore just as night came on and returned on the shallop to sleep.

tained with much courtesy in every place.[1] We found here a werowance (for so they call their kings) who sat upon a mat of reeds, with his people about him. He caused one to be laid for[2] Captain Newport, [and] gave us a deer roasted, which according to their custom they seethed again.[3] His people gave us mulberries, sodden wheat and beans, and he caused his women to make cakes[4] for us. He gave our captain his crown, which was of deer's hair dyed red. Certifying[5] him of our intention up the river, he was willing to send guides with us. This we found to be a king subject to Powhatan (the chief of all the kingdoms); his name is Arahatec, the country Arahatecoh.[6] Now as we sat merrily banquetting with them, seeing their dances, and taking tobacco, news came that the great king Powhatan was come: at whose presence they all rose off their mats (save King Arahatec), separated themselves apart in fashion of a guard, and with a long shout they saluted him. Him we saluted with silence sitting still on our mats, our captain in the midst; but presented (as before we did to King Arahatec) gifts of diverse sorts, as penny knives, shears, bells, beads, glass toys, etc. more amply than before. Now this king appointed five men to guide us up the river, and sent posts before to provide us victual. I caused now our kind consort that described the river to us, to draw it again before King Arahatec, who in every thing consented to this draft, and it agreed with his first relation.[7] This we found a faithful fellow, he was one that was appointed guide for us. Thus parting from Arahatec's Joy, we found the people on either side the river stand in clusters all along, still proferring us victuals, which of some were accepted; as our guides (that were with us in the boat) pleased, and gave them requital.[8] So after we had passed some ten miles, which (by[9] the pleasure and joy we took of[1] our kind entertainment, and for the comfort of our happy and hopeful discovery) we accounted scarce five, we came to the second islet

[1] I.e., the natives had shouted or signaled each time they came in sight of the shallop, whose upstream course they followed on land; the author adds that the natives generally were very courteous in "entertaining" (or serving as hosts for) the English.
[2] I.e., a mat to be spread out for.
[3] Boiled after having roasted it.
[4] Bread, perhaps in the shape of flat loaves.
[5] Informing.
[6] Wahunsonacock (1540s?–1618), who ruled a confederation of native groups in Virginia, took his name from his tribe's chief settlement, Powhatan, located near the present site of Richmond; it was his daughter Pocahontas who, according to a version of the story Captain John Smith told many years later, rescued that Englishman from execution after he was taken prisoner at the very end of 1607. One of the subchiefs who owed Powhatan obedience, Arahatec (or Arrohattoc), dwelled in a village downstream from Richmond, slightly inland from the northern shore site now occupied by Fort Brady and then the apparent location of "Arahatec's Joy," where Newport and his men "merrily" feasted with the natives.
[7] That is, Arahatec's account of the lay of the land agreed with that conveyed by the map drawn by the Wynauk man, who had been consorting with or accompanying Newport since first encountering the English. As the author next notes, the mapmaker was also sent on with them as a guide by Arahatec.
[8] I.e., the native guides decided which people to accept gifts from as the expedition went upstream, and gave out other gifts in return.
[9] Because of.
[1] From.

described in the river; over against which on Popham Side is the habitation of the great King Powhatan, which I call Powhatan's Tower. It is situated upon a high hill by the waterside, a plain between it and the water twelve score over, wheron he sows his wheat, beans, peas, tobacco, pompions,[2] gourds, hemp, flax, etc. And were any art used to[3] the natural state of this place, it would be a goodly habitation: Here we were conducted up the hill to the king, with whom we found our kind King Arahatec: These two sat by themselves apart from all the rest (save one who sat by Powhatan, and what he was I could not guess but they told me he was no werowance[4]). Many of his company sat on either side: and the mats for us were laid right over against the king's. He caused his women to bring us victuals, mulberries, strawberries, etc., but our best entertainment was friendly welcome. In discoursing with him, we found that all the kingdoms from the [Chesapeakes] were friends with him, and (to use his own word) "cheisc," which is "all one with him or under him." Also we perceived the Chesapeakes[5] to be an enemy generally to all these kingdoms: upon which I took occasion to signify our displeasure with them also: making it known that we refused to plant in their country; that we had wars with them also, showing hurts scarce whole[6] received by them, for which we vowed revenge, after their manner, pointing to the sun. Further we certified him that we were friends with all his people and kingdoms, neither had any of them offered us ill, or used us unkindly. Hereupon he (very well understanding by the words and signs we made the signification of our meaning) moved[7] of his own accord a league of friendship with us; which our captain kindly embraced; and for concluding therof, gave him his gown, put it on his back himself, and laying his hand on his breast saying "Wingapoh Chemuze" (the most kind words of salutation that may be)[8] he sat down. Now the day drawing on, we made sign to be gone, wherewith he was contented, and sent six men with us. We also left a man with him, and departed. But now rowing some three miles in shoal water we came to an overfall, impassable for boats any further. Here the water falls down through great main[9] rocks, from ledges of rocks above two fathom high, in which fall it maketh divers little islets, on which might be placed a hundred water mills for any uses. Our main river ebbs and flows four foot even to the skirt of this downfall.[1] Ships of two hundred or three hundred tons may come

[2]Pumpkins; twelve score over: a distance equal to 240 paces, or about six hundred to seven hundred feet.
[3]Applied to.
[4]Chief (Algonkian). In actuality, Newport's company did not meet Wahunsonacock himself here but his son Parahunt, known as Tanx ("little") Powhatan, who was the "werowance" of the village after which both of them were named.
[5]Chesapeakes: the people who lived along the Chesapeake Bay.
[6]Barely healed yet.
[7]Proposed.
[8]This Algonkian phrase might be rendered as "Greetings, good man!," though the second word is probably not properly given in the text.
[9]Large, strong.
[1]That is, the James has tides even up to the base of these falls at the site of Richmond.

to within five miles hereof, and the rest deep enough for barges,[2] or small vessels that draw not above six foot water. Having viewed this place, between content and grief we left it for this night, determining the next day to fit ourselves for a march by land. So we rode all night between Powhatan's Tower and that islet I call [left blank], whereon is six or seven families. One of our guides which we had from Arahatec's Joy, whose name was Navirans and [whom] now we found to be brother-in-law to King Arahatec, desired to sleep in the boat with us: we permitted him, and used him[3] with all the kindness we could. He proved a very trusty friend, as after is declared. Now we sent for our man to Powhatan, who coming told us of his entertainment, how they had prepared mats for him to lie on, gave him store[4] of victuals, and made as much on[5] him as could be.

Sunday, Whitsunday,[6] our captain caused two pieces of pork to be sodden ashore with peas; to which he invited King Powhatan: for Arahatec, persuading himself we would come down the river that night, went home before dinner, for preparation against our coming. But in presence of them both it fell out that we missing two bullet-bags which had shot and divers trucking toys[7] in them. We complained to these kings, who instantly caused them all to be restored, not wanting[8] anything. Howbeit, they had divided the shot and toys to (at least) a dozen several persons, and those also in the islet over the water; one also having stolen a knife, brought it again upon this command before we supposed it lost, or had made any sign for it. So Captain Newport gave thanks to the kings and rewarded the thieves with the same toys they had stolen, but kept the bullets, yet he made known unto them the custom of England to be death for such offenses.

Now Arahatec departed, and it being dinner time, King Powhatan with some of his people sat with us, brought of his diet,[9] and we fed familiarly, without sitting in his state as before; he ate very freshly of our meat, drank of our beer, aquavitæ, and sack.[1] Dinner done, we entered into discourse of the river—how far it might be to the head thereof, where they got their copper, and their iron, and how many days journey it was to Monacan, Rassawek[2] and the mountains Quirank, requesting him to have guides with us also in our intended march, for our captain determined to have travelled two or three days journey afoot up the river. But without giving any answer to our demands, he showed he would meet us himself at the overfall and so we parted. This Navirans

[2] That is, the final mile of the river below the falls is shallower, but smaller vessels still can operate there.
[3] Behaved toward him.
[4] A good helping.
[5] Of.
[6] Pentecost, the seventh Sunday after Easter in Christian practice; in this case, May 24.
[7] Cheap trading goods.
[8] Excepting.
[9] I.e., had his food brought out.
[1] Brandy or whiskey and wine; freshly: eagerly.
[2] Two towns of the Monacan people located upstream from Richmond.

accompanied us still in the boat. According to his promise he[3] met us; where the fellow whom I have called our kind consort, he that followed us from Turkey Isle, at the coming of Powhatan made sign to us we must make a shout, which we did. Now sitting upon the bank by the overfall beholding the same, he began to tell us of the tedious travel we should have if we proceeded any further, that it was a day and a half journey to Monacan, and if we went to Quirank, we should get no victuals and be tired, and [he] sought by all means to dissuade our captain from going any further. Also, he told us that the Monacan[4] was his enemy, and that he came down at the fall of the leaf and invaded his country. Now what I conjecture of this I have left to a further experience.[5] But our captain out of his discretion (though we would fain have seen further, yea and himself as desirous also) checked his intention and returned to his boat, as holding it much better to please the king (with whom and all of his command he had made so fair way) than to prosecute his own fancy or satisfy our requests.[6] So upon one of the little islets at the mouth of the falls he set up a cross with this inscription, "Jacobus Rex. 1607,"[7] and his own name below. At the erecting hereof we prayed for our king and our own prosperous success in this his action, and proclaimed him king, with a great shout. King Powhatan was now gone (and as we noted somewhat distasted[8] with our importunity of proceeding up further) and all the savages likewise save Navirans, who seeing us set up a cross with such a shout, began to admire,[9] but our captain told him that the two arms of the cross signified King Powhatan and himself, the fastening of it in the midst was their united league, and the shout the reverence he did to Powhatan, which cheered Navirans not a little. Also (which I have omitted) our captain before Powhatan departed showed him that if he would, he would give the werowance of Monacan into his hands, and make him king of that country, making signs to bring to his aid five hundred men, which pleased the king much, and upon this (I noted) he told us the time of the year when his enemies assail him.[1]

So far as we could discern the river above the overfall, it was full of huge

---

[3] I.e., Powhatan, meaning Tanx Powhatan.

[4] I.e., the leader of the Monacans.

[5] I.e., the author will decide what to think of this report when he has learned more.

[6] Both Newport and his men want to explore farther inland, but he gives up his "fancy" and his men's "requests" and accedes to the warnings of Tanx Powhatan, declining to go on.

[7] "James the King."

[8] Upset.

[9] Wonder, be awed.

[1] The author here adds an important point overlooked earlier in the narrative. Newport had offered to help (Tanx) Powhatan by capturing the werowance of Monacan, turning that enemy over to him, and installing him as ruler over the Monacans. Newport had asked in return (apparently) that Tanx Powhatan supply an army of five hundred men to accomplish this goal. Tanx Powhatan was pleased with this offer, responding with information about when the Monacan people usually raided his own country, information presumably of use in planning an offensive against them. Note, though, the author's recent point about Tanx Powhatan's "distaste" for the strong desire of the Englishmen to penetrate beyond his own territory into the hinterland where, among others, the Monacans lived.

rocks. About a mile off, it makes a pretty big island; It runs up between high hills which increase in height one above another so far as we saw. Now our kind consort's relation[2] saith (which I dare well believe, in that I found not any one report false of the river so far as we tried,[3] or that he told us untruth in anything else whatsoever) that after a day's journey or more, this river divides itself into two branches, which both come from the mountains Quirank. Here he whispered with me that their caquassan[4] was got in the bits of rocks and between cliffs in certain veins.

Having ended thus of force[5] our discovery, our captain intended to call of[6] King Powhatan, and sending Navirans up to him he came down to the waterside, where he[7] went ashore single unto him, presented him with a hatchet, and staying but till Navirans had told (as we truly perceived) the meaning of our setting up the cross, which we found did exceedingly rejoice him, he[8] came aboard, with the kindest farewell that possibly might be. Now at our putting off the boat, Navirans willed us to make a shout, which we did two several[9] times, at which the king and his company waved their skins about their heads, answering our shout with gladness in a friendly fashion.

This night (though late) we came to Arahatec's Joy, where we found the king[1] ready to entertain us, and had provided some victuals for us, but he told us he was very sick, and not able to sit up long with us, so we repaired[2] aboard.

Monday he came to the waterside, and we went ashore to him again. He told us that our hot drinks he thought caused his grief, but that he was well again, and we were very welcome.[3] He sent for another deer which was roasted and after sodden for us (as before). Our captain caused his dinner to be dressed[4] ashore also. Thus we sat banquetting all the forenoon. Some of his people led us to their houses, showed us the growing of their corn and the manner of setting[5] it, gave us tobacco, walnuts, mulberries, strawberries, and raspberries. One showed us the herb called in their tongue wisacan, which they say heals poisoned wounds; it is like liverwort or bloodwort.[6] One gave me a root wherewith they poison their arrows. They would show us anything we demanded, and labored very much by signs to make us understand their language.

---

[2] Account.
[3] I.e., as the English ascended the river to this point, he found none of what the "kind consort" had told them to be false.
[4] Apparently copper; whispered with: whispered to.
[5] Perforce, of necessity, though perhaps with a hint of Tanx Powhatan's forceful displeasure.
[6] On.
[7] Newport, to meet with "him"—i.e., Tanx Powhatan.
[8] Tanx Powhatan.
[9] I.e., twice.
[1] I.e., Arahatec.
[2] Returned.
[3] I.e., he welcomed them again; hot drinks: alcoholic beverages.
[4] Prepared.
[5] Planting.
[6] Two European medicinal plants, the first a lichen and the second either yarrow or smartweed; wisacan: an American medicinal plant with a bitter-tasting root, perhaps the milkweed.

Navirans our guide and this king's brother made a complaint to Arahatec, that one of his people pressed into our boat too violently upon a man of ours, which Captain Newport (understanding the proneness of his own men to such injuries)[7] misconstruing the matter, sent for his own man, bound him to a tree before King Arahatec, and with a cudgel soundly beat him. The king perceiving the error, stepped up and stayed our captain's hand and sitting still awhile, he spied his own man that did the injury, upon which he silently rose, and made towards the fellow. He seeing him come, run away, after ran the king, so swiftly as I assure myself he might give any of our company six score in twelve.[8] With the king ran also divers others, who all returning brought cudgels and wands in their hands all to be tewed, as if they had[9] beaten him extremely. At dinner our captain gave the king a glass and some aquavitæ therein, showing him the benefit of the water, for which he thanked him kindly, and taking our leave of him, he promised to meet us at a point not far off where he hath another house, which he performed, withal,[1] sending men into the woods to kill a deer for us if they could. This place I call "Mulbery Shade." He caused here to be prepared for us pegatewk-apoan, which is bread of their wheat made in rolls and cakes; this the women make, and are very cleanly about it; We had parched meal, excellent good,[2] sodden beans, which eat as sweet as filbert kernels in a manner, strawberries and mulberries new shaken off the tree dropping on our heads as we sat. He made ready a land turtle which we ate, and showed that he was heartily rejoiced in our company. He was desirous to have a musket shot off, showing first the manner of their own skirmishes, which we perceive is violent, cruel, and full of celerity; they use a tree to defend them in fight, and having shot an enemy that he fall,[3] they maul him with a short wooden sword. Our captain caused a gentleman discharge his piece soldier-like before him, at which noise he started, stopped his ears, and expressed much fear, so likewise all about him. Some of his people being in our boat leapt over board at the wonder hereof, but our course of kindness after, and letting him to wit that we never use this thunder but against our enemies, yea and that we would assist him with these to terrify and kill his adversaries, he rejoiced the more, and we found it bred a better affection in him towards us, so that by his signs we understood he would ere long be with us at our fort. Captain Newport bestowed on him a red waistcoat, which highly pleased him, and so departed, giving him

---

[7] Apparently Newport suspected that the English boatman in question was complaining without due cause—something the author claims his fellows were prone to do—thus perhaps putting a strain on relations with Arahatec and his people.

[8] I.e., might run half again as fast as any of the English, traveling 360 paces in the time they covered 240.

[9] Would have; tewed: worked into proper form, as with a rough raw material, by repeated and vigorous strokes.

[1] Moreover.

[2] I.e., very good.

[3] So that he falls. Considerable evidence from other early authors suggests, to the contrary, that Native American warfare was significantly less intense than that to which Europeans had become accustomed.

also two shouts as the boat went off. This night we went some miles, and anchored at a place I call "Kind Woman's Care," which is [*left blank*] mile from Mulberry Shade.[4] Here we came within night, yet was there ready for us [a meal] of bread new made, sodden wheat and beans, mulberries, and some fish undressed more than all we[5] could eat. Moreover, these people seemed not to crave anything in requital. Howbeit, our captain voluntarily distributed gifts.

Tuesday we parted from Kind Woman's Care, and by direction of Navirans (who still accompanied in the boat with us) went ashore at a place I call "Queen Apumatec's Bower."[6] He carried us along through a plain low ground prepared for seed, part whereof had been lately cropped, and ascending a pretty hill, we saw the queen of this country coming in selfsame fashion of state as Powhatan or Arahatec, yea rather with more majesty. She had an usher before her who brought her to the mat prepared under a fair mulberry tree, where she sat her down by herself with a staid countenance. She would permit none to stand or sit near her. She is a fat lusty manly woman. She had much copper about her neck, a crownet of copper upon her head; she had long black hair, which hanged loose down her back to her middle, which only part[7] was covered with a deerskin, and else all naked. She had her women attending on her adorned much like herself (save they wanted[8] the copper). Here we had our accustomed cates,[9] tobacco and welcome. Our captain presented her with gifts liberally, whereupon she cheered[1] somewhat her countenance, and requested him to shoot off a piece, whereat (we noted) she showed not near the like fear as Arahatec, though he be a goodly[2] man. She had much corn in the ground. She is subject to Powhatan as the rest are, yet within herself of as great authority as any of her neighbor werowances. Captain Newport stayed here some two hours and departed.

Now leaving her, Navirans directed us to one of King Pamunkey's houses some five miles from the Queen's Bower.[3] Here we were entertained with great joy and gladness, the people falling to dance, the women to preparing victuals, some boys were sent to dive for mussels. They gave us tobacco, and very kindly saluted us.

This king (sitting in manner of the rest) so set his countenance striving to

---

[4]Although the distance from Mulberry Shade to Kind Woman's Care is not stated by the author, both sites were located along the James downstream from Richmond.

[5]I.e., more than all of us.

[6]This village was located on the southern shore of the James near its confluence with the Appomattox River. Queen Apumatec (her proper name was Opossunoquonuske), the leader of a small village of Appamatuck Indians, was murdered in 1610 by English settlers seeking revenge for the deaths of fourteen colonists.

[7]Which part alone (i.e., only her waist was covered).

[8]Lacked.

[9]Usually, "delicacies," although here probably food in general.

[1]Brightened.

[2]Sturdy, courageous.

[3]The Pamunkey, the chief tribe of the Powhatan league, lived in the area near the head of the present York River under their king, Opechancanough, Powhatan's brother. The house in question here, however, was located on the James.

be stately, as to our seeming he became [a] fool. We gave him many presents, and certified him of[4] our journey to the falls, our league with the great king Powhatan, a most certain friendship with Arahatec and kind entertainment of the Queen, [adding] that we were professed enemies to the Chesapeakes, and would assist King Powhatan against the Monacans. With this he seemed to be much rejoiced; and he would have had our captain stay with him all night, which he refused not, but single with the king walked above two flight shot,[5] showing thereby his true meaning without distrust or fear. Howbeit, we followed aloof off,[6] and coming up to a gallant mulberry tree, we found divers preparing victuals for us, but the king seeing our intention was to accompany our captain, he altered his purpose and weaved us in kindness[7] to our boat. This Werowance Pamunkey I hold to inhabit a rich land of copper and pearl. His country lies into the land to another river, which by relation and description of the savages comes also from the mountains Quirank, but a shorter journey. The copper he had, as also many of his people, was very flexible. I bowed[8] a piece of the thickness of a shilling round about my finger, as if it had been lead. I found them nice in parting with[9] any. They wear it in their ears, about their necks in long links, and in broad plates on their heads, So we made no great inquiry of[1] it, neither seemed desirous to have it. The king had a chain of pearls about his neck thrice double,[2] the third part of them as big as peas, which I could not value less worth than three or four hundred pounds had the pearls been taken from the mussel[3] as it ought to be. His kingdom is full of deer (so also is most of all the kingdoms); he hath (as [do] the rest likewise) many rich furs. This place I call "Pamunkey's Palace," howbeit by Navirans' words the King of Wynauk is possessor hereof. The plot of ground is bare without wood, some one hundred acres, where are set beans, wheat, peas, tobacco, gourds, pompions, and other things unknown to us in our tongue.

Now having left this king in kindness and friendship, we crossed over the water to a sharp point which is part of Wynauk on Salisbury Side (this I call "Careless Point"[4]). Here some of our men went ashore with Navirans, met ten or twelve savages, who offering them neither victuals nor tobacco, they requited

---

[4] Informed him about.

[5] Twice the distance a long-distance arrow (called a "flight") might be shot, i.e., a half mile or more; single: singly, alone.

[6] A considerable distance behind.

[7] "Weave" probably suggests either a circuitous route, or a devious purpose, or both, though the force of "kindness" would seem to work the other way; the author may mean that the werowance, not pleased that Newport's men distrusted him, changed his plans to give them a feast and gradually "wove" them all back to the boat—but did so with diplomatic skill.

[8] Bent.

[9] Reluctant to give away.

[1] Request for.

[2] I.e., a double strand wrapped three times around his neck.

[3] I.e., oysters.

[4] A site perhaps five miles farther downstream from Apumatec's Bower, near Wynauk, as the author says.

their courtesy with the like, and left them. This night we came to Point Wynauk right against which we rested all night. There was an old man with King Pamunkey (which I omitted in place to specify)[5] who we understood to be one hundred and ten years old; for Navirans with[6] being with us in our boat had learned me so much of the language, and was so excellently ingenious in signing out his meaning, that I could make him understand me, and perceive him also well in anything. But this knowledge our captain got by taking a bough and singling off the leaves, let one drop after another, saying "caische," which is "ten," so first Navirans took eleven beans and told[7] them to us, pointing to this old fellow, then one hundred and ten beans, by which he answered to our demand for ten years a bean, and also every year by itself.[8] This was a lusty old man, of a stern countenance, tall and straight, had a thin white beard, his arms overgrown with white hairs, and he went[9] as strongly as any of the rest.

Wednesday we went ashore at Point Wynauk, where Navirans caused them to go a-fishing for us, and they brought us in a short space good store. These seemed our good friends but (the cause I know not) here Navirans took some conceit,[1] and though he showed no discontent, yet would he by no means go any further with us, saying he would but go up to King Arahatek, and then within some three days after he would see us at our fort. This grieved our captain very deeply, for the loving kindness of this fellow was such as he trusted himself with us out of his own country, intended to come to our fort, and as we came[2] he would make friendship for us, before he would let us go ashore at any place, being (as it seemed) very careful of our safety. So our captain made all haste home, determining not to stay in any place as fearing some disastrous hap[3] at our fort, which fell out as we expected, thus. After our departure they seldom frequented our fort, but by one or two singly now and then, practicing upon opportunity,[4] now in our absence, perceiving their secure carriage[5] in the fort, and the 26th of May, being the day before our return, there came above two hundred of them with their king and gave a very furious assault to our fort, endangering[6] their overthrow, had not the ship's ordinance with their small shot daunted them. They came up almost into the fort, shot through the tents, [and] appeared in this skirmish (which endured hot about an hour) a very valiant people. They hurt [among] us eleven men (whereof one died after) and

---

[5] I.e., which I forgot to say at the proper place.
[6] By.
[7] Counted.
[8] Navirans first used eleven beans, each representing (according to Newport's scheme) ten years, then counted out the full 110 beans, one for each of the man's years.
[9] Walked.
[1] Notion, idea.
[2] As we went along.
[3] Occurrence, accident.
[4] Looking for a chance (to do mischief).
[5] Reckless or overly secure behavior.
[6] Threatening.

killed a boy, yet perceived they not this hurt in us. We killed divers of them, but one we saw them tug off on their backs, and how many hurt we know not.[7] A little after they made a huge noise in the woods, which our men surmised was at the burying of their slain men. Four of the Council[8] that stood in front were hurt in maintaining the fort, and our president Master Wingfield (who showed himself a valiant gentleman) had one shot clean through his beard, yet escaped hurt.[9]

Thus having ended our discovery, which we hope may tend to the glory of God, his Majesty's renown, our country's profit, our own advancing, and fame to all posterity: we settled ourselves to our own safety, and began to fortify; Captain Newport worthily of his own accord causing his seamen to aid us in the best part thereof.[1]

Thursday we labored, pallisading our fort.

Friday the savages gave on[2] again, but with more fear, not daring approach scarce within musket shot. They hurt not any of us, but finding one of our dogs they killed him. They shot above forty arrows into, and about the fort.

Saturday, we were quiet.

Sunday they came lurking in the thickets and long grass, and a gentleman, one Eustace Clovell unarmed straggling without[3] the fort, [they] shot six arrows into him, wherewith he came running into the fort, crying, "Arm, Arm," these sticking still.[4] He lived eight days, and died. The savages stayed not, but ran away.

Monday some twenty appeared, shot divers arrows at random, which fell short of our fort, and ran away.

Tuesday, Wednesday: quiet and wrought upon fortification, clapboard, and setting of corn.[5]

Thursday by break of day three of them had most adventurously[6] stolen under our bulwark[7] and hidden themselves in the long grass; [they] spied a man of ours going out to do natural necessity, shot him in the head, and through the clothes in two places, but missed the skin.[8]

Friday: quiet.

---

[7] The point seems to be that although the English killed many of the attacking Paspaheghans, they only saw them carry off a single body.

[8] The governing body in the English colony.

[9] Edward Maria Wingfield (fl. 1586–1613) was the first president of the Council in Virginia. Despite the mockheroic "wound" he received here, he was an accomplished veteran of wars in Europe, but soon he fell out of favor with the colonists and in 1608 returned home to England.

[1] Christopher Newport was not a colonist but a ship's captain employed by the Virginia Company. Presumably he and his sailors did not have to help the settlers finish the fort, but volunteered.

[2] Came on.

[3] Outside.

[4] I.e., the arrows still sticking in him.

[5] Grain, not Indian corn; clapboard: split board used by coopers in making barrel staves.

[6] Boldly.

[7] Defensive wall.

[8] Apparently the man, who had gone out to "go to the bathroom," was not hit even by the arrow shot "in" (perhaps meaning "at") his head.

Saturday there being among the gentlemen and all the company a murmur and grudge against certain preposterous proceedings, and inconvenient courses,[9] put up a petition to the Council for reformation.

Sunday: no accident.[1]

Monday, Master Clovell died that was shot with six arrows sticking in him. This afternoon two savages presented themselves unarmed afar off crying "Wingapoh." There were also three more having bow and arrows. Those we conjectured came from some of those kings with whom we had perfect league. But one of our gentlemen guarding in the woods and having no commandment to the contrary[2] shot at them, at which (as their custom is) they fell down, and after[3] ran away, yet farther off we heard them cry "Wingapoh" notwithstanding.

Tuesday, in cutting down a great oak for clapboard, there issued out of the heart of the tree the quantity of two barricoes of liquor,[4] in taste as good as any vinegar, save a little smack[5] it took of the oak.

Wednesday the Council scanned[6] the gentlemen's petition, wherein[7] Captain Newport showing himself no less careful of our amity and combined friendship, than became him in the deep desire he had of our good, vehemently with ardent affection won our hearts by his fervent persuasion, to uniformity of consent, and calmed that, out of our love to him, with ease, which I doubt without better satisfaction had not contentedly been carried.[8] We confirmed faithful love one to another, and in our hearts subscribed an obedience to our superiors this day. Captain Smith was this day sworn one of the Council, who was elected in England.[9]

Thursday, articles and orders for Gentlemen and soldiers were upon the court of guard, and content was in the quarter.[1]

Friday, cutting down another tree, the like accident of vinegar proceeded.

---

[9] Plans, courses of action.

[1] I.e., nothing happened.

[2] I.e., not having been forbidden to do so.

[3] Afterward.

[4] Enough liquid to fill two small casks.

[5] Flavor.

[6] Reviewed, perhaps quickly.

[7] I.e., during the process of review.

[8] That is, because he cared so deeply for the unity of the colony, Newport eloquently argued that the Council members should bury their differences; out of their own love for him, they did just that, an amicable resolution that the author doubts they would have reached without some other, more powerful motive.

[9] John Smith had been elected in England, but the membership of the Council was kept secret until the colonists arrived in Virginia, by which point Smith, having tangled with those in charge when the ships were still on the way over, had been placed under arrest, and once they approached the West Indies he was being threatened with execution. That eventuality was avoided, however, and the subsequent discovery that he had been named to the Council caused some embarrassment for his opponents; he assumed his post, as the author here notes, just after Newport's return from his voyage upriver. By year's end, because of his force of character and his accomplishments as an explorer and fighter in Virginia, he was named the Council's "president"—in effect, the governor of the colony.

[1] In the barracks; "court of guard": guardhouse.

Saturday eight savages lay close among the weeds and long grass, and spying one or two of our mariners, Master John Cotson and Master Mathew Fitch by themselves, shot Mathew Fitch in the breast somewhat dangerously, and so ran away this morning. Our admiral's men[2] got a sturgeon of seven foot long which Captain Newport gave us.

Sunday, two savages presented themselves unarmed, to whom our president and Captain Newport went out. One of these was that fellow I call in my "Relation of Discovery" "our kind consort," being he we met at Turkey Isle. These certified us who were our friends, and who [our] foes, saying that King Pamunkey, King Arahatec, the King of Youghtanund, and the king of Mattapanieut would either assist us or make us peace with Paspahegh, Quiyoughcohannock, Wynauk, Apamatecoh, and Chescaik, our contracted enemies:[3] He counseled us to cut down the long weeds round about our fort, and to proceed in our sawing. Thus making signs to be with us shortly again, they parted.

Monday, we wrought upon clapboard for England.

Tuesday, two savages without from Salisbury Side being Quiyoughcohannock country, Captain Newport went to them in the barge imagining they had been our Sunday friends, but these were Quiyoughcohannocks and cried (treacherously) "Wingapoh," saying their king was on the other side of a point, where had our barge gone it was so shoaled water as they might have effected their villainous plot, but our admiral told them Quiyoughcohannock was matah and chirah,[4] whereat laughing they went away.

Wednesday, Thursday, Friday, Saturday: no accident.

Sunday, we had a communion. Captain Newport dined ashore with our diet,[5] and invited many of us to supper as a farewell.

[2] The admiral or chief officer of the colony's vessels was Newport.

[3] I.e., our united enemies. Among the groups named here who have not been encountered above, the Youghtanund and Mattaponient were members of the Powhatan league living, respectively, on the southern bank of the Pamunkey River and on the Mattapony. The Quiyougcohannock, also members of the Powhatan league, lived on the southern shore of the James, while the Chescaik or Kiskiack dwelled along the York.

[4] Undefined by the author, but evidently not terms of endearment; the two together may be related to the Algonkian "matchit," meaning "bad or evil."

[5] Mess; Newport was about to head back to England.

4

THE LENNI-LENAPE RECALL
HUDSON'S LANDING

THE ANNALS OF EARLY AMERICA ARE FULL OF THOSE MOMENTS OF "FIRST encounter" when the wandering, prospecting or invading Europeans ran across the local Native American population for the first time. In New England, the Pilgrims well remembered the place where they first heard and saw (and skirmished with) the natives: "So after we had given God thanks for our deliverance," wrote William Bradford, "we took our shallop and went on our journey, and called this place, *The first Encounter.* . . ." For the Native Americans the moment of encounter often proved just as memorable. Among the Lenni-Lenape, or Delaware, who in the year 1609 were living in the vicinity of the Hudson River, the story of Henry Hudson's first arrival in New York Bay proved so durable that it was passed down orally for almost two hundred years among their descendants. Sometime in the late eighteenth century a Moravian missionary from Pennsylvania, John Heckewelder, heard a version of it "from the mouth of an intelligent Delaware Indian," probably in far-off Ohio, where the land hunger of the Europeans to which the story makes reference had since driven the Lenni-Lenape.

In a manner typical of the crosscultural patterns often found in North American contexts, the story works in part by shifting its viewpoint (something Heckewelder cannot quite convey to his own readers), and by defamiliarizing European commonplaces—as when Hudson's ship was seen by the Lenni-Lenape as an "uncommonly large fish or animal" or a "big house floating on the sea." Only gradually, as the ship neared shore, did the Lenni-Lenape reshape their initial perceptions into a form the modern reader can more easily recognize, though even then the strange encounter left lingering mysteries behind. Some of these may be untangled by reference to a European account of the same events penned by the English sailor Robert Juet. Because Juet knew nothing of the way the natives saw his ship, his prose took on a relatively matter-of-fact tone at first ("This day the people of the country came aboard of us, seeming glad of our coming"), but deeper, more ominous hints also remained in his prose. He thus noted that after the visitors left the ship at night "we rode

49

very quiet, but durst not trust them," and went on to narrate several bloody exchanges as the voyagers explored the river's mouth and then sailed more than a hundred miles into the interior and returned. Both sides presumably would have agreed that the "encounter" by this point had become a kind of running war, although much of the violence has evaporated from the surviving Lenni-Lenape account.

Two further details in the Lenni-Lenape account also may be found woven into the pattern of Juet's narrative. When Hudson's ship drew close, the natives saw that it was "positively a house full of human beings, of quite a different color from that of the Indians, and dressed differently from them." In particular, they were taken with the man—was it Hudson?—"dressed entirely in red," whom they took to be their "Mannitto," or god, come to visit them. Juet knew nothing of the religious aura of the natives' vision, but he did record that during one of the encounters in the vicinity of Manhattan, Hudson took two natives hostage and—for a reason not explained, though it almost certainly had to do with the awe the Lenni-Lenape previously showed for the red-cloaked European—"put red coats on them, and would not suffer the others to come near us." The other detail in the Lenni-Lenape story that Juet's tale may explain concerns a later moment in the voyage. When the Europeans paused at the upper end of the river, near the site of the future city of Albany, the master and mate of the ship wanted to test the trustworthiness of the native leaders, perhaps Mahicans, in that vicinity. They accordingly took them down into the *Half Moon*'s cabin for a conference and proceeded to load them up with "so much wine and aqua vitae [brandy] that they were all merry. . . . In the end one of them was drunk . . . and that was strange to them; for they could not tell how to take it."

Of the request for land with which the Lenni-Lenape legend reported by Heckewelder ends, Juet said nothing, though the Lenni-Lenape may well have been condensing into a single visit events that over time reduced their hold on the river and its islands and shores. On the other hand, the Lenni-Lenape legend did not report what Juet wrote of another fatal encounter as the *Half Moon* passed back down the river on October 2, 1609. Two canoes of natives shot off arrows at the stern of the ship; the Europeans "discharged six muskets, and killed two or three of them." When a hundred of the natives crowded onto a point to shoot at the ship as it passed, Juet himself trained a cannon on them and killed two more. The natives fled into the woods, but soon another canoe came out and Juet broke it into pieces with cannonshot, killing "one of them" as his men "killed three or four more" with their muskets. That was the end of it. The ship passed downstream to Manhattan, where the men took note of "a very good piece of ground," and, Juet wrote, "saw no people to trouble us, and rode quietly all night. . . ."

John Heckewelder, who recorded the Lenni-Lenape version of events through the mist of time and the strategy of native memory, was born in Bedford, England, in 1743, and came to America at the age of eleven. Joining the Moravians, a Protestant sect that was among the first to stress the importance of mission work, Heckewelder served as a missionary in Ohio under the great David Zeisberger during the American Revolution, living with the Christian Indians there and trying to shield them from the westward push of the European settlers. He moved back to Pennsylvania after the war and survived there until 1823, publishing the book in which this story appears in 1819.

JOHN HECKEWELDER

from *History, Manners, and Customs of the Indian Nations* (1819)

THE LENNI-LENAPE CLAIM THE HONOR OF HAVING RECEIVED AND WELCOMED the Europeans on their first arrival in the country, situated between New England and Virginia. It is probable, however, that the Mahicanni or Mohicans, who then inhabited the banks of the Hudson, concurred in the hospitable act.[1] The relation I am going to make was taken down many years since from the mouth of an intelligent Delaware Indian, and may be considered as a correct account of the tradition existing among them of this momentous event. I give it as much as possible in their own language.

A great many years ago, when men with a white skin had never yet been seen in this land, some Indians who were out a fishing, at a place where the sea widens,[2] espied at a great distance something remarkably large floating on the water, and such as they had never seen before. These Indians immediately returning to the shore, apprised their countrymen of what they had observed, and pressed them to go out with them and discover what it might be. They hurried out together, and saw with astonishment the phenomenon which now appeared to their sight, but could not agree upon what it was; some believed it to be an uncommonly large fish or animal, while others were of opinion it must be a very big house floating on the sea. At length the spectators concluded that this wonderful object was moving towards the land, and that it must be an animal or something else that had life in it; it would therefore be proper to inform all the Indians on the inhabited islands of what they had seen, and put them on their guard. Accordingly they sent off a number of runners and watermen to carry the news to their scattered chiefs, that they might send off in every direction for the warriors, with a message that they should come on immediately. These arriving in numbers, and having themselves viewed the strange appearance, and observing that it was actually moving towards the entrance of the river or bay; concluded it to be a remarkably large house in

---

[1] The "River Indians" of the Hudson Valley, closely allied to the Lenni-Lenape or Delawares, and culturally one with the Pequots and Mohegans of New England.
[2] Presumably in lower New York Bay along the southeastern shore of Staten Island.

which the Mannitto (the Great or Supreme Being) himself was present, and that he probably was coming to visit them. By this time the chiefs were assembled at York island, and deliberating in what manner they should receive their Mannitto on his arrival. Every measure was taken to be well provided with plenty of meat for a sacrifice. The women were desired to prepare the best victuals. All the idols or images were examined and put in order, and a grand dance was supposed not only to be an agreeable entertainment for the Great Being, but it was believed that it might, with the addition of a sacrifice, contribute to appease him if he was angry with them. The conjurers were also set to work, to determine what this phenomenon portended, and what the possible result of it might be. To these and to the chiefs and wise men of the nations, men, women, and children were looking up for advice and protection. Distracted between hope and fear, they were at a loss what to do; a dance, however, commenced in great confusion. While in this situation, fresh runners arrive declaring it to be a large house of various colors, and crowded with living creatures. It appears now to be certain, that it is the great Mannitto, bringing them some kind of game, such as he had not given them before, but other runners soon after arriving declare that it is positively a house full of human beings, of quite a different color from that of the Indians, and dressed differently from them; that in particular one of them was dressed entirely in red, who must be the Mannitto himself. They are hailed from the vessel in a language they do not understand, yet they shout or yell in return by way of answer, according to the custom of their country; many are for running off to the woods, but are pressed by others to stay, in order not to give offence to their visitor, who might find them out and destroy them. The house (some say, large canoe) at last stops, and a canoe of a smaller size comes on shore with the red man, and some others in it; some stay with his canoe to guard it. The chiefs and wise men, assembled in council, form themselves into a large circle, towards which the man in red clothes approaches with two others. He salutes them with a friendly countenance, and they return the salute after their manner. They are lost in admiration; the dress, the manners, the whole appearance of the unknown strangers is to them a subject of wonder; but they are particularly struck with him who wore the red coat all glittering with gold lace, which they could in no manner account for. He, surely, must be the great Mannitto, but why should he have a white skin? Meanwhile, a large hackhack[3] is brought by one of his servants, from which an unknown substance is poured out into a small cup or glass, and handed to the supposed Mannitto. He drinks—has the glass filled again, and hands it to the chief standing next to him. The chief receives it, but only smells the contents and passes it on to the next chief, who does the same. The glass or cup thus passes through the circle, without the liquor being tasted by any one, and is upon the point of being returned to the red clothed Mannitto, when one of the Indians, a brave man and a great war-

---

[3] Hackhack is properly a gourd; but since they have seen glass bottles and decanters, they call them by the same name [Heckewelder's note].

rior, suddenly jumps up and harangues the assembly on the impropriety of returning the cup with its contents. It was handed to them, says he, by the Mannitto, that they should drink out of it, as he himself had done. To follow his example would be pleasing to him; but to return what he had given them might provoke his wrath, and bring destruction on them. And since the orator believed it for the good of the nation that the contents offered them should be drunk, and as no one else would do it, he would drink it himself, let the consequence be what it might; it was better for one man to die, than that a whole nation should be destroyed. He then took the glass, and bidding the assembly a solemn farewell, at once drank up its whole contents. Every eye was fixed on the resolute chief, to see what effect the unknown liquor would produce. He soon began to stagger, and at last fell prostrate on the ground. His companions now bemoan his fate, he falls into a sound sleep, and they think he has expired. He wakes again, jumps up and declares, that he has enjoyed the most delicious sensations, and that he never before felt himself so happy as after he had drunk the cup. He asks for more, his wish is granted; the whole assembly then imitate him, and all become intoxicated.

After this general intoxication had ceased, for they say that while it lasted the whites had confined themselves to their vessel, the man with the red clothes returned again, and distributed presents among them, consisting of beads, axes, hoes, and stockings such as the white people wear. They soon became familiar with each other, and began to converse by signs. The Dutch made them understand that they would not stay here, that they would return home again, but would pay them another visit the next year, when they would bring them more presents, and stay with them awhile; but as they could not live without eating, they should want a little land of them to sow seeds, in order to raise herbs and vegetables to put into their broth. They went away as they had said, and returned in the following season, when both parties were much rejoiced to see each other; but the whites laughed at the Indians, seeing that they knew not the use of the axes and hoes they had given them the year before; for they had these hanging to their breasts as ornaments, and the stockings were made use of as tobacco pouches. The whites now put handles to the former for them, and cut trees down before their eyes, hoed up the ground, and put the stockings on their legs. Here, they say, a general laughter ensued among the Indians, that they had remained ignorant of the use of such valuable implements, and had borne the weight of such heavy metal hanging to their necks, for such a length of time. They took every white man they saw for an inferior Mannitto attendant upon the supreme Deity who shone superior in the red and laced clothes. As the whites became daily more familiar with the Indians, they at last proposed to stay with them, and asked only for so much ground for a garden spot as, they said, the hide of a bullock[4] would cover or encompass, which hide was spread before them. The Indians readily granted this apparently reasonable request; but the whites then took a knife, and beginning at one end of the hide, cut it

[4] An ox or steer.

up to a long rope, not thicker than a child's finger, so that by the time the whole was cut up, it made a great heap; they then took the rope at one end, and drew it gently along, carefully avoiding its breaking. It was drawn out into a circular form, and being closed at its ends, encompassed a large piece of ground. The Indians were surprised at the superior wit of the whites,[5] but did not wish to contend with them about a little land, as they had still enough themselves. The white and red men lived contentedly together for a long time, though the former from time to time asked for more land, which was readily obtained, and thus they gradually proceeded higher up the Mahicannittuck,[6] until the Indians began to believe that they would soon want all their country, which in the end proved true.

---

[5] These Dutchmen were probably acquainted with what is related of Queen Dido in ancient history, and thus turned their classical knowledge to a good account. [Heckewelder's note. Dido, legendary founder of Carthage, was said to have tricked the natives of that vicinity by means of the same ruse.]

[6] The Hudson River.

5

THE LOST BOY OF
CAPE COD

IN MAY 1621, A YOUNG PLYMOUTH BOY BY THE NAME OF JOHN BILLINGTON, WHO
had arrived with his family on the *Mayflower* the previous fall, wandered off
from the English settlement there and was missing for some days before Governor William Bradford could learn of his whereabouts. His fellow settlers probably attributed his errancy to some inherited failing: it was the Billingtons, after
all, that Bradford later called "one of the profanest families amongst them."
Certainly they were one of the less lucky. John's younger brother Francis had
caused a potentially serious explosion of gunpowder on the vessel as it lay off
Cape Cod the past November. A couple of months later, he took off with one
of the sailors in search of "a great sea" he had glimpsed a week earlier from the
top of a tree on a hill, but it turned out to be a lake a couple miles inland and
only five or six miles around, still called in derision "Billington Sea." A later,
more serious impulse in 1630 led their father, John, to ambush and shoot dead
another settler, John Newcomen, with whom he had had a quarrel. John Billington, Sr. was found guilty of "wilful murder, by plain and notorious evidence"; he was the first English settler to be executed in the colony.

Young John's misadventures in the summer of 1621 were less extreme. He
"lost himself in the woods," Bradford wrote, "and wandered up and down some
five days, living on berries and what he could find." By that time, he managed
to "light on an Indian plantation twenty miles south of [Plymouth,] called
Manomet." The Native Americans dwelling at that site at the head of Buzzards
Bay were Wampanoags, whose leader, Massasoit, had befriended the Pilgrims
the previous year and signed a treaty with them. Nonetheless, the Indians upon
whom John Billington chanced sent him not back to Plymouth but in the
opposite direction—out onto Cape Cod, among the people with whom the
Pilgrims had clashed during their "first encounter" the previous fall, and whose
corn caches and graves they had unearthed. Whether Billington might have
figured as a hostage aimed at securing English reparations is unclear, although
the tension surrounding the arrival of his rescue party on the outer cape comes
across in the anonymous account of their expedition printed here.

ANONYMOUS

"A Voyage Made by Ten of Our Men to the Kingdom of Nauset," *from* **Mourts Relations** (1622)

THE 11TH OF JUNE [1621] WE SET FORTH, THE WEATHER BEING VERY FAIR, BUT ere we had been long at sea, there arose a storm of wind and rain, with much lightning and thunder, insomuch that a spout arose not far from us, but God be praised, it dured not long, and we put in that night for harbor at a place, called Cummaquid,[1] where we had some hope to find the boy. Two savages were in the boat with us, the one was Tisquantum our interpreter, the other Tokamahamon, a special friend.[2] It being night before we came in, we anchored in the midst of the bay, where we were dry at a low water. In the morning we espied savages seeking lobsters, and sent our two interpreters to speak with them, the channel being between them, where they told them what we were, and for what we were come, willing[3] them not at all to fear us, for we would not hurt them. Their answer was, that the boy was well, but he was at Nauset; yet since we were there they desired us to come ashore and eat with them, which as soon as our boat floated we did, and went six ashore, having four pledges[4] for them in the boat. They brought us to their sachem or governor, whom they call Iyanough, a man not exceeding twenty-six years of age, but very personable, gentle, courteous, and fair-conditioned, indeed not like a sav-

---

[1] Barnstable harbor, some thirty miles west of Nauset (Eastham).

[2] Tisquantum or Squanto (d. 1622) was apparently the last survivor of the Patuxet Indians, who had dwelled in the vicinity of what became Plymouth Plantation until a severe epidemic probably of European origin wiped them out in 1617. Squanto survived because with several other natives he had been kidnapped in 1614 by Captain Thomas Hunt, who intended to sell them into slavery in Spain. Squanto escaped and made his way to England, where he lived for a time in London before returning home in 1618 to find his people dead. He surprised the English settlers of Plymouth when they arrived two years later by his very serviceable skill in their own language. Squanto died while guiding an English expedition in the early fall of 1622; William Bradford wrote that he "fell sick of an Indian fever, bleeding much at the nose (which the Indians take for a symptom of death) and within a few days died there [on Cape Cod]; desiring the Governor [Bradford] to pray for him that he might go to the Englishmen's God in Heaven; and bequeathed sundry of his things to sundry of his English friends as remembrances of his love; of whom they had [i.e., felt] a great loss." Of Tokamahamon less is known; elsewhere in the volume in which this narrative was first published, Edward Winslow said he was appointed to serve in Squanto's stead when that guide went out on food-trading trips for the English, and was "found faithful before and after upon all occasions."

[3] Wishing.

[4] Apparently the remainder of the English party kept four Indians as hostages ("pledges") in the boat, while the other six settlers, as soon as the tide rose high enough for the boat to move, left to go ashore.

age, save for his attire;[5] his entertainment was answerable to his parts, and his cheer plentiful and various.[6]

One thing was very grievous unto us at this place. There was an old woman, whom we judged to be no less than a hundred years old, which came to see us because she never saw [any] English, yet could not behold us without breaking forth into great passion, weeping and crying excessively. We demanding the reason of it, they told us, she had three sons, who when master Hunt was in these parts went aboard his ship to trade with him, and he carried them captives into Spain (for Tisquantum at that time was carried away also) by which means she was deprived of the comfort of her children in her old age. We told them we were sorry that any Englishman should give them that offense, that Hunt was a bad man, and that all the English that heard of it condemned him for the same, but for us we would not offer them any such injury, though it would gain us all the skins[7] in the country. So we gave her some small trifles, which somewhat appeased her.

After dinner we took boat for Nauset, Iyanough and two of his men accompanying us. Ere we came to Nauset, the day and tide were almost spent, insomuch as we could not go in with our shallop,[8] but the sachem or governor of Cummaquid went ashore and his men with him. We also sent Tisquantum to tell Aspinet the sachem of Nauset[9] wherefore we came. The savages here came very thick amongst us, and were earnest with us to bring in our boat. But we neither well could,[1] nor yet desired to do it because we had least cause to trust them, being they only[2] had formerly made an assault upon us in the same place, in time of our winter discovery for habitation. And indeed it was no marvel they did so, for howsoever through snow or otherwise we saw no houses, yet we were in the midst of them.[3]

When our boat was aground they came very thick, but we stood therein

[5] Despite this warm description of Iyanough, in 1623 the English believed he was part of a conspiracy to wipe them out, which they learned of from their ally Massasoit, and they chased him from his home; taking refuge in a swamp, he soon died of illness or hunger.

[6] I.e., he offered the visitors a plentiful variety of food ("cheer"), his hospitality equaling ("answering") his personal characteristics ("parts").

[7] I.e., furs, keenly sought out by Europeans in their trade with the Native Americans.

[8] Small coasting vessel.

[9] This sachem of Nauset was leader of the people whom the English met in their "first encounter" on the Cape Cod beach in December 1620, when the English were seeking a place to spend the approaching winter. That tense episode had led to no real damage on either side, but the English clearly remembered Aspinet's domain with some dread, as the author goes on to note. On the other hand, the grief of the old woman suggests that the bad feelings of the natives in this wider region extended back before the arrival of the Pilgrims. Like Iyanough, Aspinet seems to have died as a result of the English campaign under Captain Myles Standish in 1623.

[1] I.e., it wasn't possible to bring the vessel in any closer.

[2] Perhaps the author wants to stress that the other local natives did not join in this encounter, or he may mean that the attackers had no provocation to do what they did.

[3] I.e., had the English seen evidence of thick habitation by the Nausets in this area the past winter, they might have been less startled by the attack.

upon our guard, not suffering any to enter except two, the one being of Mono-moyick, and one of those whose corn we had formerly found.[4] We promised him restitution, and desired him either to come to Patuxet for satisfaction, or else we would bring them so much corn again. He promised to come, we used him very kindly for the present. Some few skins we got there but not many.

After sunset, Aspinet came with a great train,[5] and brought the boy with him, one bearing him through the water. He had not less than a hundred with him, the half whereof came to the shallop's side unarmed with him, the other stood aloof with their bow and arrows. There he delivered us the boy, behung with beads, and made peace with us, we bestowing a knife on him, and likewise on another that first entertained the boy and brought him thither. So they departed from us.

Here we understood, that the Narragansetts had spoiled some of Massa-soit's men, and taken him. This struck some fear in us, because the colony was so weakly guarded, the strength thereof being abroad.[6] But we set forth with resolution to make the best haste home we could; yet the wind being contrary, having scarce any fresh water left, and at least sixteen leagues home,[7] we put in again for the shore. There we met again with Iyanough the sachem of Cum-maquid, and the most of his town, both men, women and children with him. He being still willing to gratify us, took a runlet[8] and led our men in the dark a great way for water, but could find none good, yet brought such as there was on his neck[9] with them. In the meantime the women joined hand in hand, singing and dancing before the shallop, the men also showing all the kindness they could, Iyanough himself taking a bracelet from about his neck, and hang-ing it upon one of us.

Again we set out but to small purpose, for we got but little homeward. Our water also was very brackish, and not to be drunk.

The next morning, Iyanough espied us again and ran after us; we being resolved to go to Cummaquid again to water, took him into the shallop, whose entertainment was not inferior unto the former.

The soil at Nauset and here is alike, even and sandy, not so good for corn as where we are. Ships may safely ride in either harbor. In the summer, they abound with fish. Being now watered, we put forth again, and by God's provi-dence, came safely home that night.

---

[4]When the Pilgrims scoured the area around Chatham (Monomoyick) the previous winter, they had unearthed some pits filled with maize, which they commandeered for their own use. One of the two men they let into their shallop on the present occasion apparently had been among those plundered of his grain.

[5]Retinue.

[6]The Narragansetts, who inhabited the bay named for them in what later became Rhode Island, were a powerful people who showed considerable resistance to English intrusion. The report of their capture of the English ally Massasoit, although apparently false, worried the travelers because with their own absence from Plymouth very few defenders were left there.

[7]I.e., to go until arriving home.

[8]Cask.

[9]I.e., Cape Cod, his "neck" of land.

6

THE MURDER OF JOHN SASSAMON

AND

THE START OF "KING PHILIP'S WAR"

QUAKER JOHN EASTON, BORN IN WALES, WAS BROUGHT TO MASSACHUSETTS with his family in 1634. His father, Nicholas Easton, left that colony four years later because of persecution for his beliefs and settled in Rhode Island, where eventually he was to serve as governor. John himself became Rhode Island's attorney general in 1653, its deputy governor in 1674, and finally its governor from 1690 to 1695. He survived until 1705. During his term as deputy governor, Rhode Island became involved in a bitter and bloody war fought largely between the united forces of the Puritan colonies of Massachusetts, Connecticut, and Plymouth and an alliance of Native Americans of the Wampanoag, Narragansett, and Nipmuc tribes. Because the territory of the first two of these native peoples adjoined Rhode Island, that colony was inevitably drawn into the conflict even though it sought to avoid bloodshed and had long endeavored to mediate differences between the natives and the Europeans.

The causes of "King Philip's War," as the conflict was to be known because its main Indian leader was the Wampanoag sachem Metacomet (named "King Philip" by the English), were many and complex. Ever since the 1630s, when the English had ruthlessly attacked and sought to exterminate the Pequot of eastern Connecticut, continued antagonisms among native groups displaced by the invading English had kept the region on edge. These outbreaks alternated with repeated rumors that several of the groups might find common cause in their collective injury at the hands of the English and form a league against the latter. For the most part, the English succeeded in keeping such a league from forming, but by the mid-1670s one seemed about to come into existence. Triggered by the suspicious death of his brother Wamsutta (or Alexander), Metacomet's anger drove him to seek allies; the English, on the other hand, saw a wider conspiracy than probably existed, and their own hasty actions against the technically neutral Narragansetts drove the remainder of that people into Philip's camp. Although the English at last "won" the war, they did so after appalling losses to themselves and the native peoples. John Easton was well placed to comment on the first parts of this war, most of which took place in the vicinity of Narragansett Bay. As a resident of Newport, located on the southern end of Aquidneck Island, and as deputy governor of the colony, Easton was privy to events in the field there as well as to diplomatic, military, and political events taking place across the wider region. Apparently he wrote his narrative during a lull in the war early in February 1676 (the date at the end, "5th : 12m : 1675," when corrected for different calendrical practices then in use, in fact means February 5th, 1676) and perhaps he intended it for Sir Edmund Andros, governor of the colony of New York and his own choice as a possible arbitrator between the Puritan authorities and the Native Americans. At the close of 1675, the English army had surprised the Narragansetts—with whom they pretended to still be negotiating—at the secret fort they had built for themselves in the Great Swamp west of Narragansett Bay. Many of the warriors were killed in the ensuing battle (the English also lost many men), but the more appalling destruction came when the village was set on fire by the English, causing the horrible deaths of perhaps several hundred native women, children, and old men. Easton's antagonism for the Puritans clearly fuels his angry narrative of these events, but it is his pacifist ideology, not just his local jealousy, that ultimately drives his historical conception. Little is more revealing on this front than his potentially dangerous embassy to the village occupied by Metacomet on Mount Hope Peninsula, where he endeavored to convince the natives that binding arbitration with the English might work if he could bring an impartial governor from outside the region to serve as one of the arbitrators. Unfortunately, this effort at peaceful negotiation was broken by the coming of an English army, and thereafter it was violence that was to decide the conflict.

JOHN EASTON

"A Relation of the Indian War" (1676)

IN THE WINTER IN THE YEAR 1674 AN INDIAN WAS FOUND DEAD, AND BY A CORONER's inquest of Plymouth Colony judged murdered. He was found dead in a hole through ice broken in a pond, with his gun and some fowl by him. Some English supposed him thrown in, some Indians that I judged intelligible[1] and impartial in that case did think he fell in and was so drowned and that the ice did hurt his throat, as the English said it was cut, but acknowledged that sometimes naughty[2] Indians would kill others but, not as ever they heard to obscure [the deed], as if the dead Indian was not murdered.[3] The dead Indian was called Sassamon and [was] a Christian that could read and write. Report was

---

[1] Intelligent.
[2] Evil.
[3] I.e., but did not conceal the fact of the murder.

he was a bad man, that King Philip got him to write his will and he made the writing for a great part of the land to be his[4] but read as if it had been as Philip would,[5] but it came to be known and then he ran away from him. Now one Indian informed that three Indians had murdered him, and showed a coat that he said they gave him to conceal them;[6] the Indians report that the informer had played away[7] his coat, and these men sent him that coat, and after[8] demanded pay, and he not to pay so accused them,[9] and knowing it would please the English so to think him a better Christian. And the report came, that the three Indians had confessed and accused Philip so to employ them, and that the English would hang Philip. So the Indians were afraid, and reported that the English had flattered them (or [cowed] by threats) to belie Philip [so] that they might kill him to have his land and that if Philip had done it, it was their law so to execute [whom] their kings judged deserved it, [and] that he had no cause to hide it.[1]

So Philip kept his men in arms. [The] Plymouth governor required him to disband his men, and informed him his jealousy[2] was false. Philip answered he would do no harm, and thanked the governor for his information. The three Indians were hung, to the last [denying] the fact, but one broke the halter as it is reported, then desired to be saved and so was a little while, then confessed they three had done the fact and then he was hanged. And it was reported Sassamon, before his death, had informed of the Indian plot and [said] that if the Indians knew it they would kill him, and that the heathen might destroy the English for their wickedness as God had permitted the heathen to destroy the Israelites of old. So the English were afraid and Philip was afraid and both increased in arms, but for forty years' time reports and jealousies of war had been [so] very frequent that we did not think that now a war was breaking forth. But about a week before it did we had cause to think it would; then to endeavor to prevent it, we sent a man to Philip [to say] that if he would come to the ferry we would come over to speak with him. About four miles we had to come

[4] Sassamon's.
[5] Wanted (it to be); read: read (the will) aloud.
[6] I.e., to conceal their murder of Sassamon; the accuser was named Patuckson and the three Wampanoag Indians he implicated were Tobias, his son Wampapaquan, and Mattashunnamo. The body was found in Assawompsett Pond, located between the village of Plymouth and Rhode Island.
[7] Lost in gambling.
[8] Later.
[9] I.e., in order to avoid paying them, he accused them of the crime; Easton goes on to add that he also thought the English would be impressed with his Christian piety if he turned the others in.
[1] Easton's points in this difficult sentence are that: the three Indians confessed but accused Metacomet of ordering them to kill Sassamon; after confessing they became afraid that the English would use their accusation of Metacomet as a pretext for executing him so that they could seize his lands; they then claimed that the English had either talked or bullied them into implicating him; and that if he indeed was to blame, Indian law was adequate to deal with him, and he would have no reason to conceal the crime.
[2] Suspicion.

thither. [When] our messenger came to them, they not [being] aware of it behaved themselves as furious,[3] but suddenly [were] appeased when they understood who he was and what he came for. He[4] called his council and agreed to come to us. [He] came himself unarmed, and about forty of his men, armed.

Then five of us went over, three [of whom] were magistrates. We sat very friendly together. We told him our business was to endeavor that they might not receive or do wrong. They said that was well, they had done no wrong, the English wronged them. We said we knew the English said the Indians wronged them and the Indians said the English wronged them but our desire was the quarrel might rightly be decided in the best way, and not as dogs decided their quarrels. The Indians owned that fighting was the worst way, then they propounded[5] how right might take place; we said by arbitration. They said all the English agreed against them, and so by arbitration they had had much wrong, many miles square of land being so taken from them. For [the] English would have English arbitrators, and once they were persuaded to give in their arms that[6] thereby jealousy might be removed . . . the English having their arms would not deliver them as they had promised, until they consented to pay a hundred pounds. And now they had not so much land or money, that they [might] as good be killed as leave all their livelihood.[7] We said they might choose an Indian king, and the English might choose the Governor of New York[8] that neither [would have] cause to say either were parties in the difference. They said they had not heard of that way[9] and said we honestly spoke, so we were persuaded if that way had been tendered[1] they would have accepted.

We did endeavor not to hear their complaints, said it was not convenient for us now to consider of,[2] but to endeavor to prevent war, said to them [that] when, in war against English, blood was spilt, that engaged all Englishmen, for we were to be all under one king. We knew what their complaints would be, and in our colony had removed some of them in sending for Indian rulers in what[3] the crime concerned Indians' lives, which they very lovingly accepted and agreed with us to their execution and said so they were able to satisfy their

---

[3] Furiously.

[4] Metacomet.

[5] Propounded the question, i.e., inquired.

[6] So that.

[7] In 1671, during an earlier tense period, the Plymouth authorities had summoned Metacomet to the town of Taunton, northwest of his domain on Mount Hope Peninsula, where they required the disarming of his followers. Although the English claimed that this edict was to cover all his people and was to be permanent, Metacomet said he thought it was merely temporary, and many of his followers not then present ultimately refused to comply. The English at last gave in, but required that he pay the sum indicated to retrieve the withheld weapons of his own smaller party at the Taunton meeting.

[8] Sir Edmund Andros; the Rhode Islanders are proposing a means to insure that the arbitrators are not interested parties in the dispute they are to resolve.

[9] I.e., the use of disinterested go-betweens.

[1] Proposed.

[2] Given consideration to.

[3] Insofar as; rulers: judges.

subjects when they knew an Indian suffered duly.[4] But [they] said in what was only between their Indians and not in townships that we had purchased, they would not have us prosecute and that they had a great fear to have[5] any of their Indians should be called or forced to be Christian Indians. They said that such were in everything more mischievous, only dissemblers, and then the English made them not subject to their kings, and by their lying [made them] to wrong their kings. We knew it to be true, and we promising them that . . . in government to Indians all should be alike, and that we knew it was our king's will it should be so, that although we were weaker than other colonies, they having submited to our king to protect them, others dared not otherwise to molest them. So they expressed they took that to be well, [and] we had little cause to doubt but that to us, under the king, they would have yielded to our determinations in what any should have complained to us against them. But Philip charged it to be dishonesty in us to put off the hearing [of] the complaints.

Therefore we consented to hear them. They said they had been the first in doing good to the English, and the English the first in doing wrong, [and] said when the English first came their king's father was as a great man and the English as a little child. He constrained other Indians from wronging the English and gave them corn and showed them how to plant and was free to do them any good[6] and had let them have a hundred times more land, than now the king had for his own people, but their king's brother when he was king came miserably to die by being forced to court as they judged poisoned.[7] And another grievance was if twenty of their honest Indians testified that a Englishman had done them wrong, it was as nothing, and if but one of their worst Indians testified against any Indian or their king when it pleased the English that was sufficient. Another grievance was when their kings sold land the English would say it was more than they[8] agreed to and a writing must be proof against all them,[9] and some of their kings had done wrong to sell so much [that] he left his people none, and some being given to drunkness the English made them drunk and then cheated them in bargains. But now their kings were forewarned not for to part with land for nothing in comparison to the value thereof. Now whom the English had owned for king or queen they would disinherit, and make another king that would give or sell them their land,[1] [so]

---

[4] According to due process.

[5] Lest.

[6] I.e., he had freely sought to do anything that was to their benefit.

[7] Metacomet's brother Wamsutta, who succeeded their father Osemaquin, or Massasoit, in 1661, was suspected of stirring up his people against the English in 1662. He died under suspicious circumstances after having been summoned by the English to Duxbury. His people believed he had been poisoned, but that seems unlikely.

[8] The kings.

[9] I.e., whatever the Indian leaders might say, the English would produce documents that would offset their testimony.

[1] I.e., the English would refuse to recognize native leaders whom they had once recognized; instead, they would set up a "puppet" chief who would give them or sell them native lands they wanted.

that now they had no hopes left to keep any land. Another grievance [was that] the English cattle and horses still increased [so] that when they removed thirty miles from where [the] English had anything to do, they could not keep their corn from being spoiled, they never being used to fence, and thought when the English bought land of them that they would have kept their cattle upon their own land.[2] Another grievance [was that] the English were so eager to sell the Indians liquors that most of the Indians spent all in drunkeness and then ravened[3] upon the sober Indians and, they did believe, often did hurt the English cattle, and their kings could not prevent it. We knew before these were their grand complaints, but then we only endeavored to persuade that all complaints might be righted without war. But [we] could have no other answer but that they had not heard of that way, [that is,] for the Governor of York and an Indian king to have the hearing of it. We had cause to think if that had been tendered it would have been accepted. We endeavored[4] that, however, they should lay down their arms, for the English were too strong for them. They said, then the English should do to them as they did when they were too strong for the English.

So we departed without any discourteousness, and suddenly had [a] letter from [the] Plymouth governor [that] they intended in arms to conform[5] Philip, but no information [regarding] what . . . they required or what terms he refused to have their quarrel decided,[6] and in a week's time after we had been with the Indians the war thus began. Plymouth soldiers were come to have their headquarters within ten miles of Philip. Then most of the English thereabout left their houses and we had [a] letter from [the] Plymouth governor to desire our help with some boats if they had such occasion[7] and for us to look to ourselves. And from the general[8] at the quarters we had [a] letter [informing us] of the day they intended to come upon the Indians and [expressing a] desire for some of our boats to attend, so we took it to be of necessity for our Islanders, one half one day and night to attend and the other half next, so by turns, for our own safety. In this time some Indians fell a-pilfering some houses that the English had left, and a old man and a lad going to one of those houses did see three Indians run out thereof. The old man bid the young man shoot, so he did, and a[n] Indian fell down but got away again. It is reported that then some Indians come to the garrison asked why they shot the Indian. They asked

---

[2] The English and the Native Americans both farmed, but as with much else in the two cultures the ways they farmed also came into conflict. The main problem was that the English were accustomed to fencing in crop fields and letting their domestic animals forage elsewhere in the landscape. The Indians originally had no livestock and therefore used no fences; as a consequence, their fields were often devastated by wandering English stock.

[3] Preyed (the raven is a carrion eater).

[4] I.e., to convince them.

[5] Bring into conformity—with English wishes.

[6] I.e., Plymouth refused to state its demands or the counterdemands it found unacceptable—leaving no hope for negotiation.

[7] I.e., occasion to employ boats in a naval operation.

[8] Major James Cudworth of Plymouth, commander in chief of the English forces.

whether he was dead. The Indians said "yea." A[n] English lad said it was no matter. The men endeavored to inform them it was but an idle lad's words but the Indians in haste went away and did not harken to them. The next day the lad that shot the Indian and his father and five English more were killed, so the war began with Philip.

But there was a queen that I knew was not a party with Philip and [the] Plymouth governor recommended[9] her that if she would come to our Island it would be well, and she desired she might, if it were but with six of her men.[1] I can sufficiently prove, but it is too large here to relate, that she had practiced much[2] the quarrel might be decided without war, but some of our English also in fury against all Indians would not consent she should be received to our island. . . . I proffered to be at all the charge to secure her and those she desired to come with her,[3] so at length prevailed we might send for her. But one day accidentally we were prevented, and then our men had seized some canoes on her side, supposing they were Philip's, and the next day a[n] English house was there burned and mischief of either side endeavored[4] to the other and much done, [and] her houses burned, so we were prevented of any means to attain her. The English army came not down as [we were] informed they would so Philip got over and they could not find him.[5] Three days after they came down [we] had a very stormy night, [so] that in the morning the foot were disabled to return before they had refreshment. They were free to accept as we were willing to relieve them, but [the] [Boston] troopers said [by] their captain they despised it and so left the foot.[6] After the foot had refreshed themselves they also returned to their headquarters, and after hunt[ing] Philip from all sea shores [so] that they could not tell what was become of him, the Narragansett kings

[9] Advised; the "queen" was Weetamoo, of Pocasset, on the mainland east of Aquidneck Island; she had been the wife of Metacomet's dead brother Wamsutta, called by the English "Alexander." The events narrated in this section can be dated with some accuracy: the pilfering of the English houses near Swansea, just north of Mount Hope, occurred on 20 June; the shooting of the looter by the young lad took place on June 23rd, while the lad in turn was killed on the 24th.
[1] I.e., as long as she could bring along six of her men.
[2] I.e., Tried very hard in order that.
[3] I.e., Easton promised that he would shoulder all the work entailed in bringing Weetamoo and her entourage to "the island." By "charge," he may or may not be referring as well to the expenses involved.
[4] Done; Easton's general point is that raids by either side antagonized both, so that no conference could take place.
[5] The "English army" sent from Boston on June 26th (three days after the "English lad" mentioned earlier was himself killed) consisted of a company of militia or foot soldiers from several Massachusetts towns, under the command of Captain Daniel Henchman, and a company of mounted "troopers" under Captain Thomas Prentice.
[6] On June 30th, after they had swept south the entire length of Metacomet's Mount Hope Peninsula (without finding any of Metacomet's people, who apparently had fled by boat), the hungry soldiers had provisions made available to them by the local Rhode Island settlers. The troopers voiced through their captain (Thomas Prentice) their contempt at the food that was provided and rode off, leaving the infantry and the accompanying Plymouth army behind. As Easton suggests below, the Rhode Islanders did not especially welcome the "English" army, so what they offered as provisions may have been intentionally meagre or unappealing.

informed us that the queen aforesaid must be in a thicket a-starving or con-
formed to Philip. But they knew she would be glad to be from them, so from
us had encouragement to get her and as many as they could from Philip.

After the English army without our consent or informing us came into our
colony, [and] brought the Narragansett Indians to articles of agreement to
them, Philip being fled, about 150 Indians came into a Plymouth garrison voluntarily. Plymouth authority sold all for slaves (but about six of them) to be
carried out of the country.[7] It is true the Indians generally are very barbarous
people, but in this war I have not heard of their tormenting any but that the
English army caught an old Indian and tormented him. He was well known to
have been a long time a very decrepit and harmless Indian of the queen's. As
Philip fled the foresaid queen got to the Narragansetts [with] as many of her
men as she could get. But one part of the Narragansetts' agreement to Boston
[being] to kill or deliver as many as they could of Philip's people, therefore
[the] Boston men demanded the foresaid queen and others that they had so
received. For which the Indians were unfree[8] and made many excuses, [such]
as that the queen was none of them and some others were but sojourners with
Philip because removed by the English having got their land and were of their
kindred, which we know is true. Not but we think they did shelter many they
should not, and that they did know some of their men did assist Philip, but
according to their barbarous rules they accounted so[9] was no wrong or they
could not help it; but some enemies' heads they did send in, and told us they
were informed that . . . when winter came they might be sure the English
would be their enemies, and so they stood doubtful for about five months.

The English were jealous that there was a general plot of all Indians
against [the] English, and the Indians were in like manner jealous of the
English. I think it was general that they were unwilling to be wronged and that
the Indians do judge the English [to be] partial against them, and among all[1]
[there was] a filthy crew that did desire and endeavor for war [while] those of
any solidity[2] were against it and endeavored to prevent the war. Concerning
Philip we have good intelligence that he advised some English to be gone from
their outplaces[3] where they lived or they were in danger to be killed, but [it is
unclear] whether it were to prevent a war, or [he was] by their priests informed
if they began they should be beaten and otherwise not[4] (so we have good intelli-

---

[7] The selling of Indian captives into slavery was a not uncommon English practice during the war:
Metacomet's own little son, whom the English seized and whom some of them wanted to execute
for his father's crimes, was given the more "lenient" punishment of being sold into slavery in the
West Indies. The "articles of agreement" referred to above constituted the Narragansett Treaty of
July 15th.
[8] Unwilling.
[9] Such.
[1] On both sides.
[2] Moral soundness; Easton's pacifism is evident here.
[3] Outlying settlements or isolated houses.
[4] I.e., if Metacomet began hostilities, he would be defeated, but if the English began them he
would win.

gence, for I do think most of them had a desire the English would begin). And if the English be not careful to [make] manifest [that] the Indians may expect equity from them, they may have more enemies than they would [want] and more cause of jealousy.[5]

The report is that to the eastward the war thus began, by supposing that some of those Indians were at a fight in these parts and that there they saw a man wounded. So [those in] authority sent some forth to discover, having before disarmed those Indians and confined them to a place, which the Indians were not offended at. But those men coming upon them in a warlike posture they fled [so] that the men caught but three of them. Those in authority sent out again to excuse themselves, but they could only come to the speech with[6] one man as he[7] kept out of their reach. They excused themselves and said his father was not hurt, [he being] one of them they had taken. [The man] said he could not believe them, for if it were so they would have brought him; they had been deceitful to disarm them and so would have killed them all. And so he ran away. And then [some] English were killed, and the report is that up in the country hereaway they had demanded the Indians' arms and went again to parley with them and the Indians by ambuscade treacherously killed eight that were going to treat with them.[8]

When winter was come we had [a] letter from Boston of[9] the United Commissioners[1] that thay were resolved to reduce the Narragansetts to conformity [so as] not to be troubled with them anymore and desired some help of boats and otherwise if we saw cause and that we should keep secret concerning it.[2] Our governor sent them word we were satisfied [the] Narragansetts were treacherous, and had aided Philip, and as we had assisted to relieve their army before so we should be ready to assist them still, and advised[3] that terms might be tendered that such[4] might expect compensation that would accept not to

---

[5] I.e., unless the English make it clear to the Indians that the latter will be treated fairly, they will make more enemies and arouse more suspicion.

[6] Manage to speak with.

[7] Evidently the peaceful Wannalancet, leader of the Pennacook in the upper Merrimack valley.

[8] I.e., try to reach a treaty with them. Wannalancet sought to keep his people out of the conflict and withdrew farther north, but in September 1675 a raiding party under the hotheaded Captain Samuel Moseley fell upon them and burned one of their villages. The authorities at Boston, chagrined at his deed, sought to make amends but the Pennacook had withdrawn even farther north and could not be contacted. Easton cannot have known much, if anything, about this situation on his own authority; his account of the one native whose father had been taken prisoner sounds circumstantial, but the report of the ambush of the Boston emissaries by the Pennacook is almost certainly without any foundation in fact.

[9] From.

[1] The New England Confederation, formed in 1643 by Massachusetts Bay, Plymouth, and Connecticut, was an organization whose six commissioners could issue directives to the constituent colonies.

[2] Rhode Island was not a member of the confederation, but the pressure that had brought a resistant Roger Williams into the war on its side obviously was being exerted in other ways, too — as through sending this letter to the authorities there.

[3] Urged, recommended.

[4] I.e., of the Narragansetts.

engage in war and that there might be a separation between the guilty and the innocent, which in war could not be expected. We not in the least expecting they[5] would have begun the war and not before proclaimed it or not given them defiance[6] (I having often informed the Indians that Englishmen would not begin a war otherwise, [for] it was brutish so to do), I am sorry so the Indians have cause to think me deceitful for the English thus began the war with the Narragansetts; we having sent off our island many Indians and informed them if they kept by the watersides and did not meddle that . . . the English would do them no harm, although it was not safe for us to let them live here.

The army first took all those prisoners, then fell upon Indian houses, burned them and killed some men. The war [began] without proclamation and some of our people did not know the English had begun mischief to the Indians. And being confident (and [having] cause therefore)[7] that the Indians would not hurt them before the English began, [they] did not keep their garrison exactly, but the Indians, having received that mischief, came unexpected upon them, destroyed [fourteen][8] of them beside other great loss, [although] the English army say they supposed Connecticut forces had been there.[9] They sold the Indians that they had taken as aforesaid, for slaves, [except for] one old man that was carried off our island upon his son's back. He was so decrepit [he] could not go[1] and when the army . . . carried him to the garrison, some

[5] The English.

[6] Seeking to pressure the Narragansetts to abide by previous agreements and to back away from supporting Metacomet, the United Commissioners issued a stern warning to the tribe on November 12th. Their expedition to the Narragansett country aimed at implementing these English demands, but in the field it soon degenerated into an army of attack on them and on various other native groups in the Narragansett Bay country. Some parties regarded the November 12th warning as in effect a declaration of war, but Easton, like others in his camp, obviously did not view it in that light and hence found the attacks on the Narragansetts to be treacherous.

[7] I.e., having good reason to be confident.

[8] Easton's figure for the English dead in this attack is variously given as 145 or fourteen; the former seems an error.

[9] In this section of the narrative the question of when Easton wrote it becomes critical. The English armies from Connecticut, Massachusetts, and Plymouth did not converge on the Narragansett country until mid-December. Easton apparently refers to the early skirmishes of their campaign in this section, including attacks on several villages on the western shore of Narragansett Bay, one of which took place on December 14th and resulted in the capture of many prisoners and the burning of many native houses. His reference to a counteroffensive by the Narragansetts may well refer to an attack on the Jireh Bull garrison house at Pettaquamscut on December 16th. He then goes on to refer to what must have been the English army's surprise attack on the Narragansett fort in the Great Swamp due west of the Bull garrison, which took place on the afternoon of December 19th, since which, he asserts, both sides had spent about six weeks regrouping themselves. If these references are the intended ones, then his date at the end of the narrative, "5th: 12m: 1675," which might seem to be the Quaker notation for December 5th, 1675, a date on which he could not have known about such events, ought instead be read as referring to February 5th of what we now reckon as 1676, since the English calendar of the time customarily began the year with March rather than January (for Easton's use of this calendar, see his opening account of the murder of Sassamon, who died in January 1675, as having happened "in the winter in the year 1674").

[1] Walk.

would have had him devoured by dogs but the tenderness of some of them prevailed to cut off his head. And [later the army] came suddenly upon the Indians where the Indians had prepared to defend themselves and so received and did much mischief and [the] six weeks since hath been spent [by] both parties to recruit. And now the English army is out to seek after the Indians but it is most likely that [those] most able to do mischief will escape and women and children and [the] impotent[2] may be destroyed and so the most able will have the less encumbrance to do mischief.

But I am confident it would be best for English and Indians that a peace were made upon honest terms for each to have a due propriety[3] and to enjoy it without oppression or usurpation by one to the other. But the English dare not trust the Indians' promises, neither the Indians . . . the English promises, and each have great cause therefore. I see no way likely but if a cessation from arms might be procured until it might be known what terms King Charles would propound, for we have great cause to think the Narragansett kings would trust our king and that they would have accepted him to be umpire if it had been tendered about any difference (for we do know the English have had much contention against those Indians to invalidate the king's determination for Narragansetts to be in our colony, and we have cause to think it was the greatest cause of the war against them). I see no means likely to procure a cessation from arms except the governor of New York can find a way so to intercede [that] it will be likely a peace may be made without troubling our king. . . . It always hath been a principle in our colony that there should be but one supreme [ruler] to Englishmen and [likewise] in our native country wherever [the] English have jurisdiction. And so we know no English should begin a war and not first tender for the king to be umpire, and [should] not persecute such that will not conform to their worship, [especially when] . . . their worship be not owned by the king.[4] [For] the king not to mind to have such things redressed, some may take [as a sign] that he hath not power, and that there may be a way for them to take power in opposition to him. I am so persuaded [that] New England priests . . . are so blinded by the spirit of persecution and [by their wish] to maintain [their] hire[5] . . . that they have been the cause that the

---

[2] I.e., the sick and the very old.

[3] I.e., proprietorship, or a clearly distinguished territory. Easton's call for more efforts at mediation may have been intended to renew a flagging general interest in peaceful solutions that lingered for a time after the Great Swamp fight. Surviving Narragansetts sent messengers to the army camped at Wickford, north of the Bull garrison house, and the army was under instructions to consider such overtures, but contacts broke off by mid-January and by the beginning of February the English army had recruited itself sufficiently to begin a new pursuit of the Narragansetts. By February 5th, the date on which Easton apparently wrote his narrative, the Massachusetts commander had returned without success to Boston and his force was disbanded.

[4] Easton's phrasing here is confusing, but what follows is an impassioned attack on the presumptuousness, as he sees it, of the New England Puritans, who persecuted the Quakers and sought to dominate Rhode Island.

[5] I.e., to maintain their (lucrative) positions. The Quakers had no "priests."

law of nations and the law of arms have been violated in this war, and that the war had not been if there had not been a hireling . . . managing what he calleth the gospel. . . .[6]

5th : 12m : 1675. *Rhode Island.*

---

[6]Perhaps Easton's particular target here was the leading Puritan preacher of Boston, Increase Mather (1639–1723).

7

FIVE LETTERS FROM
RENSSELAERSWYCK

MARIA VAN CORTLANDT, DAUGHTER OF OLOFFE STEVENSE VAN CORTLANDT AND
Anna Loockermans, was born in July 1645 in the city of New Amsterdam, which
was to become New York after the English conquest of 1664. Both sides of van
Cortlandt's family were of the merchant class; her father was one of the city's
wealthiest merchants and a holder of civic posts under both the Dutch and the
English. In Maria's generation the family witnessed signal advances in its status:
her brother Stephanus consolidated the family's political power by serving as
the first American-born mayor of the city and capped a long career in the law
with an appointment as chief justice of the provincial supreme court. Over the
course of his life, he also acquired great quantities of land and in 1697 managed
to secure a royal patent designating him lord of van Cortlandt manor, thereby
solidifying and increasing his power over the tenants on his lands. His manor
subsequently was one of the most durable of New York's quasi-aristocratic holdings, remaining in the family's hands into the nineteenth century.

For her part, Stephanus's sister Maria married into an even more distinguished manorial family, the van Rensselaers. With several minority partners,
the Amsterdam diamond merchant Kiliaen van Rensselaer (ca. 1585–1643) had
begun to develop a Dutch "patroonship" or manor called Rensselaerswyck
along the upper Hudson River from 1629 on, and during Maria's life, Kiliaen's
descendants were to come into full control of the 850,000-acre estate. Maria's
husband, Jeremias van Rensselaer (1632–1674), was not, however, the heir of
the patroonship, but as the youngest son of Kiliaen he came to New Netherland
in the 1650s to help manage the property. Following his death in 1674, Maria
remained in their home, called Watervliet, on the northern part of the
patroonship, and took over day-to-day management of Rensselaerswyck for her
husband's relatives in the Netherlands. She, too, had no clear legal title to the
property, but residence and persistence had important consequences. None of
the first three patroons in fact came in person to America until Jeremias's
nephew Kiliaen (1655–1687) arrived in 1685, long after his uncle's death. Young
Kiliaen married Jeremias and Maria's daughter Anna van Rensselaer the next

year, but with his own death in 1687, it was a second of Jeremias and Maria's children, Anna's brother, another Kiliaen (1663–1719), who emerged as the American claimant for the manor. Due to international rivalries, the English supported this American contender against his Dutch rival, his cousin—yet a fourth Kiliaen (1667–1746), who came to America in 1695 but renounced the claim of all Dutch heirs of the first patroon in return for a modest monetary settlement and the American claimant's renunciation of all claims to the family's Dutch holdings. The guardians of the "colonie" (as the enormous manor also was called) thus were vindicated by their own heirs' inheritance of it. The symbolism of it was enriched when, in 1701, their son Kiliaen, the fourth patroon and second lord of the manor, married another Maria van Cortlandt (1680–post-1744), the daughter of Stephanus, his mother's niece and namesake, and thus his own first cousin. In some sense, it was the van Cortlandt family that won out in this long transatlantic struggle. Indeed, the next three patroons, who ruled the colonie up to the anti-rent war of the 1840s, shared a telling first name—Stephen.

Stephanus van Cortlandt played a key role in his sister's management of Rensselaerswyck in the period when she wrote the following letters, including a pair to him, as he technically was the director of the manor. The supplanted Dutch legal code, which had allowed married women to control their own property, perhaps would have let Maria rule the patroonship directly—much as, under Dutch practice, she and other married women often kept their family names, or on occasion used their husbands'. Maria's letters make it increasingly clear, however, that whatever the legalities, she was on the ground along the upper Hudson and little passed there without her knowledge or approval. She had a habit of command and decisiveness that she deployed well, not only against members of the van Rensselaer clan but also, when it became necessary, against her own brother, whose ties with the Schuyler family through his wife may have led him to favor their interests over those of his sister. She deferred to Stephanus ("I have referred them to you as being the master," she remarks of two farmers trying to have a farm on the manor transferred between them), but she also let him know what she thought: "You may do therein as you please," she remarked, "but as for me, I must say that I do not know how Gerrit dares to be so bold. . . . If he did not care to stay, he might have spoken to me about it." True, she found the burdens of her position daunting at times, but that may have been owing to the tight place she occupied, with many responsibilities daily weighing on her but little ultimate power to attend to them. She complained to her father in 1681, "The least trouble makes me sick," but her further comment in that letter makes it clear that the crux of the problem was the bind that law and custom placed her in, not her own character or physical stamina: "If it should please God to have brother Rygert [van Rensselaer] or someone else come over [from the Netherlands], I should get rid of the farm, for I cannot stand it." A letter to her brother the same month, complaining of the evident bullying of her by a local official, shows her more mettlesome spirit: "Braggarts and pompous men I cannot stand." In this latter case, she deferred to Stephanus in part because she thereby could delay that official's insistence on collecting her taxes. By 1683, when her own brother's apparent manipulation of affairs against her had become clear to her, she began to outwit him by seeking out allies of her own. She wrote to her brother-in-law, "I beg you, brother, if you write about the land and the island, etc., of Thunis de Metselaer, not to write about it to my brother Steeven, for the house of Schuyler knows [what he knows] immediately and that is enough and all they are after." Because the Schuylers had a claim against the patroonship—Alida Schuyler was the widow of Jeremias's brother Nicolaes—and her own brother Stephanus was married to Alida's sister Gertruy, Maria van Cortlandt had to tread carefully in this thistle field of conflicting interests. Her son's ultimate installation as the head of the whole colonie bespeaks his mother's care and intelligence in managing what often seemed to her a very difficult business.

Jasper Danckaerts, a minister for the Labadist sect who visited New York in this period, left a portrayal of Maria van Cortlandt that speaks of her piety, but also comments on her more worldly traits. "We went to call upon a certain Madam Rentselaer, widow of the Heer Rentselaer, son of the Heer Rentselaer of . . . the colony of Rentselaerswyck. . . . She is still in possession of the place, and still administers it as *patroonesse*, until one Richard van Rentselaer, residing in Amsterdam, shall arrive in the country. . . . This lady was polite, quite well informed, and of good life and disposition." Danckaerts found her attachment to the goods of this world perhaps a bit too strong ("The breaking up of the ice [on the Hudson] once carried away her entire mansion, and every thing connected with it, of which place she had made too much account"), but he found her strong in the face of more personal suffering—her husband's death, her own partial crippling following the birth of her last child, Maria—and saw her as an active woman clearly in charge of practical matters: "We went to look at several of her mills at work, which she had there on an ever-running stream, grist-mills, saw-mills, and others." In her letters, Maria van Cortlandt offers us a glimpse of this colonial woman of affairs whom Danckaerts discovered along the banks of the Hudson. When she died in Albany in 1689 at the age of 44, her heirs were well on their way to preeminence not only in the colonie of Rensselaerswyck but also in the larger colony of New York.

Maria van Cortlandt

from her "Correspondence"

TO RYCKERT VAN RENSSELAER
[DECEMBER 1675?]

Rygart van Rensselaer

Dear Brother: Your agreeable and long awaited letter of July 5th, stating that you were heartily sorry to learn of the death of your brother, my husband,[1] was duly received by me on the 18th of November, new style. I doubt not but it has caused a great sorrow, but as it has pleased the Lord to afflict me with such a great sorrow, I must put my [trust] in God's will. May He make me patient and strengthen me in all adversity and in my infirmity, from which at present I suffer great pain, through Jesus Christ, who gives me strength and who through His mercy will further [sustain] me.

As to the coming over of brother Nicolaes,[2] you will have learned about that from my preceding letter. I had expected more from him. If it had pleased God to spare my late husband a while longer, things would not go so [badly]. And as to the colony, matters still stand as they did when my late husband was living. Could he have spoken with his Excellency, it would have gone better. I trust that before the receipt of this letter you will already have learned everything from my letter to brother Jan Baptist, to which I refer. That I should have liked to see you come over, is true, as you know the situation better than a stranger [and also know] the circumstances in which I am placed. I doubt not but you would have helped me in everything. But as it has pleased God to provide you with a family there, I cannot advise you in the matter, as the situation of the country is well known to you.

As to the government here in this country, it is, as far as I know, good. Trade is carried on as heretofore to Boston and the West Indies and the trading with the Indians goes on as while you were here. The past summer there was a lively trade. As to agriculture, it has during the last two years become so much worse on account of high water and the increase of weeds that the farmers

---

[1] Jeremias van Rensselaer (1632–1674), the youngest son of Amsterdam diamond merchant Kiliaen van Rensselaer (ca. 1585–1643), the major partner of the group of Dutch merchants who developed an estate, or patroonship (usually called Rensselaerswyck), on the upper Hudson River starting in the early 1630s. Jeremias came over to New Netherland in 1654 at the request of his older brother Jan Baptiste, who had begun managing Rensselaerswyck in 1651 and was having considerable difficulty with the task. Jan Baptiste went home to the Netherlands in 1658, leaving Jeremias as director of the 850,000-acre "colonie"; Jeremias in turn was joined by another brother, Ryckert (Maria's correspondent here; referred to as Rygart, Rygert, or Reygart) from 1664 to 1670. Jeremias, who married Maria van Cortlandt in 1662, died in October 1674, after which point she assumed her duties as de facto director of the colonie.

[2] Reverend Nicolaes van Rensselaer, an unreliable sibling of Jeremias, Jan Baptiste, and Ryckert, came over to America in 1674.

demand a reduction [in the rent]. The honorable governor[3] has prohibited the exportation of wheat flour for six months, but allowed that of bread.

As to my house and the land across [the river?], they are in the same condition as when my late husband was living. May it please the Lord that we may [possess] them in peace and have the grist-mill and sawmill also, in order that I may be able to support myself. But we live here in great fear on account of the great war between the English and the Indians around the north and of New England,[4] although, thank God, we do not yet hear of any calamities. The Indians have plundered many villages and killed many [people?]. It seems that it pleases the Lord to visit us also in this region. May God Almighty preserve us and prevent that they receive reinforcement from other nations, for they are very bold, and that they may not proceed farther. The state of religion in this country is still the same, for which mercy we cannot sufficiently thank God Almighty. Wherewith, with hearty greetings from myself and my son Kiliaen and Anna to you and your wife, I commend you to God.

TO STEPHANUS VAN CORTLANDT [NOVEMBER? 1679]

Sr Stephenes van Cortlant[5]

Dear Brother: This will serve to advise you of the condition of the colony and that last Thursday night, at about 2 or 3 o'clock, the house next to Gerrit Reyerse's burned down to the ground, but that through God's help the houses next to it were saved. But Friday, toward noon, cries were heard that the farm of the Hooge Berg[6] was on fire, so that many people at once ran toward it and found it to be true. Before any one could get there, everything was burned, the house, barn, two barracks[7] full of grain, yes, even the pig sty. The man himself was so badly burned that Master Cornelis doubts whether he will live,[8] and this because he was so busy with the animals. The woman's face is burned because she tried to get her blind mother out of the burning house, which she just managed to do. Eleven cows were burned, but the milch cows and the horses they got loose. Everything else was burned, the linen, woolens, bed and household effects, yes, even the pots and kettles were melted. Friends have taken the

---

[3] Edmund Andros (1637–1714), who served as New York governor from 1674 to 1681.

[4] "King Philip's War," on which see John Easton's "A Relation of the Indian War."

[5] Stephanus van Cortlandt (1643–1700), New York city merchant and official (he was appointed mayor in 1677, and again in 1686–87), was Maria van Rensselaer's brother and, as official director of Rensselaerswyck following her husband's death, served as her frequent advisor during her on-site management of it. Later in his life, he managed to secure a royal patent for the manor of Cortlandt in Westchester County.

[6] "High hill" (or perhaps "High hay barrack"—see next note) farm was located on the very low Papscanee (later Staats) Island, along the shore of the Hudson opposite and below the city of Albany.

[7] The Dutch stored hay in open-sided, roofed "barracks."

[8] A medical doctor, Cornelis van Dyck; the leasee of the farm, Gysbert Cornelissen van Breukelen (also called van den Berg), in fact survived at least for another decade.

old people into their houses and have asked me to assist them, so that they may again dwell there. Therefore, Marten Gerritse, with the consent of the other friends, the next day tore down the house of Scherluyn, which Hendrick van Nes was to have, and they will immediately take it to the other side and at the first opportunity put it up again.[9] The farmers will this winter do their best to haul the timber for the barn, to help the man, and Gerrit Gysbertse[1] will also put off his own building to help his father. Now, on top of this fire, there are many who complain. Piter de Vlaming has given up the lease of his farm and moves to his mill,[2] and that house must be repaired. I do not know what to do about the farm. There are tenants for it, but they do not suit me, so that you ought to write what I am to do. I shall wait until I hear from you before having it posted to be let at public bidding. . . .

Furthermore, there is a request here of Gerrit Thunisse who, subject to our approval, has turned over his farm to Klaes van Pette for 1100 bushels of wheat and the little island which lies in front of his door to one who is called Schipper, for 180 bushels.[3] Therefore, they have asked me whether I would consent to it, which I did not want to do without your knowledge and I have referred them to you as being the master thereof. You may do therein as you please, but as for me, I must say that I do not know how Gerrit dares to be so bold and is not ashamed to do so, for my late husband would never allow any one to do so, and the late Domine[4] would not allow it either that another person was to be master of the farm. If he did not care to stay, he might have spoken to me about it. But he is too proud and mighty; he wants to do it and talks big. But as for me, if brother takes the same view of it, I would not consent to it, but according to his contract cancel his lease at the end of the third year, which will expire in 1681, and according to appraisal by impartial persons let the next lessee take over what he has [built] thereon, as the contract reads: "The term of the lease will last six consecutive years, notice to be given by either party at the end of three years." Verily, it seems to me that we have reason enough to cancel his lease at the end of the third year and then [not] to place the man who leases it in such [position?]. . . .

The said Gerrit has bought the yacht of Clas van Pette, the price to be deducted from that of the farm. The said Gerrit has again sold the yacht to

---

[9] The frame of the house in question, which probably had belonged to notary Dirck van Schelluyne before that man's departure from Rensselaerswyck in 1669, was disassembled rather than destroyed.

[1] Dutch naming often involved patronymics and loconymics, or last names indicating the father of the person in question and his or her birthplace. "Gerrit Gysbertse" thus might be Anglicized as "Jared Gilbertson," while his father's name likewise would become "Gilbert Cornelison of Breukelen" (a town near Utrecht). Presumably the latter's further name denoted his residence at the burned farm on Papscanee Island.

[2] Pieter Winne de Vlaming's new lease on a farm in Bethlehem had been signed on May 1, 1678, but at the end of that month he also had leased a mill site on what is now known, after him, as Vlaman's Kill, also in Bethlehem.

[3] Gerrit Theunissen van Vechten's lease to a farm located near Papscanee Island was assigned to Klaes van Petten in the spring of 1680.

[4] Reverend Nicolaes van Rensselaer, who died in New Netherland in 1678.

Piter Schuyler, so that I do not know how it goes here with Gerrit. He still owes us nearly 900 bushels of wheat on our [account] book. Therefore, brother may well consider what he had better do in the matter, as everything depends on you.

Davit Schuyler[5] called on me this morning to buy the lot on which the house stood that is now torn down. He says that he spoke to you about it when you were here and therefore requests me to write to you about it to ask for how much it is for sale, for it can be of no use to us now that the street has been done away with. He will write to you himself.

Secretary Livingston[6] troubles me so much about the account of the late Domine and I cannot give it to him, because it is not complete. Therefore, I would ask you to write to him some time to be pleased to wait until your arrival in the spring, for I am afraid that if I give him half the account, he will after-wards have a counter account. I have at present so much to do with one thing and another that I wish that it were spring and that I might be relieved of this trouble, for it is too much for me. The grist-mill is running and grinds a good deal more than the other.

TO OLOFFE STEVENSE VAN CORTLANDT[7]
[DECEMBER 1681]

Very dear and beloved Father: These few lines will serve to inform you of the state of our health, which now, thank God, is fair. I hope that father, mother and the friends are likewise still well, which I very much long to hear. Times are bad here; [there is] little grain, so that it is again bad for the colony. I am wishing and longing for a letter from Holland, for I can no longer live in trouble and cannot stand any exertion. If I keep quiet, without exertion, I am

[5] The Schuyler family was of considerable prominence in early Albany. Pieter Schuyler, born there in 1657, was a trader and merchant who served as the town's mayor in 1686 and held many other posts, eventually that of acting governor of New York, 1719–20. He had many ties with the van Cortlandt and van Rensselaer families. His second wife (whom he married in 1691) was Maria van Cortlandt and Jeremias van Rensselaer's daughter Maria van Rensselaer. Schuyler's sister Gertruy married the elder Maria van Cortlandt's brother Stephanus van Cortlandt in 1671, his brother Brandt married Maria and Stephanus's sister Cornelia in 1683, and his sister Alida married first Jeremias van Rensselaer's brother Nicolaes and, second, Robert Livingston, whose role in Maria van Cortlandt's business affairs will be clear below. Pieter Schuyler's uncle Davit (d. 1690) was a merchant of lesser standing who had emigrated to Albany with Pieter's father Philip around 1650.

[6] Robert Livingston (1654–1728), a native of Scotland who was raised in Rotterdam, emigrated to Albany in 1674 as a merchant; he was at this time town clerk and in 1686 succeeded, like Maria's brother, in acquiring a manorial grant. From 1718 to 1725, he was speaker of the New York assembly. He wanted the account of Nicolaes van Rensselaer in order to settle the estate of the dead man, because he was the administrator of it and perhaps because he had married the widow, Alida Schuyler, in 1679.

[7] Oloffe Stevense van Cortlandt (1600–1684), the father of Maria and Stephanus, was a New York City merchant and one of the five wealthiest inhabitants there in 1674. He had immigrated to New Amsterdam in 1638 and had served in many public offices in the years since, including burgomaster and city treasurer.

reasonably well, but the least trouble makes me sick. If it should please God to have brother Rygert or someone else come over, I should get rid of the farm, for I cannot stand it.[8]

TO STEPHANUS VAN CORTLANDT
[DECEMBER 1681]

Sr Steven van Cortlant

Dear Brother: These few lines will serve to let you know the state of our health which, thank God, is fair. I hope to hear the same from you. Some time after your departure I had a talk with Marten Gerritse[9] about the tax which we must still pay for the place in addition to the 300 bushels of wheat, [saying] that we did not intend to give more and that he need not try to collect it. At first Marten Gerritse said that it could not be, that all things must stand until the governor came and that first the other commissaries must know about it. I then told him that he could tell them if he pleased. He thereupon said that they wanted to have it, to which I replied that they should wait until spring, when my brother came up the river. As a result they sent me on the 20th of November the enclosed by Marten Gerritse, from which you can see what they want and other words in addition which Marten said to me. I told him that I would write to you and that I would await your answer to it before I would pay one penny. I wish that we could manage not to pay. Braggarts and pompous men I cannot stand. I shall therefore await your orders. It has been a very bad harvest, worse than last year. Now that we come to threshing there is not 1½ bushels . . . I do not know what I shall do to get grain. The river is not yet closed. It has been covered over, but one cannot drive on it. The north wind begins to blow quite sharply and I think that the river will be closed tomorrow. We have no snow either to take a ride sometime to visit the farmers. . . .

Madam Teller has had a dispute with Master Cornelis. I think that you will hear of it, for they will write to Capt. Bro[ckholst] about it. The dispute is about the place where the powder is stored, behind brother Teller's, in an old house of Gab[riel] Tho[masse], and all the women who live thereabouts want to have the powder removed, or want to tear down the house. The people are full of fear since the fire.[1]

---

[8] Oloffe Stevense van Cortlandt answered his daughter from New York on January 12, 1682, ". . . I shall confer sometime with your brother to see what can be done to secure for you a quiet life. I have noticed for a long time that all this quarrelling is neither good for you nor profitable."

[9] An Albany merchant and evidently one of the town's commissaries, or magistrates. He leased the present Westerlo Island, then named after him, from Rensselaerswyck.

[1] A serious fire on November 10, 1681 had destroyed several houses in Albany, so the storage of gunpowder near dwellings understandably made citizens nervous. Maria Varlet, widow of Paulus Schrijk, had lived with her first husband in Hartford, where he was a merchant serving the trade with New York. Her second husband, Willem Teller, was the father of another Dutch merchant placed in New England, Andries Teller of Boston, who married Maria van Cortlandt's sister Sophia in 1671 (hence her reference to "brother Teller" in referring to the gunpowder). Willem Teller, a violent man twice charged with manslaughter, was a prominent merchant in Albany with many English ties.

Brother Teller has since your departure been drinking heavily, so that at times he was unconscious and did not behave well at all in the house and on the street. On Friday, being drunk, he went toward morning into severe convulsions. This lasted until ten o'clock in the evening, without pause, so that all of us thought that he would not recover. There was great sorrow that he would thus depart out of this world, but the great [God . . .].[2]

TO RYCKERT VAN RENSSELAER
[NOVEMBER? 1683]

Mr Reygart van Rensslaer

Dear Brother: This serves only to let you know that I have sold the farm on which Piter Winne has heretofore resided, situated near the island, to Myndert Harmse,[3] for 2000 guilders Holland money, 1000 gl. at once, according to the bill of exchange, and the other 1000 gl. next year.[4] And whereas I had written to my brother Steeven about the sale of the said farm, whether it was advisable, he wrote back that the farm must be left before the island as a place of refuge, but as the island already has a place of refuge, it does not need the said farm, for Cornelis Segerse is dead and on the little place near the island Marten Gerritse has already had a house and barn built, in which he lets his father-in-law dwell, so that my brother's letter does not please me. To pay two thousand guilders, and that in Holland money, for such poor land is a good deal. The buildings are poor and will have to be repaired in the summer, and as there is much strange talk about the purchase of the island and other land, please be careful about the sale, and as you have asked me most urgently to send over something, I have done the best I could, and although my brother has sent back the bill of exchange and postponed the sale until we receive an answer from you, I have nevertheless sent the bill of exchange to you myself, not doubting but you would be pleased to have it. And whereas I understand that the son of Madam Schuyler has said that I shall not have the land, as he has my brother's help, I beg you to be my and my children's help and advocate. I have no doubt that my brother will write to you, as I have heard that Livingston has presented a petition to the governor and council, requesting that a division might be made of the colony, in order that he might know the late Domine's interest therein.[5] Whereupon it was ordered that a copy of the petition should be sent to you and that answer to it must be made within 15 months. I trust that

---

[2] The draft of the letter stops in midsentence here.
[3] Perhaps Myndert Harmensen van den Bogaert, an Albany surgeon.
[4] The guilder was the basic unit of Dutch currency, analogous to the pound.
[5] Here van Cortlandt outlines for her brother-in-law Ryckert the political alliances that were arrayed against her, most of which are explained in notes elsewhere. Briefly, it should be recalled that Pieter Schuyler was the ally of her brother because the latter had married Pieter's sister Gertruy in 1671; that Robert Livingston, in turn, had married Pieter's sister Alida in 1679 following the death of her first husband (Maria's brother-in-law Reverend Nicolaes van Rensselaer); and that, in 1691, Pieter Schuyler was to take as his second wife Maria's fourth daughter and namesake, Maria.

the same will be delivered to you. The said Livingston is again held in as great regard as heretofore.[6] He will not write to you any more, but will write only to the co-participants.[7] I also understand that he would like to get his hands on something else, as I have been told by a person who heard it himself, namely, that they intended to let you have one-half of the money and then, when they had possession of the land above, Livingston would attach it. The rest, what there is to it, God knows. It is here at present so sad, one does not know whether one deals with friend or foe. Yes, one dares not trust one's own brother.[8] The whole country must again furnish money and all merchandise is taxed again. God knows what this arrival of the governor may yet bring us. I hope that God will make everything turn out for the best.

I beg you, brother, if you write about the land and the island, etc., of Thunis de Metselaer,[9] not to write about it to my brother Steeven, for the house of Schuyler knows that immediately and that is enough and all they are after. I shall break off here. Commending you all to the Lord, I remain with hearty greetings to yourself, your wife and your children,

> *Your faithful sister*
> *Maria van Rensselaer*

---

[6] Apparently a reference to the continuing political clout of Livingston despite the recent change in administrations, whereby Thomas Dongan replaced Edmund Andros as New York governor.

[7] The other Dutch partners in the patroonship; the partnership had not been particularly cordial (the van Rensselaers, as holders of a two-fifths interest, managed Rensselaerswyck and refused to give any accounting to the others), and in 1685 was dissolved.

[8] Given what she says earlier and later in this letter, Maria means this assertion in a quite literal sense as a comment on Stephanus van Cortlandt.

[9] Thunis the bricklayer, otherwise unidentified.

8

HANNAH JONES AND THE
STONE-THROWING DEVIL

WITCHCRAFT IS AN ENDURINGLY FAMOUS THEME OF EARLY AMERICAN SOCIAL history, although exactly what it was and how and why it arose in the seventeenth century remain tantalizing questions. Recent inquiries stress the social dynamics that underlay accusations of witchcraft, not only in Salem in 1692 but also in many other places from the 1650s into the eighteenth century; these dovetail rather well with studies in England and on the continent that trace analogous patterns of social discord that surround and may motivate such accusations. Witchcraft, in other words, often seems to have served as a cover for disagreements about quite separate issues that find in it a conveniently fear-laden vehicle. Those wishing to play a trump card against some opponent—especially some opponent they otherwise might have trouble defeating—found the cry of "Witchcraft!" a very useful ally. Once that cry was uttered, others in the community who nursed old injuries at the hands of the accused (as might be likely in tightly woven communities) would find their own antipathies organized and revived in the process. A courageous contemporary of Cotton Mather, Robert Calef, pointed out that it was a common occurrence for the testimony of one witness in the Salem trials to revive the memory of others, calling forth old tales of things that had befallen them "after some quarrel" with the accused years earlier. The minister John Hale, who had been very active in prosecuting the Salem witches but who later repented, likewise noted, "If after anger between neighbors mischief followed, this oft bred suspicion of witchcraft in the matter."

The 1682 case of the "Stone-Throwing Devil" of Great Island, in the vicinity of Portsmouth, New Hampshire, tends to support this view. As told by Richard Chamberlain, the story involves an apparent poltergeist throwing various household implements (not to mention some of New England's plentiful stones) around the home of George Walton, a prominent Quaker with whom Chamberlain was staying. Chamberlain, who held the position of secretary of the colony and also served as a magistrate or petty judge in New Hampshire, is quite specific in detailing these instances of "stonery," and he joins Walton in accusing the latter's neighbor Hannah Jones of being the instigator of them. Now it happens that Jones was not only Walton's neighbor but also, in a number of ways, his opponent, long before the stonery of 1682. As owners of adjoining real estate, the two of them might be expected to come into conflict over the lines between their respective holdings—as frequently happened in an era when boundaries were determined not by precise surveys but rather by some-times vague landmarks. But the argument in this case went deeper than bound-ary disputes: New Hampshire in this period was undergoing tumultuous change, and Jones and Walton were on opposite sides of this larger dispute. Originally given to John Mason as a royal grant, New Hampshire began its Euro-American life as a proprietary colony, although Mason barely had begun his work when he died in 1635, leaving a vacuum into which various other parties and forces proceeded to rush. His tenants and servants, who included Hannah Jones's family, exercised squatters' rights over the lands of the nascent colony at Strawberry Bank (Portsmouth) and on Great Island, while the always alert Puritans of Massachusetts Bay, glad that their potentially dangerous Angli-can opponent Mason was dead, sought to add his domains to their own once the English Civil War put their allies in power.

Hannah Jones's father, the blacksmith Thomas Walford, had been one of Mason's servants, and in the years following 1635 he had emerged as one of the more prosperous of "Masonia's" squatters. An Anglican, he had been the earli-est English settler in Charlestown, Massachusetts, but had been expelled by the Puritans because of his beliefs. Like George Walton, who as a Quaker would have had no reason to love the Puritans, Thomas Walford was opposed to the various attempts of Massachusetts to exert its power in New Hampshire. Although they shared this one ideological and personal antipathy, the two men had more points of difference than agreement. George Walton was the host of Robert Chamberlain in 1682, in fact, precisely because the latter had aligned himself not with the squatter community of which Thomas Walford and his daughter Hannah Jones were representatives, but with the resurgent claims of the Mason family to the whole of the old family estate. Robert Mason, John Mason's grandson, was seeking to reclaim that estate in just these years, over the strong objections of Massachusetts and the great majority of New Hampshire's squatters, but with the partial support of the British crown, which granted his request to appoint a royal government for the colony in 1679. It was young Mason, in fact, who had seen to it that Chamberlain, a London lawyer, was appointed as secretary to the new government. It was also Mason who ulti-mately was responsible for the shipping of a new lieutenant governor, Edward Cranfield, to rule the colony and reassert his own rights in the fall of 1682.

Mason was in the process of subduing the landholders of his grandfather's estate by exacting fees or "quitrents" on improved lands and by insisting on the retrocession of all undeveloped tracts, which he claimed the right to grant. Because most of the land titles of the colony would not hold up in court, the colony as a whole was thrown into considerable confusion, and, as one might expect, considerable competition for favor, profit, and the spoils was set in motion. That Chamberlain's presence in Walton's house signified the Masonian effort to reclaim the colony and Walton's alignment with that effort helps explain why Walton's house would be a plausible target for stones cast from angry hands in the summer of 1682. When Lieutenant Governor Cranfield arrived, as Chamberlain recalls in his narrative, he remarked that the supernatural theories of Chamberlain himself were a less likely explanation for the carryings on at Walton's than a more pragmatic cause—namely, "the waggery of some unlucky boys." Cranfield's interpretation makes a good deal of sense. We can probably assume that the first stones cast that summer were actual ones, and that they were thrown by actual hands, perhaps under the direction of Hannah Jones's brother-in-law and neighbor John Amazeen, who also served as the constable of Great Island and was very much an insider among the colony's resisters. It seems reasonable to assume, furthermore, that the literal "stonery" provided Walton and his allies (who may have included or excluded Chamberlain) with a strategy whereby Hannah Jones might be weakened and the land dispute between the two decided in Walton's favor. Surely Walton knew that Jones's mother, Jane Walford, had been twice accused of witchcraft during her life, and even though those charges had been disproved in court, the odor of unorthodoxy still hung over the family. With her husband and brother dead, Hannah Jones was also vulnerable in the way that many women accused of witchcraft in the period were: that is, she owned property in her own right and had no close male relative or guardian to deflect the attacks of other men greedy for it. It is not hard to view all of what happened in the summer of 1682 as a plot to discredit her and cause her to lose her dispute with Walton.

If there was a plot, it was probably improvised rather than concerted, much in the way that groups of people with common interests and values often act on their affinities without overtly scheming to do so. Richard Chamberlain, ideologically friendly but a stranger to the local social order, may well have been the audience for the carryings-on rather than part of the theatrical company producing them. Close readers will note that much of what he reports seems to have been calculated for his viewing as a person who, given his political connections, might have the power to influence further events. But Chamberlain still might have served his host well once the dispute with Jones came to court—indeed, as magistrate Chamberlain does seem to have acted against Jones over the summer—and in another sense Chamberlain's narrative may represent the final product of an attempt to enlist his aid in the dispute.

Lithobolia is a curious narrative in many regards. Chamberlain wrote it many years after the fact, when he was back in England and when (perhaps significantly) all the other major actors in the case, who might have contradicted or corroborated his account, were dead—Jones, Walton, Amazeen, Cranfield, Mason. Curiously, the records of Hannah Jones's trial, if there was one, do not survive (Secretary Chamberlain, who might have been the official to record such a trial, ends his narrative with the case still hanging fire), so that in this sense too Chamberlain's amusing *Lithobolia* is the last word on the whole episode. As to Chamberlain, he was the son of William Chamberlain of London, having been born in 1632, admitted to Trinity College, Cambridge, in 1648, and to the bar in 1659. *Lithobolia* was dedicated to Chamberlain's son-in-law, Martin Lumley (a brief dedication to Lumley is omitted here), apparently as an entertaining example of Chamberlain's claim that reason could not explain away all the mysteries of experience. *Lithobolia*'s own mysteries have shown themselves remarkably durable in the nearly three hundred years since its first publication.

RICHARD CHAMBERLAIN

from **Lithobolia (1698)**

SUCH IS THE SCEPTICAL HUMOR OF THIS AGE OF INCREDULITY (NOT TO SAY INFI-delity), that I wonder they do not take up and profess, in terms, the Pyrrhonian[1] doctrine of disbelieving their very senses. For that which I am going to relate happening to cease in the province of New Hampshire in America, just upon that governor's[2] arrival and appearance at the council there, who was informed by myself, and several other gentlemen of the council, and other considerable persons, of the true and certain reality hereof, yet he continued tenacious in the opinion that we were all imposed upon by the waggery of some unlucky boys; which, considering the circumstances and passages hereafter mentioned, was altogether impossible.

I have a wonder to relate; for such (I take it) is so to be termed whatsoever is preternatural, and not assignable to, or the effect of, natural causes: It is a *lithobolia*,[3] or stone-throwing, which happened by witchcraft (as was supposed) and [was] maliciously perpetrated by an elderly woman, a neighbor suspected, and (I think) formerly detected for such kind of diabolical tricks and practices; and the wicked instigation did arise upon the account of some small quantity of land in her field, which she pretended was unjustly taken into the land of the person where the scene of this matter lay, and was her right[4]; she having been often very clamorous about that affair, and heard to say, with much bitterness, that her neighbor (*innuendo*[5] the fore-mentioned person, his name George Walton) should never quietly enjoy that piece of ground. Which, as it

---

[1] Skeptical (after Pyrrho, a fourth century B.C. Greek philosopher who taught that the senses are not reliable).
[2] Edward Cranfield, a minor court figure in England, was sent over as royal lieutenant governor of New Hampshire, at Robert Mason's behest, in 1682. He at first sided with the colonists against Mason, then reversed himself and, because of his highhanded and tyrannical behavior, soon became the target of their hatred and, eventually, organized resistance; he left the province in 1685.
[3] "Stone-throwing" (Greek).
[4] I.e., the land was rightfully hers.
[5] Hinting at.

has confirmed myself and others in the opinion that there are such things as witches, and the effects of witchcraft, or at least of the mischievous actions of evil spirits; which some do as little give credit to, as in the case of witches, utterly rejecting both their operations and their beings, we having been eyewitnesses of this matter almost every day for a quarter of a year together; so it may be a means to rectify the depraved judgment and sentiments of other disbelieving persons, and absolutely convince them of their error, if they please to hear, without prejudice, the plain, but most true narration of it; which was thus.

Some time ago being in America (in His then Majesty's[6] service) I was lodged in the said George Walton's house, a planter there, and on a Sunday night, about ten o'clock, many stones were heard by myself, and the rest of the family, to be thrown, and (with noise) hit against the top and all sides of the house, after he the said Walton had been at his fence-gate, which was between him and his neighbor one John Amazeen, an Italian,[7] to view it; for it was again, as formerly it had been (the manner how being unknown) wrung off the hinges, and cast upon the ground; and in his being there, and return home with several persons of (and frequenting) his family and house, about a flight shot distant[8] from the gate, they were all assaulted with a peal of stones, (taken, we conceive, from the rocks hard by the house) and this by unseen hands or agents. For by this time I was come down to them, having risen out of my bed at this strange alarm of all that were in the house, and do know that they all looked out as narrowly[9] as I did, or any person could (it being a bright moon-light night), but could make no discovery. Thereupon, and because there came many stones, and those pretty great ones, some as big as my fist, into the entry or porch of the house, we withdrew into the next room to the porch, no person having received any hurt, (praised by Almighty Providence, for certainly the infernal agent, constant enemy to mankind, had he not been overruled, intended no less than death or maim[ing]) save only that two youths were lightly hit, one on the leg, the other on the thigh, notwithstanding the stones came so thick, and so forcibly against the sides of so narrow a room. Whilst we stood amazed at this accident,[1] one of the maidens imagined she saw them come from the hall, next to that we were in, where searching (and in the cellar, down out of the hall) and finding nobody, another and myself observed two little stones in

---

[6] I.e., Charles II.

[7] This Greek settler was married to Hannah Jones's sister-in-law; his stepson, Jeremiah Walford, was thus Jones's nephew. Aligned with the anti-Masonians, Amazeen served as constable of Great Island. Later in 1682, he arrested George Walton and several of his workers, on a warrant issued by one of Walton's opponents (Elias Stileman, mentioned later in the text), for cutting wood on what appears to have been Jones's land. Amazeen and his stepson were sued by Walton as a result, but the court, friendly to the constable, ordered that Walton pay his costs.

[8] The distance covered by a flight-arrow, a light arrow intended for long shots; approximately a quarter mile.

[9] Carefully.

[1] Event.

a short space successively to fall on the floor, coming as from the ceiling close by us, and we concluded it must necessarily be done by means extraordinary and preternatural. Coming again into the room where we first were (next the porch), we had many of these lapidary salutations,[2] but unfriendly ones; for, shutting the door, it was no small surprise to me to have a good big stone come with great force and noise (just by my head) against the door on the inside; and then shutting the other door, next the hall, to have the like accident; so going out again, upon a necessary occasion,[3] to have another very near my body, clattering against the board-wall[4] of the house; but it was a much greater, to be so near the danger of having my head broke with a maul, or great hammer brushing along the top or roof of the room from the other end, as I was walking in it, and lighting down by me; but it fell so, that my landlord had the greatest damage, his windows (especially those of the first-mentioned room) being with many stones miserably and strangely battered, most of the stones giving the blow on the inside, and forcing the bars, lead, and hasps of the casements outwards, and yet falling back (sometimes a yard or two) into the room; only one little stone we took out of the glass of the window, where it lodged itself in the breaking it, in a hole exactly fit for the stone. The pewter and brass were frequently pelted, and sometimes thrown down upon the ground; for the evil spirit seemed then to affect variety of mischief, and diverted himself at this end after he had done so much execution at the other. So were two candlesticks, after many hittings, at last struck off the table where they stood, and likewise a large pewter pot, with the force of these stones. Some of them were taken up hot, and (it seems) immediately coming out of the fire; and some (which is not unremarkable) having been laid by me upon the table along by couples, and numbered,[5] were found missing; that is, two of them, as we returned immediately to the table, having turned our backs only to visit and view some new stone-charge or window-breach; and this experiment was four or five times repeated, and I still found one or two missing of the number, which we all marked, when I did but just remove the light from off the table, and step to the door, and back again.

After this had continued in all the parts and sides of the first room (and down the chimney) for above four hours, I, weary of the noise, and sleepy, went to bed, and was no sooner fallen asleep, but was awakened with the unwelcome disturbance of another battery of a different sort, it issuing with so prodigious a noise against the thin board-wall of my chamber (which was within another)[6] that I could not imagine it less than the fracture and downfall of great part of the chamber, or at least of the shelves, books, pictures, and other things, placed on that side, and on the partition wall between the antechamber and the door

[2] I.e., "stony greetings."
[3] I.e., to use the "necessary," or pit toilet.
[4] The siding.
[5] Marked with numbers.
[6] I.e., his bedchamber could be entered only through another room (chambers were usually second-story rooms in early New England houses).

of mine. But the noise immediately bringing up the company [from] below, they assured me no mischief of that nature was done, and showed me the biggest stone that had as yet been made use of in this unaccountable accident, weighing eight pound and an half, that had burst open my chamber door with a rebound from the floor, as by the dent and bruise in it near the door I found next morning, done, probably, to make the greater noise, and give the more astonishment, which would sooner be effected by three motions, and conse- quently three several sounds, namely, one on the ground, the next to and on the door, and the last from it again to the floor, than if it had been one single blow upon the door only; which ('tis probable) would have split the door, which was not permitted, nor so much as a square of the glass-window broken or cracked (at that time) in all the chamber. Glad thereof, and desiring them to leave me, and the door shut, as it was before, I endeavored once more to take my rest, and was once more prevented by the like passage, with another like offensive weapon, it being a whole brick that lay in the antechamber chimney, and used again to the same malicious purpose as before, and in the same manner too, as by the mark in the floor, whereon was some of the dust of the brick, broken a little at the end, apparent next morning, the brick itself lying just at the door. However, after I had lain a while, harkening to their adventures below, I dropped asleep again, and received no further molestation that night.

In the morning (Monday morning) I was informed by several of the domestics of more of the same kind of trouble; among which the most signal was, the vanishing of the spit[7] which stood in the chimney corner, and the sudden coming of it again down the same chimney, sticking of it in a log that lay in the fireplace or hearth; and then being by one of the family set by on the other side of the chimney, presently cast out of the window into the back-side. Also a pressing-iron lying on the ledge of the chimney back, was conveyed invisibly into the yard. I should think it (too) not unworthy the relation, that, discoursing then with some of the family, and others, about what had past, I said, I thought it necessary to take and keep the great stone, as a proof and evidence, for they had taken it down from my chambers; and so I carried it up, laid it on my table in my chamber, and locked my door, and going out upon occasions, and soon returning, I was told by my landlady that it was, a little while after my going forth, removed again, with a noise, which they all below heard, and was thrown into the antechamber, and there I found it lying in the middle of it; thereupon I the second time carried it up, and laid it on the table, and had it in my custody a long time to show, for the satisfaction of the curious.

There were many more stones thrown about in the house that morning, and more in the fields that day, where the master of the house was, and the men at work. Some more Mr. Woodbridge,[8] a minister, and myself, in the afternoon did see (but could not any hand throwing them) lighting near, and

[7] A long thin cooking tool with a pointed end.
[8] Reverend Benjamin Woodbridge, recently minister for a congregation in Bristol, Rhode Island, was to provide the report to Reverend Joshua Moody of Portsmouth on which Increase Mather based his version of the stone-throwing story.

jumping and tumbling on the grass: so did one Mrs. Clark, and her son, and several others; and some of them felt them too. One person would not be persuaded but that the boys at work might throw them, and straight her little boy standing by her was struck with a stone on the back, which caused him to fall a-crying, and her (being convinced) to carry him away forthwith.

In the evening, as soon as I had supped in the outer room before mine, I took a little musical instrument, and began to touch it (the door indeed was then set open for air), and a good big stone came rumbling in, and as it were to lead the dance, but upon a much different account than in the days of old, and of old fabulous enchantments, my music being none of the best. The noise of this brought up the deputy-president's wife,[9] and many others of the neighborhood that were below, who wondered to see this stone followed (as it were) by many others, and a pewter spoon among the rest, all which fell strangely into the room in their presence, and were taken up by the company. And beside all this, there was seen by two youths in the orchard and fields, as they said, a black cat, at the time the stones were tossed about, and it was shot at, but missed, by its changing places, and being immediately at some distance, and then out of sight, as they related: agreeable to which, it may not be improper to insert, what was observed by two maids, grandchildren of Mr. Walton, on the Sunday night, the beginning of this *lithoboly.* They did affirm, that as they were standing in the porch-chamber[1] window, they saw, as it were, a person putting out a hand out of the hall[2] window, as throwing stones toward the porch or entry, and we all know no person was in the hall except, at that instant, myself and another, having searched diligently there, and wondering whence those should come that were about the same time dropped near us; so far we were from doing it ourselves, or seeing any other there to do it.

On Monday night, about the hour it first began, there were more stones thrown in the kitchen, and down the chimney, one Captain Barefoot,[3] of the council for that province, being present, with others; and also (as I was going up to bed) in an upper chamber, and down those stairs.

Upon Tuesday night, about ten, some five or six stones were severally[4] thrown into the maid's chamber near the kitchen, and the glass windows broke in three new places, and one of the maids hit as she lay. At the same time was heard by them, and two young men in the house, an odd, dismal sort of whis-tling, and thereupon the youths ran out, with intent to take the supposed thrower of stones, if possible; and on the backside near the window they heard the noise (as they said) of something stepping a little way before them, as it were the trampling of a young colt, as they fancied, but saw nothing; and going

---

[9] Mrs. Elias Stileman; until Cranfield arrived later in 1682, her husband remained in power.
[1] The room above the entry hall at the front of Walton's house.
[2] The ordinary living room of the house.
[3] Walter Barefoot, a famous figure in early New Hampshire history, at the time a member of that province's council and a champion of its rights against Massachusetts.
[4] One by one.

on, could discover nothing but that the noise of the stepping or trampling was ceased, and then gone on a little before.

On Saturday morning I found two stones more on the stairs; and so some were on Sunday night conveyed into the room next the kitchen.

Upon Monday following Mr. Walton going (with his men) by water to some other land, in a place called the Great Bay, and to a house where his son was placed, they lay there that night, and the next morning had this adventure. As the men were all at work in the woods, felling wood, they were visited with another set of stones, and they gathered up near upon a hatful, and put them between two trees near adjoining, and returning from carrying wood, to the boat, the hat and its contents (the stones) were gone, and the stones were presently after thrown about again, as before; and after search, found the hat pressed together, and lying under a square piece of timber at some distance from thence. They had them again at young Walton's house, and half a brick thrown into a cradle, out of which his young child was newly taken up.

Here it may seem most proper to inform the reader of a parallel passage,[5] (namely) what happened another time to my landlord in his boat; wherein going up to the same place (the Great Bay) and loading it with hay for his use at his own house, about the midway in the river (Piscataqua) he found his boat began to be in a sinking condition, at which being much surprised, upon search, he discovered the cause to be the pulling out a plug or stopple in the bottom of the boat, being fixed there for the more convenient letting out of the rainwater that might fall into it; a contrivance and combination of the old serpent and the old woman, or some other witch or wizard (in revenge or innate enmity) to have drowned both my good landlord and his company.

On Wednesday, as they were at work again in the woods, on a sudden they heard something jingle like glass, or metal, among the trees, as it was falling, and being fallen to the ground, they knew it to be a stirrup which Mr. Walton had carried to the boat, and laid under some wood; and this being again laid by him in that very boat, it was again thrown after him. The third time, he having put it upon his girdle or belt he wore about his waist, buckled together before, but at that instant taken off because of the heat of the weather, and laid there again buckled, it was fetched away, and no more seen. Likewise the graper, or little anchor of the boat, cast overboard, which caused the boat to wind up; so staying and obstructing their passage. Then the setting pole was divers times cast into the river, as they were coming back from the Great Bay, which put them to the trouble of paddling, that is, rowing about for it as often to retrieve it.

Being come to his own house, this Mr. Walton was charged again with a fresh assault in the outhouses;[6] but we heard of none within doors until Friday after, when, in the kitchen, were four or five stones (one of them hot) taken

[5] Event.
[6] Outbuildings.

out of the fire, as I conceive, and so thrown about. I was then present, being newly come in with Mr. Walton from his middle field (as he called it), where his servants had been mowing, and had six or seven of his old troublesome companions,[7] and I had one fallen down by me there, and another thin flat stone hit me on the thigh with the flat side of it, so as to make me just feel, and to smart a little. In the same day's evening, as I was walking out in the lane by the field before mentioned, a great stone made a rustling noise in the stone fence between the field and the lane, which seemed to me (as it caused me to cast my eye that way by the noise) to come out of the fence, as it were pulled out from among those stones loose, but orderly laid close together, as the manner of such fences in that country is, and so fell down upon the ground. Some persons of note being then in the field (whose names are hereunder written) to visit Mr. Walton there, are substantial witnesses of this same stonery, both in the field, and afterward in the house that night, namely, one Mr. Hussey, son of a councillor there. He took up one that having first alighted on the ground, with rebound from thence hit him on the heel; and he keeps it to show. And Captain Barefoot, mentioned above, has that which (among other stones) flew into the hall a little before supper; which myself also saw as it first came in at the upper part of the door into the middle of the room; and then (though a good flat stone, yet) was seen to roll over and over, as if trundled, under a bed in the same room. In short, these persons, being wondrously affected[8] with the strangeness of these passages, offered themselves (desiring me to take them) as testimonies;[9] I did so, and made a memorandum, by way of record, thereof, to this effect. Namely,

These persons under written do hereby attest the truth of their being eyewitnesses of at least half a score stones that evening thrown invisibly into the field, and in the entry of the house, hall, and one of the chambers of George Walton's. Namely,

Samuel Jennings, Esq; governor of West Jersey.[1]
Walter Clark, Esq; deputy governor of Rhode Island.
Mr. Arthur Cook.
Mr. Matt. Borden of Rhode Island.
Mr. Oliver Hooton of Barbados, merchant.
Mr. T. Maul of Salem in New England, merchant.
Captain Walter Barefoot.
Mr. John Hussey.
And the wife of the said Mr. Hussey.

[7] I.e., stones.
[8] Deeply moved.
[9] Witnesses.
[1] New Jersey had originally been part of the Dutch colony of New Netherland; after the English conquered the latter in 1664, they split it into New York and New Jersey, and then further subdivided New Jersey into East and West colonies. The latter was purchased by Quaker investors and settled starting in 1675. All but one of the individuals listed here were, like Jennings (and George Walton), of the Quaker faith. The exception, Walter Barefoot, was sympathetic to them.

On Saturday, June 24, one of the family, at the usual hour at night, observed some few (not above half a dozen) of these natural (or rather unnatural) weapons to fly into the kitchen, as formerly; but some of them in an unusual manner lighting gently on him, or coming toward him so easily, as that he took them before they fell to the ground. I think there was not anything more that night remarkable. But as if the malicious demon had laid up for Sunday and Monday, then it was that he began (more furiously than formerly) with a great stone in the kitchen, and so continued with throwing down the pewter dishes, etc., great part of it all at once coming clattering down, without the stroke of a stone, little or great, to move it. Then about midnight this impious operation not ceasing, but trespassing with a *continuando*,[2] two very great stones, weighing above thirty pound apiece (that used to lie in the kitchen, in or near the chimney) were in the former, wonted,[3] rebounding manner, let fly against my door and wall in the antechamber, but with some little distance of time. This thundering noise must needs bring up the men from below, as before, (I need not say to wake me) to tell me the effect, which was the beating down several pictures, and displacing abundance of things about my chamber: but the repetition of this cannon-play by these great rumbling engines, now ready at hand for the purpose, and the like additional disturbance by four bricks that lay in the outer-room chimney (one of which having been so employed the first Sunday night, as has been said) made me despair of taking rest, and so forced me to rise from my bed. Then finding my door burst open, I also found many stones, and great pieces of bricks, to fly in, breaking the glass windows, and a paper light,[4] sometimes inwards, sometimes outwards: so hitting the door of my chamber as I came through from the antechamber, lighting very near me as I was fetching the candlestick, and afterward the candle being struck out, as I was going to light it again. So a little after, coming up for another candle, and being at the stair-foot door, a wooden mortar with great noise struck against the floor, and was just at my feet, only not touching me, moving from the other end of the kitchen where it used to lie. And when I came up myself, and two more of the same house, we heard a whistling, as it were near us in the outer room, several times. Among the rest of the tools made use of to disturb us, I found an old card for dressing flax in my chamber. Now for Monday night (June 26) one of the severest. The disturbance began in the kitchen with stones; then as I was at supper above in the antechamber, the window near which I sat at table was broke in two or three parts of it inwards, and one of the stones that broke it flew in, and I took it up at the further end of the room. The manner is observable,[5] for one of the squares was broken into nine or ten small square pieces, as if it had been regularly marked out into such even squares by a workman, to the end some of these little pieces might fly in my face (as they

---

[2] I.e., "to be continued."
[3] Accustomed.
[4] A piece of paper used to fill a "light" or space in the window casement.
[5] Worthy of observation.

did) and give me a surprise, but without any hurt. In the meantime it went on in the kitchen, whither I went down, for company, all or most of the family, and a neighbor, being there; where many stones (some great ones) came thick and threefold among us, and an old hoeing iron,[6] from a room hard by, where such utensils lay. Then, as if I had been the designed object for that time, most of the stones that came (the smaller I mean) hit me (sometimes pretty hard) to the number of above twenty, near thirty, as I remember, and whether I removed, sit, or walked, I had them, and great ones sometimes lighting gently on me, and in my hand and lap as I sat, and falling to the ground, and sometimes thumping against the wall, as near as could be to me, without touching me. Then was a room over the kitchen infested, that had not been so before, and many stones greater than usual lumbering there over our heads, not only to ours, but to the great disturbance and affrightment of some children that lay there. And for variety, there were sometimes three great, distinct knocks, sometimes five such sounds as with a great maul, reiterated divers times.

On Tuesday night (June 28) we were quiet; but not so on Wednesday, when the stones were played about in the house. And on Thursday morning I found some things that hung on nails on the wall in my chamber, namely, a spherical sun-dial, etc. lying on the ground, as knocked down by some brick or stone in the antechamber. But my landlord had the worst of that day, though he kept the field,[7] being there invisibly hit above forty times, as he affirmed to me, and he received some shrewd[8] hurtful blows on the back, and other parts, which he much complained of, and said he thought he should have reason to do, even to his dying day; and I observed that he did so, he being departed this life since.[9]

Besides this, plants of Indian corn were struck up by the roots almost, just as if they had been cut with some edged instrument, whereas *re vera*[1] they were seen to be eradicated, or rooted up with nothing but the very stones, although the injurious agent was altogether unseen. And a sort of noise, like that of snorting and whistling, was heard near the men at work in the fields many times, many whereof I myself, going thither, and being there, was a witness of; and parting thence I received a pretty hard blow with a stone on the calf of my leg. So it continued that day in two fields, where they were severally at work: and my landlord told me, he often heard likewise a humming noise in the air by him, as of a bullet discharged from a gun; and so said a servant of his that worked with him.

Upon Saturday (July 1), as I was going to visit my neighbor Capt. Barefoot, and just at his door, his man saw, as well as myself, three or four stones fall just by us in the field, or close, where the house stands, and not any other person

---

[6]The iron head of a hoe.
[7]Worked in his fields—but with the second sense that he met the lithobolic "forces" directly.
[8]Hurtful, dangerous.
[9]George Walton died in 1686, still apparently suffering from the injuries Chamberlain says he received at this time, and from others mentioned at the conclusion of the narrative.
[1]In fact.

near us. At night a great stone fell in the kitchen, as I was going to bed, and the pewter was thrown down; many stones flew about, and the candles by them put out three or four times, and the snorting heard; a Negro maid hit on the head in the entry between the kitchen and hall with a porringer from the kitchen: also the pressing-iron clattered against the partition wall between the hall and a chamber beyond it, where I lay, and Mr. Randolph,[2] His Majesty's officer for the customs, etc.

Some few stones we had on Sunday morning, (July 2) none at night. But on Monday morning (the 3rd) both Mr. Walton, and five or six with him in the field, were assaulted with them, and their ears with the old snorting and whistling. In the afternoon Mr. Walton was hit on the back with stones very grievously, as he was in his boat that lay at a cove side by his house. It was a very odd prank that was practised by the devil a little while after this. One night the cocks of hay,[3] made the day before in the orchard, was spread all abroad, and some of the hay thrown up into the trees, and some of it brought into the house, and scattered. Two logs that lay at the door, laid, one of them by the chimney in the kitchen; the other set against the door of the room where Mr. Walton then lay, as on purpose to confine him therein; a form[4] that stood in the entry (or porch) was set along by the fireside, and a joint stool[5] upon that, with a napkin spread thereon, with two pewter pots, and two candlesticks; a cheese-press[6] likewise having a spit thrust into one of the holes of it, at one end; and at the other end of the spit hung an iron kettle; and a cheese was taken out, and broken to pieces. Another time, I full well remember 'twas on a Sunday at night, my window was all broke with a violent shock of stones and brickbats;[7] which scarce missed myself: among these one huge one made its way through the great square or sash of a casement, and broke a great hole in it, throwing down books by the way, from the window to a picture over against[8] it, on the other side of the chamber, and tore a hole quite through it about half a foot long, and the piece of the cloth hung by a little part of it, on the backside of the picture.

After this we were pretty quiet,[9] saving now and then a few stones marched about for exercise, and to keep (as it were) the diabolical hand in use, till July 28, being Friday, when about forty stones flew about, abroad, and in the house and orchard, and among the trees therein, and a window broke before, was

[2] Edward Randolph, royal official and opponent of Massachusetts.
[3] Small conical heaps of hay not yet "stacked."
[4] Bench.
[5] A stool made by a joiner or skilled furniture maker—i.e., one showing careful workmanship.
[6] A wooden device perforated with holes used for extracting excess liquid from newly formed cheeses.
[7] Pieces of bricks.
[8] On the opposite wall.
[9] Sometime prior to the beginning of July, Hannah Jones was put on a peace bond—that is, she was forced to give a bond that would be forfeited if Walton complained of her again. From around that time until the end of July, as Chamberlain has it, the "stonery" at Walton's house dramatically declined.

broke again, and one room where they never used[1] before.

August 1. On Wednesday the window in my antechamber was broken again, and many stones were played about, abroad, and in the house, in the daytime, and at night. The same day in the morning they tried this experiment: they did set on the fire a pot with urine, and crooked pins in it, with design to have it boil, and by that means to give punishment to the witch, or wizard (that might be the wicked procurer or contriver of this stone affliction) and take off their own;[2] as they had been advised. This was the effect of it: As the liquor begun to grow hot, a stone came and broke the top or mouth of it,[3] and threw it down, and spilt what was in it; which being made good again,[4] another stone, as the pot grew hot again, broke the handle off; and being recruited and filled the third time, was then with a third stone quite broke to pieces and spilt; and so the operation became frustrated and fruitless.

On August 2, two stones in the afternoon I heard and saw myself in the house and orchard; and another window in the hall was broke. And as I was entering my own chamber, a great square of a casement, being a foot square, was broke, with the noise as of a big stone, and pieces of the glass flew into the room, but no stone came in then, or could be found within or without. At night, as I, with others, were in the kitchen, many more came in; and one great stone that lay on a spinning wheel to keep it steady, was thrown to the other side of the room. Several neighbors then present were ready to testify [to] this matter.

Upon August 3, Thursday, the gate between my said landlord and his neighbor John Amazeen was taken off again, and thrown into Amazeen's field, who heard it fall, and averred it then made a noise like a great gun.

On Friday the 4th, the fence against Mr. Walton's neighbor's door, (the woman of whom formerly there was great suspicion, and thereupon examination had, as appears upon record;)[5] this fence being maliciously pulled down to let in their cattle into his ground; he and his servants were pelted with above forty stones as they went to put it up again; for she had often threatened that he should never enjoy his house and land. Mr. Walton was hit divers times, and all that day in the field, as they were reaping, it ceased not, and there fell (by the men's computation) above a hundred stones. A woman helping to reap (among the rest) was hit nine or ten times, and hurt to that degree, that her left arm, hip, thigh, and leg, were made black and blue therewith; which she showed to the woman,[6] Mrs. Walton, and others. Mr. Woodbridge, a divine,[7]

---

[1] I.e., where the stones never had been active before.
[2] I.e., relieve the punishment inflicted on the inhabitants of Walton's house. This simple exorcism ritual was practiced, as Chamberlain next asserts, according to the advice of someone consulted by the inhabitants.
[3] The pot.
[4] I.e., the pot was refilled and once again set on the fire.
[5] The neighbor in question here was not Amazeen but Hannah Jones.
[6] Hannah Jones.
[7] I.e., a minister.

coming to give me a visit, was hit about the hip, and one Mr. Jefferys, a merchant, who was with him, on the leg. A window in the kitchen that had been much battered before, was now quite broken out, and unwindowed, no glass or lead at all being left: a glass bottle broken to pieces, and the pewter dishes (about nine of them) thrown down, and bent.

On Saturday the 5th, as they were reaping in the field, three sickles were cracked and broken by the force of these lapidary instruments of the devil, as the sickles were in the reapers' hands, on purpose (it seems) to obstruct their labor, and do them injury and damage. And very many stones were cast about that day; insomuch, that some that assisted at that harvest-work, being struck with them, by reason of that disturbance left the field, but were followed by their invisible adversaries to the next house.

On Sunday, being the 6th, there fell nothing considerable, nor on Monday, (7th) save only one of the children [was] hit with a stone on the back. We were quiet to Tuesday the 8th. But on Wednesday (9th) above one hundred stones (as they verily thought) repeated the reapers' disquiet in the cornfield, whereof some were affirmed by Mr. Walton to be great ones indeed, near as big as a man's head; and Mrs. Walton, his wife being by curiosity led thither, with intent also to make some discovery by the most diligent and vigilant observation she could use, to obviate the idle incredulity some inconsiderate persons might irrationally entertain concerning this venefical[8] operation; or at least to confirm her own sentiments and belief of it. Which she did, but to her cost; for she received an untoward blow (with a stone) on her shoulder. There were likewise two sickles bent, cracked, and disabled with them; beating them violently out of their hands that held them, and this reiterated three times successively.

After this we enjoyed our former peace and quiet, unmolested by these stony disturbances, that whole month of August, excepting some few times; and the last of all in the month of September (the beginning thereof), wherein Mr. Walton himself only (the original perhaps of this strange adventuyre, as has been declared) was the the designed concluding[9] sufferer; who going in his canoe (or boat) from the Great Island, where he dwelt, to Portsmouth, to attend the council, who had taken cognizance of this matter, he being summoned thither, in order to his and the suspect's examination, and the court's taking order thereabout, he was sadly hit with three pebble stones as big as one's fist; one of which broke his head, which I saw him show to the president of the council; the others gave him that pain on the back, of which (with other like strokes) he complained then, and aferware to his death.

Who, that pursues these preternatural occurances, can possibly be so much an enemy to his own soul, and irrefutable reason as obstinately to oppose himself to, or confusedly fluctuate in , the opinion and doctrine of demons, or spirits,

[8]Witching, from *venefica* (Latin), "a witch."
[9]I.e., intentionally the final.

and witches? Certainly he that does so, must do two thins more; He must temerariously unhinge, or undermine the fundamentals of the best religion in the world: and he must disingenuously quit and abandon that of the three theological virtues or graces, to which the great doctor of the gentiles gave the precedence, charity, through his unchristian and uncharitable incredulity.[1]

[1] The apostle Paul, whose special charge was the gentiles (the non-Jewish population of the Mediterranean Basin, and particularly the Romans and the Greeks), viewed charity as the greatest of virtues, writing in his first letter to the Corinthians, "And now abideth faith, hope, charity, these three; but the greatest of these is charity." From Chamberlain's viewpoint here, perhaps more important was Paul's comment that charity "beareth all things, believeth all things, hopeth all things, endureth all things" (1 Cor. 13:13, 7).

9

Two French Boys Adrift
in Spanish Territory

In 1682 the explorer René Robert Cavelier, sieur de La Salle, led a small party down the Mississippi River from Illinois and took possession of the great central valley for his king, Louis XIV, after whom he named the region Louisiana. Two years later, La Salle returned via the Gulf of Mexico with four ships loaded with settlers. His scheme to establish a French province there met with many misfortunes. La Salle was intent on settling land long claimed by the Spanish and long occupied by various Native American peoples—both of whom would be unlikely to accept intruders—and he made many tactical blunders almost from the start. Unintentionally sailing past the Mississippi, which he had not approached from its tangled delta before, he eventually made a temporary camp at Matagorda Bay on the Texas coast. With their ships wrecked, lost, or run off, La Salle's three hundred colonists began succumbing to disease in alarming numbers as he, still obsessed with his original vision, kept trying to find the valley of the Mississippi. When things turned truly desperate in the spring of 1686, La Salle set out with a small party that he intended to lead overland to Canada in search of relief, but they had covered only a fraction of the enormous distance before desertions and deaths forced him to turn back. At his return to Matagorda Bay, he found only slightly more than half of the original complement of men, women, and children alive. He set out once more the following year on a desperate expedition seeking relief for the remaining settlers. For two months, the expedition struggled on until a quarrel erupted between one of La Salle's nephews and some other members of the bewildered party, who killed the young man and several others before turning on La Salle himself. The disorderly expedition fell under the sway of the man who had shot La Salle, the sieur Duhaut, until he was in turn assassinated. In time, several of the conspirators passed into Native American society, while the core of La Salle's supporters, including his brother Jean Cavelier and another of their nephews, eventually made its way to the Mississippi. From there, they went tediously up to Illinois country, arriving in Canada the following fall.

In the meantime, the colony in Texas had suffered a devastating attack at the hands of the Karankawa or Clamcoet Indians. Among those killed was a woman named Isabelle Talon, who had joined the La Salle expedition with her husband and their two daughters and four sons in France shortly after returning from Canada. Isabelle's husband, Lucien, who had been a timber worker in Quebec, perhaps had woodsman's skills that La Salle thought of potential use in the densely forested American landscape. Some of the Talon boys, in addition, would make excellent candidates to send out among the local native communities to learn their languages and thus serve the French as guides, a common practice in Canada. The Talon family, which had been in Quebec for a considerable period, likely hoped to find their fresh start in this new French colony.

The fate the Talons actually suffered was quite different from any they might have imagined while listening to La Salle's enthusiastic plans in La Rochelle. Lucien went off one day with a hunting party under La Salle, was lost or injured in the woods, and never returned; no one could tell what had become of him. One of his daughters, Marie Elizabeth, died of disease in the camp, and her brother Pierre, who accompanied La Salle on that man's fatal last journey in 1687, wound up among the Caddo or Ceni Indians, not so much to learn their language as merely to preserve his life. The other surviving children (Marie Magdelène, Jean Baptiste, Lucien, and Robert), along with a possible relative of theirs named Eustace Bréman, had remained with Isabelle at ill-fated Matagorda Bay, where Isabelle was murdered before their eyes during the Karankawa attack. The children themselves were hurried off by some of the Karankawa women to their village, where they were eventually adopted. The Spanish general Alonso de Leon, ordered to rout the remnants of La Salle's expedition from Texas, heard of their survival and came in search of them in 1690. By then, Jean Baptiste and young Bréman had moved elsewhere in the region (another Spanish expedition found them the next year), but Marie Magdelène, Lucien, and Robert were still among the Karankawa when de Leon found them. So integrated were they with the natives that the Karankawa openly cried at the sad rescue of the children.

De Leon had been told of the survival of these children by their brother Pierre, whom he already had found dwelling much farther inland with a young Parisian, Pierre Meunier, another survivor from La Salle's second relief expedition. Both Meunier and Pierre Talon resisted de Leon's efforts to hunt them down after he first heard of their presence in Texas, and they also resisted his attempt to return them from their happy exile. Like the other children located in 1690 and 1691, they were marked all over with tattoos that their Spanish liberators tried desperately and unsuccessfully to erase from the European parchment of their skin. From 1692 to 1696, the reunited Talon children lived with the Spanish viceroy in Mexico City. The three oldest boys at length were enlisted into the Spanish marine service at Vera Cruz, while their sister and young Robert remained in Mexico City. The three mariners were captured by the French at sea in 1697, at which point Pierre and Jean Baptiste successfully transferred into the French army but Lucien, judged too young for that, was sent into domestic service at Oleron, France, where the record of him ends. The two others returned to Louisiana in 1699, where they were stationed at Biloxi and Fort Maurepas, the current center of French colonization efforts under Pierre Le Moyne d'Iberville. By the early years of the new century, bad luck struck again and they were captured by the Portuguese and held prisoner for several years until at least one and perhaps both of them once more showed up on Mobile Bay. Their brother Robert, who may have made his way to Spain and from there to France with Marie Magdelène about the same time, may also have been at Mobile that early; he was listed there by 1720 as a carpenter and a married man with two children born in the vicinity. With their tattooed faces and their gift for native languages as decided advantages, Pierre and Jean Baptiste went off into Texas with a French expedition in 1714, guiding Louis Juchereau de St. Denis toward the Rio Grande before going back to Louisiana. Marie Magdelène, married in Paris in 1699, apparently moved back to Quebec, where she and her husband set about raising a family. A record of 1719 shows her son as being married there, in Charlesbourg, in his turn.

Pierre and Jean Baptiste were interviewed in France in 1698 at the insistence of Pontchartrain, soon to be minister of the navy and an avid promoter of new French enterprises in the Indies. It is through the surviving transcript of the interview that we know much of the little that survives about their family, and indeed about the Caddo who helped preserve a part of it.

THE TALON BROTHERS

from "An Account of the Interrogation of the Two Canadians" (1698)

QUESTIONS CONCERNING THE ACCOUNT FORWARDED BY MONSEIGNEUR DE Pontchartrain[1]

These soldiers are two brothers, Pierre and Jean Baptiste Talon, born in Quebec in New France, sons of Lucien Talon, a timber worker, and his wife Isabelle (both now deceased) who were inhabitants of that place. As boys the two brothers left Canada with their father and mother to return to France; they were then quite young and are unable to state precisely when this took place. They state though that it was shortly before La Salle departed on his last expedition to Louisiana; for, after coming ashore at La Rochelle and traveling to Paris, they were engaged by La Salle, together with their parents, two younger brothers, and two sisters, to accompany La Salle on that voyage. They all accordingly returned to La Rochelle where they embarked with him, without having remained in France longer than perhaps two months.

---

[1] Jérôme Phélypeaux de Maurepas, comte de Pontchartrain, soon to be appointed minister of navy as the successor of his father, Louis. The interrogation was performed in order to gather information useful for a new French effort in the lower Mississippi favored by Pontchartrain.

La Salle had three vessels: the *Joly* of about 50 guns, on which he himself sailed; the *L'Aimable*, about 20 guns, which carried the Talon brothers and their family; and a third vessel whose name the brothers do not recall. . . .

Question 4: Did they find any natives there, and did they have any communication with them?

Reply: All the region is peopled with natives, who are divided into small tribes, each having its own name as well as its own language, which differs from that of the others. The Talon brothers were in communication with two of these tribes in particular; Pierre Talon with the Ceni,[2] the mildest and best-disposed of all the tribes of which they had knowledge; they are about one hundred leagues inland. These Ceni have their own village, where they live by families in wooden houses thatched with hay. La Salle became friendly with them, sent Pierre Talon to them to try to learn their language. This he did perfectly, living with them for a period of five or six years, until the Spanish took him away, as will be related later. But he has now almost completely forgotten this language, having lived for about ten years among the Spanish in Mexico, where they took him, and where he learned Spanish.

Jean Baptiste Talon, the younger of the two brothers, together with two still younger brothers and a sister, lived for a like number of years, and indeed even longer, with the Clamcoet tribe.[3] These are a people much more cruel and barbarous than the Ceni, and indeed than any other of the native tribes. They live along the seashore, with no villages or fixed dwellings, roaming continuously, and living on game and fish. They make camp wherever the night finds them, in rude shelters improvised on the spot from two forked poles and a ridgepole that they cover with bison hides prepared for the purpose, and which they wrap themselves in during the day. They share this custom with the other nomadic tribes of the region; this includes all the tribes between the seashore and the village of the Ceni. These latter [the Ceni], on the contrary, cultivate the land, raising Indian corn, or maize. They also grow beans and squash of various types, as well as other kinds of vegetables and root plants whose names the Talon brothers do not know. They grow tobacco, but only a small amount, and that solely for their own use. They also raise horses, which they scarcely use for other purposes than to carry meat on their hunting trips; this, because the hunters have to travel a considerable distance when hunting bison. These are very wary and avoid human settlements, so that they are not to be found within a distance of fifteen or twenty leagues from the villages. It has been noted that these bison have so keen a sense of smell that they can scent hunters from some distance when they are approached from upwind, with the result that they take flight. To come near enough to them for a kill it is necessary to approach from downwind. When finally a hunter has succeeded

[2] The Caddo, a tribe then occupying villages along the Red River watershed in present-day Arkansas and Louisiana.
[3] The Karankawa, who were responsible for the massacre of most of the people left by La Salle at his fort in 1687; they inhabited a coastal region near present-day Galveston Bay.

in killing one bison in a herd, either by arrows or by a gunshot, all the others crowd around it, their attention fastened on the victim, so that one may easily kill several others before the herd takes flight. The Ceni tribe, which incidentally is one of the largest, numbers about a thousand persons.

About twelve leagues from the Ceni, advancing inland, is another village, that of the Ayenni.[4] Pierre Talon was also acquainted with this tribe and had some contact with them. The Ayenni are an ally of the Ceni, having the same language and mode of living, but are fewer in number. Talon heard from them that further inland there are several villages belonging to other tribes. The Talon brothers have no knowledge of any tribe larger than the Ceni, but Pierre Talon heard that there is another and considerably larger tribe called the Canotins,[5] which has no fixed point of habitation, and which continually wages war against the Ceni.

All the tribes that live along the seashore, and indeed as far inland as the Ceni, are extremely barbarous and cruel, and cannot be trusted except under the most favorable conditions, and when one has a stronger force than theirs. Those tribes that live further inland, and thus closer to the Ceni, are more humane and even helpful; they are easy to contact, and display hospitality to Europeans who become lost while hunting or otherwise.

These various tribes are frequently at war with each other, as will be noted further on; they have no weapons other than bows and arrows (which have, instead of iron arrowheads, points made from a kind of flint, sharpened, or from fish bones or fish teeth) and war clubs, since the use of iron is unknown. But their arrows are never poisoned, as are those of the Caribs and other savage peoples of the Antilles.[6]

All these tribes follow the custom of going at the break of dawn each morning to the nearest stream and diving into the water; they almost never fail to do this, whatever the time of year, even when the stream is ice-covered. It often happens that they have to break a hole through the ice so that they can jump into the water. They run at top speed while going to the stream and returning, after which they place themselves in front of a great fire that has been prepared for this purpose. They wipe and shake their arms, legs, and thighs for some time, until they are quite dry, after which they wrap themselves in bison hides prepared like chamois leather, which they use as a robe, and then walk for a space of time. They claim that doing this gives them strength and makes them supple and agile in running. The men are very regular in observing this custom without missing a day, when they have the opportunity to do so. The women are not so exact in the practice. They all swim like fish, both men and women.

---

[4] The Yojuane, a band of the Tonkawa people, of northern and central Texas.

[5] Actually a version of the Caddoan name ("Kanohatino") for what is now called the Red River, but the French under La Salle mistook it for a tribal name.

[6] The Carib peoples had moved out onto the Caribbean islands, including the Antilles, from South America; they were rumored by the apparently more docile Taino to indulge in cannibalism, a word said to derive from "Carib."

The Talon brothers were required to do just as the natives themselves did; they are extremely demanding that others follow their practices, and even copy them in detail, and they often tried to convince the Talon brothers and other young Frenchmen to become pagans like themselves. They never, however, prevented them from praying, but amused themselves by moving their lips in imitation, or even spending hours just holding one or another of the books that the Clamcoet had found at the French settlement, after they had massacred them (as will be related later), and making faces as though they were reading. The natives are extremely clownish and fond of ridicule; gay, and addicted to inebrity (for they prepare drinks that go to their head, almost as wine does); they dance and sing, though very crudely, having for instruments only a spe-cially-made notched stick that they rub with another stick, and gourds filled with small pebbles or grains of corn. One of their drinks is made from a red bean that they first chew, and then mix with water. They believe that its use makes them more limber, and lighter in running; as a result they drink so much of it that they vomit it up: drinking and vomiting, alternately by turns. They make still another beverage from leaves, whose name the Talon brothers do not know. They boil these leaves in water, churning it or beating it like chocolate, so that it becomes quite foamy. They drink it while it is very hot, using it principally after they have walked a great deal. . . .

Question 7: To what place did La Salle lead them?
    Reply: The explorations of La Salle did not extend further than the village of the Ceni, which, as has been stated, is about one hundred leagues inland, since he was killed on the second expedition that he undertook to that area with the intention of penetrating further. His death occurred at a point about six leagues from the village, and before he had reached there. He was killed by a Basque named Duhaut, by a gunshot in the head.[7] Duhaut killed him in revenge for the death of his elder brother, whom, he had been told, La Salle had killed on his first expedition to explore the region, immediately after he had landed. The elder Duhaut brother had accompanied La Salle, together with a number of other men, but had never returned; he was not the only one who perished, since the greater part of those who were with La Salle on that expedition, as well as on others that he made later, suffered the same fate. For on these trips of two or three months, and even on one trip of six months without returning to the settlement, he never brought back but about half of the men who set out with him. Some became lost, and died in the forests from fatigue, or were killed by the savage Clamcoet with whom they fought, while others deserted to live among the natives, by whom they were well received.

Question 8: An account of the events attending the death of La Salle.
    Reply: The younger of the Duhaut brothers, having resolved to kill La Salle, took advantage of La Salle's having sent him as one of six men in a

---

[7] Robert Cavelier, sieur de La Salle, born in Rouen in 1643, was murdered along the Brazos River in 1687 by Duhaut, who assumed control of the expedition until he in turn was assassinated.

hunting party (they were then, as has been stated, about six leagues from the village of the Ceni) to plot against him. But among the five others in the party he found only one, an Englishman named James,[8] who would fall in with his plan. This forced them to kill the four others while they slept. One of the four was an Indian named Nica, a good hunter, whom La Salle had brought with him from Canada; another, a servant of La Salle's named Sagé. The other two were Frenchmen whose names Pierre Talon, who relates these events, does not recall. Young Talon had been with La Salle since his arrival, having been brought on the expedition with the intention of being left with the Ceni, to learn their language.

La Salle, impatient that the hunters had not returned, went ahead towards the area to which he had directed them, which was not far distant, to try to find out the reason for their delay in returning. He was accompanied only by a Franciscan friar. Duhaut and James, anticipating that La Salle would do just this, placed themselves in ambush at two points along the route, so that if one should fail, the other would succeed in their plan. Duhaut, firing first, killed La Salle on the spot by putting a ball through his forehead. He then returned with James to rejoin the main party as though they had done nothing.

Duhaut told the brother of the man he had just killed, who was a fine priest, and the latter's nephew, a young lad of ten or twelve years, what he had done to avenge, as he said, the death of his brother.[9] He told them that they were free to go wherever they wished, since he could never thereafter look at them without pain. With that the griefstricken uncle and nephew left, together with the friar who had been a witness to the murder and two or three other friends of theirs, all Frenchmen, whose names Talon does not recall. They went past the village of the Ceni, where they left Pierre Talon, in accordance with La Salle's intention. They then set out to make their way through the forest and the uncharted wilderness in an attempt to reach Canada overland, having guns and ammunition for hunting, and preferring to expose themselves to all the perils that they might encounter, and place themselves at the mercy of the savage tribes through whose territories they had to pass, rather than to remain under the authority of Duhaut. For Duhaut had assumed command of the eighteen or twenty men who remained of the unfortunate party, though he did not enjoy for very long the leadership that he had assumed after his crime; a dispute broke out between the two conspirators and two or three days later James killed him with a pistol shot. James then took over command, but the jealousy of the other members of the party brought him the same fate as Duhaut's; some days afterwards he was killed by a French sailor named Rutre. He in his turn was killed by a surgeon, also a Frenchman. This surgeon, fearing that he might suffer the same fate, took refuge with a native tribe, the Toho, close neighbors of the Ceni, who received him well because he brought with him his musket and ammunition. Not long afterwards the natives took him

[8] "English Jem" was actually a German buccaneer named Hiens, who came from Würtemburg. It was Hiens who later murdered Duhaut.

[9] Abbé Jean Cavelier, a Sulpician priest, eventually led the escape party, which included his twelve-year-old nephew, to the Illinois country and from there to Canada.

with them in a war against another tribe, the Paouïtes or Temerlouans. They took with them also Pierre Talon. The surgeon was killed in this fight, having fallen behind when the Toho took flight, as the natives never fail to do when they find the enemy on guard and prepared to meet them. As these people are very agile and are swift runners, the surgeon was unable to keep up with the Toho, and accordingly fell behind and was killed. Young Talon would have suffered the same fate, had he not been mounted on a horse belonging to the surgeon who had turned the horse over to him before going into the fight to be better able to fire his musket.

Pierre Talon returned to the village of the Ceni, where he remained for the following five or six years, until the arrival of the Spanish who carried him back to Mexico, as will later be related. Pierre Talon has not heard anything since that time as to the fate of La Salle's brother, his nephew, or any of the others who accompanied them. . . .

Question 10: The part played by each of the persons who were with La Salle at the time of his death.

Reply: We have mentioned the fate of several of those who were in La Salle's company when he died, and who in turn perished, in part by killing each other. The remainder dispersed, and fled away among the natives, except for those who followed La Salle's brother and his nephew. In addition, a young Frenchman named Pierre Meunier withdrew with the Ceni, where he lived in company with Pierre Talon, and in the same manner, until they were taken by the Spanish, as will be related further on.

As for those who remained at the settlement at the time La Salle set out on the trip on which he was killed, one of these, Jean Baptiste Talon, reports that they numbered no more than twenty or twenty-five persons, including the women, a priest, and two Franciscan friars. Almost all of these were massacred by the Clamcoet, who attacked them because La Salle on his arrival had summarily seized their boats in order to move upriver and establish his settlement. Even though peace had been made with this tribe, they had no sooner learned of La Salle's death and the resulting dissension among his people than, by the greatest treason in the world, they made a surprise attack on the settlement. Believing the Clamcoet to be friendly, the camp's inhabitants were not on the alert, so that the savages had little difficulty in slaughtering all but a very few: Jean Baptiste Talon, two of his younger brothers, Robert and Lucien, their older sister, Marie Magdelène, and one other, a Parisian named Eustache Bréman, said to be a relative of theirs. They were saved by some of the native women, who, touched by their tender ages, carried them on their backs to their huts. This, while their men slaughtered the rest, and after the Talon children had seen their mother killed before their eyes. As for the Talon's father, he had become lost in the woods some time previously while on a hunting trip with La Salle, and no one ever learned how he perished. Their other sister had died of illness at the settlement.

Moved by tenderness at the sight of an infant at her mother's breast, the native women also saved in the same manner the wife of the French officer who commanded the settlement in La Salle's absence, and who was also killed in the massacre. But the natives, on returning to their homes after the slaughter, first killed the mother and then the baby, holding it by its feet and dashing it against a tree. The men did not however harm the Talons or Eustache Bréman, who were reared and cherished by the native women who had rescued them as though they were their own children. They remained with the Indians some six or seven years, living their manner of life, until the Spanish came up from Mexico to take them away, as will be described later.

Question 11: What they did, in detail.
Reply: The Talon brothers have already related some of their specific experiences; how, when they fell into the hands of the natives, they were first of all marked on the face, hands, arms, and several other parts of the body just as the natives themselves were, with various bizarre black markings. These are made using willow charcoal, powdered and stirred into water, that is introduced beneath the skin through cuts that are made with very sharp thorns, in an extremely painful process. The charcoal and water mixes with the blood that oozes from the cuts to form marks and characters that remain permanently visible, in spite of a hundred attempts by the Spanish to remove them.

The natives took their captives on the hunt and on the war trail, after having taught them to use the bow and to run as they did; the natives run so swiftly that there is no galloping horse, no matter how fast, that they cannot follow and eventually tire out. The brothers went quite naked, as the others did, and each morning at dawn they would plunge into the nearest stream, regardless of the season. The captives ate, as the natives did, meat from the hunt, either fresh or sun-dried, but more usually half raw. The only meals that horrified the captives were those of human flesh, for these natives are all cannibals, but only with respect to their native enemies. They never wished to eat any of the French that they had killed because, as they said, "They did not eat them." Jean Baptiste Talon states that at one point he went nearly three days without food because during this time they offered him only the flesh of the Ayenni that they had killed in a war raid that will be described later.

Pierre Talon, the elder of the two brothers, had been left with the Ceni, as has been noted; he remained the whole time with their chief, who appeared to have no authority over the other natives except when waging war. Even this authority was so limited that each warrior could leave the battle and return home whenever the spirit moved him, without asking the chief's leave. They made war without observing any sort of order or discipline, but only through surprise and without exposing themselves too much to danger. They never attack except at night or at the earliest point of dawn, when they believe their enemy to be deep in sleep. But when they are able to surprise and slay some of their foes they rip off the scalp with the hair attached, afterwards carefully drying it and filling it with hay. Each warrior keeps his own scalps as trophies; they are hung on sticks from the ridgepoles of their lodges. After returning from a successful war trip they carry these scalps in the hand and display them, raising them high in the air with much ostentation and ceremony, while they dance, as is their custom, singing songs that they make up to celebrate their victories. The brave with the most scalps is the most highly regarded, and their entire glory rests in their deeds.

The chief of the Ceni had an elderly father, who also carried the title of chief. They dwelt together, but it was clear that all the authority rested in the son; the father being well on in years and evidently having passed on to his son all the honor of command. They lived in an admirable harmony. For the rest, the Talons state that these savage people always treated them with the greatest humanity conceivable, and that they were never maltreated with blows or otherwise; on the contrary, their captors showed them tenderness and affection, and seemed to be upset when anyone annoyed them, and even took their part on some occasions against their own children.

Question 12: In what manner they fell into the hands of the Spanish.
Reply: The Spanish in Mexico, having been informed of La Salle's arrival, and of his plan to establish the French in Louisiana, decided to block his plan, and for this purpose they sent three expeditions into the region,[1] although to do so they had to pass through a distant and unknown land where, from what the Talons recall having heard them say, they had never previously been. The first expedition consisted of some five hundred mounted men, armed with muskets or small carbines, pistols, and swords, and all wearing coats of mail made of iron wire formed into nets of very small mesh, which protected them from the effects of the natives' arrows. But, as it was not until long after the massacre of the French that they came into the area, they found only two of those who had become scattered after La Salle's death; these were two Frenchmen with native tribes that were nearer to the Mexican border than the tribes that we have spoken of. One of these two was a young man from Bayonne named L'Archevêque, who appeared to be of good family, and well educated; the other a sailor named Grollet.[2] The Spanish took both men back to Mexico, where the Talon brothers saw them, as they will relate later.

On the second expedition, the Spanish force did not number over two

---

[1] In fact, the Spanish sent out nine expeditions in search of La Salle's colony, four by sea and five (not three) by land. The latter were all commanded by Alonso de Leon. It was on his 1689 expedition, the fourth in the sequence, that he found the site of La Salle's settlement; in 1690 he came across Pierre Talon and Pierre Meunier, and then Talon's brothers Robert and Lucien and sister Marie Magdelène.

[2] Jean L'Archevêque of Bayonne had been one of Duhaut's associates in the murder of La Salle; he escaped thereafter and took up with Jacques Grollet of La Rochelle, who had deserted the La Salle colony earlier. The two men were found by Alonso de Leon living among the natives, taken prisoner to Mexico, and transferred to Spain. They later were allowed their freedom on the provision that they would return to America, where they both became early settlers in the Spanish colony of New Mexico. L'Archevêque eventually became a prominent figure there; he was killed somewhere on the Great Plains when Pawnee Indians attacked a Spanish expedition sent out in 1720 to chase down rumors of French interlopers.

hundred men; they had reduced their strength after learning from L'Archevêque and Grollet that disaster had overtaken the French, and that only a few
remained who had escaped the many perils that they had encountered and
were now dispersed among the native tribes. Now, with the intention of placing
even this miserable remainder of the French expedition in their power, they
penetrated much further upcountry than on their first expedition.

Having learned from some natives that the Spanish were approaching in
search of them, and fearing their cruelty, Pierre Talon and Meunier sought to
avoid them by escaping further into the country, from tribe to tribe. But while
on the way they met the Spanish, who forced them to guide the expedition to
the village of the Ceni, so that they could find out if there were any other
survivors. Having found none, they remained there for several days, and finding
the Ceni more tractable and in some ways of milder temper than the other
tribes, they left with them three Spanish Franciscan friars, with some soldiers
to guard them. They built a dwelling for them in the village, and left clothing,
meal, and other provisions, which were in ample supply since the expedition
had over four hundred horses, and those which were not needed for the
mounted force carried baggage and provisions.

During the time that Talon and Meunier were with them the friars were
busy making up a glossary of native words, in order to learn the language of the
Ceni, utilizing Talon and Meunier as interpreters through the aid of the captain and the lieutenant of the Spanish force, who spoke good French. Several
times the two Frenchmen heard the Spanish officers say that they would like
to remain in that country, which belonged to them and not to the French.
They heard the same comment later from the Viceroy of Mexico.

When Pierre Talon found that the Spanish treated them very humanely,
he told them that he still had three brothers and a sister, in addition to several
other French, with the Clamcoet, so that he might have the consolation of
seeing them removed with him and returned among Christians. This indeed
occurred; the Spanish went there and brought away his sister and the two brothers, Robert and Lucien. The third brother, Jean Baptiste Talon, and Eustache
Bréman remained with the tribe—how, Pierre Talon did not know—until
about a year later when a third Spanish expedition of about two hundred and
fifty men came in search of them and took them back to Mexico. The natives
let them go with regret, and only because it was clear that the Spanish were in
a position to take them by force should they refuse to release them. On the
other hand, the Spanish did not want to create enmity in the hearts of the
natives, since they intended to establish settlements in the region, and they
offered a horse in exchange for each of the French. But when it came to the
exchange for Talon's sister,[3] the eldest of the children, who was quite a bit older
than the boys and was fully grown, the natives demanded two horses in
exchange. At this point the bargaining became heated, and the Spanish resorted
to the use of arms, with the result that two or three natives were felled by gun

[3] Marie Magdelène Talon.

shots. The others fled, being extremely fearful of firearms; eventually they yielded up the girl for one horse, as they had done with her brothers. But, to appease the natives the Spanish gave them some tobacco, which they prize so highly that there is nothing they will not do to get it. On the Spanish side one horse was wounded by the natives' arrows, which they discharged in large numbers but with no effect on the Spanish because of their coats of mail.

The simple natives feared not only the noise of firearms, but even the sound of drums. When the Clamcoet, outraged that La Salle had seized their canoes by force, assembled with the intention of destroying the French force, they were so terror-stricken by the rattle of the drums that were beaten as the French prepared for defense that they all took to flight. After that time they became somewhat more accustomed to the sounds of battle, and instead of fleeing precipitously in terror they were content to throw themselves flat on the ground as soon as they heard the first shot from cannon or musket, in the belief that this would keep them from being hit.

They displayed such regret at being separated from the brothers and the sister of Jean Baptiste Talon that he, remaining still for a time with them, reports that they all wept plentifully at their departure, and mourned them for a month—especially for the younger boys for whom they had formed a stronger and more tender attachment than for the older ones.

The natives wept no less when Jean Baptiste Talon and Eustache Bréman were taken from them, and privately urged Talon to miss no opportunity to desert the Spanish and return to them as soon as he could, with a number of horses. This he promised, without however having any intention of keeping his word, since he much preferred to be among Christians than to remain with these savage peoples.

On the second Spanish expedition, and their first penetration as far as the Clamcoet, they picked up also an Italian whom they found there, whose name the Talons do not recall. He would never admit to having been a member of La Salle's party, though the Talon brothers believe that he was, and claimed to have come to the region by land from Canada, which is impossible to believe.

10

THE BLOODY ESCAPE OF
HANNAH DUSTAN:
A CULTURAL READER

IN 1697, WHILE IN HER FORTIETH YEAR, HANNAH EMERSON DUSTAN LAY IN BED recovering from childbirth. Martha, her twelfth child, had been born on March 9th; it was now the middle of that month, and Hannah, with the help of neighbor and midwife Mary Neff, was coming along as well as could be expected in the chill late winter of rural Haverhill, Massachusetts. At least she had a snug shelter for herself and for the seven other surviving Dustan children, from two to seventeen years of age, who were still at home. Their brick house, built just the year before by bricklayer and farmer Thomas Dustan, Hannah's husband, was sturdier than the modest frame cottages of most of the neighbors, probably including the widow Neff. It was in a similar small wooden house nearby that the Dustans themselves had lived for most of the time since their marriage eighteen years earlier.

Early in the morning of this particular March day, Thomas Dustan was working outdoors, so it was he who first noticed the signs of coming trouble. Haverhill residents had good reason to be on the alert. For the past decade, New England had been embroiled in a long war against the French Canadians and their Indian allies. The New Englanders called the conflict King William's War, blaming it on the distant English monarch, but in fact relished any opportunity to trim the territories of New France. As to the Indians—any Indians, it might seem—the settlers remembered well the devastations of King Philip's War two decades earlier. That conflict was named not for a European monarch (although one nineteenth-century account of it was embellished, in fact, with a portrait of Philip II of Spain), but rather for the Wampanoag sachem Metacomet, whom the English renamed "Philip"; they similarly renamed his brother Wamsutta "Alexander." The English had defeated Metacomet, but in the process had come close to annihilation. For long decades afterward the losses on both sides lingered in bitter memory.

Haverhill, an isolated inland town founded in the early 1640s on the northern bank of the Merrimack River, had escaped devastation during King Philip's War, but with the entrance of the French into the picture thereafter such northern frontier towns were especially exposed. Thomas Dustan and his neighbors were so alert to danger in the winter of 1697 because Haverhill had been subject to raids throughout the preceding decade. What Thomas saw at seven in the morning on March 15, 1697 was a small group of Abenaki Indians, French allies from what is now Maine. He gathered the seven older Dustan children outside and sent them off toward the nearest garrison house. He then hurried inside to give the alarm to Hannah and Mary Neff and to help them, along with the infant Martha, follow after the others. The attack proceeded so quickly, however, that he soon despaired of saving those in the house. Perhaps distracted or torn between obligations; perhaps fearing for his own life and/or those of the seven fleeing children—whatever the motive, Thomas Dustan soon rode away on his horse after those children, leaving the women and the infant to fend for themselves. Fearing he could not possibly rescue all the children, he resolved to snatch up only one of them—the one his heart would direct him to—and gallop off to the garrison house, leaving the rest to the protection of Providence. In reality, he found his heart could not make that dreadful choice; joining with all of them on foot as they fled at the slow pace of the five-year-old, he kept the pursuing Abenaki at bay with his gun until he brought the whole party to safety.

Back at the Dustan house, worse luck awaited the abandoned females, who were among the many Haverhill residents taken prisoner that morning. Mary Neff was captured outside as she tried to flee with Martha in her arms. Next the Abenaki came inside and ordered Hannah to rise from her bed; she stumbled over to the large open fireplace, where she sat and looked on as the attackers rifled through her belongings and then set the new house on fire. The house was not her only loss. As she and Mary Neff were moved off with other captives by a group of about twenty Abenaki, one of the captors snatched Martha away and, swinging the infant by the feet, smashed her soft head against a tree, ending her new life.

Hannah Dustan must have been weak and distraught, maybe even in shock, but she somehow managed to keep going, and that alone may have saved her from the fate of several unfortunate neighbors, who as they tired were cut down by hatchet and left where they fell. The party covered a dozen miles by the end of the day, the first leg of a long journey that took them far, far away from Haverhill before the week was out. By then the large group had been subdivided. Hannah Dustan and Mary Neff had come under the control of one of the original attackers, a warrior who betrayed in his personal history some of the complexities of this intercultural borderground. At this point the man, under the tutelage of the Jesuit missionaries of Maine, was a practicing Catholic. Prior to King Philip's War, however, he had lived in the Massachusetts town of Lancaster and had worshipped in the English manner. In fact, he had been a "servant" of that town's Puritan minister, the Reverend Joseph Rowlandson. Nothing better illustrates the dislocations and disaffections caused by King Philip's War than the fact that Rowlandson's wife Mary was taken captive during it, and when redeemed fled the frontier with her surviving family while the Rowlandsons' Indian servant, whose name we unfortunately don't know, apparently sympathized enough with the fate of his brethren to abandon the English for the religious and political practices of the French.

The Catholic warrior planned to take his two captive Puritans, along with a young English boy named Samuel Lennardson, who had been captured a year or more before in Worcester, to a native village in the northern reaches of what the English called New Hampshire. He told them, perhaps in jest, that once there they would be stripped and whipped and forced to run the gauntlet. The prospect of this punishment moved Hannah Dustan to a desperate expedient. On the night of March 13th, on an island in the Merrimack near the junction with the Contoocook, she and the boy from Worcester, with hatchets taken from their captors, attacked the twelve sleeping Abenaki with grim determination and deadly aim. By the time they finished, ten of the Indians lay dead on the island. Another one, sorely wounded, had run away into the woods, while the twelfth, whom Dustan wanted to take back with her as a captive of her own, managed to escape in the confusion.

Having murdered ten Abenaki, Hannah proceeded to scalp them: she scalped the two dead men, her master and the other one; she scalped the two dead women as well—and she scalped all six of the dead children, one by one. Some sources assert that she scalped all of them immediately after killing them; some, that she first left the island with Mary Neff and Samuel Lennardson on their flight toward home but then came back to the island to scalp the dead as proof of her exploit. Whenever she scalped them, the bloody trophies she brought back with her convinced the incredulous; and they garnered rewards as well as belief. The general court of Massachusetts gave the three returning captives a total of fifty pounds, half to Hannah Dustan and the other half to be split by Mary Neff and Samuel Lennardson, while the governor of far-off Maryland sent Dustan what the record calls "a very generous token of his favor." There was no set scalp bounty at this time among the English; what came to the captives from the Massachusetts legislature came as an exceptional reward for an extraordinary deed. And apparently it came with broad popular support. When Hannah's husband petitioned the general court for a reward for what he called Hannah's "just slaughter of so many of the Barbarians," he noted that "it seems a matter of universal desire through the whole province that it should not pass unrecompensed."

Indian captivity narratives constituted one of the first bodies of popular literature among the European settlers of North America. The form, dealing as it does with the conflicts between Native Americans and European Americans (and more rarely African Americans), is often described as a unique invention of American culture. Aside from the fact, however, that many of its tropes come from the Bible—especially from the "Babylonian captivity" of the Israelites—it is also true that Spanish American writers such as Alvar Nuñez Cabeza de Vaca much earlier deployed an allied form of narrative to similar ends. The form is not then, distinctive of Anglo-American experience so much as characteristic and diagnostic of it; how it was used in any given instance is the issue of most importance.

Modern scholars of what Mary Louise Pratt has called "the contact zone" in North America have remarked that captivity as an actual experience was significantly transformed as it was given a narrative shape. In New England, for instance, the majority of captives (about two-thirds) were male, whereas the bulk of the narratives (in about the same proportions) concerned females. Why this disproportion should exist is a curious but not unanswerable question. In many ways, the politically ideal captive was a white girl or a mature white woman who was a mother and if possible a recent mother. Attacked while still recovering from childbirth, the latter figure served as a pitiable victim whose presence in "Indian territory" did not raise obvious doubts about the political context of Indian violence. Attacked as she performed nothing but her putatively "natural" function, the mother/captive helped obscure the fact that most of her people taken prisoner represented a more direct and menacing threat to Native Americans—and a threat less easily hidden by the twists of narrative exposition and explanation. Even many of the rare males in captivity stories (such as the Reverend John Williams, who was surprised while asleep in bed) came to occupy stereotypically female roles in their narratives. The captive's gender is determined by reference not to biographical fact but cultural meaning. The active white male warrior is rarely a captive, more often a prisoner of war, and his story is ensconced in a quite different literary form—namely, the war narrative of the sort, say, that features John Smith or Daniel Boone.

Gender, in other words, matters in these tales less for itself—that is, less to reinforce distinctions between male and female roles within European American society—than as a proxy for political disputes between European American and Native American cultures. The passive, innocent mother/captive may reinforce white values, but she more importantly serves to represent the pacific pretensions of white society as a whole. By feminizing the very image of white society, she decoys attention away from the militaristic thrust of European culture into North America.

Hannah Dustan's story has fascinated—indeed, obsessed—American audiences ever since 1697 in part because it so insistently violates or inverts the orthodox diagram of the captivity narrative as it has established itself in American culture. Here is a woman who, whatever the version of the tale, not only endured the suffering (as any mother/captive would) but also stole the weapon from the furious "savage's" hand and, turning it back on him and the other men, women, and children in the Native American party exacted revenge with a masculine insistence. While the fact that she was snatched, from childbed makes her the ideal victim, once snatched, Hannah showed no intent to remain victimized. Because at a level below the more obvious political surfaces discussed above, the captivity narrative deals with the covert appeal of Indian "freedom" to the European American settlers, especially those in stern New England, Dustan's Indianization represents not just vengeance on but amalgamation with the natives as well. Like John Smith or Daniel Boone or the fictional Natty Bumppo, Dustan is not merely captured by the Indians: she is captivated as well, her inner identity not so much imprisoned as profoundly altered. The hatchet is an implement of both revenge and transformation. One notes, too, that in Dustan's hand it threatens to destroy the very pretence to innocent suffering that the female captive embodied.

Dustan's fascination comes, too, from the fact that although she told her story orally to several people, including the Puritan preacher Cotton Mather, her own version never made it directly into print. She has figured in many accounts, including several by Mather himself, and in each succeeding age has been refigured, a perpetual captive, it would seem, of the American imagination. What follows here is a series of accounts of her experience aimed at displaying some of the shape-shifting power in her story. The first are contemporary diary references from three Massachusetts residents: the Reverend John Pike, minister of Dover; John Marshall; and Samuel Sewall, the Salem witchcraft trial judge who earlier that year had publicly recanted his role in that event. Here we see details as they were picked up by word of mouth (in Sewall's case, via a visit from Dustan herself), a pattern deepened and enriched as well in the longer narrative of Cotton Mather, since Mather, too, met with Dustan and derived his account from her. Mather's account, in several versions, is the key early document, and most later Dustan narratives betray more or less a debt to it. It also is significant in its attempt to square the powerful events of the story with the "master narratives" of Puritan (and European American) self-conception, particularly the myths of emigration and redemption derived from the Bible and, in Puritan histories, sermons, and diaries especially, transformed into a kind of American creed. Mather's reliance on the Bible is typical of much elite writing of the period, but that reliance also helps reveal the particular fault lines in the Dustan captivity and similar narratives. Mather's account will repay close attention to its language, especially its deployment of different semantic patterns for similar events, as in the following: "She thought she was not forbidden by any *law* to take away the *life* of the *murderers* by whom her child had been butchered."

Mather's influence notwithstanding, oral lore regarding Dustan apparently accounts for one of the more interesting early versions of her experience, recounted by soldier and traveler Jonathan Carver, who grew up in Weymouth, Massachusetts. Carver, whose *Travels* is famous for its thefts from other books, its lies, and its exaggerations, refers to the "annals of New England" as his vague source, but the wild trajectory of his version (which misnames Dustan "Mrs. Rowe"—perhaps by a partial confusion of her with Mary Rowlandson—omits Mary Neff, and makes the young English captive Leonardson Dustan's "imbecile" son!) suggests that he derived his narrative instead from oral sources. That possibility is important in that it suggests how much of the talk among early European Americans focused, projected, and parlayed the tales that also made their way into print. One notes that even Mary Rowlandson, the "first" of the New England captivity figures, speaks in her account of how the stories of Indian warfare had already shaped her imagination long before King Philip's War: "Now is that dreadful hour come," she writes, "that I have often heard of (in time of war as it was the case of others), but now mine eyes see it." She clearly had heard captivity stories before living one, and the oral lore—now almost completely unrecoverable—served to shape her perception of what was happening to her. The first captivity narratives passed through American culture on hurried breath, not on the pages of books; the books derived from the lore and helped to codify it.

And even in the new age of print following the American Revolution the press itself became a kind of oral medium, diffusing tales such as the Dustan narratives printed here from the nineteenth century. One finds in them—from John Greenleaf Whittier's "legend" of 1831 to Sarah Josepha Hale's poem of 1853—a fascinatingly projective quality, a desire to reshape and control meanings. In this era, gender plays a role crucially different from the one it played for the likes of Mather and Carver, both of whom after all do celebrate the feminine "hero" of their tales. Whittier and Nathaniel Hawthorne seem sentimentally concerned with the ways in which Dustan's vengeance violated her maternal "nature," though they react to that supposed violation very differently, Hawthorne with special virulence (though the possibility that his tone is at least partly ironic should not be overlooked). Hawthorne, too, gives far more attention to Dustan's husband (as if sensing, perhaps, that one of the hidden battles in this war concerned Hannah's theft of her husband's proper role and proper weapon), while in the case of Hale's poem the whole text is concerned with the husband, suggesting that it was not simply male authors who found Hannah's violence troubling. The fourth of these more recent tales, Henry David Thoreau's, shows a troubling sense of the violence, too, but it detaches the violence from Hannah's gender and connects it instead to her nationality. Her murders, as narrated by Thoreau, become the means of her expulsion from the natural world to which his tale strongly connects her victims, who in Thoreau's era have emerged as romantic "children of the forest" whose death reflects the European Americans' self-expulsion from the American garden: it is as if, at last, the vengeance dispossesses Dustan and her people spiritually from the world to which the Indian wars had guaranteed them legal title. They won the land but lost the landscape. Thoreau shows, too, the continuing importance of oral details, since his most telling innovation in the narrative tradition is apparent in the "apple tree" against which Hannah's infant's head is dashed; the detail of the apple tree derived from lore connected with Dustan in the Haverhill area, lore incorporated by Yale president Timothy Dwight's account and apparently well known to Thoreau. Thoreau puts that detail to wonderful use: for if the apple is biblical in its echoes, it also is—as the botanically acute Thoreau surely knew—an old world fruit brought to America by his European ancestors. The tragedy was planted on American ground, this subtle detail hints, by the very people who came to eat of its fruit, fertilized in a vaguely cannibal way by the dashing of the head of Dustan's child against its trunk.

Anticipating her long-lived legend, Hannah Dustan herself survived well beyond her harrowing experience. When she came home, she found her husband and their other seven children still alive and healthy. She and Thomas had two other children before his death thirty-four years later, after which Hannah lingered on another four years, living with her son Jonathan, and dying probably in 1736. As late as 1724, when she petitioned for membership in the church in Haverhill, she stated, without audible remorse or even a quaver in her voice, "I am thankful for my captivity, 'twas the comfortablest time that ever I had: in my affliction God made his word comfortable to me."

THE CONTEMPORARY RECORD

JOHN PIKE

Diary, March 15, April 28, 1697

MARCH 15, 1697. THE INDIANS FELL UPON SOME PART OF HAVERHILL, ABOUT seven in the morning, killed and carried away thirty-nine or forty persons. Two of these captive women, viz. Dustan and Neff (with another young man) slew ten of the Indians, and returned home with the scalps.[1]

JOHN MARSHALL

Diary, April 1697

AT THE LATTER END OF THIS MONTH TWO WOMEN AND A YOUNG LAD THAT HAD been taken captive from Haverhill in March before, watching their opportunity when the Indians were asleep, killed ten of them, scalped them all and came home to Boston. [They] brought a gun with them and some other things. The chief of these Indians took one of the women captive when she had lain in childbed but a few days, and knocked her child in [the] head before her eyes, which woman killed and scalped that very Indian. This was done just about the time the council of this province had concluded on a day of fasting and prayer through the province.

SAMUEL SEWALL

Diary, April 29, May 12, 1697

APRIL 29 . . . IS SIGNALIZED BY THE ACHIEVEMENT OF HANNAH DUSTUN, MARY Neff, and Samuel Lennerson, who killed two men, their masters, and two women and six others, and have brought in ten scalps. . . .

---

[1] Pike made this entry concerning Dustan in his diary late in April 1697 but dated it March 15.

May 12 . . . Hannah Dustun came to see us. . . . She saith her master, whom she killed, did formerly live with Mr. Rowlandson[2] at Lancaster. He told her, that when he prayed [in] the English way, he thought that was good: but now he found the French way was better.[3] The single man showed the night before, to Samuel Lennarson, how he used to knock Englishmen on the head and take off their scalps, little thinking that the captives would make some of their first experiment upon himself. Samuel Lennarson killed him.

COTTON MATHER

"A Notable Exploit: *Dux Fæmina Facti*,"[4]
from Magnalia Christi Americana (1702)

ON MARCH 15, 1697, THE SAVAGES MADE A DESCENT UPON THE SKIRTS OF Haverhill, murdering and captivating about thirty-nine persons, and burning about half a dozen houses. In this broil, one Hannah Dustan, having lain in[5] about a week, attended with her nurse, Mary Neff, a body of terrible Indians drew near unto the house where she lay, with designs to carry on their bloody devastations. Her husband hastened from his employments abroad unto the relief of his distressed family; and first bidding *seven* of his *eight* children (which were from *two* to *seventeen* years of age) to get away as fast as they could unto some garrison in the town, he went in to inform his wife of the horrible distress come upon them. Ere she could get up, the fierce Indians were got so near, that, utterly desparing to do her any service, he ran out after his children; resolving that on the horse which he had with him, he would ride away with *that* [one of his children] which he should in this extremity find his affections to pitch most upon, and leave the rest unto the care of the Divine Providence. He overtook his children, about forty rod[6] from his door; but then such was the *agony* of his parental affections, that he found it impossible for him to distinguish any one of them from the rest; wherefore he took up a courageous resolution to live and die with them all. A party of Indians came up with him; and now, though they fired at him, and he fired at them, yet he manfully kept at the rear of his *little army* of unarmed children, while they marched off with the pace of a child of five years old; until, by the singular providence of God, he arrived safe with them all unto a place of safety about a mile or two from his house. But his house must in the mean time have more dismal *tragedies* acted at it. The nurse, trying to escape with the new-born infant, fell into the hands

[2] Reverend Joseph Rowlandson, husband of the famous captive Mary Rowlandson and minister of Lancaster, Massachusetts, at the time of her capture in February 1676.
[3] I.e., he preferred Catholic practice to that of the Protestant Puritans.
[4] "The leader was a woman" [Latin].
[5] I.e., having been confined to bed following the birth of a child.
[6] About seven hundred feet.

of the formidable savages; and those furious tawnies coming into the house, bid poor Dustan to rise immediately. Full of astonishment, she did so; and sitting down in the chimney with an heart full of most fearful *expectation*, she saw the raging dragons rifle all that they could carry away, and set the house on fire. About nineteen or twenty Indians now led these away, with about half a score other English captives; but ere they had gone many steps, they dashed out the brains of the infant against a tree; and several of the other captives, as they began to tire in the sad journey, were soon sent unto their long home;[7] the savages would presently bury their hatchets in their brains, and leave their carcases on the ground for birds and beasts to feed upon. However, Dustan (with her nurse) notwithstanding her present condition, travelled that night about a dozen miles, and then kept up with their new masters in a long travel of an hundred and fifty miles, more or less, within a few days ensuing, without any sensible damage in their health, from the hardships of their *travel*, their *lodging*, their *diet*, and their many other difficulties.

These two poor women were now in the hands of those whose "tender mercies are cruelties;"[8] but the good God, who hath all "hearts in his own hands,"[9] heard the sighs of these prisoners, and gave them to find unexpected favor from the master who hath laid claim unto them. That Indian family consisted of twelve persons; two stout men, three women, and seven children; and for the shame of many an English family, that has the character of *prayerless* upon it, I must now publish what these poor women assure me. 'Tis this: in obedience to the instructions which the French have given them, they would have *prayers* in their family no less than thrice every day; in the morning, at noon, and in the evening; nor would they ordinarily let their children *eat* or *sleep*, without first saying their prayers. Indeed, these *idolaters* were, like the rest of their whiter brethren, *persecutors*, and would not endure that these poor women should retire to their English prayers, if they could hinder them. Nevertheless, the poor women had nothing but fervent prayers to make their lives comfortable or tolerable; and by being daily sent out upon business, they had opportunities, together and asunder, to do like another Hannah, in "pouring out their souls before the Lord."[1] Nor did their praying friends among ourselves forbear to "pour out" supplications for them. Now, they could not observe it without some wonder, that their Indian master sometimes when he saw them dejected, would say unto them, "What need you trouble yourself? If your God will have you delivered, you shall be so!" And it seems our God would have it so to be. This Indian family was now travelling with these two captive women (and an English youth taken from Worcester, a year and a half before),

[7] I.e., to heaven, from Ecclesiastes 12:5, ". . . because man goeth to his long home, and the mourners go about the streets."
[8] Proverbs 12:10, "A righteous man regardeth the life of his beast: but the tender mercies of the wicked are cruel."
[9] Proverbs 21:1, "The king's heart is in the hand of the Lord."
[1] 1 Samuel 1:15. Hannah, sorrowful because she could not have children, "pour[ed] out [her] soul before the Lord," who thereafter allowed her to give birth to Samuel.

unto a rendezvouz of savages, which they call a *town*, some where beyond Penacook;[2] and they still told these poor women that when they came to this town, they must be stripped, and scourged, and run the *gauntlet* through the whole army of Indians. They said this was the *fashion* when the captives first came to a town; and they derided some of the faint-hearted English, which, they said, fainted and swooned away under the *torments* of this discipline. But on April 30, while they were yet, it may be, about an hundred and fifty miles from the Indian town, a little before break of day, when the whole crew was in a *dead sleep*, (reader, see if it prove not so!) one of these women took up a resolution to imitate the action of Jael upon Sisera;[3] and being where she had not her own *life* secured by any *law* unto her, she thought she was not forbidden by any *law* to take away the *life* of the *murderers* by whom her child had been butchered. She heartened the nurse and the youth to assist her in this enterprise; and all furnishing themselves with hatchets for the purpose, they struck such home blows upon the heads of their sleeping oppressors, that ere they could any of them struggle into any effectual resistance, "at the feet of these poor prisoners, they bowed, they fell, they lay down; at their feet they bowed, they fell; where they bowed, there they fell down dead."[4] Only one squaw escaped, sorely wounded, from them in the dark; and one boy, whom they reserved asleep, intending to bring him away with them, suddenly waked, and scuttled away from this desolation. But cutting off the scalps of the ten wretches, they came off, and received *fifty pounds* from the General Assembly of the province, as a recompence of their action; besides which, they received many "presents of congratulation" from their more private friends: but none gave them a greater taste of bounty than Colonel Nicholson,[5] the Governor of Maryland, who, hearing of their action, sent them a very generous token of his favor.

AN EIGHTEENTH-CENTURY ECHO

JONATHAN CARVER

from **Travels Through America (1778)**

NOTWITHSTANDING SUCH PRECAUTIONS ARE USUALLY TAKEN BY THE INDIANS, IT is recorded in the annals of New England that one of the weaker sex, almost

[2] A site on the Merrimack River in central New Hampshire, north of Concord.
[3] Jael's brutal murder of the warrior Sisera is recounted in Judges 4–5.
[4] Based on Judges 5:27, which describes Sisera's death after Jael drives a tent stake through his head while he sleeps.
[5] Francis Nicholson (1655–1728), at the time governor of Maryland, had served as lieutenant governor of the Dominion of New England in the previous decade. A scalp bounty in effect in Massachusetts had been rescinded prior to Dustan's capture, but a petition to the government signed by her husband Thomas secured twenty-five pounds for Hannah and the same amount to be split by Neff and Leonardson.

alone and unassisted, found means to elude the vigilance of a party of warriors, and not only to make her escape from them, but to revenge the cause of her countrymen.

Some years ago, a small band of Canadian Indians, consisting of ten warriors attended by two of their wives, made an irruption into the back settlements of New England. They lurked for some time in the vicinity of one of the most exterior towns and, at length, after having killed and scalped several people, found means to take prisoner a woman who had with her a son of about twelve years of age. Being satisfied with the execution they had done, they retreated towards their native country which lay at three hundred miles distance, and carried off with them their two captives.

The second night of their retreat, the woman, whose name, if I mistake not, was Rowe,[6] formed a resolution worthy of the most intrepid hero. She thought she should be able to get from her hands the manacles by which they were confined, and determined if she did so to make a desperate effort for the recovery of her freedom. To this purpose, when she concluded that her conquerors were in their soundest sleep, she strove to slip the cords from her hands. In this she succeeded and cautioning her son, whom they had suffered to go unbound, in a whisper against being surprised at what she was about to do, she removed to a distance with great wariness the defensive weapons of the Indians, which lay by their sides.

Having done this, she put one of the tomahawks into the hands of the boy, bidding him to follow her example and, taking another herself, fell upon the sleeping Indians, several of whom she instantly dispatched. But her attempt was nearly frustrated by the imbecility[7] of her son who, wanting both strength and resolution, made a feeble stroke at one of them, which only served to awaken him. She however sprung at the rising warrior and, before he could recover his arms, made him sink under the weight of her tomahawk; and this she alternately did to all the rest, except one of the women who awoke in time and made her escape.

The heroine then took off the scalps of her vanquished enemies and, seizing also those they were carrying away with them as proofs of their success, she returned in triumph to the town from whence she had so lately been dragged, to the great astonishment of her neighbours who could scarcely credit their senses or the testimonies she bore of her Amazonian intrepidity.

---

[6]Carver was in error, of course, perhaps because he was recalling a story read long before—or a story he had heard rather than read.
[7]Weakness of body or mind.

NINETEENTH-CENTURY LITERARY
TREATMENTS

JOHN GREENLEAF WHITTIER

"The Mother's Revenge,"
from *Legends of New England* (1831)

WOMAN'S ATTRIBUTES ARE GENERALLY CONSIDERED OF A MILDER AND PURER character than those of man. The virtues of meek affection, of fervent piety, of winning sympathy and of that "charity which forgiveth often," are more peculiarly her own. Her sphere of action is generally limited to the endearments of home—the quiet communion with her friends, and the angelic exercise of the kindly charities of existence. Yet, there have been astonishing manifestations of female fortitude and power in the ruder and sterner trials of humanity; manifestations of a courage rising almost to sublimity; the revelation of all those dark and terrible passions, which madden and distract the heart of manhood.

The perils which surrounded the earliest settlers of New England were of the most terrible character. None but such a people as were our forefathers could have successfully sustained them. In the dangers and the hardihood of that perilous period, woman herself shared largely. It was not unfrequently her task to garrison the dwelling of her absent husband, and hold at bay the fierce savages in their hunt for blood. Many have left behind them a record of their sufferings and trials in the great wilderness, when in the bondage of the heathen, which are full of wonderful and romantic incidents, related however without ostentation, plainly and simply, as if the authors felt assured that they had only performed the task which Providence had set before them, and for which they could ask no tribute of admiration.

In 1698[8] the Indians made an attack upon the English settlement at Haverhill—now a beautiful village on the left bank of the Merrimack. They surrounded the house of one Duston, which was a little removed from the main body of the settlement. The wife of Duston was at that time in bed with an infant child in her arms. Seven young children were around her. On the first alarm Duston bade his children fly towards the garrison house, and then turned to save his wife and infant. By this time the savages were pressing close upon them. The heroic woman saw the utter impossibility of her escape—and she bade her husband fly to succor his children, and leave her to her fate. It was a moment of terrible trial for the husband—he hesitated between his affection and his duty—but the entreaties of his wife fixed his determination.

He turned away, and followed his children. A part of the Indians pursued him, but he held them at a distance by the frequent discharge of his rifle. The children fled towards the garrison, where their friends waited, with breathless

---

[8]Whittier's mistake for 1697.

anxiety, to receive them. More than once, during their flight, the savages gained upon them; but a shot from the rifle of Duston, followed, as it was, by the fall of one of their number, effectually checked their progress. The garrison was reached, and Duston and his children, exhausted with fatigue and terror, were literally dragged into its enclosure by their anxious neighbors.

Mrs. Duston, her servant girl and her infant were made prisoners by the Indians, and were compelled to proceed before them in their retreat towards their lurking-place. The charge of her infant necessarily impeded her progress; and the savages could ill brook delay when they knew the avenger of blood was following closely behind them. Finding that the wretched mother was unable to keep pace with her captors, the leader of the band approached her, and wrested the infant from her arms. The savage held it before him for a moment, contemplating, with a smile of grim fierceness the terrors of its mother, and then dashed it from him with all his powerful strength. Its head smote heavily on the trunk of an adjacent tree, and the dried leaves around were sprinkled with brains and blood.

"Go on!" said the Indian.

The wretched mother cast one look upon her dead infant, and another to Heaven, as she obeyed her savage conductor. She has often said, that at this moment, all was darkness and horror—that her very heart seemed to cease beating, and to lie cold and dead in her bosom, and that her limbs moved only as involuntary machinery. But when she gazed around her and saw the unfeeling savages, grinning at her and mocking her, and pointing to the mangled body of her infant with fiendish exultation, a new and terrible feeling came over her. It was the thirst of revenge; and from that moment her purpose was fixed. There was a thought of death at her heart—an insatiate longing for blood. An instantaneous change had been wrought in her very nature; the angel had become a demon,—and she followed her captors, with a stern determination to embrace the earliest opportunity for a bloody retribution.

The Indians followed the course of the Merrimack, until they had reached their canoes, a distance of seventy or eighty miles. They paddled to a small island, a little above the upper falls of the river. Here they kindled a fire; and fatigued by their long marches and sleepless nights, stretched themselves around it, without dreaming of the escape of their captives.

Their sleep was deep—deeper than any which the white man knows,—a sleep from which they were never to awaken. The two captives lay silent, until the hour of midnight; but the bereaved mother did not close her eyes. There was a gnawing of revenge at her heart, which precluded slumber. There was a spirit within her which defied the weakness of the body.

She rose up and walked around the sleepers, in order to test the soundness of their slumber. They stirred not limb or muscle. Placing a hatchet in the hands of her fellow captive, and bidding her stand ready to assist her, she grasped another in her own hands, and smote its ragged edge deeply into the skull of the nearest sleeper. A slight shudder and a feeble groan followed. The savage was dead. She passed on to the next. Blow followed blow, until ten out of twelve, the whole number of the savages, were stiffening in blood. One escaped with a dreadful wound. The last—a small boy—still slept amidst the scene of carnage. Mrs. Duston lifted her dripping hatched above his head, but hesitated to strike the blow.

"It is a poor boy," she said, mentally, "a poor child, and perhaps he has a mother!" The thought of her own children rushed upon her mind, and she spared him. She was in the act of leaving the bloody spot, when, suddenly reflecting that the people of her settlement would not credit her story, unsupported by any proof save her own assertion, she returned and deliberately scalped her ten victims. With this fearful evidence of her prowess, she loosed one of the Indian canoes, and floated down the river to the falls, from which place she travelled through the wilderness to the residence of her husband.

Such is the simple and unvarnished story of a New England woman. The curious historian, who may hereafter search among the dim records of our "twilight time"—who may gather from the uncertain responses of tradition, the wonderful history of the past—will find much, of a similar character, to call forth by turns, admiration and horror. And the time is coming, when all these traditions shall be treasured up as a sacred legacy—when the tale of the Indian inroad and the perils of the hunter—of the sublime courage and the dark superstitions of our ancestors, will be listened to with an interest unknown to the present generation,—and those who are to fill our places will pause hereafter by the Indian's burial-place, and on the site of the old battlefield, or the thrown-down garrison, with a feeling of awe and reverence, as if communing, face to face, with the spirits of that stern race, which has passed away forever.

Nathaniel Hawthorne

"The Duston Family," from American Magazine of Useful and Entertaining Knowledge (1836)

Goodman Duston and his wife, somewhat less than a century and a half ago, dwelt in Haverhill, at that time a small frontier settlement in the province of Massachusetts Bay. They had already added seven children to the king's liege subjects in America; and Mrs. Duston, about a week before the period of our narrative, had blessed her husband with an eighth. One day in March, 1698,[9] when Mr. Duston had gone forth about his ordinary business, there fell out an event, which had nearly left him a childless man, and a widower besides. An Indian war party, after traversing the trackless forest all the way from Canada, broke in upon their remote and defenseless town. Goodman Duston heard the war-whoop and alarm, and, being on horseback, immediately set off full speed to look after the safety of his family. As he dashed along, he beheld dark wreaths

[9] Like Whittier, Hawthorne mistakes the date.

of smoke eddying from the roofs of several dwellings near the roadside; while the groans of dying men, the shrieks of affrighted women, and the screams of children pierced his ear, all mingled with the horrid yell of the raging savages. The poor man trembled, yet spurred on so much the faster, dreading that he should find his own cottage in a blaze, his wife murdered in her bed, and his little ones tossed into the flames. But, drawing near the door, he saw his seven elder children, of all ages between two years and seventeen, issuing out together, and running down the road to meet him. The father only bade them make the best of their way to the nearest garrison, and, without a moment's pause, flung himself from his horse, and rushed into Mrs. Duston's bed-chamber.

The good woman, as we have before hinted, had lately added an eighth to the seven former proofs of her conjugal affection; and she now lay with the infant in her arms, and her nurse, the widow Mary Neff, watching by her bedside. Such was Mrs. Duston's helpless state, when her pale and breathless husband burst into the chamber, bidding her instantly to rise and flee for her life. Scarcely were the words out of his mouth, when the Indian yell was heard; and staring wildly out of the window, Goodman Duston saw that the blood-thirsty foe was close at hand. At this terrible instant, it appears that the thought of his children's danger rushed so powerfully upon his heart, that he quite forgot the still more perilous situation of his wife; or, as is not improbable, he had such knowledge of the good lady's character as afforded him a comfortable hope that she would hold her own, even in a contest with a whole tribe of Indians. However that might be, he seized his gun and rushed out of doors again, meaning to gallop after his seven children, and snatch up one of them in his flight, lest his whole race and generation should be blotted from the earth in that fatal hour. With this idea, he rode up behind them, swift as the wind. They had, by this time, got about forty rods from the house, all pressing forward in a group; and though the younger children tripped and stumbled, yet the elder ones were not prevailed upon, by the fear of death, to take to their heels and leave these poor little souls to perish. Hearing the tramp of hoofs in their rear, they looked round, and espying Goodman Duston, all suddenly stopped. The little ones stretched out their arms; while the elder boys and girls, as it were, resigned their charge into his hands; and all the seven children seemed to say,—"Here is our father! Now we are safe!"

But if ever a poor mortal was in trouble, and perplexity, and anguish of spirit, that man was Mr. Duston! He felt his heart yearn towards these seven poor helpless children, as if each were singly possessed of his whole affections; for not one among them all but had some peculiar claim to their dear father's love. There was his first-born; there, too, the little one who, till within a week past, had been the baby; there was a girl with her mother's features, and a boy, the picture of himself, and another in whom the looks of both parents were mingled; there was one child, whom he loved for his mild, quiet, and holy disposition, and destined him to be a minister; and another, whom he loved not less for his rough and fearless spirit, and who, could he live to be a man, would do a man's part against these bloody Indians. Goodman Duston looked at the poor things, one by one; and with yearning fondness, he looked at them all, together; then he gazed up to Heaven for a moment, and finally waved his hand to his seven beloved ones. "Go on, my children," said he calmly. "We will live or die together!"

He reined in his horse, and caused him to walk behind the children, who, hand in hand, went onward, hushing their sobs and wailings, lest these sounds should bring the savages upon them. Nor was it long before the fugitives had proof that the red devils had found their track. There was a curl of smoke from behind the huge trunk of a tree, a sudden and sharp report echoed through the woods, and a bullet hissed over Goodman Duston's shoulder and passed above the children's heads. The father, turning half round on his horse, took aim and fired at the skulking foe, with such effect as to cause a momentary delay of the pursuit. Another shot—and another—whistled from the covert of the forest; but still the little band pressed on, unharmed; and the stealthy nature of the Indians forbade them to rush boldly forward, in the face of so firm an enemy as Goodman Duston. Thus he and his seven children continued their retreat, creeping along, as Cotton Mather observes, "at the pace of a child of five years old," till the stockades of a little frontier fortress appeared in view, and the savages gave up the chase.

We must not forget Mrs. Duston, in her distress. Scarcely had her husband fled from the house, ere the chamber was thronged with the horrible visages of the wild Indians, bedaubed with paint and besmeared with blood, brandishing their tomahawks in her face, and threatening to add her scalp to those that were already hanging at their girdles. It was, however, their interest to save her alive, if the thing might be, in order to exact ransom.[1] Our great-great-grandmothers, when taken captive in the old times of Indian warfare, appear, in nine cases out of ten, to have been in pretty much such a delicate situation as Mrs. Duston; notwithstanding which, they were wonderfully sustained through long, rough, and hurried marches, amid toil, weariness, and starvation, such as the Indians themselves could hardly endure. Seeing that there was no help for it, Mrs. Duston rose, and she and the widow Neff, with the infant in her arms, followed their captors out of doors. As they crossed the threshold, the poor babe set up a feeble wail; it was its death cry. In an instant, an Indian seized it by the heels, swung it in the air, dashed out its brains against the trunk of the nearest tree, and threw the little corpse at the mother's feet. Perhaps it was the remembrance of that moment that hardened Hannah Duston's heart, when her time of vengeance came. But now, nothing could be done but to stifle her grief and rage within her bosom, and follow the Indians into the dark gloom of the forest, hardly venturing to throw a parting glance at the blazing cottage, where she had dwelt happily with her husband, and had borne him eight children,—the seven, of whose fate she knew nothing, and the infant, whom she had just seen murdered.

---

[1] Native Americans took captives in part from the hope of ransoming them or selling them to French settlers in Canada as servants.

The first day's march was fifteen miles; and during that, and many succeeding days, Mrs. Duston kept pace with her captors; for, had she lagged
behind, a tomahawk would at once have been sunk into her brains. More than
one terrible warning was given her; more than one of her fellow captives,—of
whom there were many,—after tottering feebly, at length sank upon the
ground; the next moment, the death groan was breathed, and the scalp was
reeking at an Indian's girdle. The unburied corpse was left in the forest, till the
rites of sepulture should be performed by the autumnal gales, strewing the
withered leaves upon the whitened bones. When out of danger of immediate
pursuit, the prisoners, according to Indian custom, were divided among different parties of the savages, each of whom were to shift for themselves. Mrs.
Duston, the widow Neff, and an English lad fell to the lot of a family consisting
of two stout warriors, three squaws, and seven children. These Indians, like
most with whom the French had held intercourse, were Catholics; and Cotton
Mather affirms, on Mrs. Duston's authority, that they prayed at morning, noon,
and night, nor ever partook of food without a prayer; nor suffered their children
to sleep till they had prayed to the Christian's God. Mather, like an old hard-
hearted, pedantic bigot as he was, seems trebly to exult in the destruction of
these poor wretches, on account of their popish superstitions. Yet what can be
more touching than to think of these wild Indians, in their loneliness and their
wanderings, wherever they went among the dark, mysterious woods, still keeping up domestic worship, with all the regularity of a household at its peaceful
fireside.

They were travelling to a rendezvous of the savages, somewhere in the
northeast. One night, being now above a hundred miles from Haverhill, the
red men and women, and the red children, and the three palefaces, Mrs. Duston, the widow Neff, and the English lad, made their encampment, and kindled
a fire beneath the gloomy old trees, on a small island in Contocook River.[2] The
barbarians sat down to what scanty food Providence had sent them, and shared
it with their prisoners, as if they had all been the children of one wigwam, and
had grown up together on the margin of the same river within the shadow of
the forest. Then the Indians said their prayers—the prayers that the Romish
priests had taught them—and made the sign of the cross upon their dusky
breasts, and composed themselves to rest. But the three prisoners prayed apart;
and when their petitions were ended, they likewise lay down, with their feet to
the fire. The night wore on; and the light and cautious slumbers of the red
men were often broken by the rush and ripple of the stream, or the groaning
and moaning of the forest, as if nature were wailing over her wild children; and
sometimes, too, the little redskins cried in sleep, and the Indian mothers awoke
to hush them. But, a little before break of day, a deep, dead slumber fell upon
the Indians. "See," cries Cotton Mather triumphantly, "if it prove not so!"

Up rose Mrs. Duston, holding her own breath, to listen to the long, deep
breathing of her captors. Then she stirred the widow Neff, whose place was by
her own, and likewise the English lad; and all three stood up, with the doubtful

[2] A tributary that joins the Merrimack near Penacook, New Hampshire.

gleam of the decaying fire hovering upon their ghastly visages, as they stared round at the fated slumberers. The next instant each of the three captives held a tomahawk. Hark! that low moan, as of one in a troubled dream—it told a warrior's death pang! Another!—Another!—and the third half-uttered groan was from a woman's lips. But, O, the children! Their skins are red; yet spare them, Hannah Duston, spare those seven little ones, for the sake of the seven that have fed at your own breast. "Seven," quoth Mrs. Duston to herself. "Eight children have I borne—and where are the seven, and where is the eighth!" The thought nerved her arm; and the copper-colored babes slept the same dead sleep with their Indian mothers. Of all that family, only one woman escaped, dreadfully wounded, and fled shrieking into the wilderness! and a boy, whom, it is said, Mrs. Duston had meant to save alive. But he did well to flee from the raging tigress! There was little safety for a redskin, when Hannah Duston's blood was up.

The work being finished, Mrs. Duston laid hold of the long black hair of the warriors, and the women, and the children, and took all their ten scalps, and left the island, which bears her name to this very day. According to our notion, it should be held accursed, for her sake. Would that the bloody old hag had been drowned in crossing Contocook River, or that she had sunk over head and ears in a swamp, and been there buried, till summoned forth to confront her victims at the Day of Judgment; or that she had gone astray and been starved to death in the forest, and nothing ever seen of her again, save her skeleton, with the ten scalps twisted round it for a girdle! But, on the contrary, she and her companions came safe home, and received the bounty on the dead Indians, besides liberal presents from private gentlemen, and fifty pounds from the Governor of Maryland. In her old age, being sunk into decayed circumstances, she claimed, and, we believe, received a pension, as a further price of blood.

This awful woman, and that tender-hearted yet valiant man, her husband, will be remembered as long as the deeds of old times are told round a New England fireside. But how different is her renown from his!

HENRY DAVID THOREAU

from *A Week on the Concord and Merrimack Rivers* (1849)

ON THE THIRTY-FIRST DAY OF MARCH, ONE HUNDRED AND FORTY-TWO YEARS before this, probably about this time in the afternoon,[3] there were hurriedly

[3] Thoreau tells this story as an aside in his account of his own boat trip on the Merrimack River with his brother John in 1839. The time of day is late afternoon or, once the story has been told, early evening, and the two brothers are looking for a spot to camp for the night.

paddling down this part of the river, between the pine woods which then fringed these banks, two white women and a boy, who had left an island at the mouth of the Contoocook before daybreak. They were slightly clad for the season, in the English fashion, and handled their paddles unskillfully, but with nervous energy and determination, and at the bottom of their canoe lay the still bleeding scalps of ten of the aborigines. They were Hannah Dustan, and her nurse, Mary Neff, both of Haverhill, eighteen miles from the mouth of this river, and an English boy, named Samuel Lennardson, escaping from captivity among the Indians. On the 15th of March previous, Hannah Dustan had been compelled to rise from childbed, and half-dressed, with one foot bare, accompanied by her nurse, commence an uncertain march, in still inclement weather, through the snow and the wilderness. She had seen her seven elder children flee with their father, but knew not of their fate. She had seen her infant's brains dashed out against an apple tree,[4] and had left her own and her neighbors' dwellings in ashes. When she reached the wigwam of her captor, situated on an island in the Merrimack, more than twenty miles above where we now are, she had been told that she and her nurse were soon to be taken to a distant Indian settlement, and there made to run the gauntlet naked. The family of this Indian consisted of two men, three women, and seven children, beside an English boy, whom she found a prisoner among them. Having determined to attempt her escape, she instructed the boy to inquire of one of the men, how he should dispatch an enemy in the quickest manner, and take his scalp. "Strike 'em there," said he, placing his finger on his temple, and he also showed him how to take off the scalp. On the morning of the 31st she arose before daybreak, and awoke her nurse and the boy, and taking the Indians' tomahawks, they killed them all in their sleep, excepting one favorite boy, and one squaw who fled wounded with him to the woods. The English boy struck the Indian who had given him the information on the temple, as he had been directed. They then collected all the provision they could find, and took their master's tomahawk and gun, and scuttling all the canoes but one, commenced their flight to Haverhill, distant about sixty miles by the river. But after having proceeded a short distance, fearing that her story would not be believed if she should escape to tell it, they returned to the silent wigwam, and taking off the scalps of the dead, put them into a bag as proofs of what they had done, and then retracing their steps to the shore in the twilight, recommenced their voyage.

Early this morning this deed was performed, and now, perchance, these tired women and this boy, their clothes stained with blood, and their minds racked with alternate resolution and fear, are making a hasty meal of parched corn and moose-meat, while their canoe glides under these pine roots whose stumps are still standing on the bank. They are thinking of the dead whom they have left behind on that solitary isle far up the stream, and of the relentless

---

[4] The apple tree is part of the oral lore surrounding Dustan in the Haverhill area; so is the image of her as having one bare foot.

living warriors who are in pursuit. Every withered leaf which the winter has left seems to know their story, and in its rustling to repeat it and betray them. An Indian lurks behind every rock and pine, and their nerves cannot bear the tapping of a woodpecker. Or they forget their own dangers and their deeds in conjecturing the fate of their kindred, and whether, if they escape the Indians, they shall find the former still alive. They do not stop to cook their meals upon the bank, nor land, except to carry their canoe about the falls. The stolen birch forgets its master and does them good service, and the swollen current bears them swiftly along with little need of the paddle, except to steer and keep them warm by exercise. For ice is floating in the river; the spring is opening; the muskrat and the beaver are driven out of their holes by the flood; deer gaze at them from the bank; a few faint-singing forest birds, perchance, fly across the river to the northernmost shore; the fish hawk sails and screams overhead, and geese fly over with a startling clangor; but they do not observe these things, or they speedily forget them. They do not smile or chat all day. Sometimes they pass an Indian grave surrounded by its paling on the bank, or the frame of a wigwam, with a few coals left behind, or the withered stalks still rustling in the Indian's solitary cornfield on the interval. The birch stripped of its bark, or the charred stump where a tree has been burned down to be made into a canoe, these are the only traces of man,—a fabulous wild man to us. On either side, the primeval forest stretches away uninterrupted to Canada or to the "South Sea;" to the white man a drear and howling wilderness, but to the Indian a home, adapted to his nature, and cheerful as the smile of the Great Spirit.

While we loiter here this autumn evening, looking for a spot retired enough, where we shall quietly rest tonight, they thus, in that chilly March evening, one hundred and forty-two years before us, with wind and current favoring, have already glided out of sight, not to camp, as we shall, at night, but while two sleep one will manage the canoe, and the swift stream bear them onward to the settlements, it may be, even to old John Lovewell's[5] house on Salmon Brook tonight.

According to the historian, they escaped as by a miracle all roving bands of Indians, and reached their homes in safety, with their trophies, for which the General Court paid them fifty pounds. The family of Hannah Dustan all assembled alive once more, except the infant whose brains were dashed out against the apple tree, and there have been many who in later times have lived to say that they had eaten of the fruit of that apple tree.

---

[5] Captain John Lovewell of Massachusetts (1691–1725), ambushed and killed along with many of his men by the Piggwackett Indians in Maine in 1725, became the subject of several early heroic ballads. His house was in Dunstable, just upriver from Haverhill.

"The Father's Choice,"
from Woman's Record (1853)

Now fly as flies the rushing wind!
   Urge, urge thy rushing steed!
The savage yell is fierce behind;
   And life is on thy speed.

And from those dear ones make thy choice!
   The group he wildly eyed;
When "Father!" burst from every side,
   And "Child!" his heart replied.

There's one will prattle on his knee,
   Or slumber on his breast;
And one whose joys of infancy
   Are still by smiles expressed.

They feel no fear while he is near;
   He'll shield them from the foe:
But, oh! his ear must thrill to hear
   Their shriekings should he go.

In vain his quivering lips would speak;
   No words his thoughts allow:
There's a burning tear upon his cheek,
   Death's marble on his brow.

And twice he smote his clinchèd hands;
   Then bade his children fly,
And turned; and even that savage band
   Cowered at his wrathful eye.

Swift as the lightning winged with death
   Flashed forth the quivering flame:
Their finest warrior bows beneath
   The father's deadly aim.

Ambition goads the conquerer on;
   Hate points the murderer's brand:
But love and duty—these alone
   Can nerve the good man's hand.

Not the wild cries that rend the skies
   His heart of purpose move:
He saves his children, or he dies
   The sacrifice of love.

The hero may resign the field,
   The coward murderer flee:
He cannot fear, he will not yield,
   That strikes, sweet Love! for thee.

They come! they come! He heeds no cry
   Save the soft child-like wail:
"O father, save!"—"My children, fly!"—
   Were mingled on the gale.

And firmer still he drew his breath,
   And sterner flashed his eye,
As fast he hurled the leaden death,
   Still shouting, "Children, fly!"

No shadow on his brow appeared,
   Nor tremor shook his frame,
Save when at intervals he heard
   Some trembler lisp his name.

In vain the foe—those fiends unchained—
   Like famished tigers chafe:
The sheltered roof is neared, is gained;
   All, all the dear ones safe!

PART TWO

1700–1800

1

A Scots-American on the Southern Frontier

THOMAS NAIRNE, A SCOTSMAN BY BIRTH, ARRIVED IN THE NEW ENGLISH COLONY of South Carolina in the late seventeenth century and soon emerged as a key player in its life. He settled on St. Helena Island, near Beaufort at the southern border of the mainland English colonies of the period, where he lived "among the Indians." Nairne became a noted military figure, helping lead a combined Native American and colonial force against the Spanish at St. Augustine in 1702, and commanding an attack on the Apalachee Indians two years later. The southern historian Verner Crane termed Nairne "the most remarkable frontier figure of the South in Queen Anne's war." Nairne's role also went beyond military exploits. An avid and active politician, he sought to regulate the Indian trade, articulating the basis of what was to become the southern model in the Indian Act of 1707. Under the terms of that act, Nairne was appointed the first Indian agent of the colony, with authority extending all the way to the Mississippi. It was in pursuit of his duties as agent that he journeyed to the Mississippi Valley in the spring of 1708. His account of the trip, in the form of letters to several other Carolina officials, provides the text printed here, a letter addressed to Indian trade commissioner Robert Fenwick.

Nairne's rise in this important area led him to articulate an imperial vision of Carolina's future aimed at dislodging the French from Louisiana and exploiting the Indian trade (including the trade in Indian slaves) as a basis for a British imperium in the region. He threw himself into the thick of factional strife in Carolina following his election to the South Carolina house of commons in 1706. Nairne sided with the "country" party against the high-handed governor, Nathaniel Johnson, and had the aid of the English writer Daniel Defoe, who brought the attack to bear on Queen Anne and parliament. Nairne was jailed in 1708 on a trumped-up charge of treason and deprived of his position as Indian agent, but he never was tried, and following a voyage to England in 1710, he gained favor with the colony's proprietors. In later years he was judge advocate for the admiralty in South Carolina and, after 1712, Indian agent once again. It was in the latter capacity that he was on a negotiating visit to the

Yemassee in 1715 just as a general war broke out, to which—seized, tortured, and at last executed—he fell victim.

THOMAS NAIRNE

Letter to Robert Fenwick, April 13, 1708, from the Chickasaw Country

SIR, DESIGNING FOR THE CHICASAWS[1] I SET OUT FROM THE OCHESES[2] WITH Mr. Welch; on Tuesday, February the 25th [we] crossed over Coosa or the main branch of Mobile river. Our company consisted only of ten Chicasaws, sixteen Tallapoosas, whom the chiefs appointed for my guard and to carry my goods, and twenty-five Apalachees[3] that were burtheners[4] for my fellow traveler, who was going a-trading. Being thus strong we went the straightest road, tho it lay along close by the Choctaw[5] country, in some places not above forty or fifty miles from their towns, yet we rather chose to venture the danger than go any of the other roundabout ways which being safer are therefore more frequented. We had in our gang likewise several women, for the savages also[6] esteeming them necessary troubles seldom travel without some of them. Among these was a young Chickasaw princess who was carrying from the English settlement two young cats to her country as a great rarity.

Nothing [is] more contrary to my inclination, than being obliged to travel so slowly, and wait the pace of the carriers. To make the time slide on as inperceivably as possible I diverted myself by accompanying the hunters at their sports, for the Chickasaws are such excellent foresters,[7] they never missed supplying the camp with meat enough, and so civil withal,[8] that whatever was killed they threw down to us, that we might order the division[9] as we pleased. Our camp was not much unlike a crew of Gypsies, only that we were all armed men. As we set out every morning, some quality[1] of the Chickasaws, who thought themselves too good to carry burthens marched at a distance from us on both sides of the path to provide wherewithal we should sup,[2] and usually came all to the place appointed well-laden.

[1] I.e., intending to go to the Chickasaw country (in what is now northeastern Mississippi).
[2] A Creek people living in the center of present-day Georgia.
[3] The Tallapoosas and Apalachees were two other peoples of the Southeast, located in Alabama and Florida respectively.
[4] Burden carriers.
[5] A people located in southern Mississippi.
[6] I.e., like the European colonists.
[7] Woodsmen.
[8] In addition.
[9] I.e., the parceling out to the several groups.
[1] I.e., some individual Chickasaw who thought themselves superior.
[2] I.e., to hunt for food.

We pitched camp always about two or three o'clock ([so] that any [straggler] might have time to come up) then the ladies went to making broth or roasting turkeys or what else we had. When the camp was placed[3] the usual diversion of the hunters was either to look for bear, fire a ring for deer[4] or go to the clay pits and shoot buffaloes, for you must observe that in the spring and all summer, these cattle eat abundance of clay. They find out such places as are saltish, which they lick up in such quantities as if some hundreds of thousands of bricks had been made out of them,[5] and the paths leading to these holes are as many and well trod, as these to the greatest cowpens in Carolina.[6] Though [now] buffalo bulls are not fit for men to eat, yet in May, June and July the buffalo bulls are very fat and good, the cows and heifers in the fall and winter. The tongues of these creatures are extraordinary fine a-tasting, like marrow, and that causes the death of many hundreds of them. Of all hunting diversions, I took most pleasure in firing rings for in that we never missed seven or ten deer. Three or four hours after the ring is fired, of four or five miles' circumference, the hunters post themselves within as nigh the flame and smoke as they can endure. The fire on each side burns in toward the center and thither the deer gather from all parts to avoid it, but striving to shun a death which they might often escape, by a violent spring, they fall into a certain one from the bullets of the hunters, who drawing nigher together, as the circle grows less, find an easy prey of the impounded deer, though [they] seldom kill all for some who find a place where the flame is less violent, jump out. This sport is the more certain the longer the ground has been unburned.[7] If it has not for two or three years there are so many dry leaves, grass and trash, that few creatures within escape, and the men are forced to go out betimes at some slack place to the leeward.[8] In killing buffaloes they aim at the yearlings and heifers, being the tenderest and indeed no beef exceeds them. After shooting three or four of these, no remonstrances can prevail with the savages to march farther that day, but the kettles and spits [go] to work. Sir, a hasty man can worst of any travel in company with them, [for] their whole discourse[9] is, "Here's excellent ground for bears or turkeys, in this canepiece[1] we shall surely meet with buffaloes," and 'twould in their opinion be perfect folly to pass by without hunting them. The heads of you Britons have in them a thousand projects and chimeras,[2] about making yourselves great, rich, and the Lord knows what, this keeps you perpetually in a hurry, which the more prudent savages avoid by making happiness

---

[3] Located.

[4] I.e., hunt deer by driving them with fires in large circles.

[5] I.e., from the resulting large pits.

[6] Early ranches on which cattle herds were overwintered.

[7] I.e., the thicker grass, once fired, ensures a better hunt.

[8] To escape being caught in the fire, the hunters must make a speedy escape where, upwind, the flames are less intense.

[9] I.e., a fast traveler would make the worst company for these Native Americans, given that their talk is always about hunting.

[1] Ground covered with thickets of cane.

[2] Illusions.

consist in a few things. They're in the highest felicity when after a prosperous morning's hunt, they sit with their mistresses, by some pretty brook under the shady trees, enjoying the fruits of their labor. When their bellies were full one or another usually entertained the company with a song and his rattle, and at nights when it is the most danger, (to show the Choctaws how little we valued[3] them) we used to pass away the time by setting up a drum and setting our fingers and dancers to work, and because I designed to promote peace, I was usually entertained with the songs belonging to the pipe of peace, which are several and the best the Chickasaws have. But after our mirth was over we always took care to lie with our guns and pistols ready by our side in case of a sudden assault from any party in the night, for the Choctaws often beat up the quarters[4] and kill travelers in this path.

Upon a night alarm in the woods, the common method is to take your arms, presently fly off from the fires and wait the issue. If the enemy advances toward the fire, then have the others a sure shot at them by the light of the fires.

About midway a little on one side of the road is a perfect salt spring, where are to be seen multitudes of buffaloes always striving for it. I saw sea coal[5] in several places of this road, which is a rarity (though of no value) in these parts of the world. I observed the more westward I went the more the country was subject to hurricanes, for betwixt the Abihkas[6] and Chickasaws, are several pieces of land laid quite level, some so lately that were yet with difficulty passable by reason of the trees fallen, others [having been] cleared by the fire. They generally run in a line from northwest to southeast three or four miles over a hundred yards long. I saw beaver dams and houses. This is the most witty creature in the world. They talk of beasts having only instinct, I wish all people had as much instinct for their own affairs as this ingenious animal has.

If then the savages of our company were cloyed with deer and buffalo, then they went a-bear-hunting. This was the time of year in which these creatures lie in their holes, for from the first of January to the middle of March they sleep and neither eat or drink. The Indian way of hunting them during that time, is only looking in holes under the roots of fallen trees, or up such trees in the swamps, which have a hollow rotten place nigh the top. In these large holes the bears make their nests and repose themselves during their sleeping season. The savages when they spy such a hole in a tree presently view it all round and [look] for the marks of the bear's claws in going up, [which] are easily seen. They either climb up some small tree that stands by together[7] and prick him out with canes, or else fire the nest, [and] as they come out of the hole, stand ready to shoot [them]. Thus I saw them take several. After the bear is skinned,

---

[3] Regarded—i.e., feared.
[4] Beat the bushes.
[5] An archaic term for coal.
[6] Creeks settled near the Upper Coosa River, Alabama.
[7] Stands nearby.

appears nothing but a mere coat of fat two or three inches thick which they likewise strip him of, and this coat of clear fat will sometimes weigh sixty, seventy, or eighty pounds but they are not so fat within[8] as hogs. They breed but once in two years, have one, two and never above three cubs, at a time. Every second or third year all the woods hereabouts swarm with these creatures. They come hither from the northern parts, when nuts are scarce there, and as soon as [they] are grown fat the strangers[9] return to the place whence they came, and leave behind them only the natives of the place. The greatest obligation an Indian can lay upon his wife and mother-in-law is to carry home good store of this fat to keep house with. They make bags of deerskins and carry [them] home full. The hunting law of the Chickasaws is, that whoever first finds the bear, has the skin and belly piece of fat, and when driving[1] a swamp he who first wounds him, has the same advantage. The rest of the fat and meat are equally divided among the fires.[2] Of no other meat they make division as not worth it, each takes what he will. I could never eat so heartily of this as of deer, or buffalo, yet 'twas mere prejudice, for this creature seldom preys on any thing, is cleanly, and eats generally grass and groundnuts, acorns, and chestnuts. The Chickasaws are so civil even among themselves that they always present the breast of bear (being the best) to the most honorable fire in the company. Accordingly, good store fell to my share. The savages in the woods sort themselves seven or eight to a fire according as they have more or less acquantance or respect for one another. Those who lodge not forty yard asunder will come [and] very formally invite one another to their fires to eat, though they're (it may be) doing nothing else at their own.

On going from Coosa[3] to the Chickasaws the rivers which we pass are the two branches of [the] Pedegoe[4] and [the] heads of Choctaw river, or the creeks belonging to one or other of them all which belong from the large river Mobile that falls into the Bay of Spirito Santo.[5] I had in this journey opportunities of seeing all the methods which the Indians use in transporting themselves and goods. I thought nothing of rafts made of dry wood or canes, of small bark canoes, these were common, but to see every man make a boat of his bed, and therein carry over clothes, arms, and ammunition very dry, was a thing I had not seen before. They take a bearskin, or large raw buckskin, without holes (or these sewed up,) this they lay up at the four corners and therein place anything of fifty, sixty or a hundred weight, their gun fastened on top of all, which they hold by the end, and therewith push the boat before themselves, swimming

[8] Inside.
[9] I.e., the northern bears.
[1] Hunting through.
[2] The subgroups of the hunt, each centered on its own fire.
[3] A branch of the Alabama River.
[4] The upper part of the Tombigbee, its branches being the Black Warrior and the Sipsey.
[5] Nairne's particular geographic points here are somewhat confused. The Tombigbee River was called the Choctaw by the Chickasaw, since it lay in the direction of that people, but the Choctaw for reverse reasons called it the Chickasaw. The Bay of Spirito Santo (Spanish) is Mobile Bay.

after [it]. Thus they transport powder, broadcloth or any other goods without taking the least wet.[6]

At leisure in the way I learned [from] Oboystabee[7] (whom you made so much of in Charleston) and who is chief warrior of the Chickasaws, the inclination of the leading men and all other of his people relating to their allegiance to our government, which the French of Mobile, by presents and promises so much shook of late. Sir, I must (by the way) inform you that the savages, especially those so remote, have not a right notion of allegiance and its being indefeasible.[8] They're apt to believe themselves at liberty, when they please to turn to those who sell them the best pennyworths,[9] and though the traders take pains to instruct them, and by good arguments endeavor to draw them from that erroneous doctrine, yet nothing but a much better trade and the reputation of far greater courage than the French could have kept this tribe in any tolerable subjection. These, with them, were motives, much more powerful than the justice of our cause.[1]

After this gentleman had informed me of most things material relating to his country, he thus went on. "About six years ago" (says he) "Tonti[2] with seven or eight Frenchmen more came up to our towns, through the Choctaw country, made peace with us, and presented[3] our chief men very liberally, invited us down to their fort, and in passing patched up a peace betwixt us and the Choctaws. To be free with you, Captain," said he, "I was one of them who was deluded, by their great promises. They bouyed us up with a mighty expectation, of what vast profit we should reap by friendship and commerce with them, so that upon their desire I killed one of your subjects the Alabamas[4] and carried them the hair. But after sufficent trial made, our people are now undeceived, and are sorry they should so lightly think of trying new friends, and do cheerfully return to their duty. It's true" (continued he) "that two old men of some note go yearly down to the French, merely for the sake of what they can get of them, and they are so silly as to believe these two can do strange feats in bringing others over to their party, when it's not in their power. These two with few refugee people who can neither hunt nor take slaves (and whom the French oblige with their awls and needles) are all that have the least regard for them among us, but entirely in the English interest are every one of the officers and military men, for they dispose of their slaves to your traders much to their

[6]Called "bullboats," these temporary craft were subject to much commentary by travelers on the frontier. They resembled the "coracles" of Britain.
[7]Described by Nairne in another letter as one of the three war chiefs of the Chickasaw.
[8]Perpetual.
[9]I.e., give them the best bargains.
[1]Nairne here describes with unusual candor the political basis of commercial competition between the British of Charleston and the French of Mobile (then their main center on the Gulf Coast; not until the 1720s did it shift to New Orleans).
[2]Henri de Tonty (ca. 1650–1704) held the French post on the upper Mississippi while waiting fruitlessly for his ill-fated associate La Salle to return upriver in the 1680s. Eventually, Tonty joined the new French colony under Iberville on Mobile Bay.
[3]Gave presents to.
[4]I.e., one member of the pro-English Alabama tribe.

advantage, and so do the hunters their skins. Of t'other sex, the beauties and fine women who are the warriors' wives and mistresses, are altogether of your party, for these ladies are so pleased to look sparkling in the dances, with the clothes bought from the English, that they would be very loath any difference should happen, lest they again be reduced to their old wear of painted buffalo calf skins."[5]

About twenty miles before our arrival at the towns the people met us, with flowers, and continued so to do in gangs, all the way to the villages, the warriors and leading men giving us the whiff[6] as their fashion is to welcome their friends. We lodged the last night of our journey, on the edge of a swamp about a mile or two from the first village, together with fifty or sixty Chickasaws who had met us. This they desired that their people might make provision to receive us in form[7] with the eagle pipe next morning, but before midnight we all repented waiting for this piece of honor, there falling a great storm of rain accompanied with violent thunder and lightning.

About twenty miles from Coosa river, we led our horses over a barren rocky hill, from the top whereof, we saw the country all about and back to the place whence they came. Most of the way continued to be miserable, barren, stony, uneven land, until I arrived within twenty miles of the Chickasaws, and then we had done with sand, stones and pines, the country being pleasant open forests of oak, chestnuts, and hickory so intermixed with savannas as if it were a made landscape.[8] These savannas are not perfectly level like ours in Carolina, but full of gentle ascents, which yet are not too steep for the plough; on the top of these knolls live the Chickasaws, their houses a gun or pistol shot asunder, with their improved ground, peach, and plum trees about them. The land from hence to the Chickasaws' country west to the great river and up its branches, some hundred miles, [is] all thus intermixed with savannas, the fittest country in the world to set up such a course of life as the present Turkomans[9] or old nomads lived; [to] remove from place to place and feed flocks. Thus happily might the inhabitants of these countries have lived, if they had not been infatuated to divide and rent themselves into so many petty tribes and by that means have endless feuds and wars one with another. This makes it just now come [into] my head, to observe to you that conquest is neither at some times nor in

[5] Oboystabee is here given a speech that reveals some of the underlying economic forces at work on the southern frontier in this period, and how the Native Americans played differing European interests off against each other. In a record of the conference in Mobile in 1702 to which reference is made by Oboystabee, Iberville noted that he told the Chickasaw and Choctaw leaders that "the English . . . have no other objective than to work their destruction by inciting [both tribes] to war on each other so that the English can get slaves, whom they send away to other countries to be sold." With more candor, he later added, "I had them told, after their manner of speaking, several other things that aimed solely at driving the English out and ruining them in the minds of the Chickasaw."
[6] I.e., filling the air with the smell of gunpowder by shooting off guns in welcome.
[7] In a proper manner.
[8] I.e., a human-made landscape or garden; savannas: open, grassy areas.
[9] A nomadic people of the Turkmen, Uzbek, Kazak, and Karakalpak republics, in the former U.S.S.R.

all cases unjust, nor unhappy for these conquered for it had been infinitely better for these infidels, if some powerful tribe had subdued the rest, and brought them under government and to a peaceable life, rather then they should thus have consumed themselves, by their savage quarrels. Thus the Incas of Peru acquired a just empire, by making war only against such as were notorious breakers of the law of nature, whom they brought to be a great nation, living peaceable and happy. Though these parts have been a little more populous than at present, yet [they] have never been thick stocked with inhabitants, and I think 'twas impossible they should by a people living without religion, law, or useful arts.

It's now that season of the year, when nature adorns the earth with a livery of verdant green, and there is some pleasure in an evening to ride up and down the savannas. When among a tuft of oaks on a rising knoll, in the midst of a large grassy plain, I revolve a thousand things about the primitive life of men and think how finely on such a small hill the tents might stand and from thence men have the agreeable sight of the flocks feeding round them. Thus lived and rambled the great patriarch in the plains of the East, thus stood the tents under and about the oaks of Mamre.[1] In this state of life it was that the bright inhabitants of the regions above designed to descend and converse with men.

The land here is a thin mold on top of a red stiff clay and white marle. The curiosity which I observed most was to see oyster shells everywhere spread over the old fields and savannas, as plentifully as if it were [an] island by the sea, especially on the declining sides of hills, where the rains had made gullies there were great beds of them, some deep, some nigher the surface, and thus it is not only here, but all over the Choctaw country. The Chickasaws beat them to pieces and mix them with clay to make earthenware. Whether these shells be like unto those of the seashore nighest to [the] place where they lie, which is the bay of Spirito Santo, I can't tell, but they're remarkably different from ours in Carolina, are far larger, the shells very much thicker, and [have] a twirl at the end. How they came there is difficult to account for, being by computation about 220 miles from the sea. I inquired if any lakes or rivers far or near yielded any [of] the like, but was satisfied there was none such. If they came by the flood it's strange that there should not be seen all the way from our country here, which is seven hundred miles, especially since nothing can be said of the height or lowness of the land here, but may [also] be said of other parts. Against their being of a spontaneous production of the earth, or play of wanton nature, it may be urged that none are found entire or increasing but all show signs of age and decay: though some are very sound, little broken and scarce perceivably moldered so that [they] may yet last many thousand years, others are the quite contrary. If nature once produced these shells, why should not such seminal principles[2] still have the like effect? It seems more easy to have recourse to

---

[1] According to Genesis, the patriarch Abraham dwelled for a time in the shady oak groves of his ally Mamre.
[2] Creative forces.

some whirlings or eddies of the flood upon its decrease. About this country are more violent lightnings and thunders than with us in Carolina, which proceeds from the moist savanna land, and great rivers. This settlement bears[3] from Charleston west a half point northerly. I see no other fruits the Chickasaws have except peaches; and plums, red, blue, and yellow. Each house hath by it a grove of these plum trees, for it seems they bear best, when run up in thickets four or five foot asunder. Over all the old fields are strawberries innumerable and that good and large. The women supplied me with these and were well pleased upon receiving two or three strings of small beads in return.

Though we saw no Choctaws in the road yet some of their hunters spied us, and ran home to tell they had seen a great company of horsemen (this was but four) besides a multitude of Indians. Sir, the Indian spies always multiply what they see at a strange rate. Upon this news the Choctaws expected a storm from the Chickasaws, which made them call in all their hunters and look out sharp. I am, worthy Sir, Your most humble servant, Thomas Nairne.

[3] Lies, by compass reading.

2

"We Are Born Free":
The Iroquois Answer the French

Cadwallader Colden, born of Scots parents in Ireland in 1688, earned a degree at Edinburgh in 1705, studied medicine in London thereafter, and by 1710 had emigrated to Philadelphia. Before that decade's end, he moved to New York, where he became intimately intertwined with that colony's history. He assumed the post of surveyor general in 1720, joined the governor's council the next year, and became lieutenant governor of the province in 1761, a post he held until his death on the eve of the Revolution in 1776. Settled for much of his life at Coldenham, Orange County, New York, Colden enjoyed the benefits of what might be termed New York's land-spoil system, which oversaw the distribution of great quantities of real estate in the Hudson Valley and the adjacent region to favored individuals; as surveyor general, Colden had a considerable part in perpetuating and exploiting that system. Colden's intellectual interests led him out into the American landscape for reasons other than economics. One of his scientific interests lay in the natural history of America, a topic on which he collaborated with his daughter Jane (1724–1766), the country's first female botanist. In addition, Colden's access to New York's records fed his curiosity about the Native Americans whose territories lay near those of the Anglo-Dutch province. Here he found fascinating transcripts of many diplomatic exchanges between the Iroquois and their various European neighbors, primarily the French of Canada and the English and Dutch of New York. From these materials more than from his own observations, Colden compiled and published his two-part *History of the Five Indian Nations Dependent on the Province of New York* (1727; 1747), leaving yet a third part in manuscript at his death.

The Iroquois attracted his attention in part because of their elaborate political league, which bound five (and, with the addition of the Tuscarora during his lifetime, six) relatively autonomous peoples into a sophisticated and powerful quasi-state. The five original members extended west from Albany in a geographical range that began with the Mohawk in the east, stretched through the Oneida, the Onondaga, and the Cayuga, and ended with the Seneca in the west. Even before the coming of the French to the northern limits of their territory and the Dutch to the eastern limits early in the seventeenth century, the Iroquois had used their political and military power to establish a growing dominance over other native peoples throughout the Northeast and the Great Lakes region. With the arrival of the European communities, they similarly exploited the nascent trade between Montreal and Albany and farther-inland tribes to solidify and extend their dominion. Although the power of the Iroquois had diminished by Colden's time, there remains an irony in the fact that the title of his book portrayed an alliance of nations that were as fiercely independent as dependent on New York. The Iroquois never missed an opportunity to assert their independence and retained their territorial sovereignty long after native peoples elsewhere in the East had suffered defeat at the hands of European American forces and had ceased to have an identifiably separate existence. Not until George Washington ordered an army into the Iroquois country in 1779 did the league suffer a genuine invasion at the hands of Anglo-colonial powers. It is worth recalling, too, that the pretext for the 1779 invasion was the fact that the Iroquois had chosen to side with the Crown in the Revolution, largely because of their long alliance with the British against their French enemies in North America.

Colden gives ample evidence in his history of the peculiar "genius" of the Iroquois, especially of their eloquence, diplomatic savvy, and independence of mind. The brief narrative presented here describes a 1684 encounter between the governor of New France, Joseph-Antoine Le Febvre de La Barre, and representatives of the Iroquois league at the mouth of the Kaihohage (or La Famine) River, along the shore of Lake Ontario in present-day New York. The French governor, having recently succeeded the comte de Frontenac, was intent on making a show of force that would subdue the Iroquois, with whom the French had had generally bad relations ever since Samuel de Champlain attacked an Iroquois party in 1609. Canada was in a very weak condition just then, and La Barre's own party had suffered from severe sickness while staying at Fort Frontenac, farther north along the lake. The Onondaga leader, Haaskouan, whom the French called "Grande Gueule" (literally, "Big Mouth," a translation of the Onondaga term; Colden, apparently unaware of its import, gives the name as "Garangula"), knew quite fully of the weak position of the French, and after La Barre made a blustering speech about how his king had ordered him to reduce the Iroquois to submission, Haaskouan arose and in his rebuttal proceeded to rub the salt of his considerable sarcasm and irony into the governor's wounds. Cadwallader Colden might be accused of taking partisan delight in this humiliation of the French leader, although in point of fact Colden himself admired the French in general for their heroic embrace of the continent, something he felt the tamer, more agriculturally inclined English had not exhibited.

CADWALLADER COLDEN

from **The History of the Five Indian Nations
Dependent on the Province of New York,
Part I (1727)**

MONSIEUR DE LA BARRE'S SPEECH TO GARANGULA

"THE KING, MY MASTER,[1] BEING INFORMED THAT THE FIVE NATIONS HAVE often infringed the peace, has ordered me to come hither with a guard, and to send Ohguesse[2] to the Onondagas, to bring the chief sachem to my camp. The intention of the great king is, that you and I may smoke the calumet[3] of peace together, but on this condition, that you promise me, in the name of the Senecas, Cayugas, Onondagas, and Mohawks, to give entire satisfaction and reparation to his subjects; and for the future never to molest them.

"The Senecas, Cayugas, Onondagas, Oneidas, and Mohawks have robbed and abused all the traders that were passing to the Illinois and Miami,[4] and other Indian nations, the children of my king. They have acted, on these occasions, contrary to the treaty of peace with my predecessor.[5] I am ordered therefore to demand satisfaction, and to tell them, that in case of refusal, or their plundering us any more, that I have express orders to declare war. This belt confirms my words.[6] The warriors of the Five Nations have conducted the English into the [Great] Lakes, which belong to the king, my master, and brought the English among the nations that are his children, to destroy the trade of his subjects, and to withdraw these nations from him. They have carried the English thither, notwithstanding the prohibition of the late governor of New York,[7] who foresaw the risk that both they and you would run. I am willing to forget these things, but if ever the like shall happen for the future, I have express orders to declare war against you. This belt confirms my words.

[1] Louis XIV (1638–1715), King of France, 1643–1715.
[2] Charles Le Moyne de Longueuil (1626–1685), called "Ohguesse" ("the partridge") by the Iroquois, was an agent for the French government and the founder of a famous Canadian family. Among his sons was Pierre Le Moyne d'Iberville, founder of the colony on Mobile Bay.
[3] "The calumet is a large smoking pipe made of marble, most commonly of a dark red, well-polished, shaped somewhat in the form of a hatchet, and adorned with large feathers of several colors. It is used in all the Indian treaties with strangers, and as a flag of truce between contending parties, which all the Indians think a very high crime to violate. These calumets are generally of nice workmanship, and were in use before the Indians knew anything of the Christians; for which reason we are at a loss to conceive by what means they pierced these pipes, and shaped them so finely, before they had the use of iron" [Colden's note].
[4] Tribes located in the region south of Lake Michigan.
[5] La Barre succeeded the comte de Frontenac in 1682.
[6] The giving of a belt of wampum, or bead and shell work, to signify the end of a speech or part of a speech, was part of Native American diplomatic ritual.
[7] Edmund Andros (1637–1714) was governor of New York from 1674 to 1681; his successor was Thomas Dongan (1634–1715), who held the position from 1682 to 1688.

Your warriors have made several barbarous incursions on the Illinois and Miami; they have massacred men, women, and children, and have made many of these nations prisoners, who thought themselves safe in their villages in time of peace. These people, who are my king's children, must not be your slaves; you must give them their liberty, and send them back into their own country. If the Five Nations shall refuse to do this, I have express orders to declare war against them. This belt confirms my words.

"This is what I have to say to Garangula, that he may carry to the Senecas, Onondagas, Oneidas, Cayugas, and Mohawks the declaration which the king, my master, has commanded me to make. He doth not wish them to force him to send a great army to Cadarackui Fort,[8] to begin a war which must be fatal to them. He would be sorry that this fort, that was the work of peace, should become the prison of your warriors. We must endeavor, on both sides, to prevent such misfortunes. The French, who are the brethren and friends of the Five Nations, will never trouble their repose, provided that the satisfaction which I demand be given, and that the treaties of peace be hereafter observed. I shall be extremely grieved if my words do not produce the effect which I expect from them; for then I shall be obliged to join with the governor of New York, who is commanded by his master to assist me, and burn the castles of the Five Nations, and destroy you. This belt confirms my words."

Garangula was very much surprised to find the soft words of the Jesuit, and of the governor's messengers,[9] turned to such threatening language. This was designed to strike terror into the Indians; but Garangula having good information from those of the Five Nations living near Cadarackui Fort, of all the sickness and other misfortunes which afflicted the French army, it was far from producing the designed effect. All the time that Monsieur de La Barre spoke, Garangula kept his eyes fixed on the end of his pipe; as soon as the governor had done speaking, he rose up, and having walked five or six times round the circle, he returned to his place, where he spoke standing, while Monsieur de La Barre kept his elbow chair.

GARANGULA'S ANSWER

"Yonnondio,[1]

"I honor you, and the warriors that are with me all likewise honor you. Your interpreter has finished your speech; I now begin mine. My words make haste to reach your ears, hearken to them.

"Yonnondio, you must have believed, when you left Quebec, that the sun had burnt up all the forests which render our country inaccessible to the French, or that the lakes had so far overflown their banks, that they had sur-

---

[8] Fort Frontenac, located on what was then known as the Cataraqui River, at the site of present-day Kingston, Ontario.
[9] Earlier, La Barre had sent a small party to convince the Iroquois to meet him.
[1] The Iroquois term for all governors of New France.

rounded our castles,[2] and that it was impossible for us to get out of them. Yes, Yonnondio, surely you must have dreamt so, and the curiosity of seeing so great a wonder has brought you so far. Now you are undeceived, since I and the warriors here present are come to assure you, that the Senecas, Cayugas, Onondagas, Oneidas, and Mohawks are yet alive. I thank you, in their name, for bringing back into their country the calumet, which your predecessor received from their hands. It was happy for you, that you left underground that murdering hatchet, that has been so often dyed in the blood of the French. Hear, Yonnondio, I do not sleep, I have my eyes open, and the sun, which enlightens me, discovers to me a great captain at the head of a company of soldiers, who speaks as if he were dreaming. He says, that he only came to the lake to smoke on the great calumet with the Onondagas. But Garangula says, that he sees the contrary, that it was to knock them on the head, if sickness had not weakened the arms of the French.

"I see Yonnondio raving in a camp of sick men, whose lives the great spirit has saved, by inflicting this sickness on them. Hear, Yonnondio, our women had[3] taken their clubs, our children and old men had carried their bows and arrows into the heart of your camp, if our warriors had not disarmed them, and kept them back, when your messenger, Ohguesse, came to our castles. It is done, and I have said it. Hear, Yonnondio, we plundered none of the French, but those that carried guns, powder, and ball to the Miami and Illinois, because those arms might have cost us our lives. Herein we follow the example of the Jesuits, who stave all the kegs of rum brought to our castles, lest the drunken Indians should knock them on the head. Our warriors have not beavers enough to pay for all these arms, that they have taken, and our old men are not afraid of the war. This belt preserves my words.

"We carried the English into our lakes, to trade there with the Ottawa and Huron,[4] as the Adirondacks[5] brought the French to our castles, to carry on a trade which the English say is theirs. We are born free, we neither depend on Yonnondio nor Corlear.[6]

"We may go where we please, and carry with us whom we please, and buy and sell what we please: If your allies be your slaves, use them as such, command them to receive no other but your people. This belt preserves my words.

"We knocked the Miami and Illinois on the head, because they had cut down the trees of peace, which were the limits of our country. They have hunted beavers on our lands; they have acted contrary to the customs of all

---

[2] Iroquois settlements were called "castles" by the English in imitation of the Dutch habit of calling them *kastelen*; both terms ultimately derive from the Latin *castellum* (a diminutive of *castrum*), which has among its meanings not only "fortress" but also "camp" and "shelter."
[3] Would have.
[4] Two Canadian nations dwelling in the upper Great Lakes area.
[5] A nation residing in the St. Lawrence Valley.
[6] The Iroquois term for the governor of New York, derived from the Schenectady trader Arent van Curler (1620–1667).

Indians, for they left none of the beavers alive, they killed both male and female. They brought the Shawnee[7] into their country, to take part with them, after they had concerted ill designs against us. We have done less than either the English or French, that have usurped the lands of so many Indian nations, and chased them from their own country. This belt preserves my words. Hear, Yonnondio, what I say is the voice of all the Five Nations; hear what they answer, open your ears to what they speak: The Senecas, Cayugas, Onondagas, Oneidas, and Mohawks say, that when they buried the hatchet at Cadarackui (in the presence of your predecessor) in the middle of the fort, they planted the Tree of Peace in the same place, to be there carefully preserved, that, in place of a retreat for soldiers, that fort might be a rendezvous for merchants; that, in place of arms and ammunition of war, beavers and merchandise should only enter there.

"Hear, Yonnondio, take care for the future, that so great a number of soldiers, as appear there, do not choke the Tree of Peace planted in so small a fort. It will be a great loss, if after it had so easily taken root, you should stop its growth, and prevent its covering your country and ours with its branches. I assure you, in the name of the Five Nations, that our warriors shall dance to the calumet of peace under its leaves, and shall remain quiet on their mats, and shall never dig up the hatchet, till their brethren, Yonnondio or Corlear, shall either jointly or separately endeavor to attack the country, which the great spirit has given to our ancestors. This belt preserves my words, and this other, the authority which the Five Nations has given me."

Then Garangula, addressing himself to Monsieur LeMoyne, said:

"Take courage, Ohguesse, you have spirit, speak, explain my words, forget nothing, tell all that your brethren and friends say to Yonnondio, your governor, by the mouth of Garangula, who loves you, and desires you to accept of this present of beaver, and take part with me in my feast, to which I invite you. This present of beaver is sent to Yonnondio on the part of the Five Nations."

When Garangula's harangue was explained to Monsieur de La Barre, he returned to his tent, much enraged at what he had heard.

Garangula feasted the French officers, and then went home, and Monsieur de La Barre set out in his way towards Montreal; and as soon as the general was embarked, with the few soldiers that remained in health, the militia made the best of their way to their own habitations, without any order or discipline.

Thus a very chargeable and fatiguing expedition (which was to strike the terror of the French name into the stubborn hearts of the Five Nations) ended in a scold between the French general and an old Indian.

---

[7]A tribe then living in the Ohio region.

3

A Quaker Captive in New France

New Hampshire Quaker Elizabeth Hanson (1684–1737) was living with her husband John in the vicinity of Dover in August 1724 when a war party of French and Indians attacked their house, plundering it and almost immediately killing two of the Hanson children. John was away just then with his oldest daughter. Elizabeth, recently delivered of an infant girl, was hurried off with the baby and three other surviving children. For the next year she dwelled with her captors until ultimately ransomed by her husband. The Hansons lost not only the two murdered children but also their oldest daughter, Sarah, who remained in New France after John and Elizabeth returned with their other offspring to New Hampshire. Ultimately, Sarah married a Frenchman and remained permanently in New France, but not until after her father had gone off again, in 1727, in search of her, only to fail in his effort, in fact dying en route.

Elizabeth's response to the experience was understandably complex. Like other New England captives, she viewed the Native Americans as "barbarous savages," and her narrative opens with a typical gesture toward biblical parallels and the spiritual improvements to be derived from such disasters. But her Quaker beliefs—which estranged her from the Puritan establishment and gave her a pacifist viewpoint—also helped shape the narrative in distinctively different ways. For one thing, they led her to seek out explanations for the behavior of her captors that were rooted in universal human needs and drives, rather than a distinctive and essential "savagery." Her text explains that scalping is a custom among the Indians, and a custom strongly influenced by the geopolitics of the Anglo-French struggle for control in North America. Similarly, another typically horrific detail of the usual captivity narrative, the act of smashing an infant's brains out, is explained as having a strategic purpose: "The Indians, to ease themselves of the [baby's] noise and to prevent the danger of a discovery that might arise from it, immediately before my face knocked its brains out." Most interestingly, Hanson attempts to explain her captor's violent designs against her later in the narrative by ascribing them to his ill luck in hunting: "I

148

always observed," she explains, "whenever he was in such a temper [that] he wanted food and was pinched with hunger." Rarely does one find such psychological insight in these wartime narratives, replete as they usually are with dehumanizing cant and partisanship. For that reason alone, Elizabeth Hanson's account is well worth careful study. In it we may observe a fuller fleshing-out of Native American character than is usually traceable elsewhere.

ELIZABETH HANSON

God's Mercy Surmounting Man's Cruelty (1728)

REMARKABLE AND MANY HAVE BEEN THE PROVIDENCES OF GOD TOWARDS His people for their deliverance in a time of trouble by which we may behold as in lively characters the truth of that saying that "He is a God nigh at hand and always ready to help assist those that fear Him and put their confidence in Him."

The sacred writings give us instances of the truth hereof in days of old as in the case of the Israelites, Job, David, Daniel, Paul, Silas, and many others. Besides which our modern histories have plentifully abounded with instances of God's fatherly care over His people in their sharpest trials, deepest distresses, and sorest exercises by which we may know He is a God that changeth not but is the same yesterday, today, and forever.

Among the many modern instances I think I have not met with a more singular one of the mercy and preserving hand of God than in the case of Elizabeth Hanson, wife of John Hanson of Knoxmarsh in Kecheachey, in Dover Township in New England, who was taken into captivity the 27th day of the 6th month called August, 1724,[1] and carried away with four children and a servant by the Indians, which relation as it was taken from her own mouth by a friend differs very little from the original copy but is even almost in her own words (what small alteration is made being partly owing to the mistake of the transcriber) which [run] as follows:[2]

As soon as they discovered themselves (having, as we understood by their discourse, been skulking in the fields some days watching their opportunity when my dear husband with the rest of our men were gone out of the way), two of these barbarous savages came in upon us; next eleven more, all naked with

---

[1] Under the Old Style dating system then in use, the year began in March, so August was the sixth month (Quakers generally avoided Roman names for the months, preferring, as here, to use just their numbers); Kecheachey: Hanson lived in Cocheco ("Kecheachey"), New Hampshire.

[2] Hanson's narrative is sometimes credited to the British Quaker preacher Samuel Bownas, among whose works it was included in 1760. The original American edition of 1728 is technically anonymous, but is signed "E.H.," presumably for Hanson.

their guns and tomahawks, came into the house in a great fury upon us and killed one child immediately as soon as they entered the door, thinking thereby to strike in us the greater terror and to make us more fearful of them.

Then in as great fury the captain[3] came up to me, but at my request he gave me quarter. There [were] with me our servant and six of our children, two of the little ones being at play about the orchard and my youngest child but fourteen days old, whether in cradle or arms I now mind not. Being in that condition, I was very unfit for the hardships I after met with, which are briefly contained in the following pages.

They next go to rifling the house in a great hurry (fearing, as I suppose, a surprise from our people, it being late in the afternoon) and packed up some linen, woolen, and what other things pleased them best. And when they had done what they would, they turned out of the house immediately and being at the door, two of my younger children, one six and the other four years old, came in sight and, being under a great surprise, cried aloud, upon which one of the Indians, running to them, takes one under each arm and brings them to us. My maid prevailed with the biggest to be quiet and still, but the other could by no means be prevailed with but continued screeching and crying very much in the fright, and the Indians, to ease themselves of the noise and to prevent the danger of a discovery that might arise from it, immediately before my face knocked its brains out. I bore this as well as I could, not daring to appear disturbed or show much uneasiness lest they should do the same to the other, but [I] should have been exceeding glad they had kept out of sight till we had been gone from our house.

Now having killed two of my children, they scalped them (a practice common with these people, which is whenever they kill any English people they cut the skin off from the crown of their heads and carry it with them for a testimony and evidence that they have killed so many, receiving sometimes a reward of a sum of money for every scalp)[4] and then put forward to leave the house in great haste without doing any other spoil than taking what they had packed together with myself and little babe fourteen days old, the boy six, and two daughters, the one about fourteen and the other about sixteen years, [and] with my servant girl.

It must be considered that, I having lain-in but fourteen days and being but very tender and weakly, being removed now out of a good room well accommodated with fire, bedding, and other things suiting a person in my condition, it made these hardships to me greater than if I had been in a strong and healthy frame, yet for all this I must go or die. There was no resistance.

In the condition aforesaid we left the house, each Indian having something, and I with my babe and three children that could go of themselves.[5] The

---

[3] Leader.

[4] This aside may have been added by the editor of Hanson's narrative.

[5] I.e., could walk under their own power. Hanson's children accompanying her were Sarah (16 years), Elizabeth (14), Ebenezer or David (6), and the infant, later baptized (as Hanson says) "Mary Ann Frossways [Françoise]" by a priest in New France.

captain, though he had as great a load as he could well carry and was helped up with it, did for all that carry my babe for me in his arms, which I took to be a favor from him. Thus we went through several swamps and some brooks, they carefully avoiding all paths of any track like a road lest by our footsteps we should be followed.

We got that night, I suppose, not quite ten miles from our house on a direct line; then, taking up their quarters, [they] lighted a fire, some of them lying down while others kept watch. I, being both wet and weary and lying on the cold ground in the open woods, took but little rest.

However, early in the morning we must go just as day appeared, traveling very hard all that day through sundry rivers, brooks, and swamps, they, as before, carefully avoiding all paths for the reason already assigned. At night I was both wet and tired exceedingly, having the same lodging on the cold ground in the open woods. Thus for twenty-six days, day by day, we traveled very hard, sometimes a little by water over lakes and ponds. And in this journey we went up some very high mountains, so steep that I was forced to creep up on my hands and knees, under which difficulty the Indian, my master, would mostly carry my babe for me, which I took as a great favor of God that his heart was so tenderly inclined to assist me though he had, as is said, a very heavy burden of his own. Nay, he would sometimes take my very blanket so that I had nothing to do but take my little boy by the hand for his help and assist him as well as I could, taking him up in my arms a little at times because [he was] so small, and when we came at very bad places, he would lend me his hand or coming behind would push me up before him. In all which he showed some humanity and civility more than I could have expected, for which privilege I was secretly thankful to God as the moving cause thereof.

Next to this we had some very great runs of water and brooks to wade through, in which, at times, we met with much difficulty, wading often to our middle and sometimes our girls were up to their shoulders and chins, the Indians carrying my boy on their shoulders. At the side of one of these runs or rivers the Indians would have my eldest daughter Sarah to sing them a song. Then was brought into her remembrance that passage in the 137th Psalm, "By the rivers of Babylon there we sat down, yea we wept when we remembered Zion; we hanged our harps on the willows in the midst thereof, for there they that carried us away captives required of us a song, and they that watched us required of us mirth."[6] When my poor child had given me this account, it was very affecting, and my heart was very full of trouble, yet on my child's account I was glad that she had so good an inclination which she yet further manifested in longing for a Bible that we might have the comfort in reading the holy text at vacant times for our spiritual comfort under our present affliction.

Next to the difficulties of the rivers were the prodigious swamps and thickets very difficult to pass through, in which places my master would sometimes lead me by the hand a great way together and give me what help he was capable

[6]A very appropriate passage, as it concerns the Babylonian captivity of the Israelites.

of under the straits we went through, and, we passing one after another, the first made it pretty passable for the hindmost.

But the greatest difficulty that deserves the first to be named was want of food, having at times nothing to eat but pieces of old beaverskin matchcoats[7] which the Indians having hid (for they came naked as is said before) in their going back again they took with them, and they were used more for food than raiment. Being cut out in long, narrow straps, they gave us little pieces which, by the Indians' example, we laid on the fire till the hair was singed away, and then we ate them as a sweet morsel, experimentally knowing that "to the hungry soul every bitter thing is sweet."[8]

It's to be considered further that of this poor diet we had but very scanty allowance so that we were in no danger of being overcharged.[9] But that which added to my troubles was the complaints of my poor children, especially the little boy. Sometimes the Indians would catch a squirrel or a beaver and at other times we met with nuts, berries, and roots they digged out of the ground, with the bark of some trees. But we had no corn for a great while together, though some of the younger Indians went back and brought some corn from the English inhabitants, the harvest not being gathered, of which we had a little allowed us. But when they caught a beaver, we lived high while it lasted, they allowing me the guts and garbage for myself and children. But not allowing us to clean and wash them as they ought made the food very irksome to us, in the conceit of our minds, to feed upon; and nothing besides pinching hunger could have made it anyway tolerable to be borne. But "that makes every bitter thing sweet."

The next difficulty was no less hard to me, for my daily travel and hard living made my milk dry almost quite up, and how to preserve my poor babe's life was no small care on my mind, having no other sustenance for it many times but cold water, which I took in my mouth and let it fall on my breast (when I gave it the teat) to suck in with what it could get from the breast. And when I had any of the broth of the beaver or other guts, I fed my babe with it as well as I could. By which means through care to keep it as warm as I could, I preserved its life till I got to Canada, and then I had some other food, of which more in its place.

Having by this time got considerably on the way, the Indians part, and we must be divided amongst them. This was a sore grief to us all. But we must submit, and no way to help ourselves. My eldest daughter was first taken away and carried to another part of the country far distant from us where for the present we must take leave of her though with a heavy heart.

We did not travel far after this before they divided again, taking my second daughter and servant maid from me into another part of the country. So, I having now only my babe at my breast and little boy six years old, we remained

[7]A Native American mantle or loose-fitting robe (from the Powhatan term *matshcore*, probably altered by reference to English "coat").
[8]Proverbs 25:7. Experimentally: experientially.
[9]Burdened, i.e., "stuffed."

with the captain still. But my daughter and servant underwent great hardships after they were parted from me, traveling three days without any food, taking nothing for support but cold water, and the third day what with the cold, the wet, and hunger the servant fell down as dead in a swoon, being both very cold and wet. At which the Indians with whom they were, were surprised, showing some kind of tenderness, being unwilling then to lose them by death, having got them so near home, hoping if they lived by their ransom to make considerable profit by them.[1]

In a few days after this they got near their journey's end where they had more plenty of corn and other food. But flesh often fell very short, having no other way to depend on for it but hunting, and when that failed, they had very short commons.[2] It was not long ere my daughter and servant were likewise parted; and my daughter's master being sick was not able to hunt for flesh. Neither had they any corn in that place but were forced to eat bark of trees for a whole week.

Being almost famished in this distress, Providence so ordered that some other Indians, hearing of their misery and want, came to visit them (these people being very kind and helpful to one another which is very commendable) and brought unto them the guts and liver of a beaver which afforded them a good repast, being but four in number, the Indian, his wife and daughter, and my daughter.

By this time my master and our company got to our journey's end where we were better fed at times, having some corn and venison and wild fowl or what they could catch by hunting in the woods. And my master, having a large family (being fifteen in number), we had at times very short commons, more especially when game was scarce.

But here our lodging was still on the cold ground in a poor wigwam (which is a kind of little shelter made with the rinds[3] of trees and mats for a covering something like a tent). These are so easily set up and taken down that they oft remove them from one place to another. Our shoes and stockings being done and our other clothes worn out in that long journey through the bushes and swamps and the weather coming in very hard, we were poorly defended from the cold for want of necessaries, which caused one of my feet, one of the little babe's, and both the little boy's to freeze. And this was no small exercise,[4] yet through mercy we all did well.

Now though we got to our journey's end, we were never long in one place but very often moved from one place to another, carrying their wigwams with

---

[1] Although ransom played some part in captivity in earlier times (Mary Rowlandson being ransomed her husband during King Philip's War), it was the Anglo-French wars of the late seventeenth and the eighteenth centuries that made it a truly important aspect of transcultural relations. As in the famous case of the Williams family in the 1720s, English captives were often sold to residents of New France as servants, and in turn some of these were ransomed by their relatives in New England.
[2] Food.
[3] Bark.
[4] Trial.

them, which they could do without much difficulty. This, being for the conveniency of hunting, made our accommodations much more unpleasant than if we had continued in one place, by reason[5] the coldness and dampness of the ground where our wigwams were pitched made it very unwholesome and unpleasant lodging.

Being now got to the Indian fort, many of the Indians came to visit us and, in their way, welcomed my master home and held a great rejoicing with dancing, firing guns, beating on hollow trees instead of drums, shouting, drinking, and feasting after their manner in much excess for several days together which, I suppose, in their thoughts was a kind of thanks to God put up for their safe return and good success. But while they were in their jollity and mirth, my mind was greatly exercised towards the Lord that I, with my dear children separated from me, might be preserved from repining against God under our affliction on the one hand and on the other we might have our dependence on Him who rules the hearts of men and can do what pleases in the kingdoms of the earth, knowing that His care is over them who put their trust in Him. But I found it very hard to keep my mind as I ought under the resignation which is proper to be in under such afflictions and sore trials as at that time I suffered, in being under various fears and doubts concerning my children that were separated from me, which helped to add to and greatly increase my troubles. And herein I may truly say my afflictions are not to be set forth in words to the extent of them.[6]

We had not been long at home ere my master went a-hunting and was absent about a week, he ordering me in his absence to get in wood, gather nuts, etc. I was very diligent, cutting the wood, and putting it in order, not having very far to carry it. But when he returned having got no prey, he was very much out of humor, and the disappointment was so great that he could not forbear revenging it on us poor captives. However he allowed me a little boiled corn for [my]self and child, but with a very angry look threw a stick or corncob at me with such violence as did bespeak he grudged our eating. At this his squaw and daughter broke out in a great crying. This made me fear mischief was hatching against us. And on it, I immediately went out of his presence into another wigwam; upon which, he comes after me and in great fury tore my blanket off my back and took my little boy from me and struck him down as he went along before him. But the poor child, not being hurt (only frightened) in the fall, he started up and ran away without crying; then the Indian, my master, left me, but his wife's mother came and sat down by me and told me I must sleep there that night. She, then going from me a little time, came back with a small skin to cover my feet withal,[7] informing that my master intended now to kill us, and I, being desirous to know the reason, expostulated that in his absence I had been diligent to do as I was ordered by him. Thus, as well as I

[5] Because.
[6] I.e., she cannot express the full extent of what she suffered.
[7] With.

could, I made her sensible how unreasonable he was. Now, though she could not understand me nor I her, but by signs, we reasoned as well as we could. She therefore makes signs that I must die, advising me by pointing up with her fingers in her way, to pray to God, endeavoring by her signs and tears to instruct me in that which was most needful, *viz.* to prepare for death, which now threatened me. The poor old squaw was so very kind and tender that she would not leave me all that night but laid herself down at my feet, designing what she could to assuage her son-in-law's wrath, who had conceived evil against me chiefly, as I understood, because the want of victuals urged him to it. My rest was little this night, my poor babe sleeping sweetly by me.

I dreaded the tragical design of my master, looking every hour for his coming to execute his bloody will upon us. But he, being weary with his hunting and travel in the woods (having toiled for nothing), went to rest and forgot it. Next morning he applied himself again to hunting in the woods, but I dreaded his returning empty and prayed secretly in my heart that he might catch some food to satisfy his hunger and cool his ill humor. He had been gone but a little time till returned with booty, having shot some wild duck, and now he appeared in a better temper, ordering the fowls to be dressed with speed, for these kind of people when they have plenty spend it as freely as they get it, spending in gluttony and drunkenness in two days' time as much as with prudent management might serve a week. Thus do they live for the most part either in excess of gluttony and drunkenness or under great straits for want of necessaries. However, in this plentiful time I felt the comfort of it in part with the family, having a portion sent for me and my little ones which was very acceptable. Now, I thinking to myself the bitterness of death was over for this time, my spirits were a little easier.

Not long after this he got into the like ill humor again, threatening to take away my life. But I always observed whenever he was in such a temper he wanted food and was pinched with hunger. But when he had success in hunting to take either bears, beavers, bucks, or fowls on which he could fill his belly, he was better humored though he was naturally of a very hot and passionate temper, throwing sticks, stones, or whatever lay in his way on every slight occasion. This made me in continual danger of my life. But that God whose Providence is over all His works so preserved me that I never received any damage from him that was of any great consequence to me for which I ever desire to be thankful to my Maker.

When flesh was scarce, we had only the guts and garbage allowed to our part, and, not being permitted to cleanse the guts any otherwise than emptying the dung without so much as washing them as is before noted, in that filthy pickle we must boil them and eat them, which was very unpleasant. But hunger made up that difficulty so that this food which was very often our lot became pretty tolerable to a sharp appetite which otherwise by no means could have been dispensed with. Thus, I considered, none knows what they can undergo till they are tried, for what I had thought in my own family not fit for food would here have been a dainty dish and sweet morsel.

By this time, what with fatigue of spirits, hard labor, mean diet, and often want of natural rest, I was brought so low that my milk was dried up, my baby very poor and weak, just skin and bone for I could perceive all its joints from one end of the babe's back to the other. And how to get what would suit its weak appetite I was at a loss, on which one of the Indian squaws perceiving my uneasiness about my child began some discourse with me in which she advised me to take the kernels of walnuts and clean them and beat them with a little water, which I did, and when I had so done, the water looked like milk. Then she advised me to add to this water a little of the finest of the Indian corn meal and boil it a little together. I did so, and it became palatable and was very nourishing to the babe so that it began to thrive and look well, which was before more like to die than live. I found that with this kind of diet the Indians did often nurse their infants. This was no small comfort to me. But this comfort was soon mixed with bitterness and trouble, which thus happened: my master, taking notice of my dear babe's thriving condition, would often look upon it and say when it was fat enough, it should be killed, and he would eat it. And pursuant to his pretense at a certain time he made me to fetch him a stick that he had prepared for a spit to roast the baby upon as he said which, when I had done, he made me sit down by him and undress the infant. When the child was naked, he felt its arms, legs, and thighs and told me it was not fat enough yet; I must dress it again until it was better in case.

Now though he thus acted, I could not persuade myself that he intended to do as he pretended but only to aggravate and afflict me. Neither ever could I think but our lives would be preserved from his barbarous hands by the overruling power of Him in whose Providence I put my trust both day and night.

A little time after this my master fell sick, and in his sickness as he lay in his wigwam, he ordered his own son to beat my son. But the old squaw, the Indian boy's grandmother, would not suffer him to do it. Then his father, my master, being provoked, catches up a stick very sharp at one end and with great violence threw it from him at my son and hit him on the breast with which my child was much bruised, and the pain, with the surprise, made him turn as pale as death. I entreated him not to cry, and the boy, though but six years old, bore it with wonderful patience, not so much as in the least complaining, so that the child's patience assuaged the barbarity of his hard heart, who, no doubt, would have carried his passion and resentment higher had the child cried, as always complaining did aggravate his passion, and his anger grew hotter upon it. Some little time after on the same day he got upon his feet [although he was] far from being well. However, though he was sick, his wife and daughter let me know he intended to kill us, and I was under a fear, unless Providence now intercepted, how it would end. I therefore put down my child and, going out of his presence, went to cut wood for the fire as I used to do, hoping that would in part allay his passion. But withal ere I came to the wigwam again, I expected my children would be killed in this mad fit, having no other way but to cast my care upon God who had hitherto helped and cared for me and mine.

Under this great feud the old squaw, my master's mother-in-law, left him, but my mistress and her daughter abode in the wigwam with my master. And when I came with my wood, the daughter came to me, whom I asked if her father had killed my children, and she made me a sign, no, with a countenance that seemed pleased it was so, for instead of his further venting his passion on me and my children, the Lord in whom I trusted did seasonably interpose, and I took it as a merciful deliverance from him, and the Indian was under some sense of the same as himself did confess to them about him afterwards.

Thus it was a little after he got up on his feet [that] the Lord struck him with great sickness and a violent pain as appeared by the complaint he made in a doleful and hideous manner which, when I understood, not having yet seen him, I went to another squaw that was come to see my master [and that] could both speak and understand English and inquired of her if my mistress (for so I always called her, and him master) thought that master would die. She answered, yes, it was very likely he would, being worse and worse. Then I told her he struck my boy a dreadful blow without any provocation at all and had threatened to kill us all in his fury and passion. Upon which the squaw told me my master had confessed the abuse he offered my child and that the mischief he had done was the cause why God afflicted him with that sickness and pain, and he had promised never to abuse us in such sort more. And after this he soon recovered but was not so passionate, nor do I remember he ever after struck either me or [my] children so as to hurt us or with that mischievous intent as before he used to do. This I took as the Lord's doing, and it was marvelous in my eyes.

Some few weeks after this my master made another remove, having as before made several. But this was the longest ever he made, it being two days' journey and mostly upon the ice. The first day's journey the ice was bare but the next day, some snow falling, made it troublesome, very tedious, and difficult traveling, and I took much damage in often falling, having the care of my babe that added not a little to my uneasiness. And the last night when we came to encamp, it being in the night, I was ordered to fetch water, but, having sat awhile on the cold ground, I could neither go nor stand but [by] crawling on my hands and knees. A young Indian squaw who came to see our people, being of another family, in compassion took the kettle and, knowing where to go, which I did not, fetched the water for me. This I took as a great kindness and favor that her heart was inclined to do me this service.

I now saw the design of this journey; my master, being, as I suppose, weary to keep us,[8] was willing to make what he could of our ransom. Therefore, he went further towards the French and left his family in this place where they had a great dance, sundry other Indians coming to our people. This held[9] some time, and while they were in it, I got out of their way in a corner of the wigwam as well as I could. But every time they came by me in their dancing, they would bow my head towards the ground and frequently kick me with as great fury as

[8] I.e., "weary of keeping us."
[9] Continued.

they could bear, being sundry of them barefoot and others having Indian moccasins. This dance held some time, and they made (in their manner) great rejoicings and noise.

It was not many days ere my master returned from the French, but he was in such a humor when he came back he would not suffer me in his presence. Therefore, I had a little shelter made with some boughs, they having digged through the snow to the ground, the snow being pretty deep. In this hole I and my poor children were put to lodge, the weather being very sharp, and hard frost in the month called January made it more tedious to me and [my] poor babes. Our stay not being long in this place, he took me to the French in order for a chapman,[1] and when we came among them, I was exposed to sale, and he asked for me 800 [French pounds]. But the French, not complying with his demand, put him in a great rage, offering him but 600. He said in a great passion if he could not have his demand, he would make a great fire and burn me and the babe in the view of the city, which was named Port Royal. The Frenchman bid the Indian make his fire. "And I will," says he, "help you if you think that will do you more good than six hundred livres," calling my master "fool" and speaking roughly to him, bid[ding] him be gone. But at the same time the Frenchman was very civil to me and for my encouragement bid me be of good cheer for I should be redeemed[2] and not go back with them again.

Retiring now with my master for this night, the next day I was redeemed for 600 pounds and in treating with my master the Frenchman queried why he asked so much for the babe's ransom, urging when it had its bellyful it would die. My master said, no, it would not die, having already lived twenty-six days on nothing but water, believing the babe to be a devil. The Frenchman told him, no, the child is ordered for longer life, and it has pleased God to preserve it to admiration.[3] My master said, no, it was a devil, and he believed it would not die unless they took a hachet and beat its brains out. Thus ended their discourse, and I was, as aforesaid, with my babe ransomed for 600 pounds; my little boy likewise at the same time for an additional sum of livres was redeemed also.

I now having changed my landlord, table, and diet, as well as my lodging, the French were civil beyond what I could either desire or expect. But the next day after I was redeemed, the Romish priests took my babe from me, and, according to their custom, they baptized it (urging if it died before that, it would be damned like some of our modern, pretended-reformed priests),[4] and they gave it a name as pleased them best which was Mary Ann Frossways, telling me my child, if it now died, would be saved, being baptized. And my landlord, speaking to the priest that baptized it, said, "It would be well now Frossways

---

[1] I.e., in order to find a merchant to purchase her.
[2] Ransomed.
[3] I.e., for the sake of causing awe. Ordered: predestined.
[4] Here, in this seeming attack on the Puritan clergy, Hanson's Quaker sympathies emerge. Quakers generally distrusted a formal, paid clergy in favor of dispersing its functions among the believers.

was baptized for it to die, being now in a state to be saved." But the priest said, "No, the child, having been so miraculously preserved through so many hardships, it may be designed by God for some great work, and, by its life being still continued, may much more glorify God than if it should now die." A very sensible remark, and I wish it may prove true.

I having been about five months amongst the Indians, in about one month after I got amongst the French, my dear husband, to my unspeakable comfort and joy, came to me, who was now himself concerned to redeem his children, two of our daughters being still captives and only myself and two little ones redeemed; and through great difficulty and trouble he recovered the younger daughter. But the eldest we could by no means obtain from their hands, for the squaw to whom she was given had a son which she intended my daughter should in time be prevailed with to marry. The Indians being very civil toward their captive women, not offering any incivility by any indecent carriage (unless they be much overgone in liquor) which is commendable in them so far.

However, the affections they had for my daughter made them refuse all offers and terms of ransom so that after my poor husband had waited and made what attempts and endeavors he could to obtain his child, and all to no purpose, we were forced to make homeward, leaving our daughter to our great grief behind us amongst the Indians and set forwards over the lake with three of our children and servant maid in company with sundry others, and, by the kindness of Providence, we got well home on the first day of the seventh month 1725.[5] From which it appears I had been from home amongst the Indians and French about twelve months and six days. In the series of which time, the many deliverances and wonderful Providences of God unto us and over us have been, and I hope will so remain to be, as a continued obligation on my mind ever to live in that fear, love, and obedience to God, duly regarding by His grace with meekness and wisdom to approve myself by His spirit in all holiness of life and Godliness of conversation to the praise of Him that hath called me, who is God blessed forever.

But my dear husband, poor man, could not enjoy himself in quiet with us for want of his dear daughter Sarah that was left behind, and, not willing to omit anything for her redemption which lay in his power, he could not be easy without making a second attempt. In order to which he took his journey about the nineteenth day of the second month[6] 1727, in company with a kinsman and his wife who went to redeem some of their children and were so happy as to obtain what they went about. But my dear husband, being taken sick on the way, grew worse and worse, as we were informed, and was sensible he should not get over it, telling my kinsman that if it was the Lord's will he must die in the wilderness, he was freely given up to it. He was under a good composure of mind and sensible to the last moment and died as near as we can guess [at] about the halfway [point] between Albany and Canada in my kinsman's arms

---

[5] Hanson uses the Quaker description (old style) for September 1, 1725.
[6] I.e., April.

and is at rest, I hope, in the Lord. And though my own children's loss is very great, yet I doubt not but his gain is much more. I, therefore, desire and pray that the Lord will enable me patiently to submit to His will in all things He is pleased to suffer to my lot while here, earnestly supplicating the God and Father of all our mercies to be a father to my fatherless children and give unto them that blessing which maketh truly rich and adds no sorrow to it, that as they grow in years they may grow in grace and experience the joy of His salvation which is come by Jesus Christ our Lord and Savior, Amen.

Now though my husband died, by reason of which his labor was ended, yet my kinsman prosecuted the thing and left no stone unturned that he thought or could be advised was proper to the obtaining my daughter's freedom, but could by no means prevail, for, as is before said (she being in another part of the country distant from where I was) and given to an old squaw who intended to marry her in time to her son, using what persuading she could to effect her end, sometimes by fair means and sometimes by severe. In the meantime a Frenchman interposed, and they by persuasion enticed my child to marry in order to obtain her freedom by reason that those captives married by the French are by that marriage made free among them, the Indians having then no pretense longer to keep them as captives. She therefore was prevailed upon, for the reasons afore assigned, to marry, and she was accordingly married to the Frenchman.[7]

Thus, as well and as near as I can from my memory (not being capable of keeping a journal), I have given a short but a true account of some of the remarkable trials and wonderful deliverances which I never purposed to expose but that I hope thereby the merciful kindness and goodness of God may be magnified, and the reader hereof provoked with more care and fear to serve Him in righteousness and humility, and then my designed end and purpose will be answered.

E.H.

---

[7] Married to Jean Baptiste Sabourin in 1727, Sarah Hanson remained in New France.

4

RESISTANCE ON A
SLAVE SHIP

WHEN HE SET OUT ON HIS SLAVE SHIP *LITTLE GEORGE* FOR THE COAST OF WEST
Africa in 1730, Rhode Islander George Scott was engaging in an act that many
of his countrymen performed almost as a routine. Rhode Island, a strong center
of maritime activity, was heavily involved in the slave trade, and the commercial richness of that colony's farmlands meant that the settlers there bought
slaves in large numbers for their own use, not just to trade elsewhere. By 1730,
very little opposition to slavery had been voiced anywhere among European
Americans, although some colonial leaders, notably the Massachusetts judge
Samuel Sewall, had protested against the inhumanity of enslaving Africans
decades earlier, and the Quakers, who were numerous in Scott's Rhode Island
as well as Pennsylvania, had already begun what later would escalate into an
anti-slavery movement. For most white Americans, however, the enslaving of
Africans (or Native Americans) seemed as much a part of the world's ordinary
economy as the many other kinds of inequality that structured their universe.
In such a hierarchically arranged society, the modern principle of equality not
only did not operate: it would have been utterly foreign to the vast majority of
people. Not until the Revolutionary era, when the patriots established an ideology of liberty as the cornerstone of the new nation, did a body of articulate
political principles exist by which, even inferentially, slavery could be legally as
well as morally challenged.

George Scott's horror at what ensued during his 1730 voyage could not,
therefore, have had much political meaning for the man who wrote it or the
readers who found it in the Boston *News Letter*. Scott tells the story of the slave
revolt on the *Little George* as a struggle between opposed forces, not principles,
in which gunpowder and other material means will play the deciding role. He
likewise insists on viewing the Africans as his subordinates even when, in fact,
he and his crew are completely at their mercy. Never does he speculate on the
motive of the Africans, or raise the least question about slavery as an increasingly important institution of his home society. Perhaps those who read his
narrative in the press felt some twinges of guilt as they did so; more likely,

though, they followed the line of threat and danger through the violent account of how the ship's company endured nine days of near-starvation in the sweltering cabin. Largely naturalistic, with a fine sense of the delicate balance that keeps the two sides from destroying each other outright, the narrative offers a grim glimpse into the netherworld of exploitation and dominance that lay beneath the surface of colonial life, and its very lack of moral insight makes it all the more telling as a document of the times.

GEORGE SCOTT

"The Voyage of the *Little George*" (1730)

I, GEORGE SCOTT (THE SCRIBER),[1] MASTER OF THE SLOOP THE *LITTLE GEORGE*, belonging to Rhode Island; sailed from the Banana Islands on the coast of Guinea,[2] the first of June 1730, having on board ninety-six slaves (thirty-five of which were men). On the 6th of said month at half an hour past four of the clock in the morning, being about 100 leagues distant from the land, the men slaves got off their irons, and making way through the bulkhead[3] of the deck, killed the watch consisting of John Harris, doctor, Jonathan Ebens, cooper, and Thomas Ham, sailor; who were, 'tis thought, all asleep. I being then in my cabin and hearing a noise upon deck (they throwing the watch overboard) took my pistol directly, and fired up the scuttle which was abaft,[4] which made all the slaves that were loose run forwards except one or two men (who seemed to laugh at the cowardice of the rest, and defiance of us, being but four men and a boy) who laid the scuttle, and kept us down confined in the cabin, and passing by the companion[5] to view us, we shot two men slaves.

On so sudden a surprise, we were at a loss what to do, but consulting together, filled two round bottles with powder, putting fuses to them, in order to send them among the slaves, with a design at the same instant of time, to issue out upon them, and either suppress them or lose our lives; but just as we were putting our design in execution, one of the slaves let fall an axe (either through accident or design) which broke the bottle as Thomas Dickinson was setting fire to the fuse, and taking fire with a keg of powder, in the cabin, raised up the deck, blew open the cabin doors and windows, discharged all our firearms but one, destroyed our clothes and burnt the man that had the bottle in his hand in a most miserable manner, and myself with the rest very much hurt thereby.

[1] Writer.
[2] Islands off the coast of present-day Sierra Leone, just south of Guinea and Guinea-Bissau on the western coast of Africa, once a center of the English slave trade.
[3] Usually a vertical partition below decks on a ship, though here apparently the deck itself.
[4] To the rear. Scuttle: hatchway in the deck.
[5] Either a glazed opening in the deck to admit light below or (more properly written "companion-way") a stairway running between decks.

Upon this unhappy accident, we expected no less than immediate death, which would have been unavoidable, had they at that juncture of time, rushed in upon us. And being in this consternation and hopeless, [we] sent up the boy in order (if possible) to bring them to terms, but they slighted our message. And soon after (the smoke clearing out of the cabin) we found the other bottle of powder which by providence had not taken fire, and which put new life and vigor into us, [so] that we were resolved to withstand them to the uttermost; and accordingly loaded our arms and shot several of the slaves, which occasioned all the men slaves to betake themselves to the quarter-deck, over our heads. The slaves then got two swivel guns, and filled them almost full with powder, which they found in the fore hold, as they were looking for provisions, and designed to blow the bulkhead in upon us, which they put fire to several times, but could not get off by reason of wet weather. We had two carriage guns in the boat, which we expected the slaves would get out, and therefore watched them very narrowly; but in a dark night they effected it, and brought them upon the quarter deck; they loaded one of the guns, and pointed it directly down the scuttle: we hearing them about the scuttle and having prepared ourselves; so soon as they lifted it up, we shot the man dead that pointed the gun. Another of the slaves standing by clapped a match to it and fired it off, which blew the scuttle all to pieces and some of the deck, but did us no damage. They then took pieces of boards and laid them over the scuttle and the hole they had made in the deck, and laid the tarpaulin, with a great weight upon them to prevent our coming up.

Then they made sail (as they thought) towards land and were continually heaving down billets of wood, and water into the cabin, with intention to disable us and spoil our small arms. And the fourth day after the rising made the same land we departed from, then stood off and on again for four or five days more, in which time the boy being forced by hunger, run up among the slaves, who immediately put him in irons. They made several attempts to come down into the cabin, but their courage failed them. I then called to them to come down to decide the matter; they answered, by and by.

Finding ourselves grow very weak, through these hardships, and for want of sustenance; we thought it proper before our strength was quite spent to take some desperate course. I proposed to cut away the ceiling and bore some holes through the vessel's bottom, which being approved on, was directly done, and let in about three feet of water. I then called to the slaves, and told them, I would drown them all, which frighted them exceedingly: they then sent the boy to the cabin door, to tell us, that they had but just made the land, and that when they got a little nearer the shore, they would take the boat and leave [us] with the young slaves: I told them if they would do that I would not sink her. (My design in letting the water in, was to force the vessel on her side that we might get some advantage.) They stood in for the land about 12 o'clock at night, struck upon the bar of Sierra Leone river, and were in great danger of being lost. The vessel [was] strong beat over the bar, and they run ashore about three leagues up the river, on the north side; [it was] then high water, and at 7 o'clock the next morning there was not above a foot of water alongside.

The natives waded from the shore with firearms, would have fain tried to overcome us, but were persuaded from it by the slaves on board, who told them we should shoot them if they appeared in our sight. They persuaded the grown slaves to go ashore, and drove the young ones overboard and then followed them, making the vessel shake at their departure. Our boy assuring us the slaves had all left the vessel, we immediately went up with our arms, and saw the slaves just ashore. We found our great guns loaded quite full. And as we hoisted out our boat, the natives mustered very thick on the shore and fired at us divers[6] time[s]. We made what haste we could to the other side of the river, where we rowed down about two leagues, and found a sloop riding in Frenchman's Bay belonging to Montserat, James Collingwood commander, where we refreshed ourselves, being all of us in a weak and miserable condition, having had nothing to subsist upon during the nine days we were under this affliction but raw rice.

[6]Several.

5

AYUBA SULEIMAN DIALLO:
AN AFRICAN'S EXILE AND RETURN

AYUBA SULEIMAN DIALLO OF BONDU, KNOWN IN THE EUROPEAN AMERICAN world as Job Ben Solomon, was a merchant and a member of the Fulbe people of sub-Saharan West Africa, born about 1701 in what is now the borderlands of Senegal and Mali. His family, several members of which were Muslim clerics, apparently was of prominence in the vicinity of Bondu on the upper Senegal River. Ayuba claimed that Bondu had been founded by his grandfather, but in fact the family was of recent standing there, having derived from Futa Toro along the lower Senegal where they claimed ties with the traditional Futa Toro rulers. The larger African region of Senegambia was at this time under dominance by European powers, especially Britain and France, which had control of the Senegal and Gambia river trade, respectively. The trade was largely confined to gum arabic (derived from the African acacia tree and used in the textile industry), gold, animal hides, elephant ivory, and beeswax; although trade in slaves was not unknown, as Ayuba Suleiman's story makes clear, it was relatively insignificant in Senegambia compared with sources farther south.

Ayuba Suleiman's exceptional experience as a slave serves to confirm this latter point. Sent by his father in February 1730 to sell two of his slaves to the English in exchange for a supply of paper and other items, he could not reach agreement with Captain Pike of the *Arabella*, which was then docked along the Gambia, so he crossed the river into hostile Mandingo territory and traded the slaves for cattle. As Ayuba Suleiman rested following this exchange, he was set upon by a party of Mandingo-speakers and promptly sold, along with his companion and interpreter, Loumein Yoas, to none other than Captain Pike. When Ayuba Suleiman convinced Pike that he was the very man who had dealt with the English a short time earlier, Pike allowed Ayuba to try to secure funds to redeem himself and Yoas. Far removed from his family, however, Ayuba was unable to make contact and effect his release before Pike sailed for America with his cargo of slaves. Ayuba and Loumein were taken with the rest to Annapolis, Maryland, where they were put into the hands of Vachell Denton, agent for the owner of the *Arabella*. Soon Ayuba was sold to a planter on Kent

Island, in the upper Chesapeake, and set to work in the tobacco fields. For obvious reasons, he did not take well to this new situation, and soon ran away through the woods until he came to the vicinity of Dover, in what is now Delaware. There he was taken up as a runaway and jailed.

At this point Ayuba's path crossed with that of Thomas Bluett, an Englishman who had heard of the captive and took an interest in his plight. Through the intercession of an old African slave who could speak the Wolof language, widely used in Ayuba's home region and known to Ayuba as well, the young man's story was secured, and Bluett, along with other Englishmen in the vicinity, made an effort to effect his ransom and release. Through a series of steps detailed in Bluett's account below, this goal was achieved, but the motives for the effort need further discussion here. Bluett clearly recognized, as did other more famous Englishmen from James Oglethorpe to Sir Hans Sloane, that Ayuba was exceptional, and it was for this reason—not out of any abstract opposition to slavery (although Oglethorpe for one certainly opposed the system)—that Ayuba drew such unusual support and ultimately was able to return to his homeland. Educated, literate, highly connected, Ayuba became an attractive object of European sympathy; that he was, as Bluett wrote, of an "exceedingly pleasant" countenance, possessed mental "ingenuity," "a solid judgment, a ready memory, and a clear head," made Ayuba readily assimilable (as the more famous Olaudah Equiano also would be later) to notions of modern individuality then emergent in European culture. That is, it was particularly hard to maintain that a man of such evident subjectivity was merely—as slaves in theory were—an object to be bought and sold like any other commodity. From a textual point of view, as well, the fact that Ayuba could tell a story of his past gave him an added sense of individuation. Although Europeans may not have been of completely open minds on the subject of Islam, that Ayuba could be understood in terms of his own culture and could furthermore demonstrate mastery of that of Europe (he amazed Bluett and others by taking apart and putting back together European tools and mechanisms for which he had not been told the use) set him apart from the mass of slaves Europeans largely did not want to know as persons.

Clearly the young Fulbe exile attracted considerable attention. Bluett apparently wrote and published his version of Ayuba's story not only because Ayuba asked him to but also because the story would appeal to an English public interested in the agon of such castaways as Daniel Defoe's Crusoe; an agon in which a key allegory of the period—the struggle of the lone self against the world—was given classic expression. For many far-flung Englishmen the prospect of being permanently torn away from the homeland was a daunting and more than theoretically possible one; in reading Ayuba's tale they could indulge not only nascent humanitarian drives but also self-centered fantasies of a safe route through the mercantile world of their era. The story also proved strikingly memorable for those who stumbled across its hero in real life. Englishman Francis Moore, stationed at James Fort at the mouth of the Gambia when Ayuba was captured and sold, noted the events in his journal at the time and later, in his *Travels* of 1738, narrated them along with Ayuba's happy return to his home. We owe to Moore some of the details of the early chapters of the story not present in Bluett, as well as the retributive ending—Ayuba's glee over Allah's punishment of his original persecutors, for instance. Whether another aspect of Ayuba's latter days is also owing at least in part to Moore— namely, the cooperative attitude toward the British attributed to him in Moore's book—is a good question, and one whose answer is almost surely affirmative. Just enough of Ayuba's canny manipulation on other issues peeks through the narratives to suggest that he may have been acting here, as elsewhere, to tell those into whose hands he had fallen precisely what they wanted to hear. Be that as it may, the onetime slave kept contact with the British along the Gambia up to his death in 1773, but by then British interests in this area of Africa had suffered several reverses, the old Royal Company was long dead, and little had come of the hope of further contact with the inner territories that Ayuba had seemed to promise.

THOMAS BLUETT

from **Some Account of the Life of Job . . . a Slave . . . in Maryland (1734)**

IN FEBRUARY, 1730, JOB'S FATHER HEARING OF AN ENGLISH SHIP AT GAMBIA River,[1] sent him, with two servants to attend him, to sell two Negroes, and to buy paper, and some other necessaries; but desired him not to venture over the river, because the country of the Mandingoes, who are enemies to the people of Futa, lies on the other side.[2] Job not agreeing with Captain Pike (who commanded the ship, lying then at Gambia, in the service of Captain Henry Hunt, brother to Mr. William Hunt, merchant, in Little Tower Street, London) sent back the two servants to acquaint his father with it, and to let him know that he intended to go farther. Accordingly having agreed with another man, named Loumein Yoas,[3] who understood the Mandingo language, to go with him as his interpreter, he crossed the River Gambia, and disposed of his Negroes for some cows. As he was returning home, he stopped for some refreshment at the house of an old acquaintance; and the weather being hot, he hung up his arms in the house, while he refreshed himself. Those arms were very valuable; consisting

---

[1] In the present country of the same name, West Africa.

[2] The Fulbe or Futa were a group of peoples, including Ayuba Suleiman's, living in Gambia; the Malinke, one of several Mandingo-speaking peoples, lived downstream along the Gambia.

[3] A member of a prominent family in the present-day Senegalese town of Bakel, north of Ayuba's home in Bondu; ultimately taken to Maryland with Ayuba, he was released for ransom and returned to Africa in 1738.

of a gold-hilted sword, a gold knife, which they wear by their side, and a rich quiver of arrows, which King Sambo[4] had made him a present of. It happened that a company of the Mandingoes, who live upon plunder, passing by at that time, and observing him unarmed, rushed in, to the number of seven or eight at once, at a back door, and pinioned Job, before he could get to his arms, together with his interpreter, who is a slave in Maryland still. They then shaved their heads and beards, which Job and his man resented as the highest indignity; though the Mandingoes meant no more by it, than to make them appear like slaves taken in war. On the 27th of February, 1730, they carried them to Captain Pike at Gambia, who purchased them; and on the first of March they were put on board. Soon after Job found means to acquaint Captain Pike that he was the same person that came to trade with him a few days before, and after what manner he had been taken. Upon this Captain Pike gave him leave to redeem himself and his man; and Job sent to an acquaintance of his father's, near Gambia, who promised to send to Job's father, to inform him of what had happened, that he might take some course to have him set at liberty. But it being a fortnight's journey between that friend's house and his father's, and the ship sailing in about a week after,[5] Job was brought with the rest of the slaves to Annapolis in Maryland, and delivered to Mr. Vachell Denton, factor[6] to Mr. Hunt, before mentioned. Job heard since, by vessels that came from Gambia, that his father sent down several slaves, a little after Captain Pike sailed, in order to procure his redemption; and that Sambo, King of Futa, had made war upon the Mandingoes, and cut off great numbers of them, upon account of the injury they had done to his schoolfellow.

Mr. Vachell Denton sold Job to one Mr. Tolsey in Kent Island in Maryland, who put him to work in making tobacco; but he was soon convinced that Job had never been used to such labour. He every day showed more and more uneasiness under this exercise, and at last grew sick, being no way able to bear it; so that his master was obliged to find easier work for him, and therefore put him to tend the cattle. Job would often leave the cattle, and withdraw into the woods to pray; but a white boy frequently watched him, and whilst he was at his devotion would mock him, and throw dirt in his face. This very much disturbed Job, and added considerably to his other misfortunes; all [of] which were increased by his ignorance of the English language, which prevented his complaining, or telling his case to any person about him. Grown in some measure desperate, by reason of his present hardships, he resolved to travel at a venture; thinking he might possibly be taken up by some master, who would use him better, or otherwise meet with some lucky accident, to divert or abate his grief. Accordingly, he travelled through the woods, till he came to the

---

[4]Samba Geladio Jegi was a ruler of limited power among the Futa, although his fame was spread by legend and his name may have been the source—perhaps in part by means of Ayuba's own narrative—of the "Sambo" of European and American stereotype.
[5]Francis Moore, whose account of Ayuba's return to Africa follows this document, confirmed the essential features of Bluett's account of Ayuba's capture.
[6]Agent.

County of Kent,[7] upon Delaware Bay, now esteemed part of Pennsylvania; although it is properly a part of Maryland, and belongs to my Lord Baltimore. There is a law in force, throughout the colonies of Virginia, Maryland, Pennsylvania, etc. as far as Boston in New England, viz. that any Negro, or white servant who is not known in the county, or has no pass, may be secured by any person, and kept in the common gaol, till the master of such servant shall fetch him. Therefore Job being able to give no account of himself, was put in prison there.

This happened about the beginning of June, 1731, when I, who was attending the courts there, and had heard of Job, went with several gentlemen to the gaoler's house, being a tavern, and desired to see him. He was brought into the tavern to us, but could not speak one word of English. Upon our talking and making signs to him, he wrote a line or two before us, and when he read it, pronounced the words Allah and Mahommed; by which, and his refusing a glass of wine we offered him, we perceived he was a Mahometan, but could not imagine of what country he was, or how he got thither; for by his affable carriage, and the easy composure of his countenance, we could perceive he was no common slave.

When Job had been some time confined, an old Negro man, who lived in that neighbourhood, and could speak the Jalloff[8] language, which Job also understood, went to him, and conversed with him. By this Negro the keeper was informed to whom Job belonged, and what was the cause of his leaving his master. The keeper thereupon wrote to his master, who soon after fetched him home, and was much kinder to him than before; allowing him a place to pray in, and some other conveniencies, in order to make his slavery as easy as possible. Yet slavery and confinement was by no means agreeable to Job, who had never been used to it; he therefore wrote a letter in Arabic to his father, acquainting him with his misfortunes, hoping he might yet find means to redeem him. This letter he sent to Mr. Vachell Denton, desiring it might be sent to Africa by Captain Pike; but he being gone to England, Mr. Denton sent the letter inclosed to Mr. Hunt, in order to be sent to Africa by Captain Pike from England; but Captain Pike had sailed for Africa before the letter came to Mr. Hunt, who therefore kept it in his own hands, till he should have a proper opportunity of sending it. It happened that this letter was seen by James Oglethorpe, Esq.,[9] who, according to his usual goodness and generosity, took compassion on Job, and gave his bond to Mr. Hunt for the payment of a certain sum, upon the delivery of Job here in England. Mr. Hunt upon this sent to Mr. Denton, who purchased him again of his master for the same money which Mr. Denton had formerly received for him; his master being very willing to part with him, as finding him no ways fit for his business.

---

[7] Now part of the state of Delaware.

[8] The language of the Wolof people, who were converted to Islam in the eighteenth century.

[9] James Edward Oglethorpe (1696–1785), soon to be governor of the new colony of Georgia, known for his opposition to slavery, also opposed the impressment of sailors into the navy and favored more lenient treatment of debtors in England.

He lived some time with Mr. Denton at Annapolis, before any ship could stir out, upon account of the ice that lay in all the rivers of Maryland at that time. In this interval he became acquainted with the Reverend Mr. Henderson,[1] a gentleman of great learning, minister of Annapolis, and commissary to the Bishop of London, who gave Job the character of a person of great piety and learning;[2] and indeed his good nature and affability gained him many friends besides in that place.

In March, 1733, he set sail in the *William*, Captain George Uriel commander; in which ship I was also a passenger. The character which the captain and I had of him at Annapolis, induced us to teach him as much of the English language as we could, he being then able to speak but few words of it, and those hardly intelligible. This we set about as soon as we were out at sea, and in about a fortnight's time, taught him all his letters, and to spell almost any single syllable, when distinctly pronounced to him; but Job and myself falling sick, we were hindered from making any greater progress at that time. However, by the time that we arrived in England, which was the latter end of April, 1733, he had learned so much of our language, that he was able to understand most of what we said in common conversation; and we that were used to his manner of speaking, could make shift to understand him tolerably well.

During the voyage, he was very constant in his devotions; which he never omitted, on any pretence, notwithstanding we had exceeding bad weather all the time we were at sea. We often permitted him to kill our fresh stock, that he might eat of it himself; for he eats no flesh, unless he has killed the animal with his own hands, or knows that it has been killed by some Mussulman.[3] He has no scruple about fish; but won't touch a bit of pork, it being expressly forbidden by their law. By his good nature and affability he gained the good will of all the sailors, who (not to mention other kind offices) all the way up the channel showed him the headlands and remarkable places; the names of which Job wrote down carefully, together with the accounts that were given him about them. His reason for so doing, he told me, was, that if he met with any Englishman in his country, he might by these marks be able to convince him that he had been in England.

On our arrival in England, we heard that Mr. Oglethorpe was gone to Georgia, and that Mr. Hunt had provided a lodging for Job at Limehouse. After I had visited my friends in the country, I went up on purpose to see Job. He was very sorrowful, and told me, that Mr. Hunt had been applied to by some persons to sell him, who pretended they would send him home; but he feared they would either sell him again as a slave, or if they sent him home would expect an unreasonable ransom for him. I took him to London with me, and waited on Mr. Hunt, to desire leave to carry him to Cheshunt in Hartfordshire; which Mr. Hunt complied with. He told me he had been applied to, as Job

---

[1] Jacob Henderson (d. 1751), a native of Ireland, the first clergyman in Annapolis.
[2] I.e., he recommended Ayuba in these terms.
[3] A follower of Islam.

had suggested, but did not intend to part with him without his own consent; but as Mr. Oglethorpe was out of England, if any of Job's friends would pay the money, he would accept of it, provided they would undertake to send him home safely to his own country. I also obtained his promise that he would not dispose of him till he heard farther from me.

Job, while he was at Cheshunt, had the honor to be sent for by most of the gentry of that place, who were mightily pleased with his company, and concerned for his misfortunes. They made him several handsome presents, and proposed that a subscription should be made for the payment of the money to Mr. Hunt. The night before we set out for London from Cheshunt, a footman belonging to Samuel Holden, Esq., brought a letter to Job, which was, I think, directed to Sir Byby Lake.[4] The letter was delivered at the African House; upon which the House was pleased to order that Mr. Hunt should bring in a bill of the whole charges which he had been at about Job, and be there paid; which was accordingly done, and the sum amounted to fifty-nine pounds, six shillings, and eleven pence half-penny. This sum being paid, Mr. Oglethorpe's bond was delivered up to the company. Job's fears were now over, with respect to his being sold again as a slave; yet he could not be persuaded but that he must pay an extravagant ransom, when he got home. I confess, I doubted much of the success of a subscription, the sum being great, and Job's acquaintance in England being so small; therefore, to ease Job's mind, I spoke to a gentleman about the affair, who has all along been Job's friend in a very remarkable manner. This gentleman was so far from discouraging the thing, that he began the subscription himself with a handsome sum, and promised his further assistance at a dead lift.[5] Not to be tedious: several friends, both in London and in the country, gave in their charitable contributions very readily; yet the sum was so large, that the subscription was about twenty pounds short of it; but that generous and worthy gentleman before mentioned, was pleased to make up the defect, and the whole sum was completed.

I went (being desired) to propose the matter to the African Company; who, after having heard what I had to say, showed me the orders that the House had made; which were, that Job should be accommodated at the African House at the company's expense, till one of the company's ships should go to Gambia, in which he should be sent back to his friends without any ransom. The company then asked me, if they could do anything more to make Job easy; and upon my desire, they ordered, that Mr. Oglethorpe's bond should be cancelled, which was presently done, and that Job should have his freedom in form, which he received handsomely engrossed,[6] with the company's seal affixed; after which the full sum of the whole charges (namely, fifty-nine pounds, six shil-

---

[4] I.e., addressed to Lake, the subgovernor of the Royal African Company, which in this period was aggressively expanding its trade in Senegal and Gambia, although overall its history since its founding in 1671 as a monopoly to exploit African commerce, including the slave trade, was a story of failure. Its headquarters were at the African House in London.

[5] I.e., if the effort at fundraising proved exceptionally difficult.

[6] Formally written out.

lings, and eleven pence half-penny) was paid in to their clerk, as was before proposed.

Job's mind being now perfectly easy, and being himself more known, he went cheerfully among his friends to several places, both in town and country. One day being at Sir Hans Sloane's,[7] he expressed his great desire to see the royal family. Sir Hans promised to get him introduced, when he had clothes proper to go in. Job knew how kind a friend he had to apply to upon occasion; and he was soon clothed in a rich silk dress, made up after his own country fashion, and introduced to their majesties, and the rest of the royal family. Her majesty was pleased to present him with a rich gold watch; and the same day he had the honor to dine with his grace the duke of Montagu,[8] and some others of the nobility, who were pleased to make him a handsome present after dinner. His grace, after that, was pleased to take Job often into the country with him, and show him the tools that are necessary for tilling the ground, both in gardens and fields, and made his servants show him how to use them; and afterwards his grace furnished Job with all sorts of such instruments, and several other rich presents, which he ordered to be carefully done up in chests, and put on board for his use. 'Tis not possible for me to recollect the many favors he received from his grace, and several other noblemen and gentlemen, who showed a singular generosity towards him; only, I may say in general, that the goods which were given him, and which he carried over with him, were worth upwards of 500 pounds; besides which, he was well furnished with money, in case any accident should oblige him to go on shore, or occasion particular charges at sea. About the latter end of July last [1734] he embarked on board one of the African Company's ships, bound for Gambia; where we hope he is safely arrived, to the great joy of his friends, and the honor of the English nation.

FRANCIS MOORE

from *Travels into the Inland Parts of Africa* (1738)

THE NEXT DAY [AUGUST 8, 1734] ABOUT NOON CAME UP THE *DOLPHIN* SNOW,[9] which saluted the fort with nine guns, and had the same number returned; after which came on shore the captain, four writers, one apprentice to the

---

[7] Scientist and at the moment president of Britain's Royal Society, Sloane (1660–1753) was intimate with George II; upon his death he bequeathed to Britain the core of what became the British Museum collections. As Francis Moore reveals below, Sloane tested Ayuba by having him translate Arabic texts and inscriptions; Ayuba impressed him as a "perfect master" of the tongue.

[8] John Montagu, second duke of Montagu (1688?–1749), took great interest in African and African Americans visiting England, including Ayuba.

[9] A kind of ship resembling a brig.

company, and one black man, by name Job Ben Solomon, a Fulbe of Bondu in Futa, who in the year 1731, as he was travelling in Jagra, and driving his herds of cattle across the countries, was robbed and carried to Joar, where he was sold to Captain Pike, commander of the ship *Arabella*, who was then trading there. By him he was carried to Maryland, and sold to a planter, with whom Job lived about a twelvemonth without being once beat by his master; at the end of which time he had the good fortune to have a letter of his own writing in the Arabic tongue conveyed to England. This letter coming to the hand of Mr. Oglethorpe, he sent the same to Oxford to be translated; which, when done, gave him so much satisfaction, and so good an opinion of the man, that he directly ordered him to be bought from his master, he soon after setting out for Georgia. Before he returned from thence, Job came to England; where being brought to the acquaintance of the learned Sir Hans Sloane, he was by him found a perfect master of the Arabic tongue, by translating several manuscripts and inscriptions upon medals: he was by him recommended to his grace the duke of Montagu, who being pleased with the sweetness of humor, and mildness of temper, as well as genius and capacity of the man, introduced him to court, where he was graciously received by the royal family, and most of the nobility, from whom he received distinguishing marks of favor. After he had continued in England about fourteen months, he wanted much to return to his native country, which is Bondu (a place about a week's travel over land from the Royal African Company's factory at Joar, on the River Gambia) of which place his father was high priest, and to whom he sent letters from England. Upon his setting out from England he received a good many noble presents from her most gracious majesty Queen Caroline, his highness the duke of Cumberland, his grace the duke of Montagu, the earl of Pembroke, several ladies of quality, Mr. [Samuel] Holden, and the Royal African Company, who have ordered their agents to show him the greatest respect. . . .

Job Ben Solomon having a mind to go up to Kau-Ur[1] to talk with some of his countrymen, went along with me. In the evening we weighed anchor, saluting the fort with five guns, which returned the same number.

On the 26th [of August, 1734] we arrived at the creek of Damasensa, and having some old acquaintances at the town of Damasensa, Job and I went up in the yawl; in the way, going up a very narrow place for about half a mile, we saw several monkeys of a beautiful blue and red, which the natives tell me never set their feet on the ground, but live entirely amongst the trees, leaping from one to another at so great distances, as any one, were they not to see it, would think improbable.

In the evening, as my friend Job and I were sitting under a great tree at Damasensa, there came by us six or seven of the very people who robbed and made a slave of Job, about thirty miles from hence, about three years ago; Job, though a very even-tempered man at other times, could not contain himself when he saw them, but fell into a most terrible passion, and was for killing

---

[1] An important market on the Gambia River.

them with his broad sword and pistols, which he always took care to have about him. I had much ado to dissuade him from falling upon the six men; but at last, by representing to him the ill consequences that would infallibly attend such a rash action, and the impossibility of mine or his own escaping alive, if he should attempt it, I made him lay aside the thoughts of it, and persuaded him to sit down and pretend not to know them, but ask them questions about himself; which he accordingly did, and they answered nothing but the truth. At last he asked them how the king their master did; they told him he was dead, and by further inquiry we found, that amongst the goods for which he sold Job to Captain Pike there was a pistol, which the king used commonly to wear slung about his neck with a string; and as they never carry arms without being loaded, one day this accidentally went off, and the ball's lodging in his throat, he died presently. At the closing of this story Job was so very much transported, that he immediately fell on his knees, and returned thanks to Mahomet for making this man die by the very goods for which he sold him into slavery; and then turning to me, he said, "Mr. Moore, you see now God Almighty was displeased at this man's making me a slave, and therefore made him die by the very pistol for which he sold me; yet I ought to forgive him, says he, because had I not been sold, I should neither have known anything of the English tongue, nor have had any of the fine, useful and valuable things I now carry over, nor have known that in the world there is such a place as England, nor such noble, good and generous people as Queen Caroline, Prince William, the duke of Montagu, the earl of Pembroke, Mr. Holden, Mr. Oglethorpe, and the Royal African Company."

On the 1st of September we arrived at Joar, the freshes[2] being very strong against us. I immediately took an inventory of the company's effects, and gave receipts to Mr. Gill for the same. After which we unloaded the sloop, and then I sent her to Yanimarew for a load of corn for James Fort, where she stayed till the 25th, and then came back to Joar, during which time I made some trade with the merchants, though at a pretty high price.

On Job's first arrival here, he desired I would send a messenger up to his own country to acquaint his friends of his arrival. I spoke to one of the blacks which we usually employ upon those occasions, to procure me a messenger, who brought to me a Fulbe, who knew the high priest his father, and Job himself, and expressed great joy at seeing him in safety returned from slavery, he being the only man (except one) that was ever known to come back to this country, after having been once carried a slave out of it by white men. Job gave him the message himself, and desired his father should not come down to him, for it was too far for him to travel; and that it was fit for the young to go to the old, and not for the old to come to the young. He also sent some presents by him to his wives, and desired him to bring his little one, which was his best-beloved, down to him. After the messenger was gone, Job went frequently along with me to Kau-Ur, and several other places about the country; he spoke always

[2] Freshets, floods.

very handsome of the English, and what he said, took away a great deal of the horror of the Fulbe for the state of slavery amongst the English; for they before generally imagined, that all who were sold for slaves, were generally either eaten or murdered, since none ever returned. His description of the English gave them also a great notion of the power of England, and a veneration for those who traded amongst them. He sold some of the presents he brought with him from England for trading-goods, with which he bought a woman-slave and two horses, which were very useful to him there, and which he designed to carry with him to Bondu, whenever he should set out thither. He used to give his country people a good deal of writing-paper, which is a very useful commodity amongst them, and of which the company had presented him with several reams. He used to pray frequently, and behaved himself with great mildness and affability to all, so that he was very popular and well-beloved. The messenger not being thought to return soon, Job desired to go down to James Fort to take care of his goods, I promising to send him word when the messenger came back, and also to send some other messengers, for fear the first should miscarry.

On the 26th [of September] I sent down the *Fame* sloop to James Fort, and Job going along with her, I gave the master orders to show him all the respect he could. . . .

On the 29th [of January, 1735] came up from Damasensa in a canoe Job Ben Solomon, who, I forgot to say, came up in the *Fame* sloop along with me from James Fort on the 26th of December last, and going on shore with me at Elephants Island, and hearing that the people of Joar were run away,[3] it made him unwilling to proceed up hither, and therefore he desired Conner to put him and his things ashore at a place called India, about six miles above Damasensa, where he has continued ever since; but now hearing that there is no farther danger, he thought he might venture his body and goods along with mine and the company's, and so came up.

On the 14th [of February] a messenger, whom I had sent to Job's country, returned hither with letters, and advice that Job's father died before he got up thither, but that he had lived to receive the letters sent by Job from England, which brought him the welcome news of his son's being redeemed out of slavery, and the figure he made in England. That one of Job's wives was married to another man; but that as soon as the husband heard of Job's arrival here, he thought it advisable to abscond: that since Job's absence from this country, there has been such a dreadful war, that there is not so much as one cow left in it, though when Job was there, it was a very noted country for numerous herds of large cattle. With this messenger came a good many of Job's old acquaintance, whom he was exceeding glad to see; but notwithstanding the joy he had to see his friends, he wept grievously for his father's death, and the misfortunes of his country. He forgave his wife, and the man that had taken her; for, says he, "Mr. Moore, she could not help thinking I was dead, for I was

[3] Owing to a war then being waged in the region.

gone to a land from whence no Fulbe ever yet returned; therefore she is not to be blamed, nor the man neither." For three or four days he held a conversation with his friends without any interruption, unless to sleep or eat. . . .

On the 8th [of April, 1735], having delivered up the company's effects to Mr. James Conner, and taken proper discharges for the same, I embarked on board the company's sloop *James*, to which Mr. Hull accompanied me, and parted with me in a very friendly manner. Job likewise came down with me to the sloop, and parted with me with tears in his eyes, at the same time giving me letters for his grace the duke of Montagu, the Royal African Company, Mr. Oglethorpe, and several other gentlemen in England, telling me to give his love and duty to them, and to acquaint them, that as he designs to learn to write the English tongue, he will, when he is master of it, send them longer epistles, and full accounts of what shall happen to him hereafter; desiring me, that as I had lived with him almost ever since he came here, I would let his grace and the other gentlemen know what he had done, and that he was the next day going with Mr. Hull up to Yanimarew, from whence he would accompany him to the gum forest,[4] and make so good an understanding between the company and his country people, that the English nation should reap the benefit of the gum trade; saying at last, that he would spend his days in endeavoring to do good for the English, by whom he had been redeemed from slavery, and from whom he had received such innumerable favors.

---

[4]A region to the north of Bondu, home of the *acacia senegal* tree, source of a material that was crucial for the expanding European textile industry; Hull: Thomas Hull, nephew of the English governor at James Fort at the mouth of the Gambia.

6

AN ENGLISH WORKER
ADRIFT IN AMERICA

IN 1729, A NO-LONGER-VERY-YOUNG ENGLISH WORKER NAMED WILLIAM MORA-ley, distressed at the lack of opportunity in his homeland, took the desperate remedy of a subsidized voyage to the American colonies. Shod in "a pair of bad new shoes" given him as part of the deal, all agog for what fortune might bring him over the sea, Moraley set sail "with a fair wind" on September 7th, the brighter prospects of his youth now completely eclipsed. He had been born in London in 1699 to a journeyman clockmaker who tried to fund his son's rise into the legal profession, but a combination of bad luck, bad relations between father and son, and William's own bad temper foreclosed that opportunity, and on the father's death in Newcastle-upon-Tyne in 1725 William was left with a token inheritance. Soon he managed to win the ill-will of his mother as well, and in 1728 he left Newcastle for London, almost thirty, at last on his own.

William's autobiography, published in Newcastle in 1743, nine years after he returned from America, does not reveal that in 1729 he was imprisoned in London for debt. Surely this was the catalyst, not the love of the "adventures" referred to in the book's title, that led him, as he put it, to "sell myself for a terms of years into the American plantations." He departed in September 1729 on the ship *Boneta* and eventually docked in Philadelphia, where his five-year indenture was purchased by a Quaker watch- and clockmaker named Isaac Pearson from nearby Burlington, New Jersey. Moraley soon began to chafe under the kind Pearson's supervision; city-bred as he had been, Moraley was mightily attracted to the nearby delights of Philadelphia (which he fully and lovingly recorded in his prose—as well as some "hammered out" verses). Moraley eventually ran away to Philadelphia, where he was ultimately captured. On his return, Pearson forgave him and allowed him to depart early from the indenture, proving that, despite his self-characterization as "the Infortunate," Moraley at times enjoyed very good luck, not the least of it involving the indulgence of other people, friends, strangers, betters, and equals, who tolerated and accepted his at times annoying and distressing behavior. An incipient con man, as occasionally his autobiography admits, Moraley seems to have had an ability to charm those who might have seen through him had they not been basically decent and trusting.

After leaving Pearson, Moraley briefly labored for two other artisans in Philadelphia, one of whom proved to be a drunk while the other soon moved to Antigua. Moraley subsequently started wandering the city and the countryside, begging or just making do, sleeping in outbuildings and cadging his meals and his drink where and from whom he might. A marriage of pure opportunism with "an old ugly maid" of modest fortune was scotched when a damaged gold ring she gave him to mend was stolen and sold (so he says) by some of his acquaintances. Set free on the roads of the middle colonies, he stumbled about physically and economically, was treed by a panther and lost in the woods, wandering between Maryland and New York, and between pillar and post, with always a crowd of debts lingering behind him and a posse of creditors close on his trail. At last, in 1734, after about a year of freedom in America, he shipped as a cook on a vessel bound for Ireland, and eventually landed in England, broke and filthy, the day after Christmas of that year. Reunited with and reconciled to his mother, he spent the next years with her, but was somewhat embittered by the manner in which she left her modest estate to him—she understood her son's weaknesses and had set up a small annuity whose principal he could not touch. Moraley lived on in Newcastle, working at his craft, until he died there in 1762.

In the account of his life that he had published two decades earlier, he claimed that his motive in writing the story was to urge others afflicted with his own weakness to learn from his mistakes. While he ate the humble pie of calling himself "the Prodigal Son" in the book, and countless times accepted some responsibility for his fate, Moraley also delighted in telling of his rascally progress through the colonies, as if his real message was not prudence but rather the opposite. He had a wanderer's love of improvised living arrangements, and probably would have found his own level regardless of how high fortune had floated him. In this sense, his lack of propagandizing talk about "Industry" makes a nice counterbalance to the nearly contemporaneous Benjamin Franklin's calculated celebration of middle-class sobriety. No emigrant's tale replete with an American dream, Moraley's modest book is a delightful wag's account of how he bumped about the world, content with what drifted near. In the section of his story printed here, Moraley, parting company with Pearson, heads off on his American wanderings, which lead him eventually to New York.

WILLIAM MORALEY

from *The Infortunate: or The Voyage and Adventures of William Moraley* (1743)

MY MASTER, AFTER WE WERE RECONCILED, BEHAVED VERY CIVILLY TO ME, AND I lived very happy, to the expiration of my servitude.[1] He had a share in an iron work at a place called Mount Holly, about seven miles from Burlington, where I was sent to work. Here I have had many a merry day. Sometimes I have acted the blacksmith; at other times, I have worked in the water, stark naked, among water snakes. Sometimes I was a cow hunter in the woods, and sometimes I got drunk for joy that my work was ended.

At last this iron work was perfected and the time of my servitude expired, and I became free. 'Tis impossible to express the satisfaction I found at being released from the precarious humor and dependence of my master. He accoutered me in an indifferent manner, and gave me my discharge, to find out a new way of living.[2] I then went to Philadelphia and served one Edmund Lewis, a brisk young clockmaker; but he being unsettled, and of a roving temper (like master, like man!), I left him, and lived with Mr. Graham, a watchmaker, newly arrived, and nephew to the famous Mr. Graham in Fleet Street.[3] With him I continued ten weeks, at ten shillings per week wages, and my board found me,[4] but he designing to settle at Antigua,[5] I left him.

Then I roamed about like a roving Tartar,[6] for the convenience of grazing, and for three weeks had no abiding place. In the nights I was forced to skulk about the extremity of the town, where I lay in a hayloft. In the daytime, I got victuals of several of my companions from London. Then, by their help, I courted an old ugly maid, who had got good store of pewter and brass. The match was agreed, and a day appointed to put me in possession of her moveables.[7] But the very night before the marriage was to be celebrated, she gave me a gold ring to take the bruises out,[8] and accidentally meeting with some of

---

[1] At this point, Moraley was indentured to Isaac Pearson (ca. 1685–1749), a Quaker artisan, particularly a clockmaker, in Burlington, New Jersey. Their reconciliation followed Moraley's escape and recapture in 1730. The indenture was set to expire in 1734, five years from its start, but Pearson forgave the final two years in exchange for Moraley's agreement to return to his service after running away, and Moraley therefore was freed from his bond late in 1732.

[2] Indentures typically required that, upon expiration, the former master provide the worker with clothes or other resources.

[3] George Graham (1673–1751) was a clockmaker, as well as an inventor and manufacturer of astronomical instruments; he was a fellow of the Royal Society; his nephew William was active in Philadelphia in the early 1730s.

[4] I.e., Moraley's food was provided as part of his pay.

[5] A British possession among the Lesser Antilles, in the Caribbean.

[6] I.e., like a nomad of the region of Tartary, in Asia.

[7] As her husband, Moraley would secure legal ownership of her property.

[8] While under his apprenticeship as a watchmaker in England and his indenture to Pearson, Moraley would have acquired experience repairing such items.

my acquaintance, they got the ring from me, sold it, and spent the money; so I lost my sweetheart.

But this life not being likely to last long, and the people's good nature beginning to cool, I set my wits to work how to get home. But not presently hearing of a ship bound for England, I was reduced to such extremity, that I looked like the picture of bad luck, and so thin, that you might have seen my ribs through my skin, and I was greatly afraid of a consumption.[9] However, having some acquaintance in the country, I went about cleaning clocks and watches, and followed the occupation of a tinker; but not being well versed in that trade, where I mended one hole, I was sure to make another.

But this life serving only for the present, did not afford me a constant supply; so in the intervals was forced to spend, when I came back, what I had earned in these sort of roamings. It never cost me any money, by way of expense; I was welcome everywhere, though unknown, and always recommended to business from place to place, where I had variety of entertainment, always endeavoring to ingratiate myself into the people's favor by a modest and decent behavior, which, with relating stories when desired, and my giving them an account of England, gained me the reputation of an intelligent man, though upon occasion I could rake[1] with the best of them, and change my note as proper time offered.

I remember I was going to a place called Crossfield, between Trenton and Burlington,[2] to mend a clock, being barefoot and barelegged; and after I had acquitted myself in the best manner, and received ten shillings for my pains, I went to Trenton, a pretty neat place, containing about two hundred houses, and lay there two nights, after I had cleaned two clocks. This town stands twenty miles from Burlington, near the River Delaware, having many handsome houses, and rich inhabitants.

Here I found out the young lady whom I saved from drowning, who, by the death of her father, was left possessed of a fortune of three thousand pounds.[3] She asked me to take a dinner with her, which I did, and after that drank tea with her, when she gave me three pound, and desired to know how things stood with me; which having satisfied her in, I took my leave of her, in order to return home.

About four miles from Trenton, passing along a spacious road, I espied a beast at a distance, and observed his eyes were fixed upon me. I was so terribly affrighted, that, to prevent any danger, I climbed up a large oak tree and secured myself in the branches. When the beast drew near, I perceived that it

[9] I.e., a wasting (or "consuming") disease, not necessarily tuberculosis.
[1] I.e., live a wild life.
[2] Probably Moraley was thinking of Crosswicks, so situated in New Jersey.
[3] Hannah Lambert was a relation of Pearson's who for a time lived in his family. Moraley described her as "a gentlewoman of beauty, good parts, and a good fortune, daughter to Mr. Thomas Lambert, a native of Yorkshire." The two were canoeing on the Delaware one day when the canoe overturned and he grasped her and swam with her to the shore. The gratitude of her wealthy family for his rescue of her, Moraley claimed, resulted in his having ready money in his pocket during the course of his indenture, normally most unusual for someone in his position.

was a panther, about the largeness of a mastiff dog. He set his forefeet against the tree, and attempted to climb up. I was so terrified at this, that I shivered, and all my passions were at work: but after he had tried to ascend in vain, by falling down twice, he roared, and gently left the place.

It was near two hours before I ventured to descend, for fear he should have concealed himself, in order to surprise me; and when I did venture down, I walked so warily, that it was near two hours more before I reached the next house, which was but two miles from the place. This proved to be the habitation of Mr. Isaac Horner, a Yorkshire gentleman of substance. I told him of this adventure, at which he laughed, and said he had been in the same circumstances. After Mr. Horner had treated me with the best his house afforded, I went to bed. In the morning I set out for home, but missed my way.

Here are so many crossroads, which makes it exceeding difficult to keep the right one; for instead of taking the right, I struck into a broad road, which, I was afterwards told, leads to a wood of pines, that grow close together, overshadows the road, and prevents any communication with the sky. In these woods, bears, wolves, and panthers range about, often putting the traveller into a fear. If I had continued this way, I should not have met with a house till I came to Salem, a town near the Capes,[4] which was near two hundred miles from me.

After I had journeyed about eight miles in the road, not finding any appearance of any house or farm to inquire of, and fearing the consequence of being lost in the woods, I returned, happily for me, and guessed at a road, which led me to Allentown, a pitiful dirty hole; where I arrived after nine hours travel, not meeting with anyone to direct me. I drank some cider, eat some hung beef,[5] and got directions to Recklesstown seated on the river, eight miles from Trenton, where I was known. Here I came and was received well. It is a pretty large neat place, of about fifty houses.

From thence I took the right road, and lost it, which so perplexed me, and being dispirited I broke out into the following expressions, *If ever I have the good fortune to reach my native country, I am resolved to reform my life and conversation, in such a manner, as not to suffer a sinful thought to harbor in my breast.* Night coming on, I was in a sad taking, reflected on my former condition of life, and, comparing it with the present, said, *I that was brought up so tenderly by my indulgent parents, am now reduced to the most deplorable circumstances.*

Thus ruminating with myself, at last I discovered a light at a great distance, and endeavored to make up to it. After some difficulty I got to it, and it proved to be the habitation of John Montgomery, a Scotchman, where I was taken up for a runaway, and detained all night.[6] However I got a good supper, consisting

---

[4] I.e., Cape May and Cape Henlopen, where Delaware Bay meets the Atlantic; Salem, New Jersey, is a rural riverside town considerably south of Trenton, and not on a direct route to the capes, so Moraley's geography here indeed seems to indicate that he was lost. His description of the landscape suggests he may be referring to the Pine Barrens of southcentral New Jersey.
[5] Air-dried.
[6] Colonel John Montgomerie (d. 1733), governor of New York and New Jersey, 1728–31.

of hot wheaten bread and milk, and a hot apple pie. In the morning I was carried on a horse by two men to Burlington, where my former master cleared me, by producing my indentures; and the men returned home, but with this difference, that they had their labor for their pains, and money out of pocket upon my account.

Three days after this adventure, I worked journey work with Peter Bishop, a blacksmith, for eight shillings a week, and necessaries found me, as lodging, meat and drink. I worked at the great hammer, in making horseshoes, horse-shoe nails, rounding of shipbolts, sharpening coulters for the plow, etc. This life I followed six week, and out of my earnings bought a fine shirt, the first I wore since my departure from England. Many a hard day I have had at this employment, but necessity enabled me to surmount all difficulties.

During this employ, my creditors at Philadelphia, where I owed trifling debts, such as three or four shillings to each, but amounted in the whole to above eight pound, found me out, and threatened me with summoning me before the magistrate. This obliged me to leave my blacksmith, for at that time I could never hear a dun with patience; so I steered my course for New York, to avoid their impertinence. After three days march, I arrived at Elizabethtown, about eighteen miles from New York. Near which place, as I was walking in the road, I espied a new brick house, and a Negro working in an adjoining field, who called to me, and asked me if I would not come and see his master, who was an Indian king.

Little persuasion served, being weary; so I went with him, and was admit-ted to the royal presence. The king was sitting by the fireside, upon a carpet, attended by two bought servants,[7] and three Negro slaves, drinking rum. His name was Yo-Taen-San-Lo, king of the Chiapase.[8] After paying him a respect due to his quality, he desired me to sit down and smoke a pipe, and ordered pipes and tobacco to be brought; and rum, a glass of which being handed to me, I soon dispatched it. He kindly asked me if I was an Englishman. I told him, I was, and born at London. Then he drank to me again, and I pledged him a second time. He invited me to dinner, and a quarter of lamb was roasted.

After dinner punch was set upon the carpet, when we drank heartily. Then he desired me to relate to him the manners and customs of the English, with the state of our king; which I did, wonderfully magnifying everything, and making our king ten times greater than he is. After drinking three or four glasses more, I would have taken my leave of him, but he desired me to stay an hour longer, which I did; and then took notice of his furniture, which was good chairs and stools, provided for strangers, for they never use any themselves, nor beds.

At last I got leave to depart, and made the best of my way to New York, where I arrived that night. In the morning I waited upon the governor, and presented to him my credentials from my first master, as to my business. He

---

[7] I.e., workers whose service had been purchased for a period of time; indentured servants.
[8] No plausible identification of the "king" or of his people is possible; Moraley may have been misremembering, fabricating, or telling of an encounter in which he played something of a dupe.

ordered me to continue at his house till further notice, and the servants helped me to what I stood in need of.

Colonel Crosby the governor,[9] was an Irishman, and formerly a common soldier; but being a graceful man, had the address to gain the affection of Lord Halifax's sister, and married her, which raised him to the posts he enjoys. He had two daughters, both handsome ladies. The eldest was married to the lord Augustus Fitzroy, second son to the duke of Grafton. The youngest is unmarried. This marriage was just then discovered, which gave a great deal of uneasiness to the family, because the father was a stranger to it; but the matter was soon made up by the lord Baltimore with the duke of Grafton.

The next day the governor ordered me two clocks to clean, for which he gave me two pistoles,[1] and recommended me to several gentlemen of figure, from whom I got money. But my creditors joining together, made one debt of it, and followed me to New York, by a letter to an attorney; which I having notice of, immediately applied to Capt. Ingoldsby, commander of the fort, and son to the late lieutenant general commander of her late majesty Queen Anne's troops in Ireland, who admitted me as a soldier: so that the attorney applying to the captain, had no remedy.

Escaping this snare, I continued at New York, and lived as a servant with a Spanish gentleman, named Don Roderigo de Almeria, of Valentia. I lived a very sober, retired life, and obtained this gentleman's favor, by my assiduity in serving him.

[9]William Cosby [not Crosby] (ca. 1690–1736), governor of New Jersey and New York, 1731–36.
[1]A Spanish gold coin worth somewhat less than a pound.

7

BRADDOCK'S DEFEAT

WHEN THE LAST CHAPTER IN THE RIVALRY BETWEEN FRANCE AND GREAT
Britain for control of North America opened in the 1750s, its setting was a then-
obscure spot at the junction of two rivers some three hundred miles inland
from Philadelphia. The French, committed to fortifying the western edge of
the British plantations so as to contain the settlers, in 1754 captured a modest
fort built there by a party of Virginians, enlarged it, and named it for Governor-
general Duquesne of New France. This was the target, the following year, of a
massive army led by the British general Edward Braddock. Braddock, despite
the fact that he had served in the British army for some forty years, knew very
little about battle; he was weakened by an adherence to textbook strategies and
a haughty disdain for the colonial components of his force. As he neared Fort
Duquesne on July 9th, 1755, the front of his drawn-out army tangled with a
scouting party of French troops and Indian warriors, and due to the element of
surprise and the confusion of his own army as it collapsed back onto itself, the
British were soon defeated, Braddock himself being mortally wounded.

There are many accounts of the events of that day from many perspectives.
The one printed here lacks the directness of many others, as it was written by a
person who never actually arrived at the scene of the battle but rather gathered
information as it hurried back, along broken lines, through an atmosphere of
fear and exaggeration. But Charlotte Brown, the author of the account, offers
many compensations for what her narrative may lack as testimony to the events
of the disastrous defeat. A widow, Charlotte Brown came over in a transport
ship, the *London*, in the late fall of 1754, accompanied by her brother, who was
a British officer, and two servants; appointed to serve as the matron of the
general hospital for Braddock's force, she was to be assisted in that task by the
nurses to whom her account refers.

Leaving the Tidewater on June 1st, Charlotte Brown followed somewhat
behind Braddock's force, along a route that led from Bellhaven, Virginia, to
Fort Cumberland in western Maryland at the confluence of Wills Creek and
the Potomac. She traveled in a fairly large and diverse party, and part of the

value of her journal lies in its depiction of the vicissitudes of life on the way. Of sprightly wit and sharp observation, she was not above poking fun at others—or at herself—but her growing sense of realism is also worthy of notice. With the dreadful news of Braddock's defeat (and the hasty word of his own death), which Brown received with others in her party just two days after it occurred, it is this realism that takes over. From that point on, the party struggled to sort rumor from more accurate reporting, and Brown and her brother and others struggled against camp illnesses that claimed him on July 17th and nearly claimed her on several occasions as well. Her account of the "Daily Occurrences at Fort Cumberland" (and of the party's disorderly retreat, begun as late as August 20th) is a gripping log of grim events on the military frontier of the great powers of her era.

CHARLOTTE BROWN

from her "Journal" (1754–56)

REMARKS ON A MARCH FROM BELLHAVEN IN VIRGINIA TO WILLS'S CREEK.

JUNE THE 1. AT 4:00 IN THE MORNING I WAS CALLED UP BY MRS. JOHNSON who came to take her leave of me and at 6:00 we marched for Wills's Creek with one officer, my brother, self and servant, two nurses, two cooks and forty men to guard us. Twelve wagons with the sick, lame, and blind, my wagon in the rear. My equipage [was] three horses and a mare good in spirit but poor in flesh, which I mentioned to Mr. Gore (my coachman), who told me that if they were right fat they would faint by the way. My brother came padding on his horse in the rear, but as my friend Gore observed, there was no fear of his fainting by the way, being very poor in flesh. We had marched three miles when my coachman was for taking a better road but the sentries forbid it; but he said it was very hard if the other wagons drove to the Old Boy[1] he must follow them. We halted at 3:00 and dined on a piece of salt pork and water to drink, and at 6:00 we came to the old court house[2] seventeen miles from Bellhaven. [We] laid in a room with but three beds in it.

June the 2. At break of day the drum beat. I was extremely sleepy but got up and as soon as our officer had eaten six eggs and drank a dram or two and some punch we marched; but my wagon being in the rear the day before, my coachman insisted that it was not right that Madam Brown should be behind and if they did not give way they should feel the soft end of his whip, [so] he gained his point and got in front. The roads are so bad that I am almost dis-

---

[1] I.e., "went to Satan."
[2] At Fairfax, Virginia.

jointed; at 12:00 we halted at Mr. Coleman's, pitched our marquees[3] and dined on salt gammon,[4] nothing better to be had.

June the 3. At 3:00 in the morning was awaked by the drum but was so stiff that I was at a loss to tell whether I had any limbs. I breakfasted in my wagon and then set off in front, at which all the rest were very much enraged, but to no purpose, for my coachman told them that he had but one officer to obey and she was in his wagon and it was not right that she should be blinded with dust. My brother the day before left his cloak behind, so [he] sent his man back for it on his horse and marched on foot and on the road met with Mr. Adams, a parson, who left his horse and padded with them on foot. We halted at Mr. Minor's. We ordered some fowls for dinner but not one [was] to be had, so [I] was obliged to set down to our old dish, gammon and greens. The officer and the parson replenished their bowl so often that they began to be very joyous until their servant told them that their horses were lost, at which the parson was much enraged and popped out an oath, but Mr. Falkner said, "Never mind your horse, Doctor, but have you a sermon ready for next Sunday?"[5] I being the doctor's countrywoman he made me many compliments and told me he should be very happy if he could be better accquainted with me but hoped when I came that way again I would do him the honor to spend some time at his house. I chatted till 11:00 and then took my leave and left them a full bowl before them.

June the 4. At break of day my coachman came and tapped at my chamber door and said, "Madam, all is ready and it is right early." I went to my wagon and we moved on. [We] left Mr. Falkner behind in pursuit of his horse, marched fourteen miles and halted at an old sage Quaker's with silver locks. His wife on my coming in accosted me in the following manner: "Welcome, Friend, set down, thou seems full bulky to travel, but thou are young and that will enable thee. We were once so ourselves but we have been married forty-four years and may say we have lived to see the days that we have no pleasure therein." We had recourse to our old dish gammon, nothing else to be had, but they said they had some liquor they called whisky, which was made of peaches. My friend Thompson being a preacher, when the soldiers came in as the spirit moved him held forth to them and told them the great virtue of temperance. They all stared at him like pigs but had not a word to say in their justification.

June the 5. My lodgings not being very clean I had so many close companions called ticks that deprived me of my night's rest, but I indulged till 7:00. We halted this day, all the nurses baking bread and boiling beef for to march tomorrow. [We had] a fine regale, two chicken with milk and water to drink, which my friend Thompson said was fine temperate liquor; several things [were] lost out of my wagon, amongst the rest they took two of my hams, which

---

[3] Large field tents.
[4] Ham.
[5] "Mr. Falkner" is mentioned earlier by Brown as "our commanding officer," but she gives no other details.

my coachman said was an abomination to him and if he could find out who took them he would make them remember taking the next.

June the 6. Took my leave of my friend Thompson, who bid me farewell. A great gust of thunder and lightning and rain so that we were almost drowned. Extreme bad roads. We passed over the Blue Ridge, which was one continual mountain. For three miles forged through two rivers. At 1:00 we halted at Mr. Key's, a fine plantation; had for dinner two chicken. The soldiers desired my brother to advance them some whisky, for they told him he had better kill them at once than to let them die by inches, for without [it] they could not live. He complied with their request and it soon began to operate, they all went to dancing and bid defiance to the French. My friend Gore began to shake a leg. I asked him if it was consistent as a member of his society[6] to dance; he told me that he was not at all united with them and that there were some of this people who called themselves Quakers and stood up for their church but had no more religion in them than his mare. I then told him I should set him down as a Ranter.[7]

June the 7. Having no room to lodge in, I laid in the chimney, so wanted no calling in the morning having no sleep all night. At 4:00 we began to march, left Mr. Falkner behind who did not choose to march with an empty stomach. Great gusts of rain, my wagon and everything in it wet and all the sick almost drowned. At 4:00 we halted at my friend Laidler's, who bid me welcome but had no whisky, which was the soldier's first inquiry for they were still in the opinion that they could not live without it. We now live high, had for dinner a quarter of lamb and a pie; to drink my friend Thompson's temperate liquor, spring water. I spent the evening very agreeable, Mr. Falkner favored me with several tunes on his flute, chatted till 10:00 and then retired.

June the 8. I slept but poorly, lying on a deal[8] feather bed. Having had no sleep for two nights did not hear the drum. We marched at 4:00; at 9:00 we halted at my friend Bellinger's, who bid me welcome. My brother set off for Winchester,[9] . . . but Mr. Falkner said he would do himself the pleasure of staying with me; we spent the day very agreeably, had for dinner some veal and greens, to drink French wine and for supper milk punch.

June the 9. Laid on some planks, halted all this day, the nurses busy baking bread and boiling beef and washing. Mr. Falkner went a shooting, returned and brought me some squirrels; dressed them for dinner. My brother returned from Winchester, there came with him Mr. Savage an officer and thirteen recruits and a wagon with a nurse and four sick men, one at the point of death.

June the 10. Up before the sun and marched till 12:00, extreme hot and very bad roads. I was obliged to walk. We halted at 7:00 at my friend Roger's, who had nothing for us to eat. Mr. Falkner and Mr. Savage went a-shooting

[6]I.e., Society of Friends, or Quakers.
[7]A member of a radical antinomian sect of the previous century, frequently the target of accusations about moral laxity.
[8]Plain lumber.
[9]In Virginia, a few miles beyond the Shenandoah River.

and brought me some pigeons; had them for supper which made us a fine regale; to drink, milk and water. At 10:00 I went to bed in my wagon but laid extremely cold. Mr. Falkner ordered a sentinel to be at my wagon all night so that no one should molest me.

June the 11. The drum beat and awaked me but I was at a loss for some time to tell where I was. My coachman put the horses to the wagon and marched on and desired me not to disturb myself. The roads were so bad that the poor horses were not able to keep on their legs, which I observed to my coachman, who said they were right tough and good and that every one was not to be taken by their looks and as to [the] black and [the] brown they were as good as ever stretched a chain. We left one of the nurses and a sick man behind, he not being able to march any further. Two of the wagons broke down, halted till they were mended, [and] I walked till my [feet] were blistered. We came to a place called Spring Mountain, and there we encamped. We drank tea and supped on the stump of an old tree; we had nothing to eat but salt pork, to drink humble grog. We chatted till 11:00 and were very merry and then retired to our respective wagons.

June the 12. At 2:00 in the morning the drum beat but I could have wished it to have stayed a few hours longer, being very sleepy. We marched but there is no describing the badness of the roads. I walked as far as I was able; the poor horses no longer regard the smack of the whip or beat of the drum, and as to [the] black, she could go no further. Two of the wagons broke down. At 10:00 we came to the river and waited six hours before we could ferry over. At 8:00 at night we halted at a rattlesnake colonel's named Crisop.[1] Had for supper some lamb, to drink some very bad wine which was but five pence a quart. I could get no bed, so went to my wagon.

June the 13. At 3:00 we marched but I was so ill I could not hold up my head. Three of the wagons broke down. At 4:00 in the afternoon Mr. Bass came to meet us and gave me some letters from England, and at 6:00 we came to Fort Cumberland,[2] the most desolate place I ever saw. I went to Mr. Cherrington, who received me kindly, drank tea and then went to the governor[3] to apply for quarters. I was put into a hole [so bad] that I could see daylight through every log, and [it had] one porthole for a window—which was as good a room as any in the fort.

---

[1] Thomas Cresap (ca. 1702–ca. 1790), a native of England, lived on the western border of Maryland, where he traded with the Indians and mediated between them and the colonial government. His son Michael (1742–1775) was later accused of brutality toward the Indians and particularly the murder of members of the Mingo chief Logan's family in 1774. Rattlesnake colonel: a term for a frontier fighter, somewhat disparaging. (The traveler Alexander Hamilton wrote in 1744, "It is a common saying here that a man has no title to that dignity [a colonel's commission]until he has killed a rattlesnake.")

[2] Located on the Potomac River, at the site of the present Cumberland, Maryland.

[3] Of the fort, Colonel James Innis.

DAILY OCCURRENCES AT FORT CUMBERLAND

June the 14. I was taken very ill with a fever and other disorders which continued ten days and [I] was not able to get out of my bed.

July the 1. My brother was taken ill with a fever and flux and fits, my maid taken ill with a fever.

July the 4. All greatly alarmed with the Indians scalping several families within ten miles of us. One poor boy brought in with his scalp off; he lived four days. Several families left their homes and came to the fort for protection.

July the 7. My brother extremely ill; he was blistered.[4] Several who called themselves friendly Indians came to the fort but the gates were ordered to be shut. They stayed four hours and then went to the camp and we had not a drop of water there being no well in the fort.

July the 8. My brother still the same, and [my] maid very ill and I can get no nurse so that I am very much fatigued.

July the 11. My brother much better; all of us greatly alarmed. A boy came from the camp and said the general was killed four miles from the French fort and that almost all Sir Peter Hacket's regiment is cut off by a party of French and Indians who were behind trees. Dunbar's regiment was in the rear so that they lost but few men.[5] It is not possible to describe the distraction of the poor women for their husbands. I packed up my things to send for we expected the Indians every hour. My brother desired me to leave the fort but I am resolved not to go, but share my fate with him.

July the 12. My brother better; no news from the camp so we hope that it is not true what the boy said.

July the 13. I am in great distress—my brother told me if he was not better he could not live but a few days. He submitted to have Mr. Tuton, one of the [doctors], to attend him. He gave him two draughts which had a surprising effect and I hope that he is better. An officer is come from the camp and confirms all [that] the boy said.

July the 14. I sat up with my brother and was much surprised in the night, he was so convulsed I thought he was dying. He dozed and I hope that he is better.

July the 15. My brother much better. Two officers came from the camp wounded, and several wagons with the sick and some at the point of death.

July the 17. Oh! how shall I express my distraction! This unhappy day at 2:00 in the afternoon deprived me of my dear brother, in whom I have lost my

---

[4] I.e., treated with a blister plaster, designed to raise a blister as a means of relief.

[5] Brown reports rumors here, but most of them proved true. Braddock's force stumbled across a party of French and Indian fighters on July 9 and was routed with heavy casualties. Braddock himself was among the wounded in the melee, but did not die until July 13, two days after this entry in Brown's journal is dated. Sir Peter Halket, with the rank of colonel, who was in command of the 44th regiment of foot, then serving as the rear guard of Braddock's drawn-out army, was killed early in the battle; Colonel Thomas Dunbar, in command of the 48th regiment of foot, was far behind Braddock at the time of the encounter, and led the army's eventual retreat.

kind guardian and protector and am now left a friendless exile from all that is dear to me.

July the 19. I am in so much grief I can think of nothing. Mr. Cherrington was so kind as to order[6] my brother's funeral.

July the 20. I was taken very ill with a fever and flux which I have had six weeks.[7]

July the 22. Very ill and in the greatest pain. I wrote the unhappy news to my brother[8] and sent [it] to England by a packet which was going.

July the 25. Very bad. My disorder still increasing, I can get no nurse. My servant is gone to her husband to the camp.

August the 1. I have got a nurse but a very bad one. I can neither eat, drink, or sleep, my mind being always on my brother.

August the 12. My fever a little better; got up but could not sit, I was so faint.

August the 15. A little better, but can get nothing that I can eat for here is nothing to be had but beef.

August the 16. Much better. The director says we must march very soon to Frederick's Town in Maryland,[9] which is 150 miles. God only knows how I shall get there, my brother having made me promise him on his death bed not to travel in a carriage as he said it would soon kill me.

August the 17. I went out of my room, supported by two [people]. The day is fixed we are to march, the 20th, and I am resolved not to stay behind if I am able to sit on a horse, which I have not been on this sixteen years.

August the 18. Very busy packing up for my march, which increased my disorder very much. Mr. Cherrington is gone so that I shall not be so happy as to go in his party. He is the only one I can call my friend. I can get no horse so fear I must be left behind.

August the 20. I happily met with a horse. I bought it and set off with my nurse walking by my side; all the gentlemen were gone before. I was so weak I could hardly sit. I met with Mr. Adair, who seeing me alone was so kind as to send his servant with me. We had marched six miles and my horse did not choose to go any further but laid down with me on his back. A servant of the general's seeing me in distress got down and set me on his horse and marched with me. We halted till 3:00 and I was so weak that I was supported by two [people] into the house. All the beds were taken up by the officers before I came so I was obliged to lie on the ground on an old hammock. I had no sleep.

August the 21. I was extremely ill but was obliged to march. My horse threw me going down a hill but happily [I] got no hurt.

August the 22. I was a little better. I had marched four miles and we came

[6]Arrange for.
[7]Brown refers here to the continuance of the illness that she first noted on June 14, some five weeks earlier.
[8]Another brother, back in England, to whom Brown sent her letter via a packet boat.
[9]Now Frederick.

to the River Potomac, in [fording] of which my horse threw me. I must have been lost had not one of the men with one arm come to my assistance. I rode in my wet clothes six miles and then came to a house but could get no bed so laid on the ground on some Indian corn.[1] I could get no sleep.

August the 23. Very ill, but was obliged to march, having a pain in my limbs. We halted at 6:00. I laid on my old lodging, the ground.

August the 24. We halted. I was very busy mending my saddle which I was at a loss to do. Very ill, I could get nothing I could eat or drink.

August the 26. I was up with sun, but was so ill I could not march fast. I halted at 3:00 in the afternoon, but could get no bed.

August the 27. Extremely ill and could not march, but at 11:00 I was a little better and marched and at 5:00 in the afternoon I halted in extreme pain.

August the 28. I halted all day; very ill, but could get no place to lie on but the ground and stayed all day.

August the 29. I was extremely [ill]; applied to the doctor, who gave [me] a bottle to take every two hours, in great distress. I lost my way in the woods for two hours and expected to be scalped every minute, but coming to several roads I let my horse go which way he chose and he carried me to a house where was Mr. Cherrington, who had heard I was coming and had provided a good bed for me, which is the first I have had since I left the fort.

August the 30. I was very ill and not able to march with the rest. Mr. Anderson was so kind as to leave his servant to attend me. We marched at 10:00 and at 6:00 arrived at Frederick's Town in Maryland. Mr. Bass came to meet me. He had taken a lodging for me at the Widow De Butts. I was very much fatigued, having marched since I left the fort 150 miles and was very ill with a fever and flux.

[1] Probably on some corn stalks.

8

PARLIAMENT DEBATES
AN AMERICAN TAX

A NATIVE OF MILFORD, CONNECTICUT, JARED INGERSOLL (1722–1781) FIRST
went to London in 1758 as an agent for his colony, serving in that post until
1761, and again after 1764. He was present as Parliament, in the wake of the
British victory over France in the Seven Years' War, sought to reduce national
debt and readjust the government's relation to its American possessions, both
old and new. As part of this effort, Parliament sought to pass the Stamp Act,
which threatened taxes on newspapers and many kinds of legal and commercial
documents. Ingersoll opposed the Stamp Act, and in February 1765, as Parliament was once more entertaining the legislation after having delayed its consideration to consult with colonial agents such as himself (and Benjamin Franklin
of Pennsylvania), Ingersoll wrote a letter to Connecticut's governor, Thomas
Fitch, detailing the debate on the bill in the House of Commons. Particularly
interesting is his reporting of an impassioned speech by radical Isaac Barré, an
Irish soldier and member of Parliament who strongly supported the American
colonies. Responding to a statement of Charles Townshend that implied the
colonies had been richly supported by the mother country, Barré replied, in
the start of what became a famous litany, "They planted by your care? No! Your
oppressions planted 'em in America. . . ." In this speech Barré coined the
phrase that was to electrify American opposition when he termed the colonists
"Sons of Liberty," and he went on to predict dire consequences should Britain
give Americans the impression that their rights had been violated. Silenced by
the speech, the House of Commons nevertheless recovered its composure and
passed the bill, which the Lords assented to without debate and which the
crown finally approved on March 22nd.

Obviously impressed by Barré and moved by the radical's logic and sense
of American history, Ingersoll nonetheless looked to his own opportunities once
the bill was law. Acting on the advice of Benjamin Franklin, he secured
appointment for himself as Stamp Act agent for Connecticut, to which he soon
returned, although mob action against him forced him to resign the post by
September. The Stamp Act itself was soon repealed, but as further difficulties

with Britain developed, Ingersoll tended to side with Britain and by the time of the war was a confirmed Loyalist. Having served the crown as judge of the vice-admiralty in the years 1768–75, from 1777 until his death he was technically on parole in New Haven from the fledging American government. In a reversal of the contrast between Benjamin Franklin and his Loyalist son William, Ingersoll's son Jared (1749–1822) served as a member of the Continental Congress and the Constitutional Convention and later had a distinguished legal career, being for many years attorney general of Pennsylvania.

JARED INGERSOLL

Letter to Governor Thomas Fitch of Connecticut, February 11, 1765

SINCE MY LAST TO YOU I HAVE BEEN HONORED WITH YOURS OF THE 7TH OF December in which you inform me that the General Assembly have been pleased to desire my assistance while here in any matters that may concern the colony. Be so good, sir, in return as to assure the Assembly that I have not only a due sense of the honor they have done me by placing this confidence in me, but that I have ever since my arrival here, from motives of inclination as well as duty, done everything in my power to promote the colony's interests.

The principal attention has been to the stamp bill that has been preparing to lay before Parliament for taxing America. The point of the authority of Parliament to impose such tax I found on my arrival here was so fully and universally yielded that there was not the least hopes of making any impressions that way. Indeed it has appeared since that the House would not suffer to be brought in, nor would any one member undertake to offer to the House any petition from the colonies that held forth the contrary of that doctrine. I own I advised the agents if possible to get that point canvassed that so the Americans might at least have the satisfaction of having the point decided upon a full debate, but I found it could not be done, and here, before I proceed to acquaint you with the steps that have been taken in this matter, I beg leave to give you a summary of the arguments which are made use of in favor of such authority.

The House of Commons, say they, is a branch of the supreme legislature of the nation, and which in its nature is supposed to represent, or rather to stand in the place of, the commons; that is, of the great body of the people who are below the dignity of peers; that this House of Commons consists of a certain number of men chosen by certain people of certain places, which electors, by the way, they insist are not a tenth part of the people, and that the laws, rules, and methods by which their number is ascertained have arose by degrees and from various causes and occasions, and that this House of Commons therefore is now fixed and ascertained and is a part of the supreme unlimited power of the nation, as in every state there must be some unlimited power and authority;

and that when it is said they represent the commons of England it cannot mean that they do so because those commons choose them, for in fact by far the greater part do not, but because by their constitution they must themselves be commoners and not peers, and so the equals, or of the same class of subjects, with the commons of the kingdom. They further urge that the only reason why America has not been heretofore taxed in the fullest manner has been merely on account of their infancy and inability; that there have been, however, not wanting instances of the exercise of this power in the various regulations of the American trade, the establishment of the post office, etc., and they deny any distinction between what is called an internal and external tax as to the point of the authority imposing such taxes. And as to the charters in the few provinces where there are any, they say in the first place the king cannot grant any that shall exempt them from the authority of one of the branches of the great body of legislation, and in the second place say the king has not done or attempted to do it. In that of Pennsylvania the authority of Parliament to impose taxes is expressly mentioned and reserved; in ours 'tis said, our powers are generally such as are *according to the course of other corporations in England* (both which instances by way of sample were mentioned and referred to by Mr. Grenville[1] in the House); in short, they say a power to tax is a necessary part of every supreme legislative authority, and that if they have not that power over America, they have none, and then America is at once a kingdom of itself.

On the other hand, those who oppose the bill say it is true the Parliament have a supreme unlimited authority over every part and branch of the king's dominions, and as well over Ireland as any other place, yet we believe a British Parliament will never think it prudent to tax Ireland. 'Tis true they say that the commons of England and of the British empire are all represented in and by the House of Commons, but this representation is confessedly on all hands by construction[2] and virtually only as to those who have no hand in choosing the representatives, and that the effects of this implied representation here and in America must be infinitely different in the article of taxation. Here in England the member of Parliament is equally known to the neighbor who elects and to him who does not; the friendships, the connections, the influences are spread through the whole. If by any mistake an Act of Parliament is made that prove injurious and hard, the member of Parliament here sees with his own eyes and is moreover very accessible to the people; not only so, but the taxes are laid equally by one rule and fall as well on the member himself as on the people. But as to America, from the great distance in point of situation, from the almost total unacquaintedness, especially in the more northern colonies, with the members of Parliament, and they with them, or with the particular ability and circumstances of one another, from the nature of this very tax laid upon others not equally and in common with ourselves, but with express purpose to ease

[1] George Grenville (1712–1770), who concurrently held the positions of prime minister, first lord of the treasury, and chancellor of the exchequer (1763–65).
[2] Interpretation.

ourselves, we think, say they, that it will be only to lay a foundation of great jealousy and continual uneasiness, and that to no purpose, as we already by the regulations upon their trade draw from the Americans all that they can spare. At least they say this step should not take place until or unless the Americans are allowed to send members to Parliament; for *who of you*, said Col. [Isaac] Barré[3] nobly in his speech in the House upon this occasion; *who of you reasoning upon this subject feels warmly from the heart* (putting his hand to his own breast) *for the Americans as they would for themselves or as you would for the people of your own native country?* And to this point Mr. Jackson produced copies of two Acts of Parliament granting the privilege of having members to the county palatine of Chester and the bishopric of Durham upon petitions preferred for that purpose in the reign of King Henry the eighth and Charles the first, the preamble of which statutes counts upon the petitions from those places as setting forth that being in their general civil jurisdiction exempted from the common law courts, etc., yet being subject to the general authority of Parliament, were taxed in common with the rest of the kingdom, which taxes by reason of their having no members in Parliament to represent their affairs, often proved hard and injurious, etc., and upon that ground they had the privilege of sending members granted them—and if this, say they, could be a reason in the case of Chester and Durham, how much more so in the case of America.

Thus I have given you, I think, the substance of the arguments on both sides of that great and important question of the right and also of the expediency of taxing America by authority of Parliament. I cannot, however, content myself without giving you a sketch of what the aforementioned Mr. Barré said in answer to some remarks made by Mr. Charles Townshend[4] in a speech of his upon this subject. I ought here to tell you that the debate upon the American stamp bill came on before the House for the first time last Wednesday, when the same was opened by Mr. Grenville, the Chancellor of the Exchequer, in a pretty lengthy speech, and in a very able, and I think, in a very candid manner he opened the nature of the tax, urged the necessity of it, endeavored to obviate all objections to it—and took occasion to desire the House to give the bill a most serious and cool consideration and not suffer themselves to be influenced by any resentments which might have been kindled from anything they might have heard out of doors—alluding, I suppose, to the New York and Boston Assemblies' speeches and votes—that this was a matter of revenue which was of all things the most interesting to the subject, etc. The argument was taken up by several who opposed the bill (viz.) by Alderman Beckford, who, and who only, seemed to deny the authority of Parliament, by Col. Barré, Mr. Jackson, Sir William Meredith, and some others. Mr. Barré, who by the way, I think, and I find I am not alone in my opinion, is one of the finest speakers that the House can boast of, having been some time in America as an officer in the

---

[3] Isaac Barré (1726–1802), who opposed British assertions of right over North America, particularly during the ministry of Frederick (Lord) North, which began in 1770.

[4] Townshend (1725–1767) had been secretary-at-war (1761–62) and was soon, once appointed chancellor of the exchequer in 1766, to achieve notoriety for the tax acts named after him.

army, and having while there, as I had known before, contracted many friendships with American gentlemen, and I believe entertained much more favorable opinions of them than some of his profession have done, delivered a very handsome and moving speech upon the bill and against the same, concluding by saying that he was very sure that most who should hold up their hands to the bill must be under a necessity of acting very much in the dark, but added, perhaps as well in the dark as any way.

After him Mr. Charles Townshend spoke in favor of the bill—took notice of several things Mr. Barré had said, and concluded with the following or like words: "And now will these Americans, children planted by our care, nourished up by our indulgence until they are grown to a degree of strength and opulence, and protected by our arms, will they grudge to contribute their mite to relieve us from the heavy weight of that burden which we lie under?" When he had done, Mr. Barré rose, and having explained something which he had before said and which Mr. Townshend had been remarking upon, he then took up the before mentioned concluding words of Mr. Townshend, and in a most spirited and I thought an almost inimitable manner, said:

"They planted by your care? No! Your oppressions planted 'em in America. They fled from your tyranny to a then uncultivated and unhospitable country where they exposed themselves to almost all the hardships to which human nature is liable, and among others to the cruelties of a savage foe, the most subtle, and I take upon me to say, the most formidable of any people upon the face of God's earth. And yet, actuated by principles of true English liberty, they met all these hardships with pleasure, compared with those they suffered in their own country, from the hands of those who should have been their friends.

"They nourished by *your* indulgence? They grew by your neglect of 'em. As soon as you began to care about 'em, that care was exercised in[5] sending persons to rule over 'em, in one department and another, who were perhaps the deputies of deputies to some member of this house, sent to spy out their liberty, to misrepresent their actions and to prey upon 'em; men whose behavior on many occasions has caused the blood of those sons of liberty to recoil within them; men promoted to the highest seats of justice; some who to my knowledge were glad by going to a foreign country to escape being brought to the bar of a court of justice in their own.

"They protected by *your* arms? They have nobly taken up arms in your defence, have exerted a valor amidst their constant and laborious industry for the defence of a country, whose frontier while drenched in blood, its interior parts have yielded all its little savings to your emolument. And believe me, remember I this day told you so, that same spirit of freedom which actuated that people at first, will accompany them still. But prudence forbids me to explain myself further. God knows I do not at this time speak from motives of party heat; what I deliver are the genuine sentiments of my heart; however

---

[5] Expressed by.

superior to me in general knowledge and experience the reputable body of this House may be, yet I claim to know more of America than most of you, having seen and been conversant in that country. The people I believe are as truly loyal as any subjects the king has, but a people jealous of their liberties and who will vindicate them if ever they should be violated; but the subject is too delicate and I will say no more."

These sentiments were thrown out so entirely without premeditation, so forcibly and so firmly, and the breaking off so beautifully abrupt, that the whole House sat a while as amazed, intently looking and without answering a word.

I own I felt emotions that I never felt before and went the next morning and thanked Col. Barré in behalf of my country for his noble and spirited speech.

However, sir, after all that was said, upon a division of the House upon the question there was about 250 to about 50 in favor of the bill.

The truth is, I believe some who inclined rather against the bill voted for it, partly because they are loath to break the measures of the ministry, and partly because they don't undertake to inform themselves in the fullest manner upon the subject. The bill comes on to a second reading tomorrow when ours and the Massachusetts petitions will be presented and perhaps [there] may be some further debate upon the subject, but to no purpose, I am very sure, as to the stopping or preventing the Act taking place.

The agents of the colonies have had several meetings, at one of which they were pleased to desire Mr. Franklin[6] and myself as having lately come from America and knowing more intimately the sentiments of the people, to wait on Mr. Grenville, together with Mr. [Richard] Jackson and Mr. [Charles] Garth, who, being agents are also members of Parliament, to remonstrate against the stamp bill, and to propose in case any tax must be laid upon America, that the several colonies might be permitted to lay the tax themselves. This we did Saturday before last. Mr. Grenville gave us a full hearing—told us he took no pleasure in giving the Americans so much uneasiness as he found he did—that it was the duty of his office to manage the revenue—that he really was made to believe that considering the whole of the circumstances of the mother country and the colonies, the latter could and ought to pay something, and that he knew of no better way than that now pursuing to lay such tax, but that if we could tell of a better, he would adopt it. We then urged the method

[6] Benjamin Franklin (1706–1790) had served as the London agent for Pennsylvania in the late 1750s and returned home in 1762. At the end of 1764, he had been sent over again on a mission concerned with the colony's charter, but he became absorbed in the debates over the Stamp Act that winter. Often politically astute, Franklin proved at first obtuse on the question of the Stamp Act, opposing it but advising his fellow countrymen to obey the law. He ran afoul of public opinion for this stand as well as for having himself purchased stamped paper and helped secure the appointment of a friend as a Stamp Act agent (as well as advising Ingersoll himself to apply for the agency for Connecticut); his appearance before the House of Commons on February 13, 1766, urging repeal of the act, helped him recoup his reputation, and by 1770 he was serving in London as agent not only for his home colony but also for Georgia, New Jersey, and Massachusetts, having emerged as the unofficial ambassador of the united colonies in London.

first mentioned as being a method the people had been used to—that it would at least seem to be their own act and prevent that uneasiness and jealousy which otherwise we found would take place—that they could raise the money best by their own officers, etc.

Mr. Jackson[7] told him plainly that he foresaw [by] the measure now pursuing, by enabling the crown to keep up an armed force of its own in America and to pay the governors in the king's governments, and all with the Americans' own money, the assemblies in the colonies would be subverted—that the governors would have no occasion as for any ends of their own or of the crown, to call 'em, and that they never would be called together in the king's governments. Mr. Grenville warmly rejected the thought, said no such thing was intended nor would, he believed, take place. Indeed, I understand since, there is a clause added to the bill applying the monies that shall be raised to the protecting and defending America *only*. Mr. Grenville asked us if we could agree upon the several proportions each colony should raise. We told him no. He said he did not think anybody here was furnished with materials for that purpose; not only so, but there would be no certainty that every colony would raise the sum enjoined and to be obliged to be at the expense of making stamps to compel some one or two provinces to do their duty, and that perhaps for one year only, would be very inconvenient; not only so, but the colonies by their constant increase will be constantly varying in their proportions of numbers and ability and which a stamp bill will always keep pace with, etc.

Upon the whole he said he had pledged his word for offering the stamp bill to the House, that the House would hear all our objections and would do as they thought best; he said he wished we would preserve a coolness and moderation in America; that he had no need to tell us that resentments indecently and unbecomingly expressed on one side the water would naturally produce resentments on tother side, and that we could not hope to get any good by a controversy with the mother country; that their ears will always be open to any remonstrances from the Americans with respect to this bill, both before it takes effect and after, if it shall take effect, which shall be expressed in a becoming manner, that is, as becomes subjects of the same common prince.

I acquainted you in my last that Mr. [Thomas] Whately, one of the secretaries of the treasury, and who had under his care and direction the business of preparing the stamp bill, had often conferred with me on the subject. He wanted, I know, information of the several methods of transfer, law process, etc., made use of in the colony, and I believe has been also very willing to hear all objections that could be made to the bill or any part of it. This task I was glad to undertake, as I very well knew the information I must give would oper-

[7]Ireland native Richard Jackson was a lawyer and a member of Parliament but had been allied with Franklin in the latter's capacity as representative of Pennsylvania in the 1750s and was himself very interested in American affairs. In 1759, Franklin had asked to have Jackson appointed as agent for the colony but the Pennsylvania Assembly denied his request and Franklin stayed on in London. Eventually, on Franklin's departure from England in 1762, Jackson did succeed him and during the Stamp Act deliberations remained the official general agent of the colony.

ate strongly in our favor; as the number of our law-suits, deeds, tavern licences, and in short, almost all the objects of the intended taxation and duties are so very numerous in the colony that the knowledge of them would tend to the imposing a duty so much the lower as the objects were more in number. This effect, I flatter myself, it has had in some measure. Mr. Whately, to be sure, tells me I may fairly claim the honor of having occasioned the duty's being much lower than was intended, and three particular things that were intended to be taxed I gave him no peace till he dropped; these were licences for marriage—a duty that would be odious in a new country where every encouragement ought to be given to matrimony, and where there was little portion; commissions of the justices of peace, which office was, generally speaking, not profitable and yet necessary for the good order and government of the people; and notes of hand which with us were given and taken so very often for very small sums.

After all, I believe the people in America will think the sums that will be raised will be quite enough, and I wish they mayn't find it more distressing than the people in power here are aware of.

The merchants in London are alarmed at these things; they have had a meeting with the agents and are about to petition Parliament upon the Acts that respect the trade of North America.

What the event of these things will be I don't know, but am pretty certain that wisdom will be proper and even very necessary, as well as prudence and good discretion to direct the councils of America.

9

THE LANGUAGE OF SLAVERY

A SHARP-TONGUED AND STILL RELATIVELY UNKNOWN SATIRIST OF THE LATE colonial era, Charles Woodmason (ca. 1720–1776?) left a bulk of manuscript writings from which little was published until the 1950s. Born in England, Woodmason emigrated to South Carolina in 1752, apparently to locate a promising situation for his family. As it happened, his estranged wife, who seems to have died around 1762, never followed him to America with their young son, perhaps because (as Woodmason confided in a letter to a friend) an injury caused by a kick from a horse to his groin had given him an "incapacity for nuptial rites." Despite this abandonment by his family, Woodmason remained in Carolina and did very well there. He accumulated lands and bought slaves to work them until by 1760 he had acquired more than two thousand acres on the north coast of the colony. In addition to running his plantations there, he engaged in trade, and by 1757 had established a frontier store just inland from his home. In the same period, he held many public positions in the church and the government, from which he gained more knowledge of the colony and its peoples. A man of many interests and powerful likes and dislikes, he lived well and enjoyed the benefits of his success.

By the early 1760s, Woodmason's scene of action had shifted to Charleston, the elegant and privileged center of the colony's trade and social and political life. Here, too, he continued his active role in public affairs. He was widely known and liked in Charleston until 1765 when, like Jared Ingersoll in Connecticut, Woodmason made the strategic mistake of securing one appointment too many—that of stamp distributor under the new and much-hated act of Parliament. Perhaps because of this quick turnaround in his reputation, or because of a spiritual unease not satisfied by his worldly prosperity, Woodmason veered sharply into a new career: he departed for London by year's end to be ordained as an Anglican priest. His plan was to return to South Carolina as a missionary to the poor settlers of the backcountry region, with whom he had become acquainted through his years as a storekeeper and merchant. Woodmason thought his new charges would be eager for the virtues of genteel urban culture, but he clearly underestimated what lay ahead, and it took him many months before he began to understand that they had their own culture—rural, economically and politically marginalized, more sympathetic to the dissenting sects than to his own Anglican creed—and that they wanted from him only what they knew would benefit them. Although he remained strongly committed to his own values, by the end of 1760s Woodmason had undergone a second, even more remarkable transformation. Finding the backsettlers oppressed by the coastal elite (of which he himself had been a member for a considerable period) he began to sympathize with them and soon emerged as their energetic and verbally talented spokesperson. As the "Regulators" sought to impose some local order on their region, beset by gangs of thieves as well as the powers that be in Charleston, Woodmason became supportive of their efforts and understanding of their views, to which he proceeded to give powerful and witty expression.

The Regulators arose at a time when Charleston's elite was carrying on its own protest against Britain. Woodmason, whose loyalty to the Crown was to strengthen as the Revolution neared, saw the Charlestonians as hypocritical, mouthing liberal pieties in their dispute with Britain but giving the common backsettlers precisely the sort of high-handed treatment they found so offensive when aimed at themselves from Britain: "Lo! such are the men who bounce, and make such noise about Liberty! Liberty! Freedom! Property! Rights! Privileges! and what not," he wrote at one particularly pungent moment, "and at the same time keep half their fellow subjects in a state of slavery."

Whig political theory, from which Woodmason drew his own argument, and which was widely adopted by colonial apologists from British sources, cast the ordinary Englishman as endowed with certain rights that were constantly under threat from forces conspiring to abridge or deny them. Its archetypal cry of "Slavery!" reflected the view of the Whigs that liberty always existed at risk in a world of "interests," and this cry echoed again and again through the halls of colonial debate and across the pages of colonial pamphleteering in the period. Hence Thomas Jefferson, in his *Summary View of the Rights of British America* (1774), spoke of Britain's "deliberate, systematical plan of reducing us to slavery." Following out this adoption of British liberal rhetoric, some Revolutionaries saw the war as aimed at defending not just American rights but the rights of all "free-born" Englishmen as well.

Only rarely did those who employed this rhetoric in an American context note the irony of doing so in a land where slavery was not just a figure of speech or a political slogan, but an actual civil condition for most African Americans and some Native Americans. Woodmason, who used the Whig rhetoric against the Charleston elite much as he saw the elite use it against Britain, showed absolutely no awareness of the irony, as when in his mock advertisement Woodmason asked, "Is it not slavery . . . that [a debtor's] slaves shall be taken and carried down [to Charleston], and sold for not one tenth of their value? . . ." To be sure, backcountry inhabitants, who owned relatively fewer slaves than the rich and powerful planters of the coastal region or the merchants of Charleston, had suffered at the hands of their "betters," but that alone did not make them slaves in the same sense as those who were legally unfree. In South Carolina, a state with the highest proportion of actual slaves, one sees how the layers of exploitation and dominance implicated in the political realities of America on the eve of the Revolution were multiple and complexly interconnected. Freedom may have been an absolute political good but it also was a relative civil condition in which not all people either shared at the moment or were thought capable of participating in the future.

As a supporter of the Crown during the early phases of the Revolution, Woodmason himself was to learn how powerful the forces of inequality might be. He moved from South Carolina to Maryland in 1773, and in his new home he continued to be controversial: when a local fund-raising effort was begun on behalf of the colonists of Massachusetts, sorely beset by a British ban on trade and an occupying British army, Woodmason staunchly refused to support it, and soon paid a price for his stance. So unpopular did he become that in 1774 he felt forced to leave America for his own safety. After preaching for a time in the vicinity of Bristol on the southwestern coast of England, in 1776 a sick and poor Woodmason, no longer a great landowner in America, requested aid as a Loyalist refugee. Apparently he died soon after.

CHARLES WOODMASON

A mock slave auction advertisement (ca. 1769)

THE WITHIN ADVERTISEMENT IS DRAWN UP IN MANNER OF THOSE COMMONLY antecedent to a sale of Negroes. It not being suffered to appear in the papers, 'twas posted up at the exchange[1] and gave great offence to the senators. It had the intended effect to gall, and spur them, and as satire oftimes effects what reason cannot, so this very pasquil[2] obtained what the Bible could not—it made many who before were indifferent to things for to interest themselves in behalf of the people. And although a bill for courts was passed and went home for the royal assent yet the lawyers prevented that being obtained for more than twelve months, till the salaries for the a[ttorne]y g[enera]l and others were settled to their satisfaction.

The governor being newly arrived, could have no perfect knowledge of these matters. To come at truth, he took a tour upwards among the people, but moved with such celerity, that none knew of his being in the country, till he was long returned back to town.[3]

---

[1] A prominent civic structure (built 1767–71) along Charleston Bay, site of many important events during the Revolution.

[2] Or pasquinade (from Italian *pasquinata*), a lampoon posted in a public place.

[3] Governor Lord Greville Montagu arrived in South Carolina in the spring of 1766, but left in 1768 and returned in the spring of 1769, when he toured the "back" or "upper" districts as Woodmason notes.

In the land of Israel, when only one woman (and her a concubine) was ravished, a whole tribe was cut off, because they would not execute justice on the ravishers. But here, vile and impudent fellows, would come to a planter's house, and tie him, lie with his wife before his face, ravish virgins, before [the] eyes of their parents, a dozen fellows in succession. Wherever they heard of a groaning, they would beset the house and lie with all the women. At one house, they tied the midwife to the bedpost, and left the poor woman helpless, who, providentially, was happily delivered, the fright effecting it.[4] They carried off above twenty of the finest girls of the country into the woods with them and kept them for many months, as their concubines in common among them till they grew past shame and never could be brought back to a life of virtue when regained by their friends. They would put irons in the fire and burn the flesh of persons to make [them] confess where they concealed their money.

All the merchants' stores were broken up, no peddlers with goods could travel, no woman venture abroad, and numbers abandoned their habitations. Sixteen or eighteen persons (at times)[5] lost their lives, in battle with these villains: and many Negroes (as well as horses) were carried off. They penetrated, at length to the lower[6] settlements and stole many Negroes, even from one of the council. And had they not so done, it was a doubt, whether they would not have reigned much longer. But when their own house was on fire, they then thought on their neighbors. Yet the goodnatured country people pursued these fellows over the mountains, and brought back their Negroes to the great people, hoping that this instance of regard would operate in their favor, but it signified very little.

The villains had their confederates in every colony—what Negroes, horses and goods was stolen southwardly, was carried northerly, and the northward, southward: the southward shipped off at New York and Rhode Island for the French and Dutch islands, the northward carried to Georgia and Florida, where smuggling sloops would barter with the rogues, and buy great bargains.

Our senators treated all representations of these things as idle tales. Nay, there were those who would assert there were not a thousand people in the backcountry. Every complaint was adjudged chimerical. Instead of attending to the internal concerns of their country, and welfare, security, and prosperity, and trade of the inhabitants, they spent seven years in wrangling and disputing about politics and privileges, and the concerns of Great Britain—and other foreign matters.

---

[4]That is, the pregnant woman attended by the midwife was so frightened that she delivered the baby unattended. Woodmason here is rehashing newspaper stories and rumors based at least in part on stereotypes of the backcountry inhabitants as subhuman.

[5]I.e., altogether, at different times.

[6]I.e., those near the coast and Charleston.

No. 3.

Advertisement

To Be disposed of
On the Congaree, Saludy, Savannah, Wateree, and Broad Rivers
A Cargo of
Fifty Thousand Prime Slaves
(Remarkably healthy, and free from the Small Pox)
Lately imported from Great Britain, Ireland, and the Northern
Colonies
In the Good Ship
CAROLINA
George Rex,[7] Master,
In a short Passage of Ten Years—The Sale will begin on Mon-
day the 17th day of April next—Credit will be Given till—Pub-
lic Good be prefered to Private Interest—

N.B. The above slaves are sold for no fault, but they being stripped of their property by thieves and vagabonds, plundered of their effects *according to law,* by mercenary demagogues, and given up as a prey to vagrants and outlaws, for to have their throats cut, their estates rifled, their families ruined, wives insulted, daughters deflowered, and their properties sacrificed and dispersed; and not having any courts of justice where to lodge complaints or proper magistrates to whom to seek for redress of injuries or rulers to notice their grievances, nor any places for public worship wherein to implore the divine protection against, and deliverance from these and other evils, renders it absolutely necessary for the above sale taking place—

Public Spirit—Love of Country—Religion—Humanity—Charity Patriotism, and such *Old-Coin,*[8] will be taken in Payment

It's greatly to be hoped, that the gentlemen of the long robe,[9] will attend, and buy away at the said sale.

Letter to John Rutledge (1769?)

**This Copy of a letter sent to J. R. Esq.
by the Regulators.**

Sir
You say, that it is very impertinent and invidious for the back inhabitants to call themselves *slaves*, when no people on earth are in so great a state of freedom, and that they turn their liberty into licentiousness. And you ask with

---

[7]I.e., George the king.
[8]Usually a reference to outmoded specie; here, the implication is clear that such virtues are no longer "in circulation."
[9]Here, lawyers (at times, ministers as well).

what consistency or propriety they presume to use the word slavery, in the advertisement posted up at the exchange.

You also say that our legislature and executive powers have done for us all services which we merit, or require, even beyond our deserts, and shewn us every possible mark of kindness and goodness, but that we take too much upon us.

Whatever you in town may fix as the criterion of things we, who *know* and *feel* where the shoe pinches, can best determine. We think ourselves in a state of servitude and those who are so, what other can they be denominated than slaves?

You say, that a *great deal* hath been *done* for us, and much more than *we merit*. If so, then much remains *undone* (as I shall note presently) to bring us on the same level (which you want not), the same foot with yourselves.

Pray, are we not all subjects of the same king? Fellow Protestants? Fellow Christians? Fellow Britons? Of the same blood and origin? Are any of your descents, greater, nobler, ancienter, more reputable than ours? Many of you (though you abound in riches) [are] far ignobler; have you more virtue, more religion, more goodness than us? Many, [have] far less; Indeed, you may be said to have more learning, politeness, wealth, slaves, and lands but we speak of intrinsic worth. All we wish is, that you had better hearts than we can boast. But what hinders[1] that we be not your equals in every respect? Nothing but your pride, vanity, selfishness, and meanspiritedness. Had you any seeds of honor, love of your country, or value for mankind, you would strive, use your utmost endeavors, exert your whole strength, strain every nerve, to render all others around you, equally easy, happy, independent, affluent, and genteel as yourselves.

You call us a pack of beggars. Pray, sir, look back to your own origin. Draw the curtain up but for one twenty years[2] only, and view persons as then, and now. It is a strange succession of fortuitous causes that has lifted up many of your heads, not your own wisdom or virtue: quite the reverse. But step back only to the beginning of this century—What then was Carolina? What Charleston? What the then settlers (your ancestors), even such as we now are.

Will you pronounce that in fifty years, our posterity may not ride in their chariots, while yours walk on foot? Or do you fear it? It seems so by your conduct towards us. Who would have dreamed fifty years past that the Prussians should be now more than a match for the House of Austria?[3]

But we will put ourselves, sir, into your hands; and as your genius and capacity is allowed to be as great as your avarice be pleased (for once without a fee) to consider the following queries—and then say, if the term *slavery*, be unapplicable to us.

(1) Is it not *slavery*, for to travel 200, or 300 miles, to sue for a debt of 21

---

[1] I.e., what is to blame for the fact.

[2] Apparently, for one twenty-year period.

[3] Woodmason refers here to the surprising rise of Prussia as a force to be reckoned with on the continent. In the Silesian War, ended by treaty in 1763, it had fought so well against a vastly superior alliance headed by Austria that the latter was ultimately forced to begin negotiations for peace. Britain was allied with Prussia; France, with Austria.

pounds (3 pounds sterling), and for to spend, six, nay ten times that sum, [in] law charges, in recovery of it? Exclusive of time, labor, application, and traveling expenses?

(2) Is [it] not *slavery*, for an officer to come with a writ (like a letter de cachet) and force us *in a moment*, from our dwelling, not give us a minute to settle our affairs, send for our friends, compound the debt,[4] or look about us, but must be hurried in an instant 200 miles down to Charleston, there thrown into a stinking gaol, and lie many months, while at same time, we know not the party who arrests us, or never had any accounts or dealings with him, or heard of him, or if [there are] any connections, possibly he may be ours, not we his debtor, and all this we must suffer except[5] we can raise bail for 10 days. Then that bail[6] must surrender us in town, where we must instantly go to gaol, if we cannot raise special bail, which not one in a hundred can do in town, where they are unknown and possibly not one in a hundred in the country will be accepted should they ride 200 miles down to town with us. To gaol we must go, and possibly after all this, the party may discontinue [the suit], never try the cause, while we lie rotting in a filthy dungeon, and after all this suffering, and being put to vast expense, we can have no reparation, no redress for such usage. The greatest stranger in the country who never saw us, may treat any one in this manner; in England there is twenty-four hours granted to the party before he can be moved to prison, but here, not a minute? Is not this as great slavery as if we lived in France?[7]

(3) Is it not slavery, that when a writ goes against me, I should oft times not know aught of the matter, and execution[8] be awarded, that my lands shall be seized and sold in Charleston unknown to me, and for nothing though of great value, that my slaves shall be taken and carried down there, and sold for not one tenth of their value; everything I have, took possession of by the provost marshall and thus for satisfying a debt of 100 pounds—I shall have effects sold worth 1,000 or 2,000 pounds: many instances of which can be given.

(4) Is it not slavery to be supoenaed to court as a witness, and travel two or three hundred miles, stay for days together in Charleston at great expense, and never [be] called on? The like[9] when summoned as a juror, and in many other instances!

(5) Is it not slavery for to be imprisoned, fettered, arraigned, put on trial on allegation or information of some villain, or by malice of some mean justice of [the] peace, and no prosecutor appear against me, no prosecutor to be found to sue for false imprisonment or to get any redress for loss of liberty, credit, fame, and fortune? Yet this often happens to many.

(6) It is not slavery to travel two or three hundred miles to procure a

---

[4] I.e., try to refinance.
[5] Unless.
[6] I.e., the individual "going bail" for the supposed debtor.
[7] Woodmason here draws on the customary English claim that the French monarchy was absolute, and French subjects thus lacked the traditional rights of Englishmen.
[8] Order to make payment as decreed by the court.
[9] I.e., the same thing happening.

licence to be married or have banns published, or my child christened or to hear a sermon, or receive the holy communion? And as for churching of women, visiting the sick, burial of the dead, and other spiritual offices we are entirely destitute, there being neither church [n]or minister among us.

(7) Is it not slavery to travel fifty, or sixty miles to find a magistrate, for to make a single affidavit, or sue for a small debt or for to be sued before magistrates, who never saw, or know anything of the provincial, or common laws?

(8) Is it not slavery to ride such lengths to appear as evidence in some trifling nonsensical suit, between two fools, about matters not worth six pence while it shall cost me ten pounds' expense beside loss of time?

(9) Is it not slavery to ride two hundred miles to give my vote for election of vestrymen, church wardens, members of assembly, etc., or to get any parochial business transacted?

(10) Is it not slavery to be burthened with vagrants, poor travelers, sick, infirm, aged, diseased, lame persons, orphans and others who by choice or accident push or force themselves on me and whom it is impossible to remove without breach of the laws of charity, humanity, and Christianity, there being no workhouse, hospital, bridewell,[1] or provision made, or the least relief established in these parts for objects of charity, paupers, orphans etc.

(11) Is it not slavery to leave my estate and children behind me in hands of executors and trustees, who shall spend my estate during the minority of my children, give them no education, and when of age, perhaps bring them in debt, for want of an orphan law?

(12) Is it not slavery for to be at the time and cost of two or three hundred miles to assist the civil officer, in conveying of criminals to gaol?

(13) Is it not slavery for to be carried a prisoner two hundred miles to C. T. [Charleston] there to lie in a filthy prison for six months at great risk, and often to loss of health and life, and this only for a simple assault, in drink, or heat of passion, not worth cognizance,[2] or because I cannot find surety for my better behavior?

(14) Is it not slavery to serve the office of constable, to be continually hurried about from one end of the province to the other, to ride one hundred miles to serve a foolish warrant without any allowance made, and to attend the courts of justice in C. T. for several days at great expense?

(15) Is it not slavery to serve the office of church warden, and ride circuits of three or four hundred miles to collect the poor tax, without any allowance for so doing? And the same when appointed collector of the public tax?

(16) Is it not slavery to be detained from business two or three months through want of roads, bridges, and ferries, or where they are laid out, for to ride one hundred miles about, to perform a journey of ten miles, many ferries being in private hands, and no attendance,[3] and several of them fifty miles asunder?

[1] Prison.
[2] Judicial hearing.
[3] I.e., without attendants.

(17) Is it not slavery to live in continual dread of villains robbing of my house, stealing my horses and cattle, ravishing my wife and daughters (so that I dare not stir from home lest they should be exposed nor they travel abroad without a guard), just as if I was in a country which was the seat of war?

(18) Is it not slavery to be exposed to the insults of any villain, or vagrant, every idle rascal who will come to my house, and there stay and make free at his pleasure, nor I able to dislodge him through fear that if I affront him, I shall have horses or cattle killed or houses burned and therefore must bear such fellows' company, insolence, and impudence, perhaps abuse, and no redress for these evils?

(19) Is it not slavery, to have the articles which I consume, taxed for the benefit of private persons, and not the public? Or to carry on works of splendor and magnificence, in which [neither] I nor my fellow public have the least concern?

(20) Is it not slavery to have the value of my flour, and other produce depressed, and foreign articles preferred to our own (equally good in quality if not better) and this to serve the interests of a few only?

(21) Is [it] not slavery to see my wife or daughters insulted, abused, exposed to the ribaldry, obscenity, audaciousness, and licentiousness of drunken, idle, worthless, scandalous, abandoned, atrocious profligates, libertines and lawless persons, who are without habitation or property, and can obtain no redress, no remedy for so great an evil, wherefrom no woman whatever durst attend musters, races, vendues[4] or any public meetings—and are not secure even going to a sermon?

(22) Is it not slavery that I cannot be master of my own house but that if I have a wedding or christianing or birthday dinner or any set entertainment for private friends, that a set of insolent wretches shall intrude on my premises, mix with, and affront my company, quarrel, riot, consume my provisions and take what liberties they please, with impunity?

(23) Is it not slavery to be under control of insolent tavern keepers where you are necessitated to quarter at, in your travels, and to be exposed to whatever charge or treatment they please for to impose?

(24) Is it not slavery to be subject to the impudence, impertinence, and insults of free Negroes and Mulattoes, who greatly abound here? and who have taken refuge in these parts, from the northern colonies, perhaps for crimes committed there?

(25) Is it not slavery to be obliged to travel two hundred miles to C.T. there to give two or three guineas to a lawyer, for to know the contents of such or such a law, when the laws say, that every act of assembly shall be printed, and sent to every parish church? Are not our laws locked up from us, as the gospel is in popish countries?

(26) Is it not slavery to be without wise magistrates, without religion, without laws, without police, without churches, without clergy, without gospel,

---

[4] Auctions.

without sacraments, without any to marry people, so that they marry each other when and how they please and separate and come together as they please, wherefrom the country is full of whores and bastards? And is it not slavery for to have no roads, ferries, or bridges, and for poor people, who quitted their native land where they lived easily and decently, for to come here to be beggars, to be employed in cutting down the woods and clearing lands to raise crops, and afterwards for to be obliged to cut roads, to carry their produce to market? If any peasants in Russia, Poland or Germany are in a worse state of servitude than this, then, sir, we will join you in that pious wish you made in the house that the backcountry was at bottom of the sea.

10

A MASSACRE IN BOSTON

BY 1768, THE BRITISH GOVERNMENT HAD STATIONED A LARGE ARMY TO ASSERT its authority over the city of Boston, a town that led American resistance to recent British-imposed regulations. Although within a year the British commander, General Thomas Gage, had withdrawn all but about six hundred of these soldiers from Boston, even this reduced presence in the city was a continuous affront to the proud and defiant population. Ceaselessly, the inhabitants taunted the soldiers and pelted them with the age-old weapons of the people—sticks, stones, and, in the chill northern winter, even snowballs—until the British regulars seemed to be always on edge. Things came to a head in early March 1770. On March 2nd, a large affray took place between workmen at the ropewalks near John Hancock's wharf in Boston's North End and some British soldiers. It began when Samuel Gray asked a passing soldier named Patrick Walker—who, like most of his comrades, was chronically short of money—whether he wanted to hire himself out. When Walker said he did and asked what the job was, Gray replied that he could clean out the latrine. A fight between the two quickly escalated as more soldiers and workmen joined it, and ultimately it was the soldiers, though many times reinforced, who retreated. A local inhabitant kept the workmen from pursuing them, but it seemed clear that the bad blood would remain as a cause of further confrontations.

The confrontations came quickly. On the night of March 5th, the weather fair but cold and the ground still covered with snow, groups of townspeople trudged about the streets armed with barrel staves and clubs. Small detachments of soldiers also were scuttling about the town, as if they, too, expected something. Clashes occurred at various places through the night, but it is not clear what exactly happened where and when. Before long the trouble thickened around an area that symbolized the points at issue between the colonists and the home government: at the head of King Street (later to be renamed State Street) stood not only the Town House, seat of the local government, but also the Custom House and the headquarters of the British forces. In the opposite direction, King Street led down to the Long Wharf, which reached far out into the very center of Boston's harbor, where so much of the commerce of North America was focused. It was near a sentry box next to the Custom House that a wigmaker's apprentice named Edward Garrick began teasing the sentry, Private Hugh White, about the unsettled debts of one of White's officers to Garrick's master. The money owed, if any, was not the issue: the issue instead was the officer's character as a gentleman—he was not one, Garrick asserted—and soon Garrick was proclaiming that none of the regiment's other officers were gentlemen, either. Private White had had enough, struck the apprentice with his gunbutt, and before long, as the scuffle continued, other townspeople were running to join the fray. Soon the city's church bells began pealing and cries of "Fire!" echoed through the chill air. As a crowd of boys circled White, they called him the worst names they could—"Bloody back," "Damned rascally scoundrel lobster son of a bitch," and so forth—and the milling crowd thickened around White, now thoroughly frightened. Some of the townspeople tried to stanch the flow of anger, including Henry Knox, the rotund Boston bookseller who was to be a general and a strategist of note in the Revolution. Before long, the officer of the day, an Irish captain named Thomas Preston, was aroused. Warned that the ringing of the church bells signaled the intention of the townspeople to storm the garrison (in fact, the Sons of Liberty who were abroad in the streets that night tried to defuse tensions), and that the sentry who had beaten Garrick was to be kidnapped and perhaps murdered, Preston also worried that the Crown's funds, kept in the Custom House, might be in jeopardy. He detached a small party of troops—six soldiers and a non-commissioned officer—to protect Private White, and soon followed himself to assure that the troubles did not worsen.

Of course, the troubles did worsen. Accounts of exactly what transpired differ markedly depending on the point of view. Those sympathetic to the townspeople repeatedly testified that the soldiers fired on Preston's orders (which he denied), and that some of the shots poured down on the crowd from the second-story windows of the Custom House, to Preston's rear, as if snipers had been stationed there on purpose beforehand. In these claims, as in much of their rhetoric, they may have been projecting onto events their Whig view of history: here was a signal example of the feared tendency of those in power to combine in an effort to extend their sway over freeborn Englishmen. The dead and wounded in the confrontation were not, however, figments of anyone's imagination, and the Boston press quickly listed them. The dead included Samuel Gray, owner of the ropewalk at which the confrontation of March 2nd had occurred; Crispus Attucks, born at Framingham, Massachusetts, around 1723, of mixed African American and Native American descent, standing six-foot-two, a slave and by some accounts a leader in the attack on Preston's men; James Caldwell, a sailor and mate on a Boston vessel; Samuel Maverick, an apprentice ivory-turner, just seventeen, who died the next day; and Patrick Carr, a thirty-year-old leather worker in nearby Queen Street, who died some nine days later. Six others were wounded by the gunfire but recovered.

Lieutenant Governor Thomas Hutchinson acted to keep the violence from spreading, promising a full inquiry and beginning the work of it the very night of the bloodshed by addressing the citizens from the Town House balcony overlooking the site of the massacre and by collecting testimony and evidence on the spot. The Boston town meeting went into a marathon session the next day, demanding that the troops be removed from Boston (they were all gone by March 16th, stationed at Castle William, on a harbor island). Quickly the word of those who had witnessed or taken part in the confrontation began to be written down, printed, and disseminated. Among the most interesting of the accounts is that which the town meeting ordered to be drawn up by three men: merchant and politician James Bowdoin, physician Joseph Warren (who was killed at Bunker Hill five years later), and Judge Samuel Pemberton. Filled with the depositions of ordinary men and women in the streets on the night of March 5th, it offers an intriguing collective portrait of the citizenry at this crucial moment in American life. It was finished by the three men in record time; presented to the town meeting on March 19th and soon printed, it was kept out of circulation until summer out of concern about its effect on potential jurors in the pending trials for Preston and his men. It is printed here in part, along with most of a newspaper story printed the week after the events and the whole of Preston's own narrative.

THE BOSTON GAZETTE AND COUNTRY JOURNAL

News report of the massacre, with list of dead and wounded (March 12, 1770)

OUR READERS WILL DOUBTLESS EXPECT A CIRCUMSTANTIAL ACCOUNT OF THE tragical affair on Monday night last; but we hope they will excuse our being so particular as we should have been, had we not seen that the town was intending an enquiry and full representation thereof.

On the evening of Monday, being the fifth current, several soldiers of the 29th Regiment were seen parading the streets with their drawn cutlasses and bayonets, abusing and wounding numbers of the inhabitants.

A few minutes after nine o'clock four youths, named Edward Archbald, William Merchant, Francis Archbald, and John Leech, Jr., came down Cornhill together, and separating at Doctor Loring's corner, the two former were passing the narrow alley leading to Murray's barrack in which was a soldier brandishing a broad sword of an uncommon size against the walls, out of which he struck fire plentifully. A person of mean countenance armed with a large cudgel bore him company. Edward Archbald admonished Mr. Merchant to take care of the sword, on which the soldier turned round and struck Archbald on the arm, then pushed at Merchant and pierced through his clothes inside the arm close to the armpit and grazed the skin. Merchant then struck the soldier with a short stick he had; and the other person ran to the barrack and brought with him two soldiers, one armed with a pair of tongs, the other with a shovel. He with the tongs pursued Archbald back through the alley, collared and laid him over the head with the tongs. The noise brought people together; and John Hicks, a young lad, coming up, knocked the soldier down but let him get up again; and more lads gathering, drove them back to the barrack where the boys stood some time as it were to keep them in. In less than a minute ten or twelve of them came out with drawn cutlasses, clubs, and bayonets and set upon the unarmed boys and young folk who stood them a little while but, finding the inequality of their equipment, dispersed. On hearing the noise, one Samuel Atwood came up to see what was the matter; and entering the alley from Dock Square, heard the latter part of the combat; and when the boys had dispersed he met the ten or twelve soldiers aforesaid rushing down the alley towards the square and asked them if they intended to murder people? They answered "Yes, by G-d, root and branch!" With that one of them struck Mr. Atwood with a club which was repeated by another; and being unarmed, he turned to go off and received a wound on the left shoulder which reached the bone and gave him much pain. Retreating a few steps, Mr. Atwood met two officers and said, "Gentlemen, what is the matter?" They answered, "You'll see by and by." Immediately after, those heroes appeared in the square, asking where were the boogers?[1] where were the cowards? But notwithstanding their fierceness to naked men, one of them advanced towards a youth who had a split of a raw stave in his hand and said, "Damn them, here is one of them." But the young man seeing a person near him with a drawn sword and good cane ready to support him, held up his stave in defiance; and they quietly passed by him up the little alley by Mr. Silsby's to King Street where they attacked single and unarmed persons till they raised much clamor, and then turned down Cornhill Street, insulting all they met in like manner and pursuing some to their very doors. Thirty or forty persons, mostly lads, being by this means gathered in King Street, Capt. Preston with a party of men with charged bayonets, came from the main guard to the commissioner's house, the soldiers pushing their bayonets, crying, "Make way!" They took place by the Custom House and, continuing to push to drive the people off, pricked some in several places, on which they were clamorous and, it is said, threw snowballs. On this, the captain commanded them to fire; and more snowballs coming, he again said, "Damn you, fire, be the consequence what it will!" One soldier then fired, and a townsman with a cudgel struck him over the hands with such force that he dropped his firelock; and, rushing forward, aimed a blow at the captain's head which grazed his hat and fell pretty heavy upon his arm. However, the soldiers continued the fire successively till seven or eight or, as some say, eleven guns were discharged.

By this fatal maneuver three men were laid dead on the spot and two more

[1] Bastards.

struggling for life; but what showed a degree of cruelty unknown to British troops, at least since the house of Hanover has directed their operations, was an attempt to fire upon or push with their bayonets the persons who undertook to remove the slain and wounded!

Mr. Benjamin Leigh, now undertaker in the Delph manufactory, came up; and after some conversation with Capt. Preston relative to his conduct in this affair, advised him to draw off his men, with which he complied.

The dead are Mr. Samuel Gray, killed on the spot, the ball entering his head and beating off a large portion of his skull.

A mulatto man named Crispus Attucks, who was born in Framingham, but lately belonged to New Providence and was here in order to go for North Carolina, also killed instantly, two balls entering his breast, one of them in special goring the right lobe of the lungs and a great part of the liver most horribly.

Mr. James Caldwell, mate of Capt. Morton's vessel, in like manner killed by two balls entering his back.

Mr. Samuel Maverick, a promising youth of seventeen years of age, son of the widow Maverick, and an apprentice to Mr. Greenwood, ivory-turner, mortally wounded; a ball went through his belly and was cut out at his back. He died the next morning.

A lad named Christopher Monk, about seventeen years of age, an apprentice to Mr. Walker, shipwright, wounded; a ball entered his back about four inches above the left kidney near the spine and was cut out of the breast on the same side. Apprehended[2] he will die.

A lad named John Clark, about seventeen years of age, whose parents live at Medford, and an apprentice to Capt. Samuel Howard of this town, wounded; a ball entered just above his groin and came out at his hip on the opposite side. Apprehended he will die.

Mr. Edward Payne of this town, merchant, standing at his entry door received a ball in his arm which shattered some of the bones.

Mr. John Green, tailor, coming up Leverett's Lane, received a ball just under his hip and lodged in the under part of his thigh, which was extracted.

Mr. Robert Patterson, a seafaring man, who was the person that had his trousers shot through in Richardson's affair, wounded; a ball went through his right arm, and he suffered a great loss of blood.

Mr. Patrick Carr, about thirty years of age, who worked with Mr. Field, leather breeches–maker in Queen Street, wounded; a ball entered near his hip and went out at his side.

A lad named David Parker, an apprentice to Mr. Eddy, the wheelwright, wounded; a ball entered in his thigh.

---

[2] I.e., it is feared that.

CAPTAIN THOMAS PRESTON

Account of the Boston Massacre (March 13, 1770)

IT IS [A] MATTER OF TOO GREAT NOTORIETY TO NEED ANY PROOFS THAT THE arrival of his Majesty's troops in Boston was extremely obnoxious to its inhabitants. They have ever used all means in their power to weaken the regiments, and to bring them into contempt by promoting and aiding desertions, and with impunity, even where there has been the clearest evidence of the fact, and by grossly and falsely propagating untruths concerning them. On the arrival of the 64th and 65th their ardor seemingly began to abate; it being too expensive to buy off so many, and attempts of that kind rendered too dangerous from the numbers. But the same spirit revived immediately on its being known that those regiments were ordered for Halifax, and has ever since their departure been breaking out with greater violence after their embarkation. One of their justices, most thoroughly acquainted with the people and their intentions, on the trial of a man of the 14th Regiment, openly and publicly in the hearing of great numbers of people and from the seat of justice, declared "that the soldiers must now take care of themselves, *nor trust too much to their arms,* for they were but a handful; that the inhabitants carried weapons concealed under their clothes, and would destroy them in a moment, *if they pleased.*" This, considering the malicious temper of the people, was an alarming circumstance to the soldiery. Since which several disputes have happened between the townspeople and the soldiers of both regiments, the former being encouraged thereto by the countenance of even some of the magistrates, and by the protection of all the party against government. In general such disputes have been kept too secret from the officers. On the 2d instant two of the 29th going through one Gray's rope-walk, the rope-makers insultingly asked them if they would empty a vault.[3] This unfortunately had the desired effect by provoking the soldiers, and from words they went to blows. Both parties suffered in this affray, and finally the soldiers retired to their quarters. The officers, on the first knowledge of this transaction, took every precaution in their power to prevent any ill consequence. Notwithstanding which, single quarrels could not be prevented, the inhabitants constantly provoking and abusing the soldiery. The insolence as well as utter hatred of the inhabitants to the troops increased daily, insomuch that Monday and Tuesday, the 5th and 6th instant, were privately agreed on for a general engagement, in consequence of which several of the militia came

[3]On the date in question, as Page Smith tells the story in *A New Age Now Begins,* "a Boston ropemaker named William Green, busy with his fellows braiding fibers on an outdoor 'ropewalk' or ropemaking machine, called to Patrick Walker, a solder of the Twenty-ninth who was passing by, and asked if he wanted work. 'Yes,' Walker replied. 'Then go and clean my shithouse,' was Green's response." When Walker returned with forty fellow soldiers, a brawl ensued in which the soldiers, in the face of an increasing number of citizens, were bested and fled.

from the country armed to join their friends, menacing to destroy any who should oppose them. This plan has since been discovered.

On Monday night about eight o'clock two soldiers were attacked and beaten. But the party of the townspeople in order to carry matters to the utmost length, broke into two meeting houses and rang the alarm bells, which I supposed was for fire as usual, but was soon undeceived. About nine o'clock some of the guard came to and informed me the town inhabitants were assembling to attack the troops, and that the bells were ringing as the signal for that purpose and not for fire, and the beacon intended to be fired to bring in the distant people of the country. This, as I was captain of the day, occasioned my repairing immediately to the main guard. In my way there I saw the people in great commotion, and heard them use the most cruel and horrid threats against the troops. In a few minutes after I reached the guard, about one hundred people passed it and went towards the Custom House, where the king's money is lodged. They immediately surrounded the sentry posted there, and with clubs and other weapons threatened to execute their vengeance on him. I was soon informed by a townsman their intention was to carry off the soldier from his post and probably murder him. On which I desired him to return for further intelligence, and he soon came back and assured me he heard the mob declare they would murder him. This I feared might be a prelude to their plundering the king's chest. I immediately sent a non-commissioned officer and twelve men to protect both the sentry and the king's money, and very soon followed myself to prevent, if possible, all disorder, fearing lest the officer and soldiers, by the insults and provocations of the rioters, should be thrown off their guard and commit some rash act. They soon rushed through the people, and by charging their bayonets in half-circles, kept them at a little distance. Nay, so far was I from intending the death of any person that I suffered the troops to go to the spot where the unhappy affair took place without any loading in their pieces; nor did I ever give orders for loading them. This remiss conduct in me perhaps merits censure; yet it is evidence, resulting from the nature of things, which is the best and surest that can be offered, that my intention was not to act offensively, but the contrary part, and that not without compulsion. The mob still increased and were more outrageous, striking their clubs or bludgeons one against another, and calling out, "Come on you rascals, you bloody backs, you lobster scoundrels, fire if you dare, G-d damn you, fire and be damned, we know you dare not," and much more such language was used. At this time I was between the soldiers and the mob, parleying with, and endeavoring all in my power to persuade them to retire peaceably, but to no purpose. They advanced to the points of the bayonets, struck some of them and even the muzzles of the pieces, and seemed to be endeavoring to close with the soldiers. On which some well-behaved persons asked me if the guns were charged. I replied yes. They then asked me if I intended to order the men to fire. I answered no, by no means, observing to them that I was advanced before the muzzles of the men's pieces, and must fall a sacrifice if they fired; that the soldiers were upon the half cock and charged bayonets, and my giving the word

"Fire" under those circumstances would prove me to be no officer. While I was thus speaking, one of the soldiers having received a severe blow with a stick, stepped a little on one side and instantly fired, on which turning to and asking him why he fired without orders, I was struck with a club on my arm, which for some time deprived me of the use of it, which blow had it been placed on my head, most probably would have destroyed me. On this a general attack was made on the men by a great number of heavy clubs and snowballs being thrown at them, by which all our lives were in imminent danger, some persons at the same time from behind calling out, "Damn your bloods—why don't you fire." Instantly three or four of the soldiers fired, one after another, and directly after three more in the same confusion and hurry. The mob then ran away, except three unhappy men who instantly expired, in which number was Mr. Gray at whose rope-walk the prior quarrels took place; one more is since dead, three others are dangerously, and four slightly wounded. The whole of this melancholy affair was transacted in almost twenty minutes. On my asking the soldiers why they fired without orders, they said they heard the word fire and supposed it came from me. This might be the case as many of the mob called out "Fire, fire," but I assured the men that I gave no such order; that my words were, "Don't fire, stop your firing." In short, it was scarcely possible for the soldiers to know who said fire, or don't fire, or stop your firing. On the people's assembling again to take away the dead bodies, the soldiers supposing them coming to attack them, were making ready to fire again, which I prevented by striking up their firelocks with my hand. Immediately after, a townsman came and told me that four or five thousand people were assembled in the next street, and had sworn to take my life with every man's with me. On which I judged it unsafe to remain there any longer, and therefore sent the party and sentry to the main guard, where the street is narrow and short, there telling them off into street firings, divided and planted them at each end of the street to secure their rear, momently expecting an attack, as there was a constant cry of the inhabitants "To arms, to arms, turn out with your guns"; and the town drums beating to arms, I ordered my drums to beat to arms, and being soon after joined by the different companies of the 29th Regiment, I formed them as the guard into street firings. The 14th Regiment also got under arms but remained at their barracks. I immediately sent a sergeant with a party to Colonel Dalrymple, the commanding officer, to acquaint him with every particular. Several officers going to join their regiment were knocked down by the mob, one very much wounded and his sword taken from him. The lieutenant-governor and Colonel Carr soon after met at the head of the 29th Regiment and agreed that the regiment should retire to their barracks, and the people to their houses, but I kept the picket to strengthen the guard. It was with great difficulty that the lieutenant-governor prevailed on the people to be quiet and retire. At last they all went off, excepting about a hundred.

A council was immediately called, on the breaking up of which three justices met and issued a warrant to apprehend me and eight soldiers. On hearing of this procedure I instantly went to the sheriff and surrendered myself, though for the space of four hours I had it in my power to have made my escape, which I most undoubtedly should have attempted and could easily executed, had I been the least conscious of any guilt. On the examination before the justices, two witnesses swore that I gave the men orders to fire. The one testified he was within two feet of me; the other that I swore at the men for not firing at the first word. Others swore they heard me use the word "fire," but whether do or do not fire, they could not say; others that they heard the word "fire," but could not say if it came from me. The next day they got five or six more to swear I gave the word to fire. So bitter and inveterate are many of the malcontents here that they are industriously using every method to fish out evidence to prove it was a concerted scheme to murder the inhabitants. Others are infusing the utmost malice and revenge into the minds of the people who are to be my jurors by false publications, votes of towns, and all other artifices. That so from a settled rancor against the officers and troops in general, the suddenness of my trial after the affair while the people's minds are all greatly inflamed, I am, though perfectly innocent, under most unhappy circumstances, having nothing in reason to expect but the loss of life in a very ignominious manner, without the interposition of his Majesty's royal goodness.

James Bowdoin, Dr. Joseph Warren, Samuel Pemberton

from *A Short Narrative of the Horrid Massacre in Boston* (1770)

The actors in this dreadful tragedy were a party of soldiers commanded by Captain Preston of the 29th Regiment. This party, including the captain, consisted of eight, who are all committed to jail.

There are depositions in this affair which mention, that several guns were fired at the same time from the Custom House; before which this shocking scene was exhibited. Into this matter inquisition is now making. In the meantime it may be proper to insert here the substance of some of those depositions.

Benjamin Frizell, on the evening of the 5th of March, having taken his station near the west corner of the Custom House in King Street, before and at the time of the soldiers firing their guns, declares (among other things) that the first discharge was only of one gun, the next of two guns, upon which he the deponent thinks he saw a man stumble; the third discharge was of three guns, upon which he thinks he saw two men fall; and immediately after were discharged five guns, two of which were by soldiers on his right hand; the other three, as appeared to the deponent, were discharged from the balcony, or the chamber window of the Custom House, the flashes appearing on the left hand, and higher than the right hand flashes appeared to be, and of which the deponent was very sensible, although his eyes were much turned to the soldiers, who were all on his right hand.

Gillam Bass, being in King Street at the same time, declares that they (the party of soldiers from the main guard) posted themselves between the Custom House door and the west corner of it; and in a few minutes began to fire upon the people: two or three of the flashes so high above the rest, that he the deponent verily believes they must have come from the Custom House windows.

Jeremiah Allen declares, that in the evening of the 5th day of March current, being at about nine o'clock in the front chamber in the house occupied by Colonel Ingersoll in King Street, he heard some guns fired, which occasioned his going into the balcony of the said house. That when he was in the said balcony in company with Mr. William Molineux, Jr., and John Simpson, he heard the discharge of four or five guns, the flashes of which appeared to be to the westward of the sentry-box, and immediately after, he the deponent heard two or three more guns and saw the flashes thereof from out of the house, now called the Custom House, as they evidently appeared to him, and which he the said deponent at the same time declared to the aforesaid Molineux and Simpson, being then near him, saying to them (at the same time pointing his hand towards the Custom House), "There they are out of the Custom House."

George Coster, being in King Street at the time above mentioned, declares that in five or six minutes after he stopped, he heard the word of command given to the soldiers, "fire"; upon which one gun was fired, which did no execution, as the deponent observed; about half a minute after two guns, one of which killed one Samuel Gray a rope-maker, the other a mulatto man, between which two men the deponent stood; after this the deponent heard the discharge of four or five guns more, by the soldiers; immediately after which the deponent heard the discharge of two guns or pistols, from an open window of the middle story of the Custom House, near to the place where the sentry-box is placed, and being but a small distance from the window, he heard the people from within speak and laugh, and soon after saw the casement[4] lowered down; after which the deponent assisted others in carrying off one of the corpses.

Cato, a negro man, servant to Tuthill Hubbart, Esq., declares that on Monday evening the 5th of March current, on hearing the cry of fire, he ran into King Street, where he saw a number of people assembled before the Custom House; that he stood near the sentry-box and saw the soldiers fire on the people, who stood in the middle of said street; directly after which he saw two flashes of guns, one quick upon the other, from the chamber window of the Custom House; and that after the firing was all over, while the people were carrying away the dead and wounded, he saw the Custom House door opened, and several soldiers (one of whom had a cutlass), go into the Custom House and shut the door after them.

Benjamin Andrews declares, that being desired by the committee of

---

[4] I.e., the sash.

inquiry to take the ranges of the holes made by musket balls, in two houses nearly opposite to the Custom House, he finds the bullet hole in the entry-door post of Mr. Payne's house (and which grazed the edge of the door, before it entered the post, where it lodged, two-and-a-half inches deep), ranges just under the stool[5] of the westernmost lower chamber window of the Custom House.

Samuel Drowne, towards the end of his deposition (which contains a pretty full account of the proceedings of the soldiers on the evening of the 5th instant), declares, that he saw the flashes of two guns fired from the Custom House, one of which was out of a window of the chamber westward of the balcony, and the other from the balcony; the gun (which he clearly discerned), being pointed through the ballusters, and the person who held the gun, in a stooping posture withdrew himself into the house, having a handkerchief or some kind of cloth over his face.

These depositions show clearly that a number of guns were fired from the Custom House. As this affair is now inquiring into, all the notice we shall take of it is, that it distinguishes the actors in it into street-actors and house-actors; which is necessary to be observed.

What gave occasion to the melancholy event of that evening seems to have been this. A difference having happened near Mr. Gray's ropewalk, between a soldier and a man belonging to it, the soldier challenged the ropemakers to a boxing match. The challenge was accepted by one of them, and the soldier worsted. He ran to the barrack in the neighborhood, and returned with several of his companions. The fray was renewed, and the soldiers were driven off. They soon returned with recruits, and were again worsted. This happened several times, till at length a considerable body of soldiers was collected, and they also were driven off, the ropemakers having been joined by their brethren of the contiguous ropewalks. By this time Mr. Gray being alarmed interposed, and with the assistance of some gentlemen prevented any further disturbance. To satisfy the soldiers and punish the man who had been the occasion of the first difference, and as an example to the rest, he turned him out of his service; and waited on Colonel Dalrymple, the commanding officer of the troops, and with him concerted measures for preventing further mischief. Though this affair ended thus, it made a strong impression on the minds of the soldiers in general, who thought the honor of the regiment concerned to revenge those repeated repulses. For this purpose they seemed to have formed a combination to commit some outrage upon the inhabitants of the town indiscriminately; and this was to be done on the evening of the 5th instant or soon after; as appears by the depositions of the following persons, namely:

William Newhall declares, that on Thursday night the 1st of March instant, he met four soldiers of the 29th Regiment, and that he heard them say, "There were a great many that would eat their dinners on Monday next, that should not eat any on Tuesday."

---

[5] Sill.

Daniel Calfe declares, that on Saturday evening the 3d of March, a camp-woman, wife to James McDeed, a grenadier of the 29th, came into his father's shop, and the people talking about the affrays at the ropewalks, and blaming the soldiers for the part they had acted in it, the woman said, "the soldiers were in the right"; adding that "before Tuesday or Wednesday night they would wet their swords or bayonets in New England people's blood."

Mary Brailsford declares, that on Sabbath evening the 4th of March instant, a soldier came to the house of Mr. Amos Thayer, where she then was. He desiring to speak with Mr. Thayer, was told by Mrs. Mary Thayer, that her brother was engaged and could not be spoke with. He said, "Your brother as you call him, is a man I have a great regard for, and I came on purpose to tell him to keep in his house, for *before Tuesday night next at twelve o'clock, there will be a great deal of bloodshed, and a great many lives lost*"; and added that "he came out of a particular regard to her brother to advise him to keep in his house, for then he would be out of harm's way." He said, "Your brother knows me very well; my name is Charles Malone." He then went away. Of the same import, and in confirmation of this declaration, are the depositions of Mary Thayer and Asa Copeland, who both live with the said Mr. Thayer, and heard what the soldier said as above mentioned. It is also confirmed by the deposition of Nicholas Ferriter.

Jane Usher declares, that about nine o'clock on Monday morning the 5th of March current, from a window she saw two persons in the habit of soldiers, one of whom being on horseback appeared to be an officer's servant. The person on the horse first spoke to the other, but what he said, she is not able to say, though the window was open, and she not more than twenty feet distant; the other replied he hoped he should see blood enough spilt before morning.

Matthew Adams declares, that on Monday evening the 5th of March instant, between the hours of seven and eight o'clock, he went to the house of Corporal Pershall of the 29th Regiment, near Quaker Lane, where he saw the corporal and his wife, with one of the fifers of said regiment. When he had got what he went for, and was coming away, the corporal called him back, and desired him with great earnestness to go home to his master's house as soon as business was over, and not to be abroad on any account that night in particular, for "the soldiers were determined to be revenged on the ropewalk people"; and that "much mischief would be done." Upon which the fifer (about eighteen or nineteen years of age), said he "hoped in God they would burn the town down." On this he left the house, and the said corporal called after him again, and begged he would mind what he said to him.

Caleb Swan declares, that on Monday night, the 5th of March instant, at the time of the bells ringing for fire, he heard a woman's voice, whom he knew to be the supposed wife of one Montgomery, a grenadier of the 29th Regiment, standing at her door, and heard her say, "*It was not fire; the town was too haughty and too proud*"; and that "*many of their arses would be laid low before the morning.*"

Margaret Swansborough declares, that a free woman named Black Peg, who has kept much with the soldiers, on hearing the disturbance on Monday evening the 5th instant, said, "the soldiers were not to be trod upon by the inhabitants, but would know before morning, whether they or the inhabitants were to be masters."

Joseph Hooton, Jr., declares, that coming from the south end of Boston on Monday evening the 5th of March instant, against Dr. Sewall's meeting he heard a great noise and tumult, with the cry of murder often repeated. Proceeding towards the Town House he was passed by several soldiers running that way, with naked cutlasses and bayonets in their hands. He asked one of them what was the matter, and was answered by him, "By God you shall all know what is the matter soon." Between nine and ten o'clock he went into King Street, and was present at the tragical scene exhibited near the Custom House; as particularly set forth in his deposition.

Mrs. Mary Russell declares, that John Brailsford a private soldier of the 14th Regiment, who had frequently been employed by her (when he was ordered with his company to the castle, in consequence of the murders committed by the soldiers on the evening of the 5th of March), coming to the deponent's house declared, that *their* regiment were *ordered* to hold themselves in readiness, and accordingly was ready *that evening*, upon the inhabitants firing on the soldiery, to come to the assistance of the soldiery. On which she asked him, if he would have fired upon any of the inhabitants of this town. To which he replied, Yes, if he had orders; but that if he saw Mr. Russell, he would have fired wide of him. He also said, "It's well there was no gun fired by the inhabitants, for had there been, *we* should have come to the soldiers' assistance."

By the foregoing depositions it appears very clearly, there was a general combination among the soldiers of the 29th Regiment at least, to commit some extraordinary act of violence upon the town; that if the inhabitants attempted to repel it by firing even one gun upon those soldiers, the 14th Regiment were ordered to be in readiness to assist them; and that on the late butchery in King Street they actually were ready for that purpose, had a single gun been fired on the perpetrators of it.

It appears by a variety of depositions, that on the same evening between the hours of six and half after nine (at which time the firing began), many persons, without the least provocation, were in various parts of the town insulted and abused by parties of armed soldiers patrolling the streets; particularly:

Mr. Robert Pierpont declares, that between the hours of seven and eight in the same evening, three armed soldiers passing him, one of them who had a bayonet gave him a back-handed stroke with it. On complaint of this treatment, he said the deponent should soon hear more of it, and threatened him very hard.

Mr. Henry Bass declares, that at nine o'clock, a party of soldiers came out of Draper's Alley, leading to and from Murray's barracks, and they being armed with large naked cutlasses, made at everybody coming in their way, cutting and slashing, and that he himself very narrowly escaped receiving a cut from the foremost of them, who pursued him.

Samuel Atwood declares, that ten or twelve soldiers armed with drawn cutlasses bolted out of the alley leading from Murray's barracks into Dock Square, and met the deponent, who asked them if they intended to murder people? They answered, "Yes, by God, root and branch," saying, "here is one of them"; with that one of them struck the deponent with a club, which was repeated by another. The deponent being unarmed turned to go off, and he received a wound on the left shoulder, which reached the bone, disabled him and gave him much pain. Having gone a few steps the deponent met two officers, and asked them, "Gentlemen, what is the matter?" They answered, "You will see by and by"; and as he passed by Col. Jackson's he heard the cry, "Turn out the guards."

Capt. James Kirkwood declares, that about nine of the clock in the evening of the 5th day of March current, he was going by Murray's barracks: hearing a noise he stopped at Mr. Rhoads's door, opposite the said barracks, where said Rhoads was standing, and stood some time, and saw the soldiers coming out of the yard from the barracks, armed with cutlasses and bayonets, and rushing through Boylston's Alley into Cornhill. Two officers, namely, Lieuts. Minchin and Dickson, came out of the mess-house, and said to the soldiers, "My lads, come into the barracks and don't hurt the inhabitants," and then retired into the mess-house. Soon after they came to the door again, and found the soldiers in the yard; and directly upon it, Ensign Mall came to the gate of the barrack-yard and said to the soldiers, "Turn out, and I will stand by you"; this he repeated frequently, adding, "Kill them! stick them! knock them down; run your bayonets through them," with a great deal of language of like import. Upon which a great number of soldiers came out of the barracks with naked cutlasses, headed by said Mall, and went through the aforesaid alley; that some officers came and got the soldiers into their barracks, and that Mall, with his sword or cutlass drawn in his hand, [just] as often had them out again, but [they] were at last drove into their barracks by the aforesaid Minchin and Dickson.

Mr. Henry Rhoads's declaration agrees with Captain Kirkwood's.

Mr. Matthias King, of Halifax, in Nova Scotia, declares that in the evening of the fifth day of March instant, about nine o'clock, he was at his lodgings at Mrs. Torrey's, near the town pump, and heard the bells ring and the cry of "fire"; upon which he went to the door and saw several soldiers come round the south side of the Town House, armed with bayonets, and something which he took to be broadswords; that one of those people came up almost to him and Mr. Bartholomew Kneeland; and that they had but just time to shut the door upon him; otherwise he is well assured they must have fell victims to their boundless cruelty. He afterwards went into the upper chamber of the said house, and was looking out of the window when the drum and the guard went into the barrack, and he saw one of the guards kneel and present his piece, with a bayonet fixed, and heard him swear he would fire upon a parcel of boys who were then in the street, but he did not. He further declares that when the body of troops was drawn up before the guard house (which was presently after the massacre), he heard an officer say to another, that this was fine work, and just what he wanted; but in the hurry he could not see him, so as to know him again.[6]

Robert Polley declares, that on Monday evening, the 5th instant, as he was going home, he observed about ten persons standing near Mr. Taylor's door; after standing there a small space of time, he went with them towards Boylston's Alley, opposite to Murray's barracks: "We met in the alley about eight or nine armed soldiers; they assaulted us, and gave us a great deal of abusive language; we then drove them back to the barracks with sticks only; we looked for stones or bricks, but could find none, the ground being covered with snow." Some of the lads dispersed, and he, the said Polley, with a few others, were returning peaceably home, when we met about nine or ten other soldiers armed: one of them said, "Where are the sons of bitches?" They struck at several persons in the street, and went towards the head of the alley. Two officers came and endeavored to get them into their barracks; one of the lads proposed to ring the bell; the soldiers went through the alley, and the boys huzzaed, and said they were gone through Royal Exchange Lane into King Street.

Samuel Drowne declares that, about nine o'clock of the evening of the fifth of March current, standing at his own door in Cornhill, he saw about fourteen or fifteen soldiers of the 29th Regiment, who came from Murray's barracks, armed with naked cutlasses, swords, etc., and came upon the inhabitants of the town, then standing or walking in Cornhill, and abused some, and violently assaulted others as they met them; most of whom were without so much as a stick in their hand to defend themselves, as he very clearly could discern, it being moonlight, and himself being one of the assaulted persons. All or most of the said soldiers he saw go into King Street (some of them through Royal Exchange Lane), and there followed them, and soon discovered them to be quarrelling and fighting with the people whom they saw there, which he thinks were not more than a dozen, when the soldiers came there first, armed as aforesaid. Of those dozen people, the most of them were gentlemen, standing together a little below the Town House, upon the Exchange. At the appearance of those soldiers so armed, the most of the twelve persons went off, some of them being first assaulted.

The violent proceedings of this party, and their going into King Street, "quarrelling and fighting with the people whom they saw there" (mentioned in Mr. Drowne's deposition), [were] immediately introductory to the grand catastrophe.

These assailants, who issued from Murray's barracks (so called), after attacking and wounding divers persons in Cornhill, as above mentioned, being armed, proceeded (most of them) up Royal Exchange Lane into King Street;

[6]That is, he saw the officer so briefly that he would not be able to recognize him at present.

where, making a short stop, and after assaulting and driving away the few they met there, they brandished their arms and cried out, "Where are the boogers! where are the cowards!" At this time there were very few persons in the street beside themselves. This party in proceeding from Exchange Lane into King Street, must pass the sentry posted at the westerly corner of the Custom House, which butts on that lane and fronts on that street. This is needful to be mentioned, as near that spot and in that street the bloody tragedy was acted, and the street actors in it were stationed: their station being but a few feet from the front side of the said Custom House. The outrageous behavior and the threats of the said party occasioned the ringing of the meeting-house bell near the head of King Street, which bell ringing quick, as for fire, it presently brought out a number of the inhabitants, who being soon sensible of the occasion of it, were naturally led to King Street, where the said party had made a stop but a little while before, and where their stopping had drawn together a number of boys, round the sentry at the Custom House. Whether the boys mistook the sentry for one of the said party, and thence took occasion to differ with him, or whether he first affronted them, which is affirmed in several depositions; however that may be, there was much foul language between them, and some of them, in consequence of his pushing at them with his bayonet, threw snowballs at him,[7] which occasioned him to knock hastily at the door of the Custom House. From hence two persons thereupon proceeded immediately to the mainguard, which was posted (opposite to the State House) at a small distance, near the head of the said street. The officer on guard was Capt. Preston, who with seven or eight soldiers, with firearms and charged bayonets, issued from the guard house, and in great haste posted himself and his soldiers in the front of the Custom House, near the corner aforesaid. In passing to this station the soldiers pushed several persons with their bayonets, driving through the people in so rough a manner that it appeared they intended to create a disturbance. This occasioned some snowballs to be thrown at them, which seems to have been the only provocation that was given. Mr. Knox (between whom and Capt. Preston there was some conversation on the spot) declares, that while he was talking with Capt. Preston, the soldiers of his detachment had attacked the people with their bayonets; and that there was not the least provocation given to Capt. Preston or his party; the backs of the people being toward them when

[7]"Since writing this narrative, several depositions have appeared, which make it clear that the sentry was first in fault. He overheard a barber's boy saying, that a captain of the 14th (who had just passed by) was so mean a fellow as not to pay his barber for shaving him. Upon this the sentry left his post and followed the boy into the middle of the street, where he told him to show his face. The boy pertly replied, 'I am not ashamed to show my face to any man.' Upon this the sentry gave him [a] sweeping stroke on the head with his musket, which made him reel and stagger, and cry much. A fellow-apprentice asked the sentry, what he meant by this abuse? He replied, 'Damn your blood, if you do not get out of the way, I will give you something'; and then fixed his bayonet and pushed at the lads, who both ran out of his way. This dispute collected a few persons about the boy, near the Custom House. Presently after this, the party above-mentioned came into King Street, which was a further occasion of drawing people thither, as above related" [note in original narrative].

the people were attacked. He also declares that Capt. Preston seemed to be in great haste and much agitated, and that, according to his opinion, there were not then present in King Street above seventy or eighty persons at the extent.

The said party was formed into a half-circle; and within a short time after they had been posted at the Custom House, began to fire upon the people.

Captain Preston is said to have ordered them to fire, and to have repeated that order. One gun was fired first; then others in succession, and with deliberation, till ten or a dozen guns were fired; or till that number of discharges were made from the guns that were fired. By which means eleven persons were killed and wounded, as above represented.

11

Two Loyalists Take Aim

THE WRITINGS OF LOYALIST CHARLES WOODMASON SUGGEST THAT SATIRE WAS a weapon peculiarly suited to the political and social situation of Americans who clung to the cause of the Crown. By relying on a core of assumed values against which the "innovations" of fashion, morals, or politics might be condemned, satire provided those distressed by the upheavals in America a means of belittling and trivializing the people they held responsible. Two of Woodmason's contemporaries showed a similar talent for such deflations. Jonathan Boucher (1738–1804) and Janet Schaw (ca. 1735–1801), both born in Great Britain (Boucher in the English north country, Schaw in Scotland) were alarmed by what they saw during their time in America (Boucher had been a tutor and an Anglican minister; Schaw was more nearly just a visitor in 1775–76), and both were at last forced into exile by the coming war. The two shared liveliness of mind, sharpness of observation and statement, and a courage that—even in the face of increasingly serious breaches between the colonies and their homeland—did not cause them to blink.

Jonathan Boucher first came to America in the 1759 as a tutor, and when offered a parish church in Virginia was ordained as an Anglican minister (like Woodmason, he had to return to England for ordination, as there were no bishops situated in the colonies), and settled down to a life as shepherd of his flock and master of his own plantation. In the year of the Boston Massacre, he relocated to Maryland, where as the political disputes heated up he became one of the most prominent of Loyalists, until (in a climax narrated in the selection given here from his memoirs) he was forced from his pulpit and from America in 1775. Resettled in England, Boucher continued his ministerial and educational activities and prepared for the press not only his memoirs but also a collection of Loyalist sermons he claimed he had preached in America. The former work, written in 1789 but not published in full until 1925, contains acerbic but humorous accounts of his last days in America, including his anecdote of how, in response to a Patriot toast ("May the Americans all hang together in accord and concord!") he replied—much to the anger of the company—"In any cord, . . . so it be but a strong cord." It details, too, his last sermon from his church in Maryland, preached with his pistols in reach because the local Patriots had threatened to remove him, or indeed to kill him, if he attempted to take the pulpit once more.

Janet Schaw's American experience was relatively brief by comparison, and it hinged on events of less personal danger. Still, this aristocratic young Scotswoman offers lively accounts of Patriot doings—such as a muster in Wilmington, North Carolina, early in 1775, during which the apparently drunken soldiers stumbled about (in her prose if not on the field) and "made indeed a most unmartial appearance." Even so, Schaw, who later reflected on the fact that she had let the word "rebels" slip out of her pen unawares, had to admit that these "soldiers, or what you please to call them," were so skilled in their own kind of "bush-fighting" that "the worst figure [among them] can shoot from behind a bush" and kill the bravest British officer. Lacking in polish or social graces as they might be, even in 1775 Schaw could see that these citizen soldiers meant business, and could carry through on their threats. In her letters to an unknown correspondent in Scotland, later collected as a "Journal," Schaw could catch the promise of the new land for visitors like herself from an old one, but in her case the promise lived on only as a memory.

JONATHAN BOUCHER

from his "Memoirs" (1786–89)

IT SHOULD HAVE BEEN MENTIONED LONG AGO THAT, WHILE I LIVED AT CASTLE Magruder,[1] some of the patriots of my parish, which swarmed with them, were for ever stirring up anybody they could find at all so disposed, to give me trouble and vexation. They made a great outcry about my refusing to receive some corn I had bought of a planter; notwithstanding that I proved that the corn he offered to deliver me was not marketable. This is mentioned only to show that among such men in such times it becomes even meritorious to injure and insult an honest man who has had the misfortune to be voted obnoxious. Among others, I fell into a dispute with a blacksmith; the consequences of which, as it happened, did me no little service. He had a cornfield adjoining to my pasture, the fence of which was so bad, that a favorite and valuable horse of mine, though fettered, got over into it. Finding him in his field, this fellow actually shot at him, and lodged several large swan-shot in different parts of his body, so that he was for ever after lame.[2] To aggravate this shocking behavior still more, it

---

[1] Boucher at this time was living in a "very tolerable house" he had rented from a Captain Magruder; the three young men whom he was tutoring, and who lived there with him, gave it this fanciful name.

[2] Boucher's outrage at this act was based in part on the general practice in the American colonies to regard the landowner as responsible for fencing out neighbors' livestock.

was done in the sight of my wife, and not without much abuse of her husband. And as if he valued himself on his feat, he soon after came swaggering up to me, swore much, and talked much impudent nonsense; adding, whilst his gun was in one hand and a large stick in the other, which he often shook at me, that by G-d he would serve me as he had served my horse. This was too much. I saw it was his plan, if possible, to provoke me to strike him, and to have a trial of strength with me; and being a stoutish fellow, and I utterly unused to boxing, no doubt he counted on gaining a cheap victory, and of course much credit. I desired him repeatedly to keep his distance, instead of which he thrust his fist in my face. No alternative seemed now to be left, and so as we were to come to blows, I determined to have the first. I struck him but once, when "prostrate he fell, and measured o'er a length of ground." No man who has never himself experienced such a state of society as then prevailed in that country, can conceive what credit I gained, and, I add, what advantage, from this lucky blow. I was looked upon and spoken of as another Broughton;[3] and it was of more advantage to me to be so thought of than to have been set down as a Newton.

In my controversy with Messrs. Chase and Paca,[4] some personalities had occurred; and in a controversy when did they not occur? The laugh was turned particularly upon Paca, who, though neither absurd nor ridiculous, was but a weakish man, and exquisitely alive to the state of the public opinion concerning him. In short, he was so hurt as to fancy it incumbent on him to give me a regular and formal challenge; and accordingly applied to my friend Mr. Smith, the secretary to the governor, to be his second. Mr. Smith with great readiness of mind and adroitness told him that I had foreseen long ago how our dispute would terminate, and accordingly had actually engaged him to attend me as my second on the occasion. This well-timed invention staggered my adversary; which Smith improved by reciting sundry imaginary instances of my astonishing courage and prowess. Thus was I without any plan or wishes of my own all at once set up as a d——d fellow, equally in favor with Mars and Minerva. And I have every reason in the world to believe that this opinion alone saved my bacon on many occasions. One only I will now set down. I dined with Mr. Addison Murdock, a gentleman of considerable respectability, and a near relation of my wife's, in a large company of men of different parties and opinions. Among others was Dr. Brookes, a well-meaning, sensible, but blundering man, and a Mr. Osborne Sprigg, a very great patriot, who had been very busy in the corn story, and who could not forgive me for having defeated him in his attempts to fasten on me suspicions of having done wrong instead of having suffered wrong. Dr. Brookes, with the best intentions I daresay, gave as a toast, "May the Americans all hang together in accord and concord!" Prompted no doubt by my evil genius, I said, before I well knew what I was saying, "in any cord, Doctor, so it be but a strong cord." It was the appearance of wit in this

---

[3] Jack Broughton, a famous British boxer who, after killing a man in a fight, in 1743 drew up the first rules for the sport.

[4] Samuel Chase (1741–1811) and William Paca (1740–1799), two prominent Maryland Patriots, both of whom were to be signers of the Declaration of Independence.

retort, I suppose, which tempted me, and which, after all, I believe may be found in Joe Miller.[5] The patriot took fire immediately; but the explanation I made satisfied everybody else, and things might again have gone on smoothly, had not the wretch, determined to quarrel with me, when his turn came, given as his toast, "Damnation to General Gage, the troops under his command, and all who wish well to them," which I refused to drink, as when I did several others also did. Mr. Sprigg now grew outrageous, blustered and threatened at a prodigious rate, and several times pretended to get up to strike me, and seemed to be unwillingly restrained by the company. I sat perfectly still and composed, till at length when there was a little pause, I just said, "Sir, I believe everybody, as well as myself, has seen that you have determined to quarrel with me; you no doubt thought the opportunity favorable for your purpose; and I have observed you swallow large draughts of wine to render you pot-valiant. But, Sir, I will again disappoint you: permit me, gentlemen, to entreat you only to sit still, and I will stake my life for it, the gentleman will not think of coming near me." This address had its effect, for he now recollected that bruising was ungentlemanly, and that as I was said to have studied under Broughton, I might possibly be an over-match for him; and therefore I should hear from him next morning *as a gentleman.* I replied, " 'Tis very well, Sir: you are no acquaintance of mine; and if those who are your friends think the retreat you are now making a handsome one, I am contented. For the rest, I never did yet hear of your having acted in any instance *as a gentleman;* and if I should tomorrow morning, all I can say is, it will exceedingly surprise me: I shall be at my own home all day." But I never heard more of him *as a gentleman.*

It was not on this occasion only that I have experienced that the true way to escape a danger is fairly to meet it. I have, I believe, a tolerably vigorous and resolute mind; but as to fighting, in every mode of it, there is nothing I so much dread and detest. Everything therefore that I did in that way was really and truly to preserve me from fighting. And it appears that I succeeded.

The principles and ways of thinking of Whigs and Tories, or of Republicans and Loyalists, are hardly more different than are their tempers. The latter have a foolish good-nature and improvidence about them which leads them often to hurt their own interests by promoting those of their adversaries, when the objects for which they contended are removed; but the former never forgives, never ceases to effect his purposes of being revenged on those he has once called his enemies. Mr. Sprigg was a thorough Whig, and I perhaps as thorough a Loyalist; as appeared on the last fracas of the kind in which I was involved, and which now soon took place.

A public fast was ordained. In America, as in the grand rebellion in England,[6] much execution was done by sermons. Those persons who have read any out of the great number of Puritan sermons that were then printed as well

---

[5] Joseph or Josias Miller (1684–1738), English comedic actor whose name was used after his death for John Mottley's vulgar collection, *Joe Miller's Jest-book* (1739).
[6] The English Civil War, 1642–48.

as preached, will cease to wonder that so many people were worked up into such a state of frenzy; and I who either heard, or heard of, many similar discourses from the pulpits in America, felt the effects of them no less than they had before been felt here. My curate was but a weak brother, yet a strong Republican, i.e. as far as he knew how. The sermon he had preached on a former fast, though very silly, was still more exceptionable as contributing to blow the coals of sedition. Its silliness perhaps made it even more mischievous; for to be very popular, it is, I believe, necessary to be very like the bulk of the people, that is, wrong-headed, ignorant, and prone to resist authority. And I am persuaded, whenever it happens that a really sensible man becomes the idol of the people, it must be owing to his possessing a talent of letting himself down to their level. It remains to be proved, however, that ever a really sensible person did take this part; I think the contrary may be proved. As, however, Mr. Harrison's practice as well as preaching were now beginning to be exceptionable, that is, by his setting about and promoting factious associations and subscriptions, it was thought necessary that on the approaching fast-day, which was a day of great expectation, I should make a point of appearing in my own pulpit; and the governor waited on me on purpose to press my doing so.

On my informing Mr. Harrison that this was my intention, he told me he had prepared a sermon for the occasion. I asked him what subject he had pitched upon, and I never shall forget his reply. He proposed, he said, to preach against *absolute monarchy*. It was impossible, I said, not to commend the judiciousness of his choice; as the times and the country in which our lot had fallen so particularly called on us to put our people on their guard against a danger into which they seemed so likely to fall. The fact was, I fancy, he had found such a sermon in Hoadly,[7] and having transcribed it, shewed it to the committee, by whom it was approved, as any and every thing was and would have been, however loose and weak, that but seemed to be against power and for liberty.

Mr. Addison, the governor,[8] and all the most judicious friends I had, looked over my sermon, and thought I had softened it down so, that it might do good, and at least could not possibly give offence. In this and everything else that I now wrote, all that I could dare to hope to effect, was the restraining the body of the people from taking any active part; and the gist of my arguments was that in taking a part they could not be sure they were right and doing good; and so their truest wisdom as well as duty in so difficult a conjecture was, as the prophet advised them, to *sit still*.[9] And sadly as things went against loyalty and loyal men, I have the comfort to reflect that some good was done by my efforts in their favor. I had some credit and character with my brethren of the clergy, many of whom were thus restrained within the bounds of duty. And as a proof that many of the people were so restrained, I may mention that when members for the provincial congress were to be chosen, as the measure was

---

[7] Benjamin Hoadly (1676–1761), a British bishop who had initiated the so-called Bangorian controversy, on the relation of the Church of England to the monarchy.
[8] Robert Eden (1741–1784), governor of Maryland, 1768–76.
[9] See, e.g., Isaiah 30:7.

quite novel and altogether unknown to our laws, I exhorted my people to abstain from it, and not one of them attended. Out of the whole county there were but thirteen electors; and in Annapolis there were but four. And it is a certain fact, of the truth of which I at least am thoroughly convinced, that nine out of ten of the people of America, properly so called, were adverse to the revolt. But how shall an historian prove so extraordinary a fact, or expect to gain credit if he should prove it?

When the fast-day came I set off, accompanied by Mr. Walter Dulany, since made a major in a provincial loyal regiment, and was at my church at least a quarter of an hour before the usual time of beginning service. But behold, Mr. Harrison was in the desk, and was expected also, as I was soon told, to preach. This was not agreeable: but of how little significance was this compared to what I next saw, viz. my church filled with not less than two hundred armed men, under the command of Mr. Osborne Sprigg, who soon let me know I was not to preach. I returned for answer that the pulpit was my own, and as such I would use it; and that there was but one way by which they could keep me out of it, and that was by taking away my life. In church I managed to place myself so as to have the command of the pulpit, and told my curate at his peril not to attempt to dispossess me. Sundry messages were sent, and applications made to me, to relinquish my purpose; but as I knew it was my duty, and thought also that it was my interest, not to relinquish it, I persisted. And so at the proper time, with my sermon in one hand and a loaded pistol in the other, like Nehemiah,[1] I prepared to ascend the steps of the pulpit, when behold, one of my friends (Mr. David Crawford of Upper Marlborough) having got behind me, threw his arms around mine and held me fast. He assured me on his honor he had both seen and heard the most positive orders given to twenty men picked out for the purpose to fire on me the moment I got into the pulpit, which therefore he never would permit me to do, unless I was stronger than he and two or three others who stood close to him. I entreated him and them to go with me into the pulpit, as my life seemed to myself to depend on my not suffering these outrageous people to carry their point; and I suppose we should all be safe while we were all together, for Mr. Crawford and those with him were rather against than for me in politics. In all these cases I argued that once to flinch was forever to invite danger; and that as I could never be out of the reach of such men till I was out of the country, my only policy was, if possible, to intimidate them, as in some degree I had hitherto done. My well-wishers however prevailed—by force rather than by persuasion; and when I was down it is horrid to recollect what a scene of confusion ensued. A large party insisted I was right in claiming and using my own pulpit; but Sprigg and his company were now grown more violent, and soon managed so as to surround me, and to exclude every moderate man. Seeing myself thus circumstanced, it occurred to me that things seemed now indeed to be growing alarming, and

---

[1] Boucher refers to Nehemiah's refusal to leave the city of Jerusalem when, on a mission from the king of Persia, he was rebuilding its walls and those who opposed his efforts tried many stratagems to remove him.

that there was but one way to save my life. This was by seizing Sprigg, as I immediately did, by the collar, and with my cocked pistol in the other hand, assuring him that if any violence was offered to me I would instantly blow his brains out, as I most certainly would have done. I then told him that if he pleased he might conduct me to my horse, and I would leave them. This he did, and we marched together upwards of a hundred yards, I with one hand fastened in his collar and a pistol in the other, guarded by his whole company, whom he had the meanness to order to play on their drums the Rogues' March all the way we went, which they did. All farther that I could then do was to declare, as loud as I could speak, that he had now proved himself to be a complete coward and scoundrel.

Thus ended this dreadful day. . . .

JANET SCHAW

from her "**Journal**" (**1774‒76**)

WILMINGTOWN

Good heavens! what a scene this town is: Surely you folks at home have adopted the old maxim of King Charles: "Make friends of your foes, leave friends to shift for themselves."

We came down in the morning in time for the review, which the heat made as terrible to the spectators as to the soldiers, or what you please to call them. They had certainly fainted under it, had not the constant draughts of grog supported them. Their exercise was that of bush-fighting, but it appeared so confused and so perfectly different from anything I ever saw, I cannot say whether they performed it well or not; but this I know that they were heated with rum till capable of committing the most shocking outrages. We stood in the balcony of Doctor Cobham's[2] house and they were reviewed on a field mostly covered with what are called here scrubby oaks, which are only a little better than brushwood. They at last however assembled on the plain field, and I must really laugh while I recollect their figures: two thousand men in their shirts and trousers, preceded by a very ill-beat drum and a fiddler, who was also in his shirt with a long sword and a cue at his hair, who played with all his might. They made indeed a most unmartial appearance. But the worst figure there can shoot from behind a bush and kill even a General Wolfe.[3]

Before the review was over, I heard a cry of tar and feather. I was ready to

---

[2] Dr. Thomas Cobham (dates uncertain) first showed up in North Carolina in the 1760s, and soon established a prominent medical practice there. He seems to have been of Loyalist sympathies, and apparently planned to leave for England at the start of hostilities, but he did not join the British forces until 1781, when the war was virtually over.

[3] General James Wolfe (b. 1727), hero of the French and Indian War, was mortally wounded on the Plains of Abraham outside Quebec City in 1759 in a battle that brought the war—and France's active role in North America—to an end.

faint at the idea of this dreadful operation. I would have gladly quitted the balcony, but was so much afraid the victim was one of my friends, that I was not able to move; and he indeed proved to be one, though in a humble station. For it was Mr. Neilson's[4] poor English groom. You can hardly conceive what I felt when I saw him dragged forward, poor devil, frighted out of his wits. However, at the request of some of the officers, who had been Neilson's friends, his punishment was changed into that of mounting on a table and begging pardon for having smiled at the regiment. He was then drummed and fiddled out of the town, with a strict prohibition of ever being seen in it again.

One might have expected, that though I had been imprudent all my life, the present occasion might have inspired me with some degree of caution, and yet I can tell you I had almost incurred the poor groom's fate from my own folly. Several of the officers came up to dine, amongst others Col. Howe, who with less ceremony than might have been expected from his general politeness stepped into an apartment adjoining the hall, and took up a book I had been reading, which he brought open in his hand into the company. I was piqued at his freedom, and reproved him with a half compliment to his general good breeding. He owned his fault and with much gallantry promised to submit to whatever punishment I would inflict. "You shall only" said I, "read aloud a few pages which I will point out, and I am sure you will do Shakespeare justice." He bowed and took the book, but no sooner observed that I had turned up for him, that part of *Henry the Fourth*, where Falstaff describes his company, than he colored like scarlet. I saw he made the application[5] instantly; however, he read it through, though not with the vivacity he generally speaks; however, he recovered himself and coming close up to me, whispered, "You will certainly get yourself tarred and feathered; shall I apply to be executioner?" I am going to seal this up. Adieu.[6]

I closed my last packet at Doctor Cobham's after the review, and as I hoped to hear of some method of getting it sent to you, stayed, though Miss Rutherfurd was obliged to go home. As soon as she was gone, I went into the town, the entry of which I found closed up by a detachment of the soldiers; but as the officer immediately made way for me, I took no further notice of it, but advanced to the middle of the street, where I found a number of the first people in town standing together, who (to use Milton's phrase) seemed much impassioned. As most of them were my acquaintances, I stopped to speak to them, but they with one voice begged me for heaven's sake to get off the street, making me observe they were prisoners, adding that every avenue of the town was shut up, and that in all human probability some scene would be acted very unfit for

---

[4] Archibald Neilson (ca. 1745–1808), a native of Scotland, had come to North Carolina in 1771 at the request of Governor Josiah Martin, with whom he lived in the gubernatorial palace in New Bern. Like Martin, he remained loyal to the Crown and fled the province in 1775, returning via Portugal to England and eventually Scotland.

[5] I.e., got the point.

[6] Schaw is ending this particular letter; her next sentence, starting a new "packet," begins by summarizing the contents of this one.

me to witness. I could not take the friendly advice, for I became unable to move and absolutely petrified with horror.

Observing however an officer with whom I had just dined, I beckoned him to me. He came, but with no very agreeable look, and on my asking him what was the matter, he presented a paper he had folded in his hand. "If you will persuade them to sign this they are at liberty," said he, "but till then must remain under this guard, as they must suffer the penalties they have justly incurred." "And we will suffer every thing," replied one of them, "before we abjure our king, our country and our principles." "This, ladies," said he turning to me, who was now joined by several ladies, "is what they call their test, but by what authority this gentleman forces it on us, we are yet to learn." "There is my authority," pointing to the soldiers with the most insolent air, "dispute it, if you can." Oh Britannia, what are you doing, while your true obedient sons are thus insulted by their unlawful brethren; are they also forgot by their natural parents?[7]

We, the ladies, adjourned to the house of a lady, who lived in this street, and whose husband was indeed at home, but secretly shut up with some ambassadors from the back settlements on their way to the governor to offer their service, provided he could let them have arms and ammunition, but above all such commissions as might empower them to raise men by proper authority. This I was presently told though in the midst of enemies, but the loyal party are all as one family.[8] Various reasons induced me to stay all night in the house I was then at, though it could afford me no resting place. I wished to know the fate of the poor men who were in such present jeopardy, and besides hoped that I should get word to my brother, or send your packet by the gentlemen who were going to the man-of-war. In the last I have succeeded, and they are so good as [to] promise to get it safely there to my brother or the governor, who would not fail to send it by first opportunity to Britain. Indeed it is very dangerous to keep letters by me, for whatever noise general warrants made in the mouths of your sons of faction at home, their friends and fellow rebels use it with less ceremony than ever it was practised in Britain, at any period.

Rebels, this is the first time I have ventured that word, more than in thought, but to proceed.

The prisoners stood firm to their resolution of not signing the test, till past two in the morning, though every threatening was used to make them comply; at which time a message from the committee compromised the affair, and they were suffered to retire on their parole[9] to appear next morning before them. This was not a step of mercy or out of regard to the gentlemen; but they under-

---

[7] Schaw is describing how the Wilmington Committee of Safety pressured all householders in the town to agree to the terms of the Continental Association, the agreement that the Congress had approved the previous fall, and that sought to coordinate American efforts against the importation of British goods.
[8] The backsettlers in question were Scots Highlanders, who despite the recent defeats of Scots forces by England, largely remained loyal to the Crown during the American Revolution.
[9] I.e., on their word.

stood that a number of their friends were arming in their defense, and though they had kept about 150 ragamuffins still in town, they were not sure even of them; for to the credit of that town be it spoke, there are not five men of property and credit in it that are infected by this unfortunate disease.

As I had nothing further to do in town, I came up to Schawfield, where Fanny[1] met me, and we will go to Point Pleasant again in a day or two, as I find this place so warm, that I shall certainly have a fever, if I stay. It is beautiful however, the garden is in great glory, tubby roses so large and fragrant, as is quite beyond a British idea, and the trumpet honeysuckle is five times as large as ours, and everything else in proportion. I particularly name these two as their bell seems the favorite bed of the dear little hummingbirds, which are here in whole flocks. The place altogether is very fine, the Indian corn is now almost ready, and makes a noble appearance. The rice too is whitening, and its distant appearance is that of our green oats, but there is no living near it with the putrid water that must lie on it, and the labor required for it is only fit for slaves, and I think the hardest work I have seen them engaged in. The indigo is now ready; it looks very pretty, but for all these I refer you to Miller's[2] description, which, on comparison, I find perfectly just. Though the watermelons here are thought particularly fine, I am not yet reconciled to them. My brother brought some cantaloupe melon seed, which was sown here; though, by what accident I cannot tell, they were all torn up while green. They must have been exquisite, but every melon except the watermelon, is indiscriminately called muskmelon and despised, which is a pity, for our good ones must be a great treat here. The cotton is now ripe, and though only annual grows to a little bush. It seems extremely good, and is very prolific. They complain much of the trouble it requires, as it must not only be weeded, but watched while green, as the bears are very fond of it in its infancy. It also is troublesome to gather and to clean from the husk, so that few housewives will venture on the task, and I am glad they do not; for under proper management, it would be an article of great consequence. Two or three score of our old women with their cards and wheels would hurt the linen manufactories. But were I a planter, I would send a son or two to be bred to the weaving and farming business, who might teach the Negroes, and I would bring out a ship loaded on my own account with wheels, reels and looms, also ploughs, harrows, drills, spades, rakes, etc. And this may all happen, when Britain *strikes home*. We set off this afternoon for the point and travel by land, so I will be able to give you some account of our journey in that way, as we must go by the great road that leads into South Carolina the one way and Virginia the other.[3] Adieu.

[1] Fanny (the "Miss Rutherfurd" mentioned earlier) was a young woman who accompanied Schaw on her voyage from Scotland and who later married Schaw's younger brother Alexander; "Schawfield," where she met Schaw in this instance, was the plantation belonging to Schaw's older brother Robert, on the river a few miles upstream from Wilmington.
[2] Philip Miller (ca. 1690–1771), whose *Gardener's Dictionary* was first published in 1731.
[3] Schaw speaks of the plantation called Point Pleasant, located on the Northeast River and belonging to Colonel James Innes (ca. 1700–1759), then in the possession of Schaw's friend, his widow, Mrs. Jean Corbin.

12

AN ORDINARY WAR:
SIX NINETEENTH-CENTURY PENSION
APPLICATION NARRATIVES

LIKE ALL WARS, THE AMERICAN REVOLUTION WAS FOUGHT BY COMMON PEOPLE who left few records of their victories or sufferings. In the case of officers and "regulars" in the Continental service, the fledging government had some modest records, but for the many who had served in the plethora of smaller units it had very few. As a result, pension acts, which were passed in 1818 and 1832, offered rewards for those who survived (or their widows), but required that applicants provide accounts of when and where they had served. Typically, applicants submitted in their own hand or through the aid of a professional scribe—lawyer, town clerk, minister—a brief but often striking account of their service and prayed for the modest relief that the government promised. The resulting records provide an intriguingly full portrait not only of what the individual soldiers had undergone, but also of how the Revolution was remembered, and transfigured, in later eras. Particularly in the late 1820s and the 1830s, under the influence of Andrew Jackson's emphasis on the worth of the ordinary citizen, the surviving Revolutionary War veterans became living memorials of the war that most of their neighbors had only heard of. Trotted out for signal events—such as the visit of the aged General Lafayette to the nation in 1824–25—these figures dramatically underscored the links between what was fast being seen as the great era of selfless patriotism and the bustling commercial, "go-ahead" culture of the United States in the 1830s. In 1830, the nation's population was twelve million, more than four times what it had been at the end of the war; and only about 5 percent of the 1830 population was old enough to even remember anything about the Revolution personally.

The pension application narratives, preserved in the National Archives and available on microfilm as well as in John C. Dann's excellently edited selection of almost eighty specimens, constitute an extraordinary oral history source. Some eighty thousand separate files leave very few byways or major battlegrounds of the war hidden, and in many instances it is possible to gain rich on-the-spot insight into particular occurrences from comparing several narratives touching on the same campaigns. Still, perhaps more important than this is the way the narratives portray the worldview of the common soldiers, as recalled and altered in later decades. Rarely do the narratives overtly spout the patriotic rhetoric that Fourth of July celebrations already had embalmed. Indeed, they show a more ambiguous sense of the conflict than later generations wanted to have, a sense of the civil conflicts that underlay and gave support to the military struggle. At the same time, they show the common soldier's enduring capacity of alternately sympathizing with or killing his enemy.

As in the case of many "told-to" documents, the narratives slip from voice to voice, frequently launching into a semiofficial depositional style but then abandoning it at the most exciting parts of the tale. In some instances, aged veterans or spouses will avow that very little in the way of sharp detail remains (and sharp detail, of course, would help the applicant prove his or her worth as a pensioner), but once the very act of verbal reconstruction begins details float to the surface as if long lost but now recovered, to the delight and perhaps amazement of the applicants themselves. And, although officially focused on the war, which by the 1820s had assumed a kind of orthodox meaning for Americans (many of the internal opponents, after all, had left the country or been forced out, and British or Canadian opinion on the subject attracted very little credence in American minds), the narratives display an endearing tendency to latch onto seemingly insignificant episodes as if the main reward for the exercise was not public acclaim or public cash but rather the more private delight (or pain) of reviving and reinterpreting the sights and sounds and feelings of long-ago youth. When Sarah Osborn tells of her faithless husband, whom she followed around the fields of war for many months only to have him run off and commit bigamy with another woman (a woman, however, who she delights in telling us later "died dead drunk, the liquor running out of her mouth after she was dead"), she is using the occasion of a public statement to explore her personal memories, tying up, as it were, the loose ends of her experience. Or when John McCasland recalls how he and a small party of other soldiers surrounded a farmhouse in Pennsylvania, then under the control of a group of Hessian mercenaries, we find a narrative less obviously "patriotic" than we might expect. When McCasland and his fellows saw a Hessian standing guard out front, they did not relish the task of shooting him, but rather drew straws to determine which of their party had to attempt it. McCasland, an excellent shot, got the fateful straw; as he took aim on the German he intended only to wound him in the flesh of his thigh, but the shot went awry and unfortunately did far more damage. This touching account of human vulnerability and shared pain is fittingly accompanied by McCasland's memory that the one of the other Hessians soon came out of the cellar of the surrounded house, bearing aloft a "large bottle of rum . . . as a flag of truce." Although McCasland does not say so, we may assume that the now-single party, with the twelve Hessians as prisoners, proceeded to down the "flag" in common.

The six narratives printed here come from a variety of regions, viewpoints, and moments in the war. There is the tale of Sylvanus Wood, a Massachusetts shoemaker who fought at Lexington on April 19; the New Jerseyan William

Lloyd's narrative of his six years of militia service, with its mention of how, exhausted during a forced march, he slipped out of the ranks one night and slept on the porch of a house the men passed, only to catch up later; and the account of McCasland, who had moved from Pennsylvania to Kentucky even before the war was over, and had seen service there and across the Ohio River with General George Rogers Clark against the hapless Shawnee. Then there is the moving application of Rhode Islander Jehu Grant, an African American slave who escaped from his Tory master in order to serve the American cause ("When I saw liberty poles and the people all engaged for the support of freedom," he remarked in a later letter, "I could not but like and be pleased with such thing[s]"); Grant's application brought no pension, only the ruling from a Washington dominated by southern interests that as he was a fugitive slave at the time of his service he was not eligible. There are also the applications of long-lived New Yorker Sarah Osborn, a remarkable woman who had an acute memory and whose perspective as a camp follower during the war is invaluable (and who claimed in an article about her in a phrenological journal in 1854 that she was 109 years old, when she probably was only 98!); and, finally, of John Suddarth, a Virginian who tells a memorable story of how he watched George Washington stand for a quarter-hour on the ramparts trying to puzzle out what the enemy was doing at Yorktown as the ground all around him was peppered with British bullets and his aides furiously tried to bring him back into the safety of the trench. Washington in fact appears in a number of these narratives, which thus reveal some of the oral basis for the man's continuing fame long after his immersion in party politics in the 1790s.

SYLVANUS WOOD (1830)

WHOEVER THESE LINES COME BEFORE MAY DEPEND UPON [THE] FACTS THAT I, Sylvanus Wood, was born in Woburn, but in that part now called Burlington, Middlesex County, Massachusetts, twelve miles from Boston, and there I learned to make boots and shoes. There I joined a minute company, disciplined with activity by a man who was in the fight on Abrahams Plains with the brave General Wolfe, and in fifteen months hostilities commenced. I was then established at my trade two miles east of Lexington meetinghouse, on west border of Woburn, and on the nineteenth morn of April, 1775, Robert Douglass and myself heard Lexington bell about one hour before day. We concluded that trouble was near.

We waited for no man but hastened and joined Captain Parker's company[1] at the breaking of the day. Douglass and myself stood together in the center of said company when the enemy first fired. The English soon were on their

---

[1] Captain John Parker, then forty-six, was a farmer and mechanic and the elected leader of Lexington's militia. He was a veteran of Wolfe's campaign against Quebec as well as the conquest of Louisbourg, and may have been one of Robert Rogers's "Rangers."

march for Concord. I helped carry six dead into the meetinghouse and then set out after the enemy and had not an armed man to go with me, but before I arrived at Concord I see one of the grenadiers standing sentinel. I cocked my piece and run up to him, seized his gun with my left hand. He surrendered his armor,[2] one gun and bayonet, a large cutlass and brass fender, one box over the shoulder with twenty-two rounds, one box round the waist with eighteen rounds. This was the first prisoner that was known to be taken that day.

I followed the enemy to Concord and to Bunker Hill that day.[3] Next morning I agreed to stay the first campaign and served as sergeant, and when my first term was expired Col. Loammi Baldwin of the same town of myself gave me an ensign's commission for 1776 and marched to New York, when General Sullivan [and] General Lord Stirling were made prisoners. I was in the reinforcement on Long Island when we evacuated the island. General McDougall commanded the flotilla when we left the island of New York. The baggage was carried to the North River,[4] with an officer and ten privates to guard the chests, but a British ship came up the river and cut off ours, and all was lost. The next day we crossed the river and went over to Fort Lee. Soon after, we crossed back and landed above Kingsbridge. We marched on and came to a place called Frog's Point. There we had a small brush with the enemy. I received a ball through my left shoulder, Colonel Shepard through his double chin. Our wounds were dressed at Dr. Graham's, White Plains.

My wound soon got well, and at the end of 1776 campaign, Colonel Baldwin leaving the army, Colonel Wesson took the command, and he placed me as first lieutenant in Capt. John Wood's company during the war. I told the colonel I would stay with all my heart if I was not overpowered at home, and when four months was elapsed I saw my parents and offered them all I was worth if they would be willing I should stay in the army. But no offer whatever would answer. I then concluded to leave the army, but with great reluctance.

Colonel Wesson asked me what I was agoing to do. I told him I did not know what to set myself about, but, having a chance to make shoes for the army, I bought leather, hired journeymen, made shoes, and delivered them for the soldiers. And after some time was elapsed I took my money, and it would not purchase my stock, so I lost my time for 1777. After this, it came into my mind to purchase a small farm about forty acres, and my custom was to make a pair of plow-joggars[5] in the forenoon and work on the farm in the afternoon, so that I got no time to go ahawking. And about thirty years ago, I becoming acquainted with the Honorable Abraham Bigelow Clarke of Middlesex County courts, he offered me a farm in the town of Woburn, 5,333 dollars purchase, about twenty-six years ago. I labored nights as well as days and have paid for the same.

---

[2] I.e., his armaments.

[3] What Wood means by the last phrase here is not clear; the Battle of Bunker Hill, of course, took place two months later, on June 17, 1775.

[4] Hudson River.

[5] Usually, a plowman, but here apparently referring to a kind of shoe or boot worn by plowmen.

It is true but my lifting logs of wood, barrels of cider, has caused a breach of body[6] which all physicians on earth cannot make whole. This infirmity I have been troubled with about fifteen years, and now I am not able to do anything by reason of the breach. I am past seventy-six years of age.

I sent an application with my commission eight or nine years ago to Congress. I am worth nothing but what has been drawn from my fingers' ends.[7] If I am favored ever with anything for service done in the army, I need it now as well as my fellow soldiers who have done no more than I have. I think I have been neglected. If I have said anything wrong, I will seal my lips and say no more, but I am willing to publish this to the United States.

WILLIAM LLOYD (1832)

[DEPONENT ASSERTS] THAT HE ENTERED THE SERVICE OF THE UNITED STATES as a militiamen in Upper Freehold in the month of July or August, 1776, according to the best of his recollection under some of the following officers (but which of them I have forgotten, but remember that the service was performed in the township of Freehold). I think at this time the regiment of Upper Freehold militia where I lived then consisted, in that part, of Col. Samuel Forman, Elisha Lawrence, Maj. William Montgomery, Gesbert Guisebertson, Joseph Copperthwaite, Nathaniel Polhemus, Peter Wikoff, John Coward; Capts. James Brewer, William Perrine, Gilbert Longstreet, Jonathan Pitman; lieutenants and inferior officers I cannot name with certainty; neither am I sure that I am correct in naming the others, there were so many changes took place shortly after the first organization of the militia in the year 1775, and continued to change till the end of the war.

I recollect serving monthly tours in particular places in Middletown and Shrewsbury for several months under Capt. Nathaniel Polhemus, Capt. William Montgomery, Capt. Joseph Copperthwaite, Capt. Jonathan Pitman, but [it was] in Freehold, Monmouth Courthouse, where a constant guard was kept and much the greater part of my services were performed. I cannot distinctly remember the company officers I served under except Capt. David Baird and Lieutenant Longstreet. The field officers I served under I believe were Maj. Thomas Seabrooks at Middletown and Col. Samuel Forman and Col. Auke Wikoff in the early part of the war, but after the winter of 1777 I think Gen. David Forman commanded the militia in Freehold until the termination of the war. He had also under his command at the same place three or four companies of enlisted men; the names of the captains were John Burrows, William Wikoff, and one other, from Maryland as I understood, his name not remembered; also Captain Huddy, who had a small company of artillery, but whether they were enlisted or not is to deponent unknown.

---

[6] A hernia.
[7] That is, all he owns has been won by the labor of his hands.

Deponent knew of the Continental officers of the Jersey line: General Maxwell, Maj. David Rhea, Capts. William Barton, Ten Broeck Stout, and Moses Sprawls, subalterns. Knew several of the officers in the Congress regiment commanded by Col. Moses Hazen, namely Lieutenant Colonel Antill, Major Reed, Captains Munson, Saterly, Duncan, Lt. William Hurst, and others. Capt. Richard Lloyd of the same regiment was my brother. He entered as such at the organization of the regiment and continued in it during the continuance of the war, and after peace he was appointed agent of the regiment to settle with Pierce, paymaster general, and received the dues of the regiment in certificates and continued I believe a year or nearly before he accomplished that service. Deponent is his representative, as eldest brother, in the Cincinnati Society[8] of New Jersey. He has been dead many years.

From the time the British army appeared off Sandy Hook in June 1776, or thereabouts, I believe the Monmouth militia were called out, one-half monthly to the end of the war, and on this point reference may be had to the corroborating testimony of the many applicants of the Monmouth militia for pensions. From the time of my first entrance in the service, I continued to serve, in monthly alternations, to the end of the war when called upon (with the exception of the year 1778, being exempted that year on account of other employments, I went out on special and emergency cases).

Besides, I very frequently turned out when not on monthly service on special occasions when the enemy were committing depredations in places not sufficiently protected on the shores in the county and once marched sixty miles to Egg Harbor in Burlington County under Maj. Elisha Lawrence and oftentimes after refugees[9] that secreted themselves in the adjacent pines in the daytime and would come out at night to steal horses (and take them to the British by the way of Sandy Hook) and rob the houses of the inhabitants of the neighborhood where I lived. And in one instance they broke in the house of one of my near neighbors and killed the man and his wife and wounded another of the family. I was generally called upon and went out on all such occasions, both night and day, and at all seasons. I was once called upon by Captain Nixon of the Brunswick light horse to go with him in pursuit of refugees in the pines. Traveled night and day through a deep snow and piercing winter's cold. We took several prisoners, and he took them to General Putnam, then at Princeton, in compliance of the instructions given from the War Department.

I will state a few out of many dangers I encountered. In June 1778, on hearing that the British army had crossed the Delaware from Philadelphia and were approaching towards Monmouth, I went as a volunteer to General Maxwell's headquarters, then at Crosswicks. The British were then at the Black Horse, better than twenty miles from Philadelphia. Their van,[1] two or three

---

[8]The Society of the Cincinnati, founded in 1783 by officers of the American army and named after the Roman dictator and patriot Cincinnatus, was intended to be a fraternal patriotic organization, but it was viewed with suspicion by those who thought it had a political agenda.
[9]The "refugees" were irregular Loyalist partisans.
[1]I.e., vanguard.

miles in advance, were posted on a high ground at the house of one Curtis near the highway. I went the same day with about one hundred footmen and perhaps twenty militia horsemen under the command of Maj. David Rhea of the Jersey line to reconnoiter the enemy. When we had approached within about a mile of the enemy, he halted the foot, and the horsemen advanced further, but did not go far when they all fell back, except one horseman and myself went near to them, and, seeing a gap in the fence upon our right, we turned through it, descended two or three hundred yards over a rough piece of ground to a tree that stood in a field within gunshot of the enemy and in open view to them. My companion dismounted whilst I held his bridle and rested his gun against the tree and fired at them. He then mounted his horse, held mine by the bridle while I did the same. He then gave me my bridle, rode off in haste, and left me alone. A troop of British light horse were then advancing in full speed towards the gap through which I had to pass. My situation at this crisis seemed inauspicious. I had a hill to rise, and the ground uneven, having been ridged with a plough, I on my feet, and the enemy not having much further to go than I had to make the gap. I might have taken a different way, but, being a stranger to the ground and not knowing what obstructions would be in my way, I thought it best to make an effort for the gap. I mounted my horse, and the first jump he made, my saddle girth broke. I instantly seized hold of the horse's mane and held the gun and bridle with one hand and with the other reached back and took hold of the saddle, which I could not release from the horse for he held the crupper with his tail. I then slipped on the horse's bare back, put my horse to his full speed, and hopped through the gap twenty or thirty yards before them. They pursued no further. Had I fallen off when the girth broke, I should probably [have] been killed by them, or had they pursued my chance would have been little better, for my horse being pushed so hard up the hill had put him very much out of wind. A soldier that was taken prisoner told me a few days after that one of the shots we had made came very near to General Clinton.[2]

General Maxwell gave me a letter to take to Colonel Nelson of the Middlesex militia of Allentown, and after my departure the British drove him out [of] the village of Crosswicks over the bridge. They then proceeded to Allentown, west about two miles further, and encamped. I then met with Colonel Morgan and his rifle company. He drove a party of the enemy out of Allentown. I pursued after [and] came near a light horseman. He advanced towards me. I fired at him. He ran and was too near their main body to pursue him.

A day or two after this, being with Colonel Morgan on his march near the pines, about a mile south of the route the British took, I rode in company with a militia horseman about a mile distant from Colonel Morgan. Met with two horsemen of the enemy armed. I supposed them to be refugees. They saw us first, turned out in the woods, and I did not discover them until I heard the

---

[2] General Sir Henry Clinton (1730–1795) was commander in chief of British forces in North America after 1778.

rustling of the leaves made by their horses. I called upon my companion in arms to pursue them with me. He refused. It was my lot again to act alone. I pursued them myself a considerable distance, came within about sixty or seventy yards of them, checked my horse in order to fire at them, but before I could be ready they took themselves behind the trees and escaped. I searched about the woods some time but could not find them.

The next morning I heard firing of cannon and small arms at Freehold. I rode immediately that way, came on the battleground, [and] was near the center of our troops that were engaged. The balls flew thick around me. I was there when the enemy advanced with charged bayonets and Colonel Monckton, their commander, was killed. I saw him as he lay lifeless on the ground. The enemy then retreated precipitately, throwing away many of their guns. I was, I believe, the foremost in following, got as many of their guns as I could conveniently manage on my horse, with their bayonets fixed upon them. Gave them to the soldiers as they stood in rank. They threw away their French pieces, preferring the British. I remember at the time one of the officers gave me his canteen of grog to take a drink. It was the most delicious to my taste of any I ever drank. I was thirsty, the day extremely hot, and no water to be got handy but warm brook water.

At another time, when on monthly duty at Freehold, the militia I believe were generally called to General Washington's headquarters on Steel's Mountain. The British army, or part of them, had marched out of Brunswick to Somerset Courthouse. I went with the militia, then on duty I believe under the command of Lt. Gilbert Longstreet. He was the only officer that I can remember with us from Upper Freehold. We marched by the way of Princeton to Sowerland Mountain. Met with General Sullivan and his command there. About sundown he ordered a fire to be made upon the mountain, and as an answering one, I supposed, appeared on Steel's Mountain, we were ordered to march. We continued marching all night (excepting a little before day, being very tired, I slipped out of my place by a house, with one or two more lay under the piazza, and went on early in the morning). I believe the others reached the mountain before they halted. About the second day after we arrived at headquarters, the British commenced a retreat from the aforesaid courthouse. I saw General Washington view them striking their tents, and by his permission I looked at them through his spyglass, and I heard him say that if he had some men near them, their baggage might be taken from them.

The next morning I volunteered to go with a larger party of militia and I believe some regulars towards Woodbridge on the left flank of the British army as they were then on their retreat from Brunswick and on their way to Amboy. We continued our march until we came opposite to the rear of the enemy within about a mile of them. They were posted on a hill said to be called Strawberry Hill (not far from Woodbridge or Amboy I believe) behind a piece [of] woods thinly timbered. The main body halted (I mean of our men), and I volunteered again with about two hundred men to make nearer recog[nizance] of the enemy, and when we came to the woods within about three hundred yards of them, as near as I can calculate the distance, they opened their fire upon us with two fieldpieces. The first shot cut the bayonet off of one of the men's gun. We marched under their fire directly towards them, but before we got out of the woods they made a hasty retreat. The officers that commanded us, who were said to be Virginia officers, estimated the number of the British to be about a thousand men and said that if they had known our small number, they would have taken us all prisoners. I suffered much fatigue, hunger, as well as danger. I had but one meal of victuals for two or three days, and that was with Captain Lloyd, my brother, on Steel's Mountain. My fare was small apples not larger than a hickory nut.

Those services that I have previously stated to have performed under the several officers named in Middletown and Shrewsbury were accompanied by particular circumstances that gave them a more definitive and lasting impression. At one time the Negro refugees[3] fired upon a sentinel, and we pursued after them near to a place called Jumping Point on Shrewsbury. Went into the river with one of the men. He got tired a considerable distance from the land and could swim no further. I swam to him, suffered him to take me by the hips, and swam to the shore with, and saved his life.

At another [time] of service, pursuing some refugees in company of three other militiamen, I, being foremost in the pursuit, was fired at by one of them from behind a tree a short distance off and at Shark River; another time of service, recollect being stationed on monthly service at Tinton Falls by the circumstance of diverting ourselves by riding horses in the millpond there and sliding off of them and taking them by the tails, and they would draw us after them. And at the time at Shark River, we dug the inlet through the beach that had been stopped up for some time in order to let the salt water into the river to make the oysters better. I recollect being quartered two months while on duty at a particular private house and near the courthouse and at another time at another private house, same village, and served another month as a light horseman at a private house near a mile from the courthouse and under the immediate command of General Forman. During that month I was sent with three or four others to Egg Harbor for a particular purpose and was once sent express with a letter to General Washington at his headquarters near Chatham in Morris County. My other service was principally performed at the courthouse, where General Forman kept his headquarters; I mean he kept his headquarters at a house near the courthouse and the militia quartered in taverns in part and in private houses.

[3] Lloyd may be referring here to the operations of the African American Loyalist named Tye, veteran of the famous Ethiopian Regiment of Virginia, in Monmouth County, New Jersey, in June 1780.

JOHN McCASLAND (1832)

[DEPONENT AFFIRMS] THAT HE WAS BORN ON THE FIRST DAY OF JUNE IN THE year 1750 in Cumberland County, in the state of Pennsylvania, and entered the service of the United States sometime in the month of August, 1776, in Captain Thomas Campbell's company of volunteers of the Seventh Regiment Pennsylvania militia (as he believes) commanded by Colonel Brown. That he was a volunteer, and after the company was made up, the officers were elected, and that he was elected an ensign.

That the company was made up in Cumberland County, Pennsylvania, and marched to Philadelphia and then went by water to Trenton, and from Trenton they marched to Perth Amboy, and while at Amboy the British lay on Staten Island. And there was occasional cannonading, but the distance was so far that no damage was done, after which time two British men-of-war went up the North River by breaking a chevaux-de-frise[4] which had been stretched across the river to prevent their passing up the North River. Said vessels were said to be laden with provisions and munitions of war. And from Perth Amboy, [we] went to Long Island under the command of General Putnam. We found troops on Long Island (American troops), and soon after our arrival an engagement took place with the British, who I think were commanded by General Howe. We were defeated with a considerable number killed and a number taken prisoners, and among the number taken prisoners by the British was Captain Campbell. We then marched to Philadelphia, were paid off and discharged, and allowed a penny a mile to take us home. We then returned home the same route we went. I do not recollect the time we were absent, but we volunteered for three months. This deponent states that he got a discharge in Philadelphia which was signed by his lieutenant, Samuel McHatton, and Colonel Brown.

This deponent states that the next tour he served was in January 1778, when he was drafted in Cumberland County, Pennsylvania, in Captain Joseph Culbertson's company of the regiment commanded by Colonel Samuel Culbertson and was an orderly sergeant in said company. That the company marched to Valley Forge, where General Washington had his headquarters. That this was the first and last time he ever saw General Washington. That he was under the command of General Lacey, who commanded the militia. The British lay in Philadelphia this winter, and the American troops lay at Valley Forge. We had no fighting, but we had to scour the country to prevent the Hessians from plundering and destroying property, who generally [went] out in small gangs. And at different times we took Hessians prisoners and delivered them to General Washington at Valley Forge.

And on one occasion, sixteen of us were ranging about hunting Hessians, and we suspected Hessians to be at a large and handsome mansion house in

---

[4]A spiked barrier usually employed against footsoldiers or cavalry.

Bucks County, Pennsylvania, about sixteen miles from Philadelphia. We approached near the house and discovered a large Hessian standing in the yard with his gun, as a sentinel we supposed, and by a unanimous vote of the company present it was agreed on that Major McCorman or myself, who were good marksmen, should shoot him (McCorman was then a private). We cast lots, and it fell to my lot to shoot the Hessian. I did not like to shoot a man down in cold blood. The company present knew I was a good marksman, and I concluded to break his thigh. I shot with a rifle and aimed at his hip. He had a large iron tobacco box in his breeches pocket, and I hit the box, the ball glanced, and it entered his thigh and scaled the bone of the thigh on the outside. He fell and then rose. We scaled the yard fence and surrounded the house. They saw their situation and were evidently disposed to surrender. They could not speak English, and we could not understand their language. At length one of the Hessians came out of the cellar with a large bottle of rum and advanced with it at arm's length as a flag of truce. The family had abandoned the house, and the Hessians had possession. They were twelve in number. We took them prisoners and carried them to Valley Forge and delivered them up to General Washington. We were drafted for two months on the twenty-second of January and was discharged about the twenty-second of March at Valley Forge, and from Valley Forge we marched home the same route we came, and I got a discharge at Valley Forge.

In April 1780 I moved from Cumberland County, Pennsylvania, to the neighborhood of the falls of Ohio in the state of Kentucky and landed at the falls of Ohio, April 16th, 1780. The Indians were very troublesome, and in the afterpart of the summer of 1780 I went out as a volunteer under General Clark[5] as a private against the Shawnee Indians and marched up the Ohio River on the southern side and crossed it at the mouth of the Miami River, thence to Chillicothe, and at Chillicothe we had an engagement with the Indians. We defeated and routed them, cut their corn down, and burnt their houses and then returned home the same route after an absence of about six weeks. I went out under Captain McClure and was paid by the United States at the falls of the Ohio and was discharged there. That no discharges were given to the volunteers.

This deponent further states that he went out another tour of duty, in 1782, against the Shawnee Indians as a private and as a volunteer under the command of General Clark in Captain Jacob Vanmeter's company. Crossed the Ohio River at the mouth of Licking River, built a blockhouse where Cincinnati now stands, and left fifteen or twenty invalids at the blockhouse to take care of such military stores as we could not take with us. We proceeded up the Miami River to the Shawnee towns, five days' march. The Indians discovered us about two miles from the towns and made their escape. We burnt their corn, which was gathered, and burnt as many as seven little towns, took five Indians (women

---

[5] General George Rogers Clark (1752–1818) was the most prominent American figure in the West during the Revolution.

and children) prisoners, and killed five or six warriors who were scouting about. We then returned home the same route after an absence of something less than two months to the falls of the Ohio, where we were paid off. And I am of the opinion that none of us got a discharge.

JEHU GRANT (1832, 1836)

[DEPONENT AFFIRMS] THAT HE WAS A SLAVE TO ELIHU CHAMPLEN WHO RESIDED at Narragansett, Rhode Island. At the time he left him his said master was called a Tory and in a secret manner furnished the enemy when shipping lay nearby with sheep, cattle, cheese, etc., and received goods from them. And this applicant being afraid his said master would send him to the British ships, ran away sometime in August 1777, as near as he can recollect, being the same summer that Danbury was burnt. That he went right to Danbury after he left his said master and enlisted to Captain Giles Galer for eighteen months. That, according to the best of his memory, General Huntington and General Meigs's brigades, or a part of them, were at that place. That he, this applicant, was put to teaming with a team of horses and wagon, drawing provisions and various other loading for the army for three or four months until winter set in, then was taken as a servant to John Skidmore, wagon master general (as he was called), and served with him as his waiter until spring, when the said troops went to the Highlands or near that place on the Hudson River, a little above the British lines. That this applicant had charge of the team as wagoner and carried the said General Skidmore's baggage and continued with him and the said troops as his wagoner near the said lines until sometime in June, when his said master either sent or came, and this applicant was given up to his master again, and he returned, after having served nine or ten months.

(1832)

Hon. J. L. Edwards, Commissioner of Pensions:
Your servant
begs leave to state that he forwarded to the War Department a declaration founded on the Pension Act of June 1832 praying to be allowed a pension (if his memory serves him) for ten months' service in the American army of the Revolutionary War. That he enlisted as a soldier but was put to the service of a teamster in the summer and a waiter in the winter. In April 1834 I received a writing from Your Honor, informing me that my "services while a fugitive from my master's service was not embraced in said Act," and that my "papers were placed on file." In my said declaration, I just mentioned the cause of leaving my master, as may be seen by a reference thereunto, and I now pray that I may be permitted to express my feelings more fully on that part of my said declaration.

I was then grown to manhood, in the full vigor and strength of life, and heard much about the cruel and arbitrary things done by the British. Their ships lay within a few miles of my master's house, which stood near the shore, and I was confident that my master traded with them, and I suffered much from fear that I should be sent aboard a ship of war. This I disliked. But when I saw liberty poles and the people all engaged for the support of freedom, I could not but like and be pleased with such thing (God forgive me if I sinned in so feeling). And living on the borders of Rhode Island, where whole companies of colored people enlisted, it added to my fears and dread of being sold to the British. These considerations induced me to enlist into the American army, where I served faithful about ten months, when my master found and took me home. Had I been taught to read or understand the precepts of the gospel, "Servants obey your masters," I might have done otherwise, notwithstanding the songs of liberty that saluted my ear, thrilled through my heart. But feeling conscious that I have since compensated my master for the injury he sustained by my enlisting, and that God has forgiven me for so doing, and that I served my country faithfully, and that they having enjoyed the benefits of my service to an equal degree for the length [of] time I served with those generally who are receiving the liberalities of the government, I cannot but feel it becoming me to pray Your Honor to review my declaration on file and the papers herewith amended.

A few years after the war, Joshua Swan, Esq., of Stonington purchased me of my master and agreed that after I had served him a length of time named faithfully, I should be free. I served to his satisfaction and so obtained my freedom. He moved into the town of Milton, where I now reside, about forty-eight years ago. After my time expired with Esq. Swan, I married a wife. We have raised six children. Five are still living. I must be upward of eighty years of age and have been blind for many years, and, notwithstanding the aid I received from the honest industry of my children, we are still very needy and in part are supported from the benevolence of our friends. With these statements and the testimony of my character herewith presented, I humbly set my claim upon the well-known liberality of government.

SARAH OSBORN (1837)

ON THIS TWENTIETH DAY OF NOVEMBER, A.D. 1837, PERSONALLY APPEARED before the Court of Common Pleas of said county of Wayne, Sarah Benjamin, a resident of Pleasant Mount in said county of Wayne, and state of Pennsylvania, aged eighty-one years on the seventeenth day of the present month, who being first duly sworn according to law, doth on her oath make the following declaration in order to obtain the benefit of the provision made by the act of Congress passed July 4, 1836, and the act explanatory of said act, passed March 3, 1837.

That she was married to Aaron Osborn, who was a soldier during the Revolutionary War. That her first acquaintance with said Osborn commenced in Albany, in the state of New York, during the hard winter of 1780. That deponent then resided at the house of one John Willis, a blacksmith in said city. That said Osborn came down there from Fort Stanwix and went to work at the business of blacksmithing for said Willis and continued working at intervals for a period of perhaps two months. Said Osborn then informed deponent that he had first enlisted at Goshen in Orange County, New York. That he had been in the service for three years, deponent thinks, about one year of that time at Fort Stanwix, and that his time was out. And, under an assurance that he would go to Goshen with her, she married him at the house of said Willis during the time he was there as above mentioned, to wit, in January 1780. That deponent was informed by said Osborn that while he was at Fort Stanwix he served under Captain James Gregg and Colonel Van Schaick, the former of whom she was informed by said Osborn was scalped by the Indians near Fort Stanwix while he was on an excursion pigeon hunting, which in the sequel proved to be true, as she will show hereafter.

That after deponent had married said Osborn, he informed her that he was returned during the war, and that he desired deponent to go with him. Deponent declined until she was informed by Captain Gregg that her husband should be put on the commissary guard, and that she should have the means of conveyance either in a wagon or on horseback. That deponent then in the same winter season in sleighs accompanied her husband and the forces under command of Captain Gregg on the east side of the Hudson River to Fishkill, then crossed the river and went down to West Point. There [they] remained till the river opened in the spring, when they returned to Albany. Captain Gregg's company was along, and she thinks Captain Parsons, Lieutenant Forman, and Colonel Van Schaick, but is not positive.

Deponent, accompanied by her said husband and the same forces, returned during the same season to West Point. Deponent recollects no other females in company but the wife of Lieutenant Forman and of Sergeant Lamberson. Deponent was well acquainted with Captain Gregg and repeatedly saw the bare spot on his head where he had been scalped by the Indians. Captain Gregg had turns of being shattered[6] in his mind and at such times would frequently say to deponent, "Sarah, did you ever see where I was scalped?" showing his head at the same time. Captain Gregg informed deponent also of the circumstances of his being scalped: that he and two more went out pigeon hunting and were surprised by the Indians, and that the two men that were with him were killed dead, but that he escaped by reason of the tomahawk glancing on the button of his hat; that when he came to his senses, he crept along and laid his [head near] one of the dead men, and while there, his dog came to his relief, and by means of his dog, [he caught the attention of] the two fishermen who were fishing near the fort.

Deponent further says that she and her husband remained at West Point till the departure of the army for the South, a term of perhaps one year and a half, but she cannot be positive as to the length of time. While at West Point,

[6] Scattered.

deponent lived at Lieutenant Foot's, who kept a boardinghouse. Deponent was employed in washing and sewing for the soldiers. Her said husband was employed about the camp. She well recollects the uproar occasioned when word came that a British officer had been taken as a spy.[7] She understood at the time that Major André was brought up on the opposite side of the river and kept there till he was executed. On the return of the bargemen who assisted Arnold to escape, deponent recollects seeing two of them, one by the name of Montecu, the other by the name of Clark. That they said Arnold told them to hang up their dinners, for he had to be at Stony Point in so many minutes, and when he got there he hoisted his pocket handkerchief and his sword and said, "Row on boys," and that they soon arrived in Haverstraw Bay and found the British ship. That Arnold jumped on board, and they were all invited, and they went aboard and had their choice to go or stay. And some chose to stay and some to go and did accordingly.

When the army were about to leave West Point and go south, they crossed over the river to Robinson's Farms and remained there for a length of time to induce the belief, as deponent understood, that they were going to take up quarters there, whereas they recrossed the river in the nighttime into the Jerseys and traveled all night in a direct course for Philadelphia. Deponent was part of the time on horseback and part of the time in a wagon. Deponent's said husband was still serving as one of the commissary's guard. A man by the name of Burke was hung about this time for alleged treason, but more especially for insulting Adjutant Wendell, the prosecutor against Burke, as deponent understood and believed at the time. There was so much opposition to the execution of Burke that it was deferred some time, and he was finally executed in a different place from what was originally intended.

In their march for Philadelphia, they were under command of Generals Washington and Clinton, Colonel Van Schaick, Captain Gregg, Captain Parsons, Lieutenant Forman, Sergeant Lamberson, Ensign Clinton, one of the general's sons. They continued their march to Philadelphia, deponent on horseback through the streets, and arrived at a place towards the Schuylkill where the British had burnt some houses, where they encamped for the afternoon and night. Being out of bread, deponent was employed in baking the afternoon and evening. Deponent recollects no females but Sergeant Lamberson's and Lieutenant Forman's wives and a colored woman by the name of Letta. The Quaker ladies who came round urged deponent to stay, but her said husband said, "No, he could not leave her behind." Accordingly, next day they continued their march from day to day till they arrived at Baltimore, where deponent and her said husband and the forces under command of General Clinton, Captain Gregg, and several other officers, all of whom she does not recollect, embarked on board a vessel and sailed down the Chesapeake. There were several vessels along, and deponent was in the foremost. General Washington was not in the

---

[7] Major John André (1751–1780) was captured on September 23, 1780 when returning from his secret meeting with Benedict Arnold at West Point and was hanged on October 2.

vessel with deponent, and she does not know where he was till he arrived at Yorktown, where she again saw him. He might have embarked at another place, but deponent is confident she embarked at Baltimore and that General Clinton was in the same vessel with her. Some of the troops went down by land. They continued [to] sail until they had got up the James River as far as the tide would carry them, about twelve miles from the mouth, and then landed, and the tide being spent, they had a fine time catching sea lobsters, which they ate.

They, however, marched immediately for a place called Williamsburg, as she thinks, deponent alternately on horseback and on foot. There arrived, they remained two days till the army all came in by land and then marched for Yorktown, or Little York as it was then called. The York troops were posted at the right, the Connecticut troops next, and the French to the left. In about one day or less than a day, they reached the place of encampment about one mile from Yorktown. Deponent was on foot and the other females above named and her said husband still on the commissary's guard. Deponent's attention was arrested by the appearance of a large plain between them and Yorktown and an entrenchment thrown up. She also saw a number of dead Negroes lying round their encampment, whom she understood the British had driven out of the town and left to starve, or were first starved and then thrown out.[8] Deponent took her stand just back of the American tents, say about a mile from the town, and busied herself washing, mending, and cooking for the soldiers, in which she was assisted by the other females; some men washed their own clothing. She heard the roar of the artillery for a number of days, and the last night the Americans threw up entrenchments, it was a misty, foggy night, rather wet but not rainy. Every soldier threw up for himself, as she understood, and she afterwards saw and went into the entrenchments. Deponent's said husband was there throwing up entrenchments, and deponent cooked and carried in beef, and bread, and coffee (in a gallon pot) to the soldiers in the entrenchment.

On one occasion when deponent was thus employed carrying in provisions, she met General Washington, who asked her if she "was not afraid of the cannonballs?"

She replied, "No, the bullets would not cheat the gallows," that "It would not do for the men to fight and starve too."

They dug entrenchments nearer and nearer to Yorktown every night or two till the last. While digging that, the enemy fired very heavy till about nine o'clock next morning, then stopped, and the drums from the enemy beat excessively. Deponent was a little way off in Colonel Van Schaick's or the officers' marquee and a number of officers were present, among whom was Captain Gregg, who, on account of infirmities, did not go out much to do duty.

The drums continued beating, and all at once the officers hurrahed and swung their hats, and deponent asked them, "What is the matter now?"

One of them replied, "Are not you soldier enough to know what it means?"

---

[8] As with most of Osborn's narratives, other sources corroborate this dreadful tale, although they suggest that the African Americans were forced out of the British camp due to short rations and then died when they were caught between the armies.

Deponent replied, "No."

They then replied, "The British have surrendered."

Deponent, having provisions ready, carried the same down to the entrenchments that morning, and four of the soldiers whom she was in the habit of cooking for ate their breakfasts.

Deponent stood on one side of the road and the American officers upon the other side when the British officers came out of the town and rode up to the American officers and delivered up [their swords, which the deponent] thinks were returned again, and the British officers rode right on before the army, who marched out beating and playing a melancholy tune,[9] their drums covered with black handkerchiefs and their fifes with black ribbands tied around them, into an old field and there grounded their arms and then returned into town again to await their destiny. Deponent recollects seeing a great many American officers, some on horseback and some on foot, but cannot call them all by name. Washington, Lafayette, and Clinton were among the number. The British general at the head of the army was a large, portly man, full face, and the tears rolled down his cheeks as he passed along. She does not recollect his name, but it was not Cornwallis.[1] She saw the latter afterwards and noticed his being a man of diminutive appearance and having cross-eyes.

On going into town, she noticed two dead Negroes lying by the market house. She had the curiosity to go into a large building that stood nearby, and there she noticed the cupboards smashed to pieces and china dishes and other ware strewn around upon the floor, and among the rest a pewter cover to a hot basin that had a handle on it. She picked it up, supposing it to belong to the British, but the governor came in and claimed it as his, but said he would have the name of giving it away as it was the last one out of twelve that he could see, and accordingly presented it to deponent, and she afterwards brought it home with her to Orange County and sold it for old pewter, which she has a hundred times regretted.

After two or three days, deponent and her husband, Captain Gregg, and others who were sick or complaining embarked on board a vessel from York-town, not the same they came down in, and set sail up the Chesapeake Bay and continued to the Head of Elk, where they landed. The main body of the army remained behind but came on soon afterwards. Deponent and her husband proceeded with the commissary's teams from the Head of Elk, leaving Philadelphia to the right, and continued day after day till they arrived at Pompton Plains in New Jersey. Deponent does not recollect the county. They were joined by the main body of the army under General Clinton's command, and they set down for winter quarters. Deponent and her husband lived a part of the time in a tent made of logs but covered with cloth, and a part of the time at a Mr. Manuel's near Pompton Meetinghouse. She busied herself during the winter in cooking and sewing as usual. Her said husband was on duty among

[9] It was "The World Turned Upside Down."

[1] Osborn is correct: Cornwallis, complaining of bad health, sent General Charles O'Hara to surrender his sword for him.

the rest of the army and held the station of corporal from the time he left West Point.

In the opening of spring, they marched to West Point and remained there during the summer, her husband still with her. In the fall they came up a little back of Newburgh to a place called New Windsor and put up huts on Ellis's lands and again sat down for winter quarters, her said husband still along and on duty. The York troops and Connecticut troops were there. In the following spring or autumn they were all discharged. Deponent and her husband remained in New Windsor in a log house built by the army until the spring following. Some of the soldiers boarded at their house and worked round among the farmers, as did her said husband also.

Deponent and her husband spent certainly more than three years in the service, for she recollects a part of one winter at West Point and the whole of another winter there, another winter at Pompton Plains, and another at New Windsor. And her husband was the whole time under the command of Captain Gregg as an enlisted soldier holding the station of corporal to the best of her knowledge.

In the winter before the army were disbanded at New Windsor, on the twentieth of February, deponent had a child by the name of Phebe Osborn, of whom the said Aaron Osborn was the father. A year and five months afterwards, on the ninth day of August at the same place, she had another child by the name of Aaron Osborn, Jr., of whom the said husband was the father. The said Phebe Osborn afterwards married a man by the name of William Rockwell and moved into the town of Dryden, Tompkins County, New York, where he died, say ten or twelve years ago, but her said daughter yet lives near the same place on the west side of Ithaca, in the town of Enfield. Her son Aaron Osborn, Jr., lived in Blooming Grove, Orange County, New York, had fits and was crazy, and became a town charge, and finally died there at the age of about thirty years.

About three months after the birth of her last child, Aaron Osborn, Jr., she last saw her said husband, who then left her at New Windsor and never returned. He had been absent at intervals before this from deponent, and at one time deponent understood he was married again to a girl by the name of Polly Sloat above Newburgh about fifteen or sixteen miles. Deponent got a horse and rode up to inquire into the truth of the story. She arrived at the girl's father's and there found her said husband, and Polly Sloat, and her parents. Deponent was kindly treated by the inmates of the house but ascertained for a truth that her husband was married to said girl. After remaining overnight, deponent determined to return home and abandon her said husband forever, as she found he had conducted [himself] in such a way as to leave no hope of reclaiming him. About two weeks afterwards, her said husband came to see deponent in New Windsor and offered to take deponent and her children to the northward, but deponent declined going, under a firm belief that he would conduct no better, and her said husband the same night absconded with two others, crossed the river at Newburgh, and she never saw him afterwards. This was about a year and a half after his discharge. Deponent heard of him afterwards up the Mohawk River and that he had married again. Deponent, after hearing of this second unlawful marriage of her said husband, married herself to John Benjamin of Blooming Grove, Orange County, New York, whose name she now bears.

About twenty years ago, deponent heard that her said husband Osborn died up the Mohawk, and she has no reason to believe to the contrary to this day. Deponent often saw the discharge of her said husband Osborn and understood that he drew a bounty in lands in the lake country beyond Ithaca, but her husband informed her that he sold his discharge and land together in Newburgh to a merchant residing there whose name she cannot recollect. Her son-in-law, said Rockwell, on hearing of the death of Osborn, went out to see the land and returned saying that it was a very handsome lot. But said Rockwell being now dead, she can give no further information concerning it. Deponent was informed more than forty years ago and believes that said Polly Sloat, Osborn's second wife above mentioned, died dead drunk, the liquor running out of her mouth after she was dead. Osborn's third wife she knows nothing about.

After deponent was thus left by Osborn, she removed from New Windsor to Blooming Grove, Orange County, New York, about fifty years ago, where she had been born and brought up, and, having married Mr. Benjamin as above stated, she continued to reside there perhaps thirty-five years, when she and her husband Benjamin removed to Pleasant Mount, Wayne County, Pennsylvania, and there she has resided to this day. Her said husband, John Benjamin, died there ten years ago last April, from which time she has continued to be and is now a widow.

JOHN SUDDARTH (1839)

[DEPONENT ASSERTS] THAT HE VOLUNTEERED IN THE ARMY OF THE UNITED States about the last of June (he recollects it was just before harvest), 1778, as a substitute for his brother James Suddarth under the command and in the company of Captain John Burley or Burleigh and in the regiment of Colonel Bland of the Virginia troops, but he cannot state whether of the state or Continental line. Under the command of these officers he was engaged as a private in guarding the prisoners in the county of Albemarle, about four miles westwardly of Charlottesville, Virginia, which prisoners had been taken by General Gates in the defeat of General Burgoyne. He continued in this service until the last of September (a period of three months), when he was relieved by the return of his brother for whom he had substituted as aforesaid and who had been compelled to leave the service in consequence of sickness. This declarant, at the time of joining the service, resided in the county of Albemarle, Virginia. He recollects that Captain Holman Rice and Captain Garland were in this service at the same time with this declarant, and that Captain Garland was shot by a sentry whilst there.

This declarant again joined the army of the Revolution from said county of Albemarle and state of Virginia about the middle of July, 1781, in the company of Captain Benjamin Harris and joined a portion of the main army at Williamsburg, which to the best of his recollection was under the command of Major Merriweather. He will not say that Merriweather was the highest officer in command there, but from his indistinct recollection, he now seems to him to have been so. From Williamsburg we marched to Travis Point, at the mouth of Queen's Creek into York River, where we remained a few days guarding a number of beeves, etc., belonging to the American army. From thence we were marched down to the main encampment before Yorktown. We were here immediately placed to work in rearing the breastworks around the town. We were put on duty during this time at eight o'clock in the morning and not relieved until the succeeding morning at eight o'clock, only taking time to eat our meals. We then rested the succeeding twenty-four hours and so on till the works were finished. He was present at the taking the two British redoubts, the one stormed by the French and the other by the Americans. He was not a participant in the storm, except so far as that he was drawn out with a large body of other troops to render such aid as might become necessary. Each man of the troops with him had a fascine,[2] and as soon as the redoubts surrendered they were thrown down and the work of circumvallation was recommenced.

Your declarant, during the progress of these works, witnessed a deed of personal daring and coolness in General Washington which he never saw equaled. During a tremendous cannonade from the British in order to demolish our breastworks, a few days prior to the surrender, General Washington visited that part of our fortifications behind which your declarant was posted and, whilst here, discovered that the enemy were destroying their property and drowning their horses, etc. Not, however, entirely assured of what they were doing, he took his glass and mounted the highest, most prominent, and most exposed point of our fortifications, and there stood exposed to the enemy's fire, where shot seemed flying almost as thick as hail and were instantly demolishing portions of the embankment around him, for ten or fifteen minutes, until he had completely satisfied himself of the purposes of the enemy. During this time his aides, etc., were remonstrating with him with all their earnestness against this exposure of his person and once or twice drew him down. He severely reprimanded them and resumed his position. When satisfied, he dispatched a flag to the enemy, and they desisted from their purpose.

Your declarant continued at Yorktown till the surrender of Cornwallis. He then marched as a guard to the prisoners as far as Nolan's Ferry on the Potomac, where we delivered them to the Maryland troops. Thence he returned and was discharged about Christmas of that year, making this period of his service five months and a half, thus making the entire period of his service eight months and a half.

---

[2]A bundle of sticks used in reinforcing earthwork defenses.

13

THE TIDE TURNS AT SARATOGA

A GERMAN LADY OF DECIDED STANDARDS, AND WIFE OF THE BARON EISENBACH, Frederika von Riedesel found herself in an increasingly ungenteel position as the confident British campaign against the middle colonies, in which her husband played an important military role, fell apart in the early fall of 1777. The famous plan to divide New England from the other colonies by means of a three-pronged invasion of upstate New York led to a series of mistakes in strategy and judgment that left General John Burgoyne, who had marched south from Quebec, squandering an early advantage after his victory at Ticonderoga in June. He was isolated and ultimately defeated near the otherwise insignificant town of Saratoga, thirty miles north of Albany, when armies intended to join him at the latter city, one coming east from Fort Stanwix (Rome) and the other coming up the Hudson from New York City, failed to arrive. Facing an American force that was ultimately twice the size of his own, Burgoyne fought two battles between September 19th and October 7th before giving way to the inevitable on the 17th.

Frederika von Riedesel was very unusual in accompanying her general husband not only to America but also on this difficult and dangerous campaign. Mere "women" were more likely to be with an army in the field than "ladies" such as Riedesel, although even in this campaign she was not the only female of her class to be present up to the end. She tells how General Burgoyne was reluctant to allow her to proceed as the army neared its objective, and for good reason—for at last, like General Riedesel, she was captured by the Americans under General Horatio Gates. Beneath her voiced concern for her husband and her sense of the pain of the wounded one can feel her anxiety about her own exposure. When a French doctor attending a wounded Brunswick officer made sexual advances toward her after the capture and would not believe her claim that she was the wife of a German general, the fact of her exposure was doubly expressed. Her relief at the entrance of General Riedesel (and the Frenchman's hasty retreat—"perhaps . . . a skilled surgeon," she wrote him off, "but otherwise . . . a young fop") expresses well her sense of her position. On the other hand, gentility was not entirely lacking in her world—the French-man's offer of his quarters to the Riedesels, and, even more, the truly kind attentions of General Philip Schuyler suggest as much—and one finds in her response to the suffering of the wounded perhaps her own sense that gentility in any case has its limits. Indeed, her prose is most remarkable for its unflinching attention to the kinds of pain to which warfare gives birth: She looks at the mangled corpses of friends or strangers and catalogs their disarray without fear or repulsion causing her to avert her eyes. After her brief stay in Albany, Riede-sel and her husband went overland to Boston, but ultimately they wound up as paroled prisoners in Virginia, where Thomas Jefferson (their landlord, in fact) befriended them. In 1780, they were exchanged for an American general, and in 1783, returned to Europe.

FREDERIKA CHARLOTTE LOUISE VON RIEDESEL

from *Journal and Correspondence of a Tour of Duty* (1800)

WHEN THE ARMY MARCHED AGAIN (SEPTEMBER 11, 1777), IT WAS AT FIRST decided that I was to stay behind, but upon my urgent entreaty, as some of the other ladies had followed the army, I was likewise finally allowed to do so. We traveled only a short distance each day and were very often sorely tried, but nevertheless we were happy to be allowed to follow at all. I had the joy of seeing my husband every day. I had sent back the greater part of my luggage and had kept only a few of my summer clothes. Everything went well at first. We had high hopes of victory and of reaching the "promised land," and when we had crossed the Hudson and General Burgoyne said, "Britons never retreat," we were all in very high spirits. It displeased me, however, that the officers' wives were familiar with all of the army's plans and seemed all the more strange to me, as during the Seven Years' War I had noticed that in Duke Ferdinand's[1] army everything was kept absolutely secret. Here, on the contrary, even the Americans were acquainted with all our plans in advance, with the result that wherever we came they were ready for us, which cost us dearly. On September 19 there was a battle, which, although it resulted in our favor, forced us to halt at a place called Freeman's Farm.[2] I saw the whole battle myself, and, knowing that my husband was taking part in it, I was filled with fear and anguish and

---

[1] Ferdinand of Brunswick (1721–1792), brother of the reigning duke, Karl I (1713–1780), and a hero of the Seven Years' War.

[2] As Marvin Brown notes in his edition of Riedesel's book, her claim that the Battle of Freeman's Farm ended in favor of the British overlooks the fact that American casualties were half those of the British.

shivered whenever a shot was fired, as nothing escaped my ear. I saw a number of wounded men, and, what was even worse, three of them were brought to the house where I was. One of them was Major Harnage, the husband of one of the ladies of our party, the second a lieutenant, whose wife was also an acquaintance of ours, and the third was a young English officer named Young. Major Harnage and his wife had the room next to mine. He had been shot in the abdomen and suffered much. A few days after our arrival I heard moaning in the other room next to mine and learned that it was the young English officer, Young, who was suffering great pain from his wound.

I was all the more interested in him as a family named Young had been very kind to me while I was in England. I sent word to him that I would be glad to do whatever I could for him and sent some food and refreshment. He expressed a great desire to see his "benefactress," as he called me. I went to him and found him lying on some straw, as he had lost all his baggage. He was a young man of about 18 or 19 years old, actually a nephew of the Mr. Young whom I had met in England, and an only son. His parents were his only concern; he uttered no complaint about his pain. He had lost a great deal of blood, and the doctors wanted to amputate his leg, but he would not let them, and now gangrene had set in. I sent him some pillows and blankets, and my maids sent a mattress. I redoubled my efforts to help him and visited him every day, for which he called down a thousand blessings upon me. In the end the amputation was attempted, but it was too late, and he died a few days later. As he lay in the room next to mine, the walls being very thin, I could hear his groaning until the end came.

The house where I was staying was fairly well built, and I had a large room. The doors and wainscot were of solid cedar, which is quite common here. It is often used for firewood, particularly when there are many insects, because they cannot bear the smell of it. It is said, though, that the smoke is bad for the nerves, and that it can even cause pregnant women to give birth prematurely. When we marched on I had a large calash[3] readied, with room for myself and the three children and my two maids; thus I followed the army right in the midst of the soldiers, who sang and were jolly, burning with the desire for victory. We passed through endless woods, and the country was magnificent, but completely deserted, as all the people had fled before and had gone to strengthen the American army under General Gates. This was a great disadvantage for us, because every inhabitant is a born soldier and a good marksman; in addition, the thought of fighting for their country and for freedom made them braver than ever.

All this time my husband, like the rest of the army, had to stay in camp. I followed at about an hour's distance and visited my husband in camp every morning. Sometimes I had dinner with him in camp, but mostly he came to my place for dinner. The army made brief attacks every day, but none of them amounted to much. My poor husband, however, was unable to go to bed, or

[3] A carriage with a folding top.

even undress a single night. As the weather was beginning to grow cool, Colonel Williams of the artillery, observing that our mutual visits were very fatiguing, offered to have a house with a chimney built for me for five to six guineas, where I could make my home. I accepted his offer, and the house, which was about twenty feet square and had a good fireplace, was begun. These houses are called log cabins. They are made by fitting together thick logs all of about the same size, which makes a sturdy building, and one that is quite warm, particularly when the roof is covered with clay. The house was ready for me to move into the next day, and I was all the more happy, because the nights were getting damp and cold, and my husband could have lived there with me, as the house was near his camp; but suddenly on October 7 my husband, with his whole staff, had to break camp. This moment was the beginning of our unhappiness! I was just taking breakfast with my husband when I noticed that something was going on. General Fraser and, I think, General Burgoyne and General Phillips[4] also were to have had dinner that same day with me. I noticed a great deal of commotion among the soldiers. My husband told me that they were to go out on a reconnaissance, of which I thought nothing, as this often happened. On my way back to the house I met a number of savages in war dress, carrying guns. When I asked them whither they were bound, they replied, "War! War!"—which meant that they were going into battle. I was completely overwhelmed and had hardly returned to the house, when I heard firing which grew heavier and heavier until the noise was frightful. It was a terrible bombardment, and I was more dead than alive!

Toward three o'clock in the afternoon, instead of my dinner guests arriving as expected, poor General Fraser, who was to have been one of them, was brought to me on a stretcher, mortally wounded. The table, which had already been set for dinner, was removed and a bed for the general was put in its place. I sat in a corner of the room, shivering and trembling. The noise of the firing grew constantly louder. The thought that perhaps my husband would also be brought home wounded was terrifying and worried me incessantly. The general said to the doctor, "Don't conceal anything from me! Must I die?" The bullet had gone through his abdomen precisely as in Major Harnage's case; unfortunately the general had eaten a heavy breakfast, so that the intestines were expanded, and, as the doctor explained, the bullet had gone through them, not between them, as in Major Harnage's case. I heard him often exclaim, between moans, "Oh, fatal ambition! Poor General Burgoyne! Poor Mrs. Fraser." Prayers were said, then he asked that General Burgoyne have him buried the next day at six o'clock in the evening, on a hill, which was a sort of redoubt. I no longer knew where to go; the whole hall and the other rooms were full of sick men, suffering from camp sickness. Finally toward evening I saw my husband coming; then I forgot all my sorrow and had no other thought but to thank God for sparing him! He ate in great haste with me and his aides behind the house. We

[4]Simon Fraser (1729?–1777) was a Scots soldier of broad experience in Britain's earlier wars; William Phillips (d. 1781) was captured at Saratoga and held until 1781, when he was exchanged for General Benjamin Lincoln.

had been told that we had gained an advantage over the enemy, but the sad, disheartened faces I saw indicated quite the contrary, and before his departure again my husband took me aside and told me that things were going badly and that I must be ready to leave at any moment, but not to let anyone notice this. On the pretext, therefore, of wanting to move into my new house I had all my things packed. Lady Acland had a tent not far from our house; she slept there at night and spent the day in camp. Suddenly a messenger came to tell her that her husband had been mortally wounded and taken prisoner. She was deeply saddened. We tried to comfort her by telling her that the wound was only a light one, and urged her to go to him, as she would surely be permitted to do, in order that he be better nursed. She loved him dearly, although he was a rough fellow who was drunk almost every day, but, nevertheless, a brave officer. She was the loveliest of women. I spent the whole night trying to comfort her and then went back to my children, whom I had put to bed. I, myself, could not sleep, as I had General Fraser and all the other gentlemen in my room, and I was constantly afraid that my children might wake up and cry, thus disturbing the poor dying man, who kept apologizing to me for causing me so much trouble. Toward three o'clock in the morning I was told that the end was near. I had asked to be told of the approach of this moment; I wrapped the children in blankets and went into the hall with them. At eight o'clock in the morning he died. His body was washed, wrapped in a sheet, and put back into the bed. Then we returned to the room and had to see this sad sight throughout the day. Moreover, wounded officers of our acquaintance kept arriving, and the bombardment was renewed again and again. There was talk of making a retreat, but no steps were taken in this direction. Toward four o'clock in the afternoon I saw flames rising from the new house which had been built for me, so I knew that the enemy was not far away.

We learned that General Burgoyne wanted to carry out General Fraser's last wish and intended having him buried in the place designated at six o'clock. This caused an unnecessary delay and served to increase the army's misfortune. At precisely six o'clock the body was actually carried away, and we saw all the generals and their staffs take part in the funeral services on the hilltop. The English chaplain, Mr. Brudenel, held the services. Cannon balls constantly flew around and over the heads of the mourners. The American general Gates[5] said later on that, had he known that a funeral was being held, he would have allowed no firing in that direction. A number of cannon balls also flew about where I stood, but I had no thought for my own safety, my eyes being constantly directed toward the hill, where I could see my husband distinctly, standing in the midst of the enemy's fire.

The command had been given for the army to withdraw immediately after

[5] Horatio Gates (1728–1806), English-born, had come to America in the army and after retiring from service in 1765 settled in Virginia. Commissioned in the fledging American army ten years later, he saw his greatest fame from his victory at Saratoga, for which Congress put him at the head of the war board; afterward, his failure at the battle of Camden and his possible involvement in behind-the-scenes maneuvers (some aimed at undermining Washington's position) led to an eclipse of his reputation.

the funeral, and our calashes were ready and waiting. I did not want to leave before the troops did. Major Harnage, miserably ill as he was, crept out of bed so that he would not be left behind in the hospital, over which a flag of truce had been raised. When he saw me standing in the midst of danger, he ordered my children and the maidservants to be brought to the calashes and told me I would have to leave immediately. When I repeated my plea to be allowed to stay, he said, "All right, then your children must go without you, so that I can at least save them from danger." He knew the weakest spot in my armor and thus persuaded me to get into the calash, and we drove away on the evening of the 8th.

We had been warned to keep extremely quiet, fires were left burning everywhere, and many tents were left standing, so that the enemy would think the camp was still there. Thus we drove on all through the night. Little Frederika was very much frightened, often starting to cry, and I had to hold my handkerchief over her mouth to prevent our being discovered.

At six o'clock in the morning we stopped, to the amazement of all. General Burgoyne ordered the cannons to be lined up and counted, which vexed everyone because only a few more good marches and we would have been in safety. My husband was completely exhausted and during this halt sat in my calash, where my maids had to make room for him and where he slept about three hours with his head on my shoulder. In the meantime Captain Willoe brought me his wallet with banknotes, and Captain Geismar brought me his beautiful watch, a ring, and a well-filled purse and asked me to take care of these things for them. I promised to do my utmost. Finally the order was given to march on, but we had hardly gone an hour when we stopped again, because we caught sight of the enemy. There were about two hundred men who had come out to reconnoiter and could easily have been taken prisoners by our troops, if General Burgoyne had not lost his head. It was pouring; Lady Acland had had her tent put up. I urged her again to go to her husband, to whom she could have been of so much help in his present condition. She finally listened to my reasoning and, through General Burgoyne's adjutant, Lord Petersham, requested permission to go. I told her she had only to insist upon being allowed to go, and, in the end, the general finally did give her permission. The English chaplain, Mr. Brudenel, accompanied her, and the two got into a boat with a flag of truce and sailed across to the enemy (there is a handsome and well-known etching of this incident). Later on I saw her again in Albany, where her husband was fully recovered, and they both thanked me for my advice. We spent the whole of the 9th in a terrible rainstorm, ready to march on at a moment's notice. The savages had lost courage, and everywhere they were seen retreating. The slightest setback makes cowards of them, especially if they see no chance of plundering. My maid did nothing but bemoan her plight and tear her hair. I begged her to quiet herself, as otherwise she would be taken for a savage. Hereupon she became still more frantic, and she asked me whether I minded her behavior, and when I answered, "Yes," she tore off her hat, let her hair hang down over her face, and said, "It is easy for you to talk! You have your husband, but we have nothing except the prospect of being killed or of losing all we have." With regard to the latter I consoled her by promising that I would compensate her and the others for anything they might lose. The other maid, my good Lena, although very much afraid, nevertheless said nothing.

Toward evening we finally reached Saratoga which is only half an hour on the way from the place where we had spent the whole day. I was wet to the skin from the rain and had to remain so throughout the night as there was no place to change into dry clothes. So I sat down before a good fire, took off the children's clothes, and then we lay down together on some straw. I asked General Phillips, who came up to me, why we did not continue our retreat while there was yet time, as my husband had promised to cover our retreat and bring the army through. "Poor woman," he said, "I admire you! Thoroughly drenched as you are, you still have the courage to go on in this weather. If only you were our commanding general! He thinks himself too tired and wants to spend the night here and give us a supper." In fact, Burgoyne liked having a jolly time and spending half the night singing and drinking and amusing himself in the company of the wife of a commissary, who was his mistress and, like him, loved champagne.[6]

On the 10th at seven o'clock in the morning I refreshed myself with a cup of tea, and we now hoped from one moment to the next that we would at last proceed. In order to cover the retreat General Burgoyne ordered fire set to the beautiful houses and mills in Saratoga belonging to General Schuyler.[7] An English officer brought a very good bouillon, which on his urgent entreaties I had to share with him, and after drinking it we continued our march; however, we got only to the next village, not far away. The greatest misery and extreme disorder prevailed in the army. The commissary had forgotten to distribute the food supplies among the troops; there were cattle enough, but not a single one had been slaughtered. More than thirty officers came to me because they could stand the hunger no longer. I had coffee and tea made for them and divided among them all the supplies with which my carriage was always filled; for we had a cook with us who, though an arch-rogue, nevertheless always knew how to get hold of something for us and, as we learned later, often crossed streams at night in order to steal from the farmers sheep, chickens, and pigs, which he sold to us at a good price.

Finally my own supplies were exhausted, and in my desperation at no longer being able to help the others I called to Adjutant-General Petersham,

[6]The identity of Burgoyne's mistress is uncertain.

[7]Philip John Schuyler (1733–1804), member of one prominent Albany family of Dutch origins and the husband of Catherine van Rensselaer, descendant of another, lost a house in Schuylerville, just north of the battleground, among other properties in the region. It had been occupied by Burgoyne himself at a happier moment in the campaign. Schuyler had been replaced by Gates only weeks prior to Saratoga, largely to appease New England critics who favored Gates, and retired from active service in 1779. Riedesel later had a touching personal encounter with Schuyler, detailed below, and accepted his offer to let her live in his family's house in Albany following the British surrender.

who was just passing by, and, as I was really very much worried, I said to him vehemently: "Come and look at these officers who have been wounded in the common cause and who lack everything they need because they are not getting their due. It is your duty to speak with the general about this." He was very much moved, and, as a result, about a quarter of an hour later General Burgoyne himself came to me and thanked me most pathetically for having reminded him of his duty. He added that a commander is very much to be pitied if he is not properly served and his orders correctly executed. I asked his pardon for having interfered in matters which I well knew were not a woman's business, but said that it had been impossible for me to keep still when I saw how these gallant persons were in need of everything and I, myself, had nothing more to give them. Thereupon he thanked me yet again (although I believe in his heart he never forgave me for this interference) and went to the officers and told them how sorry he was about what had happened; that he had, however, taken care of all by an order; but why, he asked them, had they not come to him for food, as his kitchen was at their disposal at all times? They replied that English officers were not accustomed to visiting the kitchens of their general, and that they had taken each morsel from me with pleasure, being convinced that I had given it to them from the heart. Thereupon he gave strict orders that the provisions be properly distributed. This only delayed us still further and availed us nothing. The general resumed his place at the table, and our calashes were harnessed and made ready for departure. The whole army was in favor of making a retreat, and my husband said it could be done, if only we lost no time.[8] General Burgoyne, however, who had been promised an order[9] if he succeeded in joining General Howe's army, could not make up his mind to leave and lost everything by tarrying.

Toward two o'clock in the afternoon we heard cannon and musketry again, and alarm and confusion prevailed. My husband sent me word to get immediately to a house which was not far away. I got into the calash with my children, and just as we came up to the house I saw five or six men on the other side of the Hudson, who were aiming their guns at us. Almost involuntarily I thrust my children onto the floor of the calash and threw myself over them. The same instant the fellows fired and shattered the arm of a poor English soldier behind me, who had already been wounded and was retiring into the house. Immediately after our arrival a terrifying cannonade began, which was directed principally at the house where we sought shelter, presumably because the enemy, seeing so many people fleeing thither, got the idea that the generals themselves were there. But, alas, the house contained only the wounded and women! We were finally forced to seek refuge in the cellar, where I found a place for myself and the children in a corner near the door. My children lay on the floor with their heads in my lap. And thus we spent the whole night. The horrible smell in the cellar, the weeping of the children, and, even worse, my own fear prevented me from closing my eyes.

---

[8] To the contrary, retreat for Burgoyne's army was virtually impossible at this point.
[9] I.e., an honorary distinction.

Next morning the cannonade went on again, but from the other side. I suggested that everyone leave the cellar for a while so that I could have it cleaned, because otherwise we would all become sick. My suggestion was carried out, and I got many to help, which was highly necessary for this extensive task; the women and children, afraid to go outside, had polluted the entire cellar. When everybody had gone out, I examined our place of refuge; there were three fine cellars with well-vaulted ceilings. I suggested that the most seriously wounded men be put into one cellar, the women in another, and all the others in the third, which was nearest to the door. I had everything swept thoroughly and fumigated with vinegar, when, just as everyone was about to take his place, renewed, terrific cannon fire created another alarm. Many who had no right to enter threw themselves against the door. My children had already gone down the cellar steps, and we would all have been crushed if God had not given me the strength to keep the crowd back by standing in front of the door with outspread arms; otherwise surely someone would have been injured. Eleven cannon balls flew through the house, and we could distinctly hear them rolling about over our heads. One of the poor soldiers who lay on a table, and was just about to have his leg amputated, had the other leg shot off by one of these balls. His comrades had run away from him, and when they returned they found him scarcely breathing, lying in a corner of the room, where he had rolled himself in his agony. I was more dead than alive, not so much on account of our own danger as for the danger that hung over my husband, who kept inquiring how we were and sending me word that he was all right.

Major Harnage's wife, Mrs. Reynell, who had already lost her husband, the wife of the good lieutenant who had been so kind as to share his bouillon with me the previous day, the wife of the commissary, and myself were the only ladies with the army. We were just sitting together and bewailing our fate when someone entered, whispered something to the others, and they all looked at each other sadly. I noticed this and that all eyes were upon me, although nobody said anything. This brought the horrible thought to my mind that my husband had been killed. I screamed; they assured me, however, that such was not the case but indicated with a nod that it was the poor lieutenant's wife to whom this misfortune had befallen. She was called outside a few moments later. Her husband was not yet dead, but a cannon ball had torn his arm away at the shoulder. We heard his moaning all through the night, doubly gruesome as the sound re-echoed through the cellar; the poor fellow died toward morning. However, we spent this night just as we had the previous one. In the meantime my husband visited me, which lightened my anxiety and gave me renewed courage.

Next morning we started putting things in better order. Major Harnage and his wife and Mrs. Reynell made a room for themselves in one corner by partitioning it off with curtains. They wanted to fix up another corner for me just like it, but I preferred staying near the door so that in case of fire I would be able to get out as quickly as possible. I had some straw put down, laid my bedclothes on it, and slept there with the children, with my serving women not far away. Opposite us there were three English officers who had been wounded, but who were determined, in case of retreat, not to stay behind. One of them was a Captain Green, aide to General Phillips, a very estimable and polite man. All three assured me on oath that in case of a hasty retreat they would not forsake me, but that each of them would take one of my children with him on his horse. One of my husband's horses stood saddled and ready for me all the time. My husband often wanted to send me to the Americans, in order to put me out of danger, but I told him it would be worse than anything I had had to bear heretofore to be with people to whom I should have to be polite while my husband was fighting them. He promised me, therefore, that I could continue to follow the army. Many a time in the night, however, I was seized with the fear that he had marched away, and I crept out of my cellar to see; when I saw the troops lying by the fire, as the nights had already grown cold, I was able to sleep more tranquilly again. The things which had been entrusted to me for safekeeping also worried me. I had put them all in the front of my corset because I was constantly afraid of losing part of them, and I made up my mind never again to take such a responsibility upon myself. On the third day I found the first opportunity and a moment to change my underclothing when the courtesy of a small corner was allowed me. Meanwhile, my three above-mentioned officers stood sentry not far off. One of these gentlemen could imitate most realistically the mooing of a cow and the bleating of a calf. Whenever my little daughter Frederika cried at night, he made these sounds for her, and she would become quiet again immediately, at which we all had to laugh.

Our cook brought us food, but we had no water, and I was often obliged to quench my thirst with wine and even had to give the children some. Moreover, it was almost the only drink my husband would take. This finally began to worry our faithful Rockel, who said to me one day, "I fear that the general drinks all this wine because he is afraid of being taken prisoner, and that he is tired of living." The constant danger which surrounded my husband kept me in continuous anxiety. I was the only one among all the women whose husband had not been either killed or at least wounded, and I often said to myself, "Should I be the only lucky one?"—particularly as my husband was in such great danger day and night. He did not spend a single night in the tent, but lay outside by the sentry's fire all night long. That, alone, was enough to cause his death, as the nights were so damp and cold.

Because we were badly in need of water, we finally found the wife of one of the soldiers who was brave enough to go to the river to fetch some. This was a thing nobody wanted to risk doing, because the enemy shot every man in the head who went near the river. However, they did not hurt the woman out of respect for her sex, as they told us themselves afterwards.

I tried to divert my mind by busying myself with our wounded. I made tea and coffee for them, for which I received a thousand blessings. Often I shared my dinner with them. One day a Canadian officer came into the cellar, so weak that he could hardly stand up. We finally got it out of him that he was almost starved to death. I was very happy to be able to give him my own dinner, which gave him renewed strength and won me his friendship. When we returned to Canada later on, I became acquainted with his family.

One of the worst things we had to bear was the odor which came from the wounds when they began to fester. At one time I was nursing a Major Bloomfield, aide to General Phillips, who had a bullet shot through both cheeks, smashing his teeth and grazing his tongue. He could not keep anything in his mouth; the pus almost choked him, and he could not take any nourishment at all except a little bouillon or other liquid. We had some Rhine wine. I gave him a bottle, hoping that the acid would cleanse his wounds. He took a little of it in his mouth, and this alone had such a fortunate effect that his wounds healed entirely, and I gained another friend. Thus even in these hours of suffering and sorrow I had moments of pleasure which made me very happy.

On one of these unhappy days General Phillips wanted to visit me and accompanied my husband, who came to me once or twice every day at the risk of his life. He saw our plight and heard me beg my husband not to leave me behind in case of a hasty retreat. He took my part when he saw how I hated the thought of being left with the Americans. When he left me he said to my husband, "No! I would not come here again for ten thousand guineas, for my heart is absolutely broken."

On the other hand, not all the men who were with us deserved pity. Some of them were cowards who had no reason whatever for staying in the cellar, and who later when we were taken prisoners, were well able to stand up in line and march. We were in this dreadful position six days. Finally there was talk of capitulation, as by delaying too long our retreat was now cut off. A cessation of hostilities took place, and my husband, who was completely exhausted, could sleep in a bed in the house for the first time in a long while. In order that he would be absolutely undisturbed I had a good bed made for him in a small room and slept with my children and the maids in a large hall close by. At about nine o'clock in the morning someone came and wanted to speak to my husband. With the greatest reluctance I found it necessary to wake him. I noticed that he was not pleased about the message he received and that he immediately sent the man to headquarters and lay down again, much annoyed. Shortly afterwards General Burgoyne sent for all the other generals and staff officers to attend a council of war early in the morning, during which he suggested, on the basis of a false report, that the capitulation which had already been made to the enemy be broken. However, it was finally decided that this would be neither practicable nor advisable, and that was a lucky decision for us, because the Americans told us later that, had we broken the capitulation, we would all have been massacred, which would have been an easy matter, because there were only four to five thousand of us, and we had given them time to get more than twenty thousand of their men together.[1]

On October 16 my husband had to go back on duty, and I had to return to my cellar. That day the officers, who until then had received only salted meat, which was very bad for the wounded, were given a lot of fresh meat.[2] The good woman who always got the water for us cooked a tasty soup with it. I

[1] Gates probably had fewer than half this many men under his command.
[2] That is, an "order" of meat—not necessarily a large quantity.

had lost all appetite and had eaten nothing the whole time except a crust of bread dipped in wine. The wounded officers, my companions in misfortune, cut off the best piece of beef and presented it to me with a plate of soup. I told them it was impossible for me to eat anything. Seeing, however, how much in need of nourishment I was, they declared that they would not eat a bite themselves until I had given them the pleasure of joining them. I could no longer resist their friendly pleading, whereupon they assured me that it made them most happy to be able to share with me the first good food they had received.

On October 17 the capitulation went into effect. The generals went to the American commanding general, General Gates, and the troops laid down their arms and surrendered themselves as prisoners of war. The good woman who had fetched water for us at the risk of her life now got her reward. Everyone threw a handful of money into her apron, and she received altogether more than twenty guineas. In moments like this the heart seems to overflow in gratitude.

At last my husband sent a groom to me with the message that I should come to him with our children. I got into my beloved calash again, and while driving through the American camp I was comforted to notice that nobody glanced at us insultingly, that they all bowed to me, and some of them even looked with pity to see a woman with small children there. I confess that I was afraid to go to the enemy, as it was an entirely new experience for me. When I approached the tents a very handsome man came towards me, lifted the children out of the calash, hugged and kissed them and then, with tears in his eyes, helped me out. "You are trembling," he said. "Don't be afraid." "No," I answered, "I am not, for you look so kind and were so affectionate to my children that you have given me courage." He led me to the tent of General Gates, where I found General Burgoyne and General Phillips, who were on very friendly terms with the former. Burgoyne said to me, "Have no fear, for your sufferings have now come to an end." I replied that, of course it would be wrong to be afraid any longer if our leader were not and after seeing him on such good terms with General Gates. All the generals stayed with General Gates for dinner. The same man who had welcomed me so kindly came up to me, saying "It would embarrass you to take dinner with all these gentlemen; come to my tent with your children, and although I can only give you a frugal meal, it will be given gladly." "Surely," I replied, "you are a husband and father, because you are so good to me." I learned then that he was the American General Schuyler. He treated me to delicious smoked tongue, beefsteaks, potatoes, and good bread and butter. No dinner had ever tasted better to me. I was content. I saw that all about me were likewise, and, most important of all, my husband was out of danger.

When we had finished eating, he offered to let me live in his house, which was near Albany, and told me that General Burgoyne would also come there. I sent my husband a message, asking what I should do. He told me to accept the invitation, and as it was a two-days' journey and was already five o'clock in the afternoon, he suggested that I go on ahead and spend the night at a place about three hours from there. General Schuyler was kind enough to let a French officer take me there, a very polite man, the one in command of the troops who had reconnoitered the area and whom I have already mentioned. When he had brought us to the house where we were to spend the night, he returned to camp.

I found a French doctor at this house with a mortally wounded Brunswick officer, who had been put in his care and who died a few days later. The patient was full of praise for the doctor's treatment, and perhaps he was a skilled surgeon, but otherwise he was a young fop. He was very pleased to hear that I could speak his language and began to say all sorts of sweet things and impertinences to me, among which, that he could not possibly believe that I was a general's wife, because a woman of such high rank would never have joined her husband. I should, therefore, stay with him, as it would be better to stay with victors than with the defeated. I was furious over his boldness but did not dare to show how much contempt I felt for him, because I was without protection. When night came he offered to let me share his room with him. I replied, however, that I would sit up in the room of the wounded soldier, whereupon he made me a lot of silly compliments, when suddenly the door opened and my husband and his aide entered. "Here, sir, is my husband," I said to him with a withering glance, whereupon he departed shamefacedly. Nevertheless, he was polite enough to give us his room.

The next day we arrived in Albany, where we had so often longed to be. But we did not come as victors, as we had thought. We were welcomed by good General Schuyler, his wife, and daughters not as enemies, but in the friendliest manner possible, and they were exceedingly kind to us as well as to General Burgoyne, although he had had their beautifully furnished houses set on fire, needlessly, it is said. Their behavior was that of people who can turn from their own loss to the misfortune of others. General Burgoyne, too, was very much touched by their magnanimity and said to General Schuyler, "You are so kind to me who caused you so much damage." "Such is the fate of war," the gallant man replied. "Let us not talk about it any more." We stayed with them three days, and they assured us that they regretted seeing us go.

Our cook had stayed in town with my husband's equipment. The second night after our arrival all our things were stolen, in spite of the American guard of ten to twenty men, who had been ordered to keep watch. We had nothing left except my own and the children's bedding and the few household articles which I kept with me—and this in a country where nothing could be bought at any price, and at a time when we so badly needed many things; for my husband had to furnish board for all his aides, quartermasters, and others. Our friends, the English, of whom I speak truly as friends, because throughout our stay in America they have always treated us as such, each made us a present of some article. One gave a couple of spoons, another a few plates. It was all we had for a long time, because not until three years later in New York did we have the opportunity of replacing at great cost the things we had lost. Fortunately, I had kept my little conveyance containing my own things. As it was late in the fall, and the weather was getting raw, I had made for my calash a top of coarse linen painted with oil paint. Thus we drove to Boston—a tedious and difficult journey.

I do not know whether it was my vehicle which aroused the people's curiosity, for it really looked like a wagon in which rare animals were being transported, but I was often obliged to stop, because the people wanted to see the German general's wife with her children. In order to prevent them from tearing the linen top off the carriage, I decided it was better to alight frequently, and thus I got away more quickly than otherwise. But even so, I cannot deny that the people were friendly and were particularly pleased to hear that I could speak their native language, English.

In all my suffering God blessed me with His help, so that I lost neither my gaiety, nor my courage; but my poor husband, who was consumed by sadness over everything that had happened and by his captivity, was very much annoyed by such episodes as these, and could scarcely endure them. His health had suffered greatly, especially from the many nights spent outdoors in the cold and dampness, and, accordingly, he often had to take medicine. One day when he was very weak from the effects of an emetic, he could not sleep on account of the noise made by our American guards, who never left us, and who were drinking and feasting outside our door and who became even noisier when he asked them to be quiet. I decided to go out myself, and I told them that my husband was ill and begged them, therefore, to be a bit less noisy. They ceased at once and all was quiet. Here is proof that this nation also has respect for our sex.

Some of their generals who accompanied us were shoemakers by trade, and on days when we rested made boots for our officers and also repaired the shoes of our officers. They very much prized coined money, which for them was very scarce. One of our officers' boots were completely torn. He saw that an American general was wearing a good pair and jestingly said to him, "I would gladly give you a guinea for them." The general immediately jumped off his horse, took the guinea, gave the officer his boots, and wearing the officer's torn pair, mounted his horse again.

14

THE HUMOROUS RETREAT
OF A PATRIOT

ONE OF THE MOST DELIGHTFUL DIARISTS OF THE REVOLUTIONARY WAR ERA, Quaker Sally Wister (1761–1804), of German and Welsh background, was fourteen when the Declaration of Independence was signed in her native Philadelphia and sixteen when, in exile from the city, she began keeping her journal as a long letter addressed to her girlhood friend Deborah Norris, with whom she had attended school. Young Sally's family left her birthplace on September 20, 1777 (just days before General William Howe took Philadelphia from the Americans, forcing Congress to flee farther inland, first to Lancaster and then to York) and took up residence in Gwynedd or North Wales, a Welsh settlement north of town. There the Wisters remained some ten months, comfortably ensconced in the farmhouse of widow Hannah Foulke, on the banks of the Wissahickon, isolated from the conditions prevailing not only in the city but also in nearby Valley Forge, where Washington's army was spending its doleful winter.

Wister's youthful eye caught the glitter at the edges of the conflict, as Americans from all areas began to mix together and sense their differences (as well as similarities) in a manner that had not prevailed before. She seemed particularly taken with the gallant southern officers, like Major William Truman Stoddert of Maryland, nephew of the commander of Maryland's troops, General William Smallwood, and by her account a dashing figure, much anticipated before his visit to the Foulke home and much commented upon thereafter. Wister's delight in the incidental details of social life at such a juncture reminds us that, even in the midst of great suffering, the ordinary events of life were kept up—at times, in fact, precisely because the extraordinary events were so momentous and so threatening. Hence her account of the foolery surrounding one of the visitors to the Foulke house early in the winter of 1777: Robert Tilly, a Virginian serving as paymaster of a continental regiment, handy with his flute and a jolly fellow by nature ("a wild, noisy mortal," Sally noted, "rather genteel, [with] an extremely pretty, ruddy face, hair brown, and a sufficiency of it, a very great laugher, and talks so excessively fast that he often begins sentences without finishing the last"). Apparently bashful around women, Tilly kept the whole company in good spirits but committed the unforgivable sin of not addressing "one civil thing" to Sally herself. In league with others of her party, Sally arranged a special revenge on Tilly. There stood in the Foulke house a life-sized wooden sculpture of a British grenadier, a kind of fantasy piece that normally would have attracted little notice. In the present context, however, the wooden soldier took on special meaning. With this fearsome stick figure stationed ominously at the front door of the house, Sally and her co-conspirators had the slave of one of Tilly's fellow Virginians enter the room where most of the revelers were and announce that someone was calling. The genius of the ruse lay in the pranksters' sense that Tilly would take the bait first, and he did, rising and questioning the slave, and then rushing out into the hall. From behind the threatening figure a servant called out, "Is there any rebel officers here?" Tilly bolted out of the house, and off through hedge and briar, not stopping until he had outrun the many grenadiers chasing him down in his own imagination. When he at long last came back, with "inexpressible confusion" on his once handsome face, "his fine hair hanging dishevelled down his shoulders, all splashed with mud" (but still full of "beauty," Sally had to add), he had learned not to scorn Miss Sally Wister.

We owe a debt to Sally Wister for helping to contrive this playful episode in the early winter of Valley Forge; even more, we owe her a debt for possessing precisely that "descriptive genius" she hoped for as she sat down to write, for the eventual delectation of her friend Deborah Norris, her account of "Tilly and the Grenadier."

SALLY WISTER

from her "Journal" (1777‑78)

[*Fifth day, Dec. 11, 1777*] Noon.
The major[1] gone to camp. I don't think we shall see him again.

Well, strange creature that I am; here have I been going on without giving thee an account of two officers—one who will be a principal character; their names are Captain Lipscomb[2] and a Mr. Tilly; the former a tall, genteel man,

---

[1] Major William Truman Stoddert (1759–1793), a Maryland officer, was orphaned at nine and at seventeen left what is now the University of Pennsylvania to enlist in the American army. He was at this time attached to his uncle, General William Smallwood, whom he served, wrote Wister, "as major of brigade." She had heard much of Stoddert, and introduced him to her journal as follows: "Well, here comes the glory, the major, so bashful, so famous, etc. He should come before the captain [described in the preceding paragraph of the journal], but never mind, I at first thought the major cross and proud, but I was mistaken." She found him "large in his person, manly, and [with] an engaging countenance and address."

[2] Reuben Lipscomb (d. 1778), from Virginia, was at this time an officer in the Seventh Virginia Regiment.

very delicate from indisposition, and has a softness in his countenance that is very pleasing, and has the finest head of hair that I ever saw; 'tis a light, shining auburn. The fashion of his hair was this—negligently tied, and waving down his back. Well may it be said—"Loose flow'd the soft redundance of his hair." He has not hitherto shown himself a lady's man, tho' he is perfectly polite.

Now let me attempt to characterize Tilly.[3] He seems a wild, noisy mortal, tho' I am not much acquainted with him. He appears bashful when with girls. We dissipated the major's bashfulness; but I doubt we have not so good a subject now. He is above the common size, rather genteel, an extremely pretty, ruddy face, hair brown, and a sufficiency of it, a very great laugher, and talks so excessively fast that he often begins sentences without finishing the last, which confuses him very much, and then he blushes and laughs; and in short, he keeps me in perpetual good humor; but the creature has not addressed one civil thing to me since he came.

But I have not done with his accomplishments yet, for he is a musician— that is, he plays on the German flute, and has it here.

Fifth Day Night.

The family retired; take the adventures of the afternoon as they occurred.

Seaton[4] and Captain Lipscomb drank tea with us. While we sat at tea, the parlor door was opened; in came Tilly; his appearance was elegant; he had been riding; the wind had given the most beautiful glow to his cheeks, and blowed his hair carelessly round his face.

Oh, my heart, thought I, be secure!

The caution was needless, I found it without a wish to stray.

When the tea equipage was removed, the conversation turned on politics, a subject I avoid. I gave Betsy a hint. I rose, she followed, and we went to seek Liddy.[5]

We chatted a few moments at the door. The moon shone with uncommon splendor. Our spirits were high. I proposed a walk; the girls agreed. When we reached the poplar tree, we stopped. Our ears were assailed by a number of voices.

"A party of light horse," said one.

"The English, perhaps; let's run home."

"No, no," said I, "be heroines."

At last two or three men on horseback came in sight. We walked on. The well-known voice of the major saluted our hearing with, "How do you do, ladies?"

We turned ourselves about with one accord. He, not relishing the idea of sleeping on the banks of the Schuylkill, had returned to the mill.

We chatted along the road till we reached our hospitable mansion. Stod-

---

[3] Robert Tilly, also of Virginia, was made paymaster of Grayson's Additional Continental Regiment earlier in 1777 but resigned in 1778.
[4] Alexander Seaton, another Virginian, was quartermaster in the same unit as Tilly.
[5] Sally's younger sister Elizabeth (b. 1764) and her friend Lydia Foulke (b. 1756).

dert dismounted, and went into Jesse's[6] parlour. I sat there a half hour. He is very amiable.

Seaton, Lipscomb, Tilly, and my father, hearing of his return, and impatient for the news, came in at one door, while I made my exit at the other.

I am vexed at Tilly, who has his flute, and does nothing but play the fool. He begins a tune, plays a note or so, then stops. Well, after a while, he begins again; stops again. "Will that do, Seaton? Hah! hah! hah!"

He has given us but two regular tunes since he arrived. I am passionately fond of music. How boyish he behaves.

Sixth day, December 12th, 1777.

I ran into aunt's this morn to chat with the girls. Major Stoddert joined us in a few minutes.

I verily believe the man is fond of the ladies, and, what to me is astonishing, he has not discovered the smallest degree of pride. Whether he is artful enough to conceal it under the veil of humility, or whether he has none, is a question; but I am inclined to think it the latter.

I really am of opinion that there are few of the young fellows of the modern age exempt from vanity, more especially those who are blessed with exterior graces. If they have a fine pair of eyes they are ever rolling them about; a fine set of teeth, mind, they are great laughers; a genteel person, forever changing their attitudes to show them to advantage. Oh, vanity, vanity; how boundless is thy sway!

But to resume this interview with Major Stoddert. We were very witty and sprightly. I was darning an apron, upon which he was pleased to compliment me.

"Well, Miss Sally, what would you do if the British were to come here?"

"Do," exclaimed I; "be frightened just to death."

He laughed, and said he would escape their rage by getting behind the representation of a British grenadier which you have upstairs. "Of all things, I should like to frighten Tilly with it. Pray, ladies, let's fix it in his chamber tonight."

"If thee will take all the blame, we will assist thee."

"That I will," he replied, and this was the plan.

We had brought some weeks ago a [statue of a] British grenadier from Uncle Miles's on purpose to divert us. It is remarkably well executed, six foot high, and makes a martial appearance. This we agreed to stand at the door that opens into the road (the house has four rooms on a floor, with a wide entry running through), with another figure that would add to the deceit. One of our servants was to stand behind them, others were to serve as occasion offered.

After half an hour's converse, in which we raised our expectations to the

[6]Jesse Foulke (b. 1742), Lydia's older brother and then proprietor of the family's mill, on the Wissahickon.

highest pitch, we parted. If our scheme answers, I shall communicate in the eve. Till then, adieu. 'Tis dining hour.

Sixth Day Night.

Never did I more sincerely wish to possess a descriptive genius than I do now. All that I can write will fall infinitely short of the truly diverting scene that I have been witness to tonight. But, as I mean to attempt an account, I had as well shorten the preface, and begin the story.

In the beginning of the evening I went to Liddy and begged her to secure the swords and pistols which were in their parlor. The Marylander, hearing our voices, joined us. I told him of my proposal. Whether he thought it a good one or not I can't say, but he approved of it, and Liddy went in and brought her apron full of swords and pistols.

When this was done, Stoddert joined the officers. We girls went and stood at the first landing of the stairs. The gentlemen were very merry and chatting on public affairs, when Seaton's Negro (observe that Seaton, being indisposed, was apprized of the scheme) opened the door, candle in his hand, and said, "There's somebody at the door that wishes to see you."

"Who? All of us?" said Tilly.

"Yes, sir," answered the boy.

They all rose (the major, as he afterwards said, almost dying with laughing), and walked in to the entry, Tilly first, in full expectation of news.

The first object that struck his view was a British soldier. In a moment his ears were saluted with, "Is there any rebel officers here?" in a thundering voice.

Not waiting for a second word, he darted like lightning out at the front door, through the yard, bolted o'er the fence. Swamps, fences, thorn-hedges, and ploughed fields no way impeded his retreat. He was soon out of hearing.

The woods echoed with, "Which way did he go? Stop him! Surround the house!" The amiable Lipscomb had his hand on the latch of the door, intending to attempt his escape; Stoddert, considering his indisposition, acquainted him with the deceit.

We females ran downstairs to join in the general laugh. I walked into Jesse's parlor. There sat poor Stoddert (whose sore lips must have received no advantage from this), almost convulsed with laughing, rolling in an armchair. He said nothing; I believe he could not have spoke.

"Major Stoddert," said I, "go call Tilly back. He will lose himself—indeed he will"; every word interrupted with a "Ha! ha!"

At last he rose, and went to the door, and what a loud voice could avail in bringing him back, he tried.

Figure to thyself this Tilly, of a snowy evening, no hat, shoes down at heel, hair untied, flying across meadows, creeks and mud-holes. Flying from what? Why, a bit of painted wood. But he was ignorant of what it was. The idea of being made a prisoner wholly engrossed his mind, and his last resource was to run.

After a while, we being in rather more composure, and our bursts of laughter less frequent, yet by no means subsided—in full assembly of girls and officers—Tilly entered.

The greatest part of my risibility turned to pity. Inexpressible confusion had taken entire possession of his countenance, his fine hair hanging dishevelled down his shoulders, all splashed with mud; yet his fright, confusion and race had not divested him of his beauty.

He smiled as he tripped up the steps; but 'twas vexation placed it on his features. Joy at that moment was banished from his heart. He briskly walked five or six steps, then stopped, and took a general survey of us all.

"Where have you been, Mr. Tilly?" asked one officer. (We girls were silent.)

"I really imagined," said Stoddert, "that you were gone for your pistols. I followed you to prevent danger"—an excessive laugh at each question, which it was impossible to restrain.

"Pray, where were your pistols, Tilly?"

He broke his silence by the following expression: "You may all go to the D——l." I never heard him utter an indecent expression before.

At last his good nature gained a complete ascendance over his anger, and he joined heartily in the laugh. I will do him the justice to say that he bore it charmingly. No cowardly threats, no vengeance denounced.

Stoddert caught hold of his coat. "Come, look at what you ran from," and dragged him to the door.

He gave it a look, said it was very natural, and, by the singularity of his expressions, gave fresh cause for diversion. We all retired to our different parlors, for to rest our faces, if I may say so.

Well, certainly, these military folks will laugh all night. Such screaming I never did hear. Adieu tonight.

Seventh-day Morn, December 13th.

I am fearful they will yet carry the joke too far. Tilly certainly possesses an uncommon share of good nature, or he could not tolerate these frequent teasings.

Ah, Deborah, the major is going to leave us entirely—just going. I will see him first.

Seventh Day Noon.

He has gone. I saw him pass the bridge. The woods, which you enter immediately after crossing it, hindered us from following him farther. I seem to fancy he will return in the evening.

Seventh Day Night.

Stoddert not come back. We shall not, I fancy, see him again for months, perhaps years, unless he should visit Philadelphia. We shall miss his agreeable company.

But what shall we make of Tilly? No civil things yet from him. Adieu tonight, my dear.

First Day Morn, December 14th.

The officers yet here. No talk of their departure. They are very lively. Tilly's retreat the occasion; the principal one, however [at least].

First Day Night.

Captain Lipscomb, Seaton, and Tilly, with cousin Hannah Miles,[7] dined with us today. Hannah's health seems established, to our great joy.

Such an everlasting laugher as Tilly I never knew. He caused us a good deal of diversion while we sat at table. He has not said a syllable to one of us young ladies since Sixth-day eve. He tells Lipscomb that the major had the assistance of the ladies in the execution of the scheme. He tells a truth.

About four o'clock I was standing at the door, leaning my head on my hand, when a genteel officer rode up to the gate and dismounted. "Your servant, ma'am," and gave me the compliment of his hat. Walked into Aunt's.

I went into our parlor. Soon Seaton was called. Many minutes had not elapsed before he entered with the same young fellow whom I had just seen. He introduced him by the name of Captain Smallwood.[8] We seated ourselves. I then had an opportunity of seeing him.

He is a brother to General Smallwood. A very genteel, pretty little fellow, very modest, and seems agreeable, but no personal resemblance between him and the major.

After tea, turning to Tilly, he said,

"So, sir, I have heard you had like to have been made a prisoner last Friday night!"

"Pray, sir, who informed you?"

"Major Stoddert was my author."

"I fancy he made a fine tale of it. How far did he say I ran?"

"Two mile; and that you fell into the mill-dam!"

He raised his eyes and hands, and exclaimed, "What a confounded falsehood!"

The whole affair was again revived.

Our Tillian Hero gave a mighty droll account of his retreat, as they call it. He told us that after he had got behind our kitchen he stopped for company, as he expected the others would immediately follow. "But I heard them scream, 'Which way did he go? Where is he?' 'Aye,' said I, to myself, 'he is gone where you shan't catch him,' and off I set again."

"Pray," asked mamma, "did thee keep that lane between the meadows?"

"Oh, no, ma'am; that was a large road, and I might happen to meet some of them. When I reached yon thorn hedge, I again stopped. As it was a cold

---

[7] Daughter of Samuel Miles, American officer and politician.
[8] Heabard Smallwood (d. 1778), brother of General William Smallwood, and hence another of Stoddert's uncles.

night, I thought I would pull up my shoe heels, and tie my handkerchief round my head. I then began to have a suspicion of a trick, and, hearing the major holler, I came back."

I think I did not laugh more at the very time than tonight at the rehearsal of it. He is so good-natured, and takes all their jokes with so good a grace, that I am quite charmed with him. He laughingly denounces vengeance against Stoddert. He will be even with him. He is in the major's debt, but he will pay him.

Second-day Evening, December 15th.

Smallwood has taken up his quarters with us. Nothing worth relating occurred today

3d, 4th and Fifth-day.

We chatted a little with the officers. Smallwood not so chatty as his brother or nephew. Lipscomb is very agreeable; a delightful musical voice.

Sixth-day Noon, Dec. 19th.

The officers, after the politest adieus, have left us. Smallwood and Tilly are going to Maryland, where they live; Seaton to Virginia; and Lipscomb to camp, to join his regiment. I feel sorry at their departure, yet 'tis a different kind from what I felt some time since. We had not contracted so great an intimacy with those last.

Seventh-day, December 20th.

General Washington's army have gone into winter quarters at the Valley Forge.

We shall not see many of the military now. We shall be very intimate with solitude. I am afraid stupidity will be a frequent guest.

After so much company, I can't relish the idea of sequestration.

First-day Night.

A dull round of the same thing over again. I shall hang up my pen till something offers worth relating.[9]

---

[9]True to this world-weary comment, Wister's next entry is dated more than a month later.

15

A Black Loyalist's Escape

Boston King, the son of slaves, was born around 1760 on the plantation of Richard Waring in South Carolina. His father, "stolen away from Africa when he was young," rose to be "beloved by his master" (as King himself put it), and was given "the charge of the plantation as a driver for many years"; he was literate, and served the slave community as a minister. King's mother, also relatively privileged, spent much of her time as a seamstress or "attending upon those that were sick, having some knowledge of the virtue of herbs, which she learned from the Indians." King himself worked first in the house, but when he was nine he began to "mind the cattle," and at sixteen—in the early years of the Revolution, which Waring favored—was bound out by Waring as an apprentice to a Charleston carpenter. The latter man at first treated King poorly (on one occasion when he was wrongfully accused of stealing some precious iron nails, the man "beat and tortured [King] most cruelly") until at King's urging Waring intervened and the physical mistreatment ceased. At some point prior to the British seizure of Charleston in May 1780, the carpenter, fearing the attack, moved forty miles out into the countryside, taking King with him. While there, King took advantage of an altercation involving the carpenter's son and, knowing that as the legal property of a Patriot he would be welcomed by the British in Charleston, he fled thither. "They received me readily," he later wrote, "and I began to feel the happiness of liberty, of which I knew nothing before, although I was much grieved at first, to be obliged to leave my friends, and reside among strangers."

It was not his first uprooting and would not be his last. The hospitality of the British toward escaping African Americans, strategic rather than humanitarian, wore thin; like other liberty-seeking refugees, King lived under conditions that led him to catch smallpox, after which he was isolated from the British soldiers: "for all the blacks affected with that disease, were ordered to be carried a mile from the camp. . . . This was a grievous circumstance to me and many others. We lay sometimes a whole day without anything to eat or drink. . . ." King managed to survive through the special kindness of a British soldier (which King later was able to repay with dividends when he nursed that man back to health after he was wounded), but King was not well enough when the British left their camp to go with them. At this point, he feared the worst from the advancing Patriots, but smallpox now proved his ironic savior, forcing the Americans to shun the fugitive-slave encampment, vengeful as they otherwise may have felt toward it. Along with two dozen other victims, King soon was conveyed back across the lines, closer to the British but still a distance off from the army's hospital near Charleston. After his full recovery, King served the British interests well, nominally as a servant to a captain, but actually as a soldier staunchly committed to the cause of the Loyalists, who after all had come nearer than the Patriots to acknowledging his own rights.

His fear of retribution from his old masters and their fellow Patriots was well-founded. As the Americans retook Charleston and its environs in 1782, during the last, chaotic months of the war, following Cornwallis's surrender at Yorktown but prior to the signing of the Treaty of Paris in 1783, King left with the British army for New York City, still held by the Crown. There King met and married a woman named Violet, like him a runaway from a Carolina master. For some months King sought support through employment as a free carpenter, but without much success. Eventually he must have found work on a pilot boat, for it was from such a vessel that he was taken prisoner when, as it languished at sea off New York, it was intercepted by some American sailors; the latter conveyed him ashore in New Jersey, where he once more found himself reduced to slavery. Although he was to comment on the relatively "better" treatment accorded northern slaves, he had no intention of reconciling himself to his new fate and sought new means to liberty. He went about the town of Brunswick, and having noticed that the Raritan River at low tide was fordable, though guarded by sentinels on the lookout for escaped slaves and war prisoners, he managed to elude them late one night and went over the Arthur Kill at Perth Amboy in a stolen boat. Once on Staten Island, he procured a pass from a British officer and made his way back to New York City, where his wife and family awaited him.

As the time for the British to evacuate the city drew near, rumors circulated regarding the fate of the two thousand Loyalist ex-slaves among them. King reported that southern masters visited New York in this period, seeking out, seizing, and returning to slavery in the South their old "property." But Sir Guy Carleton, head of the British forces in North America since May 1782, at last reassured the remaining black Loyalists that the British would indeed guarantee their freedom, and Carleton had the commander in New York, General Samuel Birch, issue King and his compatriots certificates to that effect. As the white Loyalists boarded ships for Nova Scotia in the summer of 1783, King and many other blacks joined them. Arriving there in August, the ex-slaves soon were settled in Birchtown, a new settlement named for General Birch and provided for them—with a mixture of charity and condescension—six miles from the white town of Shelburne on Nova Scotia's southern shore. By early 1784, it was the largest community of free blacks on the continent.

Once settled in Birchtown with his family, King found work at his trade in Shelburne, but tensions between the poorly paid black workers and the jealous whites soon led to unacceptable conditions there. Along with his wife, King had been converted to Methodism by the efforts of Reverend Moses Wilkinson, another black Loyalist, and himself began preaching to congregations in the vicinity. Dissatisfaction with the prospects of his fellows in the vicinity of Shelburne led King to try his hand as a fisherman elsewhere in Nova Scotia, but it was his appointment as a minister near Halifax that led to the next, decisive chapter of his life. Recruited to help plant a colony of free blacks in Sierra Leone, he sailed there in 1792, spent time at school in England from 1794 to 1796 (during which period he composed the narrative of his life, published in the British *Methodist Magazine* in 1798), and on his return to Africa in 1796 resumed his religious work. His wife Violet died in Sierra Leone shortly after their first arrival there: King remarried, and he and his second wife, living in the Sherbro region on the central coast, both survived until 1802.

BOSTON KING

from "Memoirs of the Life of Boston King, a Black Preacher" (1798)

IT IS BY NO MEANS AN AGREEABLE TASK TO WRITE AN ACCOUNT OF MY LIFE, YET my gratitude to Almighty God, who considered my affliction, and looked upon me in my low estate, who delivered me from the hand of the oppressor, and established my goings, impels me to acknowledge his goodness—and the importunity of many respectable friends, whom I highly esteem—have induced me to set down, as they occurred to my memory, a few of the most striking incidents I have met with in my pilgrimage. I am well aware of my inability for such an undertaking, having only a slight acquaintance with the language in which I write, and being obliged to snatch a few hours, now and then, from pursuits, which to me, perhaps, are more profitable. However, such as it is, I present it to the friends of religion and humanity, hoping that it will be of some use to mankind.

I was born in the province of South Carolina, twenty-eight miles from Charleston. My father was stolen away from Africa when he was young. I have reason to believe that he lived in the fear and love of God. He attended to that true light which lighteth every man that cometh into the world. He lost no opportunity of hearing the gospel, and never omitted praying with his family every night. He likewise read to them, and to as many as were inclined to hear. On the Lord's Day he rose very early, and met his family, after which he worked in the field till about three in the afternoon, and then went into the woods and read till sunset, the slaves being obliged to work on the Lord's Day to procure such things as were not allowed by their masters. He was beloved by his master, and had the charge of the plantation as a driver for many years. In his old age he was employed as a mill-cutter. Those who knew him, say, that they never heard him swear an oath, but on the contrary, he reproved all who spoke improper words in his hearing. To the utmost of his power he endeavored to make his family happy, and his death was a very great loss to us all. My mother was employed chiefly in attending upon those that were sick, having some knowledge of the virtue of herbs, which she learned from the Indians. She likewise had the care of making the people's clothes, and on these accounts was indulged with many privileges which the rest of the slaves were not.

When I was six years old I waited in the house upon my master. In my ninth year I was put to mind the cattle. Here I learnt from my comrades the horrible sin of swearing and cursing. When twelve years old, it pleased God to alarm me by a remarkable dream. At midday, when the cattle went under the shade of the trees, I dreamt that the world was on fire, and that I saw the supreme judge descend on his great white throne! I saw millions of millions of souls; some of whom ascended up to heaven, while others were rejected, and fell into the greatest confusion and despair. This dream made such an impression upon my mind, that I refrained from swearing and bad company, and from that time acknowledged that there was a God, but how to serve God I knew not. Being obliged to travel in different parts of America with racehorses, I suffered many hardships. Happening one time to lose a boot belonging to the groom, he would not suffer me to have any shoes all that winter, which was a great punishment to me.

When sixteen years old, I was bound apprentice to a trade. After being in the shop about two years, I had the charge of my master's tools, which being very good, were often used by the men, if I happened to be out of the way. When this was the case, or any of them were lost, or misplaced, my master beat me severely, striking me upon the head, or any other part without mercy. One time in the holidays, my master and the men being from home, and the care of the house devolving upon me and the younger apprentices, the house was broken open, and robbed of many valuable articles, through the negligence of the apprentice who had then the charge of it. When I came home in the evening, and saw what had happened, my consternation was inconceivable, as all that we had in the world could not make good the loss. The week following, when the master came to town, I was beaten in a most unmerciful manner, so that I was not able to do anything for a fortnight. About eight months after, we were employed in building a store house, and nails were very dear at that time, it being in the American war, so that the workmen had their nails weighed out to them; on this account they made the younger apprentices watch the nails while they were at dinner. It being my lot one day to take care of them, which I did till an apprentice returned to his work, and then I went to dine. In the meantime he took away all the nails belonging to one of the journeymen, and he being of a very violent temper, accused me to the master with stealing them. For this offense I was beaten and tortured most cruelly, and was laid up three weeks before I was able to do any work. My proprietor, hearing of the bad usage

I received, came to town, and severely reprimanded my master[1] for beating me in such a manner, threatening him, that if he ever heard the like again, he would take me away and put me to another master to finish my time, and make him pay for it. This had a good effect, and he behaved much better to me, the two succeeding years, and I began to acquire a proper knowledge of my trade.

My master being apprehensive that Charleston was in danger on account of the war, removed into the country, about thirty-eight miles off. Here we built a large house for Mr. Waters, during which time the English took Charleston. Having obtained leave one day to see my parents, who lived about twelve miles off, and it being late before I could go, I was obliged to borrow one of Mr. Waters's horses; but a servant of my master's, took the horse from me to go a little journey, and stayed two or three days longer than he ought. This involved me in the greatest perplexity, and I expected the severest punishment, because the gentleman to whom the horse belonged was a very bad man, and knew not how to show mercy. To escape his cruelty, I determined to go to Charleston, and throw myself into the hands of the English. They received me readily, and I began to feel the happiness of liberty, of which I knew nothing before, although I was much grieved at first, to be obliged to leave my friends, and reside among strangers. In this situation I was seized with the smallpox, and suffered great hardships; for all the blacks affected with that disease, were ordered to be carried a mile from the camp, lest the soldiers should be infected, and disabled from marching. This was a grievous circumstance to me and many others. We lay sometimes a whole day without anything to eat or drink; but Providence sent a man, who belonged to the York volunteers whom I was acquainted with, to my relief. He brought me such things as I stood in need of; and by the blessing of the Lord I began to recover.

By this time, the English left the place,[2] but as I was unable to march with the army, I expected to be taken by the enemy. However when they came, and understood that we were ill of the smallpox, they precipitately left us for fear of the infection. Two days after, the wagons were sent to convey us to the English army, and we were put into a little cottage (being twenty-five in number) about a quarter of a mile from the hospital.

Being recovered, I marched with the army to Chamblem.[3] When we came to the headquarters, our regiment was thirty-five miles off. I stayed at the head-quarters three weeks, during which time our regiment had an engagement with the Americans, and the man who relieved me when I was ill of the smallpox, was wounded in the battle, and brought to the hospital. As soon as I heard of his misfortune, I went to see him, and tarried with him in the hospital six weeks, till he recovered, rejoicing that it was in my power to return him the kindness he had showed me. From thence I went to a place about thirty-five

[1] King makes a distinction between his legal *proprietor* and the *master* to whom he was apprenticed.
[2] The British took Charleston on May 12, 1780 and did not leave until December 13, 1782, well after Cornwallis's defeat at Yorktown.
[3] Unidentified, and perhaps a misprint in the original.

miles off, where we stayed two months, at the expiration of which, an express came to the colonel to decamp in fifteen minutes. When these orders arrived I was at a distance from the camp, catching some fish for the captain that I waited upon; upon returning to the camp, to my great astonishment, I found all the English were gone, and had left only a few militia. I felt my mind greatly alarmed, but Captain Lewes, who commanded the militia, said, "You need not be uneasy, for you will see your regiment before seven o'clock tonight." This satisfied me for the present, and in two hours we set off. As we were on the march, the captain asked, "How will you like me to be your master?" I answered, that I was Captain Grey's servant. "Yes," said he; "but I expect they are all taken prisoners before now; and I have been long enough in the English service, and am determined to leave them." These words roused my indignation, and I spoke some sharp things to him. But he calmly replied, "If you do not behave well, I will put you in irons, and give you a dozen stripes every morning." I now perceived that my case was desperate, and that I had nothing to trust to, but to wait the first opportunity for making my escape. The next morning, I was sent with a little boy over the river to an island to fetch the captain some horses. When we came to the island we found about fifty of the English horses, that Captain Lewes had stolen from them at different times while they were at Rockmount. Upon our return to the captain with the horses we were sent for, he immediately set off by himself.

I stayed till about ten o'clock, and then resolved to go to the English army. After traveling twenty-four miles, I came to a farmer's house, where I tarried all night, and was well used. Early in the morning I continued my journey till I came to the ferry, and found all the boats were on the other side of the river. After anxiously waiting some hours, Major Dial crossed the river, and asked me many questions concerning the regiment to which I belonged. I gave him satisfactory answers, and he ordered the boat to put me over. Being arrived at the headquarters, I informed my captain that Mr. Lewes had deserted. I also told him of the horses which Lewes had conveyed to the island. Three weeks after, our light horse went to the island and burnt his house; they likewise brought back forty of the horses, but he escaped. I tarried with Captain Grey about a year, and then left him, and came to Nelson's Ferry.[4] Here I entered into the service of the commanding officer of that place.

But our situation was very precarious, and we expected to be made prisoners every day, for the Americans had 1600 men, not far off; whereas our whole number amounted only to 250, but there were 1200 English about thirty miles off, only we knew not how to inform them of our danger, as the Americans were in possession of the country. Our commander at length determined to send me with a letter, promising me great rewards, if I was successful in the business. I refused going on horseback, and set off on foot about three o'clock in the afternoon; I expected every moment to fall in with the enemy, whom I well knew would show me no mercy. I went on without interruption, till I got

---

[4]Near present Eutawville, South Carolina.

within six miles of my journey's end, and then was alarmed with a great noise a little before me. But I stepped out of the road, and fell flat upon my face 'till they were gone by. I then arose, and praised the name of the Lord for his great mercy, and again pursued my journey, till I came to Mum's Corner tavern. I knocked at the door, but they blew out the candle. I knocked again, and entreated the master to open the door. At last he came with a frightful countenance, and said, "I thought it was the Americans, for they were here about an hour ago, and I thought they were returned again." I asked, "How many were there?" He answered, "About one hundred." I desired him to saddle his horse for me, which he did, and went with me himself. When we had gone about two miles, we were stopped by the picketguard, till the captain came out with thirty men. As soon as he knew that I had brought an express from Nelson's Ferry, he received me with great kindness, and expressed his approbation of my courage and conduct in this dangerous business. Next morning, Colonel Small gave me three shillings, and many fine promises, which were all that I ever received for this service from him. However he sent 600 men to relieve the troops at Nelson's Ferry.

Soon after I went to Charleston, and entered on board a man-of-war. As we were going to Chesapeake Bay, we were at the taking of a rich prize. We stayed in the bay two days, and then sailed for New York, where I went on shore. Here I endeavored to follow my trade, but for want of tools was obliged to relinquish it, and enter into service. But the wages were so low that I was not able to keep myself in clothes, so that I was under the necessity of leaving my master and going to another. I stayed with him four months, but he never paid me, and I was obliged to leave him also, and work about the town until I was married. A year after I was taken very ill, but the Lord raised me up again in about five weeks. I then went out in a pilotboat. We were at sea eight days, and had only provisions for five, so that we were in danger of starving. On the ninth day we were taken by an American whaleboat. I went on board them with a cheerful countenance, and asked for bread and water, and made very free with them. They carried me to Brunswick,[5] and used me well. Notwithstanding which, my mind was sorely distressed at the thought of being again reduced to slavery, and separated from my wife and family;[6] and at the same time it was exceeding difficult to escape from my bondage, because the river at Amboy was above a mile over, and likewise [there was] another to cross at Staten Island. I called to remembrance the many great deliverances the Lord had wrought for me, and besought him to save me this once, and I would serve him all the days of my life. While my mind was thus exercised, I went into the jail to see a lad whom I was acquainted with at New York. He had been taken prisoner, and attempted to make his escape, but was caught twelve miles off. They tied him to the tail of a horse, and in this manner brought him back to Brunswick. When I saw him, his feet were fastened in the stocks, and at night both his

[5] New Brunswick, New Jersey.
[6] In New York, King married a woman named Violet, who herself had run away from a master in Wilmington, North Carolina.

hands. This was a terrifying sight to me, as I expected to meet with the same kind of treatment, if taken in the act of attempting to regain my liberty. I was thankful that I was not confined in a jail, and my master used me as well as I could expect; and indeed the slaves about Baltimore, Philadelphia, and New York, have as good victuals as many of the English, for they have meat once a day, and milk for breakfast and supper, and what is better than all, many of the masters send their slaves to school at night, that they may learn to read the scriptures. This is a privilege indeed. But, alas, all these enjoyments could not satisfy me without liberty! Sometimes I thought, if it was the will of God that I should be a slave, I was ready to resign myself to his will; but at other times I could not find the least desire to content myself in slavery.

Being permitted to walk about when my work was done, I used to go to the ferry, and observed, that when it was low water the people waded across the river; though at the same time I saw there were guards posted at the place to prevent the escape of prisoners and slaves. As I was at prayer one Sunday evening, I thought the Lord heard me, and would mercifully deliver me. Therefore putting my confidence in him, about one o'clock in the morning I went down to the river side, and found the guards were either asleep or in the tavern. I instantly entered into the river, but when I was a little distance from the opposite shore, I heard the sentinels disputing among themselves. One said, "I am sure I saw a man cross the river." Another replied, "There is no such thing." It seems they were afraid to fire at me, or make an alarm, lest they should be punished for their negligence. When I had got a little distance from the shore, I fell down upon my knees, and thanked God for this deliverance. I traveled till about five in the morning, and then concealed myself till seven o'clock at night, when I proceeded forward, through bushes and marshes, near the road, for fear of being discovered. When I came to the river, opposite Staten Island, I found a boat; and although it was very near a whaleboat, yet I ventured into it, and cutting the rope, got safe over. The commanding officer, when informed of my case, gave me a passport, and I proceeded to New York.

When I arrived at New York, my friends rejoiced to see me once more restored to liberty, and joined me in praising the Lord for his mercy and goodness. But notwithstanding this great deliverance, and the promises I had made to serve God, yet my good resolutions soon vanished away like the morning dew: the love of this world extinguished my good desires, and stole away my heart from God, so that I rested in a mere form of religion for near three years. About which time (in 1783), the horrors and devastation of war happily terminated, and peace was restored between America and Great Britain, which diffused universal joy among all parties, except us, who had escaped from slavery, and taken refuge in the English army; for a report prevailed at New York, that all the slaves, in number 2000, were to be delivered up to their masters, although some of them had been three or four years among the English. This dreadful rumor filled us all with inexpressible anguish and terror, especially when we saw our old masters coming from Virginia, North Carolina, and other parts, and seizing upon their slaves in the streets of New York, or even dragging them out of their beds. Many of the slaves had very cruel masters, so that the thoughts of returning home with them embittered life to us. For some days we lost our appetite for food, and sleep departed from our eyes. The English had compassion upon us in the day of distress, and issued out a proclamation [of the import] that all slaves should be free, who had taken refuge in the British lines, and claimed the sanction and privileges of the proclamations respecting the security and protection of Negroes. In consequence of this, each of us received a certificate from the commanding officer at New York, which dispelled all our fears, and filled us with joy and gratitude.[7] Soon after, ships were fitted out, and furnished with every necessary[8] for conveying us to Nova Scotia. We arrived at Birchtown[9] in the month of August, where we all safely landed. Every family had a lot of land, and we exerted all our strength in order to build comfortable huts before the cold weather set in.

[7] Sir Guy Carleton (1724–1808), who was appointed to head the British army in North America in May 1782, resisted American attempts to secure the return of escaped slaves.
[8] I.e., necessity.
[9] Birchtown was named in honor of General Samuel Birch, the last British commandant of New York City, who gave the fleeing, freed blacks certificates guaranteeing their liberty. The town was laid out near Port Roseway (later Shelburne), on the southern tip of Nova Scotia, in August 1783; by January of the following year, with a population of 1,521, it was the largest free black settlement in North America.

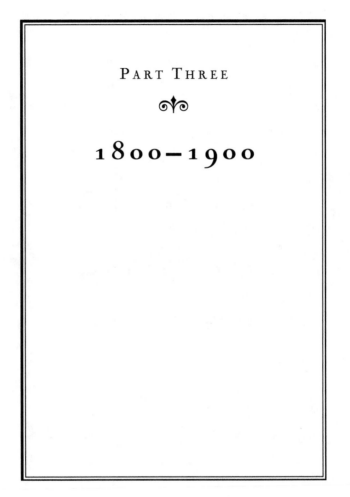

PART THREE

❧

1800–1900

1

FOUR ITINERANTS IN THE
LAND OF THE FREE

AMONG THE MANY SOCIAL CHANGES THAT SWEPT OVER AMERICA IN THE WAKE
of the Revolution was a new, often intense interest in the narrated details and
significance of ordinary lives. The present selections from four ordinary narratives published from 1798 to 1815 reveal not only the intensity of that interest,
but also the range of the lives open to scrutiny.

The first narrative, written by Stephen Burroughs (1765–1840), is the classic account of a charming but troubling scalawag who cut a broad path through
American society in the 1780s and 1790s. The son of a Presbyterian minister in
Hanover, New Hampshire, Burroughs was born in the year of the Stamp Act
crisis, and thus was only eleven when the colonies declared their independence
from Britain. Despite his youth, he soon began a series of attempts to join
the American army, succeeding at last when he was just fourteen. Burroughs's
reputation as "the worst boy in town" may help explain his desire to jump into
the fray, though he certainly was familiar with the standard rhetoric of the
revolutionaries and was adept at using it to defend a life that was morally thread-
bare: "I am so far a republican," he remarked disingenuously on the opening
page of his personal narrative (written just after his release from jail on a counterfeiting conviction), "that I consider a man's merit to rest entirely with himself, without any regard to family, blood, or connection." For those who had
encountered him or simply reflected on what they read, Burroughs's gesture
toward sturdy independence was not all that it seemed to be. Indeed, his life
was a fabric of imposture, swindling, misrepresentation, and imposition on the
good will and property of others. Not even his closest relatives were immune to
his worst behavior. When nineteen, Burroughs stole his father's sermon books
and ran off to Pelham, Massachusetts, to set himself up—until he was
unmasked—as a minister. His masquerade in Pelham was, too, merely the latest
of a series of morally troubling "reverses" in the young man's career. Just before
his stint as a preacher, Burroughs had left the army in 1781 for the life of a
scholar at Dartmouth College, which abruptly expelled him during his sopho-
more year; thereafter, in 1783, he had sailed out of Newburyport on a Yankee
packet bound for France—as the ship's physician.

When narrating his imprisonment for counterfeiting (the selection given here concerns his arrest and trial), Burroughs had sufficient audacity to complain that he was shut out from "tasting the sweets of liberty, for which we had so lately fought and bled." "How is this," he went on, ". . . that a country which has stood the foremost in asserting the cause of liberty, that those who have tasted the bitter cup of slavery, and have known from hence the value of liberty, should so soon after obtaining that blessing themselves, deprive others of it?" By then, of course, as Burroughs had the temporary honesty to go on and admit, his actions had forfeited his claim to rights, but there was enough force to his rhetoric at a time when the treatment of criminals was under hot debate that he could exude a certain tone of just indignation. Part of the legacy of the Revolution was an uncertain sense of where the boundaries between political liberty and personal indulgence lay, and how the new governments in the states and nation were to establish authority among a populace that had just shown itself resistant to external control. Burroughs fascinated his contemporaries in part because he expressed their own obsession with liberty and restraint.

The roots of his fascination also stretched in other directions. In dislodging the hierarchies of colonial society, Americans had undermined a social order that tended to certify the identity of individuals by reference to their "place" (both geographical and hierarchical) and relied on institutions and on the word of others to vouch for their character. With the wholesale migration that began after the war, and the social mobility that accompanied it, the moral geography of American life became considerably more complicated. The same fluidity that allowed some people to seek honest improvement in their condition elsewhere allowed others, such as Burroughs, to exploit the new openness of the landscape for illicit ends. Counterfeiting was such a typical crime in the postwar years partly for economic reasons but partly, too, because it was served by the new mobility that allowed the circulation of unknown "outsiders" such as Burroughs all across the landscape. His initial success as a preacher in Pelham depended on his ability to show up in the town and pass himself off—as he later was to pass off coins—as the real thing.

Burroughs's daring as a writer shows why he could so easily chat his way into positions of trust during his early life. Although a violent will underpinned his seductive surface, he evidently could seem to be a man of plausible, even likable qualities, one who became what others wanted him to be precisely because they projected their wishes onto him and had few reliable means of checking his stories. In a culture that had weakened all forms of social deference in displacing monarchy, Burroughs may have worked his magic most of all by playing on anxieties about self-presentation and the forms of social vouching that more traditionally had cushioned and contained it. First and last, he vouched for himself, and his self-confidence may have helped him persuade those whom he tricked that he was precisely who he said he was. He was obviously talented in deception, but that Burroughs was arrested in 1790 on rape charges (on one of which he was convicted) suggests that not everything was a matter of manipulated surfaces and misemployed genius. Exploits and exploitation were close kin in his experience.

After many other episodes, including time spent on Long Island and in Georgia, and another tour as a counterfeiter of United States money (this time from across the border in Canada, in the service of Britain), Burroughs pioneered the archetypal confidence man's final stance of contrite repentance: converted to Roman Catholicism, he wound up as a school teacher in Trois-Rivières, Quebec, where he died obscurely in 1840 even as his wonderfully seductive book kept pouring off the presses, in edition after edition—a total of thirty by the end of the century.

Our second narrator, Venture Smith, pursued a vastly different career. Born in Guinea, Africa, around 1729, "Smith" was in fact Broteer, eldest son of "Saungm Furro, prince of the tribe of Dukandarra." When Broteer was about six, Saungm Furro's people were conquered by nearby enemies whom "some white nation . . . equipped and sent . . . to subdue and possess the country." Broteer soon became a slave, purchased by "one Robertson Mumford," steward of a Rhode Island vessel. That vessel stopped first at the island of Barbados, by which point almost a quarter of the human cargo had died of smallpox. All the remaining slaves were sold to the planters there, except "Venture" and three others, who were carried back to Rhode Island by Captain Collingwood.

Venture's master lived on Fisher's Island, now a part of New York though located immediately adjacent to the Connecticut and Rhode Island coasts. Mumford at first employed the young slave at relatively mild work, but by the time Smith was nine years old he was heavily burdened. He also was soon caught between the wills of Robertson Mumford and Robertson's son James—who, Venture wrote many years later with a sarcastic tone, "came up to me in the course of [one] day, big with authority, and commanded me very arrogantly to quit my present business and go directly about what he should order me." When Venture replied that he already had his orders for the day, young Mumford came at him with a pitchfork; Venture snatched up another and parried, at which point his "upstart master" called in a number of other workers and told them to tie Venture up. When he proved too powerful for them, young Mumford ran home weeping to his mother. Venture, who calmly let himself be taken before her, was strung up on a butcher's "gallows" for an hour for defending his own rights. It was the same calm sense of his due (and, in several senses, self-possession) that led him soon afterward to turn in an Irishman with whom he tried to run away when that man betrayed his fellow escapees by stealing their few belongings. One can begin to see in this case why Venture was to be famous among the inhabitants of the region long after his death for his physical strength and his strength of character.

A man of such forcefulness was not long for such a place. Even while confined in slavery, Venture sought to construct a world within the world his master made for him. At twenty-two he married a young woman named Meg, another of Mumford's slaves. Soon Venture, the father of month-old Hannah, was sold by Mumford to a mainland farmer named Thomas Stanton. Through labor in his "free" time, Venture Smith had already accumulated capital, a modest sum at first, but soon enough that he could loan more than twenty pounds to Stanton's brother. The Stantons seem to have been a difficult lot, at one time pushing Venture so far that he went to the law over his mistreatment. This was always a risky recourse for a slave, and Venture was paid for it with new beatings and by being defrauded of the loan by the Stantons. At the same time, however, he conspired with a man named Hempsted Miner to make life so difficult for the Stantons that they would gladly sell him below his value— to none other than Miner, who in turn promised Venture that he would, as Venture put it, "give me a good chance to gain my freedom when I came to live with him."

Miner proved an unreliable partner in this last effort, but Venture's next master, Colonel Oliver Smith, agreed to the project in earnest, and in time Venture was able (as fisherman and farmer and woodchopper in Connecticut and on Long Island) to buy himself at the age of thirty-six, three decades after his original capture in Guinea. Thereafter, taking Colonel Smith's name as his own, he lived a life of extreme simplicity, saving all he could toward the purchase of his two sons, Solomon and Cuff, and at last (when Venture himself was forty-four) his wife Meg, then pregnant with their fourth child. He also redeemed from slavery three other black men whom he purchased from their masters. Not until he was forty-six did he manage to buy Hannah, who by that time must have been in her twenties, and as it happened, sadly was soon to die. Although Venture Smith managed by hard work and sharp attention to his property to acquire land and some wealth, he had to keep an eye out for the deceits of those whites who still thought him fair game. His description of the chicanery of Captain Elisha Hart, that "white gentleman" of Saybrook, is particularly worth attention. Long-lived, Venture Smith labored to the century's end, still living with his wife Meg at their farm in East Haddam, Connecticut, when, at the age of sixty-nine, his story was published in New London. Smith was to live on there until his death in 1805.

Venture Smith's narrative stretches back well before the Revolution, in which Venture's son Cuff fought, but the war is never mentioned by Venture himself, who had bought his own freedom during the Stamp Act crisis and that of his daughter Hannah in 1776. Still, the book's appearance in 1798, vouched for by five white Stonington residents, surely was owing to the new interest in "obscure" and ordinary lives that was one product of the war and to the rising tide of early abolitionism. The man to whom Venture Smith dictated the story, schoolteacher Elisha Niles, himself a veteran of the Revolution, remarked in his preface to the narrative that the sufferings of Venture Smith were pitiable and scandalous. And he drew a lesson only this post-Revolutionary age was prepared to find in such stories: "The reader may here see a Franklin and a Washington, in a state of nature, or rather in a state of slavery"—a man of "honesty, prudence and industry" regardless of the extraordinary oppressions he had suffered. In this sense, as the hero of his own account, Venture Smith was a strange legatee of the war he never mentioned.

The same war mattered in a very different way for the third narrator, John Robert Shaw (1761–1813). Born in Yorkshire, Shaw had a youth that rivaled that of Stephen Burroughs, and he also capped it by running away to be a soldier—though for the king. That was in 1776 or early 1777, before Saratoga, when the British prospects in the war were bright, though by the time he actually shipped for America in April 1778, Burgoyne's disaster had already happened, and once in New York, Shaw's own experience was hardly brilliant. Early on, he found himself sent across the river to Elizabeth, New Jersey, where he and his fellows were "in woeful pickle, all bedaubed with mud and mire, as black as chimney sweepers," more likely to frighten the residents by their looks than their arms. Although the town fell to the British, who proceeded to burn down the American barracks there (with a dozen sick soldiers inside), almost immediately the Americans countered and thrust them back. Other engagements, some successful and some not, followed in the North until Shaw went south on Sir Henry Clinton's expedition against Charleston in May 1780. He later was involved in the famous battle at Cowpens (January 1781), and ultimately was taken prisoner by some of Lighthorse Harry Lee's men when out on a search for food with several fellow redcoats in March 1781. Moved north with other prisoners, Shaw finally wound up in Lancaster, Pennsylvania, where he escaped from his confinement, only to join the army again—but the American army this time, motivated by the bounty money and by the thought that he thus could make a clean break with the British service. He claimed that many of the men in his American unit, including the recruiter who enlisted him, were British deserters such as himself.

Discharged in May 1784, Shaw drank away the proceeds of his service and then reenlisted for a second tour before ultimately settling down into the new career that was to support him and bring him, between further alcoholic "frolics," the considerable fame he enjoyed during his life—namely, the excavation, quarrying, and especially the digging (and blasting out) of wells. Aided by his small stature, which had almost kept him out of the British army in the first place, the itinerant Shaw dug his way across Pennsylvania into the Ohio Valley, and particularly Kentucky. He always supplemented this work with many other kinds, from basket-weaving to agricultural day labor, but the thousands of feet of wells that he dug and kept careful record of clearly were his greatest works. With a flair for self-promotion to match his talent for self-destruction, Shaw was also a "bletonist," touting and practicing the art of dowsing (finding underground water by means of a divining rod or dowsing stick), associated in his day with a French practitioner named Bleton. Alternately impressed by a need to reform his moral character and a wholehearted devotion to debauchery, he had the risk-taker's habitual carelessness. When he wrote and published his life story in his long-time hometown, Lexington, Kentucky, in 1807, he was recovering from injuries suffered—this was the fourth such occurrence—in one of his explosions ("I have lost no less than one eye, four fingers, one thumb, and seven toes," he wrote with evident pride in his ever-diminishing substance). Widely subscribed to by readers in several states who knew him or had heard of him, the book played on his swagger and his apparent luck. Miraculously, although it took several months, Shaw recovered to the point that he could again take up a shovel. The fifth time he was not so fortunate: an accidental gunpowder explosion during a well excavation in August of 1813 claimed his life.

The final narrative, that of Abigail Abbot Bailey (1746–1815), was published after her death, edited by her onetime minister, Reverend Ethan Smith, but based soundly on an autobiographical record composed in the 1790s. It was a record that Mrs. Bailey had good reason to compose. Born in Concord, New Hampshire, and raised there and to the north in Coos County, Abigail Abbot came from a large, actively religious family. Religion is one key to her life and narrative, but the *Memoirs of Mrs. Abigail Bailey* is no ordinary account of conversion and piety. It is an exceptionally rare candid account of how Abigail's husband, Asa Bailey, physically and psychologically abused his wife and, more importantly, sexually abused their third daughter, Phebe. A man of outward wealth and respectability in his community, Asa Bailey obviously led a troubled life; lacking the religious guidance possessed by his wife, and driven by strong emotional dependencies and a fierce temper, he began abusing Abigail shortly after their marriage in 1767, carried on a sexual affair with their hired girl within two years of the marriage, tried to rape another woman soon thereafter, and, after the couple had been together twenty-one years and had had fourteen children, started to pay undue attentions to Phebe, whom he alternately courted and chastised until he had reduced her to his will.

Abigail, devastated by Asa's earliest violence toward her but apparently raised in a family where anger played little part, seems not to have known how to deal with him. She persisted in the relationship, enduring and accommodating her husband (whose mercurial temperament made him at times exceptionally tender toward her) until it became clear to her that his treatment of Phebe was not just unfortunate—as she had viewed her own case earlier—but outrageous and not to be borne. Hence she confronted her husband in a moment of exquisite strength, and, in a kind of allegory of the Revolution, stood her ground and told him things *would* change. "He flew into a passion, was high, and seemed to imagine he could at once frighten me out of my object. But I was carried equally above fear, and above temper. Of this I soon convinced him, I let him know, that the business I now had taken in hand, was of too serious a nature, and too interesting, to be thus disposed of, or dismissed with a few angry words. . . . I would not suffer him to go on any longer as he had done." Asa was taken aback by her staunch defiance, and though he tried his hardest to temporize, plead, whine, beg forgiveness—and at last, kidnap her and take her to New York, where the laws were less friendly to women—Abigail persisted, had her way, and divorced him. The unfortunate truth remained that the crime he had committed was, by contemporary law, against Abigail rather than Phebe (it was considered adultery, rather than incest). Not surprisingly, Phebe left both her parents on her eighteenth birthday, never to return and never to definitively resurface. For her mother, at the least, the lessons of the tragedy were clear. She had stood her ground, defying her husband's authority, and had emerged—through pain, embarrassment, economic loss, isolation—justified and relieved. To the women who read her book the grief would be evident, but the guidance was also firm. Abigail had confronted her personal devil, called him what he was, and named him and his crime to a public much wider than the one that was privy to it during her life in New Hampshire. Here was a new use to which personal narrative might be put in the nation, a use to which many others were to resort in coming decades.

STEPHEN BURROUGHS

from Memoirs of Stephen Burroughs (1798)

IN ORDER TO GIVE ME SOME CONSOLATION FOR THE DISAPPOINTMENT WHICH I had suffered, Lysander told me he had a plan in agitation which would operate nearly as well as we expected the other would have done. "Glazier Wheeler," said he, "is a man who can be depended on for his honesty to those for whom he undertakes to work, and he can make one silver dollar into three counterfeits, which will pass as well as any. And it will be in our power to prosecute our intended expedition to the Isle of Sable upon this scheme, with nearly as great profit as we expected from transmuting metals. We shall not be with the old man a great while, before we shall be able to work at that business as well as he; and should we find it necessary, can hire a number of hands, and drive the business, at this place to a great extent; as we shall be retired from the observations of the world, and can carry on the business without molestation."[1]

My answer to Lysander was to this purport.—"You are sensible that counterfeiting the coin of any country is contrary, not only to the laws of that country, but likewise to the laws of our own minds, having implicitly engaged to observe and protect those laws, when we once take advantage of their efficacy to protect us in the enjoyment of our rights and privileges; therefore, should the business succeed according to our most sanguine wishes, and the coin pass to the end of time as standard silver, yet we should as really violate the simple principles of justice, as though we should be detected in passing coin so base as to serve

---

[1] "Lysander" is the name Burroughs gave to a friend who lived in Pelham, Massachusetts, where Burroughs, using his mother's maiden name (Davis), had falsely assumed the role of a minister of the gospel. Prior to Burroughs's flight from Pelham after the discovery of his fraud, Lysander had proposed that the two of them go to the Isle of Sable, off the coast of Nova Scotia, to counterfeit U.S. coins by "transmuting" copper into silver. The process to be used, demonstrated to them by a confidence man named Philips, an associate of Glazier Wheeler, was itself an imposture; hence the new plan, involving Wheeler himself, was to involve the use of real silver coins.

only a temporary purpose, and die in the hands of an innocent person. The transgression would be as absolute, should it never transpire[2] to the world, or be attended with any personal injury, as though it should be proclaimed to the universe; therefore, this reason alone would be sufficient to deter me from wishing such a thing to take place. Another very powerful reason is, the danger we run in prosecuting such a matter, and the ruin which would inevitably follow a detection. Glazier Wheeler it appears, has followed this business for fifty years constantly; yet he never could bring his art to such perfection as to have his money pass undetected. How often has he been confined, pilloried, cropped[3] and whipped for this business? How many have been involved in this same difficulty, who embarked in this dangerous voyage with him? How then can we expect to share a better fate? And what would be the consequence of a detection? The property which you now possess would be swept away; your children would cry in vain for bread; your reputation, which you now hold so dear, would be lost forever; and you would entail misery and infamy on your posterity. You must then be separated from your companion, from your children, from your friends; confined in a jail, a receptacle for the off-scourings of nature; treated with contempt; injured without pity; made the scoff and jeer of fools. This, sir, is a scene for a mind of sensibility."

The wife of Lysander heard this discourse with the utmost attention. Her countenance was a strong index to the feelings of her mind. Her color went and came. She now grew pale with apprehension, and now her cheeks reddened with the flush of desire, to prevent her beloved husband from rushing into dangers so desperate. She remonstrated. She expostulated. She entreated. But all to no purpose. Lysander was fixed, and nothing was able to remove his resolution. He turned to his wife with a look of that ineffable sweetness which overpowers the mind, and said, "My dear, I wish very much to see you in possession of a coach, which I shall send you in a few months."

"As to the objections which you offer, Mr. Burroughs," said Lysander, "I will endeavor to answer them in such a manner as to give you full satisfaction on that subject. If mankind had no disposition to infringe upon the rights of each other, there would be no need of law; and the whole nature, design and spirit of law is to protect each other from injury; and where no injury is intended, nor in fact done, the whole essence of law is attended to. I know the law speaks in general terms, because it cannot descend to particulars, there being such an infinity, as to put it beyond the power of man to comprehend the whole in a system; therefore, general principles must direct us in our interpretation of law. We ought in our conduct, to act as men possessing reason sufficient to direct us under the various occurrences of life, so as to vary our conduct according as circumstances shall point out, keeping in view, and practising upon the spirit of law, and when we attend to this, we cannot be said in

[2] Be revealed.
[3] To have the top of his ears trimmed off so as to make him easily identifiable as a convicted felon.

reality, to transgress the laws of the land, nor indeed the laws of our minds, because we in fact do fulfill our compact with society, namely, protect each other from injury.

"From what I have observed, I believe you will readily agree with me, that I am right in prosecuting my present plan, if I can make it evident, that no danger of injury will arise to anyone from it, and that by it, many will be made better. Money, of itself, is of no consequence, only as we, by mutual agreement, annex to it a nominal value, as the representation of property. Anything else might answer the same purpose, equally with silver and gold, should mankind only agree to consider it as such, and carry that agreement into execution in their dealings with each other. We find this verified in fact, by those bills of credit which are in circulation through the world. Those bills, simply, are good for nothing; but the moment mankind agree to put a value on them, as representing property, they become of as great consequence as silver and gold, and no one is injured by receiving a small insignificant piece of paper for a hundred bushels of wheat, when mankind stamp that value upon it, by agreeing to receive it for that amount. Therefore, we find the only thing necessary to make a matter valuable, is to induce the world to deem it so; and let that esteem be raised by any means whatever, yet the value is the same, and no one becomes injured by receiving it at the valuation. Hence, we find the world putting an enormous value upon certain stones, which intrinsically are of no use; as for instance, the diamond, the carbuncle, etc. These stones cannot be made use of in any pursuit of life. They will not serve for food, for raiment, or for any instrument of any kind whatever; therefore, of what real use can they be? Their scarcity, and certain peculiarites, have induced mankind to esteem them; and this esteem stamps a value upon them, so that they pass from one to another as the representation of property; hence, the holders of them always have a valuable possession, and probably always will have, which they at any time can exchange for property of more immediate consequence to their support. Had I the art of making diamonds, do you suppose I should transgress the laws of equity in putting that art into practice? except I should fill the world with them, so as to destroy their scarcity, and hence depreciate their value in the hands of others. To put this art into practice, so as to enrich myself, and not destroy that due proportion between representative property and real property, is doing myself a favor, and injuring none. Gold and silver are made use of for convenience, to transact our business of barter and exchange with each other, as the representation of property, it being less cumbersome, and more easy to communicate from one to another, than real property of any kind; hence, when there is a due proportion of representative property, business can be transacted to the greatest advantage, and with the greatest ease. And when the public experience a scarcity or redundancy, they of course suffer an inconveniency; therefore, that person who contributes his mite to keep the balance between those two species of property just poised, is a blessing to himself and to the community of which he is a member. That an undue scarcity of cash now prevails, is a truth too obvious for me to attempt to prove.[4] Your own observation will convince you of it. Hence, whoever contributes, really to increase the quantity of cash, does not only himself, but likewise the community an essential benefit. And, that this can be done, in the pursuit which I have undertaken, and without endangering the safety of any one, I will convince you by ocular demonstration."

He then presented me with a bag of dollars, which he said were made by Glazier Wheeler. I poured them all out; I examined them with care, as I then thought; I compared them with other dollars, which were good. I could discover no difference.

His arguments now stood all plain before me; they were collected in a line; and what do you think was the consequence? I blush to tell you the truth!—I feel ashamed of my own weakness!—My great want of solid judgment at that time, almost persuades me to hide the relation of this fact. These arguments convinced me, unfounded as they were.

Lysander told me his intentions were to pay strict attention to the business, and did not doubt his finally raising himself and family to a state of the greatest affluence. He had already obtained a sufficiency to answer present purposes. He should soon obtain much more. The business was at a stand, just at present, for want of drugs[5] proper for carrying it forward. He intended soon to go to Springfield, where he should obtain whatever he wanted for such a purpose.

Lysander had not yet passed, or attempted to pass, any of his money. As I expected to leave his house the next night, on my route to Danbury, and to pass through Springfield in my way, he agreed to set out with me, and go his route in my company. His wife had ever felt dissatisfied about this business; being easily alarmed with the least appearance of danger, towards one in whom her happiness was so essentially embraced; but when I drew the dreadful picture of a detection, she grew almost frantic with fear; and when she saw that no entreaties would prevail over his determination, she embraced the first opportunity of conversing with me alone; and besought me in those moving terms which would have melted a savage, to use my influence to prevent him from prosecuting his present undertaking.

Her grief spoke more powerfully for her, than all the oratory of a Burke.[6] I could not resist her importunity. The language of her countenance and actions [was] irresistible. When Lysander came into our company, I began the attack in the most vulnerable part of his fortress. I endeavored to set the distress

---

[4] "Lysander's" Lockean sophistries do point here to a very real contemporary issue. In the very town where Burroughs had worked in 1785 as "Rev. Davis," Pelham, Massachusetts, Daniel Shays the next year was to begin his short-lived "Rebellion." Shays roused the area's heavily indebted farmers, who felt themselves oppressed by a shortness of money, and led them in attacks on the courts and, in 1787, the state arsenal at Springfield.

[5] I.e., chemicals.

[6] Edmund Burke (1729–1797), British statesman whose eloquence was especially noted by Americans because he supported the colonies in their dispute with Britain.

of his wife in its true light before him. I recapitulated his own arguments, which he had before used, in order to induce me, "to be contented with a bare competeney." I repeated to him emphatically the words of Young, in his "Night Thoughts":[7]

> Why all this toil for triumphs of an hour?
> What tho' we wade in wealth, or soar in fame,
> Earth's highest station ends in "Here he lies."

I told him I knew perfectly well his sincere affections for his wife, and his ambition of seeing her become possessed of an equipage, etc. "But believe me, sir, not all the pomp and splendor of riches will repay her for the pain and anxiety she will endure on your account, for the space of one day, when you have absolutely launched into this dangerous ocean; therefore, sir, inasmuch as her happiness is a leading motive in your pursuits in life, you will make a most egregious blunder in your calculations, even provided you are ever so successful in your undertakings."

The feelings of Lysander were moved. The struggle in his breast was apparent in his countenance. He sat in silence a while, then burst into a flood of tears, and retired into another room. Not many minutes had elapsed before he returned. His countenance wore a more settled aspect. He mentioned his weakness with some confusion. He said he was ashamed of being seen in tears, especially on such an occasion, not having resolution sufficient to withstand our united attacks. "But," said he, "the business is fixed—the die is cast—I have pledged my faith—I have given my word to procure those articles at Springfield. Not only myself, but more than a dozen others, are now waiting for me to fulfill my engagements. Shall I, of all others, after having agreed in the most solemn manner to yield my aid in the prosecution of this business, now in open violation of faith, retreat and leave them in suspense?

"I feel the emotions of gratitude towards you, Mr. Burroughs, for the warmth of your feelings in my concerns; but this truth is manifest to me, that the enthusiasm of your feelings as well as my wife's, does not give you an opportunity of reasoning coolly and candidly upon this subject. Enough has been said. These articles must be obtained; and no entreaties shall deter me from paying attention to it."

What could be done? what more could be said? Lysander's wife I saw was inconsolable. What would you have done, had you been in my situation? Words had now become entirely out of the question, and only one thing remained to be done; and that I determined to do.

I told Lysander I would take his money; go to Springfield, purchase all the articles, and return with them immediately. With some reluctance he consented, gave me twenty dollars for the business, made out his account of the

[7]Edward Young (1683–1765) published his *Night Thoughts* in 1742–45.

articles wanted, and directed me to the apothecary's shop, to whom I must apply for them. At night I left them with ten thousand blessings accompanying me.

Riding alone through the dreary night, reflection would make me a visit. The scenes through which I had passed had been so rapid, and filled with the emotions of sensibility,[8] to that degree, as to leave but little room for reflection.

I have now, said I, set out to perform that business, which, two days since, I do not believe the art of man could have persuaded me to.

It is a new undertaking; but I believe not attended with danger; for the money is executed so well, as to prevent any man from distinguishing it from standard silver: at least it looks as well to me as any money; and I do not see why I cannot distinguish counterfeit from true money, as well as others.

I think my motive for this undertaking is founded on the principles of uprightness. I think the sentiment of friendship is the uppermost object in this undertaking. Possibly a species of vanity might have some influence on my mind; and that I might wish to show the wife of Lysander how ready I was to undertake such a desperate business to befriend her; though, in reality, the danger consisted chiefly in her own fancy.

What would be the consequence, should one among the ten thousand events, which daily occur, serve to reveal the part, which I am now about to act? What would be the opinion of people concerning me, but of the most disagreeable kind, after having passed the ordeal of Pelham reports, founded on facts, which, to the world at large, would appear very unfavorable? They would undoubtedly form their opinion from ostensible facts, that I was divested of honesty, uprightness and integrity. And even should I declare to the world, that my intentions were not against the good of society, this declaration would fall upon the unbelieving hearts of a multitude, prone to place confidence in an evil report, and difficult in giving credit to that which is favorable.

These circumstances would, moreover, be attended with the following disagreeable events, namely, reports of my misfortunes, or crimes, would spread and probably be attended with that exaggeration, of which reports of that kind generally partake, and reach my friends, connections and enemies; and of misfortunes, that which gives triumph to an enemy is the most keenly felt. My friends would mourn, my enemies would rejoice.

A view of these disagreeable events, which probably might happen, made a very deep impression on my mind. I was almost ready to faint under the trial, and thought to relinquish my undertaking. But again, said I, should I fail upon this first trial, what a pitiful appearance should I make in my own eyes? I set out on this expedition with an idea that my friendship would carry me any length. I have pledged my friendship for the performance of this business; and shall this be said of Burroughs, that in fair weather he was possessed with

---

[8]Burroughs draws on the language of "sensibility" as articulated by various eighteenth-century thinkers and writers. The opposite of rationality, and associated with benevolence and innocence, it usually, as here, suggests a primarily emotional response to experience.

friendly sentiments, but the moment the prospect became overcast with clouds, his friendship failed? How shall it be known whether I really possess those sentiments of benevolence, of which I have made such a pompous display, otherwise than by standing the trial in time of adversity? If the feelings of Damon and Pythias[9] were graduated upon that scale of cool deliberation, which has appeared in my reasoning upon this subject, those God-like acts of benevolence towards each other would never have been recorded of them, which not only made Dionysius stand in mute astonishment, but left a memento to the end of time, to what an amazing height virtuous friendship may arise.

Contemplating upon matters, in this point of view, it gave me pain to think that I had even hesitated about my performing the engagements which I had entered into. I felt a degree of guilt, which I wished to hide from my own view; it produced a mortification which was exceedingly painful; therefore, I determined in my own mind, never again to allow myself to [question] the propriety of my undertaking, but to pursue it with unremitting attention, till it was accomplished.

About 11 o'clock, A.M. I arrived at Springfield; made application at the shop where I was directed; told the shopkeeper my demands; and received from him the articles according to the bill. I delivered him his money and departed. Stepping into the printing-office, across the way, to do some business, I was there, in a few minutes arrested by an officer of justice. The business at the apothecary's had made so little impression on my mind, that I could not conceive what could be the cause of my being arrested, at the time when the officer made me a prisoner. He informed me; and in an instant the whole view of my desperate situation opened upon me. I was taken before justice Pincheon, who treated the business with a great degree of candor. However, a company of attorneys, clerks, etc. being called together by this event, were very active in making observations against me, and hunting for evidence, for fear I should not be committed for trial. After all circumstances had been attended to with care, on both sides of the question, and the justice was about to give his final decision on the business, a part of the before mentioned clerks came into the office, hauling after them a man, like the Trojans, when they had found the Greek Sinon, vociferating, "here is a man who knows him! here is a man who knows him!"[1]

When the stranger was introduced, and silence prevailed, Justice Pincheon asked what he knew concerning me? The answer was, that I was the greatest villain in the world; had come to Pelham under a fictitious name; had

[9]Actually, Damon and Phintias (corrupted to Pythias), two residents of Syracuse, on Sicily, in the fourth or fifth century B.C.; Phintias, who had been sentenced to death by the tyrant Dionysius, was released just in time for him to save Damon, who had pledged himself as bail for his friend.
[1]Daniel A. Cohen writes, "On August 23, 1785, Burroughs was arrested in the town of Springfield, Massachusetts, for attempting to pass two counterfeit coins." Greek Sinon: Sinon pretended to desert from the Greek forces besieging Troy so that he could sneak his comrades into the city inside their "Trojan horse."

there preached, when I was unworthy of the business; had endeavored to kill a number of men in Pelham; had cheated them out of their money, etc.

This man you will readily understand, was a Pelhamite. He rode post from Springfield to Pelham, constantly once a week. He felt all the prejudice incident to that people. He gave his testimony in a very categorical manner. It was now determined that I must take up my abode in jail, and there continue till the session of the Supreme Court, when I should take my trial for passing counterfeit money. I was accordingly committed. And now sir, I believe I have brought your patience to a very severe trial, by the length of my tedious narrative; therefore I will leave the business here till tomorrow; for I feel almost sick myself, with ruminating upon the gloomy scenes through which I soon passed after this.

As the apothecary was the only witness against me, which could be produced at court, I entertained warm expectations of being acquitted on my trial.

In the state of Massachusetts, many inconveniences had been experienced from the frequent circulation of counterfeit money; therefore, the governor had offered a reward of twenty-five pounds, L. M.[2] to any person, who should detect another in making or passing counterfeit money, knowing it to be such. Hence, the complainant became interested in the issue on trial, and of course, ought to be excluded from giving his testimony.

The apothecary, it is evident, would be entitled to his reward from government the moment I became convicted of the crime for which I remained confined. Hence, I felt confident that his testimony could not, according to every principle of justice, and would not, be admitted.

In cases where not more than one dollar is in dispute, this regulation is invariably and sacredly adhered to, namely, that no one shall be admitted a witness in a case wherein he is mediately or immediately concerned; and certainly, said I, where character, liberty and property are at stake, they will not dare to deviate from this rule of impartiality.

Those who would plead for the propriety of the apothecary's being admitted a witness in this cause, must either deny this general rule, namely, "that a man interested in a cause, ought to be excluded from bearing testimony in that cause," or else the being entitled to twenty-five pounds, in case of my conviction, did not make the apothecary interested in the case.

Immediately after my confinement, a number of speculative geniuses resorted to me, expecting I would turn evidence for the state, and involve many more in the situation to which I was reduced; they therefore were anxious to improve this time of harvest, and enrich themselves with the bounty of government. Hence, they offered me their exertions in my behalf, and moreover half of the reward which should be received, in case of the conviction of others, from government.

Had these speculators known with what contempt I viewed their conduct, they might have saved themselves considerable trouble. To speculate in human

[2] "Legal money"—not, that is, counterfeit.

woe, and barely for the sake of enriching themselves, reduce others to a state of wretchedness and misery, is an object so detestable as to excite horror in every feeling breast. Had their real motive been the good of society, their object would have been laudable; but it was a matter of public notoriety, that Glazier Wheeler had wrought openly for months past in New Salem; but these heroes took no notice of him, until the moment it was known that a reward was to be obtained for prosecuting money-makers to conviction, then all their ardor was in action; and this too, for the benefit of government.

Those who applied to me, found their expectations frustrated; that I had no design to communicate to them any knowledge I possessed concerning others; therefore they turned their course to different objects; and determined, since I would not further their designs, that I should suffer the effects of popular prejudice.

The printer, in Springfield, inserted a paragraph in his weekly publication, not calculated to fix the most pleasing idea upon the minds of people through the country, namely, that I had been to a clergyman under pretence of coming from a mission among the Indians, and being poorly clothed, had stated to the clergyman, that my clothes had been worn out during my continuance among them. That the clergyman had invited me to preach, and in order to my appearing in character, offered me a suit of clothes; that I had accepted the offer; and in order to prepare myself for the exercises of the next day, had retired into his study, begging the favor of his watch, to know how long I might allow myself to study previous to my retiring to rest. That after the clergyman and his family had retired to rest, I had silently left the house; carrying with me at the same time, watch, clothes, etc. And leaving this text written on paper, and folded as for a sermon, "You shall seek me early and shall not find me."

These matters were all calculated to fix an invincible prejudice against me, in the minds of those people by whom I must ultimately be tried; and consequently deprived me of that favor which every person ought to have, upon a matter of such infinite consequence to his prosperity in life. I saw these matters and what would be the probable event.

I expected application would be made to me, for a discovery of my confederate, or confederates, at the session of the Supreme Court; and therefore, ought to form some system in my own mind, to regulate my conduct upon such an occasion. I ought either to discover the person of whom I received the money, and for whom I had acted in passing it, or else I ought to exonerate him entirely from incrimination, or even suspicion; and in order to weigh these matters in the balance of justice, it will naturally arise into view, what is his situation contrasted with my situation and circumstances? The connections which have existed between us, and our views and expectations under that connection?

True it is, that this act was performed solely for his advantage, not having my own emolument in view, either directly or indirectly; therefore, ought he not to suffer the consequence of this business? Moreover, his character stands as fair in this county, as any man's whatever, and of consequence, he would stand a better chance on trial, in the prejudices of people, than I should. He is likewise a man of property, and can of consequence make arrangements for assistance, by counsel and friends, which I cannot expect; and even should he be convicted, the exertions of government may be more mild towards him, than they would towards me; for judges are but men, and are subject to like passions and prejudices, with other men; and it is not impossible but that they may feel the operation of prejudice in a trial respecting me, as well as others, which I daily see are governed by it.

These were the arguments in favor of my making a discovery of the person from whom I had received the money. The arguments on the other side were, that Lysander, it is true, has a character, property, etc. to lose, and which he moreover must lose, in a great measure, should he be subjected to trial. He has a family, a description of which I have already given you, which must share his fortune in the world; therefore his ruin must bring ruin likewise on his family. A wife, possessed of every tender feeling, must suffer more than is possible for a man to suffer, who is calculated by nature, to endure the robust toils of pain and hardship; and as she must suffer with her husband, in feelings, at least, it will be involving two in misery, as great as what I can endure, should I reveal this business respecting Lysander.

It will likewise involve those who are perfectly innocent, in difficulty, as well as the guilty, namely, Lysander's wife and children; therefore, whether will it be better to meet the impending storm alone and unsupported, or else to exculpate myself, by throwing the same burthen upon six others, and all of them entirely innocent, excepting one? Moreover, why did I undertake this business, unless it was to hazard the danger myself, which attended this undertaking? I am determined. The arguments are more against me than they are for me, and I must stand the power of this storm, thick and fast gathering over my head.

Happy was it for me, that I was ignorant at that time of the dreadful trials and miseries which I had to encounter, before I was released from a state of confinement; otherwise, my courage must have sunk; my resolution must have failed.

My blood, at this distant period of time, runs cold, at taking a retrospective view of those scenes. Since I have been writing this narrative, necessity has compelled me to have recourse to minutes, which brought those scenes into view, which have been a great tax on my tranquillity. I cannot now close my eyes in sleep, without being called to act these things over again in imagination. I start from sleep often, sweating with agony of mind, under the apprehensions which those images present to my view.[3]

My determination being fixed, I laid my account to conduct accordingly. Many people visited me daily, out of curiosity, to see a character entirely new;

---

[3] "These observations, the writer of this note has often heard Burroughs repeat with emotion, even since writing his second volume [i.e., 1804]. How then is it possible he could have again plunged himself headlong, and with his eyes open, into the same gulf of misery!" [Note in 1832 text.]

the public being fully possessed with the belief, that I had absolutely stolen a watch and suit of clothes from a clergyman, and had left him the text before mentioned; and all I could say or do, had no influence to make them believe to the contrary.

Some said this clergyman was Dr. Huntington of Coventry, and some said it was Mr. Trumbull, of North Haven; but those two gentlemen denying any such transaction towards them, said the matter was a fact, but who the clergyman was was unknown. It appeared that the world were determined not to give up any unfavorable idea which had once been broached concerning me, let it be ever so unfounded or improbable. Therefore their ears were open to every breath of slander which was puffed against me. My visitants would often look at me, when relating matters of fact, with an arch significance, declarative of their knowing the bottom of the business, notwithstanding all my plausible declarations. I do believe, if I had set out with warmth, to prove to the world that I was a man, and not a woman, that a great number, from that circumstance, would have been able at once to look through the deception which I was endeavoring to lay them under, and known for certainty that I was, in reality, a woman; so strong was the desire of mankind, at that day, to elude my deceptions, which they thought I was master of, to the utmost degree.

In this situation, you will readily conceive it could hardly be expected that I should run clear of a verdict against me, let the proof be ever so inadequate; for the wisest and most considerate of men will be influenced in their reasonings by those popular clamors, more or less; and they cannot avoid it, so liable is human nature to err in the devious path of life.

The speculators in government bounties had now taken Glazier Wheeler, who was likewise committed for trial. This man you will likely have a curiosity to be made more minutely acquainted with, as he will make somewhat of a figure in this narrative. He was a man tottering under the weight of years, having long since, to all appearance, been a presumptive candidate for the grave. He was a man of small mental abilities, but patient and persevering in any manual pursuit, to admiration. Credulous in the extreme, which subjected him to the duplicity of many who had resorted to him for his work: inoffensive and harmless in his manners, simple in his external appearance, and weak in his observations on men and manners. He had spent all his days in pursuit of the knowledge of counterfeiting silver, so as to bear the test of assays. He had always been unfortunate, and always lived poor.

This was the man concerning whom the world had said so much, and who was to take his trial at the same time with me. One other, by the name of Jones, was likewise committed, either for counterfeiting or passing counterfeit money, which I do not recollect. Likewise one by the name of Cook was in confinement, to take his trial for burglary. These were the men who waited for the approach of the court with fearful apprehensions of the event.

Many circumstances had taken place whilst I lay confined here, which served to give me a pretty sanguine dependance on my own abilities. I had written a scrawl of ribaldry, and entitled it "The Hay-Mow Sermon," representing my exploits in Pelham, at Rutland, etc. and delivered this often to those who came to see me as a phenomenon.[4] I found many applauded this as a witty thing, until I finally began to think it so myself. The flattery of those who were willing to alleviate the miseries of my situation, by making me at peace with myself, had such an operation on my mind, that I seriously began to think myself a man of some consequence, and was determined to let this circumstance be fully known at court, when I should have an opportunity of displaying all my abilities in such a conspicuous manner as to create admiration in the minds of all.

This was the state of things when I was called to the bar, and my indictment read. The judges on the bench, at this time, if I remember right, were Messrs. Cushing, Sargent, Sumner and Dana. The attorney general was Robert Treat Paine, of whom you have heard much mention made.[5]

In the indictment, I was charged with passing two pieces of base metal, the counterfeit of Spanish milled dollars,[6] knowing them to be such, etc. To the indictment I pleaded not guilty. I had no counsel at this time, owing to the following reason: when I was first committed to confinement, I expected to be in want of more money than what I had on hand, for expenses in jail, attorney's fees at trial, etc. Therefore, [I] sold my horse, saddle and bridle, and had a promise of the money in ten days, but to my no small disappointment, have not received my pay to this day: of course at the time of trial, [I] was entirely destitute of money.

Being wholly unacquainted with the practice of the gentlemen of the bar at that time, I had embraced the opinion that they never would attend to the application of any, without an advanced fee. This idea I afterwards found to be entirely groundless. Under this apprehension, I applied for no help, having no money to remunerate a counsellor for his assistance. This being the case, I stood alone in the business, which communicated an idea to the gentlemen of the bar, that a confidence in my own abilities induced me to look with indifference upon their assistance. This, of consequence, did not serve to ingratiate myself into their favor. This was not all. In my address to the jury I flung out some hard expressions against them, owing to my mistaken idea of their venal practice; all which served to create myself enemies, without the least apparent advantage arising from it.

I have often thought that a retrospective view of a thousand foolish calculations which people make in the days of youthful inexperience, and the thought-

---

[4]This "sermon," published in 1798 in Hanover, New Hampshire, purported to be the one Burroughs said he had delivered to the Pelhamites when they cornered him in a Rutland, Vermont, barn. As Philip Gura has pointed out in his edition of the *Memoirs*, however, Burroughs there refers to events that took place during Shays's Rebellion two years after the Pelhamites cornered him.

[5]Burroughs here indicated that his original manuscript contained an extended discussion of Paine (1731–1814), but in a note added that it was being cut from the published version.

[6]A Spanish coin "milled" in a screw press; also known as a "piece of eight," it circulated widely in the United States at the time.

less, unmeaning impetuosity, with which they pursue these objects of calculation, would serve greatly to lessen the resentment which the wiser part of mankind often feel towards them.

After I had pled to the indictment, the attorney general arose and opened the cause to the jury, stating in the course of his observations, that I had been a most abandoned character, leading a life of iniquity from the beginning; that I had been a counterfeiter not only of the coin of the country, but had also counterfeited a name, a character, a calling, all which seemed to communicate this idea to the world, that I had given a loose to the practice of every enormity; that my wickedness had at length found me out; and that I should now suffer a punishment due to my long course of crimes.

After he had closed, he proceeded to call on his evidences. When the apothecary came on to the stand, I objected to the court against his being admitted, being a person interested in the business. After hearing the arguments pro and con the bench took the matter under consideration, and determined that his evidence might be taken; giving for reason, that it had before been determined; and that the reward which government had offered, would militate against the conviction of crimes of that nature, rather than promote it, if the complainant should be excluded from giving testimony.

As soon as this determination of the court was declared, I pretty much gave up the idea of being acquitted. However, I thought it necessary to make the last defense I was able to; therefore, after the witnesses were examined, I began my address to the jury, and in the course of my observations, took notice of the remarks of the attorney general; that he had, contrary to every principle of law and justice, asserted facts in open court, apparently with a wicked design, to fix a prejudice in their minds, in order to prevent my trial being impartial, not even attempting to produce evidence to support the base assertions which he had made.

I continued still further: "I am astonished," said I, "to see all justice and virtue fled from the bench. That those characters whom we are taught to revere, on account of their eminent station, should so far debase their own importance, as to remain in silence, when the most flagrant violations of all rules of order are perpetrated before them in open court; therefore, gentlemen of the jury, I turn to you as the only support, which now may be depended on, for the enjoyment of our just rights and privileges."

And now sir, what do you think of this rant? I know what you will say, namely, that it is the ebullition of a mad, hair-brained fellow. My feelings, it is true, were wounded by the observations of the attorney general, and I verily expected to punish all those whom I thought to blame in the business; but how weak was my reasoning upon such a subject! How mad the part which I acted! I soon found to my cost, that in the room of[7] punishing others, I was irritating that power in whose grasp I was embraced.

I continued my remarks to the jury, upon the evidence which had been

_____
[7] Instead of.

exhibited against me, with as much argument as the case would admit of. The attorney general answered my remarks, and the judges summed up the evidence, and stated the business to the jury not in a very impartial manner. The jury retired, and in about one hour returned with the verdict of GUILTY!

The sentence was soon pronounced, which was to this effect, namely, that I should stand one hour in the pillory, and remain three years confined to the house of correction, without the corporal punishment which generally is inflicted on those who are sentenced to said house. Glazier Wheeler's sentence was the same, excepting an addition of twenty stripes, and to be cropped. Jones was sentenced for two years to the house of correction, and twenty stripes. Cook, for burglary, was sentenced to two years to the house of correction, an hour in the pillory, and ten stripes.

I was remanded to jail, there to contemplate the gloomy prospect before me, of spending three years in a state of close confinement. I expected this state of imprisonment would be in the common jail of the county, there being no other house of correction provided. Here the horrors of my situation began to open to my view! I saw an eternity in miniature before me, consisting of one continued scene of gloomy horrors. Shut from the enjoyment of society, from performing a part among the rest of my fellow mortals, to make some establishment for myself, in this state of dependence; and from tasting the sweets of liberty, for which we had so lately fought and bled.

How is this said I to myself, that a country which has stood the foremost in asserting the cause of liberty, that those who have tasted the bitter cup of slavery, and have known from hence the value of liberty, should so soon after obtaining that blessing themselves, deprive others of it? I know that it will be said, that for my crimes I am deprived of liberty, which is according to every dictate of justice; whereas America was only struggling for her natural rights, when exercising the principles of virtue.

I have no idea of calling in question the justice of the American cause, but only advert to the situation and feelings of the people in this state, to show that they feelingly knew the value of liberty; and therefore, it appears more strange that they should wantonly trifle with this valuable treasure. It has been abundantly said by the leading men in this state, that life without liberty is not worth the possessing. This was abundantly urged to the people in the time of war; and it was urged with great truth and propriety; therefore that the same characters upon a revision of the criminal code, with a pretence of mollifying those laws which were sanguinary and cruel, should substitute slavery for death,[8] is to me conduct, truly enigmatical.

---

[8] I.e., substitute long-term imprisonment for capital punishment.

VENTURE SMITH

from *A Narrative of the Life and Adventures of Venture, a Native of Africa* (1798)

AFTER ALL THE BUSINESS WAS ENDED ON THE COAST OF AFRICA, THE SHIP SAILED from thence to Barbados.[9] After an ordinary passage, except great mortality by the smallpox, which broke out on board, we arrived at the island of Barbados, but when we reached it, there were found out of the two hundred and sixty that sailed from Africa, not more than two hundred alive. These were all sold, except myself and three more, to the planters there.

The vessel then sailed for Rhode Island, and arrived there after a comfortable passage. Here my master sent me to live with one of his sisters, until he could carry me to Fisher's Island,[1] the place of his residence. I had then completed my eighth year. After staying with his sister some time I was taken to my master's place to live.

When we arrived at Narragansett, my master went ashore in order to return a part of the way by land, and gave me the charge of the keys of his trunks on board the vessel, and charged me not to deliver them up to anybody, not even to his father without his orders. To his directions I promised faithfully to conform. When I arrived with my master's articles at his house, my master's father asked me for his son's keys, as he wanted to see what his trunks contained. I told him that my master entrusted me with the care of them until he should return, and that I had given him my word to be faithful to the trust, and could not therefore give him or any other person the keys without my master's directions. He insisted that I should deliver to him the keys, threatening to punish me if I did not. But I let him know that he should not have them, let him say what he would. He then laid aside trying to get them. But notwithstanding he appeared to give up trying to obtain them from me, yet I mistrusted[2] that he would take some time when I was off my guard, either in the daytime or at night to get them; therefore I slung them round my neck, and in the daytime concealed them in my bosom, and at night I always lay with them under me, that no person might take them from me without [my] being apprised of it. Thus I kept the keys from everybody until my master came home. When he returned he asked where Venture was. As I was then within hearing, I came, and said, "Here sir, at your service." He asked me for his keys, and I immediately took them off my neck and reached them out to him. He took

---

[9] Smith refers to his account, in the narrative's first chapter, of the war in his father's country around the year 1735, which resulted in his own capture and sale to a ship's steward. The ship, captained by a man named Collingwood, departed from Guinea and sailed to Barbados, in the West Indies.

[1] Now part of New York, Fisher's Island lies near New London, Connecticut; and Napatree Point, Rhode Island.

[2] Suspected.

them, stroked my hair, and commended me, saying in presence of his father that his young Venture was so faithful that he never would have been able to have taken the keys from him but by violence; that he should not fear to trust him with his whole fortune, for that he had been in his native place so habituated to keeping his word, that he would sacrifice even his life to maintain it.

The first of the time of living at my master's own place, I was pretty much employed in the house at carding wool and other household business. In this situation I continued for some years, after which my master put me to work out of doors. After many proofs of my faithfulness and honesty, my master began to put great confidence in me. My behavior to him had as yet been submissive and obedient. I then began to have hard tasks imposed on me. Some of these were to pound four bushels of ears of corn every night in a barrel for the poultry, or be rigorously punished. At other seasons of the year I had to card wool until a very late hour. These tasks I had to perform when I was about nine years old. Some time after I had another difficulty and oppression which was greater than any I had ever experienced since I came into this country. This was to serve two masters. James Mumford, my master's son, when his father had gone from home in the morning, and given me a stint to perform that day, would order me to do *this* and *that* business different from what my master directed me. One day in particular, the authority which my master's son had set up, had like to have produced melancholy effects. For my master having set me off[3] my business to perform that day and then left me to perform it, his son came up to me in the course of the day, big with authority, and commanded me very arrogantly to quit my present business and go directly about what he should order me. I replied to him that my master had given me so much to perform that day, and that I must therefore faithfully complete it in that time. He then broke out into a great rage, snatched a pitchfork and went to lay me over the head therewith; but I as soon got another and defended myself with it, or otherwise he might have murdered me in his outrage. He immediately called some people who were within hearing at work for him, and ordered them to take his hair rope and come and bind me with it. They all tried to bind me but in vain, though there were three assistants in number. My upstart master then desisted, put his pocket handkerchief before his eyes and went home with a design to tell his mother of the struggle with young Venture. He told her that their young Venture had become so stubborn that he could not control him, and asked her what he should do with him. In the meantime I recovered my temper, voluntarily caused myself to be bound by the same men who tried in vain before, and carried before my young master, that he might do what he pleased with me. He took me to a gallows made for the purpose of hanging cattle on,[4] and suspended me on it. Afterwards he ordered one of his hands to go to the peach orchard and cut him three dozen of whips to punish me with. These were brought to him, and that was all that was done with them, as I was

---

[3] I.e., having indicated to Venture.
[4] A "meat gallows," a device used for suspending the bodies of slaughtered animals.

released and went to work after hanging on the gallows about an hour.

After I had lived with my master thirteen years, being then about twenty-two years old, I married Meg, a slave of his who was about my age. My master owned a certain Irishman, named Heddy, who about that time formed a plan of secretly leaving his master. After he had long had this plan in meditation he suggested it to me. At first I cast a deaf ear to it, and rebuked Heddy for harboring in his mind such a rash undertaking. But after he had persuaded and much enchanted me with the prospect of gaining my freedom by such a method, I at length agreed to accompany him. Heddy next inveigled two of his fellow servants to accompany us. The place to which we designed to go was the Mississippi. Our next business was to lay in a sufficient store of provisions for our voyage. We privately collected out of our master's store, six great old cheeses, two firkins of butter, and one whole batch of new bread. When we had gathered all our own clothes and some more, we took them all about midnight, and went to the waterside. We stole our master's boat, embarked, and then directed our course for the Mississippi River.

We mutually confederated not to betray or desert one another on pain of death. We first steered our course for Montauk Point, the east end of Long Island. After our arrival there we landed, and Heddy and I made an incursion into the island after fresh water, while our two comrades were left at a little distance from the boat, employed at cooking. When Heddy and I had sought some time for water, he returned to our companions, and I continued on looking for my object. When Heddy had performed his business with our companions who were engaged in cooking, he went directly to the boat, stole all the clothes in it, and then traveled away for East Hampton, as I was informed. I returned to my fellows not long after. They informed me that our clothes were stolen, but could not determine who was the thief, yet they suspected Heddy as he was missing. After reproving my two comrades for not taking care of our things which were in the boat, I advertised Heddy[5] and sent two men in search of him. They pursued and overtook him at Southampton and returned him to the boat. I then thought it might afford some chance for my freedom, or at least a palliation for my running away, to return Heddy immediately to his master, and inform him that I was induced to go away by Heddy's address.[6] Accordingly I set off with him and the rest of my companions for our master's, and arrived there without any difficulty. I informed my master that Heddy was the ringleader of our revolt, and that he had used us ill. He immediately put Heddy into custody, and myself and companions were well-received and went to work as usual.

Not a long time passed after that, before Heddy was sent by my master to New London jail. At the close of that year I was sold to a Thomas Stanton, and had to be separated from my wife and one daughter, who was about one month old. He resided at Stonington Point. To this place I brought with me from my

---

[5] I.e., posted an advertisement describing him as a runaway.
[6] Persuasion.

late master's, two Johannes, three old Spanish dollars, and two thousand of coppers, besides five pounds of my wife's money.[7] This money I got by cleaning gentlemen's shoes and drawing boots, by catching muskrats and minks, raising potatoes and carrots, etc. and by fishing in the night, and at odd spells.

All this money, amounting to near twenty-one pounds York currency, my master's brother, Robert Stanton, hired of[8] me, for which he gave me his note. About one year and a half after that time, my master purchased my wife and her child, for seven hundred pounds old tenor.[9] One time my master sent me two miles after a barrel of molasses, and ordered me to carry it on my shoulders. I made out[1] to carry it all the way to my master's house. When I lived with Captain George Mumford, only to try my strength, I took up on my knees a tierce[2] of salt containing seven bushels, and carried it two or three rods. Of this fact there are several eyewitnesses now living.

Towards the close of the time that I resided with this master, I had a falling out with my mistress. This happened one time when my master was gone to Long Island a-gunning. At first the quarrel began between my wife and her mistress. I was then at work in the barn, and hearing a racket in the house, induced me to run there and see what had broken out. When I entered the house, I found my mistress in a violent passion with my wife, for what she informed me was a mere trifle; such a small affair that I forbear to put my mistress to the shame of having it known. I earnestly requested my wife to beg pardon of her mistress for the sake of peace, even if she had given no just occasion for offence. But whilst I was thus saying, my mistress turned the blows which she was repeating on my wife to me. She took down her horsewhip, and while she was glutting her fury with it, I reached out my great black hand, raised it up and received the blows of the whip on it which were designed for my head. Then I immediately committed the whip to the devouring fire.

When my master returned from the island, his wife told him of the affair, but for the present he seemed to take no notice of it, and mentioned not a word about it to me. Some days after his return, in the morning as I was putting on a log in the fireplace, not suspecting harm from anyone, I received a most violent stroke on the crown of my head with a club two feet long and as large round as a chair post. This blow very badly wounded my head, and the scar of it remains to this day. The first blow made me have my wits about me you may suppose, for as soon as he went to renew it, I snatched the club out of his hands and dragged him out of the door. He then sent for his brother to come and assist him, but I presently left my master, took the club he wounded me with, carried it to a neighboring justice of the peace, and complained of my master.

---

[7] Coins with a variety of sources: the Johannes (or "half joe") is a Portuguese gold coin named for the king who first issued it in the eighteenth century; Spanish dollars are the familiar "pieces of eight"; coppers, of several potential sources, are coins of modest worth; and the pounds are, of course, standard British currency.

[8] Borrowed from.

[9] Currency officially replaced by newer issues (often of different value), but still circulating.

[1] Managed to.

[2] Cask (usually of forty-two-gallon capacity).

He finally advised me to return to my master, and live contented with him till he abused me again, and then complain. I consented to do accordingly. But before I set out for my master's, up he come and his brother Robert after me. The justice improved this convenient opportunity to caution my master. He asked him for what he treated his slave thus hastily and unjustly, and told him what would be the consequence if he continued the same treatment towards me. After the justice had ended his discourse with my master, he and his brother set out with me for home, one before and the other behind me.

When they had come to a by-place,[3] they both dismounted their respective horses, and fell to beating me with great violence. I became enraged at this and immediately turned them both under me, laid one of them across the other, and stamped both with my feet what I would.[4]

This occasioned my master's brother to advise him to put me off.[5] A short time after this I was taken by a constable and two men. They carried me to a blacksmith's shop and had me handcuffed. When I returned home my mistress inquired much of her waiters, whether Venture was handcuffed. When she was informed that I was, she appeared to be very contented and was much transported with the news. In the midst of this content and joy, I presented myself before my mistress, showed her my handcuffs, and gave her thanks for my gold rings. For this my master commanded a Negro of his to fetch him a large ox chain. This my master locked on my legs with two padlocks. I continued to wear the chain peaceably for two or three days, when my master asked me with contemptuous hard names whether I had not better be freed from my chains and go to work. I answered him, "No." "Well then," said he, "I will send you to the West Indies or banish you, for I am resolved not to keep you." I answered him, "I crossed the waters to come here, and I am willing to cross them to return."

For a day or two after this not anyone said much to me, until one Hempsted Miner, of Stonington, asked me if I would live with him. I answered him that I would. He then requested me to make myself discontented and to appear as unreconciled to my master as I could before he bargained with him for me; and that in return he would give me a good chance to gain my freedom when I came to live with him.[6] I did as he requested me. Not long after, Hempsted Miner purchased me of my master for fifty-six pounds lawful. He took the chain and padlocks from off me immediately after.

It may here be remembered, that I related a few pages back, that I hired out a sum of money to Mr. Robert Stanton, and took his note for it. In the fray between my master Stanton and myself, he broke open my chest containing his brother's note to me, and destroyed it. Immediately after my present master

[3] An out-of-the-way place.
[4] I.e., as much as he wished.
[5] I.e., to sell him.
[6] A revealing passage that suggests how free whites might compete with each other through the medium of enslaved blacks. Miner thus wanted Venture to give Stanton a hard time so that Stanton would be motivated to get rid of him at a lower price. In return, Miner promised to reward Venture for cooperating by making it easier for him to gain his freedom.

bought me, he determined to sell me at Hartford. As soon as I became apprised of it, I bethought myself that I would secure a certain sum of money which lay by me, safer than to hire it out to a Stanton. Accordingly I buried it in the earth, a little distance from Thomas Stanton's, in the road over which he passed daily. A short time after my master carried me to Hartford, and first proposed to sell me to one William Hooker of that place. Hooker asked whether I would go to the German Flats[7] with him. I answered, "No." He said I should; if not by fair means I should by foul. "If you will go by no other measures, I will tie you down in my sleigh." I replied to him, that if he carried me in that manner, no person would purchase me, for it would be thought that he had a murderer for sale. After this he tried no more, and said he would not have me as a gift.

My master next offered me to Daniel Edwards, Esq., of Hartford, for sale. But [Edwards] not purchasing me, my master pawned me to him for ten pounds, and returned to Stonington. After some trial of my honesty, Mr. Edwards placed considerable trust and confidence in me. He put me to serve as his cup-bearer and waiter. When there was company at his house, he would send me into his cellar and other parts of his house to fetch wine and other articles occasionally for them. When I had been with him some time, he asked me why my master wished to part with such an honest Negro, and why he did not keep me himself. I replied that I could not give him the reason, unless it was to convert me into cash, and speculate with me as with other commodities. I hope that he can never justly say it was on account of my ill conduct that he did not keep me himself. Mr. Edwards told me that he should be very willing to keep me himself, and that he would never let me go from him to live, if it was not unreasonable and inconvenient for me to be parted from my wife and children; therefore he would furnish me with a horse to return to Stonington, if I had a mind for it. As Miner did not appear to redeem me I went, and called at my old master Stanton's first to see my wife, who was then owned by him. As my old master appeared much ruffled at my being there, I left my wife before I had spent any considerable time with her, and went to Colonel O. Smith's. Miner had not as yet wholly settled with Stanton for me, and had before my return from Hartford given Colonel Smith a bill of sale of me. These men once met to determine which of them should hold me, and upon my expressing a desire to be owned by Colonel Smith, and upon my master's settling the remainder of the money which was due to Stanton for me, it was agreed that I should live with Colonel Smith. This was the third time of my being sold, and I was then thirty-one years old. As I never had an opportunity of redeeming myself whilst I was owned by Miner, though he promised to give me a chance, I was then very ambitious of obtaining it. I asked my master one time if he would consent to have me purchase my freedom. He replied that he would. I was then very happy, knowing that I was at that time able to pay part of the purchase money, by means of the money which I some time since bur-

---

[7] In the western Mohawk Valley of New York, so called from the settlement of Germans there early in the eighteenth century.

ied. This I took out of the earth and tendered to my master, having previously engaged a free Negro man to take his security for it, as I was the property of my master, and therefore could not safely take his obligation myself.[8] What was wanting in redeeming myself, my master agreed to wait on me for, until I could procure it for him. I still continued to work for Colonel Smith. There was continually some interest accruing on my master's note to my friend the free Negro man above named, which I received, and with some besides which I got by fishing, I laid out in land adjoining my old master Stanton's. By cultivating this land with the greatest diligence and economy, at times when my master did not require my labor, in two years I laid up ten pounds. This my friend tendered my master for myself, and received his note for it.

Being encouraged by the success which I had met in redeeming myself, I again solicited my master for a further chance of completing it. The chance for which I solicited him was that of going out to work the ensuing winter. He agreed to this on condition that I would give him one quarter of my earnings. On these terms I worked the following winter, and earned four pounds sixteen shillings, one quarter of which went to my master for the privilege, and the rest was paid him on my own account. This added to the other payments made up forty-four pounds, eight shillings, which I had paid on my own account. I was then about thirty-five years old.

The next summer I again desired he would give me a chance of going out to work. But he refused and answered that he must have my labor this summer, as he did not have it the past winter. I replied that I considered it as hard that I could not have a chance to work out when the season became advantagous, and that I must only be permitted to hire myself out in the poorest season of the year. He asked me after this what I would give him for the privilege per month. I replied that I would leave it wholly with his own generosity to determine what I should return him a month. "Well then," said he, "if so two pounds a month." I answered him that if that was the least he would take I would be contented.

Accordingly I hired myself out at Fisher's Island, and earned twenty pounds, thirteen pounds six shillings of which my master drew for the privilege, and the remainder I paid him for my freedom. This made fifty-one pounds two shillings which I paid him. In October following I went and wrought six months at Long Island. In that six month's time I cut and corded four hundred cords of wood, besides threshing out seventy-five bushels of grain, and received of my wages down only twenty pounds, which left remaining a larger sum. Whilst I was out that time, I took up on my wages only one pair of shoes.[9] At night I lay on the hearth, with one coverlet over and another under me. I returned to my master and gave him what I received of my six months labor. This left only thirteen pounds eighteen shillings to make up the full sum for

---

[8] That is, with few or no legal rights, Venture protected his financial interest by having the "free Negro man" technically receive Stanton's "note of obligation."
[9] That is, he "charged" only this one item against his promised wages.

my redemption. My master liberated me, saying that I might pay what was behind if I could ever make it convenient, otherwise it would be well. The amount of the money which I had paid my master towards redeeming my time, was seventy-one pounds two shillings. The reason of my master for asking such an unreasonable price, was, he said, to secure himself in case I should ever come to want. Being thirty-six years old, I left Colonel Smith once for all. I had already been sold three different times, made considerable money with seemingly nothing to derive it from, been cheated out of a large sum of money, lost much by misfortunes, and paid an enormous sum for my freedom.

My wife and children were yet in bondage to Mr. Thomas Stanton. About this time I lost a chest, containing besides clothing, about thirty-eight pounds in paper money. It was burnt by accident. A short time after I sold all my possessions at Stonington, consisting of a pretty piece of land and one dwelling house thereon, and went to reside at Long Island. For the first four years of my residence there, I spent my time in working for various people on that and at the neighboring islands. In the space of six months I cut and corded upwards of four hundred cords of wood. Many other singular and wonderful labors I performed in cutting wood there, which would not be inferior to those just recited, but for brevity sake I must omit them. In the aforementioned four years what wood I cut at Long Island amounted to several thousand cords, and the money which I earned thereby amounted to two hundred and seven pounds ten shillings. This money I laid up carefully by me. Perhaps some may enquire what maintained me all the time I was laying up money. I would inform them that I bought nothing which I did not absolutely want. All fine clothes I despised in comparison with my interest, and never kept but just what clothes were comfortable for common days, and perhaps I would have a garment or two which I did not have on at all times, but as for superfluous finery I never thought it to be compared with a decent homespun dress, a good supply of money and prudence. Expensive gatherings of my mates I commonly shunned, and all kinds of luxuries I was perfectly a stranger to; and during the time I was employed in cutting the aforementioned quantity of wood, I never was at the expense of six-pence worth of spirits. Being after this labor forty years of age, I worked at various places, and in particular on Ram Island, where I purchased Solomon and Cuff, two sons of mine, for two hundred dollars each.

It will here be remembered how much money I earned by cutting wood in four years. Besides this I had considerable money, amounting in all to near three hundred pounds. When I had purchased my two sons, I had then left more than one hundred pounds. After this I purchased a Negro man, for no other reason than to oblige him, and gave for him sixty pounds. But in a short time after he run away from me, and I thereby lost all that I gave for him, except twenty pounds which he paid me previous to his absconding. The rest of my money I laid out in land, in addition to a farm which I owned before, and a dwelling house thereon. Forty-four years had then completed their revolution since my entrance into this existence of servitude and misfortune. Solomon my eldest son, being then in his seventeenth year, and all my hope and dependence for help, I hired him out to one Charles Church, of Rhode Island, for one year, on consideration of his giving him twelve pounds and an opportunity of acquiring some learning. In the course of the year, Church fitted out a vessel for a whaling voyage, and being in want of hands to man her, he induced my son to go, with the promise of giving him on his return, a pair of silver buckles, besides his wages. As soon as I heard of his going to sea, I immediately set out to go and prevent it if possible.—But on my arrival at Church's, to my great grief, I could only see the vessel my son was in almost out of sight going to sea. My son died of the scurvy in this voyage, and Church has never yet paid me the least of his wages. In my son, besides the loss of his life, I lost equal to seventy-five pounds.

My other son being but a youth, still lived with me. About this time I chartered a sloop of about thirty tons burthen, and hired men to assist me in navigating her. I employed her mostly in the wood trade to Rhode Island, and made clear of all expenses above one hundred dollars with her in better than one year. I had then become something forehanded,[1] and being in my forty-fourth year, I purchased my wife Meg, and thereby prevented having another child to buy, as she was then pregnant. I gave forty pounds for her.

During my residence at Long Island, I raised one year with another, ten cart loads of watermelons, and lost a great many every year besides by the thievishness of the sailors. What I made by the watermelons I sold there, amounted to nearly five hundred dollars. Various other methods I pursued in order to enable me to redeem my family. In the night time I fished with set-nets and pots for eels and lobsters, and shortly after went a whaling voyage in the service of Colonel Smith.—After being out seven months, the vessel returned, laden with four hundred barrels of oil. About this time, I become possessed of another dwelling-house, and my temporal affairs were in a pretty prosperous condition. This and my industry was what alone saved me from being expelled that part of the island in which I resided, as an act was passed by the selectmen of the place, that all Negroes residing there should be expelled.

Next after my wife, I purchased a Negro man for four hundred dollars. But he having an inclination to return to his old master, I therefore let him go. Shortly after I purchased another Negro man for twenty-five pounds, whom I parted with shortly after.

Being about forty-six years old, I bought my oldest child Hannah, of Ray Mumford, for forty-four pounds, and she still resided with him. I had already redeemed from slavery, myself, my wife and three children, besides three Negro men.

About the forty-seventh year of my life, I disposed of all my property at Long Island, and came from thence into East Haddam. I hired myself out at first to Timothy Chapman, for five weeks, the earnings of which time I put up carefully by me. After this I wrought for Abel Bingham about six weeks. I then put my money together and purchased of said Bingham ten acres of land,

---

[1] I.e., prudently supplied with future resources.

lying at Haddam Neck, where I now reside.—On this land I labored with great diligence for two years, and shortly after purchased six acres more of land contiguous to my other. One year from that time I purchased seventy acres more of the same man, and paid for it mostly with the produce of my other land. Soon after I bought this last lot of land, I set up a comfortable dwelling-house on my farm, and built it from the produce thereof. Shortly after I had much trouble and expense with my daughter Hannah, whose name has before been mentioned in this account. She was married soon after I redeemed her, to one Isaac, a free Negro, and shortly after her marriage fell sick of a mortal disease; her husband, a dissolute and abandoned wretch, paid but little attention to her in her illness. I therefore thought it best to bring her to my house and nurse her there. I procured her all the aid mortals could afford, but notwithstanding this she fell a prey to her disease, after a lingering and painful endurance of it.

The physician's bills for attending her during her illness amounted to forty pounds. Having reached my fifty-fourth year, I hired two Negro men, one named William Jacklin, and the other Mingo. Mingo lived with me one year, and having received his wages, run in debt to me eight dollars, for which he gave me his note. Presently after he tried to run away from me without troubling himself to pay up his note. I procured a warrant, took him, and requested him to go to Justice Throop's of his own accord, but he refusing, I took him on my shoulders, and carried him there, distant about two miles. The justice asking me if I had my prisoner's note with me, and replying that I had not, he told me that I must return with him and get it. Accordingly I carried Mingo back on my shoulders, but before we arrived at my dwelling, he complained of being hurt, and asked me if this was not a hard way of treating our fellow creatures. I answered him that it would be hard thus to treat our honest fellow creatures. He then told me that if I would let him off my shoulders, he had a pair of silver shoe-buckles, one shirt and a pocket handkerchief, which he would turn out to me. I agreed, and let him return home with me on foot; but the very following night, he slipped from me, stole my horse and has never paid me even his note. The other Negro man, Jacklin, being a comb-maker by trade, he requested me to set him up, and promised to reward me well with his labor. Accordingly I bought him a set of tools for making combs, and procured him stock. He worked at my house about one year, and then run away from me with all his combs, and owed me for all his board.

Since my residence at Haddam Neck, I have owned of boats, canoes and sail vessels, not less than twenty. These I mostly employed in the fishing and trafficking business, and in these occupations I have been cheated out of considerable money by people whom I traded with taking advantage of my ignorance of numbers.

About twelve years ago, I hired a whaleboat and four black men, and proceeded to Long Island after a load of round clams. Having arrived there, I first purchased of James Webb, son of Orange Webb, six hundred and sixty clams, and afterwards, with the help of my men, finished loading my boat. The same evening, however, this Webb stole my boat, and went in her to Connecticut River, and sold her cargo for his own benefit. I thereupon pursued him, and at length, after an additional expense of nine crowns, recovered the boat; but for the proceeds of her cargo I never could obtain any compensation.

Four years after, I met with another loss, far superior to this in value, and I think by no less wicked means. Being going to New London with a grandchild, I took passage in an Indian's boat, and went there with him. On our return, the Indian took on board two hogsheads of molasses, one of which belonged to Captain Elisha Hart, of Saybrook, to be delivered on his wharf. When we arrived there, and while I was gone, at the request of the Indian, to inform Captain Hart of his arrival, and receive the freight for him, one hogshead of the molasses had been lost overboard by the people in attempting to land it on the wharf. Although I was absent at the time, and had no concern whatever in the business, as was known to a number of respectable witnesses, I was nevertheless prosecuted by this conscientious gentleman (the Indian not being able to pay for it) and obliged to pay upwards of ten pounds lawful money, with all the costs of court. I applied to several gentlemen for counsel in this affair, and they advised me, as my adversary was rich, and threatened to carry the matter from court to court till it would cost me more than the first damages would be, to pay the sum and submit to the injury; which I according did, and he has often since insultingly taunted me with my unmerited misfortune. Such a proceeding as this, committed on a defenseless stranger, almost worn out in the hard service of the world, without any foundation in reason or justice, whatever it may be called in a Christian land, would in my native country have been branded as a crime equal to highway robbery. But Captain Hart was a *white gentleman*, and I a *poor African*, therefore it was *all right, and good enough for the black dog.*

I am now sixty-nine years old. Though once straight and tall, measuring without shoes six feet one inch and an half, and every way well-proportioned, I am now bowed down with age and hardship. My strength which was once equal if not superior to any man whom I have ever seen, is now enfeebled so that life is a burden, and it is with fatigue that I can walk a couple of miles, stooping over my staff. Other griefs are still behind; on account of which some aged people, at least, will pity me. My eyesight has gradually failed, till I am almost blind, and whenever I go abroad one of my grandchildren must direct my way; besides for many years I have been much pained and troubled with an ulcer on one of my legs. But amidst all my griefs and pains, I have many consolations; Meg, the wife of my youth, whom I married for love, and bought with my money, is still alive. My freedom is a privilege which nothing else can equal. Notwithstanding all the losses I have suffered by fire, by the injustice of knaves, by the cruelty and oppression of false-hearted friends, and the perfidy of my own countrymen whom I have assisted and redeemed from bondage, I am now possessed of more than one hundred acres of land, and three habitable dwelling-houses. It gives me joy to think that I have and that I deserve so good a character, especially for truth and integrity. While I am now looking to the grave as my home, my joy for this world would be full—IF my children, Cuff for whom I paid two hundred dollars when a boy, and Solomon who was born soon after I purchased his mother—If Cuff and Solomon—O! that they had walked in the way of their father. But a father's lips are closed in silence and in grief! — Vanity of vanities, all is vanity!

JOHN ROBERT SHAW

from **A Narrative of the Life and Travels of the Well-Digger (1807)**

MY COMRADE AND I STARTED ON OUR ROAD TO FRANKFORT, CALLING AT GENeral Wilkinson's,[2] who politely treated us to a grog and advised us to go to the salt works; he likewise generously put us across the river.

After we crossed the river the first house we stopped at proved to be a particular acquaintance of mine from Pittsburgh (Mr. Haymaker), who treated us with kind hospitality, advising us not to go to the salt works; for, said he, "It is a hell on earth."

From his house we started in the morning with grateful hearts for Arnold's Station (making inquiry on the road for Jersey and Pennsylvania people). When we arrived at Captain Arnold's house, he generously invited us to dinner, which was truly acceptable.[3]

My comrade inquired if there were any Jersey people convenient to there. Captain Arnold observed his father came from Jersey, and he made no doubt that he would give him work; upon which we started on to Baker's tavern, where we had not been long before some men came to the house, amongst whom were old Mr. Arnold, and with whom my comrade soon made a bargain to work, and trudged off, leaving poor old Shaw to shift as well as he could.

I proceeded to Mr. McGuire's, who lived in the vicinity, and asked for quarters, which was granted.

Soon after my arrival my landlord inquired which way I was traveling. I told him I could not tell how far, but that I was in pursuit of work, which I was willing to do for my victuals and whatever other compensation my employer thought proper. He told me I need go no further, asking me what I could do; to which I answered a number of domestic affairs, such as to wait on his lady, etc.

The following morning after breakfast my employer walked to a new improvement (a handsome situation)[4] where he had built a double log house after the Virginia fashion (without a cellar). I asked the cause of his so doing, he observed that the foundation was a solid rock, and that the cellar would cost him more than the house.

---

[2]General James Wilkinson (1757–1825), who in 1791 was not yet the infamous associate of Aaron Burr. He owned a good deal of Frankfort and, as Shaw notes, controlled the ferry across the Kentucky River there.

[3]Captain William Arnold, whose "station" was located southwest of the Kentucky River.

[4]An "improvement" was a new settlement.

I told him provided he furnished me with some powder and the necessary tools, that I would blow him out a cellar, for a shirt and a pair of shoes; to which he agreed, and accordingly furnished me with a set of new-fashioned tools indeed. Suffice it to say that by the dint of assiduity and elbow grease, I soon earned my shirt and shoes, and that much to the satisfaction of my employer; after which I built him a lime kiln.

Mr. McGuire, observing a number of his hogs to be badly torn, naturally conjectured it must have been done by a panther,[5] therefore proposed a hunting frolic to me, to which I readily agreed.

We started and had not traveled far before we came on the track of two panthers; proceeding on about a quarter of a mile, I observed one of them on the limb of a large tree; calling out to McGuire (and being entirely unacquainted with the different quadrupeds), "Yonder is a deer on the limb of that tree," which deer or rather panther, he observing, immediately fired and wounded it, after which it jumped down and pursued different directions, receiving three different wounds before we killed it; and out of his skin I made myself a good pair of shoes.

On the first day of March (1792) I started from Mr. McGuire's, who satisfied me well for my winter's work, pursuing my way across Steel's ferry, and along the north side of the Kentucky River, until I came to Joseph McLain's, where I blew some rocks for him.

After which I proceeded to one Abraham Morten's (Jessamine)[6] with whom I agreed to split 5,000 rails. Here was the first place I understood that cutting and splitting one hundred rails per day was not thought a day's work for a man, being the second time I undertook such a job. I first began with 40, but soon found that I could easily accomplish 200, and could do were I acquainted with the different sorts of timber, a fourth more in a day.

I then commenced with a certain captain—to blow rocks and quarry stone, and after working with him a considerable time, he insidiously endeavored to defraud me out of my hire; and with a great deal of persuasion [I] prevailed with him to pay me half of it, considering half a loaf better than no bread.

After receiving my half stipend, I proceeded to the mouth of Hickman,[7] where I got pretty well fuddled, and went to the boat intending to cross, but Mr. Ballenger, the ferryman, observing my intoxication, would not admit me into the boat, consequently [I] returned to the ferry house (Mr. Scott's) where I spent the remainder of my hard-earned money; the result of which was a violent attack of the bottle fever, but the commiseration, assiduity and kind attention of Mr. and Mrs. Scott to me at that time shall always be impressed on my heart, therefrom never to be erased.

After recovering from my indisposition I commenced digging a well for

[5] I.e., puma or mountain lion.
[6] Jessamine County, Kentucky, southwest of Lexington.
[7] A creek in Jessamine County.

John Biswell, four miles from Mr. Scott's ferry; a storm coming on prevented me from progressing; therefore [I] turned to my old trade of frolicking, the result as usual—the bottle fever.

Afflicted with it, I was one night lying in the tavern before the fire, when I was disturbed by a parcel of ruffians, consisting of Major Mastin Clay, Lieutenant Spence, a Mr. Moss and [Mr.] Sow. They entered the house and had not been there long before making inquiry of the landlord who I was.

He answered, "Old Shaw the well-digger, who is very sick."

"Damn him," observed Clay, "let us have a little fun with him."

With that he laid a chunk of fire on my leg, which burnt me severely.

I jumped on my feet requesting of them to let me alone, saying I was then sick and [had] no person to take my part, but even so, I would try the best of them singly; this exasperated them, and Clay being the greatest scoundrel among them, urged the rest to lay hold of me, which they did, compelling a Negro who was in the house to butt me with his head and gouge me severely.

I observed to Clay that if ever an opportunity offered I should pay him off in equal coin, which I fortunately did. For shortly after, meeting him at Taylor's tavern in Lexington, I demanded satisfaction for the brutal treatment I had received from him; however, by the intercession of some friends, and his making ample concessions, we compromised the matter amicably.

I started from Jessamine (County) in the spring of 1793, and proceeded on to Clear Creek, where I worked for Mr. Ephraim, James January, Joseph Wood, James Dunn, and William and Joseph Hughes, by all of whom I was well treated.

Leaving Clear Creek, I went to Lexington where I engaged with one Trainer (a sort of tavern keeper) to quarry stone for him at two shillings per day—low wages but he still wanted me for less, and strove by every means in his power to take advantage of me.

His foreman, one Johnson, informed me that three blasts a day, from ten to twelve inches deep, was a good day's work for a man. I observed to him that such a man was not fit to work in a quarry, and bet him a wager of a bottle of whiskey that I could blow three blasts before breakfast, which I won.[8] After which Mr. Trainer offered me a share in the quarry, which I refused, observing at the same time that I had not seen a man in Kentucky that I would join in that line of business with.

Shortly after, I commenced digging a well for one Samuel Lamb on Clear Creek, who generously supplied me with money to buy tools; he likewise furnished me with a horse to ride to Lexington in order to purchase them, which I did, and on my return fell off the horse and had a very narrow escape for my life. The well I finished for Mr. Lamb, for which I was honorably paid.

It was about this time that I dreamed a singular dream, which was that I

---

[8]The reason for the challenge here is the fact that the charges were "from ten to twelve inches deep"—that is, the quarry worker had to drill or chisel holes that deep by hand into the rock so as to accommodate the charges.

thought I heard a voice calling to me saying, "Shaw! Shaw! Repent or you will be damned." And in the course of a few weeks after, I dreamed another, in which I thought I heard the same voice saying, "Shaw! Shaw! Repent and you will be saved."

This last dream alarmed me so much that I awoke the family and communicated my dream to them.

There was in the house at that time a certain Andrew Ward, supposed to be a pious man, who exhorted me seriously to reform from the mode of life which I was in the habit of pursuing, and pointed out to me what must be the inevitable result of my perseverance therein, which I took extremely kind.

Leaving Mr. Lamb's, I came to Black's Station;[9] and so on to Lexington, where I again commenced my mad career; falling in company with one Prothroe, who assiduously assisted in distributing my money.

My money being expended and having no place to stay, I requested liberty of this Prothroe to lie in a corner of his shop (he being a cabinet maker) until I got better (being at the time of course afflicted with my old complaint the bottle fever).

This he refused, observing I had no money, and therefore wished to have nothing to do with me, but immediately observing that if I would sign my name to a piece of blank paper, he would give me a dram; thinking no harm, I accordingly did, after which he insisted on my leaving the house, which I did in a very distressed situation, and went out to Maxwell's Spring.[1]

There I drank a quantity of water, which occasioned me to vomit a quantity of blood.

Night coming on I walked along intending to take up my quarters in a friend's house, but growing weary and sick, I lay down in the woods, and shortly fell asleep, continuing so until midnight, when being awakened by a noise which I could not account for, I jumped up rather amazed, and within nine or ten feet of me saw a ball of fire, apparently as large as a bushel, and at the same time heard a voice over my head crying, "Shaw! Shaw! Will you not speak to me?"

A thousand conjectures now began to float in my head; I began to reflect on my former dreams—I rose and began to pray fervently, in which posture I did not long continue before those gloomy visions totally vanished.

I then proceeded further into the woods, but did not continue long there before I heard the voice and saw the fire as plain as before; however, day appearing, I felt relieved, and proceeded on the road, where I had not long continued before I observed a man walking alongside of me. On a close view of him, I found it to be the exact likeness of Prothroe, imagining in myself that he was killed, and that this my companion must be his ghost.

I then observed to him that I never did him any harm, therefore requested

[9] A settlement northwest of Lexington.
[1] According to Oressa M. Teagarden and Jeanne L. Crabtree in their edition of Shaw's book, Maxwell Spring "was a favorite spot for political rallies and debates, in which Henry Clay, John Breckinridge, George Nicholas, and others took part."

of him in God's name to leave me; at the name of God he immediately disappeared, and I continued on my journey, hoping the worst was over; but shocking to relate, I did not go far before he met me full in the face, in quite a different dress, when again using my former argument he again disappeared, and I proceeded to the five-mile cabin, where lo! Again appeared my visitant dressed in black.

Being determined to ascertain whether or not it was substance, I made a grasp at him, and wonderful to relate! It vanished like an airy vision, but again appeared behind some logs, which lay convenient, beckoning me to come to him; I did and followed him from log to log until he vanished and left me extremely exhausted.

I then proceeded to the five-mile cabin [and] got the man of the house to accompany me part of the road towards Lexington. Passing by a house, the woman gave me some breakfast, after which observing some drovers going by, with [them] I traveled on to Lexington, my visiting ghost appearing to me in different shapes, forms, attitudes and dress, still beckoning me to approach him, which I now dreaded as he frequently appeared besmeared with blood. However, I found the name of God was my only safeguard, which I continually kept repeating to him, and he as continually disappearing until I arrived in Lexington.

When I arrived in Lexington, I immediately went to the house of Prothroe, and told him what I had seen, exhorting him to reform and strive to live a better life, observing to him that I feared something extraordinary would shortly happen from the omens that were portending.

He answered saying, "I am determined to live a more regular and Christian life, for indeed I had shocking dreams lately, which induce me to take up the resolution of becoming a better man."

I left the house and proceeded up the hill, and meeting with Mr. Patterson and [Mr.] Ellison, who earnestly entreated me to quit the company of Prothroe, and to endeavor to lead a better and more uniform life.

Mr. Ellison politely invited me to his house, it being in the evening. After prayers, Mrs. Ellison made a pallet bed for me, where I had not long lain before I was astonished with the sight of the ball of fire and the voice calling me, "Shaw, won't you speak to me?"

I jumped on my feet, calling to Mr. Ellison, requesting of him for God's sake to go to prayer.

He immediately took a religious book and began reading. I seated myself alongside of him, with my head between my knees, when I thought I observed the hand of a man stretched towards me.

I then got up requesting him to let me read—he accordingly gave me the book, and rising up in order to bring another candle out of the next room, when I thought I observed a venerable old man standing between me and the door, with his gray locks hanging over his ears.

Mr. Ellison returned and remained with me some time, whilst I read. But growing sleepy, he called up two of his apprentices and then retired to bed. I continued reading until between the hours of twelve and one, in company with the boys, when I imagined that I beheld rising at the end of the table, a head like a man's and eyes like two balls of fire, glaring me full in the face.

My astonishment at the horrid sight can be better imagined than expressed. However, I summoned fortitude enough to say, "Begone, Satan, or I'll shoot you with the Word of God," when immediately it disappeared, leaving behind a smoke similar to that which is produced by sulphur, which induced me to think it was the devil, and consequently no hopes for me.

My lost state appeared so apparent to me that I requested of Mr. Ellison to summon all the profligate youth and old drunkards in the town, in order to take warning by me and to avoid if possible the life I had pursued, and which brought me to this truly distressing situation. It being an unseasonable hour, Mr. Ellison declined calling them.

I continued in extreme distress, the devil (as I supposed) appearing to me in various forms too horrid to mention, until at length day appeared, to my inexpressible pleasure, which relieved me in part from my fancy-raised vision.

I requested Mr. Ellison to call in some pious men in order that I might converse and advise with them, amongst whom was a Mr. Adams (a Scotchman and a good one) who strenuously advised me to study the scriptures and to abide invariably [by] the precepts therein laid down. During the day my disturbed imagination still continued to raise up ideal apparitions, but at night when bedtime came on, I implored fervently the aid of that Supreme Being, who is the defender and support of all us miserable mortals, from which I felt relieved.

I tied a handkerchief around my eyes, went to bed and enjoyed as comfortable a night's rest as ever I experienced, after which I enjoyed a calm serenity, for the describing of which words are here denied me, and for which, my kind and candid readers will I hope excuse me. Suffice it to say that I turned in to work for Mr. Ellison and made him a compensation for the trouble he had been at with me.

After compensating Mr. Ellison with my labor, for his trouble with me, Mr. James Parker asked me to finish a well that had been begun by Trainer, who refused giving it up, but Mr. Parker told him that he would not employ him any longer, as he considered him a troublesome, inattentive man, upon which Trainer gave up the well.

Accordingly I commenced digging at a dollar per day. I had not worked long at this well when I was visited by Prothroe, requesting me to fulfill the contents of an indenture which he said he held against me. I will here beg leave to trespass a little on my reader's patience, in order to be particular in developing fully the character of this nefarious swindler.

The reader must recollect reading in one of the preceding pages of my signing a blank paper at the request of Prothroe, which blank he filled up with an indenture binding me as a servant to him for three months, witnessed by some of his comrades of equal "honesty" with himself.

On his producing this indenture I was astonished, and thinking there was no alternative quitted my well and commenced working for him. However, taking into consideration that he acquired this instrument of writing unlawfully,

I consulted some of my friends, who advised me to compromise the matter with him, which I did after paying him four pounds ten shillings in merchandise.

And now I call that Being to witness, who is and will be the eventual judge of all things, that I never directly nor indirectly owed this Prothroe one cent in my life.

I then returned to Mr. Parker's, where I had not worked long before I got ready for a blast, when throwing down the fire twice, and the shot not going off, I went down to prime afresh, but was not careful in scraping the coals away, and leaving some tow round the touch hole, which occasioned the priming to catch.

The blast went off with about three-quarters of a pound of powder in my hand, which consequently left me for dead in the bottom of the well, but shortly recovering and the neighbors assembling, who hauled me up, and after getting bled and drinking a little spirits and water, [I] felt tolerably well recovered, and in the course of eight days after, went to work. Though feeling rather disagreeable, being both burnt and lame, . . . I soon accomplished the well for which I was well paid.

I then with some of my companions repaired to Wood's tavern, got groggy, after which [I] was standing in the street, when a shop boy (Samuel Combs) threw a handful of lime mortar into my eyes, by which means notwithstanding every remedy connected with the assistance of doctors was made use of, I lost my right eye.

I applied to the boy's father for assistance, but never received any satisfaction. However, by the assistance of some worthy gentlemen in Lexington, viz. Messrs. James, William and Alexander Parker, John Bradford and William Leavy, there was a subscription raised for me, which assisted me much in my then distressed situation.

Mr. Castleman (tanner) of Woodford county, came to me, observing that his tanyard had gone dry, requesting me to go with him and procure him water. I accordingly went, but immediately on my arrival there was taken ill, owing to a cold I got, which struck into my eyes, but by the medical aid of Dr. Ridgely was soon relieved, and shortly after satisfied Mr. Castleman with water.

I then dug a well for Mr. Symmes near Woodford Courthouse.

I fell in with a man of the name of Wright, with whom I agreed to dig wells in partnership. Going to Woodford Courthouse we first commenced partnership in a drinking frolic, which continued until our money was all spent, and then observed by the landlord's looks that it was full time to decamp.

Fortunately a gentleman of the name of Sharp coming to the house, invited us home, where we were treated very politely.

Leaving there we started for Frankfort, but my being taken with my old complaint (the bottle fever) occasioned my quartering under a tree. My comrade proceeded to the house of a Mr. Reeves, who kindly sent for me and had me conveyed to an outhouse[2] prepared for my reception, where I got bled and

---

[2] Outbuilding.

continued for some days, being extremely well treated.

During my illness my comrade went on to Frankfort. For Frankfort I started likewise after recovering, but did not get beyond the crossroads before a Mr. Samuel made application, requesting me to find water for him. Here proved a fine opportunity of proving the infallible doctrine of bletonism,[3] there being at least one hundred people present, a number of whom disbelieved the accuracy of said doctrine; but I soon opened their eyes to the truth of it, for laying off three different places which I marked, and being then carried into the house and there blindfolded, and then led out the same direction, I came within six inches of the above mentioned marks without the least variation, which correctness proved the infallibility of bletonism, and caused the astonished crowd to become proselyted to the doctrine.

I then proceeded to Frankfort, where I laid off a number of wells, and being called on by a Daniel Weisiger to judge a well he had on hand, which I did with my forket[4] switch and condemned it, but on further examination found there was water to be got in his garden, and [I] offered to dig him a well for forty dollars, which he refused, though since [he has] acknowledged to me that he wished he had embraced my offer.

I then returned to Lexington. My fame as a well-digger being established so thoroughly, that applications were coming to me every day from every part of the country, which encouraged me entering on a scene of intemperance, dissipation and extravagance, the consequence of which was going in debt in Lexington, particularly to Mr. Hugh MacIllvain, merchant in said town, to whom I owed one hundred dollars.[5]

It may perhaps be entertaining to the reader to know how I contracted part of this debt, which is as follows:

One court day in particular, getting a little as usual about half seas over, and dashing thro' and fro among the crowd, I happened to meet with an old woman and her daughter, informing them that I had been a widower nine years, and my attachment always being great for women, I promised them considerable presents provided the young one would grant me certain favors, to which she agreed.

I accordingly carried them to the store, where the young one first supplied herself with a handsome gown pattern, and immediately slipped out the door; after which the old one received her fee, observing me talking to the storekeeper, she took the advantage and stepped out at the blind side of me, leaving me as usual in the lurch.

During the summer I made my home at a certain Mr. Kelley's, a brother well-digger, convenient to whose house lived a young woman, to whom I got particularly attached. She being but indifferently clad, I supplied her with gen-

[3] Named for a M. Bleton, a famous French practitioner in the period, this was the ability to locate subterranean water by physically sensing its presence—that is, "witching" or "dowsing."
[4] I.e., forked.
[5] Shaw's point here is that the prospect of success led him to celebrate so much that he drank himself into debt.

teel apparel, and likewise paid a doctor for attending her during a severe fit of sickness, after recovering from which she married and left me as usual like the done-over tailor.

I was sent for by a Mr. Elisha Winter living on Tates Creek, whom I assisted to dig a mill race, and for which I was well paid. After that, being sent for by a Mr. Anderson, who had a large cave on his land and was desirous of ascertaining whether or not there was water in it. I told him there was, but he wished to have it ascertained by someone going down.

A number being present, they all refused the disagreeable undertaking; however, for the honor of bletonism, I resolved on venturing down.

Immediately ropes and every necessary apparatus were prepared and then I made my gloomy exit; at the termination of my career[6] I found what I was certain of before, a fine body of water, a bottle of which I brought up to satisfy the credulous expectants of my resurrection and doctrine—true I was much bruised in body and limbs, all of which I was willing to bear for the honor above mentioned.

I then commenced well-digging for a certain Joel Hill, in part payment for which I agreed to take a wool hat, which I accordingly did, from a hatter, Mr. Hill sending his son with me when I got it.

But Mr. Hill neglecting to pay or rather would not pay for it, consequently it fell as usual upon Jonas.

I then started and came to a Mr. Redman's tavern, where I took a good jorum.[7] I then proceeded on to Mr. Hubbard Taylor's, living in Clark County, for whom I dug a well and for which he honorably paid me.

At Strode's Station[8] I met a soldier who was amongst those who took me prisoner, and whom I treated kindly, as he was in part the means of my continuing in a land of liberty.

Taking up goods in Cock and Lytle's store, to the amount of eighteen pounds, I jogged on with them to Clark Courthouse, and there commenced a roaring frolic with a set of as jovial fellows as ever sat over a half pint of whiskey, amongst whom was a jolly Irishman, who cut as many didos[9] as I could for the life of me; consequently he and I became the butts of the company, and at length began to wrestle, he being booted and spurred, and being likewise dexterous at the fun, had greatly the advantage of me, who had no shield against his steel but a thin pair of trousers and nothing to oppose his dexterity but strength.

However, by repeating our wrestling, I gained some knowledge of the art, and ultimately got the better of my old Hibernian, though not before I had my legs properly indented with the steel gaffs; the only recompence I could make for which was to lay him on his back in the fire to dry, as it were.

[6] At the end of the process.
[7] Jonas: That is, like the blameless Jonah, Shaw was the unfortunate victim of other people's deeds. Good jorum: A large quantity of drink.
[8] A small settlement near modern Winchester (then called Clark's Courthouse), Kentucky.
[9] Capers.

Here I exchanged all my goods for whiskey, then turned to jobbing about the town, and showing Mr. Baker, the proprietor of the land, a number of places where water might be found. He kept me there a considerable time, endeavoring all in his power to acquire of me some knowledge of bletonism, after which he sent me off without either fee or reward.

I now started for Lexington, frolicking as usual, and took up goods in Thomas Hart's store to the amount of four pounds eight shillings. I put up at Gabriel Poindexter's tavern, still continuing my intemperance until stopped in my career by a severe fit of sickness, in which I lay suspended between life and death for some considerable time, and were it not for the skill and kind attention of Dr. Ridgley, would never have recovered, it being full two months before I was capable of doing a stroke of work.

My first job after recovering was to wall a well for Mr. Wood, and by working for some time up to my middle in water, I unfortunately contracted a cold, which settled in my eyes, by which I became totally blind, but was restored to sight again by that humane and skillful physician, Doctor Ridgley.

I now began to take a retrospect of my past life, considering maturely the sums of money and the precious time which I had misspent; therefore, resolving with the assistance of Divine Providence to amend my conduct, and be circumspect in my future deportment; as a prelude to which I commenced barkeeping for my landlord, Gabriel Poindexter, during the continuance of which no solicitations whatever could induce me to violate the bonds of sobriety.

In 1795 I commenced partnership in the stone-quarrying business with a Mr. John Cock, and continued with him until the season for well-digging came on, which was the means of my partly paying off my debts; for in this same John Cock I found a father, friend, and partner, a good citizen and an honest man.

After the conclusion of my partnership I commenced well-digging and dug nineteen that season, besides three more which I dug for Captain John Fowler, [and I] quarried stone and walled them in.

In quarrying this stone I had the misfortune to be blown up again; for whilst I was ramming, the blast went off, blew the hammer out of one hand and the rammer out of the other to a considerable distance; however, I came off unhurt, a few scattering splinters excepted.

The winter coming on, I gave up well-digging for the season, and shortly after got acquainted with a young woman by the name of Susanna Bell (living in Colonel Patterson's family) and to whom I was married by the Rev. Henry Toulmin.

The spring following, I purchased two lots of James Johnson, on one of which I built myself a new log house, into which I moved and in the course of the summer rented a quarry from John McConnel, and then carried on stone-quarrying and lime-burning very extensively.

I shortly thereafter engaged with Captain Fowler to go to Bank Lick to dig for salt water, under the superintendence of Captain Alexander, and during my absence on the 11th day of October, had a son born, whom I called Henry Robert Shaw. I continued at the Bank Lick until driven away by a storm.

The year following, 1797, I engaged again with Captain Fowler to go to the Bank Lick and was to start on the first of August. I thought it best to move my family also, and accordingly sold my house and lot, and at an under[1] price.

But when the time approached that we were to depart, Captain Fowler, to my loss, was elected to Congress, which entirely defeated my plan, which occasioned me being under the necessity of renting a house for myself and family.

I was at this time under the necessity of contracting an unavoidable debt, which was utterly out of my power to pay immediately. One of my creditors came to me and observed that a pretended friend of mine advised him to sue me.

This with some other crosses began to make me very uneasy, but my distresses reaching the ears of Captain Fowler, he immediately came to town and desired me to bring him an account of the different debts which I owed; accordingly I did, and he became responsible for them all.

Here I cannot help digressing from the thread of my narrative to introduce an apostrophe of gratitude to that kind, that generous, and to me that incomparable friend; but panegyric must be thrown away on him; because his virtues as a man, as a citizen, and to sum up the whole, as an enlightened and disinterested patriot, are so universally known.

Colonel Patterson observing likewise the distressed situation of myself and family, humanely gave me a house to live in rent-free, with as much fuel as I could consume, for which I shall ever retain a grateful sense.

On the 11th day of April, 1798, I had a daughter born to me, whom I called Nancy Robert Shaw. At the same time I entered into partnership with Colonel Patterson, in the stone-quarrying and lime-burning business, and likewise leased two acres of land from him, for six years at forty shillings per year.

On the 12th day of October, 1799, of glorious memory, I had a son born, whom I called John Robert Shaw, a chip of the old block; and with this pleasing intelligence, to you reader, I shall close this interesting chapter.

ABIGAIL ABBOT BAILEY

from **Memoirs of Mrs. Abigail Bailey** (1815)

DECEMBER, 1788. MR. B. BEGAN TO BEHAVE IN A VERY UNCOMMON MANNER: HE would rise in the morning, and after being dressed, would seat himself in his great chair, by the fire, and would scarcely go out all day. He would not speak, unless spoken to; and not always then. He seemed like one in the deepest study.

---

[1] Low.

If a child came to him, and asked him to go to breakfast, or dinner, he seemed not to hear: then I would go to him, and must take hold of him, and speak very loudly, before he would attend; and then he would seem like one waking from sleep. Often when he was eating, he would drop his knife and fork, or whatever he had in his hand, and seemed not to know what he was doing. Nor could he be induced to give any explanation of his strange appearance and conduct. He did not appear like one senseless, or as though he could not hear, or speak. His eyes would sparkle with the keen emotions of his mind.

I had a great desire to learn the cause of this strange appearance and conduct. I at first hoped it might be concern for his soul; but I was led to believe this was not the case. He continued thus several days and nights, and seemed to sleep but little.

One night, soon after we had retired to bed, he began to talk very familiarly, and seemed pleasant. He said, "Now I will tell you what I have been studying upon all this while: I have been planning to sell our farm, and to take our family and interest, and move to the westward, over toward the Ohio country, five or six hundred miles; I think that is a much better country than this; and I have planned out the whole matter. Now I want to learn your mind concerning it; for I am unwilling to do anything contrary to your wishes in things so important as this." He said he wished to gain my consent, and then he would consult the children, and get their consent also. I was troubled at his proposal; I saw many difficulties in the way. But he seemed much engaged, and said he could easily remove all my objections. I told him it would be uncertain what kind of people we should find there; and how we should be situated relative to gospel privileges.[2] He said he had considered all those things; that he well knew what kind of minister, and what people would suit me; and he would make it his care to settle where those things would be agreeable to me, and that in all things he would seek as much to please me, as himself. His manner was now tender and obliging: and though his subject was most disagreeable to me, yet I deemed it not prudent to be hasty in discovering too much opposition to his plans. I believe I remarked, that I must submit the matter to him. If he was confident it would be for the interest of the family, I could not say it would not be thus; but really I could not at present confide in it.

He proceeded to say, that he would take one of our sons, and one daughter, to go first with him on this tour, to wait on him;[3] and that he probably should not return to take the rest of the family under a year from the time he should set out. He said he would put his affairs in order, so that it should be as easy and comfortable for me as possible, during his absence.

Soon after, Mr. B. laid this his pretended plan before the children; and after a while he obtained their consent to move to the westward. They were not pleased with the idea, but wished to be obedient, and to honor their father.

[2] I.e., the availability of a proper church.
[3] To attend and serve him.

Thus we all consented, at last, to follow our head and guide, wherever he should think best; for our family had ever been in the habit of obedience: and perhaps never were more pains taken to please the head of a family, than had ever been taken in our domestic circle.

But alas! Words fail to set forth the things which followed! All this pretended *plan* was but a specious cover to infernal designs. Here I might pause, and wonder, and be silent, humble, and astonished, as long as I live! A family, which God had committed to my head and husband, as well as to me, to protect and train up for God, must now have their peace and honor sacrificed by an inhuman parent, under the most subtle and vile intrigues, to gratify a most contemptible passion! I had before endured sorrowful days and years, on account of the follies, cruelties, and the base incontinency of him who vowed to be my faithful husband. But all past afflictions vanish before those which follow. But how can I relate them? Oh tell it not in Gath![4] Must I record such grievousness against the husband of my youth?

> Oft as I try to tell the doleful tale,
> My quivering lips and faltering tongue do fail:
> Nor can my trembling hand, or feeble pen,
> Equal the follies of this worst of men!

I have already related that Mr. B. said he would take one of our sons, and one daughter, to wait on him in his distant tour, before he would take all the family. After he had talked of this for a few days, he said he had altered his plan. He would leave his son, and take only his daughter: he would hire what men's help he needed; his daughter must go and cook for him. He now commenced a new series of conduct in relation to this daughter, whom he selected to go with him, in order (as he pretended) to render himself pleasing and familiar to her; so that she might be willing to go with him, and feel happy: for though, as a father, he had a right to command her to go, yet (he said) he would so conduct toward her, as to make her cheerful and well-pleased to go with him. A great part of the time he now spent in the room where she was spinning, and seemed shy of me, and of the rest of the family. He seemed to have forgotten his age, his honor, and all decency, as well as all virtue. He would spend his time with this daughter, in telling idle stories, and foolish riddles, and singing songs to her, and sometimes before the small children, when they were in that room. He thus pursued a course of conduct, which had the most direct tendency to corrupt young and tender minds, and lead them the greatest distance from every serious subject. He would try to make his daughter tell stories with him, wishing to make her free and sociable, and to erase from her mind all that fear and reserve, which he had ever taught his children to feel toward him. He had ever been sovereign, severe and hard with his children, and they stood in the greatest fear of him. His whole conduct,

---

[4]See 2 Samuel 1:19–20.

toward this daughter especially, was now changed, and became most disagreeable.

For a considerable time I was wholly at a loss what to think of his conduct, or what his wish or intentions could be. Had such conduct appeared toward any young woman beside his own young daughter, I should have had no question what he intended: but as it now was, I was loth to indulge the least suspicion of base design. His daily conduct forced a conviction upon my alarmed and tortured mind, that his designs were the most vile. All his tender affections were withdrawn from the wife of his youth, the mother of his children. My room was deserted, and left lonely. His care for the rest of his family seemed abandoned, as well as all his attention to his large circle of worldly business. Everything must lie neglected, while this one daughter engrossed all his attention.

The black cloud, rising like a storm of hail, had rolled on, and had gathered over my head. I clearly saw that Mr. B. entertained the most vile intentions relative to his own daughter. Whatever difficulty attended the obtaining of legal proof, yet no remaining doubt existed in my mind, relative to the existence of his wickedness. And I had no doubt remaining of the violence, which he had used; and that hence arose his rage against her. It must have drawn tears of anguish from the eyes of the hardest mortals, to see the barbarous corrections, which he, from time to time, inflicted on this poor young creature, and for no just cause. Sometimes he corrected her with a rod, and sometimes with a beech stick, large enough for the driving of a team; and with such sternness and anger sparkling in his eyes, that his visage seemed to resemble an infernal, declaring, that if she attempted to run from him again, she should never want but one correction more, for he would whip her to death! This his conduct could be for no common disobedience, for she had ever been most obedient to him in all lawful commands. It seemed as though the poor girl must now be destroyed under his furious hand. She was abashed, and could look no one in the face.

Among the many instances of his wickedly correcting her, I shall mention one. One morning Mr. B. rose from bed while it was yet dark. He immediately called this daughter and told her to get up. She obeyed. And as she knew her daily business, she made up her fire in her room, and sat down to her work. He sat by the fire in the kitchen. As my door was open, I carefully observed his motions. He sat looking into the fire for some time, as though absorbed in his thoughts. It soon grew light. The small children arose, and came round the fire. He looked round like one disappointed and vexed. He sprang from his chair, and called his daughter, whom he first called. She left her work in her room, and came immediately to him. In great rage, and with a voice of terror, he asked why she did not come to him when he first called her? She respectfully told him that he called her to get up, which she immediately did, and went to her work. But she said she did not hear him call her to come to him. He seized his horsewhip, and said, in a rage, he would make her know that when he called her, she should come to him. He then fell to whipping her without mercy. She cried, and begged, and repeated her assertion, that she did not know he called her to come to him. She had done as he told her. She got up, and went to her work. But he was not in the least appeased. He continued to whip her, as though he were dealing with an ungovernable brute, striking over her head, hands, and back; nor did he spare her face and eyes, while the poor girl appeared as though she must die. No proper account could he ever be prevailed on to give of this conduct.

None can describe the anguish of my heart on the beholding of such scenes. How pitiful must be the case of a poor young female, to be subjected to such barbarous treatment by her own father, so that she knew of no way of redress!

It may appear surprising that such wickedness was not checked by legal restraints. But great difficulties attend in such a case. While I was fully convinced of the wickedness, yet I knew not that I could make legal proof. I could not prevail upon this daughter to make known to me her troubles, or to testify against the author of them. Fear, shame, youthful inexperience, and the terrible peculiarities of her case, all conspired to close her mouth against affording me, or any one, proper information. My soul was moved with pity for her wretched case: and yet I cannot say I did not feel a degree of resentment, that she would not, as she ought, expose the wickedness of her father, that she might be relieved from him, and he brought to due punishment. But no doubt his intrigues, insinuations, commands, threats, and parental influence, led her to feel that it was in vain for her to seek redress.

My circumstances, and peculiar bodily infirmities,[5] at that time, were such as to entitle a woman to the tenderest affection and sympathies of a companion. On this account, and as Mr. B. was exceeding stern, and angry with me for entertaining hard thoughts of him, I felt unable to do anything more for the relief of my poor daughter. My hope in God was my only support. And I did abundantly and earnestly commit my cause to him. I felt confident that he would, in his own time, and as his infinite wisdom should determine, grant relief.

Sept. 15, 1789. A son and daughter, twins, were added to our family. The son lived but seventeen days. The distresses of the poor helpless babe were dreadful while he lived. I did hope that his dreadful fits, and his death, might be a means of awakening the conscience of his father. But alas, the father seemed to be given over to a reprobate mind indeed. He seemed wholly unaffected, as if his heart had been made of stone. And he proceeded in his wickedness.

After a while, through the mercy of God, my health was restored. One Sabbath morning, Mr. B. talked of going to meeting. He seemed in good health, and in earnest to attend, that day, on public worship. I was glad, and told him I wished to go with him. But before meeting time he said he had a headache, and could not accompany me to meeting that day.

He told an older daughter (beside his favorite one) that she might have his

---

[5] At this time, Bailey was pregnant with twins, Judith and Simon, whose birth is noted below.

horse, and ride to meeting. I was sorry for his concluding not to go. For I wished to go, and the riding was bad. We had a bad river to ford, and I wanted his company and aid. But he pretended to be unable to go.

The next morning I took an opportunity with Mr. B. alone to have solemn conversation. My health being now restored, I thought it high time, and had determined, to adopt a new mode of treatment with Mr. B. I calmly introduced the subject, and told him, plainly and solemnly, all my views of his wicked conduct, in which he had long lived with his daughter. He flew into a passion, was high, and seemed to imagine, he could at once frighten me out of my object. But I was carried equally above fear, and above temper. Of this I soon convinced him, I let him know, that the business I now had taken in hand, was of too serious a nature, and too interesting, to be thus disposed of, or dismissed with a few angry words. I told him I should no longer be turned off in this manner, but should pursue my object with firmness, and with whatever wisdom and ability God might give me; and that God would plead my cause, and prosper my present undertaking, as he should see best. I reminded Mr. B. of my long and unusually distressing illness; how he had treated me in it; how wicked and cruel he had been to the wife of his youth; how unable I had been to check him in that awful wickedness, which I knew he had pursued; that all my inexpressible griefs and solemn entreaties had been by him trampled under foot.

I therefore had not known what to do better than to wait on God as I had done, to afford me strength and opportunity to introduce the means of his effectual control. This time, I told him, had arrived. And now, if God spared my life, (I told Mr. B.) he should find a new leaf turned over, and that I would not suffer him to go on any longer as he had done. I would now soon adopt measures to put a stop to his abominable wickedness and cruelties. For this could and ought to be done. And if I did it not, I should be a partaker of his sins, and should aid in bringing down the curse of God upon our family.

By this time Mr. B. had become silent. He appeared struck with some degree of fear. He, by and by, asked me what I intended or expected to do, to bring about such a revolution as I had intimated? whether I knew what an awful crime I had laid to his charge? Which [crime] he said could not be proved. He wished to know whether I had considered how difficult it would be for me to do any such thing against him, as I was under his legal control and he could overrule all my plans as he pleased. I told him, I well knew I had been placed under his lawful government and authority, and likewise under his care and protection. And most delightful would it have been to me, to have been able quietly and safely to remain there as long as I lived. Gladly would I have remained a kind, faithful, obedient wife to him, as I had ever been. But I told Mr. B. he *knew* he had violated his marriage covenant, and hence had forfeited all legal and just right and authority over me, and I should convince him that I well knew it. I told him I was not in any passion. I acted on principle, and from long and mature consideration. And though it had ever been my greatest care and pleasure (among my earthly comforts) to obey and please him, yet by his most wicked and cruel conduct, he had compelled me to undertake this most undesirable business—of stopping him in his mad career; and that I now felt strength, courage and zeal to pursue my resolution. And if my life was spared, he would find that I should bring something to pass, and probably more than he now apprehended.

As to what I could prove against him I told Mr. B. he knew not how much evidence I had of his unnatural crimes, of which I had accused him, and of which *he knew he was guilty.* I asked him why he should not expect that I should institute a process against him, for that most horrid conduct, which he had long allowed himself to pursue, and with the most indecent and astonishing boldness?

I told him I well knew that he was naturally a man of sense, and that his conscience now fully approved of my conduct.

Mr. B. seeing me thus bold and determinate, soon changed his countenance and conduct. He appeared panic-struck; and he soon became mild, sociable and pleasant. He now made an attempt, with all his usual subtlety, and flatteries to induce me to relinquish my design. He pretended to deny the charge of incest. But I told him I had no confidence in his denial of it; it was therefore in vain! Upon this he said, he really did not blame, or think hard of me, for believing him guilty of this sin. He said, he knew he had behaved foolishly, and had given me full reason to be jealous of him; and he repeated that he did not at all think hard of me for entertaining the views which I had of him. He then took the Bible, and said, he would lay his hand on it, and swear that he was not guilty of the crime laid to his charge. Knowing what I did, I was surprised and disgusted at this impious attempt. I stepped towards him, and in a resolute and solemn manner begged of him to forbear! assuring him, that such an oath could not undo or alter real facts, of which he was conscious. And this proceeding, I assured him, would be so far from giving me any satisfaction, that it would greatly increase the distress of my soul for him in his wickedness. Upon this he forbore, and laid his Bible aside.

Mr. B. said he believed there never before was any man, who was so great a fool as he had been! That, after I had so kindly settled with him for his past offences, and upon such low and reasonable terms, he should again move me to jealousy, and thus destroy all my confidence in him. He said he wished he could be set back on the ground he had left, or had remained on so favorable a footing, as that on which I had placed him in our settlement. I replied, that I really thought too, that he was one of the most foolish of men; that I had long been constrained to view him not only extremely *wicked*, but extremely *foolish!*

I told him he had truly been a wonder to me; I had looked upon him with astonishment. He was naturally, I added, a man of sense; he was a man of much knowledge, had acquired property, and had been a man of considerable note. And that he should thus degrade and ruin himself, soul and body, and destroy a large promising family, as he had done, it was indeed most astonishing! I reminded him that he had been much in good company, and many gentlemen had honored him with their friendly attention. I asked, if any sum of money would induce him to be willing that those gentlemen should know that of him, which I knew? And, that though he seemed to be too willing to throw himself away, as though he were of no worth, I assured him, I did yet set something more by myself, than to be viewed as capable of conniving at such detestable conduct.

Mr. B. replied, that if I had made up my mind no longer to live with him, I need not be at any trouble to obtain a legal separation. For he would depart to some distant country, where I should be troubled with him no more. I remarked, that when Abraham's wife was dead, he wished, however well he had loved her, to have her now buried out of his sight.[6] And, though I could by no means compare him to the pious Sarah, yet, if true virtue and friendship in my husband were dead, I did truly wish him to be removed from my sight. And that true virtue and friendship were indeed dead in him, I thought I had the most melancholy and incontestable evidence.

Our unhappy daughter now became eighteen years of age, and thus legally free from her father. She immediately left us, and returned no more.[7] As she was going, I had solemn conversation with her relative to her father's conduct. She gave me to understand that it had been most abominable. But I could not induce her to consent to become an evidence against him. I pleaded with her the honor and safety of our family, the safety of her young sisters, and her own duty; but she appeared overwhelmed with shame and grief, and nothing effectual could yet be done.

I hence saw, that in relation to commencing a legal process, God's time seemed not yet to have arrived. I must still wait and look to him to open the path of my duty. . . .

Monday, March 19. We again moved forward upon my gloomy and sorrowful journey. After a while a man fell in company with us, travelling on foot. Mr. B. had been some acquainted with him. They fell into conversation. After a while the man remarked, that he had walked that day ten or twelve miles, from Captain Gould's of Granville.[8] This struck my mind as a strange thing, that we were going to this very place (Capt. Gould's), [and] that this man had come from there; had come ten or twelve miles; and was now going on the same way with us! I asked Mr. B. how this was? "Oh," he said, "we must go to Granville through Rupert, and come in at the lower end of the town, because of a great mountain, which we could not pass with a sleigh. But this man came over across on foot." Mr. B. added, that we should be there by noon, or a little after.

After we had proceeded several miles, Mr. B. threw off the mask at once, and kept me no longer in the dark, at least relative to what was *not* the object of his journey, that it was not what he had ever said. He told me, we are now

<hr />

[6] See Genesis 23.

[7] Ann Taves, editor of a modern reprint of Bailey's book, notes that little is conclusively known of Phebe Bailey's life after her eighteenth birthday (April 20, 1790). A report that she died among the celibate and egalitarian Shakers has not been confirmed.

[8] Captain Ebenezer Gould, of Killingly, Connecticut, settled in Granville, New York, near the Vermont border, at the time of the Revolution.

in the state of New York, and now you must be governed by the laws of this state, which are far more suitable to govern such women as you, than are the laws of New Hampshire.[9] He added, that he was not going to Granville; nor had he ever intended to go thither, or to trade with Capt. Gould. But all this plan, he said, he had laid, to lead me off from home, that he might get me away from the circle of the Abbots, and Brocks, and my connections, and then see if he could not bring me to terms, that would better suit himself.[1] And now, if I would drop all that was past, and concerning which I had made so much noise, and would promise never to make any more rout about any of those things, and to be a kind and obedient wife to him, without any more ado—it was well! If not, he would proceed accordingly. He said, unless I would thus engage, he would drive on among strangers, till that sleigh and those horses were worn out! He went on conversing in this way. Sometimes he would speak of carrying me to the Ohio; sometimes of taking me among the Dutch people, where, he said, I could not understand a word of their language. And then he would talk of taking me to Albany, or where he could sell me on board a ship. He assured me that I should never return home again. He said he had been cunning enough to get me away from home; and now he believed he should be crafty enough to keep me away. I might *cry*, he added, as much as I pleased; but I could not help myself. If I should try to escape from him, he said, he was as long-headed as I was, and I might well expect that he could outwit me. Mr. B. said that his brothers,[2] D. and F. and also E. F. were all confederate with him in this plan. And if I should by any means escape from him, and get home, he had empowered his brother D. to keep all the interest out of my hands, and to advertise me in his name, forbidding all persons harboring or trusting me.[3]

Thus, Mr. B. said, he had not been idle, but had been planning to take care of himself. And he thought he had got things in a very good way!

I now, for once, had full confidence in the truth of what Mr. B. had said. I believed he had, at last, told me the truth. I could now place some dependence on his words. But Oh, the terrors of such truth as this! My mind was astonished! My heart was broken! My thoughts immediately flew to my poor forsaken children. My grief for them was truly inexpressible. I can only say, my sorrow was complete. My grief arose to the highest pitch that I thought my nature could endure. Everything in the whole scene appeared to me calculated to overwhelm the soul with horror, grief and distress.

As to my own person, I thought little or nothing of any tortures, or miseries,

---

[9]Ann Taves reports that "no divorces were granted in New York from 1675 until 1787 when the state enacted a law which allowed for divorce on the grounds of adultery." In Puritan New England, where marriage was a civil ceremony (rather than a sacrament of the church), divorce was more easily obtained.

[1]Abigail's birth family (including her married sister Judith Brock) lived in the adjoining towns of Newbury, Vermont, and Haverhill, New Hampshire.

[2]Actually, kinsmen—only D[aniel Bailey] was literally Asa's brother; the other two individuals soon referred to, as Taves identifies them, were [Reuben] F[oster], his brother-in-law, and E[dward] F[oster], his nephew.

[3]A typical ploy in the event a woman left her husband, who would post advertisements or run them in papers warning creditors not to extend credit to her.

that Mr. B. might inflict on my mortal part. If he should kill the body, he could do no more. But I had other things on my mind, which were far more dreadful to me than bodily tortures, or even death. 1. The miseries of my dear children. 2. The infinite dishonor my leaving them and going off with Mr. B. would do to religion, in the view of those who knew not the circumstances which had led me away. The latter, as well as the former, appeared to me insupportable. And the situation of my family—Oh my children, my dear, unhappy, forsaken children!—the thought of their case would rend my heart with the keenest distress.

I had in seasons past, after the commencement of my peculiar troubles, been greatly tried, for fear I should not exercise suitable wisdom and discretion, under my difficulties, so as to do honor to the cause of virtue and religion. And now I thought that I had exceedingly erred in judgment, and had been very unwise indeed, in thus far hearkening to Mr. B's stories, and being led off by him from all my friends.

I had, after all my knowledge of Mr. B's falsehood and wickedness, been in the habit of placing some dependence on his most solemn assertions. He had promised so fair and so much to me relative to my having half the interest;[4] and I had been so much in the habit of fearing him; and such too was the delicate nature of our difficulties; that I had been very cautious and sparing, as to conversing freely with any, even my familiar connections, upon my difficulties. I ever meant to let all my friends, and the public, by and by, know the uttermost of my trials. But I was led to think it would be well to get my concerns with Mr. B. (as to the property) first settled. I meant they should understand (and I supposed they did understand) that I never designed to live with Mr. B. anymore. But I had not been very explicit with them relative to this thing.

I now felt that I had greatly erred, in not having opened my mind more fully to them, and sought their advice in everything, and particularly relative to this journey. They would now see, that I was gone off with Mr. B. and did not return, as I promised my family. They would not know where I had gone with him, nor the true reason. And now I thought that people, and even my friends among the rest, must think that I had not only been very unwise in going off with such a man, but that I had been deceitful. I well knew that appearances against me (if I did not soon return) must be exceedingly dark. And as I had professed religion, and had been a great advocate for experimental[5] and practical piety, I thought this appearance of absconding with Mr. B. and leaving my family, would bring a great wound on the cause of Christ. This I knew not how to endure. I thought people would be led to apply to me what is said of the ostrich, that "she leaveth her eggs in the earth, and forgetteth that the foot may crush them, or the wild beasts devour them; that she hardeneth herself against her young ones, as though they were not hers." "Even the sea monsters draw out their breasts to give suck to their young ones; but the daughter of my people

---

[4] Under New Hampshire law, Abigail was entitled to a full half share of the couple's property; this was one of the obligations he hoped to avoid by kidnapping her and taking her to New York.
[5] Based on experience.

is become cruel." "Can a mother forget her sucking child, that she should not have compassion on the son of her womb? Yea, they may forget."[6] Those and similar texts ran in my mind. It seemed as though people, my friends, and even my children too, must be led to think that I had thus become cruel as the ostrich, and hardened against my own dear offspring, now like tender helpless orphans, exposed to a thousand evils. If they could see what was in my heart, they would see that those children were dearer to me than my life. But the appearance was altogether against me. Oh, what a monster of a mother must I appear to them, when they find that I do not return! How would the friends of religion mourn, that I had given such occasion to the enemy to reproach! And how would the enemies of religion triumph, and say, "Ah, so we would have it!" I now thought, how little have I done for Christ in my day! How little has God been glorified by me! And now so worthless a creature has suffered herself to be so strangely deceived, and led off from her young helpless family, under circumstances so dubious, in appearance, so inexpressibly mortifying, and so calculated to wound that cause, which I have earnestly longed to see built up. Oh, every thought of these things cut my soul to the quick, and filled me with unutterable pain.

The following sacred passage ran in my mind; "Died Abner as a fool dieth. Thy hands were not bound, nor thy feet put in fetters. As a man falleth before wicked men, so fellest thou."[7] It seemed to me wonderful, that I had been so deluded by Mr. B. I was astonished to think I had suffered myself to be so deceived and fooled by such a man, and led off thus from my family and home! It seemed as though I could not have conceived that he could have got me away, unless he had bound me, and taken me by force. David, when lamenting over Abner, said, "The Lord shall reward the doer of evil according to his wickedness." And so in the present case, I did believe that God would reward the man, who had thus injured and imposed on innocence and credulity; who had exercised such monstrous falsehood and cruelty against me and our poor young children, taking me from them in such treachery. This act of Mr. B. I truly thought (inasmuch as it was in such wanton violation of so many promises, and oaths voluntarily made) exceeded all his antecedent barbarities toward his children or me. I had once in a dream (as formerly hinted) beheld this man deliberately murdering the younger part of his family, because by his crimes he was forced to flee to a great distance, and could not take them with him![8] Yes, and had seen myself pursuing, with him, a strange and doleful journey, for an

---

[6] For these three biblical quotations, see Job 39:13–17, Lamentations 4:3, and Isaiah 49:15.

[7] Abner, of the house of Saul, warred against David until he was treacherously murdered by Joab, after which David lamented over him in the words quoted by Bailey (see 2 Samuel 3).

[8] Earlier, Abigail wrote, "One night I dreamed of seeing Mr. B. in the horrid act of murdering his children in cold blood. I thought I screeched, and begged of him to forbear. He said he knew what he was doing. He knew that everybody in these parts had become his enemy; and that those who used to be his friends, who respected and honored him, were now turned against him. And he was determined to leave the country, and go to a great distance. And as he could not carry his small children, so he would not leave them among his enemies."

unaccountable something, having left my family, and not knowing how they could live, or what would become of them! Ah, too late is the recollection of the premonition! I am caught in the toils. Might but the sequel be verified also, that I escaped from him, and flew upon the wings of the wind, till I reached my friends! The God of salvation can effect this also.

Having thus, in silent astonishment, and for a considerable time, revolved such things in my mind, I began to fill my mouth with arguments, and to try what I could effect, in exciting the feelings, pity and compassion of Mr. B. toward our own dear offspring, our young, helpless, deserted children and babes. For it seemed to me impossible that he should be wholly destitute of any feelings toward them. I now adopted every tender consideration and expression, that I could use; (and surely these flowed with great ease from my wounded and bleeding heart!) to excite some parental feeling in him. I attempted to address his natural good sense, and that he must know that our poor little family, left as they were, must greatly suffer, in body and mind, if not die, unless I returned to them. Their hearts broken—their cries and sobs continuing—till their ruin might close the wretched scene! I thus pleaded their lamentable case, in the most melting manner of which I was capable. But all my expressions and arguments fell as far short of exciting the least apparent feeling in his heart, as they did of equalling the anguish of mine! He appeared to me to have become totally destitute of natural affection, and even for his youngest children.

When I found that this argument was utterly in vain, I adopted another. I began once more to labor to move his compassion toward himself. I most solemnly entreated him to have mercy on himself, and no longer to carry on a cruel warfare against his own interests, temporal and eternal. I told him he was certainly operating against himself; and if he had any regard to his own honor, peace and happiness, he ought immediately to discover it by helping me home again to our poor children, and by afflicting them and me no more. As for my own life, I told Mr. B. that I did now regard it for my children's sakes, much more than for my own. I told him he could do nothing more to me than to kill my body, even should God suffer him to do his worst. But to himself he was doing an infinitely greater injury. For he was taking the most direct way, not only to destroy his honor and peace in time, but to bring himself, body and soul, into everlasting destruction.

Thus I reasoned and expostulated with the father of my children in the most rational, tender, pathetic manner I was possibly able. But alas, I had the distressing mortification to find, that all was in vain. He appeared totally destitute of all feeling upon these subjects.

Although I had lost all affection for Mr. B. as a husband, or a friend, yet I had much feeling for him as a fellow creature. When he exulted in the thought of his being "long-headed," and of his having so completely outwitted me, I saw that he felt very strong in himself. He seemed to imagine that he had done all those feats by his own mighty wisdom—that he now had me in his power, and could do in all things according to his own will. I pitied the poor man, and felt a desire that he might see his own weakness, and nothingness, and that all these things were overruled by God in infinite wisdom, to effect his own purposes. Hearing the boastings of self-importance, I groaned, and said, "O poor creature, I wonder you can feel so strong in yourself!" I told him it appeared so clear to me, that God governed everything, even his present wickedness, and that he could do no more than God would overrule for his own glory; that he now appeared no more than a moth, or a worm. And I longed to have him know that he was no more in the hands of God, than the least insect. And unless he repented and turned, he would ere long find that the arm of the Lord, whom he was condemning, was infinitely strong, and that it is a fearful thing to fall into the hands of the living God![9] And as he was now pursuing so cruel and wicked a course, and seemed so disposed to boast and exult in his own wit and power to bring wicked devices to pass, fearless of the indignation of righteous heaven, so it seemed to me his case was but little short of desperate.

I had, at that time, such a sense of the wretched state and condition of this poor miserable man, who was thus rushing on to his own disgrace and eternal ruin, as words cannot express. I viewed him in the hands of an incensed God, and yet stout-hearted and stupidly unconcerned, [and] glorying in his shame and cruelty. I can truly say that for sometime my thoughts were carried away from my own momentary affliction (though it was now so severe) and absorbed in the view of *his* infinitely more dreadful wretchedness. I realized his accountability to God, and eternity looked near. His awful case made my soul to tremble for him.

But waving the farther consideration of the guilt and spiritual wretchedness of him who had thus betrayed me, I told Mr. B. that if his two brothers, whom he had named, and Mr. E. F. had indeed conspired with him against me, as he had said, I thought I might say with Job, "My brethren have dealt deceitfully as a brook,"[1] and that with Job I might add, "God hath delivered me to the ungodly, and turned me over into the hands of the wicked." But I further remarked to him, if it were indeed the case, that four cunning men had, by putting their heads together, planned the ruin of one poor feeble woman, half distracted with cares and troubles, which his wickedness had brought upon her—if I had really been deceived by his horrid lies and false oaths, I thought he had [nothing], of which to boast! If he had laid any plan (I told him) which would have been called fair dealing or manly, I should not so much have blamed him. But as the case was, his conduct was most criminal, horrid and insufferable; and that he was still persisting in it in carrying me further from home, and refusing to let me return. On this I told him he might depend, that should the merciful God ever again deliver me out of his cruel hands, and set my feet on the ground of liberty, he would want four times four as cunning men as himself, again to decoy me away. But as the case now was with me, I told him, I knew no better way than to submit to him as a captive. But though

[9] See Hebrews 10:31.
[1] Job 6:15, 16:11.

he had brought me to such a distance "from all the Abbots, and Brocks, and my other friends," as he was pleased to call them, yet one thing he might depend on—he had not yet deprived me of an honest and firm heart. I was yet, as much as ever, disposed to avoid wrong, and do right. And hence I could not, and would not, ever submit to his proposals, to bury past matters, and live with him as his wife, in future. He might carry me, if he was able, to the ends of the earth, or sell me as a slave, as he had proposed, on board a ship. But this should never alter my mind in relation to living with him, the rest of our days, as he wished. I would make no such agreement, let come what would. But I would yield as a captive to his violent hands, till the Lord should see fit to deliver me. I told Mr. B. I could, through Christ's strengthening me, endure sufferings. But the thought of wickedly yielding to his proposals, was to me insupportable. And that I did earnestly pray to God for grace never to comply with this or any wicked proposal; and that God would hold up my goings in his ways, that my footsteps slip not.[2]

[2] See Psalms 17:5.

2

JUDGE COOPER OF
COOPERSTOWN

Born in a log house in rural Philadelphia in 1754 to "extremely poor" Quaker farmers, William Cooper grew up with very few advantages, including only minimal education. By the time of his death late in 1809, however, he had been a merchant, a member of Congress, a judge, and, most importantly, owner and developer of literally hundreds of thousands of acres of land, mostly in central and northern New York. His most important efforts centered on a beautiful azure lake embowered in old hills at the center of what was to become Otsego County. Here, where Lake Otsego's water poured out to give rise to the Susquehanna River, there sprang up in the 1780s a village first known quite unpretentiously as Foot of the Lake, but eventually called, for its owner and founder, Cooperstown. It grew rapidly, as did the whole county, until by 1810 Otsego was the second most populous county in the whole state; only New York County (Manhattan) exceeded it.

Its phenomenal growth was owing to several causes. Many of its settlers came from New England when, after the Revolution, Yankees poured out of their own region seeking elbow room for a population that had been growing steadily for generations and by 1765 was already in need of land. They came to many areas of New York, and to Otsego in particular because some Yankee soldiers passing down Lake Otsego with General James Clinton in 1779 during his brutal invasion of the Iroquois country noted Otsego's potential. When Cooper secured control of the land immediately after the war, he was more fortunate than he might have imagined, as it lay precisely across the route of the immigrants soon to head to this first of many "Wests." He also was wise enough, at least initially, to approach these and other immigrants with open arms. His policy of helping poor families to establish themselves on land they owned outright (rather than, as was especially the practice in older New York regions, renting it on long-term leases) contributed to the rapid growth of his settlement and its surrounding farmlands, even if in the end the wealth he thought he was leaving to his heirs was swallowed up in part by the collapse of land prices after the War of 1812, which left the mortgages he willingly extended to settlers in areas more remote from Cooperstown next to worthless. By 1820, in fact, the judge's family was fractured, diminished, and deep in debt. While they had contributed to the problem by their wasteful spending of an inheritance that seemed immense (and secure), in point of fact that inheritance was mostly a shadow.

The later fate of the Cooper family was chronicled in part by the judge's son James Fenimore Cooper in novels such as *The Pioneers* (1823), which recounts the story of Cooperstown's founding with an ironic sense of how events often undercut human expectation. Cooper's novel, portraying the settlers as wasteful and petty and the settlement as ill-formed and noisy, makes the exuberant optimism of the judge himself in his own version of that story, published in 1810, sound both a bit naive and a bit too hopeful. But William Cooper knew quite well that all was not as grand as he might wish to make it sound: "In bonds and mortgages," he wrote in 1804, "I am rich, in money poor," even if he probably viewed this fact as a temporary financial condition rather than a true reflection of his worth. It was a period when great fortunes, many much greater than Cooper's, in fact vanished in a collapse of debts and demands, but it was a time, too, when a person of Cooper's modest background, if he was to accomplish anything, had to risk everything. Indeed, Cooper found risk essential to the nation's expansion, and at least in print he took comfort in such ideals as cooperation, neighborliness, and association. A thoroughgoing capitalist and a fierce partisan of the Federalist party, which in theory was distrustful of the common citizens, he yet trusted to the social nature of the species to provide not only pleasure but also support. Hence his belief in helping the poor—of which he had quite recently been one—to achieve a stable if modest success. Cooper, bound upward on his own trajectory toward wealth and gentility, as historian Alan Taylor has argued recently, did not court the poor politically— as his diehard Republican opponents did. Nonetheless, he articulated a vision of economic democracy that the Yankee settlers found appealing and supportive, and he thus helped to extend the implications of the Revolution into new domains of society. That New York State was particularly burdened with landholding systems (descended from colonial patroonships and manors) that did not uplift the poor made his economic principles even more attractive to his customers and clients.

Judge Cooper wrote *A Guide in the Wilderness* sometime prior to 1807 in response to a request from an Irish-American friend, William Sampson, who wished to help his compatriots prepare for and succeed at emigration to America. Sampson, an Irish lawyer seized in the 1790s for his involvement with the patriotic Society of United Irishmen, had been exiled to Portugal in 1799 and came to America in 1806, soon establishing himself as a staunch proponent of individual rights and a pro-labor attorney. He sought to publish the pamphlet first in New York City, but failing that, had recourse to his brothers still in Ireland and arranged for it to be issued, the year after Cooper's death, in Dublin.

WILLIAM COOPER

---

from A Guide in the Wilderness (1810)

LETTER FROM JUDGE COOPER TO WILLIAM SAMPSON, ESQ.

Sir,

I SHALL CHEERFULLY ANSWER THE QUERIES YOU HAVE PUT TO ME. THE manly way in which you have challenged me, and the good sense you have shown upon a subject of which you can have no experience, and the object I perceive you have at heart, that of procuring information in a matter interesting to your countrymen, does you honor, and makes it a pleasure for me so satisfy so fair a curiosity. I shall answer each query in the order you have proposed them; and, although that knowledge acquired by practice alone, cannot well be imparted, yet I feel, I believe, the bent of your inquiries, and shall do all in my power to make my answers useful, as well to your countrymen as to my own.

I shall first make the general supposition, that either a wealthy individual, or else a company, purchase a large tract of land, say 50,000 acres. The purchaser, or someone strongly interested in the purchase, should go upon the spot, and give public notice of the day when he means to open the sales. The conditions should be advertised, and notice given, that every person desirous of buying, should have as much or as little as he choose, on a credit of seven or ten years, paying annual interest. The price will naturally vary according to soil and situation.

It should be distinctly understood, that the whole tract is open for settlement, without any reserve on the part of the landlord, as nothing is more discouraging than any appearance in him of views distinct from the prosperity of the whole; and this would be evident, if in the very outset he reserved any part in contemplation of a future advance, at the expence of the labor of the original settlers, to whose advantage these reserved tracts had not contributed. The reason is plain: The first difficulties are the greatest, and it is only by combination and cooperation that they can be surmounted. The more the settlers are in number, the more hands can be brought to effect those works which cannot be executed by a few; such are the making of roads and bridges, and other incidents to the cultivation of the wilderness, which are impossible to individuals, but which numbers render practicable and easy.

Besides, he who comes to better his condition, by embarking in such an enterprise, would find it no relief from his present poverty, to be doomed to a life of savage solitude; he will still desire the society of his species, and the ordinary comforts of life; he will look for some religious institution, some school for his children. There must be mechanics to build houses, and erect mills, and other useful or necessary purposes. Where there are a number of settlers, each bearing his proportion of the labor, and contributing to the expense, these things arise almost of course; but it would be very discouraging to a few scattered settlers to reflect, that they were toiling under all the hardships and disadvantages of a new and arduous undertaking, whilst others, who had contributed nothing, should afterwards come in and reap all the advantages of their activity. The reserved tracts, therefore, serving only to separate them from each other, and depriving them of the comforts of society, and the advantage of cooperation, would be sources of just discontent, and the landlord who seemed to harbor the ungenerous project of trafficking with the future profits of their industry, and to give all his care to his own interest, without any sympathy with them, would become deservedly an object of distrust and jealousy: his influence would cease, and that confidence, which could alone animate and invigorate a difficult enterprise, once vanishing, nothing but failure could ensue.

Thus the advantage of the landlord is to reserve no part, if he can possibly dispose of it. Sometimes a man of large property with an enterprising spirit, will seek for a tract suitable to his means and his ambition. Such a one may have friends and connections, who may want courage to face the first difficulties, or venture on untried ways, but whom he hopes to draw after him by example. It is of great importance to promote the success of such a person, and he will be justly entitled to kindness and support. His task will be to smooth the way for others. As soon as he is himself seated, his next wish will be to draw around him a neighborhood of relatives and friends, whose habits are congenial to his own. He will be repaid for his labor and risk, by selling at a small advance beyond the price he paid, and the interest upon it. Such, besides that he will come provided with stock and capital, will be useful, as it were, to sound the horn and proclaim the settlement, and will be a new center of attraction.

But whilst we acknowledge the importance of the wealthy undertaker,[1] we must not despise the offer of the poor man. He can never be insignificant, who is willing to add his labor to the common stock: for the interest of every individual, from the richest landholder to the poorest settler, conspires and contributes to the great primary object, to cause the wilderness to bloom and fructify, and each man prospers in proportion as he contributes to the advantage of his neighbor.

With respect to the lands: although they will naturally vary in quality, I never in the first instance make any difference in price, but leave that matter to regulate itself. In the beginning the poorer settler will refuse the rougher spots, and rightly, as they will yield him no immediate subsistence. I therefore leave them until that period, when the timber they afford shall become valuable for the purposes of fencing and of fuel. And by the simple measure of letting things take their own course, I find my interest and that of the whole community promoted, [so that] in no instance have the rough grounds and the swamps failed to be eventually most profitable to me: nay, in fifteen years' time their value has increased to sevenfold.

The poor man, and his class is the most numerous, will generally undertake about one hundred acres. The best mode of dealing with him, is to grant

[1] I.e., investor, promoter.

him the fee simple by deed, and secure the purchase money by a mortgage on the land conveyed to him.[2] He then feels himself, if I may use the phrase, as a man upon record. His views extend themselves to his posterity, and he contemplates with pleasure their settlement on the estate he has created, a sentiment ever grateful to the heart of man. His spirit is enlivened; his industry is quickened; every new object he attains brings a new ray of hope and courage. He builds himself a barn and a better habitation, plants his fruit trees, and lays out his garden; he clears away the trees, until they, which were the first obstacles to his improvement, becoming scarcer, become more valuable, and he is at length as anxious to preserve, as he was at first to destroy them. He no longer feels the weight of debt, for having the fee, he can sell at an improved value, nor is he bound to remain against his will.

Not so if he had been bound by special contracts and conditions, subjecting him to the forfeiture of his land, and with it of his labor. Gloomy apprehensions then seize upon his mind; the bright view of independence is clouded; his habits of thought become sullen and cheerless, and he is unable to soar above the idea of perpetual poverty.

Thus, by the adoption of a rational plan, it appears that the interests of all parties are made to coincide. The settler sleeps in security, from the certainty of his possession, and the landlord is safe in the mortgage he holds, and the state profits by the success of each in the increase of its wealth and population.

A moderate price, long credit, a deed in fee, and a friendly landlord are infallible inducements to a numerous settlement: and where there is much people there will be trade; and where there is trade there will be money; and where there is money the landlord will succeed; but he should be ever in the midst of the settlers, aiding and promoting every beneficial enterprise.

In this point of view I have often compared the dealer in land to a ship. Money is the element he swims in; without money, he is aground; and as a ship that is not afloat is no better than a wreck, so when he ceases to have money, his activity and usefulness are gone.

So, in rural phrase, may we compare the poor settler to the creature of draft. Unsustained, overloaded, and oppressed, he yields no profit; well-treated, in good heart, and gently driven, his labor is lighter, and his profit more. It is no otherwise with man. He can bear so much, and no more. If forced beyond that, his spirits will finally sink under oppression; whereas, by timely aids [and] encouraging words from a landlord who has his confidence and whom he feels to be his friend, he will perform wonders, and exceed his own hopes.

You have desired to know something of my own proceedings, and since I

---

[2] That is, Cooper urges the landowner to sell parcels outright ("in fee simple") to ordinary farmers, a practice that he followed, often taking the mortgages for payment of the purchase price himself. By contrast, some New York landowners refused to sell land, preferring to let it out on long-term leases. While Cooper's preference certainly offered poor settlers greater opportunity, in practice his own heirs found that many of the mortgages they inherited were not honored. By 1820, the surviving heirs had lost control of most of the father's land and wealth.

am to speak of myself, I can nowhere better introduce that subject than now, in proof of what I have asserted.

I began with the disadvantage of a small capital, and the incumbrance of a large family, and yet I have already settled more acres than any man in America. There are forty thousand souls now holding directly or indirectly under me, and I trust, that no one amongst so many can justly impute to me any act resembling oppression. I am now descending into the vale of life, and I must acknowledge that I look back with self-complacency upon what I have done, and am proud of having been an instrument in reclaiming such large and fruitful tracts from the waste of the creation. And I question whether that sensation is not now a recompense more grateful to me than all the other profits I have reaped. Your good sense and knowledge of the world will excuse this seeming boast; if it be vain, we all must have our vanities, let it at least serve to show that industry has its reward, and age its pleasures, and be an encouragement to others to persevere and prosper.

In 1785 I visited the rough and hilly country of Otsego, where there existed not an inhabitant, nor any trace of a road. I was alone, three hundred miles from home, without bread, meat, or food of any kind; fire and fishing tackle were my only means of subsistence. I caught trout in the brook, and roasted them on the ashes. My horse fed on the grass that grew by the edge of the waters. I laid me down to sleep in my watchcoat, nothing but the melancholy wilderness around me. In this way I explored the country, formed my plans of future settlement, and meditated upon the spot where a place of trade or a village should afterwards be established.

In May 1786, I opened the sales of 40,000 acres, which, in sixteen days, were all taken up by the poorest order of men. I soon after established a store, and went to live among them, and continued so to do till 1790, when I brought on my family. For the ensuing four years the scarcity of provisions was a serious calamity; the country was mountainous, there were neither roads nor bridges.

But the greatest discouragement was in the extreme poverty of the people, none of whom had the means of clearing more than a small spot in the midst of the thick and lofty woods, so that their grain grew chiefly in the shade. Their maize did not ripen, their wheat was blasted, and the little they did gather they had no mill to grind within twenty miles distance—not one in twenty had a horse, and the way lay through rapid streams, across swamps, or over bogs. They had neither provisions to take with them, nor money to purchase them; nor if they had [money], were any to be found on their way. If the father of a family went abroad to labor for bread, it cost him three times its value before he could bring it home, and all the business on his farm stood still till his return.

I resided among them, and saw too clearly how bad their condition was. I erected a storehouse, and during each winter filled it with large quantities of grain, purchased in distant places. I procured from my friend Henry Drinker a credit for a large quantity of sugar kettles; he also lent me some potash kettles, which we conveyed as we best could, sometimes by partial roads on sleighs, and sometimes over the ice. By this means I established potash works among the settlers, and made them debtor for their bread and laboring utensils. I also gave them credit for their maple sugar and potash, at a price that would bear transportation, and the first year after the adoption of this plan I collected in one mass forty-three hogsheads of sugar, and three hundred barrels of pot and pearl ash, worth about nine thousand dollars.[3] This kept the people together and at home, and the country soon assumed a new face.

I had not funds of my own sufficient for the opening of new roads, but I collected the people at convenient seasons, and by joint efforts we were able to throw bridges over the deep streams, and to make, in the cheapest manner, such roads as suited our then humble purposes.

In the winter preceding the summer of 1789, grain rose in Albany to a price before unknown. The demand swept the whole granaries of the Mohawk country. The number of beginners who depended upon it for their bread greatly aggravated the evil, and a famine ensued, which will never be forgotten by those who, though now in the enjoyment of ease and comfort, were then afflicted with the cruelest of wants.

In the month of April I arrived amongst them with several loads of provisions, destined for my own use and that of the laborers I had brought with me for certain necessary operations; but in a few days all was gone, and there remained not one pound of salt meat nor a single biscuit. Many were reduced to such distress, as to live upon the roots of wild leeks; some more fortunate lived upon milk, whilst others supported nature by drinking a syrup made of maple sugar and water. The quantity of leeks they ate had such an effect upon their breath, that they could be smelled at many paces distance, and when they came together, it was like cattle that had pastured in a garlic field. A man of the name of Beets mistaking some poisonous herb for a leek, ate it, and died in consequence. Judge of my feelings at this epoch, with two hundred families about me, and not a morsel of bread.

A singular event seemed sent by a good Providence to our relief. It was reported to me that unusual shoals of fish were seen moving in the clear waters of the Susquehanna. I went and was surprised to find that they were herrings. We made something like a small net, by the interweaving of twigs, and by this rude and simple contrivance, we were able to take them in thousands. In less than ten days each family had an ample supply with plenty of salt. I also obtained from the legislature, then in session, seventeen hundred bushels of corn. This we packed on horses' backs, and on our arrival made a distribution among the families, in proportion to the number of individuals of which each was composed.

This was the first settlement I made, and the first attempted after the Revo-

---

[3] Potash and pearl ash (potassium carbonate) were produced by partly refining the wood ashes that came from trees burned in opening farmland. Used in the production of glass, soap, and wool, potash or pearl ash sometimes gave settlers their first ready money, the price in December 1807, for instance, being 225 dollars per ton in New York City.

lution. It was, of course, attended with the greatest difficulties; nevertheless, to its success many others have owed their origin. It was besides the roughest land in all the state, and the most difficult of cultivation of all that has been settled, but for many years past it has produced everything necessary to the support and comfort of man. It maintains at present eight thousand souls, with schools, academies, churches, meeting-houses, turnpike roads, and a market town. It annually yields to commerce large droves of fine oxen, great quantities of wheat and other grain, abundance of pork, potash in barrels, and other provisions; merchants with large capitals, and all kinds of useful mechanics reside upon it; the waters are stocked with fish, the air is salubrious, and the country thriving and happy. When I contemplate all this, and above all, when I see these good old settlers meet together, and hear them talk of past hardships, of which I bore my share, and compare the misery they then endured with the comforts they now enjoy, my emotions border upon [a] weakness, which manhood can scarcely avow. One observation more on the duty of landlords shall close my answer to your first inquiry.[4]

If the poor man who comes to purchase land has a cow and a yoke of cattle to bring with him, he is of the most fortunate class, but as he will probably have no money to hire a laborer, he must do all his clearing with his own hands. Having no pasture for his cow and oxen, they must range the woods for subsistence; he must find his cow before he can have his breakfast, and his oxen before he can begin his work. Much of the day is sometimes wasted, and his strength uselessly exhausted. Under all these disadvantages, if in three years he attains a comfortable livelihood, he is pretty well off; he will then require a barn, as great losses accrue from the want of shelter for his cattle and his grain. His children, yet too young to afford him any aid, require a school, and are a burden upon him; his wife, bearing children, and living poorly in an open house, is liable to sickness, and doctors' bills will be to pay. If then, in addition to all this, he should be pressed by his landlord, he sinks under his distress; but if, at this critical moment, he be assisted and encouraged, he will soon begin to rise. The landlord should first give him a fair time. If after that he cannot pay the principal money, he may take from him a release of the equity of redemption, and then grant him a lease forever with a clause of fee on payment of the principal, and the rent reserved, which it would be well to make payable in wheat, with a moderate advance on the first price and interest.[5]

Indeed justice and policy combine to point out the duty of the landlord; for if a man has struggled ten years in vain, and is, at the end of that time,

---

[4]William Sampson's first query was: "Which is the best way for the purchaser of a large tract of forest or unsettled lands, to bring it into a productive state? What profit he ought reasonably to expect whilst he leaves to the tenant or settler the means of settling himself? In short, what is the interest, and what the duty of such landlord?"

[5]As an alternative to foreclosure, Cooper describes a means of salvaging the farmer who cannot pay off his mortgage by exchanging it for a lease, always holding out the chance for him to purchase the land by paying the principal at some future point. These are exceptionally generous terms.

unable to pay, not only humanity, but self-interest dictates another course, and some new expedient for reciprocal advantage. So here, the tenant instead of being driven for the principal, will not only keep his possession, but retain the privilege of re-acquiring the principal at a future day, by the very produce of the lands. He will be happy in the idea of still preserving his home, will pay his rent with cheerfulness, and the landlord has so much certainly added to his capital, whether the tenant re-purchases the fee or not—the improvements[6] if he does not purchase it, and if he does, the price agreed upon.

Therefore, independently of the reasons above given, it is better for the landlord to accept of the poorest settler, than to reserve tracts in his own hands, because every part of the land by this means is made to contribute to the common stock of labor, cooperation, and general improvement, and because he has a better profit by the consent of the individual, and consistent with the advantage of all.

For example: if you sell one hundred acres for one hundred pounds, with interest at the end of ten years, it will amount to one hundred and seventy pounds; and though the tenant cannot presently pay this sum (at least without selling his farm), yet the landlord has his security for it in his mortgage-deed, and the improved value of the land, and is therefore no loser by the delay. In most instances the tenant will be very unwilling to sell the farm he has reclaimed with so much pains, and, worn with years and labor, to enter upon the hardships of a new undertaking. He sees that his land is now in good order and productive, and that he will be able easily to pay the yearly rent of fourteen pounds in produce, and that he can always acquire the disposal of the [fee] simple upon performance of the condition.

Having now given you an idea of the difficulties of our first settlement, it is right I should observe to you, that the settlement of lands in general is not at this day attended with such obstacles. In many parts of the state the soil is so fine, and so many settlements are already formed throughout, that the rest will follow of course. But still the landlord who resides on the spot, and pursues such a track as I have pointed out, will succeed with much the most certainty, and will gain many years of time.

Some rich theorists let the property they purchase lie unoccupied and unproductive, and speculate upon a full indemnity from the future rise in value, the more so as they feel no want of the immediate profits. But I can assert from practical experience, that it is better for a poor man to pay forty shillings an acre to a landlord who heads the settlement, and draws people around him by good plans for their advancement and arrangements for their convenience, than to receive a hundred acres gratis from one of these wealthy theorists. For if fifty thousand acres be settled, so that there is but one man upon a thousand acres, there can be no one convenience of life attainable; neither road, school, church, meeting, nor any other of those advantages, without which man's life would resemble that of a wild beast.

---

[6] The buildings, clearings, fences, and so forth.

Of this I had full proof in the circumstances of the Burlington company.[7] They were rich, and purchased a tract of sixty-nine thousand acres, and made a deed of gift of one hundred acres out of each thousand to actual settlers; and this they were bound to do in compliance with a condition in the king's patent. They provided these settlers with many articles of husbandry under the particular agency of Mr. Nathaniel Edwards. But he very soon returned, and not long afterwards the settlers followed, stating, that they could not support themselves so far in the woods in that scattered situation.

I then resided in Burlington, and when I undertook to make the settlement on those very lands, where so rich a company had failed, it was thought a romantic undertaking for a man unprovided with funds, to attempt what gratuitous donations had not been able to achieve. Nevertheless I succeeded, and for the very reason that I made no partial gifts, but sold the whole at a moderate price with easy payments, having for myself a handsome profit; and people were readily induced to come when they saw a number of cooperators, and the benefits of association.

You have now before you, as well as I can explain, the advantages and the difficulties which belong to an enterprise in new lands. But let me be clearly understood in this, that no man who does not possess a steady mind, a sober judgment, fortitude, perseverance, and above all, common sense, can expect to reap the reward, which to him who possesses those qualifications, is almost certain.

W. C.

---

[7]This company of investors from Cooper's previous hometown, Burlington, New Jersey, had owned the land in Otsego County that Cooper was to develop. It was to investigate the land, in fact, that Cooper undertook the 1785 journey described in his letter to Sampson.

3

THE SONS OF LIBERTY AND
A SON OF THE FOREST

WHAT WILLIAM APESS REVEALS ABOUT HIS BACKGROUND, EXPERIENCE, AND aspirations in his brief autobiography, *A Son of the Forest* (1829), forms the basic framework for what little we know of him. Born in the western Massachusetts town of Colrain in 1798, but relocated soon afterward to the vicinity of New London, Connecticut, he claimed descent through his paternal grandmother from King Philip, the great Pokanoket leader, but also showed strong affiliations with the Pequot, a people distinct from the Pokanoket of what is now Rhode Island, and had European American and probably African-American ancestors as well. These ties, along with an increasingly urgent need to address the position of Native Americans within United States society, gave him a unique perspective. Almost alone among his Native American brethren in New England in the early nineteenth century, Apess conceived of new ways to understand—and especially to articulate for Native Americans and non–Native Americans alike—the distinctive points of view which his people had come to occupy. His use of writing to codify his views and to spread them in print is particularly important.

Apess spent his boyhood in a liminal region between races, classes, families, and places. When his parents separated around 1801, he was placed in the home of his impoverished, alcoholic maternal grandparents, of Pequot descent, who horribly abused him; when perhaps five, he was indentured to a poor white master named Furman, who treated him somewhat better, allowing him modest education and introducing him to Christianity, which was to be of utmost importance to Apess both personally and as a means of coming to terms with his own past and the present and future prospects of Native Americans. During his time with the Furmans he was certainly better off in material ways—indeed, it seems likely that he would not have survived much longer with his grandparents—but he also suffered a feeling of alienation from his Indian heritage. He touchingly tells how the stories of Indian "savagries" he heard among the whites left him deathly afraid of the Natives—later he wrote that if he'd known the real story he would have dreaded the whites—and he seems to have felt an inner struggle between aspects of his larger, complex identity.

Perhaps such inner conflicts led him to be difficult for the Furmans to control; when he was around eleven or twelve, Apess's indenture was transferred to two other masters in rather quick succession. Despondent over his loneliness and probably over his dependency on others, as well, Apess was much soothed by the religious teachings he encountered at this time, and in March 1813 he experienced the "perfect freedom" provided by a conversion to Methodism, a creed especially attuned to the poor and the outcasts. His present master, however, soon forbade him to continue attending the services, which he thought were deluding and confusing the boy. Before long Apess and a poor white friend, John Miner, ran away from home. They traveled to New York City, where Miner shipped on a privateer and Apess, befuddled by drink offered by a recruiter, joined the American army and, at fifteen, was bound for service along the Canadian border. It is at this point that the selection from *A Son of the Forest* printed below begins.

Apess was not unaware of the ironies revealed by his service in the name of a government that did not recognize the citizenship of Native Americans, as his ironic uses of Republican rhetoric suggests, but he also was not insensitive to the thrills (and terrors) of warfare. His experience on Lake Champlain and in the vicinity of Plattsburgh—at a time when the American forces there, until the very end, seemed unable to achieve victory or even a decent struggle—matured his viewpoint and helped activate his political awareness. Aside from one attempt at escaping the service (given his young age, his recruitment had been technically illegal anyway), Apess served to the seriocomic end, usually in camp or in retreat, with blustering officers, poor food, and the "sublime horrors" occasionally visited on the hapless soldiers. After he left the army, Apess went to Canada, where he lived in a series of contexts, including among Native communities along Lake Ontario in the winter of 1815–16. He eventually returned to the States through upstate New York to Connecticut. Working at various jobs and alternately seeking God and drinking rum, he emerged in the 1820s as an itinerant preacher all over the Northeast, to white audiences, black audiences, and mixed audiences from Portland, Maine, to Albany, New York. In Albany, however, where he had particular success, he nonetheless recalled that "crowds flocked out, some to *hear* the truth and others to *see* 'the Indian.' " Because he understood Christianity as egalitarian and radical, the irony in his comment was of course deep. To hear the truth was precisely to *see* the Indian, not to refuse to recognize the latter's suffering presence in the midst of white "Christian" America.

In 1830, Apess showed up in the census as living in New York City, but it wasn't until 1833 that his work acquired special significance when he visited the Native American community at Mashpee, on the inner stretch of Cape Cod. Soon he was deeply entangled in the Mashpee attempt to acquire control over their lives, and he came to serve them—with his deepening talent for oratory and writing and his political sense—as spokesperson, composing the powerful and timely tract *Indian Nullification of the Unconstitutional Laws of the Commonwealth of Massachusetts* (1835), its very title suggesting how he typically sought to intersect his own arguments with the dominant strands of European-

American cultural and political concern. Nullification in the 1830s was the slogan of states' rights advocates in the South, especially South Carolina, who held that state governments could ignore federal laws with which they did not agree. In adopting this principle for his own defense of Mashpee rights, Apess cannily parodied white-on-white rhetoric at that same time that he suggested that some kinds of oppression were more severe than others. Tapping European-American memories of the civil conflicts that had torn apart white society, Apess wrote, regarding attempts to force the Mashpee into compliance with Massachusetts orders that the Natives regarded "all who opposed our freedom, as Tories, hostile to the Constitution and the liberties of the country." Again and again he cast his own campaigns against white domination as part of the whites' own cherished Revolution. The next year, the 160th anniversary of the start of King Philip's War, Apess published the eulogy on King Philip that he had delivered at the Odeon Theater in Boston. Here he equated Philip with the whites' great hero Washington, and toyed with the declamatory presumption of white orators such as Daniel Webster, whose famous Plymouth Rock oration of 1820 Apess now respoke and rewrote by unraveling European-American history and reweaving the threads with a Native design: "December . . . 1620, the Pilgrims landed at Plymouth," he wrote, "and without asking liberty from anyone they possessed themselves of a portion of the country, and built themselves houses, and then made a treaty, and commanded [the Natives] to accede to it. This, if now done, it would be called an insult, and every white man would be called to go out and act the part of a patriot to defend their country's rights; and if every intruder were butchered, it would be sung upon every hilltop in the Union that victory and patriotism was the order of the day. And yet the Indians (though many were dissatisfied), without the shedding of blood or imprisoning anyone, bore it. And yet for their kindness and resignation toward the whites, they were called savages and [were said to have been] made by God on purpose for [the whites] to destroy."

    With such promise and power, it is tragic that Apess died, of alcoholism, in New York City in early 1839. Although his memory was not lost—the standard *Dictionary of American Biography* (1928–37) included a brief sketch of Apess— it was not until the late 1980s that the precise scope of his talent and the significance of his life began to be appreciated.

WILLIAM APESS

from **A Son of the Forest** (1829)

I WAS THUS LEFT ENTIRELY ALONE IN A STRANGE CITY.[1] WANDERING ABOUT, I fell in company with a sergeant and a file of men who were enlisting soldiers

---

[1] Apess has just told how he had run away from home, probably in March 1813, with John Miner, a poor white boy from near Stonington. The two made their way to New York City, where they split up, John enlisting for a cruise on a privateer.

for the United States Army. They thought I would answer their purpose, but how to get me was the thing. Now they began to talk to me, then treated me to some spirits, and when that began to operate they told me all about the war and what a fine thing it was to be a soldier. I was pleased with the idea of being a soldier, took some more liquor and some money, had a cockade fastened on my hat, and was off in high spirits for my uniform. Now, my enlistment was against the law, but I did not know it;[2] I could not think why I should risk my life and limbs in fighting for the white man, who had cheated my forefathers out of their land. By this time I had acquired many bad practices. I was sent over to Governor's Island, opposite the city, and here I remained some time. Too much liquor was dealt out to the soldiers, who got drunk very often. Indeed, the island was like a hell upon earth, in consequence of the wickedness of the soldiers. I have known sober men to enlist, who afterward became confirmed drunkards, and appeared like fools upon the earth. So it was among the soldiers, and what should a child do, who was entangled in their net? Now, although I made no profession of religion, yet I could not bear to hear sacred things spoken of lightly, or the sacred name of God blasphemed; and I often spoke to the soldiers about it, and in general they listened attentively to what I had to say. I did not tell them that I had ever made a profession of religion. In a little time I became almost as bad as any of them, could drink rum, play cards, and act as wickedly as any. I was at times tormented with the thoughts of death, but God had mercy on me and spared my life, and for this I feel thankful to the present day. Some people are of opinion that if a person is once born of the spirit of God he can never fall away entirely, and because I acted thus, they may pretend to say that I had not been converted to the faith. I believe firmly that, if ever Paul was born again, I was; if not, from whence did I derive all the light and happiness I had heretofore experienced? To be sure it was not to be compared to Paul's—but the change I felt in my very soul.

I felt anxious to obtain forgiveness from every person I had injured in any manner whatever. Sometimes I thought I would write to my old friends and request forgiveness—then I thought I had done right. I could not bear to hear any order of Christians ridiculed, especially the Methodists—it grieved me to the heart.

It appeared that I had been enlisted for a musician, as I was instructed while on the island in beating a drum. In this I took much delight. While on the island I witnessed the execution of a soldier who was shot according to the decision of a court martial. Two men had been condemned for mutiny or desertion. It is impossible for me to describe the feelings of my heart when I saw the soldiers parade and the condemned, clothed in white, with Bibles in their hands, come forward. The band then struck up the dead march, and the procession moved with a mournful and measured tread to the place of execution, where the poor creatures were compelled to kneel on the coffins, which were alongside two newly dug graves. While in this position the chaplain went forward and conversed with them—after he had retired, a soldier went up and

[2] Apess was then fifteen.

drew the caps over their faces; thus blindfolded, he led one of them some distance from the other. An officer then advanced and raised his handkerchief as a signal to the platoon to prepare to fire—he then made another for them to aim at the wretch who had been left kneeling on his coffin, and at a third signal the platoon fired and the immortal essence of the offender in an instant was in the spirit land. To me this was an awful day—my heart seemed to leap into my throat. Death never appeared so awful. But what must have been the feelings of the unhappy man who had so narrowly escaped the grave? He was completely overcome and wept like a child, and it was found necessary to help him back to his quarters. This spectacle made me serious; but it wore off in a few days.

Shortly after this we were ordered to Staten Island, where we remained about two months. Then we were ordered to join the army destined to conquer Canada. As the soldiers were tired of the island, this news animated them very much. They thought it a great thing to march through the country and assist in taking the enemy's land. As soon as our things were ready we embarked on board a sloop for Albany and then went on to Greenbush, where we were quartered. In the meantime I had been transferred to the ranks. This I did not like; to carry a musket was too fatiguing, and I had a positive objection to being placed on the guard, especially at night. As I had only enlisted for a drummer, I thought that this change by the officer was contrary to law and, as the bond was broken, liberty was granted me; therefore, being heartily tired of a soldier's life, and having a desire to see my father once more, I went off very deliberately. I had no idea that they had a lawful claim on me and was greatly surprised as well as alarmed when arrested as a deserter from the army. Well, I was taken up and carried back to the camp, where the officers put me under guard. We shortly after marched for Canada, and during this dreary march the officers tormented me by telling me that it was their intention to make a fire in the woods, stick my skin full of pine splinters, and after having an Indian powwow over me, burn me to death. Thus they tormented me day after day.

We halted for some time at Burlington but resumed our march and went into winter quarters at Plattsburgh. All this time God was very good to me, as I had not a sick day. I had by this time become very bad. I had previously learned to drink rum, play cards, and commit other acts of wickedness, but it was here that I first took the name of the Lord in vain, and oh, what a sting it left behind. We continued here until the ensuing fall, when we received orders to join the main army under General Hampton.[3] Another change now took place: We had several pieces of heavy artillery with us, and of course horses were necessary to drag them, and I was taken from the ranks and ordered to take charge of one team. This made my situation rather better. I now had the privilege of riding. The soldiers were badly off, as the officers were very cruel to them, and for every little offense they would have them flogged. One day the officer of our company got angry at me and pricked my ear with the point of his sword.

---

[3] Wade Hampton (1751–1835), a Revolutionary veteran and major general in the War of 1812, was in command of the American force on Lake Champlain in 1813.

We soon joined the main army and pitched our tents with them. It was now very cold, and we had nothing but straw to lie on. There was also a scarcity of provisions, and we were not allowed to draw our full rations. Money would not procure food—and when anything was to be obtained the officers always had the preference, and they, poor souls, always wanted the whole for themselves. The people generally have no idea of the extreme sufferings of the soldiers on the frontiers during the last war; they were indescribable; the soldiers ate with the utmost greediness raw corn and everything eatable that fell in their way. In the midst of our afflictions, our valiant general ordered us to march forward to subdue the country in a trice. The pioneers[4] had great difficulty in clearing the way—the enemy retreated, burning everything as they fled. They destroyed everything, so that we could not find forage for the horses. We were now cutting our way through a wilderness and were very often benumbed with the cold. Our sufferings now for the want of food were extreme—the officers, too, began to feel it, and one of them offered me two dollars for a little flour, but I did not take this money, and he did not get my flour; I would not have given it to him for fifty dollars. The soldiers united their flour and baked unleavened bread; of this we made a delicious repast.

After we had proceeded about thirty miles, we fell in with a body of Canadians and Indians—the woods fairly resounded with their yells. Our "brave and chivalrous" general ordered a picked troop to disperse them. We fired but one cannon, and a retreat was sounded to the great mortification of the soldiers, who were ready and willing to fight. But as our general did not fancy the smell of gunpowder, he thought it best to close the campaign by retreating with seven thousand men, before a "host" of seven hundred. Thus were many a poor fellow's hopes of conquest and glory blasted by the timidity of one man. This little brush with an enemy that we could have crushed in a single moment cost us several men in killed and wounded. The army now fell back on Plattsburgh, where we remained during the winter; we suffered greatly for the want of barracks, having to encamp in the open fields a good part of the time.[5] My health, through the goodness of God, was preserved notwithstanding many of the poor soldiers sickened and died. So fast did they go off that it appeared to me as if the plague was raging among them.

When the spring opened, we were employed in building forts. We erected three in a very short time. We soon received orders to march and joined the army under General Wilkinson, to reduce Montreal.[6] We marched to Odletown in great splendor, "heads up and eyes right," with a noble commander at our head and the splendid city of Montreal in our view. The city, no doubt,

---

[4] I.e., the vanguard of the army.

[5] In part because of possible confusion in Apess's loose dating of events, the exact battle referred to here is not clear. He may be speaking of the unsuccessful attempt on Canada that General Hampton made shortly after his posting on Champlain early in 1813.

[6] General James Wilkinson (1757–1825), having hardly recovered from the scandals arising from his association with Aaron Burr, was moved from a post at Mobile to the St. Lawrence in 1813. As Apess goes on to relate, he dismally failed in attempts on Canada.

presented a scene of the wildest uproar and confusion; the people were greatly alarmed as we moved on with all the pomp and glory of an army flushed with many victories. But when we reached Odletown, John Bull met us with a picked troop. They soon retreated, and some took refuge in an old fortified mill, which we pelted with a goodly number of cannonballs. It appeared as if we were determined to sweep everything before us. It was really amusing to see our feminine general with his nightcap on his head and a dishcloth tied round his precious body, crying out to his men, "Come on, my brave boys, we will give John Bull a bloody nose." We did not succeed in taking the mill, and the British kept up an incessant cannonade from the fort. Some of the balls cut down the trees, so that we had frequently to spring out of their way when falling. I thought it was a hard time, and I had reason too, as I was in the front of the battle, assisting in working a twelve-pounder, and the British aimed directly at us. Their balls whistled around us and hurried a good many of the soldiers into the eternal world, while others were most horribly mangled. Indeed, they were so hot upon us that we had not time to remove the dead as they fell. The horribly disfigured bodies of the dead—the piercing groans of the wounded and the dying—the cries for help and succor from those who could not help themselves—were most appalling. I can never forget it. We continued fighting till near sundown, when a retreat was sounded along our line, and instead of marching forward to Montreal we wheeled about, and, having once set our faces toward Plattsburgh and turned our backs ingloriously on the enemy, we hurried off with all possible speed. We carried our dead and wounded with us. Oh, it was a dreadful sight to behold so many brave men sacrificed in this manner. In this way our campaign closed. During the whole of this time the Lord was merciful to me, as I was not suffered to be hurt. We once more reached Plattsburgh and pitched our tents in the neighborhood. While here, intelligence of the capture of Washington was received. Now, says the orderly sergeant, the British have burnt up all the papers at Washington, and our enlistment for the war among them; we had better give in our names as having enlisted for five years.[7]

We were again under marching orders, as the enemy, it was thought, contemplated an attack on Plattsburgh. Thither we moved without delay and were posted in one of the forts. By the time we were ready for them, the enemy made his appearance on Lake Champlain, with his vessels of war. It was a fine thing to see their noble vessels moving like things of life upon this mimic sea, with their streamers floating in the wind. This armament was intended to cooperate with the army, which numbered fourteen thousand men, under the command of the captain general of Canada, and at that very time in view of our troops.[8] They presented a very imposing aspect. Their red uniforms, and the instru-

---

[7] Using as a pretext the fact that American forces had burned the parliament building in York (Toronto), the British invaded the District of Columbia in August 1814 and burned several public buildings there.

[8] Sir George Prevost (1767–1816), governor general of Canada at the time, was repulsed in his 1814 attack on Plattsburgh by American general Alexander Macomb (1782–1841).

ments of death which they bore in their hands, glittered in the sunbeams of heaven, like so many sparkling diamonds. Very fortunately for us and for the country, a brave and noble commander was placed at the head of the army. It was not an easy task to frighten him. For notwithstanding his men were inferior in point of number to those of the enemy, say as one to seven, yet relying on the bravery of his men, he determined to fight to the last extremity. The enemy, in all the pomp and pride of war, had sat down before the town and its slender fortifications and commenced a cannonade, which we returned without much ceremony. Congreve rockets,[9] bombshells, and cannonballs poured upon us like a hailstorm. There was scarcely any intermission, and for six days and nights we did not leave our guns, and during that time the work of death paused not, as every day some shot took effect. During the engagement, I had charge of a small magazine. All this time our fleet, under the command of the gallant MacDonough, was lying on the peaceful waters of Champlain.[1] But this little fleet was to be taken, or destroyed: It was necessary, in the accomplishment of their plans. Accordingly, the British commander bore down on our vessels in gallant style. As soon as the enemy showed fight, our men flew to their guns. Then the work of death and carnage commenced. The adjacent shores resounded with the alternate shouts of the sons of liberty and the groans of their parting spirits. A cloud of smoke mantled the heavens, shutting out the light of day—while the continual roar of artillery added to the sublime horrors of the scene. At length, the boasted valor of the haughty Britons failed them—they quailed before the incessant and well-directed fire of our brave and hardy tars and, after a hard-fought battle, surrendered to that foe they had been sent to crush. On land the battle raged pretty fiercely. On our side the Green Mountain boys[2] behaved with the greatest bravery. As soon as the British commander had seen the fleet fall into the hands of the Americans, his boasted courage forsook him, and he ordered his army of heroes, fourteen thousand strong, to retreat before a handful of militia.

This was indeed a proud day for our country. We had met a superior force on the lake, and "they were ours."[3] On land we had compelled the enemy to seek safety in flight. Our army did not lose many men, but on the lake many a brave man fell—fell in the defense of his country's rights. The British moved off about sundown.

We remained in Plattsburgh until the peace. As soon as it was known that the war had terminated, and the army disbanded, the soldiers were clamorous

[9] Named for the inventor, Sir William Congreve (1772–1828).
[1] Although Macomb's conduct of the land battle against the superior British forces was notable, especially against the background of earlier American incompetence on the Canadian frontier of upper New York, he could not have carried the day without the signal aid of Captain Thomas MacDonough (1783–1825). Since 1812, MacDonough had constructed or otherwise obtained a fleet of thirteen ships on Champlain under great difficulties, and brilliantly defeated a superior British force on the lake at the time of the invasion by Prevost, who consequently withdrew.
[2] Many of the men who served in Hampton's force had been recruited from Vermont.
[3] Oliver Hazard Perry (1785–1819) sent this famous report to W. H. Harrison following his signal victory in the battle of Lake Erie in September 1813.

for their discharge, but it was concluded to retain our company in the service—I, however, obtained my release. Now, according to the act of enlistment, I was entitled to forty dollars bounty money and one hundred and sixty acres of land. The government also owed me for fifteen months' pay. I have not seen anything of bounty money, land, or arrearages, from that day to this. I am not, however, alone in this—hundreds were served in the same manner. But I could never think that the government acted right toward the "Natives," not merely in refusing to pay us but in claiming our services in cases of perilous emergency, and still denying us the right of citizenship; and as long as our nation is debarred the privilege of voting for civil officers, I shall believe that the government has no claim on our services.[4]

No doubt there are many good people in the United States who would not trample upon the rights of the poor, but there are many others who are willing to roll in their coaches upon the tears and blood of the poor and unoffending natives—those who are ready at all times to speculate on the Indians and defraud them out of their rightful possessions. Let the poor Indian attempt to resist the encroachments of his white neighbors, what a hue and cry is instantly raised against him. It has been considered as a trifling thing for the whites to make war on the Indians for the purpose of driving them from their country and taking possession thereof. This was, in their estimation, all right, as it helped to extend the territory and enriched some individuals. But let the thing be changed. Suppose an overwhelming army should march into the United States for the purpose of subduing it and enslaving the citizens; how quick would they fly to arms, gather in multitudes around the tree of liberty, and contend for their rights with the last drop of their blood. And should the enemy succeed, would they not eventually rise and endeavor to regain liberty? And who would blame them for it?

When I left the army, I had not a shilling in my pocket. I depended upon the precarious bounty of the inhabitants, until I reached the place where some of my brethren dwelt. I tarried with them but a short time and then set off for Montreal. I was anxious, in some degree, to become steady and went to learn the business of a baker. My bad habits now overcame my good intentions. I was addicted to drinking rum and would sometimes get quite intoxicated. As it was my place to carry out the bread, I frequently fell in company, and one day, being in liquor, I met one of the king's soldiers, and after abusing him with my tongue, I gave him a sound flogging. In the course of the affair I broke a pitcher which the soldier had, and as I had to pay for it, I was wicked enough to take my master's money, without his knowledge, for that purpose. My master liked me, but he thought, if I acted so once, I would a second time, and he very properly discharged me. I was now placed in a bad situation—by my misconduct, I had lost a good home! I went and hired myself to a farmer, for four dollars per month. After serving him two months, he paid me, and with the

---

[4] Barry O'Connell, in his edition of Apess's writings, reports that Apess may have been denied his due because he deserted from the service sometime prior to September 14, 1815.

money I bought some decent clothes. By spells, I was hired as a servant, but this kind of life did not suit me, and I wished to return to my brethren. My mind changed, and I went up the St. Lawrence to Kingston, where I obtained a situation on board of a sloop, in the capacity of a cook, at twelve dollars per month. I was on board the vessel some time, and when we settled the captain cheated me out of twelve dollars. My next move was in the country; I agreed to serve a merchant faithfully, and he promised to give me twelve dollars a month. Everything went on smooth for a season; at last I became negligent and careless, in consequence of his giving me a pint of rum every day, which was the allowance he made for each person in his employment.

While at this place, I attended a Methodist meeting—at the time I felt very much affected, as it brought up before my mind the great and indescribable enjoyments I had found in the house of prayer, when I was endeavoring to serve the Lord. It soon wore off, and I relapsed into my former bad habits.

I now went again into the country and stayed with a farmer for one month; he paid me five dollars. Then I shifted my quarters to another place and agreed with a Dutch farmer to stay with him all winter [1815–16?] at five dollars a month. With this situation I was much pleased. My work was light—I had very little to do except procuring firewood. I often went with them on hunting excursions; besides, my brethren were all around me, and it therefore seemed like home. I was now in the Bay of Quinte;[5] the scenery was diversified. There were also some natural curiosities. On the very top of a high mountain in the neighborhood there was a large pond of water, to which there was no visible outlet—this pond was unfathomable. It was very surprising to me that so great a body of water should be found so far above the common level of the earth. There was also in the neighborhood a rock that had the appearance of being hollowed out by the hand of a skillful artificer. Through this rock wound a narrow stream of water: It had a most beautiful and romantic appearance, and I could not but admire the wisdom of God in the order, regularity, and beauty of creation. I then turned my eyes to the forest, and it seemed alive with its sons and daughters. There appeared to be the utmost order and regularity in their encampment.

Oh, what a pity that this state of things should change. How much better would it be if the whites would act like a civilized people and, instead of giving my brethren of the woods "rum!" in exchange for their furs, give them food and clothing for themselves and children. If this course were pursued, I believe that God would bless both the whites and natives threefold. I am bold to aver that the minds of the natives were turned against the gospel and soured toward the whites because *some* of the missionaries have joined the unholy brethren in speculations to the advantage of themselves, regardless of the rights, feelings, and interests of the untutored sons of the forest. If a good missionary goes among them, and preaches the pure doctrine of the gospel, he must necessarily

---

[5] In the vicinity of present Belleville, Ontario, on the northern shore of Lake Ontario. O'Connell reports that both Mohawk and Mississauga communities existed there at the time.

tell them that they must "love God and their neighbor as themselves—to love men, deal justly, and walk humbly." They would naturally reply, "Your doctrine is very good, but the whole course of your conduct is decidedly at variance with your profession—we think the whites need fully as much religious instruction as we do." In this way many a good man's path is hedged up, and he is prevented from being useful among the natives, in consequence of the bad conduct of those who are, properly speaking, only "wolves in sheep's clothing." However, the natives are on the whole willing to receive the gospel, and of late, through the instrumentality of pious missionaries, much good has been done—many of them have been reclaimed from the most abandoned and degrading practices and brought to a knowledge of the truth as it is in Jesus!

4

THE RETURN OF AN
AMERICAN HERO

IN 1777, A NINETEEN-YEAR-OLD FRENCH ORPHAN NAMED MARIE JOSEPH PAUL Yves Roch Gilbert du Motier, marquis de Lafayette, arrived in America to throw himself into its fight against Britain, France's enemy as well as America's. The son of an officer killed in France's last war with England, the shy young man had been a member of the king's musketeers since 1771, and a captain since 1774. In America, he was quickly commissioned a major general, assigned to Washington's staff, and by the year's end had his own command. Except for a period of time spent back in France, where he continued to serve American interests, he remained in the field to the war's end. He was a member of the court martial held after Benedict Arnold's treason, voting eventually for the British spy Andre's death, and later pursued but could not catch Arnold himself. It was Lafayette who trapped Cornwallis at Yorktown in 1781 and then held him in place until Washington's and Rochambeau's armies and the French navy under De Grasse arrived to force his surrender and the war's end. Slightly wounded in 1777 at the Battle of Brandywine Creek, Lafayette represented to his American hosts the perfectly disinterested devotion to liberty that they thought their revolt from Britain at its best called into being. Back in France soon after the English surrendered, Lafayette eventually became immersed in attempts to spread the same lofty doctrine in his homeland. At first a keen supporter of this new Revolution, he later became alarmed at its excesses, was condemned by the national assembly in 1791 and forced to flee the country. After being jailed for a time for his views, he returned home in 1799, opposed to Napoleon and for a long time out of political life. By 1820 he had reemerged as a member of the Chamber of Deputies.

In 1824, at the suggestion of President Monroe, Lafayette returned in triumph to the United States, which he had last seen forty years earlier. As he visited every one of the now twenty-three states, massive public crowds greeted him with a warmth he found touching. As "the Nation's Guest," he roused memories not only of his own sacrifices but also of those of the many Americans who had fought and suffered in the war. At Mount Vernon his prayerful silence before the tomb of George Washington (after whom his only son, who accompanied him on the visit, had been named) struck just the right note; when he visited the aged Jefferson, fifteen years his senior, at Monticello, the two tearfully clasped each other in their arms again and again. Over and over, not only in such relatively private moments (many of these, though, were reported quickly in the press) but also in large, outdoor, public fetes, the best of feelings were indulged.

Not that there were not more somber undertones to the festivities. Surprisingly, crime attended the god of liberty: Pickpockets were as common as mosquitoes, and no part of the nation seemed exempt from them. (One southern newspaper, injecting a sectional note, reported that "a set of pickpockets seem to have followed General Lafayette from Boston.") Amid all this backward-looking celebration, too, Lafayette himself did not avoid the work liberty still had to accomplish in the nation. He focused particularly on slavery and its evils, making a point of greeting in public in Richmond an African American ex-slave who had served him as a spy, and in Ohio complimenting the French settlers of Gallipolis for having situated themselves on free soil. Lafayette, who had been adopted by the Mohawk during the Revolution, likewise made a point of visiting Native Americans during his tour, particularly in the Gulf States (part of his southern tour, along with his visit to Natchez and St. Louis, is described in the selection given here from his secretary's account of the whole visit). His tour was a triumph, but hardly a mindless self-congratulation on the part of the nation that, in turning out in such numbers to see him, was reflecting on its own emerging maturity, its ever-dimming past, and its persistently troubling problems. The year after Lafayette returned to France (where, as the forces of oppression once more arose, he sought to champion liberty even up to his death in 1834), an event occurred in America that soberly underscored how finally Americans' ties with the past were being severed: On the Fourth of July 1826 Jefferson and John Adams both died, reminding the residents in this "new" land that the world that Lafayette represented to them would not always exist, even in their memories.

Just a year prior to this ominous coincidence, on the Fourth of July 1825, Lafayette had been in New York, helping to lay the cornerstone of a new library for apprenticed workers in Brooklyn; he paused to assist several young children standing nearby up to a position from which they might observe the ceremony. "Happening to stand near," one of the boys later wrote of the experience, "I remember I was taken up by Lafayette in his arms and held a moment—I remember that he pressed my cheek with a kiss as he set me down—the childish wonder and nonchalance during the whole affair at the time,—contrasting with the indescribable preciousness and of the reminiscence since." It was just this sort of passing on of memory that made the visit of this extraordinary friend of the nation so important, not just for this one little boy, who in time became the poet Walt Whitman, but for the maturing nation as well.

Auguste Levasseur

from *Lafayette in America* (1829)

ON THE 29TH OF MARCH [1825], AFTER HAVING TAKEN LEAVE OF THE CITIZENS of Milledgeville, and expressed our thanks to the committee of arrangement, the authorities of the town and the state, for the kindnesses with which we had been loaded, we resumed our route with some aides-de-camp of Governor Troup,[1] who, with a skillful foresight, had previously arranged everything, so that the general should experience the inconveniences inevitably to be encountered, as little as possible, in a journey across a country without roads, towns, and almost without inhabitants; for, to enter the state of Alabama, we had to traverse that vast territory which separates it from Georgia, and which is inhabited by the Creek nation; a people which civilization has blighted with some of its vices, without having been able to win them from the habits of a wandering and savage life.

The first day, after travelling for some hours, we arrived at Macon to dinner, where the general was received with enthusiasm by the citizens, and a number of ladies, whose elegance and manners formed a singular contrast to the aspect of the country we had traversed. Macon, which is a small and handsome village, tolerably populous, did not exist eighteen months since; it has arisen from the midst of the forests as if by enchantment. It is a civilized speck lost in the yet immense domain of the original children of the soil. Within a league of this place, we are again in the bosom of virgin forests; the summits of these aged trees, which appear as records of the age of the world, waved above our heads, and, when agitated by the winds, gave rise alternately to that shrill or hollow tone, which Chateaubriand[2] has termed the voice of the desert. The road we pursued was a kind of gully or fissure, over the bottom of which the general's carriage was with difficulty drawn, and often at the risk of being shattered in pieces; we followed on horseback, and arrived in the evening at the Indian agency.

This is an isolated habitation in the midst of the forests, built during the last year for the conferences between the Indian chiefs and the commissioners of the United States. It was there that the treaty was formed, by which the tribes inhabiting the left bank of the Mississippi consented to retire to the right bank, on the payment of a considerable sum of money to them. The year 1827 was assigned as the time for their evacuation, and it is not without sorrow that the Indians find that it is drawing near. They will relinquish with regret the neighborhood of civilized man, although they detest him, and accuse their chiefs of having betrayed them in making this cession, which, it is said, has

---

[1] George M. Troup (1780–1856) served as governor of Georgia from 1823 to 1827.
[2] Vicomte François René de Chateaubriand (1768–1848), author of several very popular romances concerning Native Americans, including *Atala* (1801) and *Les Natchez* (1826).

already cost the life of McIntosh, one of the chiefs who signed the treaty.[3]

We passed the night at the Indian agency; we had been expected the evening before by about a hundred Indians, among whom the name of Lafayette has existed by tradition for fifty years, but the delays we had met with had exhausted their patience, and they had gone to prepare for our reception elsewhere. On the second day we had to traverse thirty-two miles over a road which became more and more difficult. A storm, such as is never seen in Europe, and which, however, I cannot pause to describe, now assailed us, and forced us to halt for some hours. Happily we found a shelter in a cabin built by an American, not far distant from the road. Some Indian hunters, accustomed, no doubt, to seek refuge here, were drying their garments around a large fire; we took our place among them without being known, or attracting any particular attention. Mine, on the contrary, was strongly excited by this interview, the first of the kind I had met with. I had heard much of the manners of these sons of nature, and, like every inhabitant of a civilized country, I entertained such singular ideas respecting them, that the slightest of their gestures, and every minutiæ of their dress and accoutrements, induced an astonishment which the Indians did not appear to share in seeing us. As far as I could, by signs, I proposed a multitude of questions, to which they replied by a pantomime, which was at once expressive and laconic. I had heard much of the apathy of Indians as a natural faculty, but also singularly augmented in them by education. I wished to make a few experiments on this point, but did not know how they would receive them. I provoked one of them by hostile gestures; but my anger, though tolerably well-assumed, did not appear to excite more emotion than the tricks of a child would have done. He continued his conversation without attending to me, and his countenance expressed neither fear nor contempt.

After some other trials of the same kind, always received with the same calm indifference, I recurred to signs of kindness. I offered to the Indians a glass of brandy: this succeeded better. They emptied it. I showed them some pieces of money, which they took without ceremony. I soon quitted them, and it appeared to me that we separated very good friends. The termination of the storm now permitted us to resume our route, and we arrived at a resting place rather better than that of the preceding evening. This was a group of cabins constructed of logs, and covered with bark. The owner was an American, whom a reverse of fortune had forced to take refuge here, where he carried on a lucrative trade with the Indians by exchanging goods from the coast for furs. His small farm was composed of some acres in tolerable cultivation, a well-furnished poultry yard, and the dwelling I have spoken of above. On arrival, we found two Indians seated before his door, one young, the other middle-aged, but both remarkable for their beauty and form. They were dressed in a short

[3] The Treaty of Indian Springs (1825) was negotiated for the Creeks by a pro-removal group led by William McIntosh (1775–1825), a half-British Creek chief and cousin of Governor Troup of Georgia, in violation of a Creek law prohibiting, on pain of death, any cession of tribal land without due authority. McIntosh and some of his allies were put to death as a consequence.

frock, of a light material, fastened around the body by a wampum belt. Their heads were wrapped with shawls of brilliant colors, their leggings of buckskin reached above the knee. They arose on the approach of the general, and saluted him, the youngest, to our great astonishment, complimenting him in very good English. We soon learnt that he had passed his youth in college in the United States, but that he had withdrawn several years before from his benefactor, to return among his brethren, whose mode of life he preferred to that of civilized man. The general questioned him much as to the state of the Indian nations. He replied with much clearness and precision. When the last treaty of the United States was spoken of, his countenance became somber, he stamped on the ground, and, placing his hand upon his knife, murmured the name of McIntosh in such a manner, as to make us tremble for the safety of that chief. And when we appeared to be astonished, "McIntosh," exclaimed he, "has sold the land of his fathers, and sacrificed us all to his avarice. The treaty he has concluded in our name, it is impossible to break, but the wretch!" He stopped on making this violent exclamation, and shortly afterwards quietly entered on some other topic of conversation.

Hamley (the name of the young Indian), when he found we were somewhat rested, proposed to us to visit his house, which he pointed out to us on the slope of a hill at a little distance. Two of the governor's aides-de-camp and myself accepted the invitation, and followed the two Indians. On our route they showed to us a fenced enclosure, filled with deer and fawns, which they called their reserve, and which served them for food when they had been unsuccessful in the chase. Hamley's cabin adjoined this enclosure. We entered it. There was a large fire on the hearth, and evening having commenced, the whole building was illuminated by the flame of the burning pine wood. The furniture consisted of two beds, a table, some rude chairs, whilst wicker baskets, firearms, and bows and arrows, with a violin, were hanging on the walls. The whole arrangement indicated the presence of man in a half-civilized state. Hamley's companion took down the violin, and handling the instrument with vigor rather than lightness and grace, played some fragments of Indian airs, which induced a desire of dancing in Hamley, but whether from courtesy, or from a wish of inducing a comparison which would result to his own credit, he begged us to begin. The grave Americans who accompanied me, excused themselves. Being younger, or less reserved, I did not wait for a second invitation, and executed some steps of our national dances; this was all that Hamley desired. I saw him throw off everything that might embarrass him, seize a large shawl, and triumphantly spring into the center of the apartment, as if he would say, it is now my turn. His first movements, slow and impassioned, gradually became animated, his movements, incomparably bolder and more expressive than those of our opera dancers, soon became so rapid that the eye could scarcely follow them. In the intervals, or when he halted for breath, his steps softly beating time to the music, his head gently inclined, and gracefully following the movements of his pliant body, his eyes sparkling with an emotion which reddened the coppery hue of his complexion, the cries that he uttered when he awoke from this reverie in order to commence his rapid evolutions,[4] had the most striking effect upon us, which it is impossible to describe.

Two Indian women, whom I afterwards learned were Hamley's wives, approached the house, during the time that it resounded with his exertions and our plaudits, but they did not enter, and I therefore merely saw them. They had the usual beauty of this race; their dress was composed of a long white tunic, and a scarlet drapery thrown over their shoulders; their long black hair was wholly unconfined. On their neck, they had a necklace of four or five strings of pearls, and in their ears, those immense silver rings so generally worn by Indian women. I believed, from their reserve, that Hamley had forbidden them to enter, and therefore made no inquiries respecting them. There were also some Negroes about the house, but they did not appear to be slaves. They were fugitives to whom he had granted an asylum, and who repaid his hospitality by their labor.

I would willingly have remained several days as Hamley's guest and companion in the chase, but we were obliged to continue our journey. We retired, and the next day, the 31st [of] March, resumed our route. As we plunged deeper into this country of forests, the Indian soil seemed to efface from our minds those prejudices which induce civilized man to endeavor to impose his mode of life on all those nations who still adhere to primitive habits, and to consider the invasion of districts in which this pretended barbarity still exists, as a noble and legitimate conquest. It must, however, be stated, to the praise of the Americans, that it is not by extermination or war, but by treaties, in which their intellectual superiority, it is true, exercises a species of gentle violence, that they pursue their system of aggrandizement against the Indian tribes to the west and north. With them, civilization is not sullied by crimes to be compared with those of Great Britain in India, but in rendering this justice to them, we, at the same time, cannot help feeling a strong interest in the fate of the unhappy Indians. Thus, in meeting at every turn the bark cabin of the Creek hunter, now the habitation of peace and savage yet happy ignorance, we could not think without sorrow how soon it might be overthrown and replaced by the farm of the white settler. It was on the banks of the Chattahoochee that we met with the first assemblage of Indians, in honor of the general. A great number of women and children were to be seen in the woods on the opposite bank, who uttered cries of joy on perceiving us. The warriors descended the side of a hill at a little distance, and hastened to that part of the shore at which we were to disembark. The variety and singular richness of their costumes presented a most picturesque appearance. Mr. George Lafayette,[5] who was the first that landed, was immediately surrounded by men, women, and children, who danced and leaped around him, touched his hands and clothes with an air of surprise and

---

[4] Movements.

[5] Lafayette's only son, George Washington Lafayette (1779–1849), was a military officer and statesman.

astonishment, that caused him almost as much embarrassment as pleasure. All at once, as if they wished to give their joy a grave and more solemn expression, they retired, and the men ranged themselves in front. He who appeared to be the chief of the tribe, gave, by an acute and prolonged cry, the signal for a kind of salute, which was repeated by the whole troop, which again advanced towards the shore. At the moment the general prepared to step on shore, some of the most athletic seized the small carriage we had with us, and insisted that the general should seat himself in it, not willing, as they observed, that their father should step on the wet ground. The general was thus carried in a kind of palanquin[6] a certain distance from the shore, when the Indian whom I have spoken of as the chief, approached him and said in English, that all his brothers were happy in being visited by one who, in his affection for the inhabitants of America, had never made a distinction of blood or color; that he was the honored father of all the races of men dwelling on that continent.[7] After the chief had finished his speech, the other Indians all advanced and placed their right arm on that of the general, in token of friendship. They would not permit him to leave the carriage, but dragging it along, they slowly ascended the hill they had previously left, and on which one of their largest villages was situated.

During our progress I drew near to the Indian chief; I supposed that as he spoke English, he, like Hamley, had been educated in the United States, and this I found to be the case. He was about twenty-eight years of age, of a middle height; but the symmetry of his limbs was perfect, his physiognomy noble, his expression mournful. When he was not speaking he fixed his large black eyes, shaded by a heavy brow, steadfastly on the ground. When he told me that he was the eldest son of McIntosh,[8] I could not recall, without emotions of sorrow, the imprecations I had heard poured forth against this chief, on the preceding evening. This, in all probability, occasioned the air of depression and thoughtfulness I remarked in the young man, but what I afterwards learned in conversation with him explained it still more satisfactorily: his mind had been cultivated at the expense of his happiness. He appreciated the real situation of his nation, he saw it gradually becoming weaker, and foresaw its speedy destruction. He felt how much it was inferior to those which surrounded it, and was perfectly aware that it was impossible to overcome the wandering mode of life of his people. Their vicinity to civilization had been of no service to them; on the contrary, it had only been the means of introducing vices to which they had hitherto been strangers. He appeared to hope that the treaty which removed them to another and a desert country, would re-establish the ancient organiza-

[6] An enclosed litter or elaborate sedan chair.
[7] The comment was not entirely an effort at flattery. During the Revolution, Lafayette had been adopted by the Mohawk, whom he visited in an attempt to keep them from siding with Britain; he also opposed slavery, and after the war purchased a plantation in Cayenne solely as an experiment in educating and emancipating the slaves on it. During his tour of the United States, he pointedly sought to include African Americans whenever possible; at New Orleans he thus remarked, "I have often during the War of Independence seen African blood shed with honor in our ranks for the cause of the United States."
[8] This was Chief Chilly McIntosh.

tion of the tribes, or at least preserve them in the state in which they now were.

When we arrived at the brow of the hill we perceived the glitter of helmets and swords; troops were drawn up in line along the road. These were not Indians, they were civilized men, sent by the state of Alabama to escort the general. The singular triumphal march to which he had been obliged to submit, now ceased. The Indians saw with some jealousy the American escort range themselves round the general, but we approached the village, and they ran on in order to precede us. We there found them on our arrival, with their garments thrown off, and prepared to afford us a sight of their warlike games.

We arrived on a large plain, around which were situated about a hundred Indian huts, crowned by the rich verdure of the dense thickets. One house was distinguished for its greater size; it was that of the American agent. He also kept an inn, and his wife superintended a school for the instruction of the Indian children. All the men were assembled, deprived of a part of their dress, their faces painted in a grotesque manner, and some wearing feathers in their hair, as a mark of distinction. They then announced to us that there would be a mock fight in honor of their white father. In fact, we soon perceived them separate into two divisions, and form two camps at the two extremities of the place, appoint two leaders, and make preparations for a combat. The cry that was uttered by each of these troops, and which we were told was the war-whoop of the Indian tribes, is, perhaps, the most extraordinary modulation of the human voice that can be conceived, and the effect it produced on the combatants of all ages, was still more so. The sport began.[9] They explained the plan to us as follows: Each party endeavored to drive a ball beyond a certain mark, and that which attained this object seven times would be the victor. We soon saw the combatants, each armed with two long rackets, rush after the light projectile, spring over each other in order to reach it, seize it in the air with incredible dexterity, and hurl it beyond the goal. When the ball was missed by a player, it fell to the ground, when every head was bent, a scene of great confusion ensued, and it was only after a severe struggle that the players succeeded in again throwing it up. In the midst of one of these long combats, whilst all the players were bent around the ball, an Indian detached himself from the group to some distance, returned on a run, sprung into the air, and after making several somersets, threw himself on the shoulders of the other players, leaped into the circle, seized the ball, and for the seventh time cast it beyond the mark. This player was McIntosh. The victory was obtained by the camp which he commanded; he advanced to receive our congratulations under a shower of applause from a part of the Indian women, whilst the wives of the vanquished appeared to be endeavoring to console them.

The general, after this game, which much amused him, visited the interior of some of the huts, and the Indian school. When we were ready to resume our journey, young McIntosh reappeared dressed as a European. He requested permission from the general to accompany him to Montgomery, where he

---

[9] It was a version of lacrosse.

wished to carry his brother, who was about ten years of age, in order to place him under the care of a citizen of Alabama, who had generously offered to educate him. The general consented to it, and we all set out for Uchee Creek, an American tavern,[1] situated on the banks of a creek of that name. We arrived at that place at an early hour, and visited the neighborhood, which was charming. Accompanied by McIntosh, I soon made an acquaintance with the Indians of that district. We found them exercising with the bow. I wished to try my skill. McIntosh likewise armed himself; he had the arm and eye of William Tell. Some proofs of his skill would scarcely be credited were I to relate them. I was most struck with the skill with which, whilst lying on the ground, he discharged an arrow, which, striking the ground at a few paces distance, made a slight rebound, and flew to an immense distance. This is the mode employed by the Indians when they wish to discharge their arrows to a great distance without discovering themselves. I tried in vain to accomplish it; each time my arrow, instead of rebounding, buried itself in the earth.

We returned to Uchee Creek, and met an Indian chief on his way to the tavern. He was on horseback, with a woman behind him. When he arrived within a few paces of the house, he dismounted and went forward to salute the general, and to make some purchases. During this time his wife remained with the horse, brought it to him when he wished to depart, held the bridle and stirrup when he mounted, and afterwards sprung up behind him. I asked my companions if this woman was the wife of the Indian, and if such was the condition of the females of the nation. They replied, that in general they were treated as we had seen; in the agricultural districts they cultivated the ground, among the hunters they carried the game, the culinary utensils, and other necessary articles, and thus loaded could travel great distances, that even maternal cares scarcely exonerated them from these laborious occupations. However, in the excursions I afterwards made in the environs of Uchee Creek, the condition of the women did not appear to me as unhappy as I was led to expect. I saw before almost all the houses the women sitting in circles, engaged in weaving baskets or mats, and amusing themselves with the games and exercises of the young men, and I never remarked any signs of harshness on the part of the men, or of servile dependence on the part of the women. I was so hospitably received in all the Indian cabins at Uchee Creek, and the country around was so beautiful, that it yet appears to me as the most beautiful spot I ever visited. From Uchee Creek to the cabin of Big Warrior, which is the nearest resting place, is about a day's journey, through a country inhabited by Indians. We several times met parties of them, and were greatly assisted by them in extricating ourselves from dangerous places in the road, for the storm had encumbered them, and swelled the streams. On one of these occasions, the general received a touching specimen of the veneration these sons of nature held him in. One

---

[1] Crabtree Tavern, located in what William Bartram called "Uche town" in his *Travels* (1791); Bartram described the Native American settlement of Uche with an enthusiasm similar to Levasseur's.

of the torrents we were to cross had risen above the unnailed wooden bridge over which the carriage of the general was to proceed. What was our astonishment, on arriving at the stream, to find a score of Indians, who, holding each other by the hand, and breast deep in water, marked the situation of the bridge by a double line. We were well pleased at receiving this succor, and the only recompense demanded by the Indians, was to have the honor of taking the general by the hand, whom they called their white father, the envoy of the Great Spirit, the great warrior from France, who came in former days to free them from the tyranny of the English. McIntosh, who interpreted their discourse to us, also expressed to them the general's and our own good wishes. The village of the Big Warrior is thus named on account of the extraordinary courage and great stature of the Indian who was its chief. We arrived there at a late hour; the chief had been dead some time; the council of old men had assembled to name his successor, and had designated one of his sons, remarkable for the same strength of body, as worthy of filling his place. This son had much conversation with Mr. George Lafayette; he expressed himself in English, and astonished us by the singular apathy with which he spoke of the death of his father. But the Indians have not the slightest idea of what we call grief and mourning. Death does not appear an evil to them, either as regards the person who has quitted this life, or those who are thus separated from him. The son of Big Warrior only appeared to regret that the death of his father, which had occurred a short time before, did not permit him to dispose of his inheritance, and to present one of the dresses of this celebrated chief to the general.

We only passed one night with the family of Big Warrior; the next day we arrived at Line Creek, that is to say, at the frontier of the Indian country. We were received there by an American who had married the daughter of a Creek chief, and had adopted the Indian mode of life. He was a Captain Lewis, formerly in the army of the United States; his house was commodious, and was furnished with elegance for an Indian cabin. Captain Lewis, who is distinguished for his knowledge and character, appeared to us to exercise great influence over the Indians. He had assembled a great number, well-armed and mounted, to act as an escort to the general. One of the neighboring chiefs came at the head of a deputation to compliment the general. His discourse, which appeared studied, was rather long, and was translated to us by an interpreter. He commenced by high eulogiums on the skill and courage the general had formerly displayed against the English; the most brilliant events of that war were recalled and recounted in a poetical and somewhat pompous strain. He terminated somewhat in these words: "Father, we had long since heard that you had returned to visit our forests and our cabins; you, whom the Great Spirit formerly sent over the great lake to destroy those enemies of man, the English, clothed in bloody raiment. Even the youngest amongst us will say to their descendants, that they have touched your hand and seen your figure, they will also behold you, for you are protected by the Great Spirit from the ravages of age—you may again defend us if we are attacked. . . ."

On Monday, the 18th of April, some distant discharges of cannon, which we heard at dawn, announced our approach to a city. Some minutes afterwards, the first rays of the sun gilding the shores of the Mississippi, which, in this place, rose a hundred and fifty feet above the surface of the water, showed us the tops of the houses in Natchez. Our steamboat stopped a little while previous to arriving opposite the town, and we went on shore at Bacon's landing, where the citizens, with a calash and four horses, and an escort of cavalry and volunteer infantry, were waiting for the general. We might have landed a little higher up and entered the city by a more direct road, but the members of the committee of arrangement had the address to conduct us by a devious[2] road, along which our eyes were presented with all the beauties of the country. In proportion as we advanced, the escort increased. It consisted of citizens on horseback, militia on foot, ladies in carriages, and nearly the whole population, who came in a crowd to see their beloved and long expected guest. Two addresses were made to the general: one by the president of the committee of arrangement, on entering the city; the other by the mayor, on one of the most elevated spots on the banks of the Mississippi, within view of the town and the river, its source of prosperity. At the moment the general finished his reply, a man suddenly emerged from the crowd, approached the calash, waving his hat in the air, and cried out, "Honor to the commander of the Parisian national guard! I was under your orders in '91, my general, in one of the battalions of the Filles-Saint-Thomas. I still love liberty as I loved it then: Live, Lafayette!"[3] The general was agreeably surprised to meet, on the shores of a distant country, one of his old citizen-soldiers, who recalled to him in so touching a manner the happy times when he could rationally think of the happiness and liberty of his country. He affectionately offered him his hand, and expressed to him the pleasure he felt in thus meeting him in a land of liberty and hospitality.

At the moment we were preparing to enter our hotel, we observed a long procession of children of both sexes approaching us. They were led by Colonel Marshall, who requested of the general for them, and in their name, permission to shake hands with him. The general willingly complied with this wish of the children of Natchez, who marched in order before him, placing successively one of their little hands in that which had fought for the liberty of their fathers. The parents, spectators of this scene, contemplated it with silence and emotion. On its termination, I heard them congratulate each other on the happy influence which this day would have upon the future characters of their children. "When they have grown up," said they, "and come to read their country's history, they will find the name of Lafayette intimately connected with all the events which led to the freedom of their fathers, they will recall the gentleness of his manners, the mildness of his voice, when he received them in their infancy, and will feel an increased love for a liberty won by such a man."

[2] Roundabout; address: adroitness.
[3] The French National Guard, organized in the early phase of the French Revolution, was intended to replace the old royalist army with a citizen force; Lafayette assumed command of it on July 15, 1789, the day after the fall of the Bastille.

The inhabitants of Natchez neglected nothing which could contribute to the pleasure of their guest during the twenty-four hours he remained with them. The public dinner concluded with toasts, *To the Nation's Guest—The triumph of Yorktown—France fighting for the liberty of the world—The victory of New Orleans*—in fact to all glorious and patriotic American recollections. It was not until after the ball which closed about daybreak, that the general could think of embarking. The ladies employed all the charms of mind and person to retain him as long as possible, but our minutes were counted; and six o'clock in the morning found us again on board our vessel.

At the moment when the general was about to leave the shore, an old revolutionary soldier presented himself, and uncovering his breast marked with scars, "These wounds," said he, "are my pride. I received them fighting by your side for the independence of my country. Your blood, my general, flowed the same day at the battle of Brandywine, where we were so unfortunate."[4] "It was indeed a rough day," said the general to him, "but have we not since been amply indemnified?"—"Oh! that is very true," replied the veteran, "at present we are happy beyond our furthest wishes. You receive the blessings of ten millions of freemen, and I press the hand of my brave general! virtue always has its reward!" Every one applauded the enthusiasm and frankness of the old soldier, whom the general cordially greeted. . . .

On the morning of the 29th of April, Governor Clark, of Missouri, Governor Coles of Illinois, and Colonel Benton, came on board; who all three came to accompany the general to St. Louis.[5] Some minutes after, the steamboat *Plough Boy*, having on board a great number of citizens, ranged alongside the *Natchez*, and the nation's guest was saluted by three cheers, which made the forests of the Missouri resound with *Welcome, Lafayette*. We then weighed anchor, and at nine o'clock saw a large number of buildings whose architecture was very fantastical, rising from the midst of beautiful green shrubbery and smiling gardens, commanding distant views of the river. This was the city of St. Louis. Its name, and the language of a great portion of its inhabitants, soon informed us of its origin. But if we were struck with the diversity of languages in which General Lafayette was saluted, we were not less so by the unity of sentiment which they manifested. The shore was covered by the whole population, who mingled their cries of joy with the roar of the cannon of our two vessels. The moment the general stepped on shore, the mayor, Dr. Lane,[6] presented himself at the head of the municipal authorities, and greeted him with an address.

---

[4] During the American defeat at Brandywine Creek, Pennsylvania (September 11, 1777), the twenty-year-old Lafayette was wounded.

[5] William Clark (1770–1838), Meriwether Lewis's partner, was governor of Missouri Territory, 1813–21; Edward Coles (1786–1868), an abolitionist, was governor of Illinois, 1822–26; Thomas Hart Benton (1782–1858), lawyer and newspaperman, was United States senator from Missouri, 1821–50.

[6] Dr. William Carr Lane (1789–1863), elected St. Louis's first mayor in 1823 and reelected many times thereafter.

As the general concluded his reply to the mayor, an elegant calash drawn by four horses approached the shore, to conduct him to the city, through all the streets of which he was drawn in the midst of the acclamations of the people. He was attended by Mr. Augustus Chouteau,[7] a venerable old gentleman by whom St. Louis was founded, Mr. Hempstead, an old soldier of the revolution, and the mayor. These gentlemen conducted him to the house of the son of Mr. Chouteau, prepared for his reception, which was thrown open to all citizens without distinction, who desired to visit the national guest. Among the visitors, the general met with pleasure Mr. Hamilton, son of General Alexander Hamilton, the former aide-de-camp to Washington, whom be so much loved, and an old French sergeant of Rochambeau's army named Bellissime. This last could not restrain the joy he felt on seeing a countryman thus honored by the American nation.

The inhabitants of St. Louis knew that General Lafayette could only remain a few hours with them, and they took advantage of the short time he had to dispose of to show him everything which their city and its environs contained worthy of notice. While dinner was preparing at Mr. Peter Chouteau's, we rode out in a carriage to visit on the banks of the river those remains of ancient Indian monuments which some travellers call tombs, whilst others regard them as fortifications or places for the performance of religious ceremonies. All these opinions are unfortunately equally susceptible of discussion, for these monuments have not preserved any sufficiently well-marked characters to afford foundation for satisfactory deductions. Those near St. Louis are nothing but mounds covered with green turf, the ordinary shape of which is an oblong square. Their common height is little more than eight feet, but must have been much greater before the earth they are built of was thrown down during the lapse of ages. Their sides are inclined, and the mean length of their base is from eighty to a hundred feet, their width varying from thirty to sixty feet. What leads me to believe that these fabrics of earth have never been used as strongholds in war, is, that not one of them is surrounded by ditches, and they are placed too near together. These mounds are not only met with in the environs of St. Louis, but all over the states of Missouri, Indiana, and upon the borders of Ohio, where, we are informed, they meet with much more interesting traces of the greatest antiquity, indicating that this world which we call *new*, was the seat of civilization, perhaps long anterior to the continent of Europe.

From the mounds of St. Louis to the junction of Mississippi and Missouri, we should only have had two or three hours' ride, but the time of the general was so calculated that we were obliged to forego the pleasure we should have derived from visiting the union of these two rivers, which have their sources in countries where nature yet reigns undisturbed. Returned to town, we went to

---

[7] René Auguste Chouteau (1749–1829), fur trader and associate of Pierre Laclede in founding St. Louis. Later, Levasseur may mistake one of his nephews, Auguste Pierre or more likely Pierre, as his son.

see the collection of Indian curiosities made by Governor Clark, which is the most complete that is to be found. We visited it with the greater pleasure from its being shown us by Mr. Clark, who had himself collected all the objects which compose it, while exploring the distant western regions with Captain Lewis. Specimens of all the clothing, arms, and utensils for fishing, hunting, and war, in use among the various tribes living on the sources of the Missouri and Mississippi, are here to be found. Among the articles commonly worn by the Indian hunters, collars made of claws of prodigious size, particularly struck our attention. These claws, Governor Clark informed us, are from that most terrible of all the animals of the American continent, the grizzly bear of the Missouri, the ferocious instinct of which adds still more to the terror inspired by its enormous size and strength. The bears of this species meet together to the number of ten or twelve, and some times more, to chase and make a common division of their prey. Man is their favorite prey, and when they fall upon his track, they chase him with outcries like those made by our hounds in coursing a hare, and it is difficult to escape the steadiness of their pursuit. This animal is altogether unknown in Europe, even in the largest menageries. The London Cabinet of Natural History possesses only a single claw, which is regarded as a great rarity.[8] Governor Clark has visited, near the sources of the Missouri and Mississippi, Indian tribes which, previous to his visit, had never seen a white man; but among whom he nevertheless discovered traces of an ancient people more civilized than themselves. Thus, for example, he brought away with him a whip which the riders of these tribes do not understand the mode of using on their horses at the present time. The knots of this are very complex, and actually arranged like the *knout* of the Cossacks. He presented General Lafayette with a garment bearing a striking resemblance to a Russian riding coat. It is made of buffalo skin, prepared so as to retain all its pliancy, as if dressed by the most skillful tanner. From these and some other facts, Mr. Clark, and Captain Lewis, his companion, concluded that there formerly existed, near the pole, a communication between Asia and America. These two intrepid travellers published in 1814, an interesting account of the journeys made by them in 1804, 1805, and 1806, by order of the American government, the object being to explore the sources of the Missouri, and the course of the Columbia River, till it reaches the Pacific Ocean.

We could have remained a considerable longer time in Governor Clark's museum, listening to the interesting accounts which he was pleased to give us relative to his great journeys, but were informed that the hour for dinner had arrived, and we went to the house of Mr. Peter Chouteau. On our way we visited a portion of the town which we had not before seen, and were surprised at the whimsical manner in which some of the houses, apparently the most ancient, were constructed. They generally consisted of a single story, sur-

---

[8] Levasseur here added a note to his text indicating that Governor Clark had more recently sent a live specimen of a young grizzly to Lafayette, who promptly conveyed it to the zoo at the Jardin du Roi in Paris. The translator of the book, in another note, took exasperated issue with Levasseur's fables about grizzlies hunting humans down in packs, yelping all the while like dogs.

rounded by a gallery covered with a wide projecting roof.[9] Someone pointed out to us, that formerly the basement was not inhabited, and that the stairway leading to the upper story was moveable at pleasure. This precaution was used by the first inhabitants of St. Louis for the purpose of guarding against the insidious nocturnal attacks of the Indians, who saw with jealousy the whites making permanent settlements among them. When St. Louis, then a feeble village, passed under the Spanish authority, the neighboring Indians were still so numerous and enterprising, that the inhabitants could scarcely resist them, or even venture abroad. It is related, that, in 1794, an Indian chief entered St. Louis, with a portion of his tribe, and having demanded an interview, spoke as follows: "We come to offer you peace. We have made war against you for a great many moons, and what has been the result? Nothing. Our warriors have used every means to fight with yours, but you will not, and dare not meet us! You are a pack of old women! What can be done with such people, since they will not fight, but make peace? I come therefore to you to bury the hatchet, brighten the chain, and open a new communication with you."

Since that time the tribes have greatly diminished, and most of them departed. Those still remaining in the vicinity show the most peaceable disposition towards the white inhabitants, with whom they carry on a considerable trade in furs. The inhabitants of St. Louis are, besides, sufficiently numerous no longer to fear such neighbors. The population amounts to nearly six thousand souls, which number will probably be doubled in a few years, for this city has the prospect of a brilliant destiny in these vast regions, in the midst of which civilization, under the guidance of American liberty and industry, must run a giant's course. St. Louis is already the grand storehouse of all the commerce of the countries west of the Mississippi. It is situated near the junction of four or five great rivers, all of whose branches, which spread to the most distant extremities of the Union, furnish an easy and rapid communication with all those places which can contribute to the wants or luxuries of its happy inhabitants. Into what astonishment is the mind thrown on reflecting that such a height of prosperity is the result of but a few years, and that the founder of so flourishing a city still lives, and, for a long time, has been in the enjoyment of the results which he neither could have hoped for, nor anticipated, had it been predicted to his young and ardent imagination on first approaching the solitary shores of the Mississippi. This enterprising man, who, with his axe, felled the first tree of the ancient forest on the place where the city of St. Louis stands, who raised the first house, about which, in so short a time, were grouped the edifices of a rich city; who, by his courage and conciliating spirit, at first repressed the rage of the Indians, and afterwards secured their friendship; this happy man is Mr. Augustus Chouteau. I have already named him among those appointed by the inhabitants of St. Louis to do the honors of their city to the guest of the Ameri-

[9]The picturesque houses of French Louisiana, of which a few specimens survive in villages such as Ste. Geneviève, Missouri, actually have at their center a quite "grammatical" French house; they gain their peculiarity from having wide porches (galleries) placed all around this core, the whole covered with one large, double-pitched hipped roof.

can nation. It was at the house of his son, Mr. Peter Chouteau, that we partook of the feast of republican gratitude. It was highly interesting to behold seated at the table the founder of a great city, one of the principal defenders of the independence of a great nation, and the representatives of four young republics, already rich from their industry, powerful from their liberty, and happy from the wisdom of their institutions. As might be readily supposed, the conversation was highly interesting. Mr. Augustus Chouteau was asked a great many questions respecting his youthful adventures and enterprises. The companion in arms of Washington was requested to relate some details of the decisive and glorious campaign of Virginia, and the members of the different deputations of Louisiana, Mississippi, Tennessee, and Missouri, drew a pleasing picture of the prosperous advancement of their respective states. In this company, that which touched General Lafayette most was the prevailing unanimity among the guests, who, though they did not all speak one language, agreed perfectly in respect to the excellence of those republican institutions under which it was their happiness to live. Before leaving the banquet in order to attend the ball which the ladies were so kind as to prepare for us, some toasts were exchanged, all of which bore the impression of the harmony existing between the old French and the new American population. Mr. Delassus, formerly lieutenant-governor of Louisiana,[1] drank, *"The United States and France!* May these two countries produce another Washington and another Lafayette, to emancipate the rest of the world!" Governor Coles drank, *"France!* dear to our hearts from so many recollections, and above all for having given birth to our Lafayette." General Lafayette finished by drinking the health of the venerable patriarch, who, in 1763, founded the town of St. Louis, and immediately afterwards we left the table for the ball, where we found the most numerous and brilliant company assembled, as we were informed, that had ever been seen upon the western shore of the Mississippi. The splendid decorations of the room, and the beauty of the ladies who graced it, made us completely forget that we were on the confines of a wilderness which the savages themselves consider as insufficient for the supply of their simple wants, since they only frequent it occasionally. We partook of the pleasures of the evening until near midnight, the hour at which we were to return on board the *Natchez*, for the purpose of taking some rest before daylight, when we were to depart. At the moment we were about to embark, many citizens of St. Louis had the goodness to offer us several objects of curiosity, such as bows, arrows, calumets, and dresses of the Missouri Indians. We accepted with gratitude these testimonies of benevolence, which we have preserved as agreeable remembrancers of happy occurrences so far from our country.

---

[1] Carlos Dehault Delassus (dates uncertain) was the lieutenant governor of Louisiana under the Spanish regime.

5

A PATRIOT'S LAMENT

WHEN, IN 1818 AND ESPECIALLY 1832, CONGRESS PASSED THE PENSION LAWS allowing small annual payments to veterans of the Revolution, it stimulated a large outpouring of applications—and, as we have seen earlier in this book, wide-ranging recollections. A great many of the eighty thousand veterans who eventually applied for support focused on the task in hand—securing modest support for their last years—and tended to stress the events of the past rather than their own present feelings, conditions, or recollective efforts. As a result, the narratives give one the impression (finally an illusion, of course) that they represent a continuity of action and word from the 1770s into the second third of the following century. Hence, with the provisos just indicated, they can as easily be used as sources about the war as they can about the pension movement that they also, and more immediately, document.

The pension process also stimulated, however, a mood of vociferous protest in some quarters. Not only in some of the applications but even more so in separately penned narratives published in the period, veterans poured forth the bottled-up resentment they felt about the ingratitude of the public toward the individuals who had suffered to secure the blessings others enjoyed. None of these veterans complained more passionately than Joseph Plumb Martin, who in 1830 issued his *Narrative* from a small press in Hallowell, Maine. With a populist's sense of rectitude and indignation, Martin detailed his long service in the rebel army—from his enlistment at the age of seventeen as a private in his native Connecticut through Valley Forge, on to Yorktown, and to his final mustering out as a sergeant in 1783. The son of a Congregational minister who lost his parish and had to struggle along at the cooper's trade, Martin himself came out of the war with nearly-worthless paper certificates from the government representing his "pay." He soon migrated north to New England's frontier, Maine, in search of what he hoped would be free land in a country he himself had helped to liberate. After a long, fruitless protest against the "great proprietors" who had gained control of much land in the region, Martin in 1797 finally gave in and secured a toehold on a hundred-acre tract in the town of Stockton

Springs for a price of 170 dollars. Time was not, however, to be kind to him. His sick wife and retarded son required extra care and he himself, weakened by his exposure during six years of military service under very bad conditions, could not make a go of his farm, at least not with the purchase price hanging over him. In 1801, with the time for his payment nearing, he humbly asked Henry Knox (who by marriage, contrivance, and investment had managed to gain control of an empire in land in Maine) to give him compassion and an extension on his debt. Historian Alan Taylor, in his study of the Maine frontier at this time, writes of the results: "By 1811 [Martin's] farm had shrunk to fifty acres—only eight improved—that yielded but ten bushels of grain and supported only three steers and two swine. . . . By 1818 Martin had lost his homestead." Because he had served in the Continental army during the war, Martin was eligible under the first pension act of that same year; he applied and received the guarantee of eight dollars monthly.

To judge by his *Narrative* of twelve years later, the pension obviously had not soothed Martin's anger over the mistreatment he felt the nation had visited on himself and his fellow veterans. Throughout the story, but particularly at the end (reprinted here), we hear the bitter voice of a man who believes that his better feelings were exploited for the good of others—others who had not the least sense of obligation or thanks, but instead gloried in his duping. Eloquently, he details all the promises the government made and broke, asking why this was so and answering with sharp political savvy, "One reason was, because she had all the power in her own hands, and I had none." Short rations, bad clothing, and dismal living conditions might on their own have created this bitter perspective, but perhaps, too, as Taylor suggests, the fact that Henry Knox, the great proprietor of the Waldo Patent in Maine, was also the great General Henry Knox of the Continental army helped to give Joseph Plumb Martin the sense that the Revolution had displaced one hierarchy only to erect another one on the necks of the ordinary citizens who had fought in it. Martin's indictment of his nation's ingratitude at the end of his *Narrative* thus resonates with the cultural themes of the period when it was written; his book is not just about how the war was won in the 1770s and 1780s, but also about how, for people such as himself in any case, it seemed to be lost in the decades following.

JOSEPH PLUMB MARTIN

from *A Narrative of Some of the Adventures, Dangers, and Sufferings of a Revolutionary Soldier* (1830)

I NOW BID A FINAL FAREWELL TO THE SERVICE. I HAD OBTAINED MY SETTLEMENT certificates and sold some of them, and purchased some decent clothing, and then set off from West Point. I went into the highlands, where I accidentally came across an old messmate, who had been at work there ever since he had left the army in June last, and, as it appeared, was on a courting expedition. I stopped a few days with him and worked at the farming business; I got acquainted with the people here, who were chiefly Dutch, and as winter was approaching, and my friend recommended me to them, I agreed to teach a school amongst them—A fit person!—I knew but little and they less, if possible. "Like people, like priest." However, I stayed and had a school of from twenty to thirty pupils, and probably I gave them satisfaction; if I did not, it was all one; I never heard anything to the contrary. Anyhow, they wished me to stay and settle with them.

When the spring opened I bid my Dutch friends adieu, and set my face to the eastward, and made no material halt till I arrived in the, now, state of Maine,[1] in the year 1784, where I have remained ever since, and where I expect to remain so long as I remain in existence, and here at last to rest my warworn weary limbs. And here I would make an end of my tedious narrative, but that I deem it necessary to make a few short observations relative to what I have said; or a sort of recapitulation of some of the things which I have mentioned.

When those who engaged to serve during the war, enlisted, they were promised a hundred acres of land, each, which was to be in their own or the adjoining states. When the country had drained the last drop of service it could screw out of the poor soldiers, they were turned adrift like old worn-out horses, and nothing said about land to pasture them upon. Congress did, indeed, appropriate lands under the denomination of "soldier's lands," in Ohio state, or some state, or a future state; but no care was taken that the soldiers should get them. No agents were appointed to see that the poor fellows ever got possession of their lands; no one ever took the least care about it, except a pack of speculators, who were driving about the country like so many evil spirits, endeavoring to pluck the last feather from the soldiers. The soldiers were ignorant of the ways and means to obtain their bounty lands, and there was no one appointed to inform them. The truth was, none cared for them; the country was served, and faithfully served, and that was all that was deemed necessary. It was, "Soldiers, look to yourselves, we want no more of you." I hope I shall one day find land enough to lay my bones in. If I chance to die in a civilized country, none will deny me that. A dead body never begs a grave;—thanks for that.

They were likewise promised the following articles of clothing per year:[2] one uniform coat, a woollen and a linen waistcoat, four shirts, four pair of shoes, four pair of stockings, a pair of woollen, and a pair of linen overalls, a hat or a leather cap, a stock for the neck,[3] a hunting shirt, a pair of shoebuckles and a blanket. Ample clothing, says the reader; and ample clothing, say I. But what did we ever realize of all this ample store:—why, perhaps, a coat (we generally did get that) and one or two shirts, the same of shoes and stockings, and, indeed, the same may be said of every other article of clothing—a few

---

[1] Until 1820, Maine remained part of Massachusetts.
[2] That is, during their active duty in the war.
[3] A wide cloth band or scarf to be wrapped twice around the neck and tied or pinned, common in the eighteenth century.

dribbled out in a regiment, two or three times in a year, never getting a whole suit at a time, and all of the poorest quality; and blankets of thin baize,[4] thin enough to have straws shot through without discommoding the threads. How often have I had to lie whole stormy cold nights in a wood, on a field, or a bleak hill, with nothing but the canopy of the heavens to cover me, all this too in the heart of winter, when a New England farmer, if his cattle had been in my situation, would not have slept a wink from sheer anxiety for them. And if I stepped into a house to warm me, when passing, wet to the skin and almost dead with cold, hunger and fatigue, what scornful looks and hard words have I experienced.

Almost everyone has heard of the soldiers of the Revolution being tracked by the blood of their feet on the frozen ground. This is literally true; and the thousandth part of their sufferings has not, nor ever will be told. That the country was young and poor, at that time, I am willing to allow; but young people are generally modest, especially females. Now, I think the country (although of the feminine gender, for we say, "she," and "her," of it) showed but little modesty at the time alluded to, for she appeared to think her soldiers had no private parts; for on our march from the Valley Forge, through the Jerseys, and at the boasted Battle of Monmouth, a fourth part of the troops had not a scrip[5] of anything but their ragged shirt-flaps to cover their nakedness, and were obliged to remain so long after. I had picked up a few articles of light clothing during the past winter, while among the Pennsylvania farmers, or I should have been in the same predicament. "Rub and go," was always the Revolutionary soldier's motto.[6]

As to provision of victuals, I have said a great deal already; but ten times as much might be said and not get to the end of the chapter. When we engaged in the service we were promised the following articles for a ration: one pound of good and wholesome fresh or salt beef, or three-fourths of a pound of good salt pork, a pound of good flour, soft or hard bread, a quart of salt to every hundred pounds of fresh beef, a quart of vinegar to a hundred rations, a gill of rum, brandy or whiskey per day; some little soap and candles, I have forgot how much, for I had so little of these two articles, that I never knew the quantity. And as to the article of vinegar, I do not recollect ever having any except a spoonful at the famous rice and vinegar Thanksgiving in Pennsylvania, in the year 1777.[7] But we never received what was allowed us. Oftentime I have gone

[4] A coarsely woven, napped wool or cotton cloth, resembling felt.
[5] Scrap; Battle of Monmouth: on June 28, 1778 Washington and Sir Henry Clinton fought to no decisive conclusion at Monmouth Courthouse, in New Jersey.
[6] That is, lacking sufficient clothes, they needed to rub heat back into their limbs on occasion, then keep on marching.
[7] Martin earlier explained this reference. In the fall of 1777, Congress ordered the army to observe a day of thanksgiving. "We must now have what Congress said," Martin wrote, "a sumptuous Thanksgiving to close the year of high living we had now seen brought nearly to a close. . . . Our country, ever mindful of its suffering army, opened her sympathizing heart so wide, upon this occasion, as to give us something to make the world stare. And what do you think it was, reader? Guess. You cannot guess. . . . I will tell you; it gave each and every man *half a gill* of rice and a *tablespoonful* of vinegar."

one, two, three, and even four days without a morsel, unless the fields or forests might chance to afford enough to prevent absolute starvation. Often, when I have picked the last grain from the bones of my scanty morsel, have I eaten the very bones, as much of them as possibly could be eaten, and then have had to perform some hard and fatiguing duty, when my stomach has been as craving as it was before I had eaten anything at all.

If we had got our full allowance regularly, what was it? A bare pound of fresh beef, and a bare pound of bread or flour. The beef, when it had gone through all its divisions and subdivisions, would not be much over three-quarters of a pound, and that nearly or quite half bones. The beef that we got in the army, was, generally, not many degrees above carrion; it was much like the old Negro's rabbit, it had not much fat upon it and but a very little lean. When we drew flour, which was much of the time we were in the field, or on marches, it was of small value, being eaten half-cooked, besides a deal of it being unavoidably wasted in the cookery.

When in the field, and often while in winter quarters, our usual mode of drawing our provisions (when we did draw any) was as follows: a return[8] being made out for all the officers and men, for seven days, we drew four days of meat, and the whole seven days of flour. At the expiration of the four days, the other three days' allowance of beef. Now, dear reader, pray consider a moment, how were five men in a mess, five hearty, hungry young men to subsist four days on twenty pounds of fresh beef (and I might say, twelve or fifteen pounds) without any vegetables or any other kind of sauce to eke it out? In the hottest season of the year it was the same, though there was not much danger of our provisions putrifying—we had none on hand long enough for that; if it did, we were obliged to eat it, or go without anything. When General Washington told Congress, "the soldiers eat every kind of horse fodder but hay," he might have gone a little farther, and told them, they eat considerable hog's fodder, and not a trifle of dog's—when they could get it to eat.

We were, also, promised six dollars and two-thirds a month, to be paid us monthly; and how did we fare in this particular? Why, as we did in every other. I received the six dollars and two-thirds, till (if I remember rightly) the month of August, 1777, when paying ceased. And what was six dollars and sixty-seven cents of this "Continental currency" as it was called, worth? It was scarcely enough to procure a man a dinner. Government was ashamed to tantalize the soldiers any longer with such trash, and wisely gave it up for its own credit. I received one month's pay in specie while on the march to Virginia, in the year 1781, and except that, I never received any pay worth the name while I belonged to the army. Had I been paid as I was promised to be at my engaging in the service, I needed not to have suffered as I did, nor would I have done it—there was enough in the country, and money would have procured it if I had had it. It is provoking to think of it. The country was rigorous in exacting my compliance to *my* engagements to a punctilio,[9] but equally careless in performing her

8 An accounting.
9 A fine point of conduct.

contracts with me; and why so? One reason was, because she had all the power in her own hands, and I had none. Such things ought not to be.

The poor soldiers had hardships enough to endure, without having to starve; the least that could be done was to give them something to eat. "The laborer is worthy of his meat" at least, and he ought to have it for his employer's interest, if nothing more. But, as I said, there were other hardships to grapple with. How many times have I had to lie down like a dumb animal in the field, and bear "the pelting of the pitiless storm," cruel enough in warm weather, but how much more so in the heart of winter. Could I have had the benefit of a little fire, it would have been deemed a luxury. But when snow or rain would fall so heavy that it was impossible to keep a spark of fire alive, to have to weather out a long wet, cold, tedious night in the depth of winter, with scarcely clothes enough to keep one from freezing instantly—how discouraging it must be, I leave to my reader to judge. It is fatiguing, almost beyond belief, to those that never experienced it, to be obliged to march twenty-four or forty-eight hours (as very many times I have had to) and often more, night and day without rest or sleep, wishing and hoping that some wood or village I could see ahead, might prove a short resting place, when, alas, I came to it, almost tired off my legs, it proved no resting place for me. How often have I envied the very swine their happiness, when I have heard them quarrelling in their warm dry sties, when I was wet to the skin, and wished in vain for that indulgence. And even in dry, warm weather, I have often been so beat out with long and tedious marching, that I have fallen asleep while walking the road, and not been sensible of it till I have jostled against someone in the same situation. And when permitted to stop and have the superlative happiness to roll myself in my blanket, and drop down on the ground, in the bushes, briars, thorns, or thistles, and get an hour or two's sleep, O! how exhilarating. Fighting the enemy is the great scarecrow to people unacquainted with the duties of an army. To see the fire and smoke, to hear the din of cannon and musketry, and the whistling of shot— they cannot bear the sight or hearing of this. I never was killed in the army; I never was wounded but once; I never was a prisoner with the enemy; but I have seen many that have undergone all these; and I have many times run the risk of all of them myself; but, reader, believe me, for I tell a solemn truth, that I have felt more anxiety, undergone more fatigue and hardships, suffered more every way, in performing one of those tedious marches, than ever I did in fighting the hottest battle I was ever engaged in, with the anticipation of all the other calamities I have mentioned added to it. . . .

But the poor old decrepit soldiers, after all that has been said, to discourage them, have found friends in the community, and I trust there are many, very many, that are sensible of the usefulness of that suffering army, although, perhaps, all their voices have not been so loud in its praise as the voice of slander has been against it. President Monroe was the first of all our presidents, except President Washington, who ever uttered a syllable in the "old soldiers" ' favor. President Washington urged the country to do something for them and not to forget their hard services, but President Monroe told them how to act; he had been a soldier himself in the darkest period of the war, that point of it that emphatically "tried men's souls"; was wounded, and knew what soldiers suffered. His good intentions being seconded by some revolutionary officers, then in Congress, brought about a system by which, aided by our present worthy vice president,[1] then secretary [of] war, heaven bless him, many of the poor men who had spent their youthful, and consequently, their best days in the hard service of their country, have been enabled to eke out the fag end of their lives a little too high for the grovelling hand of envy or the long arm of poverty to reach.

Many murmur now at the apparent good fortune of the poor soldiers. Many I have myself seen, vile enough to say, that they never deserved such favor from the country. The only wish I would bestow upon such hard-hearted wretches, is, that they might be compelled to go through just such sufferings and privations as that army did. And then if they did not sing a different tune, I should miss my guess.

But I really hope those people will not go beside themselves. Those men whom they wish to die on a dunghill; men, who, if they had not ventured their lives in battle, and faced poverty, disease and death for their country, to gain and maintain that independence and liberty, in the sunny beams of which, they like reptiles are basking, they would, many or the most of them, be this moment, in as much need of help and succor, as ever the most indigent soldier was before he experienced his country's beneficence.

The soldiers consider it cruel to be thus vilified, and it is cruel as the grave, to any man, when he knows his own rectitude of conduct, to have his hard services, not only debased and underrated, but scandalized and vilified. But the revolutionary soldiers are not the only people that endure obloquy, others as meritorious, and perhaps more deserving than they, are forced to submit to ungenerous treatment.

But if the old revolutionary pensioners are really an eyesore, a grief of mind, to any man, or set of men (and I know they are), let me tell them that if they will exercise a very little patience, a few years longer will put all of them beyond the power of troubling them; for they will soon be "where the wicked cease from troubling, and the weary are at rest."[2]

---

[1] John C. Calhoun (1782–1850); here and in the following lines, Martin is discussing the Pension Act of 1818, passed when Monroe was president and Calhoun was secretary of war.
[2] Job 3:17.

6

REVOLT IN SOUTHAMPTON

NAT TURNER WAS A MAN WHO BY HIS OWN ADMISSION HAD A SPECIAL DESTINY thrust upon him. Sitting in the jail in Southampton County, Virginia, in November 1831, he told a local lawyer named Thomas R. Gray that ever since his boyhood he knew something different was intended for him. Playing with a group of other slave children on the Turner plantation when he was three or four years old, he was telling them about something he remembered happening when his mother overheard him and said that he was right, it had happened, but it had happened before he was born. She doubted what he was saying at first, doubted his truthfulness, but he persisted, adding more details, until she and then other adults who gathered around were astonished and concluded that young Nat was going to be a prophet. His parents from that point on kept insisting that he was meant for some great purpose, and they said that some marks on his body—strange growths more than birthmarks—also confirmed that conclusion. As he grew older, it was apparent that Nat Turner was unusual in other ways; he had a mind that was "restless, inquisitive and observant of everything that was passing." He was much attracted to religion, as befit his vocation as a prophet, but his talents spread over all creation. He picked up reading and writing with such ease that he told Gray he did not recall ever actually learning the alphabet, it was so natural to him, but just one day when a book was shown to him to quiet him he looked at it and "began spelling the names of different objects." When older, he experimented making different things—paper and gunpowder, for two—and when Gray questioned him as to how they were made he offered well-informed explanations. Aware of his special calling, he held himself aloof from others, disciplining himself for the task that would come to him.

Only slowly did the purpose emerge. As he told Gray, he ran away from his master and hid in the woods for a month, but then came back. The other slaves distrusted him at that point, wondering why anyone able to escape from slavery would return. But Nat Turner was already hearing voices that directed him in these things, and the voices told him to go back. Soon he had an ominous, powerful vision; in 1825, he told Gray, "I saw white spirits and black spirits engaged in battle, and the sun was darkened—the thunder rolled in the heavens, and blood flowed in streams—and I heard a voice saying, 'Such is your luck, such you are called to see, and let it come rough or smooth, you must surely bear it.' "

And bear it he did. On the night of August 21, 1831, with several other men gathered to his purpose, Nat Turner led an attack on the slave-owners of his county that was to electrify the South. By the time the attack ended, several dozen whites, men, women, children, grandparents, lay dead, many horridly gashed, and the living were roused and rushing about to find the perpetrators and stanch the larger wound in the white body politic. Many of the slaves responsible for the political uprising, for such it clearly was, were soon in custody, and tried and executed with dispatch. Nat himself hid out until the end of October but was found and seized and with similar speed tried and executed.

The details of what happened in August are given in Nat Turner's *Confessions* to Gray, the full text of which follows. But that brief book is a difficult item, and more needs to be said here about Turner and how the book came to be written, and also about Gray. Thomas R. Gray, a lawyer in the town of Jerusalem (renamed Courtland in 1888), had been one of the appointed counsel for the men previously arrested and tried in the case, but had no official role in Nat Turner's trial. A friend of Turner's jailer, he succeeded in gaining access to the prisoner over a three-day period (November 1st to 3rd)—prior to the trial, which occurred on November 5th—and, with another person taking down Turner's statements, sought to gratify what he called "public curiosity" (*obsession* might be a better word) with regard to the origins of the uprising. Gray was in his sixties then, married to a woman in her thirties who had had no children, and the owner of as many as thirty-three slaves (the man who tried Turner, Jeremiah Cobb, owned thirty-two). While we should not overlook the fact that Gray's defense of others in the trials was not without its risks to a man situated as he was, it is fairly clear that his interest in Turner's story sprang from something other than sympathy with the man. Indeed, certain particulars in the document that are attributable only to him show his own stance: whereas the court record, for instance, has Justice Cobb stating the sentence of Turner in relatively unemotional language (Turner was to be "taken by the Sheriff to the usual place of execution and then and there hanged by the neck until he be dead"), Gray elaborated this into an expression of outrage on the part of the white community—the justice addresses Turner directly, for one thing, and says "you [are to] . . . be hung by the neck until you are dead! dead! dead! And may the Lord have mercy on your soul." Even the little religious flourish at the end of Gray's version has no counterpart in the trial record, which ends with the far more pragmatic (though still horrific in another sense) valuation of Turner, necessary because the state had to pay their owners for all executed slaves, one of the few things that militated against even more executions in the case: "And the Court values the said slave to the sum of three hundred and seventy-five dollars." Adding to the dead-level tone of that final line is the fact that the amount of compensation was originally stated at 350 dollars but apparently was modestly increased due to second thoughts or to protest from the heirs of Turner's most recent owner, Joseph Travis, who with his wife and three children was among those murdered.

Most of Gray's interpolations into the text of the *Confessions* are apparent, and are made clear in the editing of the text here. It should be also pointed out, however, that his motives in compiling the document were at least in part commercial. He secured a copyright for the small book as early as November 10th, a week after he finished his interviews with Turner, only five days after Turner's conviction, and just a day prior to the execution. The book appeared in Baltimore before the month was out (a Richmond paper noticed it on November 22nd) and in Richmond the following year a second edition appeared. Thomas Wentworth Higginson, the abolitionist, wrote in 1861 that some forty thousand copies of the book had been circulated; that figure may be off, but to judge from the number of contemporary references to it (Harriet Beecher Stowe used it, for instance, in composing part of her novel *Dred* [1856]) the *Confessions* clearly must have entered the public consciousness as a key document in the history of slavery. How accurate it is in its portrayal of Turner is a very complicated question. Gray's emphasis on the man's evident skills, sense of vocation, and charismatic power cannot be seen as contributing to a "savagist" reading of the Southampton revolt (that is, the view that African Americans, even with the "advantages" of slavery, were incapable of civilization—and hence, of course, incapable of emancipation) but these aspects of the portrait of Turner at the same time might be seen as deflecting attention—consciously or not—from the ultimate cause of such violence, which was the violence of slavery itself. William Lloyd Garrison pointed to the scars described on Nat Turner's body as the source of his uprising, but this, too, personalized more than was warranted the final cause of the revolt. When we read Turner's sense of mission in social rather than religious terms, or read the religion as being socially *active*, we may be closer to the truth. We should not take Gray's book as simply his, or as naïvely Turner's; but if we read shrewdly between the lines of force that gave structure to the occasion of its birth, we can read its dynamics as themselves part of Turner's story.

THOMAS R. GRAY, ED.

The Confessions of Nat Turner (1831)

TO THE PUBLIC

THE LATE INSURRECTION IN SOUTHAMPTON HAS GREATLY EXCITED THE PUBLIC mind, and led to a thousand idle, exaggerated and mischievous reports. It is the first instance in our history of an open rebellion of the slaves, and attended with such atrocious circumstances of cruelty and destruction, as could not fail to leave a deep impression, not only upon the minds of the community where this fearful tragedy was wrought, but throughout every portion of our country, in which this population is to be found. Public curiosity has been on the stretch to understand the origin and progress of this dreadful conspiracy, and the motives which influence its diabolical actors. The insurgent slaves had all been destroyed, or apprehended, tried and executed (with the exception of the leader), without revealing anything at all satisfactory, as to the motives which governed them, or the means by which they expected to accomplish their object. Everything connected with the sad affair was wrapped in mystery, until Nat Turner, the leader of this ferocious band, whose name has resounded throughout our widely extended empire, was captured. This "great bandit" was taken by a single individual, in a cave near the residence of his late owner, on Sunday, the thirtieth of October, without attempting to make the slightest resistance, and on the following day safely lodged in the jail of the county. His captor was Benjamin Phipps, armed with a shotgun well charged. Nat's only weapon was a small light sword which he immediately surrendered, and begged that his life might be spared. Since his confinement, by permission of the jailer, I have had ready access to him, and finding that he was willing to make a full and free confession of the origin, progress and consummation of the insurrectory movements of the slaves of which he was the contriver and head, I determined for the gratification of public curiosity to commit his statements to writing and publish them, with little or no variation, from his own words. That this is a faithful record of his confessions, the annexed certificate of the county court of Southampton, will attest. They certainly bear one stamp of truth and sincerity. He makes no attempt (as all the other insurgents who were examined did) to exculpate himself, but frankly acknowledges his full participation in all the guilt of the transaction. He was not only the contriver of the conspiracy, but gave the first blow towards its execution.

It will thus appear, that whilst everything upon the surface of society wore a calm and peaceful aspect; whilst not one note of preparation was heard to warn the devoted inhabitants of woe and death, a gloomy fanatic was revolving in the recesses of his own dark, bewildered, and overwrought mind, schemes of indiscriminate massacre to the whites, schemes too fearfully executed as far as his fiendish band proceeded in their desolating march. No cry for mercy penetrated their flinty bosoms. No acts of remembered kindness made the least impression upon these remorseless murderers. Men, women and children, from hoary age to helpless infancy were involved in the same cruel fate. Never did a band of savages do their work of death more unsparingly. Apprehension for their own personal safety seems to have been the only principle of restraint in the whole course of their bloody proceedings. And it is not the least remarkable feature in this horrid transaction, that a band actuated by such hellish purposes, should have resisted so feebly, when met by the whites in arms. Desperation alone, one would think, might have led to greater efforts. More than twenty of them attacked Dr. Blunt's house on Tuesday morning, a little before daybreak, defended by two men and three boys. They fled precipitately at the first fire, and their future plans of mischief were entirely disconcerted and broken up. Escaping thence, each individual sought his own safety either in concealment, or by returning home, with the hope that his participation might escape detection, and all were shot down in the course of a few days, or captured and brought to trial and punishment. Nat has survived all his followers, and the gallows will speedily close his career. His own account of the conspiracy is submitted to the public, without comment. It reads an awful, and it is hoped, a useful lesson, as to the operations of a mind like his, endeavoring to grapple with things beyond its reach: how it first became bewildered and confounded, and finally corrupted and led to the conception and perpetration of the most atrocious and heartrending deeds. It is calculated also to demonstrate the policy of our laws in restraint of this class of our population, and to induce all those entrusted with their execution, as well as our citizens generally, to see that they are strictly and rigidly enforced. Each particular community should look to its own safety, whilst the general guardians of the laws, keep a watchful eye over all. If Nat's statements can be relied on, the insurrection in this county was entirely local, and his designs confided but to a few, and these in his immediate vicinity. It was not instigated by motives of revenge or sudden anger, but the results of long deliberation, and a settled purpose of mind. [It was] the offspring of gloomy fanaticism, acting upon materials but too well prepared for such impressions. It will be long remembered in the annals of our country, and many a mother as she presses her infant darling to her bosom, will shudder at the recollection of Nat Turner and his band of ferocious miscreants.

Believing the following narrative, by removing doubts and conjectures from the public mind which otherwise must have remained, would give general satisfaction, it is respectfully submitted to the public by their obedient servant,

T. R. *Gray.*

Jerusalem, Southampton, Va. November 5, 1831

We the undersigned, members of the court convened at Jerusalem, on Saturday, the 5th day of November 1831, for the trial of Nat, *alias* Nat Turner, a Negro slave, late the property of Putnam Moore, deceased, do hereby certify, that the confessions of Nat, to Thomas R. Gray, was read to him in our presence, and that Nat acknowledged the same to be full, free, and voluntary; and that furthermore, when called upon by the presiding magistrate of the court, to state if he had anything to say, why sentence of death should not be passed upon him, replied he had nothing further than he had communicated to Mr. Gray. Given under our hands and seals at Jerusalem, this 5th day of November, 1831.

Jeremiah Cobb, [Seal]
Thomas Pretlow, [Seal]
James W. Parker [Seal]
Carr Bowers, [Seal]
Samuel B. Hines, [Seal]
Orris A. Browne, [Seal]

State of Virginia, Southampton County, to wit:

I, James Rochelle, clerk of the county court of Southampton in the state of Virginia, do hereby certify, that Jeremiah Cobb, Thomas Pretlow, James W. Parker, Carr Bowers, Samuel B. Hines, and Orris A. Browne, esquires, are acting justices of the peace, in and for the county aforesaid, and were members of the court which convened at Jerusalem, on Saturday the 5th day of November, 1831, for the trial of Nat *alias* Nat Turner, a Negro slave, late the property of Putnam Moore, deceased, who was tried and convicted, as an insurgent in the late insurrection in the county of Southampton aforesaid, and that full faith and credit are due, and ought to be given to their acts as justices of the peace aforesaid.

    [Seal]

In testimony whereof, I have hereunto set my hand and caused the seal of the court aforesaid, to be affixed this 5th day of November, 1831
James Rochelle,

C. S. C. C.

CONFESSION

Agreeable to his own appointment, on the evening he was committed to prison, with permission of the jailer, I visited Nat on Tuesday the 1st [of] November, when, without being questioned at all, he commenced his narrative in the following words:

"Sir,—You have asked me to give a history of the motives which induced me to undertake the late insurrection, as you call it. To do so I must go back to the days of my infancy, and even before I was born. I was thirty-one years of age the 2nd of October last, and born the property of Benjamin Turner, of this county. In my childhood a circumstance occurred which made an indelible impression on my mind, and laid the groundwork of that enthusiasm,[1] which has terminated so fatally to many, both white and black, and for which I am about to atone at the gallows. It is here necessary to relate this circumstance—trifling as it may seem, it was the commencement of that belief which has grown with time, and [which] even now, sir, in this dungeon, helpless and forsaken as I am, I cannot divest myself of. Being at play with other children, when three or four years old, I was telling them something, which my mother overhearing, said it had happened before I was born. I stuck to my story, however, and related some things which went, in her opinion, to confirm it. Others being called on were greatly astonished, knowing that these things had happened, and caused them to say in my hearing, I surely would be a prophet, as the Lord had shewn me things that had happened before my birth. And my

---

[1] In the special eighteenth-century sense—that is, characterized by a mental state distorted by strong emotion.

father and mother strengthened me in this my first impression, saying in my presence I was intended for some great purpose, which they had always thought from certain marks on my head and breast.[2] My grandmother, who was very religious and to whom I was much attached, my master, who belonged to the church, and other religious persons who visited the house and whom I often saw at prayers, noticing the singularity of my manners, I suppose, and my uncommon intelligence for a child, remarked I had too much sense to be raised (and if I was, I would never be of any service to anyone) as a slave. [In respect] to a mind like mine, restless, inquisitive and observant of everything that was passing, it is easy to suppose that religion was the subject to which it would be directed, and although this subject principally occupied my thoughts, there was nothing that I saw or heard of to which my attention was not directed.

"The manner in which I learned to read and write . . . had great influence on my own mind, as I acquired it with the most perfect ease, so much so that I have no recollection whatever of learning the alphabet, but to the astonishment of the family one day, when a book was shown to me to keep me from crying, I began spelling the names of different objects. This was a source of wonder to all in the neighborhood, particularly the blacks, and this learning was constantly improved at all opportunities. When I got large enough to go to work, while employed, I was reflecting on many things that would present themselves to my imagination, and whenever an opportunity occurred of looking at a book, when the school children were getting their lessons, I would find many things that the fertility of my own imagination had depicted to me before. All my time, not devoted to my master's service, was spent either in prayer, or in making experiments in casting different things in molds made of earth, in attempting to make paper, gunpowder, and many other experiments, that although I could not perfect [them], yet convinced me of [their] practicability if I had the means.[3] I was not addicted to stealing in my youth, nor have ever been. Yet such was the confidence of the Negroes in the neighborhood, even at this early period of my life in my superior judgment, that they would often carry me with them when they were going on any roguery, to plan for them. Growing up among them with [their] confidence in my superior judgment (and when this, in their opinions, was perfected by divine inspiration, from the circumstances already alluded to in my infancy, and which belief was ever afterwards zealously inculcated by the austerity of my life and manners), [I] became the subject of remark by white and black. Having soon [been] discovered to be great, I must appear so, and therefore studiously avoided mixing in society, and wrapped myself in mystery, devoting my time to fasting and prayer.

"By this time, having arrived to man's estate, and hearing the scriptures commented on at meetings, I was struck with that particular passage which

---

[2] "A parcel of excrescences which I believe are not at all uncommon, particularly among Negroes, as I have seen several with the same. In this case he has either cut them off or they have nearly disappeared" [Gray's aside in the original text].

[3] "When questioned as to the manner of manufacturing those different articles, he was found well-informed on the subject" [Gray's footnote].

says: 'Seek ye the kingdom of heaven and all things shall be added unto you.'[4] I reflected much on this passage, and prayed daily for light on this subject. As I was praying one day at my plough, the spirit spoke to me, saying "Seek ye the kingdom of Heaven and all things shall be added unto you" (*Question*—What do you mean by the spirit. *Answer*—The spirit that spoke to the prophets in former days)[5]—and I was greatly astonished, and for two years prayed continually, whenever my duty would permit—and then again I had the same revelation, which fully confirmed me in the impression that I was ordained for some great purpose in the hands of the Almighty. Several years rolled round, in which many events occurred to strengthen me in this my belief. At this time I reverted in my mind to the remarks made of me in my childhood, and the things that had been shown me, and [that] it had been said of me in my childhood by those by whom I had been taught to pray, both white and black, and in whom I had the greatest confidence, that I had too much sense to be raised (and if I was, I would never be of any use to anyone) as a slave. Now finding I had arrived to man's estate, and was a slave, and these revelations being made known to me, I began to direct my attention to this great object, to fulfil the purpose for which, by this time, I felt assured I was intended. [I knew] the influence I had obtained over the minds of my fellow servants (not by the means of conjuring and such like tricks—for to them I always spoke of such things with contempt) but by the communion of the spirit whose revelations I often communicated to them, and they believed and said my wisdom came from God. I now began to prepare them for my purpose, by telling them something was about to happen that would terminate in fulfilling the great promise that had been made to me. About this time I was placed under an overseer, from whom I ran away, and after remaining in the woods thirty days, I returned, to the astonishment of the Negroes on the plantation, who thought I had made my escape to some other part of the country, as my father had done before. But the reason of my return was, that the spirit appeared to me and said I had my wishes directed to the things of this world, and not to the kingdom of heaven, and that I should return to the service of my earthly master—'For he who knoweth his master's will, and doeth it not, shall be beaten with many stripes, and thus have I chastened you.'[6] And the Negroes found fault, and murmured against me, saying that if they had my sense they would not serve any master in the world. And about this time I had a vision—and I saw white spirits and black spirits engaged in battle, and the sun was darkened, the thunder rolled in the heavens, and blood flowed in streams—and I heard a voice saying, 'Such is your luck, such you are called to see, and let it come rough or smooth, you must surely bear it.'

"I now withdrew myself as much as my situation would permit, from the intercourse of my fellow servants, for the avowed purpose of serving the spirit more fully—and it appeared to me, and reminded me of the things it had

---

[4] Luke 12:31.
[5] Here and later, these parenthetical exchanges represent Gray's interrogations of Turner.
[6] See Luke 12:47.

already shown me, and that it would then reveal to me the knowledge of the elements, the revolution of the planets, the operation of tides, and changes of the seasons. After this revelation in the year of 1825, and the knowledge of the elements being made known to me, I sought more than ever to obtain true holiness before the great day of judgment should appear, and then I began to receive the true knowledge of faith. And from the first steps of righteousness until the last, was I made perfect; and the holy ghost was with me, and said, 'Behold me as I stand in the heavens,' and I looked and saw the forms of men in different attitudes, and there were lights in the sky to which the children of darkness gave other names than what they really were—for they were the lights of the Savior's hands, stretched forth from east to west, even as they were extended on the cross on Calvary for the redemption of sinners. And I wondered greatly at these miracles, and prayed to be informed of a certainty of the meaning thereof, and shortly afterwards, while laboring in the field, I discovered drops of blood on the corn as though it were dew from heaven, and I communicated it to many, both white and black, in the neighborhood, and I then found on the leaves in the woods hieroglyphic characters and numbers, with the forms of men in different attitudes, portrayed in blood, and representing the figures I had seen before in the heavens. And now the holy ghost had revealed itself to me, and made plain the miracles it had shown me—for as the blood of Christ had been shed on this earth, and had ascended to heaven for the salvation of sinners, and was now returning to earth again in the form of dew; and as the leaves on the trees bore the impression of the figures I had seen in the heavens, it was plain to me that the Savior was about to lay down the yoke he had borne for the sins of men, and the great day of judgment was at hand. About this time I told these things to a white man (Etheldred T. Brantley) on whom it had a wonderful effect, and he ceased from his wickedness, and was attacked immediately with a cutaneous eruption, and blood oozed from the pores of his skin, and after praying and fasting nine days, he was healed, and the spirit appeared to me again, and said, as the Savior had been baptized so should we be also. And when the white people would not let us be baptized by the church, we went down into the water together, in the sight of many who reviled us, and were baptized by the spirit. After this I rejoiced greatly, and gave thanks to God. And on the 12th of May, 1828, I heard a loud noise in the heavens, and the spirit instantly appeared to me and said the serpent was loosened, and Christ had laid down the yoke he had borne for the sins of men, and that I should take it on and fight against the serpent, for the time was fast approaching when the first should be last and the last should be first[7] (*Question*—Do you not find yourself mistaken now? *Answer*—Was not Christ crucified?) And by signs in the heavens [it informed me] that it would make known to me when I should commence the great work, and until the first sign appeared, I should conceal it from the knowledge of men, and on the appearance of the sign (the eclipse of the sun last February) I should arise and prepare

[7] See Matthew 19:30.

myself, and slay my enemies with their own weapons. And immediately on the sign appearing in the heavens, the seal was removed from my lips, and I communicated the great work laid out for me to do, to four in whom I had the greatest confidence (Henry, Hark, Nelson, and Sam). It was intended by us to have begun the work of death on the 4th [of] July last. Many were the plans formed and rejected by us, and it affected my mind to such a degree, that I fell sick, and the time passed without our coming to any determination how to commence, still forming new schemes and rejecting them, when the sign appeared again, which determined me not to wait longer.

"Since the commencement of 1830, I had been living with Mr. Joseph Travis, who was to me a kind master, and placed the greatest confidence in me; in fact, I had no cause to complain of his treatment to me. On Saturday evening, the 20th of August, it was agreed between Henry, Hark and myself, to prepare a dinner the next day for the men we expected, and then to concert a plan, as we had not yet determined on any. Hark on the following morning brought a pig, and Henry brandy, and being joined by Sam, Nelson, Will and Jack, they prepared in the woods a dinner, where about three o'clock I joined them. (*Question*—Why were you so backward in joining them? *Answer*—The same reason that had caused me not to mix with them for years before.) I saluted them on coming up, and asked Will how came he there; he answered, his life was worth no more than others, and his liberty as dear to him. I asked him if he thought to obtain it? He said he would, or lose his life. This was enough to put him in full confidence. Jack, I knew, was only a tool in the hands of Hark. It was quickly agreed we should commence at home (Mr. J. Travis') on that night, and until we had armed and equipped ourselves, and gathered sufficient force, neither age nor sex was to be spared (which was invariably adhered to). We remained at the feast, until about two hours in the night, when we went to the house and found Austin; they all went to the cider press and drank, except myself. On returning to the house, Hark went to the door with an axe, for the purpose of breaking it open, as we knew we were strong enough to murder the family, if they were awaked by the noise; but reflecting that it might create an alarm in the neighborhood, we determined to enter the house secretly, and murder them whilst sleeping. Hark got a ladder and set it against the chimney, on which I ascended, and hoisting a window, entered and came downstairs, unbarred the door, and removed the guns from their places. It was then observed that I must spill the first blood. On which, armed with a hatchet, and accompanied by Will, I entered my master's chamber. It being dark, I could not give a death blow; the hatchet glanced from his head, he sprang from the bed and called his wife. It was his last word: Will laid him dead with a blow of his axe, and Mrs. Travis shared the same fate as she lay in bed. The murder of this family, five in number, was the work of a moment. Not one of them awoke. There was a little infant sleeping in a cradle, that was forgotten, until we had left the house and gone some distance, when Henry and Will returned and killed it.

"We got here, four guns that would shoot, and several old muskets, with a pound or two of powder. We remained some time at the barn, where we paraded; I formed them in a line as soldiers, and after carrying them through all the maneuvers I was master of, marched them off to Mr. Salathul Francis', about six hundred yards distant. Sam and Will went to the door and knocked. Mr. Francis asked who was there, Sam replied it was him, and he had a letter for him, on which he got up and came to the door. They immediately seized him, and dragging him out a little from the door, he was dispatched by repeated blows on the head. There was no other white person in the family. We started from there for Mrs. Reese's, maintaining the most perfect silence on our march. Finding the door unlocked, we entered, and murdered Mrs. Reese in her bed, while sleeping; her son awoke, but it was only to sleep the sleep of death;[8] he had only time to say 'Who is that?' and he was no more. From Mrs. Reese's we went to Mrs. Turner's, a mile distant, which we reached about sunrise, on Monday morning. Henry, Austin, and Sam, went to the still, where, finding Mr. Peebles, Austin shot him, and the rest of us went to the house. As we approached, the family discovered us, and shut the door. Vain hope! Will, with one stroke of his axe, opened it, and we entered and found Mrs. Turner and Mrs. Newsome in the middle of a room, almost frightened to death. Will immediately killed Mrs. Turner, with one blow of his axe. I took Mrs. Newsome by the hand, and with the sword I had when I was apprehended, I struck her several blows over the head, but [was] not able to kill her, as the sword was dull. Will turning around and discovering it, despatched her also.

"A general destruction of property and search for money and ammunition, always succeeded the murders. By this time my company amounted to fifteen, and nine men mounted, who started for Mrs. Whitehead's (the other six were to go through a byway to Mr. Bryant's, and rejoin us at Mrs. Whitehead's). As we approached the house we discovered Mr. Richard Whitehead standing in the cotton patch, near the lane fence; we called him over into the lane, and Will the executioner was near at hand with his fatal axe to send him to an untimely grave. As we pushed on to the house, I discovered someone run round the garden, and thinking it was some of the white family, I pursued them, but finding it was a servant girl belonging to the house, I returned to commence the work of death. But they whom I left, had not been idle; all the family were already murdered, but Mrs. Whitehead and her daughter Margaret. As I came round to the door I saw Will pulling Mrs. Whitehead out of the house, and at the step he nearly severed her head from her body, with his broad axe. Miss Margaret, when I discovered her, had concealed herself in the corner, formed by the projection of cellar cap from the house. On my approach she fled, but was soon overtaken, and after repeated blows with a sword, I killed her by a blow on the head, with a fencerail. By this time, the six who had gone by Mr. Bryant's rejoined us, and informed me they had done the work of death assigned them.

"We again divided, part going to Mr. Richard Porter's and from thence to

---

[8] See Psalms 13:3.

Nathaniel Francis', the others to Mr. Howell Harris' and Mr. T. Doyles. On my reaching Mr. Porter's, he had escaped with his family. I understood there that the alarm had already spread, and I immediately returned to bring up those sent to Mr. Doyles and Mr. Howell Harris'; the [other] party I left going on to Mr. Francis', having told them I would join them in that neighborhood. I met these sent to Mr. Doyles' and Mr. Harris' returning, having met Mr. Doyle on the road and killed him; and learning from some who joined them, that Mr. Harris was from home, I immediately pursued the course taken by the party gone on before. But knowing they would complete the work of death and pillage at Mr. Francis' before I could get there, I went to Mr. Peter Edwards', expecting to find them there, but they had been here also. I then went to Mr. John T. Barrow's; they had been here and murdered him. I pursued their track to Capt. Newit Harris', where I found the greater part mounted, and ready to start. The men, now amounting to about forty, shouted and hurrahed as I rode up; some were in the yard, loading their guns, others drinking. They said Captain Harris and his family had escaped, [but] the property in the house they [had] destroyed, robbing him of money and other valuables. I ordered them to mount and march instantly (this was about nine or ten o'clock, Monday morning).

"I proceeded to Mr. Levi Waller's, two or three miles distant. I took my station in the rear, and as it was my object to carry terror and devastation wherever we went, I placed fifteen or twenty of the best-armed and most-relied on, in front, who generally approached the houses as fast as their horses could run. This was for two purposes, to prevent escape and strike terror to the inhabitants, [and] on this account I never got to the houses, after leaving Mrs. Whitehead's, until the murders were committed, except in one case. I sometimes got in sight in time to see the work of death completed, viewed the mangled bodies as they lay, in silent satisfaction, and immediately started in quest of other victims. Having murdered Mrs. Waller and ten children, we started for Mr. William Williams's. [We] killed him and two little boys that were there, [and while we were] engaged in this, Mrs. Williams fled and got some distance from the house; but she was pursued, overtaken, and compelled to get up behind one of the company, who brought her back, and after showing her the mangled body of her lifeless husband, she was told to get down and lay by his side, where she was shot dead. I then started for Mr. Jacob Williams's, where the family were murdered. Here [I] found a young man named Drury, who had come on business with Mr. Williams—he was pursued, overtaken and shot.

"Mrs. Vaughan's was the next place we visited, and after murdering the family here, I determined on starting for Jerusalem. Our number amounted now to fifty or sixty, all mounted and armed with guns, axes, swords and clubs. On reaching Mr. James W. Parker's gate, immediately on the road leading to Jerusalem, and about three miles distant, it was proposed to me to call there, but I objected, as I knew he was gone to Jerusalem, and my object was to reach there as soon as possible; but some of the men having relations at Mr. Parker's it was agreed that they might call and get his people. I remained at the gate on the road, with seven or eight, the others going across the field to the house, about half a mile off. After waiting some time for them, I became impatient, and started to the house for them, and on our return we were met by a party of white men, who had pursued our blood-stained track, and who had fired on those at the gate, and dispersed them, which I knew nothing of, not having been at that time rejoined by any of them. Immediately on discovering the whites, I ordered my men to halt and form, as they appeared to be alarmed. The white men, eighteen in number, approached us [with]in about one hundred yards, when one of them fired[9] and I discovered about half of them retreating. I then ordered my men to fire and rush on them; the few remaining stood their ground until we approached within fifty yards, when they fired and retreated. We pursued and overtook some of them who we thought we left dead;[1] after pursuing them about two hundred yards, and rising a little hill, I discovered they were met by another party, and had halted, and were reloading their guns.[2] [I thought] that those who retreated first, and the party who fired on us at fifty or sixty yards distance, had all fallen back to meet others with ammunition. I saw them reloading their guns, and more coming up than I saw at first; and several of my bravest men being wounded, the others became panic-struck and squandered[3] over the field, [and] the white men pursued and fired on us several times. Hark had his horse shot under him, and I caught another for him as it was running by me; five or six of my men were wounded, but none left on the field. Finding myself defeated here, I instantly determined to go through a private way, and cross the Nottoway River at the Cypress Bridge, three miles below Jerusalem, and attack that place in the rear, as I expected they would look for me on the other road, and I had a great desire to get there to procure arms and ammunition. After going a short distance in this private way, accompanied by about twenty men, I overtook two or three who told me the others were dispersed in every direction.

"After trying in vain to collect a sufficient force to proceed to Jerusalem, I determined to return, as I was sure they would make back to their old neighborhood, where they would rejoin me, make new recruits, and come down again. On my way back, I called at Mrs. Thomas's, Mrs. Spencer's, and several other places, [but] the white families having fled, we found no more victims to gratify our thirst for blood. We stopped at Major Ridley's quarter for the night, and being joined by four of his men, with the recruits made since my defeat, we mustered now about forty strong. After placing out sentinels, I laid down to

---

[9]"This was against the positive orders of Captain Alexander P. Peete, who commanded, and who had directed the men to reserve their fire until within thirty paces" [Gray's aside in the text].

[1]"They were not killed" [Gray's aside in the text].

[2]"This was a small party from Jerusalem who knew the Negroes were in the field, and had just tied their horses to await their return to the road, knowing that Mr. Parker and family were in Jerusalem, but knew nothing of the party that had gone in with Captain Peete; on hearing the firing they immediately rushed to the spot and arrived just in time to arrest the progress of these barbarous villains, and save the lives of their friends and fellow citizens" [Gray's aside in the text].

[3]I.e., scattered themselves.

sleep, but was quickly roused by a great racket; starting up, I found some mounted, and others in great confusion. One of the sentinels having given the alarm that we were about to be attacked, I ordered some to ride round and reconnoiter, and on their return the others being more alarmed, not knowing who they were, fled in different ways, so that I was reduced to about twenty again. With this I determined to attempt to recruit,[4] and proceed on to rally in the neighborhood I had left. Dr. Blunt's was the nearest house, which we reached just before day; on riding up the yard, Hark fired a gun. We expected Dr. Blunt and his family were at Major Ridley's, as I knew there was a company of men there. The gun was fired to ascertain if any of the family were at home; we were immediately fired upon and retreated, leaving several of my men. I do not know what became of them, as I never saw them afterwards.

"Pursuing our course back and coming in sight of Captain Harris's, where we had been the day before, we discovered a party of white men at the house, on which all deserted me but two (Jacob and Nat). We concealed ourselves in the woods until near night, when I sent them in search of Henry, Sam, Nelson, and Hark, and directed them to rally all they could at the place we had had our dinner the Sunday before, where they would find me. I accordingly returned there as soon as it was dark and remained until Wednesday evening, when discovering white men riding around the place as though they were looking for someone, and none of my men joining me, I concluded Jacob and Nat had been taken, and compelled to betray me. On this I gave up all hope for the present, and on Thursday night after having supplied myself with provisions from Mr. Travis's, I scratched a hole under a pile of fence rails in a field, where I concealed myself for six weeks, never leaving my hiding place but for a few minutes in the dead of night to get water, which was very near. Thinking by this time I could venture out, I began to go about in the night and eavesdrop [on] the houses in the neighborhood, pursuing this course for about a fortnight and gathering little or no intelligence, afraid of speaking to any human being, and returning every morning to my cave before the dawn of day. I know not how long I might have led this life, if accident had not betrayed me. A dog in the neighborhood passing by my hiding place one night while I was out, was attracted by some meat I had in my cave, and crawled in and stole it, and was coming out just as I returned. A few nights after, two Negroes having started to go hunting with the same dog, and passed that way, the dog came again to the place, and having just gone out to walk about, discovered me and barked, on which thinking myself discovered, I spoke to them to beg concealment. On making myself known they fled from me. Knowing then they would betray me, I immediately left my hiding place, and was pursued almost incessantly until I was taken a fortnight afterwards by Mr. Benjamin Phipps, in a little hole I had dug out with my sword, for the purpose of concealment, under the top of a fallen tree. On Mr. Phipps' discovering the place of my concealment, he cocked his gun and aimed at me. I requested him not to shoot and I would

[4]Recover.

give up, upon which he demanded my sword. I delivered it to him, and he brought me to prison. During the time I was pursued, I had many hair-breadth escapes, which your time will not permit you to relate. I am here loaded with chains, and willing to suffer the fate that awaits me."

I here proceeded to make some inquiries of him, after assuring him of the certain death that awaited him, and that concealment would only bring destruction on the innocent as well as guilty of his own color, if he knew of any extensive or concerted plan. His answer was, "I do not." When I questioned him as to the insurrection in North Carolina happening about the same time,[5] he denied any knowledge of it; and when I looked him in the face as though I would search his inmost thoughts, he replied, "I see sir, you doubt my word; but can you not think the same ideas, and strange appearances about this time in the heavens might prompt others, as well as myself, to this undertaking?" I now had much conversation with and asked him many questions, having forborne to do so previously, except in the cases noted in parentheses; but during his statement, I had, unnoticed by him, taken notes as to some particular circumstances, and having the advantage of his statement before me in writing,[6] on the evening of the third day that I had been with him I began a cross-examination, and found his statement corroborated by every circumstance coming within my own knowledge or the confessions of others who had been either killed or executed, and whom he had not seen nor had any knowledge [of] since 22d of August last.

He expressed himself fully satisfied as to the impracticability of his attempt. It has been said he was ignorant and cowardly, and that his object was to murder and rob for the purpose of obtaining money to make his escape. It is notorious, that he was never known to have a dollar in his life; to swear an oath, or drink a drop of spirits. As to his ignorance, he certainly never had the advantages of education, but he can read and write (it was taught him by his parents) and for natural intelligence and quickness of apprehension, is surpassed by few men I have ever seen. As to his being a coward, his reason as given for not resisting Mr. Phipps, shows the decision of his character. When he saw Mr. Phipps present his gun, he said he knew it was impossible for him to escape as the woods were full of men; he therefore thought it was better to surrender, and trust to fortune for his escape. He is a complete fanatic, or plays his part most admirably. On other subjects he possesses an uncommon share of intelligence, with a mind capable of attaining anything, but warped and perverted by the influence of early impressions. He is below the ordinary stature, though strong and active, having the true Negro face, every feature of which is strongly marked. I shall not attempt to describe the effect of his narrative, as told and

---

[5] Not only in North Carolina, but in other southern states, reports of uprisings in this period were rife, some of them based on actual happenings.

[6] Gray's implication is that an official scribe took down Nat Turner's statement while he, Gray, listened and occasionally took notes. Note that the end of this complicated sentence is somewhat garbled in the original.

commented on by himself, in the condemned hole of the prison. The calm, deliberate composure with which he spoke of his late deeds and intentions, the expression of his fiend-like face when excited by enthusiasm, still bearing the stains of the blood of helpless innocence about him; clothed with rags and covered with chains; yet daring to raise his manacled hands to heaven, with a spirit soaring above the attributes of man: I looked on him and my blood curdled in my veins.

I will not shock the feelings of humanity, nor wound afresh the bosoms of the disconsolate sufferers in this unparalleled and inhuman massacre, by detailing the deeds of their fiend-like barbarity. There were two or three who were in the power of these wretches, had they known it, and who escaped in the most providential manner. There were two whom they thought they left dead on the field at Mr. Parker's, but who were only stunned by the blows of their guns, as they did not take time to reload when they charged on them. The escape of a little girl who went to school at Mr. Waller's, where the children were collecting for that purpose, excited general sympathy. As their teacher had not arrived, they were at play in the yard, and seeing the Negroes approach, she ran up on a dirt chimney (such as are common to log houses)[7] and remained there unnoticed during the massacre of the eleven that were killed at this place. She remained on her hiding place till just before the arrival of a party, who were in pursuit of the murderers, when she came down and fled to a swamp, where, a mere child as she was, with the horrors of the late scene before her, she lay concealed until the next day, when seeing a party go up to the house, she came up, and on being asked how she escaped, replied with the utmost simplicity, the Lord helped her. She was taken up behind a gentleman of the party, and returned to the arms of her weeping mother. Miss Whitehead concealed herself between the bed and the mat that supported it, while they murdered her sister in the same room, without discovering her. She was afterwards carried off, and concealed for protection by a slave of the family, who gave evidence against several of them on their trial. Mrs. Nathaniel Francis, while concealed in a closet, heard their blows, and the shrieks of the victims of these ruthless savages; they then entered the closet where she was concealed, and went out without discovering her. While in this hiding place, she heard two of her women in a quarrel about the division of her clothes. Mr. John T. Baron, discovering them approaching his house, told his wife to make her escape, and scorning to fly, fell fighting on his own threshold. After firing his rifle, he discharged his gun at them, and then broke it over the villain who first approached him, but he was overpowered and slain. His bravery, however, saved from the hands of these monsters, his lovely and amiable wife, who will long lament a husband so deserving of her love. As directed by him, she attempted to escape through the garden, when she was caught and held by one of her servant girls, but another coming to her rescue, she fled to the woods,

---

[7]A chimney laid up in sticks, log cabin fashion, and coated inside with mud so as to protect against fire.

and concealed herself. Few indeed, were those who escaped their work of death. But fortunate for society, the hand of retributive justice has overtaken them; and not one that was known to be concerned has escaped.

The Commonwealth,

vs.

Nat Turner

Charged with making insurrection, and plotting to take away the lives of divers free white persons, etc. on the 22d of August, 1831.

The court composed of ———, having met for the trial of Nat Turner, the prisoner was brought in and arraigned, and upon his arraignment pleaded *Not guilty*; saying to his counsel, that he did not feel so.

On the part of the Commonwealth, Levi Waller was introduced, who being sworn, deposed as follows: *(agreeably to Nat's own "Confession.")*[8] Colonel Trezvant was then introduced, who being sworn, narrated Nat's "Confession" to him, as follows: *(his "Confession" as given to Mr. Gray.)* The prisoner introduced no evidence, and the case was submitted without argument to the court, who having found him guilty, Jeremiah Cobb, Esq., chairman, pronounced the sentence of the court, in the following words: "Nat Turner! Stand up. Have you any thing to say why sentence of death should not be pronounced against you?"

Ans. "I have not. I have made a full confession to Mr. Gray, and I have nothing more to say."

"Attend then to the sentence of the court. You have been arraigned and tried before this court, and convicted of one of the highest crimes in our criminal code. You have been convicted of plotting in cold blood, the indiscriminate destruction of men, of helpless women, and of infant children. The evidence before us leaves not a shadow of doubt, but that your hands were often imbrued in the blood of the innocent, and your own confession tells us that they were stained with the blood of a master [who was], in your own language, too indulgent. Could I stop here, your crime would be sufficiently aggravated. But the original contriver of a plan, deep and deadly, one that never can be effected, you managed so far to put it into execution, as to deprive us of many of our most valuable citizens; and this was done when they were asleep, and defenseless, under circumstances shocking to humanity. And while upon this part of the subject, I cannot but call your attention to the poor misguided wretches who have gone before you. They are not few in number—they were your bosom associates; and the blood of all cries aloud, and calls upon you, as the author of their misfortune. Yes! You forced them unprepared, from time to eternity. Borne down by this load of guilt, your only justification is, that you were led away by fanaticism. If this be true, from my soul I pity you; and while

---

[8]That is, in this case and that of Magistrate Trezvant immediately following, the 1831 text does not give the testimony verbatim, but asserts that in each case it agreed essentially with the text of the preceding *Confessions.*

you have my sympathies, I am, nevertheless called upon to pass the sentence of the court. The time between this and your execution, will necessarily be very short, and your only hope must be in another world. The judgment of the court is, that you be taken hence to the jail from whence you came, thence to the place of execution, and on Friday next, between the hours of 10 A.M. and 2 P.M. be hung by the neck until you are dead! dead! dead! And may the Lord have mercy upon your soul."

A LIST OF PERSONS MURDERED IN THE INSURRECTION, ON THE 21ST AND 22ND OF AUGUST, 1831

Joseph Travers and wife and three children, Mrs. Elizabeth Turner, Hartwell Prebles, Sarah Newsome, Mrs. P. Reese and son William, Trajan Doyle, Henry Bryant and wife and child, and wife's mother, Mrs. Catharine Whitehead, son Richard and four daughters and grandchild, Salathiel Francis, Nathaniel Francis' overseer and two children, John T. Barrow, George Vaughan, Mrs. Levi Waller and ten children, William Williams, wife and two boys, Mrs. Caswell Worrell and child, Mrs. Rebecca Vaughan, Ann Eliza Vaughan, and son Arthur, Mrs. John K. Williams and child, Mrs. Jacob Williams and three children, and Edwin Drury—amounting to fifty-five.

7

THE SAC LEADER
HEADS EAST

BORN IN A SAC VILLAGE ALONG THE ROCK RIVER IN THE FUTURE STATE OF Illinois in 1767, Makataimeshekiakiak (known to European Americans as Black Hawk) grew up in a world that was rapidly changing. France had barely lost control of its tenuous "empire" in the upper Mississippi country at the conclusion of the Seven Years' War with Britain and its American colonies in 1763, and the fur trade it had carried on in the Great Lakes basin was in profound transition, with British and American investors vying with the old French merchants of Montreal for control of a vast hinterland whose Native American inhabitants had become more or less dependent on European trade goods. More changes rapidly followed. By the time Makataimeshekiakiak was fifteen, Britain had lost control of the lower reaches of his familiar world, though new rivalries with the United States government and with independent American traders along the upper lakes were to continue for decades. The Sac and their closely related Fox kin had been remote from the seat of the conflict during the American Revolution, but remoteness was now only a memory. By 1804, the aggressive Americans, having just purchased France's rights to Louisiana (preserved by a subterfuge from British control in 1763), had become a strong presence in the region. Illinois, no longer the outer limit of American territory, emerged as a way-station to an enormous new "West" quickly forming itself on the map and in the American mind.

William Henry Harrison (1773–1841), then governor of Indiana Territory but authorized by President Jefferson to deal broadly on questions of native lands and boundaries, forced a treaty of cession on the Sac and Fox in St. Louis on November 3rd, 1804, which in Black Hawk's later view would be "the origin of all [their] difficulties." Several of the peoples' leaders had gone to that old French city in order to resolve a fairly minor dispute, but in an atmosphere of mutual misunderstanding wound up agreeing to a cession of all tribal lands east of the Mississippi, including that on which Black Hawk's village stood. Because immediate withdrawal was not expected, at the time little disagreement arose; however, following the end of the War of 1812 the influx of Americans from the East and a large readjustment of Anglo-American tensions in the upper Midwest brought the issue to a head, and the United States government required compliance.

For Black Hawk, a minor political figure in his tribe but long recognized as a warrior, the troubles preceded the War of 1812. Unlike the powerful chief Keokuk, who was loyal to the United States during the war (even though he also did not like the 1804 treaty), Black Hawk sided with and fought for the British. Following the latter's defeat and the rising tide of American immigration, Keokuk favored appeasing the United States government by withdrawing across the Mississippi into Iowa. In violation of a treaty he himself signed in 1831, Black Hawk refused to abandon the Illinois country permanently, and early the next year organized a small band of his people and sought an alliance with the Winnebago, Potawatomi, and Kickapoo—as well as the British once more—so that he could dislodge the Americans from his ancestral lands. Chief Keokuk pleaded forcefully against the desperate intent of this "British band" of his people, and offered to go to Washington to negotiate a peaceful solution with the Jackson administration; former explorer and then Indian superintendent William Clark declined his offer. Black Hawk reentered Illinois in April, conducted a desultory war for the next fifteen weeks, and eventually was trapped at the juncture of Bad Axe River and the Mississippi, near present-day La Crosse, Wisconsin, as he sought to escape westward from pursuing American forces. By September a new treaty had been signed and sealed (with Keokuk: Black Hawk, jailed at Jefferson Barracks, Missouri, was not allowed to participate) and even more Sac and Fox land, this time in what was to become Iowa, fell into the hands of the government.

Black Hawk might have become an obscure footnote to history had the United States government not forced him to go east after his imprisonment, first to Washington (where he met and was impressed by Jackson, but also was held as a prisoner for a time), and then, as if to overwhelm him with the power and scope of the nation that had defeated him, on a tour through the great cities of the Northeast. The defeated warrior was duly affected: "astonished" by the size of Baltimore, "surprised" that Philadelphia was so much larger, and amazed by all he saw in New York, from a balloon ascension the first day to the fireworks at Castle Garden, the railroads, and everything else. While he did maintain his cultural distance, drawing some favorable comparisons between his people's ways and those of the Americans, his tour remains as one of the best-documented examples of how Americans used their material development as a potent argument against would-be opponents to their march across the continent.

And it is, in Black Hawk's case, the documentation that is especially important. When he returned to the Mississippi in the summer of 1833, he told the Sac and Fox interpreter, Franco-Potawatomi Antoine LeClaire (an associate of Clark and later a very wealthy man, whose face appeared on the first five-dollar bill issued in Iowa), that he wished to write his own history so that "the people of the United States . . . might know the *causes* that had impelled him to act as he had done, and the *principles* by which he was governed." LeClaire claimed that he interpreted Black Hawk's oral narrative as it was taken down, in English, by Virginia-born Illinois printer John B. Patterson. Some contemporaries doubted the book's authenticity, but LeClaire and Patterson staunchly defended it, as did James Hall, coauthor of the famous *History of the Indian Tribes of North America* (1836–40), who knew Black Hawk and wrote that the Sac himself had acknowledged the book's authenticity. While its style shows some attempt to make Black Hawk sound rough and "Indian" at times, and alternately shows a desire to make him seem "noble" by giving him locutions he certainly did not use (as he did not, after all, dictate it in English), the book has come to assume its proper place as the nearest thing to an autobiography that any Native American situated as Black Hawk was in 1833 could have produced. In the selections printed here, his account of the eastern "tour" offers fascinating commentary on the clash of worlds within which his whole life had been shaped. If Black Hawk was no Tecumseh, as historian Donald Jackson wrote in his new edition of the book, no great orator like Keokuk, and no great spiritual figure in Native American history, what he was is no less instructive: "a stubborn warrior brooding upon the certainty that his people must fight to survive." Although after his defeat in 1832 he no longer fought, he surely kept on brooding at his new home in Iowa, where he died in 1838.

BLACK HAWK

from Life of Makataimeshikiakiak or Black Hawk (1833)

ON OUR ARRIVAL AT JEFFERSON BARRACKS, WE MET THE GREAT WAR CHIEF, [White Beaver,] who had commanded the American army against my little band.[1] I felt the humiliation of my situation: a little while before, I had been the leader of my braves, now I was a prisoner of war! but had surrendered myself. He received us kindly, and treated us well.

We were now confined to the barracks, and forced to wear the ball and chain! This was extremely mortifying, and altogether useless. Was the White Beaver afraid that I would break out of his barracks, and run away? Or was he ordered to inflict this punishment upon me? If I had taken him prisoner on the

---

[1] The time was early autumn, 1832; Black Hawk and his party had just arrived at Jefferson Barracks, St. Louis, as prisoners under the conduct of Lieutenant Jefferson Davis (1808–1889). There they were turned over to the commander, General Henry Atkinson ("White Beaver," 1782–1842). There, too, the writer Washington Irving, on his way back from the prairies late in 1832, found the Sacs "a forlorn crew, emaciated and dejected" and Black Hawk "a meager old man upwards of seventy"—though he thought Black Hawk exhibited "a fine head, a Roman style of face, and a prepossessing countenance."

field of battle, I would not have wounded his feelings so much, by such treatment—knowing that a brave war chief would prefer death to dishonor! But I
do not blame the White Beaver for the course he pursued—it is the custom
among white soldiers, and, I suppose, was a part of his duty.

The time dragged heavily and gloomy along throughout the winter,
although the White Beaver [did] everything in his power to render us comfortable. Having been accustomed, throughout a long life, to roam the forests
o'er—to go and come at liberty—confinement, and under such circumstances,
could not be less than torture!

We passed away the time making pipes, until spring, when we were visited
by the agent, trader, and interpreter, from Rock Island, Keokuck,[2] and several
chiefs and braves of our nation, and my wife and daughter. I was rejoiced to
see the two latter, and spent my time very agreeably with them and my people,
as long as they remained.

The trader presented me with some dried venison, which had been killed
and cured by some of my friends. This was a valuable present; and although he
had given me many before, none ever pleased me so much. This was the first
meat I had eaten for a long time, that reminded me of the former pleasures of
my own wigwam, which had always been stored with plenty.

Keokuck and his chiefs, during their stay at the barracks, petitioned our
Great Father, the president, to release us, and pledged themselves for our good
conduct. I now began to hope that I would soon be restored to liberty, and the
enjoyment of my family and friends, having heard that Keokuck stood high in
the estimation of our Great Father, because he did not join me in the war. But
I was soon disappointed in my hopes. An order came from our Great Father to
the White Beaver, to send us on to Washington.

In a little while all were ready, and left Jefferson barracks on board of a
steamboat, under charge of a young war chief, whom the White Beaver sent
along as a guide to Washington. He carried with him an interpreter and one
soldier. On our way up the Ohio, we passed several large villages, the names of
which were explained to me. The first is called Louisville, and is a very pretty
village, situated on the bank of the Ohio River. The next is Cincinnati, which
stands on the bank of the same river. This is a large and beautiful village, and
seemed to be in a thriving condition. The people gathered on the bank as we
passed, in great crowds, apparently anxious to see us.

On our arrival at Wheeling, the streets and river's banks were crowded
with people, who flocked from every direction to see us. While we remained
here, many called upon us, and treated us with kindness—no one offering to
molest or misuse us. This village is not so large as either of those before mentioned, but is quite a pretty village.

We left the steamboat here, having travelled a long distance on the pretti-

---

[2] The trader was the English-born George Davenport (1783–1845), whose post was on Rock Island;
Sac leader Keokuk (ca. 1790–1842) consistently favored government policy.

est river (except our Mississippi) that I ever saw, and took the stage. Being unaccustomed to this mode of travelling, we soon got tired, and wished ourselves seated in a canoe on one of our own rivers, that we might return to our friends. We had travelled but a short distance, before our carriage turned over, from which I received a slight injury, and the soldier had one arm broken. I was sorry for this accident, as the young man had behaved well.

We had a rough and mountainous country for several days, but had a good trail for our carriage. It is astonishing to see what labor and pains the white people have had to make this road, as it passes over an immense number of mountains, which are generally covered with rocks and timber, yet it has been made smooth and easy to travel upon.[3]

Rough and mountainous as is this country, there are many wigwams and small villages standing on the roadside. I could see nothing in the country to induce the people to live in it, and was astonished to find so many whites living on the hills!

I have often thought of them since my return to my own people; and am happy to think that they prefer living in their *own* country, to coming out to *ours*, and driving us from it, that they might live upon and enjoy it—as many of the whites have already done. I think, with them, that wherever the Great Spirit places his people, they ought to be satisfied to remain, and thankful for what He has given them; and not drive others from the country He has given them, because it happens to be better than theirs! This is contrary to our way of thinking; and from my intercourse with the whites, I have learned that one great principle of their religion is, "to do unto others as you wish them to do unto you!" Those people in the mountains seem to act upon this principle; but the settlers on our frontiers and on our lands, seem never to think of it, if we are to judge by their actions.

The first village of importance that we came to, after leaving the mountains, is called Hagerstown. It is a large village to be so far from a river, and is very pretty. The people appear to live well, and enjoy themselves much.

We passed through several small villages on the way to Fredericktown,[4] but I have forgotten their names. This last is a large and beautiful village. The people treated us well, as they did at all the other villages where we stopped.

Here we came to another road, much more wonderful than that through the mountains. They call it a railroad! I examined it carefully, but need not describe it, as the whites know all about it. It is the most astonishing sight I ever saw. The great road over the mountains will bear no comparison to it— although it has given the white people much trouble to make. I was surprised to see so much labor and money expended to make a good road for easy travelling. I prefer riding on horseback, however, to any other way; but suppose that these people would not have gone to so much trouble and expense to make a

---

[3] Black Hawk is here describing the "National Road," which first reached Wheeling in 1818 from Cumberland, Maryland. In 1833, its western terminus was Columbus, Ohio.

[4] Frederick, Maryland, about fifty miles due west of Baltimore.

road, if they did not prefer riding in their new-fashioned carriages, which seem to run without any trouble. They certainly deserve great praise for their industry.

On our arrival at Washington, we called to see our Great Father, the president.[5] He looks as if he had seen as many winters as I have, and seems to be a great brave! I had very little talk with him, as he appeared to be busy, and did not seem much disposed to talk. I think he is a good man; and although he talked but little, he treated us very well. His wigwam is well furnished with everything good and pretty, and is very strongly built.

He said he wished to know the cause of my going to war against his white children. I thought he ought to have known this before; and, consequently, said but little to him about it—as I expected he knew as well as I could tell him.

He said he wanted us to go to Fortress Monroe, and stay awhile with the war chief who commanded it.[6] But, having been so long from my people, I told him that I would rather return to my nation—that Keokuck had come here once on a visit to see him, as we had done, and he let him return again, as soon as he wished; and that I expected to be treated in the same way. He insisted, however, on our going to Fortress Monroe, and as our interpreter could not understand enough of our language to interpret a speech, I concluded it was best to obey our Great Father, and say nothing contrary to his wishes.

During our stay at the city, we were called upon by many of the people, who treated us well, particularly the squaws! We visited the great council house of the Americans—the place where they keep their big guns—and all the public buildings, and then started to Fortress Monroe. The war chief met us, on our arrival, and shook hands, and appeared glad to see me. He treated us with great friendship, and talked to me frequently. Previous to our leaving this fort, he gave us a feast, and made us some presents, which I intend to keep for his sake. He is a very good man, and a great brave! I was sorry to leave him, although I was going to return to my people, because he had treated me like a brother during all the time I remained with him.

Having got a new guide, a war chief,[7] we started for our own country, taking a circuitous route. Our Great Father being about to pay a visit to his children in the big towns towards sunrising, and being desirous that we should have an opportunity of seeing them, directed our guide to take us through.

On our arrival at Baltimore, we were much astonished to see so large a village; but the war chief told us that we would soon see a *larger one*. This surprised us more. During our stay here, we visited all the public buildings and places of amusement, saw much to admire, and were well entertained by the people, who crowded to see us. Our Great Father was there at the same time, and seemed to be much liked by his white children, who flocked around him

[5] Andrew Jackson and Black Hawk were the same age.
[6] At Old Point Comfort, Hampton, Virginia; commanded at the time by Colonel Abraham Eustis, who had fought against the Sac in the war.
[7] Brevet Major John Garland.

(as they had done us) to shake him by the hand. He did not remain long, having left the city before us.

We left Baltimore in a steamboat, and travelled in this way to the big village, where they make medals and money.[8] We again expressed surprise at finding this village so much larger than the one we had left; but the war chief again told us, that we would soon see another much larger than this. I had no idea that the white people had such large villages, and so many people. They were very kind to us, showed us all their great public works, their ships and steamboats. We visited the place where they make money, and saw the men engaged at it. They presented each of us with a number of pieces of the coin as they fell from the mint, which are very handsome.

I witnessed a militia training in this city, in which were performed a number of singular military feats. The chiefs and men were well-dressed, and exhibited quite a warlike appearance. I think our system of military parade far better than that of the whites—but, as I am now done going to war, I will not describe it, or say anything more about war, or the preparations necessary for it.

We next started to New York, and on our arrival near the wharf, saw a large collection of people gathered at Castle Garden.[9] We had seen many wonderful sights in our way—large villages, the great national road over the mountains, the railroads, steam carriages, ships, steamboats, and many other things; but we were now about to witness a sight more surprising than any of these. We were told that a man was going up into the air in a balloon! We watched with anxiety to see if it could be true, and to our utter astonishment, saw him ascend in the air until the eye could no longer perceive him. Our people were all surprised, and one of our young men asked the prophet[1] if he was going up to see the Great Spirit?

After the ascension of the balloon, we landed, and got into a carriage, to go to the house that had been provided for our reception. We had proceeded but a short distance, before the street was so crowded that it was impossible for the carriage to pass. The war chief then directed the coachman to take another street, and stop at a different house from the one he had intended. On our arrival here, we were waited upon by a number of gentlemen, who seemed much pleased to see us. We were furnished with good rooms, good provisions, and everything necessary for our comfort.

The chiefs of this big village, being desirous that all their people should have an opportunity to see us, fitted up their great council house for this purpose, where we saw an immense number of people, all of whom treated us with friendship, and many with great generosity.

The chiefs were particular in showing us everything that they thought would be pleasing or gratifying to us. We went with them to Castle Garden to

[8] Philadelphia.
[9] This round masonry fort off the tip of Manhattan had become a key celebration ground for New Yorkers; it was here that Lafayette was received in 1824.
[1] Among those accompanying Black Hawk was Wabokieshiek or White Cloud, known as "the Prophet," half Sac and half Winnebago, known for his closeness to the spirit world.

see the fireworks, which was quite an agreeable entertainment—but to the whites who witnessed it, less magnificent than the sight of one of our large prairies would be when on fire.

We visited all the public buildings and places of amusement, which to us were truly astonishing, yet very gratifying.

Everybody treated us with friendship, and many with great liberality. The squaws presented us many handsome little presents, that are said to be valuable. They were very kind, very good, and very pretty—for palefaces!

Among the men who treated us with marked friendship, by the presentation of many valuable presents, I cannot omit to mention the name of my old friend, Crooks,[2] of the American Fur Company. I have known him long, and have always found him to be a good chief, one who gives good advice, and treats our people right. I shall always be proud to recognize him as a friend, and glad to shake him by the hand.

Having seen all the wonders of this big village, and being anxious to return to our people, our guide started with us for our own country. On arriving at Albany, the people were so anxious to see us, that they crowded the street and wharves, where the steamboat landed, so much, that it was almost impossible for us to pass to the hotel which had been provided for our reception.

We remained here but a short time, and then started for Detroit. I had spent many pleasant days at this place; and anticipated, on my arrival, to meet many of my old friends, but in this I was disappointed. What could be the cause of this? Are they all dead? Or what has become of them? I did not see our old father[3] there, who had always gave me good advice, and treated me with friendship.

After leaving Detroit, it was but a few days before we landed at Prairie du Chien. The war chief at the fort treated us very kindly, as did the people generally. I called on the father of the Winnebagoes, to whom I had surrendered myself after the battle at the Bad Axe, who received me very friendly.[4] I told him that I had left my great medicine bag with his chiefs before I gave myself up; and now that I was to enjoy my liberty again, I was anxious to get it, that I might hand it down to my nation unsullied!

He said it was safe; he had heard his chiefs speak of it, and would get it and send it to me. I hope he will not forget his promise, as the whites generally do, because I have always heard that he was a good man, and a good father and made no promises that he did not fulfill.

Passing down the Mississippi, I discovered a large collection of people in

[2] Scotsman Ramsay Crooks (1787–1859), partner of John Jacob Astor.
[3] Lewis Cass (1782–1866), governor of Michigan Territory, 1813–31, and Jackson's secretary of war, 1831–36.
[4] Joseph Montfort Street (1782–1840), agent to the Winnebago since 1827 and brigadier general in the Illinois militia, had been present at the Battle of Bad Axe (August 3, 1832) at the juncture of Bad Axe River and the Mississippi, which he described as follows; "The Indians were pushed literally into the Mississippi, the current of which was at one time perceptibly tinged with the blood of the Indians who were shot on its margin and in the stream."

the mining country, on the west side of the river, and on the ground that we had given to our relation, Dubuque,[5] a long time ago. I was surprised at this, as I had understood from our Great Father, that the Mississippi was to be the dividing line between his red and white children, and that he did not wish either to cross it. I was much pleased with this talk, as I knew that it would be much better for both parties. I have since found the country much settled by the whites further down, and near to our people, on the west side of the river. I am very much afraid, that in a few years, they will begin to drive and abuse our people, as they have formerly done. I may not live to see it, but I feel certain that the day is not distant.

When we arrived at Rock Island, Keokuck and the other chiefs were sent for. They arrived the next day with a great number of their young men, and came over to see me. I was pleased to see them, and they all appeared glad to see me. Among them were some who had lost relations during the war the year before. When we met, I perceived the tear of sorrow gush from their eyes at the recollection of their loss; yet they exhibited a smiling countenance, from the joy they felt at seeing me alive and well.

The next morning the war chief, our guide, convened a council at Fort Armstrong. Keokuck and his party went to the fort; but, in consequence of the war chief not having called for me to accompany him, I concluded that I would wait until I was sent for. Consequently the interpreter came, and said they were ready, and had been waiting for me to come to the fort. I told him I was ready, and would accompany him. On our arrival there, the council commenced. The war chief said that the object of this council was to deliver me up to Keokuck. He then read a paper, and directed me to follow Keokuck's advice, and be governed by his counsel in all things! In this speech he said much that was mortifying to my feelings, and I made an indignant reply.

I do not know what object the war chief had in making such a speech, or whether he intended what he said, but I do know, that it was uncalled for, and did not become him. I have addressed many war chiefs, and have listened to their speeches with pleasure—but never had my feelings of pride and honor insulted on any former occasion. I am sorry that I was so hasty in reply to this chief, because I said that which I did not intend.[6]

In this council, I met my old friend, a great war chief,[7] whom I had known about eighteen years. He is a good and brave chief. He always treated me well, and gave me good advice. He made a speech to me on this occasion, very different from that of the other chief. It sounded [as if it was] coming from a brave! He said he had known me a long time—that we had been good friends during that acquaintance—and, although he had fought against my braves, in

[5] Canadian-born Julien Dubuque (1762–1810) had established himself in Prairie du Chien in the 1780s and gained the permission of the Fox to work the lead deposits in Iowa in 1788.
[6] This was Major Garland, who later wrote that "Black Hawk showed some emotion" when Keokuk's authority was affirmed by the Americans, and rose in anger to speak passionately on the question, but could not continue, and later apologized.
[7] Colonel William Davenport, then commander of Fort Atkinson.

our late war, he still extended the hand of friendship to me, and hoped, that I was now satisfied, from what I had seen in my travels, that it was folly to think of going to war against the whites, and would ever remain at peace. He said he would be glad to see me at all times and on all occasions would be happy to give me good advice.

If our Great Father were to make such men our agents, he would much better serve the interests of our people, as well as his own, than in any other way. The war chiefs all know our people, and are respected by them. If the war chiefs, at the different military posts on the frontiers, were made agents, they could always prevent difficulties from arising among the Indians and whites; and I have no doubt, had the war chief above alluded to, been our agent, we never would have had the difficulties with the whites which we have had. Our agents ought always to be braves! I would, therefore, recommend to our Great Father, the propriety of breaking up the present Indian establishment, and creating a new one—and of making the commanding officers, at the different frontier posts, the agents of the government for the different nations of Indians.[8]

I have a good opinion of the American war chiefs, generally, with whom I am acquainted; and my people, who had an opportunity of seeing and becoming well acquainted with the great war chief who made the last treaty with them, in conjunction with the great chief of Illinois,[9] all tell me that he is the greatest brave they ever saw, and a good man—one who fulfills all his promises. Our braves speak more highly of him, than any chief that has ever been among us, or made treaties with us. Whatever he says, may be depended upon. If he had been our Great Father, we never would have been compelled to join the British in their last war with America—and I have thought that, as our Great Father is changed every few years, his children would do well to put this great war chief in his place as they cannot find a better chief for a Great Father anywhere.

I would be glad if the village criers in all the villages I passed through, would let their people know my wishes and opinions about this great war chief.

During my travels, my opinions were asked on different subjects, but for want of a good interpreter, were very seldom given. Presuming that they would be equally acceptable now, I have thought it a part of my duty, to lay the most important before the public.

The subject of colonizing the Negroes was introduced, and my opinion asked, as to the best method of getting clear of these people. I was not prepared, at the time, to answer, as I knew but little about their situation. I have since made many inquiries on the subject—and find that a number of states admit no slaves, whilst the balance hold these Negroes as slaves, and are anxious (but do not know how) to get clear of them. I will now give my plan, which, when understood, I hope will be adopted.

[8] This passage and the following paragraph nicely emphasize the complex attitude of Native leaders toward members of the U.S. army.
[9] John Reynolds (1788–1865), governor of Illinois 1830–34, also commanded the Illinois militia during the war.

Let the free states remove all the male Negroes within their limits, to the slave states—then let our Great Father buy all the female Negroes in the slave states, between the ages of twelve and twenty, and sell them to the people of the free states, for a term of years: say, those under fifteen, until they are twenty-one, and those of, and over fifteen, for five years; and continue to buy all the females in the slave states, as soon as they arrive at the age of twelve, and take them to the free states, and dispose of them in the same way as the first—and it will not be long before the country is clear of the black skins, about which, I am told, they have been talking, for a long time; and for which they have expended a large amount of money.

I have no doubt but our Great Father would willingly do his part in accomplishing this object for his children, as he could not lose much by it, and would make them all happy. If the free states did not want them all for servants, we would take the balance in our nation, to help our women make corn!

I have not time now, nor is it necessary, to enter more into detail about my travels through the United States. The white people know all about them, and my people have started to their hunting grounds, and I am anxious to follow them.

Before I take leave of the public, I must contradict the story of some village criers, who (I have been told,) accuse me of "having murdered women and children among the whites!" This assertion is false! I never did, nor have I any knowledge that any of my nation ever killed a white woman or child. I make this statement of truth, to satisfy the white people among whom I have been travelling (and by whom I have been treated with great kindness) that, when they shook me by the hand so cordially, they did not shake the hand that had ever been raised against any but warriors.

It has always been our custom to receive all strangers that come to our village or camps, in time of peace, to share with them the best provisions we have, and give them all the assistance in our power: if on a journey, or lost, to put them on the right trail; and if in want of moccasins, to supply them. I feel grateful to the whites for the kind manner they treated me and my party, whilst travelling among them—and from my heart I assure them, that the white man will always be welcome in our village or camps, as a brother. The tomahawk is buried forever! We will forget what has passed—and may the watchword between the Americans and Sacs and Foxes, ever be—"*Friendship!*"

I am now done. A few more moons, and I must follow my fathers to the shades! May the Great Spirit keep our people and the whites always at peace— is the sincere wish of

Black Hawk.

8

FOUR FOURTHS AND
FOUR NEW DECLARATIONS

THE NATIONAL FESTIVAL OF THE FOURTH OF JULY BEGAN TO BE OBSERVED EVEN during the Revolution, but it was the nineteenth century that converted the celebration into a pious occasion that the soldiers and victims of the American Revolution, the first American civil war, would not have recognized. Increasingly the Revolution was emerging in official rhetoric as a grand national moment that had given birth to America's touted freedoms. Events such as the return of Lafayette to America in 1824–25 and the widespread patriotic displays it encouraged helped solidify this image of the war in American minds. It was at a celebration of the Fourth in New York City in 1825, as noted in connection with Lafayette's tour, that the young Walt Whitman was swept up into a sense of nationalism that was never to leave him. Although American writers have not been particularly eager to sail their muse directly out upon the waters of the Fourth, much of their writing is saturated with its sentiment: It was on the Fourth, we recall, that Henry Thoreau went out to undertake his own, quieter revolution at Walden Pond.

If high art has been relatively absent on this national day, oratory has been drunk with its solemn excitement. Thousands upon thousands of Fourth of July orations have floated on the air and poured from the press seemingly everywhere—even among expatriate communities in Germany, Italy, Britain, and France, where the idea of American freedom was for obvious reasons rarefied and abstract. Along with other, more literally explosive sounds, the addresses served as the secular sermons of America's civil religion—that is, the body of beliefs, centered on liberal notions of political and economic rights, that in many ways bound together the otherwise heterogeneous mass.

But of course the heterogeneity resulted, in part, from the diverse states of freedom within the country. Freedom, contrary to much theory, was not an absolute principle that could exist in perfect abundance. Freedom as it evolved in practice in the United States in these years was contingent and relative, and it acted in the social marketplace like a commodity. Those who were free were so in part because others were not: Slave-owners enjoyed their exalted positions

419

precisely because their slaves were so debased from a civil point of view; Native Americans were removed from the East in large numbers and quite literally kept off the lands to which, afterwards, white men had enhanced access. The reality of freedom was that as a social principle it was inherently limited, and its limitations served certain interests and disserved others.

Not surprisingly, the standard Fourth of July oration did not dwell on the dynamics by which the free gained their privileges in America. At the same time, however, the Fourth of July became a natural occasion for measuring how close the nation had come in realizing its potential. Abolitionists such as Frederick Douglass (who in his famous 1852 speech "What to the Negro Is the Fourth of July?" asked difficult, pointed questions) punctured the pious balloon of America's liberal rhetoric. Even those with no overt political agenda could discuss the holiday with a certain amount of satire and irony in face-to-face addresses or in published accounts. Because the festival tended to be noisy, raucous, dangerous, fueled by alcohol and other dangerous chemicals such as gunpowder, its very excesses lent an air of sober truth to the most satiric of descriptions. Frontier realist Caroline Kirkland included in her quasi-fictional *Western Clearings* (1845) a piece entitled "A Forest Fete" that is rich with petty rivalries and bathos, and almost empty of nobility. She noted that "the passion for showing joy and gratitude through the medium of gunpowder seems to increase and strengthen with every recurrence of our national festival, till as much 'villainous saltpeter' is expended on a single celebration as would have sufficed our revolutionary forefathers to win a pitched battle." No idealists, her celebrants preferred a sail on "Onion Lake" to a reading of the Declaration of Independence. When those responsible for packing the boating party's picnic failed to coordinate their efforts, the heat melted enough of their butter "to have smoothed the lake in case of a tempest," while the celebrants, overstocked with "acres of pie," had "very few plates to eat it from; teakettles and teapots, but no cups and saucers." The effect resembles that of Grant Wood's tart painting of 1932, *Daughters of Revolution:* Wood's viewer is led to wonder whether his three self-satisfied women who peer out from in front of a small print of Leutze's famous *Washington Crossing the Delaware* are adequate to bear the burden of which they are so mindlessly proud.

The Fourth of July also provided the context for more searching critiques of the American "system." As Frederick Douglass did, countless other individuals and groups used the moment to measure America's potential against its actualities, its prescriptive documents against its descriptive realities. It was not just the occasion of the Fourth that provided a context for criticism in these other cases. Instead, the very documents at the core of national memory, the Constitution and especially the Declaration of Independence, became models for a reiteration of American ideals. Starting in the 1820s, a whole new genre of what we might call "re-declarations of independence" thus emerged, a genre that continues to flourish today. Although at times these redeclarations have had a lighter tone, in most instances the intent has been serious and the language formal. There is no unitary political slant to the effort: Northern abolitionists appealed to the founding documents as a justification of their cause, but so did Southern secessionists. In most cases, however, the very act of measuring contemporary conditions against the principles of the nation's founding documents implies a consistent utopian standard. In this world of imagined polities, the original documents provide a means for evoking a golden age in the future or, less often, the past. The four instances of the redeclaration genre given below thus present an array of more or less radical proposals urging the restoration or the extension of original promise.

These redeclarations derive from across the nineteenth century, but they reflect a pair of purposes for which the form was often employed: the rights of labor and the rights of women. In the first, published in 1829, the English radical George Henry Evans, who immigrated to the United States in 1820 and became the founder of the labor press here, probes how class issues—all but unstated in the original document—might be attended to. Evans, influenced by Thomas Paine's writings, sought to improve the lot of the ordinary worker, but shunned the means promoted by contemporary socialists, favoring instead the individualist assumptions already present in the Declaration of Independence. It is interesting in his case, as in the other three, to trace precisely how his own language interacts with that of the original. Quoting key phrases, Evans applied them to new purposes; he also inserted into the original text by judicious political editing a new agenda of issues. When the original twisted away from his purposes (as in his first two lines) he stopped quoting and rewrote the Jeffersonian document so as to force a new intention into its very text. By the end of the century, in the more radical text of labor activist Daniel De Leon, the disparity between the original text and his own aspirations was so great that Jefferson provided De Leon with only a point of departure: "When, in the course of human progression," De Leon's text begins, and from that point on a new ideology takes over and a new language replaces the old one almost completely. Still, it is intriguing that De Leon found the rhetoric of redeclaration fitting for his own purposes. So potent were the occasion and the act that even De Leon, a staunch socialist and thoroughgoing doctrinaire, found the opportunity to employ them irresistible. One of his real accomplishments in the American labor movement was to forge connections, previously overlooked, between a domestic radical tradition and European ideology, and how he did so can be seen in his own "Declaration of Interdependence."

Editor of the Socialist Labor party's paper, *The People*, De Leon published his text in the Fourth of July issue for 1895. In a great many instances, redeclarations have been timed to coincide with the great American holiday. As such, their very seriousness has tended to undercut (or perhaps deepen) the satire of Kirkland and others who emphasized the boozy mindlessness of the occasion. Even when the calendar has not been cooperative, however, the actual holiday always has been implicit in such declaratory acts, since the very posture of the speaker or writer and the language employed invoke it. The Seneca Falls women's rights convention of 1848 took place later in July, so an exact coincidence of its "Declaration of Sentiments and Resolutions" with the national fete that year was not possible, but the coincidence in mood and form remains unmistakable. Elizabeth Cady Stanton framed her text as a close updating of the original, following it line by line and phrase by phrase. Here one finds the revisionary intent at its best, with the stylistic alterations funded by a reenvisioning of the basic social contract on which the 1776 document was based. Particularly nice is Stanton's use of the bill of indictments portion of Jefferson's original, in which George III was charged with the crimes and misdeeds that became the justification for separation; by means of this close parody, Stanton could lay at the feet of *the* American "HE" a similar, and similarly disturbing, list of crimes. The Fourth of July hovers over the whole effort like a ritual moment rather than a secular holiday. By contrast, the "Declaration of Rights for Women" of 1876, although presented on July 4th, shows only the vaguest of connections to the original document. The committee bearing this "declaration" interrupted the august celebration of the centennial at Philadelphia in order to present the document publicly, but in the main its text paraphrased arguments in the 1776 one, or applied its doctrines to new circumstances rather than directly engaging it on a line-by-line basis. The 1848 and 1876 women's rights "Declarations" thus give a nice example of how wide the range of engagement with the Declaration of Independence could be.

Interspersed among the four redeclarations given here is a quartet of texts, including part of Frederick Douglass's, that depict in a variety of ways the nation's sacred holiday. The gathering tends toward the militant and the satiric. The Reverend Nathaniel Paul's July 5th address in Albany, New York, was in celebration not of the general holiday so much as the specific occasion associated with it that year: namely, the completion of New York's gradualist abolition of slavery. Oregon Trail pioneer Catherine Haun's narrative, written some years after her crossing with her family in 1849, tells of the celebration of her wagon party—consisting of a bit of pageantry, an attempt to recite the original Declaration (truncated by the fact that nobody could remember very much of the text), a couple of gunshots, songs, and something of an oration, all of it presided over by a most uncanny "Goddess of Liberty" in the person of a young woman named America West. Exercising a kind of tangible freedom, the Americans in Haun's narrative differed from Reverend Paul and Frederick Douglass, who probed the very roots of the American social contract and the ideology that it pretended to implement.

Perhaps the most fascinating of all these documents is that of the French baron Edmond Mandat-Grancey, who chanced to be in Deadwood City, South Dakota, during that town's amusing celebration of the national holiday in 1883. With the outsider's complete disregard for anything but the observably true, he nailed Americans dead to rights. His opening summary of the glorious Revolution shows his deflationary intent from the outset: "One hundred and seven years ago today the thirteen English colonies in America, feeling annoyed at the policy of the English minister, Lord North, in still compelling them to pay a petty duty on tea, proclaimed their independence"—an independence whose costs he goes on to detail in an equally maddening way. When, at the end of the selection, he floors a drunken cowboy who comes seeking him out, he suggests precisely his own general, pistol-toting take on American pretension. He could have found many other little episodes from his trip across the country from which to develop such themes, but his choice of the Fourth shows how that holiday was recognized as the very apex—or nadir—of American liberalism in the period. While it is tempting to dismiss Mandat-Grancey as a European aristocrat who came armed with intent into the western democracy, his book offers an intriguing glimpse into the diminished expectations many Americans themselves felt during the Gilded Age. Whereas Reverend Paul and Frederick Douglass both entertained the assumption that the ideals about which they had profound quarrels at least *mattered* to "free" Americans, the proto-populists of Mandat-Grancey's Deadwood had been diverted enough from previous ideals that monarchy, at least so he reports, was for some a viable option for the country. His irony, after all, reflects not just on his own reportage and angle of view; it reflects as well on an America where corruption (such as the "Star Routes" scandal he mentions) precisely underscored the relative nature of "freedom."

1827: ALBANY, NEW YORK

Rev. Nathaniel Paul, *from* An Address Delivered on the Celebration of the Abolition of Slavery . . . July 5, 1827

WE LOOK FORWARD WITH PLEASING ANTICIPATION TO THAT PERIOD, WHEN IT shall no longer be said that in a land of freemen there are men in bondage, but when this foul stain will be entirely erased, and this worst of evils will be forever done away. The progress of emancipation, though slow, is nevertheless certain. It is certain because that God who has made of one blood all nations of men, and who is said to be no respecter of persons, has so decreed; I therefore have no hesitation in declaring from this sacred place, that not only throughout the United States of America, but throughout every part of the habitable world where slavery exists, it will be abolished. However great may be the opposition of those who are supported by the traffic, yet slavery will cease. The lordly planter who has his thousands in bondage, may stretch himself upon his couch of ivory, and sneer at the exertions which are made by the humane and benevolent, or he may take his stand upon the floor of Congress, and mock the pitiful generosity of the East or West for daring to meddle with the subject, and attempting to expose its injustice; he may threaten to resist all efforts for a general or a partial emancipation even to a dissolution of the union. But still I declare that slavery will be extinct. A universal and not a partial emancipation must take place, nor is the period far distant.

The indefatigable exertions of the philanthropists in England to have it abolished in their West India islands, the recent revolutions in South America, the catastrope and exchange of power in the isle of Haiti, the restless disposition of both master and slave in the southern states, the constitution of our government, the effects of literary and moral instruction, the generous feelings of the pious and benevolent, the influence and spread of the holy religion of the cross of Christ, and the irrevocable decrees of Almighty God, all combine their efforts and with united voice declare, that the power of tyranny must be subdued, the captive must be liberated, the oppressed go free, and slavery must revert back to its original chaos of darkness, and be forever annihilated from the earth.

Did I believe that it would always continue, and that man to the end of time would be permitted with impunity to usurp the same undue authority over his fellow, I would disallow any allegiance or obligation I was under to my fellow creatures, or any submission that I owed to the laws of my country. I would deny the superintending power of divine providence in the affairs of this life. I would ridicule the religion of the Savior of the world, and treat as the worst of men the ministers of an everlasting gospel. I would consider my Bible as a book of false and delusive fables, and commit it to the flames. Nay, I would still go farther; I would at once confess myself an atheist, and deny the existence of a holy God. But slavery will cease, and the equal rights of man will be universally acknowledged. Nor is its tardy progress any argument against its final accomplishment. But do I hear it loudly responded—this is but a mere wild fanaticism, or at best but the misguided conjecture of an untutored descendant of Africa. Be it so, I confess my ignorance, and bow with due deference to my superiors in understanding; but if in this case I err, the error is not peculiar to myself. If I wander, I wander in a region of light from whose political hemisphere the sun of liberty pours forth his refulgent rays, around which dazzle the star-like countenances of Clarkson, Wilberforce, Pitt, Fox and Grenville, Washington, Adams, Jefferson, Hancock and Franklin;[1] if I err, it is their sentiments that have caused me to stray. . . .

We do well to remember, that every act of ours is more or less connected with the general cause of emancipation. Our conduct has an important bearing, not only on those who are yet in bondage in this country, but its influence is extended to the isles of India, and to every part of the world where the abomination of slavery is known. Let us then relieve ourselves from the odious

---

[1] The first five of these figures were the British abolitionist Thomas Clarkson (1760–1846); British statesman William Wilberforce (1759–1833), who won abolition of the slave trade in Parliament in 1807; William Pitt the Younger (1759–1806), British prime minister who supported Wilberforce's early efforts at abolishing the slave trade; British statesman Charles James Fox (1749–1806), also an abolitionist; and William Wyndham Grenville (1759–1834), who as leader of the coalition government formed after Pitt's death in 1806 saw to the passage of the Wilberforce abolition bill. Reverend Paul also shrewdly picked Britons who in many cases had favored the American side in the Revolution.

stigma which some have long since cast upon us, that we were incapacitated by the God of nature, for the enjoyment of the rights of freemen, and convince them and the world that although our complexion may differ, yet we have hearts susceptible of feeling; judgment capable of discerning, and prudence sufficient to manage our affairs with discretion, and by example prove ourselves worthy the blessings we enjoy.

1829: NEW YORK CITY

George Henry Evans, "The Working Men's Declaration of Independence"

"WHEN, IN THE COURSE OF HUMAN EVENTS, IT BECOMES NECESSARY" FOR ONE class of a community to assert their natural and unalienable rights in opposition to other classes of their fellow men, "and to assume among" them a political "station of equality to which the laws of nature and of nature's God," as well as the principles of their political compact, "entitle them; a decent respect to the opinions of mankind," and the more paramount duty they owe to their own fellow citizens, "requires that they should declare the causes which impel them" to adopt so painful, yet so necessary, a measure.

"We hold these truths to be self-evident, that all men are *created equal*; that they are endowed by their creator with certain unalienable rights; that among these are *life, liberty,* and the *pursuit of happiness*; that to secure these rights" against the undue influence of other classes of society, prudence, as well as the claims of self-defence, dictates the necessity of the organization of a party, who shall, by their representatives, prevent dangerous combinations to subvert these indefeasible and fundamental privileges. "All experience hath shown, that mankind" in general, and *we as a class in particular,* "are more disposed to suffer, while evils are sufferable, than to right themselves," by an opposition which the pride and self interest of unprincipled political aspirants, with more unprincipled zeal or religious bigotry, will wilfully misrepresent. "But when a long train of abuses and usurpations" take place, all invariably tending to the oppression and degradation of one class of society, and to the unnatural and iniquitous exaltation of another by political leaders, "it is their right, it is their duty," to use every constitutional means to *reform* the abuses of such a govern-ment, and to provide new guards for their future security. The history of the political *parties* in this state, is a history of political *iniquities,* all tending to the enacting and enforcing oppressive and unequal laws. To prove this, let facts be submitted to the candid and impartial of our fellow citizens of all parties.

1. The laws for levying taxes are all based on erroneous principles, in con-sequence of their operating most oppressively on one class of society, and being scarcely felt by the other.

2. The laws regarding the duties of jurors, witnesses, and militia trainings,[2] are still more unequal and oppressive.

3. The laws for private incorporations are all partial in their operations; favoring one class of society to the expense of the other, who have no equal participation.

4. The laws incorporating religious societies have a pernicious tendency, by promoting the erection of magnificent places of public worship by the rich, [which exclude] others and which others cannot imitate; consequently engendering spiritual pride in the clergy and people, and thereby creating odious distinctions in society, destructive to its social peace and happiness.

5. The laws establishing and patronizing seminaries of learning are unequal, favoring the rich, and perpetuating imparity,[3] which natural causes have produced, and which judicious laws ought, and can, remedy.

6. The laws and municipal ordinances and regulations, generally, besides those specially enumerated, have heretofore been ordained on such principles, as have deprived nine-tenths of the members of the body politic, who are *not* wealthy, of the *equal means* to enjoy *"life, liberty, and the pursuit of happiness,"* which the *rich* enjoy exclusively; but [which] the federative compact[4] intended to secure to all, indiscriminately. The lien law in favor of landlords against tenants,[5] and all other honest creditors, is one illustration among innumerable others which can be adduced to prove the truth of these allegations.

We have trusted to the influence of the justice and good sense of our political leaders, to prevent the continuance of these abuses, which destroy the natural bands[6] of equality so essential to the attainment of moral happiness, "but they have been deaf to the voice of justice and of consanguinity."

Therefore, we, the working class of society, of the city of New York, "appealing to the supreme judge of the world," and to the reason, and consciences of the impartial of all parties, "for the rectitude of our intentions, do, in the spirit, and by the authority," of that political liberty which has been promised to us equally with our fellow men, solemnly publish and declare, and invite all under like pecuniary circumstances, together with every liberal mind, to join us in the declaration, "that we are, and of right ought to be," entitled to EQUAL MEANS to obtain equal moral happiness, and social enjoyment, and that all lawful and constitutional measures ought to be adopted to the attainment of those objects. "And for the support of this declaration, we mutually pledge to each other" our faithful aid to the end of our lives.

---

[2] Laws requiring compulsory annual militia service or the payment of a fine had unequal impact on the poor and the rich.

[3] I.e., inequality.

[4] I.e., the United States Constitution.

[5] Under the terms of leases that were common in New York prior to the revision of the state constitution in the 1840s, manorial landlords had the right to confiscate tenants' property to recover payments due to them.

[6] Bonds.

Elizabeth Cady Stanton, "Declaration of Sentiments and Resolutions"

DECLARATION OF SENTIMENTS

WHEN, IN THE COURSE OF HUMAN EVENTS, IT BECOMES NECESSARY FOR ONE portion of the family of man to assume among the people of the earth a position different from that which they have hitherto occupied, but one to which the laws of nature and of nature's God entitle them, a decent respect to the opinions of mankind requires that they should declare the causes that impel them to such a course.

We hold these truths to be self-evident: that all men and women are created equal; that they are endowed by their Creator with certain inalienable rights; that among these are life, liberty, and the pursuit of happiness; that to secure these rights governments are instituted, deriving their just powers from the consent of the governed. Whenever any form of government becomes destructive of these ends, it is the right of those who suffer from it to refuse allegiance to it, and to insist upon the institution of a new government, laying its foundation on such principles, and organizing its powers in such form, as to them shall seem most likely to effect their safety and happiness. Prudence, indeed, will dictate that governments long established should not be changed for light and transient causes; and accordingly all experience hath shown that mankind are more disposed to suffer, while evils are sufferable, than to right themselves by abolishing the forms to which they were accustomed. But when a long train of abuses and usurpations, pursuing invariably the same object evinces a design to reduce them under absolute despotism, it is their duty to throw off such government, and to provide new guards for their future security. Such has been the patient sufferance of the women under this government, and such is now the necessity which constrains them to demand the equal station to which they are entitled.

The history of mankind is a history of repeated injuries and usurpations on the part of man toward woman, having in direct object the establishment of an absolute tyranny over her. To prove this, let facts be submitted to a candid world.

He has never permitted her to exercise her inalienable right to the elective franchise.

He has compelled her to submit to laws, in the formation of which she had no voice.

He has withheld from her rights which are given to the most ignorant and degraded men—both natives and foreigners.

Having deprived her of this first right of a citizen, the elective franchise, thereby leaving her without representation in the halls of legislation, he has oppressed her on all sides.

He has made her, if married, in the eye of the law, civilly dead.

He has taken from her all right in property, even to the wages she earns.

He has made her, morally, an irresponsible being, as she can commit many crimes with impunity, provided they be done in the presence of her husband. In the covenant of marriage, she is compelled to promise obedience to her husband, he becoming, to all intents and purposes, her master—the law giving him power to deprive her of her liberty, and to administer chastisement.

He has so framed the laws of divorce, as to what shall be the proper causes, and in case of separation, to whom the guardianship of the children shall be given, as to be wholly regardless of the happiness of women—the law, in all cases, going upon a false supposition of the supremacy of man, and giving all power into his hands.

After depriving her of all rights as a married woman, if single, and the owner of property, he has taxed her to support a government which recognizes her only when her property can be made profitable to it.

He has monopolized nearly all the profitable employments, and from those she is permitted to follow, she receives but a scanty remuneration. He closes against her all the avenues to wealth and distinction which he considers most honorable to himself. As a teacher of theology, medicine, or law, she is not known.

He has denied her the facilities for obtaining a thorough education, all colleges being closed against her.

He allows her in church, as well as state, but a subordinate position, claiming apostolic authority for her exclusion from the ministry, and, with some exceptions, from any public participation in the affairs of the church.

He has created a false public sentiment by giving to the world a different code of morals for men and women, by which moral delinquencies which exclude women from society, are not only tolerated, but deemed of little account in man.

He has usurped the prerogative of Jehovah himself, claiming it as his right to assign for her a sphere of action, when that belongs to her conscience and to her God.

He has endeavored, in every way that he could, to destroy her confidence in her own powers, to lessen her self-respect, and to make her willing to lead a dependent and abject life.

Now, in view of this entire disfranchisement of one-half the people of this country, their social and religious degradation—in view of the unjust laws above mentioned, and because women do feel themselves aggrieved, oppressed, and fraudulently deprived of their most sacred rights, we insist that they have immediate admission to all the rights and privileges which belong to them as citizens of the United States.

In entering upon the great work before us, we anticipate no small amount of misconception, misrepresentation, and ridicule; but we shall use every instrumentality within our power to effect our object. We shall employ agents, circulate tracts, petition the state and national legislatures, and endeavor to enlist the pulpit and the press in our behalf. We hope this convention will be followed by a series of conventions embracing every part of the country.

RESOLUTIONS

WHEREAS, THE GREAT PRECEPT OF NATURE IS CONCEDED TO BE, THAT "MAN shall pursue his own true and substantial happiness." Blackstone in his *Commentaries*[7] remarks, that this law of nature being coeval with mankind, and dictated by God himself, is of course superior in obligation to any other. It is binding over all the globe, in all countries and at all times; no human laws are of any validity if contrary to this, and such of them as are valid, derive all their force, and all their validity, and all their authority, mediately and immediately, from this original; therefore,

Resolved, That such laws as conflict, in any way, with the true and substantial happiness of woman, are contrary to the great precept of nature and of no validity, for this is "superior in obligation to any other."

Resolved, That all laws which prevent woman from occupying such a station in society as her conscience shall dictate, or which place her in a position inferior to that of man, are contrary to the great precept of nature, and therefore of no force or authority.

Resolved, That woman is man's equal—was intended to be so by the Creator, and the highest good of the race demands that she should be recognized as such.

Resolved, That the women of this country ought to be enlightened in regard to the laws under which they live, that they may no longer publish[8] their degradation by declaring themselves satisfied with their present position, nor their ignorance, by asserting that they have all the rights they want.

Resolved, That inasmuch as man, while claiming for himself intellectual superiority, does accord to woman moral superiority, it is pre-eminently his duty to encourage her to speak and teach, as she has an opportunity, in all religious assemblies.

Resolved, That the same amount of virtue, delicacy, and refinement of behavior that is required of woman in the social state, should also be required of man, and the same transgressions should be visited with equal severity on both man and woman.

Resolved, That the objection of indelicacy and impropriety, which is so often brought against woman when she addresses a public audience, comes with a very ill grace from those who encourage, by their attendance, her appearance on the stage, in the concert, or in feats of the circus.

---

[7] William Blackstone (1723–1780) published his very influential *Commentaries on the Laws of England* from 1765 to 1769.
[8] I.e., publicly acknowledge.

Resolved, That woman has too long rested satisfied in the circumscribed limits which corrupt customs and a perverted application of the scriptures have marked out for her, and that it is time she should move in the enlarged sphere which her great Creator has assigned her.

Resolved, That it is the duty of the women of this country to secure to themselves their sacred right to the elective franchise.

Resolved, That the equality of human rights results necessarily from the fact of the identity of the race in capabilities and responsibilities.

Resolved, therefore, That, being invested by the Creator with the same capabilities, and the same consciousness of responsibility for their exercise, it is demonstrably the right and duty of woman, equally with man, to promote every righteous cause by every righteous means; and especially in regard to the great subjects of morals and religion, it is self-evidently her right to participate with her brother in teaching them, both in private and in public, by writing and by speaking, by any instrumentalities proper to be used, and in any assemblies proper to be held; and this being a self-evident truth growing out of the divinely implanted principles of human nature, any custom or authority adverse to it, whether modern or wearing the hoary sanction of antiquity, is to be regarded as a self-evident falsehood, and at war with mankind.

1849: LARAMIE RIVER, WYOMING

Catherine Haun, *from* "A Woman's Trip Across the Plains"

IT WAS THE FOURTH OF JULY WHEN WE REACHED THE BEAUTIFUL LARAMIE River. Its sparkling, pure waters were full of myriads of fish that could be caught with scarcely an effort. It was necessary to build barges to cross the river and during the enforced delay our animals rested and we had one of our periodical "house cleanings." This general systematic readjustment always freshened up our wagon train very much, for after a few weeks of travel things got mixed up and untidy and often wagons had to be abandoned if too worn for repairs, and generally one or more animals had died or been stolen.

After dinner that night it was proposed that we celebrate the day and we all heartily joined in. America West was the Goddess of Liberty,[9] Charles Wheeler was orator and Ralph Cushing acted as master of ceremonies. We sang patriotic songs, repeated what little we could of the Declaration of Independence, fired off a gun or two, and gave three cheers for the United States and California Territory in particular!

---

[9] Unlikely as it sounds, America West was the name of a eighteen-year-old fellow emigrant on Haun's journey, the daughter of a couple from Peoria, Illinois.

The young folks decorated themselves in all manner of fanciful and grotesque costumes—Indian characters being most popular. To the rollicking
music of violin and Jew's harp we danced until midnight. There were Indian
spectators, all bewildered by the (to them) weird war dance of the Pale Face
and possibly they deemed it advisable to sharpen up their arrow heads. During
the frolic when the sport was at its height a strange white woman with a little
girl in her sheltering embrace rushed into the corral. She was trembling with
terror, tottering with hunger. Her clothing was badly torn and her hair dishev-
eled. The child crouched with fear and hid her face within the folds of her
mother's tattered skirt. The woman could give no account of her forlorn condition but was only able to sob: "Indians," and "I have no body nor place to go
to." After she had partaken of food and was refreshed by a safe night's rest she
recovered and the next day told us that her husband and sister had contracted
cholera[1] on account of which her family, consisting of husband, brother, sister,
herself and two children, had stayed behind their train. The sick ones died and
while burying the sister the survivors were attacked by Indians, who, as she
supposed, killed her brother and little son. She was obliged to flee for her life,
dragging with her the little five-year-old daughter.

She had been three days walking back to meet a train. It had been necessary, in order to avoid Indians, to conceal herself behind trees or boulders much
of the time and although she had seen a train in the distance before ours she
feared passing the Indians that were between the emigrants and herself. She
had been obliged to go miles up the Laramie to find a place where she could
get across by wading from rock to rock and the swift current had lamed her and
bruised her body.

Raw fish that she had caught with her hands and a squirrel that she killed
with a stone had been their only food. Our noise and campfire had attracted
her and in desperation she braved the Indians around us and trusting to the
darkness ventured to enter our camp. Martha, for that was her name, had emigrated from Wisconsin and pleaded with us to send her home; but we had now
gone too far on the road to meet returning emigrants so there was no alternative
for her but to accept our protection and continue on to California. When she
became calm and somewhat reconciled to so long and uncertain a journey
with strangers she made herself useful and loyally cast her lot with us. She
assisted me with the cooking for her board; found lodgings with the woman
whose husband was a cripple and in return helped the brave woman drive the
ox team. Mr. and Mrs. Lamore kept her little girl with their own. . . .

---

[1] Fast-acting Asiatic cholera, first noted in this country in 1832, broke out again in 1848 and at the
time Haun migrated (1849) was a serious threat to overland emigrants. Some wagon trains that
year lost two-thirds of their members, and overall the mortality may have been as high as 6
percent. Disease and accident remained the leading causes of death among all emigrants across
the plains.

1852: ROCHESTER, NEW YORK

Frederick Douglass, *from* "What to the Slave Is the Fourth of July?"

FELLOW CITIZENS: PARDON ME, AND ALLOW ME TO ASK, WHY AM I CALLED UPON to speak here today? What have I or those I represent to do with your national independence? Are the great principles of political freedom and of natural justice, embodied in that Declaration of Independence, extended to us? And am I, therefore, called upon to bring our humble offering to the national altar, and to confess the benefits, and express devout gratitude for the blessings resulting from your independence to us?

Would to God, both for your sakes and ours, that an affirmative answer could be truthfully returned to these questions. Then would my task be light, and my burden easy and delightful. For who is there so cold that a nation's sympathy could not warm him? Who so obdurate and dead to the claims of gratitude, that would not thankfully acknowledge such priceless benefits? Who so stolid and selfish that would not give his voice to swell the hallelujahs of a nation's jubilee, when the chains of servitude had been torn from his limbs? I am not that man. In a case like that, the dumb might eloquently speak, and the "lame man leap like a hart."[2]

But such is not the state of the case. I say it with a sad sense of disparity between us. I am not included within the pale of this glorious anniversary! Your high independence only reveals the immeasurable distance between us. The blessings in which you this day rejoice are not enjoyed in common. The rich inheritance of justice, liberty, prosperity, and independence bequeathed by your fathers is shared by you, not by me. The sunlight that brought life and healing to you has brought stripes and death to me. This Fourth of July is *yours*, not *mine. You* may rejoice, *I* must mourn. To drag a man in fetters into the grand illuminated temple of liberty, and call upon him to join you in joyous anthems, were inhuman mockery and sacrilegious irony. Do you mean, citizens, to mock me, by asking me to speak today? If so, there is a parallel to your conduct. And let me warn you, that it is dangerous to copy the example of a nation whose crimes, towering up to heaven, were thrown down by the breath of the Almighty, burying that nation in irrecoverable ruin. I can today take up the lament of a peeled and woe-smitten people.[3]

"By the rivers of Babylon, there we sat down. Yea! We wept when we remembered Zion. We hanged our harps upon the willows in the midst thereof.

---

[2] Isaiah 35:6.

[3] See Isaiah 18:2, "Go, ye swift messengers, to a nation scattered and peeled, to a people terrible from their beginning hitherto; a nation meted out and trodden down, whose land the rivers have spoiled!" (More recent translations offer quite different readings—for instance, the *New English Bible* speaks of "a people tall and smooth-skinned, a people dreaded near and far, a nation strong and proud, whose land is scoured by rivers").

For there they that carried us away captive, required of us a song; and they who wasted us, required of us mirth, saying, 'Sing us one of the songs of Zion'. How can we sing the Lord's song in a strange land? If I forget thee, O Jerusalem, let my right hand forget her cunning. If I do not remember thee, let my tongue cleave to the roof of my mouth."[4]

Fellow citizens, above your national, tumultuous joy, I hear the mournful wail of millions, whose chains, heavy and grievous yesterday, are today rendered more intolerable by the jubilant shouts that reach them. If I do forget, if I do not remember those bleeding children of sorrow this day, "may my right hand forget her cunning, and may my tongue cleave to the roof of my mouth!" To forget them, to pass lightly over their wrongs, and to chime in with the popular theme, would be treason most scandalous and shocking, and would make me a reproach before God and the world. My subject, then, fellow citizens, is "American Slavery." I shall see this day and its popular characteristics from the slave's point of view. Standing here, identified with the American bondman, making his wrongs mine, I do not hesitate to declare, with all my soul, that the character and conduct of this nation never looked blacker to me than on this Fourth of July. Whether we turn to the declarations of the past, or to the professions of the present, the conduct of the nation seems equally hideous and revolting. America is false to the past, false to the present, and solemnly binds herself to be false to the future. Standing with God and the crushed and bleeding slave on this occasion, I will, in the name of humanity, which is outraged, in the name of liberty, which is fettered, in the name of the Constitution and the Bible, which are disregarded and trampled upon, dare to call in question and to denounce, with all the emphasis I can command, everything that serves to perpetuate slavery—the great sin and shame of America! "I will not equivocate; I will not excuse";[5] I will use the severest language I can command, and yet not one word shall escape me that any man, whose judgment is not blinded by prejudice, or who is not at heart a slave-holder, shall not confess to be right and just.

But I fancy I hear some of my audience say it is just in this circumstance that you and your brother abolitionists fail to make a favorable impression on the public mind. Would you argue more and denounce less, would you persuade more and rebuke less, your cause would be much more likely to succeed. But, I submit, where all is plain there is nothing to be argued. What point in the antislavery creed would you have me argue? On what branch of the subject do the people of this country need light? Must I undertake to prove that the slave is a man? That point is conceded already. Nobody doubts it. The slave-holders themselves acknowledge it in the enactment of laws for their govern-

---

[4] Psalms 137:1–6. See also verses 8 and 9, surely in Douglass's mind: "O daughter of Babylon, who art to be destroyed: happy shall he be, that rewardeth thee as thou hast served us. Happy shall he be, that taketh and dasheth thy little ones against the stones."

[5] From a famous utterance of William Lloyd Garrison (1805–1879) in the first issue of his abolitionist paper, *The Liberator* (1831–65): "I am in earnest—I will not equivocate—I will not excuse—I will not retreat a single inch—and *I will be heard*."

ment. They acknowledge it when they punish disobedience on the part of the slave. There are seventy-two crimes in the state of Virginia, which, if committed by a black man (no matter how ignorant he be), subject him to the punishment of death; while only two of these same crimes will subject a white man to like punishment. What is this but the acknowledgment that the slave is a moral, intellectual, and responsible being? The manhood of the slave is conceded. It is admitted in the fact that Southern statute-books are covered with enactments, forbidding, under severe fines and penalties, the teaching of the slave to read and write. When you can point to any such laws in reference to the beasts of the field, then I may consent to argue the manhood of the slave. When the dogs in your streets, when the fowls of the air, when the cattle on your hills, when the fish of the sea, and the reptiles that crawl, shall be unable to distinguish the slave from a brute, then I will argue with you that the slave is a man!

For the present it is enough to affirm the equal manhood of the Negro race. Is it not astonishing that, while we are plowing, planting, and reaping, using all kinds of mechanical tools, erecting houses, constructing bridges, building ships, working in metals of brass, iron, copper, silver, and gold; that while we are reading, writing, and ciphering,[6] acting as clerks, merchants, and secretaries, having among us lawyers, doctors, ministers, poets, authors, editors, orators, and teachers; that while we are engaged in all the enterprises common to other men—digging gold in California, capturing the whale in the Pacific, feeding sheep and cattle on the hillside, living, moving, acting, thinking, planning, living in families as husbands, wives, and children, and above all, confessing and worshipping the Christian God, and looking hopefully for life and immortality beyond the grave—we are called upon to prove that we are men?

Would you have me argue that man is entitled to liberty? That he is the rightful owner of his own body? You have already declared it. Must I argue the wrongfulness of slavery? Is that a question for republicans? Is it to be settled by the rules of logic and argumentation, as a matter beset with great difficulty, involving a doubtful application of the principle of justice, hard to understand? How should I look today in the presence of Americans, dividing and subdividing a discourse, to show that men have a natural right to freedom, speaking of it relatively and positively, negatively and affirmatively? To do so would be to make myself ridiculous, and to offer an insult to your understanding. There is not a man beneath the canopy of heaven who does not know that slavery is wrong *for him.*

What! Am I to argue that it is wrong to make men brutes, to rob them of their liberty, to work them without wages, to keep them ignorant of their relations to their fellow men, to beat them with sticks, to flay their flesh with the lash, to load their limbs with irons, to hunt them with dogs, to sell them at auction, to sunder their families, to knock out their teeth, to burn their flesh, to starve them into obedience and submission to their masters? Must I argue that a system thus marked with blood and stained with pollution is wrong? No;

---

[6]I.e., calculating.

I will not. I have better employment for my time and strength than such arguments would imply.

What, then, remains to be argued? Is it that slavery is not divine; that God did not establish it; that our doctors of divinity are mistaken? There is blasphemy in the thought. That which is inhuman cannot be divine. Who can reason on such a proposition? They that can, may; I cannot. The time for such argument is past.

At a time like this, scorching irony, not convincing argument, is needed. Oh! had I the ability, and could I reach the nation's ear, I would today pour out a fiery stream of biting ridicule, blasting reproach, withering sarcasm, and stern rebuke. For it is not light that is needed, but fire; it is not the gentle shower, but thunder. We need the storm, the whirlwind, and the earthquake. The feeling of the nation must be quickened; the conscience of the nation must be roused; the propriety of the nation must be startled; the hypocrisy of the nation must be exposed; and its crimes against God and man must be denounced.

What to the American slave is your Fourth of July? I answer, a day that reveals to him more than all other days of the year, the gross injustice and cruelty to which he is the constant victim. To him your celebration is a sham; your boasted liberty an unholy license; your national greatness, swelling vanity; your sounds of rejoicing are empty and heartless; your denunciation of tyrants, brass-fronted impudence; your shouts of liberty and equality, hollow mockery; your prayers and hymns, your sermons and thanksgivings, with all your religious parade and solemnity, are to him mere bombast, fraud, deception, impiety, and hypocrisy—a thin veil to cover up crimes which would disgrace a nation of savages. There is not a nation of the earth guilty of practices more shocking and bloody than are the people of these United States at this very hour.

Go where you may, search where you will, roam through all the monarchies and despotisms of the Old World, travel through South America, search out every abuse and when you have found the last, lay your facts by the side of the everyday practices of this nation, and you will say with me that, for revolting barbarity and shameless hypocrisy, America reigns without a rival.

1876: PHILADELPHIA

National Woman Suffrage Association, "Declaration of Rights for Women"

WHILE THE NATION IS BUOYANT WITH PATRIOTISM, AND ALL HEARTS ARE attuned to praise, it is with sorrow we come to strike the one discordant note, on this one-hundredth anniversary of our country's birth. When subjects of kings, emperors, and czars, from the old world join in our national jubilee, shall the women of the republic refuse to lay their hands with benedictions on the nation's head? Surveying America's exposition, surpassing in magnificence those of London, Paris, and Vienna, shall we not rejoice at the success of the youngest rival among the nations of the earth? May not our hearts, in unison with all, swell with pride at our great achievements as a people; our free speech, free press, free schools, free church, and the rapid progress we have made in material wealth, trade, commerce and the inventive arts? And we do rejoice in the success, thus far, of our experiment of self-government. Our faith is firm and unwavering in the broad principles of human rights proclaimed in 1776, not only as abstract truths, but as the cornerstones of a republic. Yet we cannot forget, even in this glad hour, that while all men of every race, and clime, and condition, have been invested with the full rights of citizenship under our hospitable flag, all women still suffer the degradation of disfranchisement.

The history of our country the past hundred years has been a series of assumptions and usurpations of power over woman, in direct opposition to the principles of just government, acknowledged by the United States as its foundation, which are:

First—The natural rights of each individual.

Second—The equality of these rights.

Third—That rights not delegated are retained by the individual.

Fourth—That no person can exercise the rights of others without delegated authority.

Fifth—That the non-use of rights does not destroy them.

And for the violation of these fundamental principles of our government, we arraign our rulers on this Fourth day of July, 1876—and these are our articles of impeachment:

Bills of attainder[7] have been passed by the introduction of the word "male" into all the state constitutions, denying to women the right of suffrage, and thereby making sex a crime—an exercise of power clearly forbidden in article I, sections 9, 10, of the United States Constitution.

The writ of habeas corpus, the only protection against *lettres de cachet*[8] and all forms of unjust imprisonment, which the Constitution declares "shall not be suspended, except when in cases of rebellion or invasion the public safety demands it," is held inoperative in every state of the Union, in case of a married woman against her husband—the marital rights of the husband being in all cases primary, and the rights of the wife secondary.

The right of trial by a jury of one's peers was so jealously guarded that states refused to ratify the original Constitution until it was guaranteed by the Sixth Amendment. And yet the women of this nation have never been allowed a jury

[7]An official extinguishment of an individual's civil rights, usually for a serious crime such as treason; as noted, the United States Constitution, Article 1 Section 9, forbids the passing of bills of attainder by Congress and by state legislatures.

[8]Habeas corpus: a legal right, guaranteed by Article 1 Section 9 of the Constitution, that limits wrongful imprisonment except in times of rebellion or invasion by requiring that an imprisoned individual be brought promptly into court so that the case against him or her may be examined; lettres de cachet: official documents authorizing illegal imprisonment.

of their peers—being tried in all cases by men, native and foreign, educated and ignorant, virtuous and vicious. Young girls have been arraigned in our courts for the crime of infanticide; tried, convicted, hanged—victims, perchance, of judge, jurors, advocates—while no woman's voice could be heard in their defense. And not only are women denied a jury of their peers, but in some cases, jury trial altogether. During the war, a woman was tried and hanged by military law, in defiance of the Fifth Amendment, which specifically declares: "No person shall be held to answer for a capital or otherwise infamous crime, unless on a presentment or indictment of a grand jury, except in cases . . . of persons in actual service in time of war." During the last presidential campaign, a woman, arrested for voting, was denied the protection of a jury, tried, convicted, and sentenced to a fine and costs of prosecution, by the absolute power of a judge of the Supreme Court of the United States.

Taxation without representation, the immediate cause of the rebellion of the colonies against Great Britain, is one of the grievous wrongs the women of this country have suffered during the century. Deploring war, with all the demoralization that follows in its train, we have been taxed to support standing armies, with their waste of life and wealth. Believing in temperance, we have been taxed to support the vice, crime and pauperism of the liquor traffic. While we suffer its wrongs and abuses infinitely more than man, we have no power to protect our sons against this giant evil. During the temperance crusade, mothers were arrested, fined, imprisoned, for even praying and singing in the streets, while men blockaded the sidewalks with impunity, even on Sunday, with their military parades and political processions. Believing in honesty, we are taxed to support a dangerous army of civilians, buying and selling the offices of government and sacrificing the best interests of the people. And, moreover, we are taxed to support the very legislators and judges who make laws, and render decisions adverse to woman. And for refusing to pay such unjust taxation, the houses, lands, bonds, and stock of women have been seized and sold within the present year, thus proving Lord Coke's[9] assertion, that "The very act of taxing a man's property without his consent is, in effect, disfranchising him of every civil right."

Unequal codes for men and women. Held by law a perpetual minor, deemed incapable of self-protection, even in the industries of the world, woman is denied equality of rights. The fact of sex, not the quantity or quality of work, in most cases, decides the pay and position; and because of this injustice thousands of fatherless girls are compelled to choose between a life of shame and starvation. Laws catering to man's vices have created two codes of morals in which penalties are graded according to the political status of the offender. Under such laws, women are fined and imprisoned if found alone in the streets, or in public places of resort, at certain hours. Under the pretense of regulating public morals, police officers seizing the occupants of disreputable houses, march the women in platoons to prison, while the men, partners in their guilt,

---

[9] Edward Coke (1552–1634), English jurist who opposed the Crown at many junctures.

go free. While making a show of virtue in forbidding the importation of Chinese women on the Pacific Coast for immoral purposes, our rulers, in many states, and even under the shadow of the national capitol, are now proposing to legalize the sale of American womanhood for the same vile purposes.

Special legislation for woman has placed us in a most anomalous position. Women invested with the rights of citizens in one section—voters, jurors, office-holders—crossing an imaginary line, are subjects in the next. In some states, a married woman may hold property and transact business in her own name; in others, her earnings belong to her husband. In some states, a woman may testify against her husband, sue and be sued in the courts; in others, she has no redress in case of damage to person, property, or character. In case of divorce on account of adultery in the husband, the innocent wife is held to possess no right to children or property, unless by special decree of the court. But in no state of the Union has the wife the right to her own person, or to any part of the joint earnings of the co-partnership during the life of her husband. In some states women may enter the law schools and practice in the courts; in others they are forbidden. In some universities girls enjoy equal educational advantages with boys, while many of the proudest institutions in the land deny them admittance, though the sons of China, Japan and Africa are welcomed there. But the privileges already granted in the several states are by no means secure. The right of suffrage once exercised by women in certain states and territories has been denied by subsequent legislation. A bill is now pending in Congress to disfranchise the women of Utah, thus interfering to deprive United States citizens of the same rights which the Supreme Court has declared the national government powerless to protect anywhere. Laws passed after years of untiring effort, guaranteeing married women certain rights of property, and mothers the custody of their children, have been repealed in states where we supposed all was safe. Thus have our most sacred rights been made the football of legislative caprice, proving that a power which grants as a privilege what by nature is a right, may withhold the same as a penalty when deeming it necessary for its own perpetuation.

Representation of woman has had no place in the nation's thought. Since the incorporation of the thirteen original states, twenty-four have been admitted to the Union, not one of which has recognized woman's right of self-government. On this birthday of our national liberties, July Fourth, 1876, Colorado, like all her elder sisters, comes into the Union with the invidious word "male" in her constitution.

Universal manhood suffrage, by establishing an aristocracy of sex, imposes upon the women of this nation a more absolute and cruel despotism than monarchy; in that, woman finds a political master in her father, husband, brother, son. The aristocracies of the old world are based upon birth, wealth, refinement, education, nobility, brave deeds of chivalry; in this nation, on sex alone, exalting brute force above moral power, vice above virtue, ignorance above education, and the son above the mother who bore him.

The judiciary above the nation has proved itself but the echo of the party in power, by upholding and enforcing laws that are opposed to the spirit and letter of the Constitution. When the slave power was dominant, the Supreme Court decided that a black man was not a citizen, because he had not the right to vote; and when the Constitution was so amended as to make all persons citizens, the same high tribunal decided that a woman, though a citizen, had not the right to vote. Such vacillating interpretations of constitutional law unsettle our faith in judicial authority, and undermine the liberties of the whole people.

These articles of impeachment against our rulers we now submit to the impartial judgment of the people. To all these wrongs and oppressions woman has not submitted in silence and resignation. From the beginning of the century, when Abigail Adams, the wife of one president and mother of another, said, "We will not hold ourselves bound to obey laws in which we have no voice or representation,"[1] until now, woman's discontent has been steadily increasing, culminating nearly thirty years ago in a simultaneous movement among the women of the nation, demanding the right of suffrage. In making our just demands, a higher motive than the pride of sex inspires us; we feel that national safety and stability depend on the complete recognition of the broad principles of our government. Woman's degraded, helpless position is the weak point in our institutions today: a disturbing force everywhere, severing family ties, filling our asylums with the deaf, the dumb, the blind; our prisons with criminals, our cities with drunkenness and prostitution; our homes with disease and death. It was the boast of the founders of the republic, that the rights for which they contended were the rights of human nature. If these rights are ignored in the case of one-half the people, the nation is surely preparing for its downfall. Governments try themselves. The recognition of a governing and a governed class is incompatible with the first principles of freedom. Woman has not been a heedless spectator of the events of this century, nor a dull listener to the grand arguments for the equal rights of humanity. From the earliest history of our country woman has shown equal devotion with man to the cause of freedom, and has stood firmly by his side in its defense. Together, they have made this country what it is. Woman's wealth, thought and labor have cemented the stones of every monument man has reared to liberty.

And now, at the close of a hundred years, as the hour hand of the great clock that marks the centuries points to 1876, we declare our faith in the principles of self-government; our full equality with man in natural rights; that woman was made first for her own happiness, with the absolute right to herself—to all the opportunities and advantages life affords for her complete development; and we deny that dogma of the centuries, incorporated in the codes of all nations—that woman was made for man—her best interests, in all cases, to be sacrificed to his will. We ask of our rulers, at this hour, no special favors,

---

[1] Paraphrased from a famous letter written by Abigail to John Adams on March 31, 1776.

no special privileges, no special legislation. We ask justice, we ask equality, we ask that all the civil and political rights that belong to citizens of the United States, be guaranteed to us and our daughters forever.

1883: DEADWOOD CITY, SOUTH DAKOTA

Galiot François Edmond, Baron de Mandat-Grancey, *from* Cowboys and Colonels (1887)

JULY 4TH.—ONE HUNDRED AND SEVEN YEARS AGO TODAY THE THIRTEEN English colonies in America, feeling annoyed at the policy of the English minister, Lord North, in still compelling them to pay a petty duty on tea, proclaimed their independence, which has cost them, to begin with, an eight years' war, and subsequently another of five years, in which a million men at least have perished, in order to get rid of slavery. And in return for these sacrifices the Americans have enabled themselves to become, indisputably, the most pilfered and the worst administered of all nations, whilst their neighbors of Canada, or their cousins of Australia, though they are still subjects of Her Majesty, Queen Victoria—whom God preserve!—do not pay so dear for their tea, are not plundered by anybody, and are ruled admirably by themselves alone—facts that would lead one to infer that the Yankees, with all their shrewdness, have seized the shadow and let others enjoy the substance.

In order to celebrate this glorious anniversary, all the inhabitants of Deadwood and the neighborhood have been thronging since six o'clock this morning in the bars or in the barbers' shops, saturating their stomachs with ardent spirits or smearing their hands with highly odoriferous pomatums and oils, for without these two preliminary operations there is no good fête in America. When we make our appearance in the street, they are snatching up the newspapers giving a program of the ceremony. The morning edition announces that a new element is to contribute to the interest of the spectacle. The miners of the Caledonia, it seems, are in rivalry with those of the other four mines under the united management of Mr. Gregg. Hitherto this pot-valiant party spirit has manifested itself simply in a few shots from revolvers, exchanged after "a drop" of whiskey, and no one has paid much attention to the diversion. But now today the Caledonians have set forth in the newspapers a proclamation, announcing that they challenge all the others, not to single combat, but to a simple trial of proficiency in mining work. It is the question to determine which gang of miners can break down the most mineral in a given time. The stake is sixty dollars a head. This is an affair quite to the American taste, and bets are being booked on both sides. The first cowboy I meet, "a little elevated," will absolutely give me the Caledonians at three to one.

The procession is not to be formed until nine o'clock, but the first rôles are already on the ground. First there are the *marshals*. They are gentlemen in black frock-coats on horseback, with a great sword, the hilt of which is in the form of a cross, and a chain around their neck, and they are galloping frantically up and down the street, admonishing some, and trying to arrange others in file, without producing any appreciable effect. They remind us a little of the *Cirque*. There are also firemen in red shirts; a few Indian hunters, great brawny fellows with faces by no means reassuring, their hair falling over their back, and clad in doeskin jackets and moccasins prepared by their Indian wives—for it seems they are all married to two or three squaws of different tribes, in order to multiply their relations, and are accordingly called Indian scouts or squaw-men, but they are not held in high estimation. They are the chief personages in the Indian wars; they fire the first shots, and when hostilities are once engaged, they betray alternately both parties, acting as spies on each for the account of the other; but, after all, they have more affinity with the redskins, whose mode of life they have adopted, and generally adhere to, taking care at the same time to fleece them well of their horses, their buffaloes, and even to the hair of their heads.

At last, about half-past eight, the *marshals* succeed in obtaining some appearance of order, putting themselves at the head of the procession, which begins to move. First, there is the inevitable fireman, who, in this country, no more resembles the active little soldier which one sees behind the scenes of our theatres, making love to the supernumerary actresses, than the puppet with the enormous helmet in the pantomime. In America the fireman is an institution; the smallest button of his uniform, as well as the pettiest hose-screw of his pump, is the product of the meditations of all the sagacious bigwigs of the country. All these admirable precautions, unfortunately, are invariably useless; nowhere are the people so well provided against fire, and nowhere else does it make such ravage. I have never seen a city that has not, once or twice at least, been almost totally burnt down.

Behind these comes our friend, Judge MacLaughlin,[2] he who is to deliver the *oration*. He comes in a buggy, which he drives himself; beside him is seated the other heroine of the fête, Mrs. P———, whose rôle is to read the Declaration of Independence.

After them follows the military band mentioned in the newspapers. It is a flourish that recalls that of French villages. They play different airs, which should be national, but which are difficult to distinguish, each performer being too deeply penetrated with the principles of independence that are glorified this day, not to play his own little favorite melody, without troubling himself about the notes produced by his comrades. The great drum here makes an imposing figure. The unhappy individual that bears it, a German emigrant recently arrived, moves one's heart with compassion to look at him. His poor battered felt [hat], his long faded black coat all frayed and fringed, shining with

[2] Mandat-Grancey earlier described the judge as "a man already aged, grave and earnest, possessing, it seems, a considerable fortune and a high reputation." Although Catholic, he had lived among the Mormons for years; his son was reportedly about to become a Jesuit.

grease and riddled with holes, his begrimed trousers and shapeless shoes, his haggard, flabby face—all this forlorn figure, from top to toe, is oozing with misery, with that dire misery of the dark alleys of Berlin, with that misery which, from the time of Aristotle to our days, has provoked those risings of peoples who, emerging from the "off-scourings of nations," as mentioned by Tacitus, have thrown themselves on the south of Europe in search of all those enjoyments refused to them by a sterile earth and a sunless sky. Here they are now flowing into America, and all the efforts of the great chancellor[3] will be powerless to arrest the tide of emigration. We next see passing a triumphal car containing about forty little girls in white frocks singing *Hail, Columbia*; each of these represents a state or a territory. After these come a straggling crowd of good simple people belonging to different societies.

In about half an hour the head of the procession reappears. Judge MacLaughlin gallantly aids Mrs. P———to mount a stage, erected almost facing our hotel. Many persons and the band of music install themselves there in their turn. One of the eaglets we saw selling last evening is perched on the rail.[4] A shrivelled old gentleman, whom they call the "president," then rises and begins to speak.

"Gentlemen," he says, "you have all, no doubt, taken notice of the program of the day in the newspapers. However, I think I had better read it to you. Will you, then listen to me?

"At half-past nine, procession.

"At ten o'clock, after a prayer said by the Reverend X———, speech by Judge MacLaughlin.

"At eleven o'clock, reading of the Declaration of Independence by Mrs. P———."

Mrs. P———, a pale-looking little lady in a white dress and with a great hat, puts on charming little ways, agitating a roll of paper she is holding in her hand. The crowd is evidently thoroughly sympathetic.

The president continues—

"At half-past eleven, luncheon. Those who belong to Deadwood will go and take their meal at home; strangers who have friends here can go and enjoy their hospitality, if they are invited; the others will find in the hotels, and especially at the Wentworth House, a meal as abundant as delicate, provided, however, they have the means of paying for it, which they should be sure about previously on examining their pockets. If not, they would do better to keep away."

An allusion of this kind would be considered with us in the worst possible taste. Here it produces no unfavorable impression, it is simply a joke. Poverty is not, as in Europe, an habitual condition, involving a kind of degradation in the eyes of those who suffer, as well as for the public. It is here a situation that

---

[3] Otto von Bismarck (1815–1898), first chancellor of the German empire, 1871–90.
[4] Mandat-Grancey noted of the previous evening, "The lovers of patriotic emblems are crowding round a workman who is selling a nest of eaglets. It strikes me, by-the-bye, that this bird personifies admirably the American race; they are always eating and are ever lean."

may be prolonged, but which is only transitory; the man who today has nothing to eat is quite convinced that, one day or other, in "prospecting," he will find a mine as magnificent as the treasure of Monte Cristo, and this, perhaps, is already come to his hand. With these sentiments, an allusion to his poverty, however coarse and heartless it may be, does not hurt his feelings, for he no more takes it seriously than the young scapegraces of the Latin Quarter of Paris in their "vie de bohème."

While the president is speaking, one of the marshals comes to invite us to take a place on the platform; but as our costumes are too *négligés*,[5] and we do not intend to remain long, and, besides, fearing I shall be booked for a speech if I put my foot on it, I decline the proffered honor.

Judge MacLaughlin rises afterwards, and begins to speak. His speech, from the commencement, appeared to me so remarkable, that I have taken notes, and if I am not quite sure of the exact words, I am at least of their purport.

"My dear fellow citizens," he begins, "we are assembled to celebrate the hundred-and-seventh anniversary of the day on which our ancestors proclaimed their independence. On a day like this it is good to commune with oneself, and, while returning thanks to God for the unparalleled prosperity which He has deigned to grant us, to ask ourselves what are the moral and material causes that have led to this prosperity. Some attribute it to that republican form that has been given to our government. But this is an opinion manifestly false. In ancient times, as in our days, in the old continent as in the new world, nations of different race have had the same experience, but very unequal success. Let us consider, in fact, what has taken place in the old Spanish colonies, which, in proclaiming their independence, have desired to adopt a constitution modelled on that of ours. Everywhere we see nothing but civil wars, oppression of the feeble by the strong, a violent suppression of all liberty, and a fatal return to barbarism. The same experience has been tested in Spain; in France at three different times, and with what signal failure I have no need to tell you.

"It is not, therefore, to the republican form that we are indebted for this prosperity of which we are so proud. What, then, is it due to? Gentlemen, I am going to tell you: we owe it, in the first place, to the divine providence, who has led us by the hand like the Hebrews on coming out of Egypt, in order to bring us into the land of plenty.

"But we owe it also to the circumstance, that labor among us has always been honorable, that everyone was ready to sacrifice his life and his fortune to defend the life and fortune of his brethren; that, when poor, we were frugal, pure-living, and laborious, and having become rich, we have not given way to the allurements of luxury, but, in retaining all the virtues of our poverty, we have employed the acquired riches simply in the development of civilization in the immense continent that has fallen to us as an inheritance.

"There, gentlemen, these are the causes of our prosperity: it is not the republic that has given us all these qualifications; it is all these qualifications

---

[5] Careless, informal.

that have rendered us capable of living under a republic. Now, those virtues of our youth, do we possess them still? It is with profound sadness that I put this question to myself; for, in truth, when one sees what is passing around us today, we no longer know whether it is with an affirmation that we should reply: when one sees the fortune of the nation in the hands of a few shameless speculators; when the public coffers are pilfered by the very hands entrusted with them, as we have just seen in the affair of the Star Routes; when the Jay Goulds[6] are in power; when the elections are no longer free, but are disposed of by the railway companies at their free will in trafficking with the public conscience, and when justice is powerless to suppress abuses of this kind; then, gentlemen, it is urgent to recognize, if the republican form is incapable of arresting such a disorganization of the social body, that the time is not far off when we shall be obliged to demand, in another form of government, both liberty and security."

I was astounded on hearing these words: had they been pronounced at New York or Washington I should have been less astonished.

When I left Paris, a few weeks ago, the *directeur* of one of the great Paris newspapers had asked me to procure an American correspondent for him. On my arrival in New York I spoke to several persons of this commission, one that drew on me, during my entire sojourn at Fifth Avenue Hotel, a long file of journalists who came to offer their services for this post so highly esteemed there. They all naturally spoke of political matters. At this time, the acquittal of the accused in the Star Routes case deeply interested public opinion.

One of the first who came to see me, said to me quite naturally:

"Oh! things cannot go on in this way much longer: the acquittals at present are nothing more than a question of money. In the country, security is still guaranteed in a certain way by the good custom the inhabitants have adopted of administering justice themselves by means of lynch law. But this reaches hardly any other than ruffians; with a little money the rest are quite sure of escape. If this sort of thing goes on, we shall soon be obliged to resort to monarchy."

"You are joking," I said; "to talk about monarchy in America is almost a heresy; if there is in the world any nation republican by tradition, by experience, and by instinct, it is surely yours."

"But, not at all, I am not jesting. What you say is true, we are all that, but we are eminently a practical people. We are not bamboozled with fine phrases, and be sure, the day, when it will be proved that the republic and security are become incompatible, that it will not be security we shall sacrifice; only," he added, smiling, "if we must have a king, I do not know very well where we shall find him. We shall be obliged to resort to the productive capabilities of foreign countries, for we have not got the homemade article."

---

[6]Jay Gould (1836–1892), unscrupulous financier especially known for his involvement in railroad investments and his manipulations of various markets. A "star route" is a postal route, usually rural, over which mail is carried by private, contracted carrier—so named because it is marked in postal schedules with an asterisk; during the later 1870s and early 1880s, a famous corruption scandal involved such routes.

I thought he was only in a jesting humor, and simply laughed at it. Still, wishing to confirm what I suspected, I had the curiosity to lead the conversation to the same subject with another. To my great astonishment, the idea did not at all seem new to him; he discussed it. I tried others in the same way, always journalists. Everyone of them spoke to me like people who had already well considered the question. A certain number, a few only, said openly, that at some time or other the form of government would be modified in the direction of monarchy. Others, and these seemed to me they must be right, simply regretted that the thing was little possible; a very few declared themselves absolutely opposed to the idea.

Politics are of all subjects of conversation the most agreeable to Americans. If there is an opportunity for the topic they will impose it on you, and they are always ready to listen to and discuss, with the most perfect courtesy, ideas quite opposed to their own. In this we are bound to recognize a great superiority of education over ours. It is therefore never inopportune nor disagreeable in a discussion of this kind to touch on subjects that may seem the most delicate or dangerous.

If, however, by chance, rare indeed, your adversary loses his *sang-froid*, he would immediately be called to order by those present, whatever class of society they may belong to. I well remember an incident in which I was struck by a fact of this nature.

One day, while travelling by rail, a stranger came to sit beside me, and began to relate that he was going to France with his brother-in-law, who was a deserter from the French navy. I replied, that if the said brother-in-law was not disposed to serve his country for three years at a third of the pay, he would do well to deny himself the pleasure of this little voyage.

Upon this, my man got into a rage, declared to me that his brother-in-law having become naturalized, 50,000 Americans would invade France and beat them into a jelly in a trice, if they tried to meddle with his liberty. I replied that his brother-in-law was quite free to remain in America so long as he liked, but if he came back to France, the *Commissaire d'inscription maritime* of his quarter[7] would be pleased to have the opportunity of getting him arrested by two gendarmes, without thinking of the 50,000 Americans; and that it would be far too easy a matter to elude the laws of his country, if a young man of eighteen had only to make a voyage to America for a month, in order to escape subsequently the military service.

I touched there as I well knew, I must admit, a particularly sensitive point. The question interests so many people yonder, especially among the German population, that it was discussed under a variety of forms, and always with much warmth. From all corners of the carriage, adversaries sprang up. The discussion lasted a full hour, but was always perfectly courteous; and strange to say—a thing that would never happen in France—in the end many of my interlocutors were of my opinion.

[7] I.e., commissioner of the regional ship's registry.

In these conversations on politics, which are impossible to avoid in America, I always took pleasure in leading on, by some means or other, to a discussion on the subject of the form of government, repeating the views of the journalists of New York. So long as we were in the eastern states, and even at Chicago, it excited no astonishment, but in proportion as I advanced further into the West, it was not the same; and this was the reason I was so much surprised at Judge MacLaughlin's speech, and especially at the reception so evidently sympathetic the crowd gave to his ideas. I believe, however, that these are shared here by a very small minority, while they become more general as one advances into the East beyond the Mississippi.

And the reason is very simple. In the states of the East, a middle class is rapidly forming, composed of people who have not themselves made their fortune, but who have inherited one made by their parents, and this they will by all means enjoy in peace.

These people have no longer the energy, somewhat stern if not fierce, of their ancestors; they are not rich enough to be confident of their ability to "grease the paw" sufficiently of the first elected judge, who might take it into his head to set a ransom upon them. Below them exist the populace, constantly fed by fresh arrivals from Europe, chiefly Irish and Germans, who sometimes become for the moment absolute masters by reason of their number, and who feel themselves constantly menaced by these evildoers; for in the cities, bands of malefactors are constantly formed that are openly protected by the magistrates, elected by their votes, and there is no other way of dealing with these vagabonds than a summary execution by lynch law. Now, it is not at all agreeable for a good, peaceful citizen to go away some fine night with a hundred others to besiege the prison, and take and hang at the first telegraph pole some scoundrel who, in a well-ordered country, would, years ago, have infallibly figured at the end of a rope.

This middle class will certainly, in the long run, impose its will, for, besides having the advantage of number, it contains all the living strength of the nation. This class clearly sees that, however good a thing liberty may be, security is far better, and it is quite ready to sacrifice so much of the former as may be necessary to obtain the latter in all its plenitude.

But will the people go so far as a monarchy? I think not. It is, however, a fact that some think it possible. At all events, they will surely modify the form of the government with the object of securing more executive authority.

In the West the conditions are quite different.

It is generally imagined in Europe that it is the vast solitudes of the prairie that absorb all the emigrants which one sees, at certain periods of the year, encumbering the quays of Liverpool and Havre. I once thought so too myself, but it is an error. In the Far West I have hardly seen any of them. All the farmers, all the miners I have met, were, with three or four exceptions, Americans. The poor creatures, broken down with misery, which old Europe sends across the Atlantic, have nothing like the energy requisite for a life of the frontiers.

They nearly all stop short of the great manufacturing centres of the East, where they take precisely the places of those who are led by a love of adventure, or driven by a hatred of the restraint of civilization, to seek more freedom in the Far West. The old farmer of Arkansas, whom I met on the way to Pierre, setting out for the Yellowstone, expressed the idea that led them forward. He told me that the country he quitted had decidedly become *too crowded*.[8]

A population recruited with such elements has necessarily the taste for liberty, and for equality also, strained even to excess. In the matter of security, they are satisfied with that which can be guaranteed by a revolver of large calibre. The existing régime, which allows them to live absolutely as they like, delights them. To be free to lynch, from time to time, some lubber or miscreant they have the good luck to catch, is for them a refreshing diversion, and they take good care not to miss an opportunity of sharing in the enjoyment.

During my sojourn yonder, I have never taken up a newspaper without reading in it [of] some execution of this sort.

Between two populations of a turn of mind and aspirations so different, there cannot exist much sympathy. Hitherto the West has been too thinly peopled that much notice should be taken of this feeling in a country where number imposes the law, but I fancy that the state of things as they exist will, before very long, be singularly modified. I have an idea that the first question cropping up will be that of the capital. In a federation of states, where its *rôle* is so important, the metropolis should exist nearly in the center of the agglomeration. Washington has, for a long time, tolerably well fulfilled these conditions. At present the Californians begin to find it rather hard to be obliged to send their senators and deputies to a city from which they are separated by an eight days' journey by railway. The prizes of good places besides fall too much to the share of the old states: therefore, all the politicians of the West are not backward in declaring that some day or other it will be necessary to rebuild the White House on the right bank of the Mississippi.[9] When this question arrives at a stage when its solution can no longer be deferred, great complication may be expected, and the separation of states, which could not be effected for the benefit of the South in taking a line from east to west, may still be accomplished in favor of the western states and territories by drawing a line from north to south.

All these fine speculations have taken me far away from Deadwood and the fête of the Fourth of July. When Judge MacLaughlin had finished his speech, he turned round, making a gallant bow to Mrs. P————, who, rising in her turn, began reading the Declaration of Independence. Unfortunately, this excellent lady, who, on getting up, revealed to us a situation generally agreed to be held interesting from their point of view—though we much need a better term that would express also the sentiments of the disinterested[1]—this

---

[8] Earlier in the book, Mandat-Grancey does relay this comment from the Arkansas traveler, though it suspiciously resembles widely circulating (but largely fabulous) accounts of how the famous Daniel Boone would "retire" whenever other people came too close to him.

[9] I.e., the right as one faces downstream—in this case, then, the west bank.

[1] That is, she looked pregnant.

excellent lady, I say, did not seem to be much accustomed yet to speak in public. It is certainly not I who am going to find fault with her for it, nor with the worthy Mr. P———, who, standing up at the foot of the platform, was looking most tenderly on his wife. But the result was, that, not having heard a word of what she said, it is impossible to state here precisely of what Mrs. P——— and the inhabitants of Deadwood have declared themselves independent; at all events, the list of their liberties is long, for it took twenty minutes to read it. It might, perhaps, have been shorter and more useful to have read an enumeration of their duties.

When Mrs. P———sat down, I expected an explosion of cheers, but, to my great astonishment, there was no greeting from anyone. American crowds are remarkably silent. The president merely rose at once to announce that the ceremony was going to end with a prayer, to be delivered by the Reverend X———. We then see a stout man in a black frock coat, who, in very good terms, improvises a prayer, which is listened to most reverently. One detail, however, makes us smile a little; it is the care with which the reverend minister enumerates the various things on which he appeals for the divine blessing. "Bless, O Lord," he exclaims, "the standing crops and those that are in the ground; multiply the flocks and herds; may our mines, which are being worked, continue to give dividends more and more considerable; help us to discover new lodes; may the rain be abundant without having any inundation . . ." and so forth. If, after this, the good God does not specially watch over the inhabitants of the Black Hills (Dakota), which, by-the-bye, must not be confounded with other Black Hills that exist elsewhere, it certainly will not be through any fault of the reverend gentleman, who evidently took scrupulous care that every *i* should have its dot.

During a good part of the ceremony, Monsieur Bouverie[2] abandoned me; perched on the balcony of Wentworth House, he has been photographing the scene, and has obtained two or three very good negatives, and when I rejoin him I find he has already made up his luggage. Satisfied that we have the requisite money in our pockets, we run down to the dining room, where we are lucky enough to find room, notwithstanding the crowding. We devour something, take leave of Mr. Dickerman, who is come to say goodbye, and hurry to the livery stable to saddle our horses and start.

While I am just putting the bridle on *Jean-Leblanc*, a drunken cowboy comes reeling into the stable, screaming with all his might.

"They tell me there's a curséd French baron here, and I want to see a curséd French baron."

Upon this, he stumbles against me. I seize him by the belt of his trousers and send him rolling into an empty stall, where he sits on the straw with his legs apart, holding in his hand a big revolver, which he has not the strength to lift, repeating, with persistence, the same phrase.

We set out now with the conviction of having contributed our part, in his case, to the rejoicings of the Fourth of July.

---

[2] Mandat-Grancey's companion on the journey.

Daniel De Leon,
"Declaration of Interdependence by the Socialist Labor Party"

WHEN IN THE COURSE OF HUMAN PROGRESSION, THE DESPOILED CLASS OF wealth producers becomes fully conscious of its rights and determined to take them, a decent respect to the judgment of posterity requires that it should declare the causes which impel it to change the social order.

More truly can we say of our plutocracy than our forefathers did of the British crown that "its history is one of repeated injuries and usurpations, all having in direct object the establishment of an absolute tyranny over these states." Let the facts speak.

The foundation of the Union was coeval with the birth of the modern system of production by machinery. No sooner was the federal Constitution adopted than the spirit of capitalism began to manifest its absorbing tendency and corrupting influence. Every new invention was looked upon, not as a means of promoting the welfare of all, but as an instrument of private profit. Every tract of fertile land belonging to the states was appropriated by individuals, regardless of the rights of future generations. Every public franchise of any value was given away to "enterprising" persons and companies.

Thus was already formed in those early days, a privileged class, whose wealth was derived from the labor of others; this growing monopoly of the means of production and exchange, by placing a steadily increasing number of disinherited workers in its dependence for employment, strengthened its hold upon the public powers, which it used more and more unscrupulously for its own aggrandizement.

Even such a public calamity as war was turned by that selfish and unpatriotic class to its own enrichment. By their labor alone the working people not only provided their own sustenance but supplied the means of supporting armies, recruited from their own ranks. Yet, from the fact that the instruments of production were the private property of individuals, the product itself was also the property of those individuals, who stood between the people and their government. For that part of the product which was required to carry on the war, the nation, therefore, became indebted to capitalists, who availed themselves of the public needs to exact exorbitant prices, further increased by the depreciation of the currency or of the interest-bearing bonds in which the war supplies were paid for, and which would some day have to be redeemed at par. In other words, during and after a war the capitalist class cost to the country several times as much as the enemy.

So did the promises and purposes of the Revolution immediately prove abortive. While the fundamental law declared that the Union was formed "to establish justice, insure domestic tranquillity, promote the general welfare, and secure the blessings of liberty," free scope was given to an economic system replete with injustice, pregnant with the seeds of domestic strife, destructive of every true element of happiness, and fatally tending to class tyranny.

Under that system men, proclaimed free and equal, were soon made to realize that they were only labor power in human form, to be sold in the market for what it could fetch, and to be consumed in the production of wealth for the exclusive benefit of those who already had wealth.

Under that system the value of a man, and, therefore, his remuneration, were not to be measured by the extent to which his industry and intelligence benefited his fellows. They were to be gauged by the necessities of his competitors on the "labor market"; so that, as the competition increased, the tendency of his wages was constantly downward, until it reached the minimum required to keep alive his flesh-and-bone machine while it was hired to an employer, who thus became the absolute owner of the net product, or, "surplus value," created by that human machine.

Under that system the toiling masses, hungry and despised, turned the wilderness into a garden, the stones, the clay, the trees into resplendent cities, the ore and the coal into new organs of motion, through which human strength, speed and skill were multiplied a thousandfold, the lightning itself into an obedient messenger; they built factories, ships, docks and warehouses; constructed railroads, bridged rivers and pierced mountains; then descended into their nameless graves, leaving all in the hands of their despoilers, to further oppress and degrade the inheritors of their misery.

Under this system society, so called, became a worse pandemonium than it had ever been. Each looked upon his neighbor as a legitimate prey or a dangerous antagonist. The laborer viewed with dismay the appearance of another laborer, while the employer of both plotted the ruin of a rival employer. And this horrible struggle for life among the weak, for dominion among the powerful, ever more intense as the means of life became greater and as the dominion of man over nature grew more extensive, was glorified by sophists as the providential law of human progress!

From this state of anarchy emerged at last the plutocracy of our day. How and at what cost we shall now see.

For a century or more anarchy reigned supreme in all the branches of production. At times, without definite or approximate knowledge of actual conditions, but stimulated by a reckless desire for gain, every "captain of industry" went on "rushing business" to the utmost capacity of his means and credit, until the market was "overstocked"; that is, until he found by the event what he might have learned before by a timely use of common sense, namely:

1. That since, under the wage system the people can only buy back a portion of their product, the profit-making class must depend on itself alone for the consumption of the remainder.

2. That insofar, then, as the overproduction, so called, consists of such necessaries as the wage-earning masses require, it must either be sold at a great sacrifice or remain in store until the workers engaged in the production of

things exclusively used by the said profit-making class can gradually absorb it.

3. That in the meantime the production of necessaries must stop and the adventurous "captains" who have incurred obligations beyond their means are necessarily bankrupted.

4. That a large number of the very people who purchase those necessaries from retailers are consequently thrown out of employment, and that the current stock of those traders is thereby converted into an overstock, with the inevitable result of widespread failure, reaching at last the industries affected to the production of capitalist commodities.

And then must the strange spectacle be afforded, of a whole people—with the exception of a few drones for whom the sun of prosperity never sets—reduced to the utmost destitution in the midst of the plenty of their own creation; men, women and children starving, apparently, because there is too much wheat and meat; ragged and shoeless, apparently because there is too much clothing and footwear; idle, and therefore miserable, actually because there stands between them and the idle machine, as also between them and busy nature, a paper wall of private ownership, stamped "sacred" by the hand of imposture.

At such times those social functions only which have escaped individual covetousness—those public services like the post office, education, and other departments of national, state and municipal administration which have remained socialized—are entirely free from the general paralysis, insofar at least as their working force is involved. And although tainted with the corruption that capitalism imparts to government, they shine in the night of economic chaos as vivid illustrations of individual security and public benefit in social cooperation. By the contrast of their normal activity with the intermittent palsy of all the capitalized organs of the social body, they plainly show that individual suffering is the natural punishment inflicted upon men for their disregard of the fundamental law of social existence—the law of interdependence—or solidarity.

Every such crisis reduced the number of capitalistic combatants and left the survivors stronger than formerly. It also left the wage-workers weaker in proportion.

The time at last came when the powerful had more to gain by combination among themselves than by internecine war. They became class-conscious, and, therefore, interdependent, as against the individualistic and, therefore, turbulent class from which they had now emerged. The era of capitalistic competition was fast passing away, to be succeeded by the era of plutocratic concentration.

In all the chief branches of production the TRUST made its appearance, spreading its devilfish tentacles in the corresponding channels of distribution.

The effects of this new movement were multiple and ominous. They may, in part, be enumerated as follows:

First—Simplification of administrative methods and consequent reduction of the clerical force.

Second—Application of labor-saving machinery and processes on an unprecedented scale of magnitude and efficiency.

Third—Consequent increase of productive power without a proportionate increase, and in many instances with an actual decrease, in the number of employees.

Fourth—Reduction, at first, of the wholesale price of the product to the point where the smaller competitors still in the field must abandon it, and subsequent enforcement of a monopoly price by the victorious combination or "trust."

Fifth—Hence destruction of the middle class at an accelerating rate (which, since 1889, has reached an annual average of 11,000 failures), and consequent displacement, partly temporary, chiefly permanent, of the labor previously employed by the bankrupted firms.

Sixth—Therefore, decreased competition among capitalists, increased competition among workers.

Seventh—Steady fall of the wage rate; that is, curtailment of the purchasing power of the masses, resulting in a lesser increase in the production of necessaries than in the number of the population.

Eighth—Enlargement of the purchasing power of the capitalist class, resulting in a prodigious development of the industries affected to the production of luxuries and to the creation of new capital, yet insufficient to absorb the labor displaced by mechanical, administrative and other improvements in all the industries.

Ninth—Introduction of the contract or "sweating" system wherever practicable; so that, by abandoning an insignificant portion of his fleecings to a contractor, or "sweater," the capitalist may relieve himself of all the care and odium incident to the superintendence of wage labor, while securing at the same time from every wage slave in his direct or indirect employment the highest degree of efficiency and the most merciless intensity of toil.

Tenth—Consequent widening of the distance between capitalist and laborer, until both have become actually invisible and personally unknown to each other, although mutually felt across the dividing chasm, not as interdependent human beings, but as brute forces in constant opposition, the weaker of which (namely, labor) must yield more and more to the stronger (namely, capital).

To all those effects, already well developed, may be added a still more portentous one, now in course of development, as follows:

Growing insufficiency of the domestic markets to meet the enlarging capacities, and practically unlimited possibilities, of domestic production. Therefore, international competition; that is, huge masses of national labor hurled against each other in the international conflict between mighty capitalists for supremacy in the world's market. Logically, in the end, the trusts are to become international and capital will lose entirely its national character, while any sentiment of patriotism remaining in the workers will have been used to stimulate competition among them, prevent their international organization, and thus reduce them, all over the world, to the same level of misery and degradation.

Of course, all the social and political evils already developed by the capitalistic system in its primary stage of competition were further intensified by the first effects of plutocratic concentration. With the steady growth of enforced idleness and destitution, ever more productive of disorganization, ignorance and immorality, came naturally a greater servility of the politicians to a class now possessed of overwhelming economic power, thoroughly united and determined to compel obedience. "The perversion of democracy to the ends of plutocracy" went on unchecked by any consideration of statesmanship or by any crude manifestation of public discontent. The powers of government so long used legislatively to confer privileges upon the capitalist class were at last used arbitrarily, and even murderously, to establish the absolute dominion of the plutocracy. And, blind to the true cause of its sufferings, lacking in the knowledge and spirit of interdependence, hopelessly divided against itself, the multitude stupidly sanctioned at the polls the economic despotism and political corruption which its own venal misleaders affected to denounce in bombastic phrases at public assemblies.

Of those misleaders, the most effectively treacherous were prominent in the organizations of labor, which it was their disgusting function to keep from uniting politically against the political machines of the plutocratic class. It was, indeed, plain enough that thus united, and only thus, could organized labor rally to its standard the masses of the people, and by one strike at the ballot box, costless and bloodless, achieve the emancipation of the working class. Therefore, "No politics in trade unions," was the cry of those traitors; and it was re-echoed by every thoughtless man, who, proudly holding in his left hand a full-paid union card, with his right voted himself and his fellows into slavery on election day.

But throughout the civilized world the wage workers are asserting their interdependence—the natural dependence of every man upon his fellows, of every nation upon all other nations; and under the banner of international socialism millions of them are now marching to the conquest of the public powers.

They recognize that the social body is an organism, and, as such, is subject in its life, health and development to the general law which governs organic nature; that the more highly it is developed, the more interdependent are all its members; that the very extent of this mutual dependence of parts determines the amount of freedom and the degree of perfection with which they respectively perform their natural functions, ever so diverse, yet all tending usefully and harmoniously to the common end.

They realize also that the capitalist is no more a legitimate member of the social organism than a parasite in the human body is a necessary part of the organ upon which it feeds, and upon the proper working of which all the other organs depend for support and vigor. And they are determined to expel him.

The class struggle has reached its climax. With the triumph of the united toilers over their combined despoilers will end class privilege and class rule.

Americans, fall into line! Onward to the Cooperative Commonwealth!

To the industrious the tools of industry; to the laborer the fruits of his labor; to mankind the earth!

9

A HARDSCRABBLE BOYHOOD

IN THE WINTER OF 1891–92, LIVING ALONE AS A CARETAKER AT AN ADIRONDACK hunting lodge, Henry Conklin (1832–1915) wrote down a modest narrative of his boyhood and youth. Born to a poor family of tenant farmers then living in Schenectady County, New York, he was one of fifteen children, growing up "in poverty's vale, and the wilderness of want." Although resources were scant, Conklin took solace from his strong family and seems never to have resented his poverty or felt deprived, for from his still-premodern perspective poverty was something of a virtue—or at least was productive of virtue and not shameful. Had he been inclined toward it, he might have offered a pretty convincing indictment of his father, Samuel, an ex-sailor who came ashore with a taste for grog (which was dispensed on ships, naval and otherwise, in prodigious quantities) and did a stint in the army during the War of 1812. It was his father's weakness for alcohol, Henry states, that led to the family's perpetual wanderings, since he was easily taken advantage of and probably lacked the kind of application necessary to make a go of the few farms that passed through his ownership. But Henry, who states that his father was not violent, obviously was prepared to forgive him for a weakness all too commonly seen in the period.

By the time Henry, the ninth child, was born, the Conklins had lived in at least a dozen different houses, mostly rented, scraping out a bare living in New York's chill St. Lawrence region before moving down to the Mohawk Valley and the highlands to its south—the region just east of William Cooper's Otsego County. Although New York, due in large part to the Erie Canal, was in the midst of a long sustained growth, the Conklins did not share in the prosperity. Along with many other rural families on hill farms too far from the canal for it to matter to them, they lived a life of almost unimaginable spareness. As the editor of Conklin's memoir, Wendell Tripp, has written, "What is interesting about Conklin's experience is that it took place in the midst of plenty, for New York State in the 1830s and 1840s was settled and prosperous. It held the nation's largest city and several lesser metropolises; farms in the Hudson, Mohawk, and Genesee valleys created a prosperous agricultural civilization; the Erie Canal was a thriving commercial artery; railroads crossed the state; schools, resorts, factories dotted the land. But rural families like the Conklins, living in semi-settled pockets, away from the main routes of commerce, were still facing the pioneer problems of clearing land, scrabbling for a cash crop, and struggling each day for clothing to cover their nakedness and food to sustain their lives." Henry Conklin never had shoes until he was almost twelve, not even in the winter. When his clothes needed washing, he had to stay in bed while his mother washed them, for he had only one set. He received minimal schooling and had few opportunities in life.

In the selection from his narrative given here, Henry reflects on his thin past and describes a moment of special hope in 1839 as the family moved to fifty or sixty acres of land they had managed to purchase and built a new house. Of particular interest is his description of the family's economic life, with its reliance not just on farming but also on weaving, gathering, and on shingle-making—a marginal activity of the time, which usually was performed by people of precisely the Conklins' background and prospects but which became key to the Conklins' economic identity. Henry was six when the great move described in the selection occurred and stayed on the new place for the rest of his childhood—till he was twelve—when the family moved again, further west to Herkimer County. There they lived in a series of makeshift houses the first year until settling onto a bit of marginal land along West Canada Creek, where the family was to remain for some time. Their closeness there to the great forest of the Adirondacks was a key fact in the evolution of the family's economic life. Not only did shingle-making assume a greater role in the experience of the family members, female and male alike; Henry and his many brothers also became lumbermen, and in time Henry and particularly his own son Burton James became famous for their work in the increasingly popular Adirondacks. Burt Conklin became a celebrated Adirondack guide and especially trapper, and Henry was staying the winter of 1891–92 at the hunting camp precisely because his own life, which included farming as well, had become so well identified with the region. Conklin spent that winter making shingles on contract with the camp's owner—and writing out his very unusual narrative.

HENRY CONKLIN

from his "Memoirs" (1891–92)

THE LAND OF YOUTH. WE STILL LIVED IN JOHN PERRY'S HOUSE.[1] THE FALL before I was six years old was spent at home scarcely going to school any as I

---

[1] This part of Conklin's story opens in 1838, just as his family is preparing to move from a house located in the town of Blenheim, Delaware County, New York. This was the last of a string of rented homes they occupied prior to building themselves a new house on a fifty- or sixty-acre farm they had recently purchased in nearby Fulton township. The new place, about which the selection printed here has much to say, was the fifth place that six-year-old Henry lived in since birth and at least the fifteenth his parents occupied since their marriage twenty years before.

had no shoes to wear and my time was spent mostly helping mother and sister Ruth at spinning and weaving, for the fall was a busy time with them, while Julia Ann did the housework. James was now old enough to help Father and John about the work on the farm. Julius and Samuel were away from home at their adopted places, and Abiah worked out, for in fact he was a money grabber, always working out and always had good luck in getting his pay. He carefully saved all of his wages and in the fall brought home his earnings to share them with Mother, his brothers and sisters.[2]

He went to school winters, paying for his own schooling. On days when there was no school, he used to help Father and John get up wood in great big logs that a team could hardly draw, and he and John used to race chopping to see who could beat one another—that is, to see who could cut off the butt log first. It was about an even race but John generally came out ahead. Wood was all chopped in those days, for they knew nothing about sawing off a hardwood log with a crosscut saw. Crosscut saws were not yet invented for sawing hard-wood.[3]

That winter wore away as usual with our fun of riding downhill and brother John [was] now on hand again, making us boys hand sleighs. Evenings when he had nothing else to do he would tinker away by the great blazing fire for hours making or repairing a sled. And such hand sleds, we thought they were splendid. No wonder we all loved John.

Early in the spring sister Ruth went away to work at Uncle Tom Peaslee's, a farmer living a few miles west of us. His farm was next joining where Uncle Joe Curtis lived. Ruth never came home again to stay but frequently was home on a visit and brought us lots of presents. Dear sister Ruth, how much she loved my mother. How sweet she looked in her womanly Christian beauty for she had long before experienced religion and was now a respected and faithful member of the Methodist church. How we used to cling to her whenever she was home. But now she had found a good place to work, plenty to wear, plenty to eat and was now fairly on the road that finally led her out of poverty's vale.[4]

After Ruth went away to work sister Julia had to take her place at the wheel and loom and I was old enough to help them to do chores about the house. My work was sweeping, washing dishes and helping mother to wash and do most all kinds of indoor work as my sisters older than I were occupied elsewhere and sister Mary was not old enough to do much. In fact I was my mother's boy-girl and I believed it for Mother said so. If she went away anywhere I had to go with her to help about something, to keep the snakes away while picking huckleberries and when visiting to either carry the bundle or the baby. I could

---

[2] Henry's surviving siblings included: John (b. 1819); Ruth (b. 1822); Abiah (b. 1823); Julia Ann and Julius (b. 1825); Samuel Jr. (b. 1828); James (b. 1830); Mary Elizabeth (b. 1834); Casandana or Cassie (b. 1835); and Amy Catherine (b. 1838). One infant had died in 1821; a final brother, Leonard, was to be born in 1840, and two sisters: Lydia, in 1843, and Merinda, in 1844.

[3] Although crosscut saws certainly predated Conklin's youth, he was very familiar with the lumber business and may well be right with regard to the particular type he had in mind.

[4] Conklin's fondness for sentimental-moral sayings such as this marks both his passing acquaintance with genteel culture and his willingness to employ formulaic language.

carry Cassie, as we always called her, for she was so little. I was then nimble and stout with curly brown hair, blue eyes and rosy cheeks and in my own eyes quite a lad, just blooming into youth. Although we were poor I was blithesome and gay, caring not for poverty or care or trouble, happy-go-lucky in the morning of the sweet time of youth. Oh how glorious and bright and happy seemed the hours and days and the sweet slumber at night. No brainracking or planning, [no] restless, uneasy, sleepless nights, but calm and sweet were my slumbers as a summer evening.

Well I remember this season. Father, John and James worked hard but did not seem to get along well. Crops were poor and everything went wrong while hiring places. So Father said they would look around to buy a place somewhere. They went over into what was called Tompkins Hollow in the town of Fulton, ten or twelve miles north of Blenheim Hill, and here they found and bought a small place of fifty or sixty acres with no buildings on it and most all woods. Now we were to move again as soon as they could fix a place to move into. So whenever Father and John could get away for two or three days at a time, they used to drive over and work, taking some lumber each time, for we were to live in grand style in a frame house. Father was quite a carpenter, for he had worked at the trade when a young man while living on Long Island. Father hewed the timber and John drew some logs up to a sawmill in the hollow about a mile above our new place towards Rosman Hill. In this way they gathered lumber to start the building. Mother was well pleased with the undertaking and did all she could to help them along by cooking up a basket of provisions each time they went over to work at the house. They had what they called their dinner basket. It was made of wide splints, round like a cheesebox and a high cover on it made of splints also. The cover was fastened on with splint hinges. In my imagination it would hold a bushel.

Oh what El Dorado stories they told of our new home. Such nice spring water near the house and what a lovely brook full of trout running right past the door. It was nothing but talk of the new home and moving over to it, all in the latter part of the summer or late in the fall, and to hurry matters along one day it was finally decided that Father and John should go over and get their new neighbors together and make a bee to put up the house. So over they went and let the people know what they wanted and they soon got enough together, some bringing nails, some shingles, and some lumber and some of this and some of that, anything that was needed to carry it along and they set at it old-fashioned bee style, with a basket of dinner and a jug of old rye whiskey and before night they had the house so far constructed that Father thought it would do to move into.

The next thing was to pack up and move. They had taken over a part of their old useless truck and traps, what they could, every time they went over, so there was not so much to move when the family went over. It was late in the fall and it was getting cold weather and it was hurry up, hurry up. Finally there was a day set to go. Father and Mother made all preparations and the day before we were to start they packed up everything except what we needed that night.

I was old enough now to assist and entered into the business of moving most heartily for I longed to get over in the new frame house and see the brook where the trout were. At last the morning came for us to start and it was all hurly-burly. John, Father, Mother, Julia Ann and James were all at work. There were not so many this time to go as usual, for Ruth, Julius, Samuel and Abiah were away at work but there were six besides Father and Mother, making eight in all to go. My father had a team and one of our neighbors had volunteered to come over and take a load. The loom and all its relative traps had gone on the advance a few days before, for I remember it stood in a pile in the new house when we got there.

At last we got started, two loads of us in the clumsy old-fashioned high-box wagons without springs and the road was rough and stony and it was jolty, jolty, jolt as we went. We had to go down through Darling Hollow past where we had once lived on the same road where I saw the elephant, then down through those crooked dugway hills[5] that I had traveled many times, then from Darling Hollow northeast down and down great long hills until we came to Patchin Hollow. Here was a little hamlet, a post office, store, hotel, gristmill and a few other dwellings. From here our road turned toward the northwest up the hills again through small clearings and pieces of woods for three or four miles and then we came to a big piece of woods three or four miles long. While going up the last hills John, James and I had been walking for the wagons were heavy-loaded.

Brother James had on his feet a pair of Father's old worn out shoes that were too large for his feet but he had managed to get on stockings and old rags enough to fill them up and they were tied on with tow[6] strings and so he went skuff, skuff with these great shoes swabbing over the frozen hubs. I had on my feet a pair of old stockings with two or three thicknesses of cloth of some kind sewed on the bottom which mother had fixed for me to wear while moving. My feet were good and warm at first, but after leaving Patchin Hollow the boys had to walk most of the way, and before we got up the hills my moccasins were worn to tatters on the bottom and my bare toes were on the frozen hubs. But what did I care then for any such a thing! I had been used to it all through childhood.

Happy, oh I was happy now for we were on our way to the new home over in the promised land. Well, when we came to the woods how dark and dismal they looked. They were second-growth pine and great towering dark hemlocks. In the center of these woods was a great swamp and it was called Wolf Swamp because in the early days of settlement it was a rendezvous and hiding place for wolves. While going through the swamp my brother John and Father were telling some awful wolf stories and I got so scairt I clumb on the wagon until I

---

[5] Region where roads have been sharply cut into steep terrain; elephant: As recounted earlier in the book, when Henry was three his sister Julia Ann took him to see a passing circus, which included "a great old elephant with his majestic tread and great ears flopping and long round tail switching from side to side."
[6] Rough cloth made from partially finished flax; Conklin describes the process later.

got past it. On we went and out of the woods to a clearing where lived a man by the name of Boyd and from his house it was only half a mile across down a great steep hill through a piece of woods and then over the brook to our new house. This was a footpath and I traveled it hundreds of times after. John, James and I went across to build a fire while the teams had to go by the road which led towards the west for about half a mile and then turned and wound around down the hill on the flats, then east by another new house and our nearest neighbor, Jay Tompkins. One half mile east was our new house.

After we left the teams we boys skipped pretty lively down the hill through the woods to an old clearing of two or three acres. Here was the brook and when we crossed it John says, "Here boys is where the trout are." I looked in the deep holes as we crossed over on a log but did not see any. We soon got to the new house and John went to work with a flint, a piece of steel and some punk and there he sat over a pile of dry sticks and slivers. Whackety whack, click, click, click, and at last he struck fire and soon had a good blaze. For good old brother John had prepared for this beforehand by getting a lot of pitch-pine slivers. We soon had a roaring fire but had to watch the chimney and boards above the fireplace for they had only time enough to build up the back of the chimney with stone as far as the chamber floor, and above there and out of the roof were tacked on temporarily a few boards for the smoke to go up out until they had more time to complete it. The door was not hung yet and there was only one window in and only a part of the chamber floor was laid yet. We got the castle good and warm and along about dark on come the rest of them, and then it was unload and carry in the truck.

The lower part of the house was all in one room and before the teams had got along we carried the old loom, wheels and warping bars to the farthest corner from the fire so as to give room for the family by the fireplace. After we had all gotten in and settled and warm the next thing was supper. Mother had prepared for this by baking some great loaves of rye and Indian bread baked in the big iron baking kettle. We also had tea, cold meat and potatoes—baked in the ashes, for they had not gotten the trammel pole[7] up yet and so could not boil them in the dinner pot. What a good supper it was to us hungry movers as we had not stopped to get dinner on the way except to eat a lunch while the teams were being fed.

That night Jay Tompkins came down to see us and I never shall forget him. What a rollicsome funloving fellow he was and what hours of fun and laughter he made for us for years after. He would heat the fire shovel red hot, then lick it with his tongue and not get burned and then he said he could swallow us if he had some grease to grease our heads with. Many and many a time he used to come over to have fun with us, chasing us around the house to swallow us. That night he and my brother John got to singing songs. Oh happy, happy John. He was happy that night, and why should he not be? He had hacked and jogged and toted about as the mainstay of the family through Jeffer-

[7]The horizontal pole placed in a fireplace to hold the trammel, a notched adjustable pothook.

son, Schenectady and Schoharie counties all his life and now they had got and were going to have a home of their own where Mother should have a little rest.

That night we all slept on the floor, not having time to put up the bedsteads. The trundle bedsteads were left outdoors that night. We had old-fashioned cord bedsteads made of four-by-four hardwood scantling big enough for barn timber and great ropes for bedcords. I remember how we looked that night in beds scattered over the floor with the great shadows of the fire flickering over our heads on the beams and rafters and roof inside.

Time went on and Father and John finished the chimney by lathing the inside of the boards and plastering them with mud and clay mixed together. Then they finished the chamber floor and put in two more windows and hung the door on great wooden hinges that John had manufactured. Then they made a pair of stairs for the chamber in one corner by the chimney, and in the other corner they made a cupboard, and by banking[8] the house on the outside up to the windows we were quite comfortable for the winter.

After they got the house fixed they put up a sort of barn or shed of logs for the team and a place for hay, and during the winter Father and John used to go over on Blenheim Hill and draw their hay over on a slight for the teams.

Abiah came home as usual this winter, and he and Julia Ann went to school part of the time. They had to go over two miles away over towards West Gilboa or Rosman Hill. It was so far I could not go.

Towards spring Abiah bought a cow out of his last summer earnings and gave it to Mother. I do not remember that we had ever owned a cow before but I presume we had. How proud Mother felt with her cow. She was a great big nice one, spotted red, white and cream color and what a pet we all made of her. That spring when she gave milk I used to go with Mother and watch her milk.

I was then seven years old and I thought that if I could only milk I would soon be a man and sometimes after Mother would get her milked she would let me strip her out.[9] In this way I soon learned to milk and then I used to milk her all the time. I was so small I could not carry in the pail of milk alone and when I got her milked I would call for Mother or someone to carry in the milk. The milk pail was made of wooden staves with three or four large wooden hoops on it and a wooden bail, and in good feed the cow would fill this pail.

We called our house a frame house. Well, it was a frame house of hewn timber just put together with pins enough to keep the wind from blowing it over. It was double-boarded up and down, and for the time being they had made the roof of boards, but in the spring Father and John made some pine shingles and shingled it.

The farm was in a narrow valley running east and west perhaps thirty or forty rods wide. This was good rich tillable land and partly cleared. Through this valley ran a nice gravelly brook where the trout lived and they were quite

[8] Insulating the foundation on the outside with straw or earth.
[9] Drain the udder.

plentiful when we first came there. The brook ran within twenty feet of the door and just over the brook in a little bank was a clear cold crystal spring. We had a little bridge over the brook to get to it. On the south side of the valley was a very steep hill covered with forest growth running the whole length of the farm. This too was good land but a terrible place to get crops off of. On the north side of the valley was a sloping side hill just steep enough to ride downhill on, and here was our coasting ground in winter with our hand sleds. But this side hill was very poor land. The soil was a sort of clay and it was mostly barren with the exceptions of a few second-growth pine, oak bushes, sweet ferns and huckleberry bushes, and up in here were the rattlesnakes. Our land on the west joined Jay Tompkins and they had cleared down to our line perhaps fifty rods from our house, and we could see up to their house. Across here we had a footpath to their house but the wagon road ran along the south side of the valley and that was further around.

Father and John went to work in the spring that year clearing land, and with what help James, Mother and I were to them, they cleared most of the flats west of the house and got it into spring wheat, corn, potatoes and flax. Our folks most always raised flax and while living here I first learned how to help take care of it from the time it was pulled, dried and thrashed, then retted in water and dried again and stored away in the barn or shed. Then in winter or stormy weather it went through the process of breaking and hatcheling[1] until it was ready for the wheel and then Mother would spin it for towels and cloth- ing. The tow was made into coarse cloth for bags, towels and our summer pants. The fine flax was spun and wove into fine linen for sheets, shirts, table- cloths, dresses and Sunday pants. In this way my mother supplied the house- hold with linen until she got so old, worn out and feeble with hard work that she had to give it up, and then we also stopped raising flax.

Down along the brook east of the house on the flats we had a good sugar bush, and Father and John made quite a lot of sugar that spring. Down on these flats we gathered leeks, cowslips, and adder tongues for greens. That summer we got along quite well for we could live on most anything in the summer. And trout, we had never had such nice trout to eat as we got from the brook, and we used to fish down a mile or two to where there were some great deep holes in the gorge.

When the berries came it was nothing but pick berries with Mother and the children that were old enough to go. The berries were picked and dried for winter use and to sell. The huckleberries were most always sold for they brought the most in the market. I went many and many a day with Mother taking our dinner and picking berries to dry.

We used to go northwest of us to a place called huckleberry plains. There were hundreds of acres with nothing but scrub oak, pine, white birch, elders, sweet fern and berry bushes, and in berrying time there were a good many

---

[1] Combing out with a hatchel; the point of the whole process is to separate the long fibers in the flax stalks from the softer material.

people there picking berries. And the snakes, I killed many a rattler for I carried an oak stick five or six feet long, and when one made his appearance I went for him with a vengeance. I was spry then and could get around quite lively. One or two walloping blows would lay them out. When we came to a nice patch of berries I ran around it poking my stick in under and around to see if there were any snakes under the bushes and ferns before Mother would go picking. Brother James used to go with us when he could be spared at home, and Mother would send him after water in some ravine, for he knew where the good springs were. Thus it went year after year while we lived in Tompkins Hollow. How we enjoyed the dried fruit in the cold winters when other luxuries were scarce.

I think sister Julia worked out the first summer we lived here. But when at home she used to go with us to pick berries or took care of the house and our two younger sisters, Mary and Cassie, still our little fairy, as we called her. I remember how she looked, so fat and chubby trying to walk and talk. She was the pet of all the household. I don't know but I must have felt a little jealous, for most of the kisses were lavished on the younger ones and I thought I was slighted. The kisses now for me were few and far between but I knew where my kisses came from and a good rousing kiss and a hug from Mother made it all up, and I was old enough now to appreciate them too. Oh those sweet kisses, love tokens of the dearest one on earth I knew at that time.

That summer we raised quite a lot of wheat, some corn and potatoes and buckwheat, and we also had quite a garden. Mother did most of the garden work with James and my help weeding the beds. Before this I did not know much about garden work. Our garden was just over across the brook by the spring. After this year I always was my mother's helper in the garden and became quite an expert in the business.

That fall Father and John built an addition to the barn. It was a threshing floor to thresh grain on. I remember also raking buckwheat up in bunches for sister Julia to set up. After the corn was husked it was set in pans around the fire to dry so we could get an early grist.[2] One evening we had a shelling bee to shell corn. We all sat in a ring before the fire. I remember John sitting on a barn shovel using the blade to tear off the corn. This was glorious fun for us as we talked of what nice johnny cake we were going to have and [how] we would live now on the fat of the land. Only think, wheat and corn of our raising and just going to the mill.

That night we got the grist ready, put up in bags and set in the corner by the door, and next morning Father and John started off to the mill. I think the name of the place was Cobleskill, and they went northwest over the hills by Rosman Hill schoolhouse and then down through Sapbush Hollow and so on to Cobleskill. It was late when they got home and I was in bed and to sleep. Next morning Mother had a rousing big sweetened johnny cake, sweetened with maple sugar. And the wheat flour, what nice sweet bread it made, but

[2] A batch of grain ready to be ground ("grist for her mill").

rather dark. And the wheat kernel, what lovely pancakes baked on Mother's great big round griddle with a bail on and a swivel in the top so she could turn it around to turn the cakes as it hung over the fireplace. Then we had good sweet milk. Johnny cake, milk and pancakes of our own raising. What jolly treats they were to us then. Yet perhaps no better than we had had at other times, but we had all been more or less interested in the first crops on our new farm.

On the twenty-ninth day of September 1838, another little sister was born. They named her Amy Catherine after our aunt Amy Curtis. She was not so tiny and small as Cassie but large and fleshy with large bright blue eyes and light hair. Now we had another one to love and caress. Another one to provide for and go with us along down through the vale of poverty. Another one to share our joys and sorrows through life's uneven way.

None of us went to school this winter, for the schoolhouse was too far off. Abiah was away from home this winter working for his board and going to school. My brother James and I were setting snares for rabbits. Down below our house along the road that leads to the Schoharie Flats or Creek was a large piece of second-growth timber of birches, oak and pine, and here the rabbits had their runways. Early in the winter there came quite a deep snow, almost knee deep. We started out one day to look for the rabbits with our snares made of linen thread good and stout. We had no shoes nor boots to wear on our feet so we contrived a plan to go and not freeze our feet. We took a great big sheepskin that Father had tanned with the wool on and started running as far as we could without freezing our feet, then we would lay it down wool side up, get onto it and pull it up around our feet until they got warm. Then we went on again and so on until we set a few snares with spring poles. On going back to the house we did not stop so often.

The next morning bright and early we went to the snares, taking the sheepskin for a footwarmer. Sure enough we had one in a snare. He was caught around the middle and was alive, jumping about like a horse, but we had him all the same and quickly dispatched him with a club. How proud we felt carrying him home. Our feet were not cold now running through the snow. One had the rabbit and the other the sheepskin, whirling them around our heads in the air. Oh what a feast we would have now. We decided before we got home it should be a potpie, and potpie it was, made by Mother's own hands, cooked in the big dinner pot. And such dumplings—none but a mother knew how to make such dumplings. So we thought then, and many and many a rabbit did we get after that in winters while we lived there. It helped us along quite well through poverty's vale. But the sheepskin we never used after that winter. We managed to get some old cast-off shoes given us by some of the neighbors and if we did not get old shoes we sewed rags on our feet to tramp in the snow.

The next spring and summer went along as usual only I had gotten more acquainted with most all our new neighbors. Mr. Tompkin's family were the nearest and we went there the most. There was old Mr. and Mrs. Tompkins or

Aunt Peggy as we called her. She was a great big fat good-natured old lady most always out to work in the lots. She had two great big dogs and she would take them and go up in the lots on the side hill and dig out woodchucks. The dogs would hole one and then the fun would begin. The dogs both digging and she with a hoe or shovel. I tell you, the dirt would fly. When she got after a woodchuck everyone in the neighborhood knew it by the noise she made yelling, "Sic 'em Tige, sic 'em Tige." Brother James and I used to skin up across lots to help her and see the fun, and fun it was. The fat old woman would work and dig until the sweat ran off her face to get a woodchuck for a roast, for they used to eat them.

The old lady kept guinea pigs. They were a little chunk of an animal about half as large as a rabbit with short legs, short ears and short tails and a nose like a little pig. They were fed on grass and clover winter and summer. They were spotted, black and white. In summer she kept them in a large tight yard outdoors, and in winter she kept them in boxes or cages in the house under her bed. She raised them for the Albany market, taking them there every fall, all but two or three pairs to breed from the next year. The rich people in Albany bought them and kept them in great cages for pets just the same as people now keep canary birds. She used to get as high as five dollars a pair and that would depend on their beauty as to the spots. She made more clean money out of her guinea pigs than they did off the farm. I have stayed over there many an hour to look at the guinea pigs and help her pick clover to feed them on.

The old gentleman was a very quiet sort of an easygoing worker, always busy and always quiet. But there was their son Jay. As I told you before, he was full of fun and frolic. He used to come down to our house to torment us children. He would open his great wide mouth and chase us around the house to swallow us, and he said many a time he could do it if our heads were greased.

His wife Elizabeth was as full of fun as Jay only not quite so noisy. They had two children, Joshua and Hannah. Hannah was the baby, and when she was little Jay come over one day and flattered me up to go and work for him until I was twenty-one years old. He was to give me Hannah for a wife, a pair of guinea pigs and an old frozen-footed hen that he said went thump, thump across the barn floor. So I went over with him and stayed all night but I did not sleep much. Next morning he set me to rocking the cradle that Hannah laid in. He said if she was to be my wife I must begin to take care of her now, and after breakfast he would show me the old hen.

When breakfast was ready he said I could go to the brook and wash. So I went out and the minute his back was turned I scud for home. I got some ways before he saw me and he hooted but I did not stop until I got home. I left my hat behind and sent James over after it. But how he did plague me after that. I never heard the last of it.

The Tompkins people were always good to us and ever ready to help in time of need.

Directly south of us up a great steep hill one half mile through the woods lived the Boyds. Their farm and ours joined. They were good neighbors also and quite well off. Mr. Boyd was a carpenter by trade, and they had a nice frame house and barn. There were four in the family: Mr. and Mrs. Boyd, a girl named Ann Eliza and a boy named Henry.

I took a great notion to both of these children, and boy-style, I fell in love with Ann at first sight and Henry was my best chum. After this I went to Mr. Boyd's more than anywhere else. I thought at first that Ann was dreadful homely with her big brown eyes and long nose, but when I got more acquainted with her I did not notice her nose and her eyes became more beautiful. Her beauty was her kind ways, gentle manners and good behavior. I was always happy in her presence and will tell you more further on. It is enough to say now that I loved her and she was my angel.

The second summer we lived there Father and John went to making pine shingles to take to market. A little east of the house, they built a shingle camp[3] of old pine logs and made a fireplace in it. The timber for the shingles was taken from old pine tops that had lain there for years. The butts of the trees had been taken away for lumber, leaving the tops to rot and waste. The heart of these were good yet, although the moss was growing over some of them. They dug these out and between the rows of knots they would get two or three good shingle cuts.

James and I were busy now helping them, as we were as much interested in the shingle business as the older ones, for the shingles were to go to the Albany market to be traded for some things for winter. All through the summer and rainy weather and odd spells we worked at the shingles, and in the fall they had enough made for two loads. They got Jay Tompkins to go with one load and our own team took the other. They were gone four days and when coming home my father's old team tuckered out and had to be left several miles back at one of our neighbors, and Jay brought my father's stuff as far as his house. It was late at night when they got home but not so late but that us children heard what they had to say about the trip.

Among the articles they had gotten was a barrel of wheat flour raised out west somewhere and ground in the new style.[4] We had never seen at any one time a whole barrel of flour and packed in a barrel too. How they did talk about that barrel of flour that night, and they decided to go over early in the morning and carry it home across lots so some of it could be baked for breakfast. Early in the morning they started. All of us children that could walk had to go along to see the curiosity. There was Father and John, Julia Ann, James, Mary and Cassie, the little fairy, and myself, and how we looked stringing along cross lots, and when we got over there, Father and John tied some ropes around the barrel of flour and put in two long sticks so they could carry it.

---

[3] Cabin, perhaps open on one side and with a shed (or single pitch) roof.
[4] Barreled flour was known much earlier in New York, as that was the common means for shipping it, but for a poor rural family like the Conklins this "new" product—especially because it was associated with new milling processes such as that invented by Oliver Evans—was an "urban" wonder.

Among the things they got that time was a new tin baker constructed like an open camp with a cover to turn back.[5] This they let Julia Ann carry and she carried it on her shoulder. When all was ready we started, Father ahead and John behind carrying the flour. I shall never forget how we looked running along beside them gabbing and talking all the way, and then when we came to the fences (there were three) they would stop to rest while James and I would lay off the top rails so they could step over, and in this way they lugged the flour home.

We were rich then for we had a whole barrel of flour and a new tin baker to bake biscuit in. What a wonder the new tin baker was and who could be smart enough to invent such a thing. The barrel was soon opened and the tin baker in position before the fire, and for breakfast (though rather late) we had some splendid white biscuit almost as white as snow. How we did live then and how the neighbors came to visit us and have a taste, as I thought of the biscuits made of boughten flour put up in barrels and brought from Albany. Mother prized the tin baker very highly as it was so nice to bake pie in. Pie was another luxury Mother learned to make and bake in the new tin baker, but the pies were not so big and thick as those baked in the iron bake kettle.

[5] The tin bakers common at the time were open-fronted boxes, with flat or sloping tops, designed to be placed in front of an open fire so as to catch and reflect the heat. The "open camp" Conklin compares this one to is of the sort described in note 3 above.

10

THE "STONE WORK" OF A
NEW ENGLAND FARMER

SECURE IN HIS VALUES AND HIS SENSE OF SKILL, ASA G. SHELDON (1788–1870), a native of Lynnfield, Massachusetts, learned early in his life that essential avocation of the Yankee farmer: how to lay up stones. Therein lay one secret to his success in life. The typical Yankee moved stones to get them out of the way, even though their stony siblings and cousins seemed to fill in the vacancies with uncanny speed. Asa Sheldon learned how to move them so as to make something out of them—not just the lovely stone walls that knit together the New England landscape even today, but monuments to his own skill and the physical and financial ambition of the nascent corporations he worked for—especially the railroad companies that needed embankments and culverts and bridges put up if their aim to speed the nation's commerce (while lining their own pockets) was to be realized. Rather like John Robert Shaw, the excavator and well-digger of the Ohio Valley, Sheldon built his life out of an elemental substance; unlike Shaw, he did so with sober application and a sense of the shifting ground of the construction trades as large corporations and massive projects began to demand less flair and idiosyncracy and more rationality from those who moved the earth.

Sheldon was a farmer first and last. His skill with stones came out of the farmer's necessities, and the profits of his stone work—when they actually came to him—were ploughed back into his agricultural pursuits. True, he added to his agricultural pursuits a litany of other economic roles—he was a cattle drover, a teamster, and a sawyer as well—but this was the coin of the farmer's complex realm in those days, when fractional occupations in fact made up a whole economic life. It is Sheldon's detailed record of his many activities that gives his humble life story a great deal of its interest.

The narrative has other appeals as well. Sheldon recorded, particularly in his account of his "stone work" that is printed here, the complicated process by which a rural society made its transition to industrial means of production and, more importantly, industrial patterns of relationship. Sheldon's work for the railroads, especially the Boston and Maine, placed him often enough not only in harm's way but also at the crossroads where a population concerned about the enormous changes being worked in its ways of life and work gathered to consider, express their doubts about, and sometimes oppose those changes. He must have been a master of negotiating amicable ends to difficult conflicts, as his tales about how he finessed any number of impasses suggest. Time after time, local residents opposed—with their bodies, their guns, their pungent opinions—the route by which he was attempting to run through some new rail development. Sheldon more often than not used an ingenious combination of patience, cajolery, flattery, and neighborliness to achieve his goals, applying old values and processes to very new situations and a new order of relations. Ironically, his story in the selection printed here focuses not only on how he managed to preserve a sense of community while easing large material and cultural changes into place, but also on how the corporation that he served so well attempted to cheat him out of his due. The faceless corporate shilly-shallying does not hold up well in contrast to the personal responsibility that was Sheldon's hallmark. Whereas he flattered his way to the dinner table of a woman who at first opposed a rail line, the railroad company disregarded his own honorableness and tried every means at its disposal to reduce his just bill. As a result, Sheldon was nearly ruined, for it was his own credit—financial and moral, one feels—that allowed him to secure the materials needed for the jobs he did, and the railroad's dishonesty left him nearly broke with his credit under a cloud for a long time and his spirit sorely tried. Sheldon's usefulness lies partly in his framing of modernization as a moral question. He avoided the law except as a last resort, preferring to talk things through as his ancestors had long done, and if the typical "Yankee" of American folklore is a sharp bargainer— here, the part played by the railroad magnates—Sheldon reminds us that the bedrock of a moral vision underlay the shrewdness. Like the unpromising, even intractable material out of which he so cannily made a living, Sheldon's core had a shape and heft that wears very well. His account of honest labor nobly pursued and competently performed is the sort of story for which there is always room.

ASA G. SHELDON

from Life of Asa G. Sheldon (1862)

IN THE YEAR 1809, PASSING THROUGH SQUIRE WILLIAM BLANCHARD'S FARM, I observed his three men laying stone wall, Charles Burt being foreman. I noticed he tried a stone several ways, and then about to throw it aside in a pet, said, "It won't lay no way."

"Hold on, Burt," said I, "There is one way that stone will lay and make good work."

"I should like to know which way?"

Putting my hand to the stone, I said, "make that the bed and lay it over the joint of those two."

He did so, and it made solid work without a pinner.[1] The squire stood by, puffing a cigar, and said, "Young man what shall I give you to work for me three hours?" This was the first time I had ever spoken with him.

"One shilling[2] per hour," said I, having no idea he would give it, eight cents being the common price.

"Now," said he, "I want you to pick out every stone and direct how it shall be laid, and I will give you your price."

An hour or so afterwards, the squire appeared again with something to cheer the hands and quench thirst.

"Burt, how do you get along?" said he.

"Faster than we have done, and easier too," said Burt.

Again the squire came, saying, "Young man, your three hours are out. Walk up to the house and I will pay you, but you must stop and take a cup of tea with me and my wife first."

At that time I should rather "take a licking," as boys say, than sit down to tea with them, but I soon found myself introduced to the most amiable and social of women. And since that time I never regretted my acquaintance with the Blanchard family. To this time, whenever opportunity offers, I can spend an hour very agreeably with any of the descendants of that couple. After this occurrence whenever there was a culvert to be built in the highway, Sheldon was called on to take charge of it.

The first year of my residence on the Flint farm [I] built a stone wall around his family graveyard, near his house. He wished a permanent wall, that would stand the lapse of centuries, as he might leave his farm. I made inquiries in that respect a few days since, and was informed that not a stone had fallen from its place, neither from the graveyard or hog-sty wall that I built. People had told him, no man could lay a wall that hogs would not throw down. So well pleased was he that no other man was employed to lay stone for him while I occupied his farm, a period of thirteen years.

During the first year of my railroad experience, when Deacon Addison Flint had charge of the stone work, and I of the earth, as I chanced to be looking at the stone layers, they turned an uncouth stone weighing more than three tons round and round, and were about casting it aside when I ventured to say, "Hold on, I can see a way for it."

"How is that?" said the foreman.

I told them, and the trial satisfied all parties. John Haggins, department engineer, being present, soon brought about an exchange. Flint was put on the earth, and I upon the stonework.

---

[1] A small stone used to support larger ones. Sheldon also demonstrates here the key principle of laying a stable wall: put one stone over the joint between two, and abut two over the center of one.

[2] The English coin was carried over in various parts of the United States, with varying values ranging from twelve-and-a-half cents to around sixteen cents.

I wish to avoid the imputation of egotism in saying that my abutments of bridges stood só well that I have since been employed to rebuild abutments to bridges built by others, on the Boston and Lowell Railroad, to the number of fourteen. . . .

During all this reconstruction of bridges, the business was so managed that the cars were never delayed one moment, much to the gratification of the agents.

For Patrick T. Jackson, Charles S. Storrow, Waldo Higginson, William Parker, agents, and Benjamin F. Baldwin, engineer, I have done work to the amount of over 100,000 dollars. And all this without any written contract, neither of us being bound by writing, and I ever found their memorandum of the agreement proved as strong as any bond could make it. I thank God that he has raised up these honest, fair-dealing, upright men. But to my sorrow, on one other railroad I found both engineer and agents to be men of a very different character.

I was once invited to take the job of constructing several miles of railroad in company with two others. I had about concluded to engage, when one of them said to me, "If you do take the stone work, I don't want you should do it as you did the Boston and Lowell, to stand forever, but get it done as cheap as we can and get it accepted, and secure our pay for it, and then I don't care if it all goes to destruction the next day."

"Then I will have nothing to do with it," said I, "for I have never yet laid a stone on the railroad that I thought likely to endanger any man's life and I never mean to."

The road was built, and soon after I heard of the stonework giving way, the engine falling through, bringing one man to a most excruciating death.

In the year 1839, I was employed in making an abutment for the Boston and Maine railroad, at the bridge over the Merrimac River on the Bradford side. I likewise teamed[3] rails and ties for nine miles of road, of which a man named Clark was agent. He told me in the commencement that they, the company, had no right to the land; I must beg my way along as well as I could. And sure I did have to beg my way. One amusing circumstance I will relate. As we approached land belonging to a middle-aged widow, in depositing our rails, the neighbors mustered their heavy teams and built a wall across the track completely blocking up our way. I informed Clark of the circumstance when he gave orders to have the wall taken out of the way. Jacob Morey's team was the first to start on to forbidden ground. Just as he started I espied a woman hurrying across the field toward us, who proved to be the rightful owner of the land.

Some hundreds had collected to see the "fight," as they termed it. To Morey I said, "Don't stop for any man, but be sure not drive over a woman."

She did not happen to be quick enough to get ahead of the oxen, and so ran in between the off ox and the load. This chanced to be the worst ox to kick

---

[3] Carried by teams of oxen.

I ever owned; I should not have dared to stand there myself. I hastened to the spot with all eagerness and warned the woman of her danger, but I presume she did not believe one word I told her. That he did not kick was truly a wonder, but he stood passive as a lamb. On looking round I saw that her son had placed a long wagon crosswise ahead of the other teams and blockaded them. A hand was dispatched to get some hay for Morey's team, with orders for the other teamsters to do the same, "for if we must stand here, they must have something to eat," I said.

It being the month of March, it was all mud and water where she stood. I then brought a plank and laid it carefully in for her to stand upon, saying, "If you will stand there, I will make you as comfortable as I can." I was just as sociable as lay in my power, but not a word could I get out of her, or a smile from her lips until Squire Tilton from Exeter, then treasurer of the railroad, said, "Sheldon, I have always heard that you were a smart man; I am surprised that you let one woman stop all this work. Why don't you drive over her?"

"Squire," said I, "for more than twenty years I have not been in the habit of driving more than half way over so handsome a woman as that."

This brought a smile to her face and loosened her tongue.

"How long are you going to keep your oxen here?" asked she.

"If I can't go ahead I shall keep my cattle here till twelve o'clock Saturday night, and bring them back Sunday night at twelve o'clock; and as I have not engaged to board anywhere, [I] should like to board with you. Now if you will go up and get supper I will come and help you eat it. What time do you have supper?"

"We eat our supper at six o'clock," said she.

She then stepped out, and I helped her up the bank with what politeness I was master of, and for once I must say I was glad to see one of the fair sex walking from me. She had stood there at least half an hour.

When six o'clock came, I made my way up to the house, entered without rapping as if it had been my boardinghouse. I found all seated at table but one who waited and was detained. I took the chair appropriated to her, and said, "I suppose this chair is reserved for me."

"If you are determined you will eat supper with us, you may sit in that chair."

"Madam, I am not only determined to eat supper with you, but I am determined to board with you while my work continues in this neighborhood."

While eating she asked, "Do you intend to keep those teams where my son is, as long as you proposed to keep the other team?"

"Yes, certainly I do."

"Then I will send for him to drive his team home."

We grew quite sociable before supper was finished, and could talk about the railroad pleasantly. She asked me, "Was that a real kicking ox of yours, or did you say so to frighten and drive me away?"

"Oh, it was a real kicking ox; and it is an astonishment to me that he did not kick you under the wheels."

I boarded with her as long as I pleased, and found it a good boarding place.

After the consummation of this job the same company advertised for proposals for laying nine miles of rails, and eight miles of stone work. I, with five others, carried in proposals for the rail-work, and I by myself carried in proposals for the stonework. The directors voted to accept of both, and we met to make the contracts. The contract for the rail-work was made, but Bailey's name stood first, although mine was first on the proposal. This done, Squire Clark, the agent, wished to see me alone. When by ourselves, he said, "I wish to say to you in confidence, I don't know how far we shall go with our road, or when we shall be obliged to stop. I don't want to make any contract for the stonework, but I want you to go there and work when I say so, and do as I say, and I will see you well paid for it."

After a while, Haywood, the engineer, came and said to me, "How soon can you be at Exeter, ready to work at Captain Fernald's bridge?"

"How soon do you want me if I could be there?"

"I want you to be there very much tomorrow morning at eight o'clock."

"I think I can be there at that time," I replied.

We loaded our stone tools and set out at midnight; travelled fourteen miles before sunrise; stopped and breakfasted at Dodge's tavern, and proceeded to the ground and were ready there at eight o'clock.

While waiting, I put up four stakes at the four corners where I judged the bridge ought to be. At nine o'clock, Haywood and Clark arrived.

"Mr. Haywood, where shall I put in this bridge?" I asked.

"Where do you think it best to put it in?" said he.

"Where those four stakes stand."

"Then put it there," said he.

"I don't know whether you will or not," said an unknown gentleman.

"Is this Captain Fernald?" said Mr. Haywood.

"Fernald is my name," he answered.

"I am very happy to see you, Captain Fernald," said Haywood.

The parties, after talking together a few minutes, told me that I might go to work.

A number of walls meeting here, just where I wanted to work, I asked, "Who owns these walls?"

"I own them," said F.

"These walls will serve for backers; I would like to buy them. What will you take for them?"

"Thirty dollars," said the Captain.

"Captain Fernald, they are not worth ten dollars for you to move away."

He started quick, a characteristic of a sea captain. "It is nothing to you what they are worth to me; if I sell them to you I want what they are worth to you."

"Captain Fernald, if you will allow me to make remarks five minutes, I will then hear you an hour if you wish me to. We will suppose these stones to be worth thirty dollars to me, but only ten dollars to you, would it not be more just to divide and call it twenty dollars, giving me ten dollars and you ten dollars, than it would be to take either extreme?"

"You have convinced me; you shall have them for twenty dollars. You and I are friends now." And pointing to two lots of land, he said, "I own that land and if you want any stone there, you are welcome to get them."

This bridge was finished without any special trouble, and about ten rods further up we put in an abutment on Fernald's land, close to the line, intending to build another on the other side, owned by a man named Swasey, to accommodate both in their farm operations. I had no acquaintance with Swasey but hoped to get along without difficulty. The morning came and we started as usual to commence our work. I saw a man coming across the field with a gun in his hand, and when he came up, he said, "What are you going to do here?"

"I am going to dig away and put in a abutment on this side for a bridge to accommodate Captain Fernald and Mr. Swasey."

"I will put a ball through the heart of the first man who takes a stone from this wall."

I saw there was a dead set, and turning to the stone layers, said, "Go up into Judge Smith's pasture to splitting stone; I have bought the privilege of taking out all the stone I wished. And you teamsters, go and draw them and lay them on the highway, handy to be used, if we are ever allowed to do the work."

My boarding place was Dodge's tavern, where Swasey made his appearance every evening and held converse with me. It soon become apparent that he was smoothing down, and in about a week he said to me, "Mr. Sheldon, we think about here that you know more concerning railroads than we do, and some think that you will say just what you think about it. Now tell me, had I better let the road pass through my land or not."

"Certainly, you had," said I. "You told me the other night that you had three thousand cords of standing wood, and as soon as the railroad is in operation, every cord of that wood will be worth fifty cents more than it now is. They are now buying wood at Wilmington for three dollars per cord, to run their engine to East Kingston; and as soon as the cars run wood will be worth as much here as it is in Wilmington. The cut is already made through your farm, and if you could stop the work from going further, you could never get one cent of damages, and I advise you to take stock in the road for damages."

"When do you want to go to work on that abutment, if I would let you?"

"Tomorrow morning at sunrise," said I.

"Then you may go on," he replied.

We were on the work at sunrise, and soon Mr. Swasey made his appearance with his team. His first question was, "Where shall I begin to work?" I told him, and he worked all day like a hero, as he was, and at night he pulled off his hat and, bowing low, said, "You are welcome to this day's work, because you would not be mad even though I threatened your life. Sheldon, when I came out here with my gun, it was loaded with two balls, and I certainly should have put them through your heart had you attempted to move a stone."

Pretty much after this fashion we worked our way along through all this section. Sometimes we were not able to lay a stone for a week, being obliged to move back and forth and work a few days in a place when and where we could get a chance. When we could get no opportunity to lay stone we employed ourselves in getting them out and drawing them near where we hoped to lay them. These delays certainly impeded the work more than thirty-three percent, or nearly one-half; and besides the workmen began to grow uneasy and fretful at moving about so much and not being able to show more for their work.

One day I met the agent and engineer in a sleigh on Kingston Plain. "Clark," said I, "hadn't we better leave the work and go home, for certainly some days we do not earn twenty-five cents where we spend a dollar."

"Haven't I said to you times enough, stay there and do what I want you to, and I will see you well paid. Don't say anything more to me about leaving unless I tell you to."

So poor was the credit of the corporation at that time, that not a stick of timber could be bought for a temporary bridge, unless Edward Crane or I would promise to see it paid for. Crane was on the earth and I on the stonework; we were the only two undertakers[4] on the ground.

As a palliation for the seeming insanity that prevailed among the landowners, I would say that there was a prevailing belief that the road would never be finished. The stock was as low as sixty percent,[5] and they feared they would not get damages.

When the work was all completed, they owed me 8,500 dollars as honestly as ever one man owed another. I sent an order to the treasurer for 45 dollars and he refused to pay it, saying he owed me nothing.

When it was announced that the corporation "owed me nothing," there were forty writs levied upon my property within twenty-four hours, for the announcement was made in the long entry of the largest hotel in Exeter. In this situation, the reader can well judge what a waste was made of my property. One instance I will here mention. About a fortnight prior to this there was a large sale of chestnut timber in New Hampshire, at auction. I attended and bought 1650 dollars worth; paid 150 dollars cash and gave three notes of 500 dollars each, one to be paid in six months, one in one year and one in eighteen months. In a few days a large timber dealer offered me 500 dollars for the bargain. Knowing it was the best bargain of timber I ever bought in my life, and wanting winter work for my oxen and men, I thought it not wise to accept the offer, not doubting but that I should receive my pay for that job and could handle it to my liking and turn it at last to more advantage. The money being withheld, and all my property attached, I lost not only the bargain but the 150 dollars previously paid. The man who offered me 500 dollars for the bargain, afterwards bought the lot, and I have been informed by good authority that he

---

[4] Contractors.
[5] I.e., of its original or face value.

cleared 3,000 dollars on the bargain. Great numbers of chestnut ties, from this lot, were carried on the railroad to Boston and then shipped to R.

Hon. Thomas West succeeded Mr. Clark in office, and became agent of the road. I made him the offer to leave the case to three men, who were directors of the road when the work was done. This was not accepted. I then offered to leave it to Patrick T. Jackson, James F. Baldwin and Chas. S. Storrow. This offer did not meet their approbation. I then commenced a suit against them. After several months I received a communication by letter to meet the directors at Dover on a specified day. On arriving at Andover, I was introduced to one of the directors by the name of Weld. On the way, we talked over the matter, and he said he had understood that I had once offered to leave it to three men who were directors on the road when the work was done.

"I did," said I.

"Will you renew that offer?" he asked.

"I will," was my answer.

When we arrived at Haverhill, Mr. West came into the cars, and Mr. Weld related the conversation that had taken place between us on the road, and expressed his surprise that the corporation should suffer themselves to be sued when I had made them so fair an offer.

"I don't know," said Mr. West, "but he has made them an offer that they would rather accept of than that. I believe he has offered to leave it to Jackson, Baldwin and Storrow."

"I did make that offer."

"Will you renew it?" said Mr. Weld.

"I will renew both offers, and you may take your choice."

"It shall be done; it shall be settled without going further in court."

On going into the room with the directors, they said that there was nothing in the way of settlement; if I would retire, Mr. West and I could talk it over in the cars on our way home. When the subject was introduced, Mr. West said, "The directors all meet at Boston tomorrow. If you will come and bring your bill, and we do not pay it, Jackson, Baldwin and Storrow shall settle it."

To Boston I went, and met West in State Street, when he accosted me thus, "Sheldon, they will not have Jackson on this reference at any rate."

"You have already agreed to have him," said I.

"Well go in and see what they say."

When in, it was soon announced that Mr. Jackson could not be allowed to serve as referee.

"Gentlemen," I said, "if you will give me any reason why Mr. Jackson cannot be admitted to serve, I will be content with another man."

"Sheldon," said Mr. Weld, "we find, here in Boston, that you have done so much work for Mr. Jackson, and have been with him so much that he will believe every word you say, and we may as well leave the case to him."

My answer was, "It is no disgrace to me after being with him, and doing as much for him as I have done, to have him believe all I say."

The chairman then said, "Name a man living somewhere between Boston and Dover, within three miles of our road."

I then named twenty men, all of whom were rejected as soon as named. "Gentlemen," said I, "it is of no use for me to pick out a man; name one yourselves."

"Colonel Duncan, of Haverhill," said Mr. Weld.

"I do not want a better man," said I, "he is one of the first three that I offered to leave it to."

As the cars were about to leave, they decided that John Flint, of Andover, should write notices to the several gentlemen, and I should see that they had them.

So early was I up the next morning that I travelled eight miles before John Flint was out of bed. He wrote the notices and I flew up and down on the railroad and carried them to the respective gentlemen that same day. But strange to believe, before the specified day came, I received a letter from Duncan that they would have neither of the Boston gentlemen at any rate to sit on the case between me and the corporation.

Here the case hung until Colonel Duncan was appointed auditor by the court. He appointed a meeting at Andover, to which the several parties repaired. After Mr. Haywood's testimony, Mr. West advanced a proposal to give me 7000 dollars if I would take 1000 dollars in their railroad stock. After a little deliberation I decided to accept it, for this reason. The bargain was made privately between me and Mr. Clark, on that account I had no evidence of it and Mr. Haywood said on the stand, he could not recollect the conversation between Clark and me on Kingston Plain. Furthermore, the same gentleman came to me and said the stone work referred to as a sample for me was not good enough but was filling, and asked what way it could be made better. I informed him by splitting out the stone with wedges instead of powder,[6] but it would cost more. He asked, "How much more?"

"One dollar per yard,"[7] was the answer.

"Well," said he, "get them out with wedges."

On the stand he acknowledged the work was one dollar per yard better, but he *could not recollect* ever giving any order for that course.

About three years after commencing my suit, when I received from the corporation 7000 dollars, I made the best settlement with [my] creditors circumstances would permit, and began life again with only 75 dollars.

I would like to say distinctly to every stockholder of the Boston and Maine railroad, that when your corporation was in a sinking condition I did what I could to further on the work, day and night, some nights going without any

---

[6] The distinction here is between an older method of breaking stone with gunpowder and a more expensive but better method that came into use in the late eighteenth century. The latter involved the use of rows of splitting pins into which wedges or "feathers" were fit. As the wedges were hit with a hammer, they expanded the pins, thereby producing a clean, smooth break.

[7] I.e., per cubic yard of cut stone.

sleep. And now knowing how I have been treated, are there not some lovers of justice among you who are willing to make some recompense in view of the faithfulness with which I have served you? Some may say, why did you risk so much without a written contract? I would state in reply, I had done more than 100,000 dollars worth of work for men who were agents, and always found their word to be good as their bond; this gave me too much confidence in men.

To Mr. West I would say, you have had a long time to reflect, that you once agreed to let Jackson, Baldwin and Storrow settle the case between me and your corporation. Then you refused to let Mr. Jackson act, and Colonel Duncan's name was substituted in his stead. The next thing, you refused to let Mr. Baldwin and Mr. Storrow act. By so doing I consider you ruined a man who had served your corporation faithfully. After so long a time if you have repented of what I consider a great sin, I trust you will set about making some recompense. But if your heart is yet hardened, I pray God, when your eyes are closed in death, to have mercy on your soul.

11

FUGITIVES

BORN IN 1814 NEAR LEXINGTON, KENTUCKY, THE SLAVE WILLIAM WELLS BROWN was the son of a slave woman named Elizabeth and a white man called George Higgins. Higgins, Brown wrote in his *Narrative* (first published in 1847), was "connected with some of the first families of Kentucky" and was a relative of Brown's master, Dr. John Young, whom Brown indicted in the court of natural rights as "the man who stole me as soon as I was born." Of light complexion, Brown was to show himself especially attuned to the ironies of the color line as an absolute in American racial "thought"; in the appendix to his narrative, particularly in its later versions, he was to include newspaper advertisements for runaway slaves that played precisely on this point: "I will give ten dollars for the apprehension of William Dubberly," ran one. "William is about nineteen years old, QUITE WHITE, and would not readily be mistaken for a slave." Brown might himself have been this "William," except that Dr. Young never would have advertised for him under that name. His mother had called him William (as she had called her other children Solomon, Leander, Benjamin, Joseph, Milford, and Elizabeth) but his childless master had a nephew named William Moore and would not tolerate Brown's bearing the same given name: "My mother," Brown wrote with his characteristically dry sarcasm, "was ordered to change my name to something else," and thenceforth he was known as "Sandford." Not until his escape could he defiantly reassume his old identity, adding to it the name of the Ohio Quaker who aided his escape, Wells Brown. His acceptance of Brown's name surely was meant as a tribute to that man, and as a memorial token of the fugitive's own history; but, given the importance of color in William Wells Brown's work, we may see it as a ironic touch as well.

Dr. Young moved to Missouri shortly after the birth of William. When old enough to work, William served first as a house servant on Young's plantation, where his mother labored as a field hand. When Young moved into St. Louis, the boy was hired out as a servant in a tavern run by "Major Freeland":

He was formerly from Virginia, and was a horseracer, cockfighter, gambler, and withal an inveterate drunkard. There were ten or twelve servants in the house, and when he was present, it was cut and slash—knock down and drag out. In his fits of anger, he would take up a chair and throw it at a servant; and in his more rational moments, when he wished to chastise one, he would tie them up in the smokehouse, and whip them; after which, he would cause a fire to be made of tobacco stems, and smoke them. This he called "*Virginia play.*"

Mistreatment by Freeland led to William's first attempt to escape; he was hunted down by dogs in the woods outside St. Louis and taken back to Freeland, who in retribution "smoked" him. Only when Freeland failed in business did William get away from him, being successively rented out to work on steamboats or on land for a variety of more or less harsh masters, including James Walker, a slave-trader whom Brown accompanied ("heartsick," he said, at what happened and his own hand in it) on three "dealing" trips down the Mississippi. At length, instructed by Dr. Young to seek out a new master who might be persuaded to buy him, Brown took advantage of the opportunity and made another attempt to escape, trying this time to take his mother—whom Young had since sold off to another master—with him. "Advertised" by the two masters, the two runaways were seized by a trio of slavehunters and thrown in jail. Informed that his master was sick, Brown prayed "not for his recovery, but for his death," but Young indeed got better and sold Brown to a merchant tailor in St. Louis named Samuel Willi. Brown had been rented to Willi previously; now, ignorant that Brown had just tried to escape and been caught, Willi intended to rent him out in turn. Brown was soon working on a steamboat amid the horrors of the slave market again, for the boat carried many gangs of slaves from Missouri southward. It was on this broad experience as well as on his own tough life that Brown was to base his effective anti-slavery campaign in later years.

Samuel Willi eventually sold Brown as a house slave to a steamboat captain named Enoch Price, from whom Brown was at last able to escape—alone this time, his mother having been sold down the river by her master—on New Year's Day, 1834. Once in Ohio, he was befriended by Wells Brown (the selection from his narrative printed here concerns this part of his life), and from the Cincinnati region made his way to Lake Erie. He spent the next several years as a free laborer based in Buffalo, working on Great Lakes boats and endeavoring to aid other fugitives passing through to Canada. In 1842, for instance, he "conveyed, from the first of May to the first of December, sixty-nine fugitives over Lake Erie to Canada." It was in the next year that Brown, who had heard nothing about "antislavery" prior to his escape to the North, became a lecturer for the Western New York Anti-Slavery Society, and from then on he devoted his efforts to the cause. He moved east to Boston in 1847, where he wrote his *Narrative* "in sight of Bunker Hill Monument," conscious that he was still technically a slave, unprotected by any law, "even in Massachusetts." A work of witness as well as of self-presentation, the book told of the lives of many others in addition to Brown; in later editions, he lengthened an appendix (for the most part included in the selection here) that graphically demonstrated how the "peculiar institution" of slavery depended on a brutal code and a brutal language. The book was very successful, issued in nine editions by 1850, and led to Brown's voyage to Europe in 1849 as a delegate to the International Peace Conference being held in Paris that August. After that event, he rallied antislavery forces as a journalist in Great Britain and Ireland, seeking to counter the publicity efforts of what he called the "dominant oligarchy in the United States," the slave-holders, whose agents were very active there. "Slavery," Brown remarked in a note to the London edition of his *Narrative*, "cannot be let alone. It is aggressive, and must either be succumbed to, or put down." The passage of the Fugitive Slave Law in 1850 in the United States led Brown, still a fugitive himself, to extend his stay abroad until 1854, when several British friends purchased his freedom for him and he came home.

While remaining a staunch activist in the antislavery effort in both hemispheres, William Wells Brown also pursued a new career as author. He published the first African American travel book, entitled *Three Years in Europe*, in 1852; his soon-famous "Jeffersonian" novel *Clotel; or the President's Daughter* the next year; a play, *The Escape; or, A Leap for Freedom*, in 1858; *The Black Man: His Antecedents, His Genius, and His Achievements* (1862); *The Negro in the American Rebellion* (1867); *The Rising Sun* (1873); and *My Southern Home; or, The South and Its People* (1880), an astute analysis of race and racism in the United States both before and after the Civil War. Active not only as a writer but also as a temperance worker and lecturer, Brown died in Chelsea, Massachusetts, in November 1884.

WILLIAM WELLS BROWN

from *Narrative of William Wells Brown, an American Slave* (1847)

BUT THE MORE I THOUGHT OF THE TRAP LAID BY MRS. PRICE TO MAKE ME satisfied with my new home, by getting me a wife, the more I determined never to marry any woman on earth until I should get my liberty.[1] But this secret I

---

[1] Enoch Price of St. Louis, a steamboat captain and commission merchant, had owned Brown, who was called "Sanford" or "Sandford," for only three months prior to the escape that he soon details. In the chapters immediately preceding this selection, Brown tells how his former owner, Dr. Young, had sent him off to find a new master for himself; Brown took advantage of this opportunity and ran away with his mother, but was caught and jailed. Young subsequently sold Brown to a merchant tailor named Samuel Willi, who in turn sold him to Price. Price had purchased Brown to use him as a carriage driver, largely for Mrs. Price. Mrs. Price, who prided herself on the appearance and condition of her slaves, tried to convince Brown that he should marry another Price slave named Maria; when he balked at this, she purchased another slave, named Eliza, whom she thought Brown was interested in. Hence his opening point about Mrs. Price's marriage "trap."

was compelled to keep to myself, which placed me in a very critical position. I must keep upon good terms with Mrs. Price and Eliza. I therefore promised Mrs. Price that I would marry Eliza; but said that I was not then ready. And I had to keep upon good terms with Eliza, for fear that Mrs. Price would find out that I did not intend to get married.

I have here spoken of marriage, and it is very common among slaves themselves to talk of it. And it is common for slaves to be married; or at least to have the marriage ceremony performed. But there is no such thing as slaves being lawfully married. There has never yet a case occurred where a slave has been tried for bigamy. The man may have as many women as he wishes, and the woman as many men; and the law takes no cognizance of such acts among slaves. And in fact some masters, when they have sold the husband from the wife, compel her to take another.

There lived opposite Captain Price's, Doctor Farrar, well known in St. Louis. He sold a man named Ben, to one of the traders. He also owned Ben's wife, and in a few days he compelled Sally (that was her name) to marry Peter, another man belonging to him. I asked Sally why she married Peter so soon after Ben was sold. She said, because master made her do it.

Mr. John Calvert, who resided near our place, had a woman named Lavinia. She was quite young, and a man to whom she was about to be married was sold, and carried into the country near St. Charles, about twenty miles from St. Louis. Mr. Calvert wanted her to get a husband; but she had resolved not to marry any other man, and she refused. Mr. Calvert whipped her in such a manner that it was thought she would die. Some of the citizens had him arrested, but it was soon hushed up. And that was the last of it. The woman did not die, but it would have been the same if she had.

Captain Price purchased me in the month of October, and I remained with him until December, when the family made a voyage to New Orleans, in a boat owned by himself, and named the *Chester*. I served on board as one of the stewards. On arriving at New Orleans, about the middle of the month, the boat took in freight for Cincinnati; and it was decided that the family should go up the river in her, and what was of more interest to me, I was to accompany them.

The long-looked-for opportunity to make my escape from slavery was near at hand.

Captain Price had some fears as to the propriety of taking me near a free state, or a place where it was likely I could run away, with a prospect of liberty. He asked me if I had ever been in a free state. "Oh yes," said I, "I have been in Ohio; my master carried me into that state once, but I never liked a free state."

It was soon decided that it would be safe to take me with them, and what made it more safe, Eliza was on the boat with us, and Mrs. Price, to try me, asked if I thought as much as ever of Eliza. I told her that Eliza was very dear to me indeed, and that nothing but death should part us. It was the same as if we were married. This had the desired effect. The boat left New Orleans, and proceeded up the river.

I had at different times obtained little sums of money, which I had reserved for a "rainy day." I procured some cotton cloth, and made me a bag to carry provisions in. The trials of the past were all lost in hopes for the future. The love of liberty, that had been burning in my bosom for years, and had been well-nigh extinguished, was now resuscitated. At night, when all around was peaceful, I would walk the decks, meditating upon my happy prospects.

I should have stated, that, before leaving St. Louis, I went to an old man named Frank, a slave, owned by a Mr. Sarpee. This old man was very distinguished (not only among the slave population, but also the whites) as a fortune-teller. He was about seventy years of age, something over six feet high, and very slender. Indeed, he was so small around his body, that it looked as though it was not strong enough to hold up his head.

Uncle Frank was a very great favorite with the young ladies, who would go to him in great numbers to get their fortunes told. And it was generally believed that he could really penetrate into the mysteries of futurity. Whether true or not, he had the *name*, and that is about half of what one needs in this gullible age. I found Uncle Frank seated in the chimney corner, about ten o'clock at night. As soon as I entered, the old man left his seat. I watched his movement as well as I could by the dim light of the fire. He soon lit a lamp, and coming up, looked me full in the face, saying, "Well, my son, you have come to get Uncle to tell your fortune, have you?" "Yes," said I. But how the old man should know what I came for, I could not tell. However, I paid the fee of twenty-five cents, and he commenced by looking into a gourd, filled with water. Whether the old man was a prophet, or the son of a prophet, I cannot say; but there is one thing certain, many of his predictions were verified.

I am no believer in soothsaying, yet I am sometimes at a loss to know how Uncle Frank could tell so accurately what would occur in the future. Among the many things he told was one which was enough to pay me for all the trouble of hunting him up. It was that I *should be free!* He further said, that in trying to get my liberty I would meet with many severe trials. I thought to myself any fool could tell me that!

The first place in which we landed in a free state was Cairo, a small village at the mouth of the Ohio River. We remained here but a few hours, when we proceeded to Louisville. After unloading some of the cargo, the boat started on her upward trip. The next day was the first of January. I had looked forward to New Year's Day as the commencement of a new era in the history of my life. I had decided upon leaving the peculiar institution that day.

During the last night that I served in slavery I did not close my eyes a single moment. When not thinking of the future, my mind dwelt on the past. The love of a dear mother, a dear sister, and three dear brothers, yet living, caused me to shed many tears. If I could only have been assured of their being dead, I should have felt satisfied; but I imagined I saw my dear mother in the cottonfield, followed by a merciless taskmaster, and no one to speak a consoling word to her! I beheld my dear sister in the hands of a slave-driver, and compelled to submit to his cruelty! None but one placed in such a situation can for a moment imagine the intense agony to which these reflections subjected me.

At last the time for action arrived. The boat landed at a point which appeared to me the place of all others to start from. I found that it would be impossible to carry anything with me but what was upon my person. I had some provisions, and a single suit of clothes, about half worn. When the boat was discharging her cargo, and the passengers engaged carrying their baggage on and off shore, I improved the opportunity to convey myself with my little effects on land. Taking up a trunk, I went up the wharf, and was soon out of the crowd. I made directly for the woods, where I remained until night, knowing well that I could not travel, even in the state of Ohio, during the day, without danger of being arrested.

I had long since made up my mind that I would not trust myself in the hands of any man, white or colored. The slave is brought up to look upon every white man as an enemy to him and his race; and twenty-one years in slavery had taught me that there were traitors even among colored people. After dark, I emerged from the woods into a narrow path, which led me into the main travelled road. But I knew not which way to go. I did not know north from south, east from west. I looked in vain for the North Star; a heavy cloud hid it from my view. I walked up and down the road until near midnight, when the clouds disappeared, and I welcomed the sight of my friend—truly the slave's friend—the North Star!

As soon as I saw it, I knew my course, and before daylight I travelled twenty or twenty-five miles. It being in the winter, I suffered intensely from the cold, being without an overcoat, and my other clothes rather thin for the season. I was provided with a tinderbox, so that I could make up a fire when necessary. And but for this, I should certainly have frozen to death; for I was determined not to go to any house for shelter. I knew of a man belonging to General Ashley,[2] of St. Louis, who had run away near Cincinnati, on the way to Washington, but had been caught and carried back into slavery; and I felt that a similar fate awaited me, should I be seen by any one. I travelled at night, and lay by during the day.

On the fourth day my provisions gave out, and then what to do I could not tell. Have something to eat I must, but how to get it was the question! On the first night after my food was gone, I went to a barn on the roadside and there found some ears of corn. I took ten or twelve of them, and kept on my journey. During the next day, while in the woods, I roasted my corn and feasted upon it, thanking God that I was so well provided for.

My escape to a land of freedom now appeared certain, and the prospects of the future occupied a great part of my thoughts. What should be my occupation, was a subject of much anxiety to me; and the next thing, what should be my name? I have before stated that my old master, Dr. Young, had no children of his own, but had with him a nephew, the son of his brother, Benjamin

---

[2] Probably William H. Ashley (ca. 1778–1838), fur trader and politician, lieutenant governor of Missouri, 1820, and United States representative, 1831–37.

Young. When this boy was brought to Dr. Young, his name being William, the same as mine, my mother was ordered to change mine to something else. This, at the time, I thought to be one of the most cruel acts that could be committed upon my rights; and I received several very severe whippings for telling people that my name was William, after orders were given to change it. Though young, I was old enough to place a high appreciation upon my name. It was decided, however, to call me "Sandford," and this name I was known by, not only upon my master's plantation, but up to the time that I made my escape. I was sold under the name of Sandford.

But as soon as the subject came to my mind, I resolved on adopting my old name of William, and let Sandford go by the board, for I always hated it. Not because there was anything peculiar in the name, but because it had been forced upon me. It is sometimes common, at the south, for slaves to take the name of their masters. Some have a legitimate right to do so.[3] But I always detested the idea of being called by the name of either of my masters. And as for my father, I would rather have adopted the name of "Friday," and been known as the servant of some Robinson Crusoe, than to have taken his name. So I was not only hunting for my liberty, but also hunting for a name; though I regarded the latter as of little consequence, if I could but gain the former. Travelling along the road, I would sometimes speak to myself, sounding my name over, by way of getting used to it, before I should arrive among civilized human beings. On the fifth or sixth day, it rained very fast, and froze about as fast as it fell, so that my clothes were one glare of ice. I travelled on at night until I became so chilled and benumbed—the wind blowing into my face— that I found it impossible to go any further, and accordingly took shelter in a barn, where I was obliged to walk about to keep from freezing.

I have ever looked upon that night as the most eventful part of my escape from slavery. Nothing but the providence of God, and that old barn, saved me from freezing to death. I received a very severe cold, which settled upon my lungs, and from time to time my feet had been frostbitten, so that it was with difficulty I could walk. In this situation I travelled two days, when I found that I must seek shelter somewhere, or die.

The thought of death was nothing frightful to me, compared with that of being caught, and again carried back into slavery. Nothing but the prospect of enjoying liberty could have induced me to undergo such trials, for

> Behind I left the whips and chains,
> Before me were sweet Freedom's plains!

This, and this alone, cheered me onward. But I at last resolved to seek protection from the inclemency of the weather, and therefore I secured myself behind some logs and brush, intending to wait there until some one should

---

[3] I.e., because their masters are their fathers. Brown was the son of George Higgins of Kentucky, a relation of Dr. Young.

pass by, for I thought it probable that I might see some colored person, or, if not, someone who was not a slaveholder. For I had an idea that I should know a slaveholder as far as I could see him.

The first person that passed was a man in a buggywagon. He looked too genteel for me to hail him. Very soon another passed by on horseback. I attempted to speak to him, but fear made my voice fail me. As he passed, I left my hidingplace, and was approaching the road, when I observed an old man walking towards me, leading a white horse. He had on a broad-brimmed hat and a very long coat, and was evidently walking for exercise. As soon as I saw him, and observed his dress, I thought to myself, "You are the man that I have been looking for!" Nor was I mistaken. He was the very man!

On approaching me, he asked me if I was not a slave. I looked at him some time, and then asked him if he knew of any one who would help me, as I was sick. He answered that he would; but again asked, if I was not a slave. I told him I was. He then said that I was in a very pro-slavery neighborhood, and if I would wait until he went home, he would get a covered wagon for me. I promised to remain. He mounted his horse, and was soon out of sight.

After he was gone, I meditated whether to wait or not; being apprehensive that he had gone for someone to arrest me. But I finally concluded to remain until he should return, removing some few rods to watch his movements. After a suspense of an hour-and-a-half or more, he returned with a two-horse covered wagon, such as are usually seen under the shed of a Quaker meetinghouse on Sundays and Thursdays, for the old man proved to be a Quaker of the George Fox[4] stamp.

He took me to his house, but it was some time before I could be induced to enter it. Not until the old lady came out, did I venture into the house. I thought I saw something in the old lady's cap that told me I was not only safe, but welcome, in her house. I was not, however, prepared to receive their hospitalities. The only fault I found with them was their being too kind. I had never had a white man to treat me as an equal, and the idea of a white lady waiting on me at the table was still worse! Though the table was loaded with the good things of this life, I could not eat. I thought if I could only be allowed the privilege of eating in the kitchen I should be more than satisfied!

Finding that I could not eat, the old lady, who was a "Thompsonian," made me a cup of "composition," or "number six,"[5] but it was so strong and hot, that I called it *"number seven!"* However, I soon found myself at home in this family. On different occasions, when telling these facts, I have been asked how I felt upon finding myself regarded as a man by a white family, especially just having run away from one. I cannot say that I have ever answered the question yet.

---

[4] George Fox (1624–1691), founder of Quakerism, renowned for the strength of his convictions despite being often imprisoned by the authorities.
[5] "Number six" was a popular mixture or "composition" marketed in the period; Brown jokes that the mixture prepared here was more potent still. Thompsonian: Or Thomsonian, after Samuel Thomson (1769–1843), Massachusetts botanic physician who stressed vegetable treatments.

The fact that I was in all probability a freeman, sounded in my ears like a charm. I am satisfied that none but a slave could place such an appreciation upon liberty as I did at that time. I wanted to see mother and sister, that I might tell them "I was free!" I wanted to see my fellow slaves in St. Louis, and let them know that the chains were no longer upon my limbs. I wanted to see Captain Price, and let him learn from my own lips that I was no more a chattel, but a man! I was anxious, too, thus to inform Mrs. Price that she must get another coachman. And I wanted to see Eliza more than I did either Mr. or Mrs. Price!

The fact that I was a freeman—could walk, talk, eat and sleep, as a man, and no one to stand over me with the blood-clotted cow-hide—all this made me feel that I was not myself.

The kind friend that had taken me in was named Wells Brown. He was a devoted friend of the slave, but was very old, and not in the enjoyment of good health. After being by the fire awhile, I found that my feet had been very much frozen. I was seized with a fever, which threatened to confine me to my bed. But my Thompsonian friends soon raised me, treating me as kindly as if I had been one of their own children. I remained with them twelve or fifteen days, during which time they made me some clothing, and the old gentleman purchased me a pair of boots.

I found that I was about fifty or sixty miles from Dayton, in the state of Ohio, and between one and two hundred miles from Cleveland, on Lake Erie, a place I was desirous of reaching on my way to Canada. This I know will sound strangely to the ears of people in foreign lands, but it is nevertheless true. An American citizen was fleeing from a democratic, republican, Christian government, to receive protection under the monarchy of Great Britain. While the people of the United States boast of their freedom, they at the same time keep three millions of their own citizens in chains; and while I am seated here in sight of Bunker Hill Monument, writing this narrative, I am a slave, and no law, not even in Massachusetts, can protect me from the hands of the slave-holder!

Before leaving this good Quaker friend, he inquired what my name was besides William. I told him that I had no other name. "Well," said he, "thee must have another name. Since thee has got out of slavery, thee has become a man, and men always have two names."

I told him that he was the first man to extend the hand of friendship to me, and I would give him the privilege of naming me.

"If I name thee," said he, "I shall call thee Wells Brown, after myself."

"But," said I, "I am not willing to lose my name of William. As it was taken from me once against my will, I am not willing to part with it again upon any terms.

"Then," said he, "I will call thee William Wells Brown."

"So be it," said I; and I have been known by that name ever since I left the house of my first white friend, Wells Brown.

After [he gave] me some little change, I again started for Canada. In four days I reached a public house, and went in to warm myself. I there learned that some fugitive slaves had just passed through the place. The men in the barroom were talking about it, and I thought that it must have been myself they referred to, and I was therefore afraid to start, fearing they would seize me; but I finally mustered courage enough, and took my leave. As soon as I was out of sight, I went into the woods, and remained there until night, when I again regained the road, and travelled on until next day.

Not having had any food for nearly two days, I was faint with hunger, and was in a dilemma what to do, as the little cash supplied me by my adopted father, and which had contributed to my comfort, was now all gone. I however concluded to go to a farmhouse, and ask for something to eat. On approaching the door of the first one presenting itself, I knocked, and was soon met by a man who asked me what I wanted. I told him that I would like something to eat. He asked me where I was from, and where I was going. I replied that I had come some way, and was going to Cleveland.

After hesitating a moment or two, he told me that he could give me nothing to eat, adding that if I would work, I could get something to eat.

I felt bad, being thus refused something to sustain nature, but did not dare tell him that I was a slave.

Just as I was leaving the door, with a heavy heart, a woman who proved to be the wife of this gentleman came to the door and asked her husband what I wanted. He did not seem inclined to inform her. She therefore asked me herself. I told her that I had asked for something to eat. After a few other questions, she told me to come in and she would give me something to eat.

I walked up to the door, but the husband remained in the passage, as if unwilling to let me enter.

She asked him two or three times to get out of the way, and let me in. But as he did not move, she pushed him on one side, bidding me walk in! I was never before so glad to see a woman push a man aside! Ever since that act, I have been in favor of "woman's rights!"

After giving me as much food as I could eat, she presented me with ten cents, all the money then at her disposal, accompanied with a note to a friend, a few miles further on the road. Thanking this angel of mercy from an overflowing heart, I pushed on my way, and in three days arrived at Cleveland, Ohio.

Being an entire stranger in this place, it was difficult for me to find where to stop. I had no money, and the lake being frozen, I saw that I must remain until the opening of the navigation, or go to Canada by way of Buffalo. But believing myself to be somewhat out of danger, I secured an engagement at the Mansion House, as a table waiter, in payment for my board. The proprietor, however, whose name was E. M. Segur, in a short time hired me for twelve dollars a month; on which terms I remained until spring, when I found good employment on board a lake steamboat.

I purchased some books and at leisure moments perused them with considerable advantage to myself. While at Cleveland, I saw, for the first time, an antislavery newspaper. It was the *Genius of Universal Emancipation*, published by Benjamin Lundy;[6] and though I had no home, I subscribed for the paper. It was my great desire, being out of slavery myself, to do what I could for the emancipation of my brethren yet in chains, and while on Lake Erie, I found many opportunities of "helping their cause along."

It is well known that a great number of fugitives make their escape to Canada, by way of Cleveland; and while on the lakes, I always made arrangement to carry them on the boat to Buffalo or Detroit, and thus effect their escape to the "promised land." The friends of the slave, knowing that I would transport them without charge, never failed to have a delegation when the boat arrived at Cleveland. I have sometimes had four or five on board at one time.

In the year 1842, I conveyed, from the first of May to the first of December, sixty-nine fugitives over Lake Erie to Canada. In 1843, I visited Malden, in Upper Canada, and counted seventeen in that small village, whom I had assisted in reaching Canada. Soon after coming north I subscribed for the *Liberator*, edited by that champion of freedom, William Lloyd Garrison.[7] I had heard nothing of the antislavery movement while in slavery, and as soon as I found that my enslaved countrymen had friends who were laboring for their liberation, I felt anxious to join them, and give what aid I could to the cause.

I early embraced the temperance cause, and found that a temperance reformation was needed among my colored brethren. In company with a few friends, I commenced a temperance reformation among the colored people in the city of Buffalo, and labored three years, in which time a society was built up, numbering over five hundred out of a population of less than seven hundred.

In the autumn, 1843, impressed with the importance of spreading antislavery truth, as a means to bring about the abolition of slavery, I commenced lecturing as an agent of the Western New York Anti-Slavery Society, and have ever since devoted my time to the cause of my enslaved countrymen. . . .

APPENDIX

In giving a history of my own sufferings in slavery, as well as the sufferings of others with which I was acquainted, or which came under my immediate observation, I have spoken harshly of slaveholders, in church and state.

Nor am I inclined to apologize for anything which I have said. There are exceptions among slaveholders, as well as among other sinners; and the fact that a slaveholder feeds his slaves better, clothes them better, than another, does not alter the case; he is a slaveholder. I do not ask the slaveholder to feed, clothe, or to treat his victim better as a slave. I am not waging a warfare against the collateral evils, or what are sometimes called the abuses, of slavery. I wage

---

[6]Lundy (1789–1839), a New Jersey native of Quaker background, had moved to Ohio in 1815; a saddler by trade, he published his abolitionist newspaper from 1821 until 1835, and then revived it in Illinois in 1839.

[7]Garrison (1805–1879) had been recruited to the antislavery party by Benjamin Lundy, in whose paper he published many denunciations of the system before he launched *The Liberator* in 1831.

a war against slavery itself, because it takes man down from the lofty position which God intended he should occupy, and places him upon a level with the beasts of the field. It decrees that the slave shall not worship God according to the dictates of his own conscience; it denies him the word of God; it makes him a chattel, and sells him in the market to the highest bidder; it decrees that he shall not protect the wife of his bosom; it takes from him every right which God gave him. Clothing and food are as nothing compared with liberty. What care I for clothing or food, while I am the slave of another? You may take me and put cloth upon my back, boots upon my feet, a hat upon my head, and cram a beefsteak down my throat, and all of this will not satisfy me as long as I know that you have the power to tear me from my dearest relatives. All I ask of the slaveholder is to give the slave his liberty. It is freedom I ask for the *slave*. And that the American slave will eventually get his freedom, no one can doubt. You cannot keep the human mind forever locked up in darkness. A ray of light, a spark from freedom's altar, the idea of inherent right, each, all, will become fixed in the soul; and that moment his "limbs swell beyond the measure of his chains," that moment he is free; then it is that the slave dies to become a freeman; then it is felt that one hour of virtuous liberty is worth an eternity of bondage; then it is, in the madness and fury of his blood, that the excited soul exclaims,

> From life without freedom, oh! who would not fly;
> For one day of freedom, oh! who would not die?

The rising of the slaves in Southampton, Virginia, in 1831, has not been forgotten by the American people. Nat Turner, a slave for life—a Baptist minister—entertained the idea that he was another Moses, whose duty it was to lead his people out of bondage. His soul was fired with the love of liberty, and he declared to his fellow slaves that the time had arrived, and that "They who would be free, themselves must strike the blow." He knew that it would be "liberty or death" with his little band of patriots, numbering less than three hundred. He commenced the struggle for liberty; he knew his cause was just, and he loved liberty more than he feared death. He did not wish to take the lives of the whites; he only demanded that himself and brethren might be free. The slaveholders found that men whose souls were burning for liberty, however small their numbers, could not be put down at their pleasure, that something more than water was wanted to extinguish the flame. They trembled at the idea of meeting men in open combat, whose backs they had lacerated, whose wives and daughters they had torn from their bosoms, whose hearts were bleeding from the wounds inflicted by them. They appealed to the United States government for assistance. A company of United States troops was sent into Virginia to put down men whose only offence was, that they wanted to be free. Yes! northern men, men born and brought up in the free states, at the demand of slavery, marched to its rescue. They succeeded in reducing the poor slave again to his chains, but they did not succeed in crushing his spirit.

Not the combined powers of the American Union, not the slaveholders, with all their northern allies, can extinguish that burning desire of freedom in the slave's soul! Northern men may stand by as the bodyguard of slaveholders. They may succeed for the time being in keeping the slave in his chains; but unless the slaveholders liberate their victims, and that, too, speedily, some modern Hannibal will make his appearance in the southern states, who will trouble the slaveholders as the noble Carthaginian did the Romans. Abolitionists deprecate the shedding of blood; they have warned the slaveholders again and again. Yet they will not give heed, but still persist in robbing the slave of liberty.

"But for the fear of northern bayonets, pledged for the master's protection, the slaves would long since have wrung a peaceful emancipation from the fears of their oppressors, or sealed their own redemption in blood." To the shame of the northern people, the slaveholders confess that to them they are "indebted for a permanent safeguard against insurrection"; that "a million of their slaves stand ready to strike for liberty at the first tap of the drum"; and but for the aid of the North they would be too weak to keep them in their chains. I ask in the language of the slave's poet,

> What! shall ye guard your neighbor still,
> While woman shrieks beneath his rod,
> And while he tramples down at will
> The image of a common God?
> Shall watch and ward be 'round him set,
> Of northern nerve and bayonet?

The countenance of the people at the North has quieted the fears of the slaveholders, especially the countenance which they receive from northern churches. "But for the countenance of the northern church, the southern conscience would have long since awakened to its guilt: and the impious sight of a church made up of slaveholders, and called the church of Christ, been scouted from the world." So says a distinguished writer.

Slaveholders hide themselves behind the church. A more praying, preaching, psalm-singing people cannot be found than the slaveholders at the South. The religion of the South is referred to every day, to prove that slaveholders are good, pious men. But with all their pretensions, and all the aid which they get from the northern church, they cannot succeed in deceiving the Christian portion of the world. Their child-robbing, man-stealing, woman-whipping, chain-forging, marriage-destroying, slave-manufacturing, man-slaying religion, will not be received as genuine; and the people of the free states cannot expect to live in union with slaveholders, without becoming contaminated with slavery. They are looked upon as one people; they *are* one people; the people in the free and slave states form the "American Union." Slavery is a national institution. The nation licenses men to traffic in the bodies and souls of men; it supplies them with public buildings at the capital of the country to keep their victims in. For a paltry sum it gives the auctioneer a license to sell American men, women, and children, upon the auction-stand. The American slavetrader, with the Constitution in his hat and his license in his pocket, marches his gang of chained men and women under the very eaves of the nation's capitol. And this, too, in a country professing to be the freest nation in the world. They profess to be democrats, republicans, and to believe in the natural equality of men; that they are "all created with certain inalienable rights, among which are life, liberty, and the pursuit of happiness." They call themselves a Christian nation; they rob three millions of their countrymen of their liberties, and then talk of their piety, their democracy, and their love of liberty; and, in the language of Shakspeare, say,

> And thus I clothe my naked villany,
> And seem a saint when most I play the devil.

The people of the United States, with all their high professions, are forging chains for unborn millions, in their wars for slavery. With all their democracy, there is not a foot of land over which the "stars and stripes" fly, upon which the American slave can stand and claim protection. Wherever the United States Constitution has jurisdiction, and the American flag is seen flying, they point out the slave as a chattel, a thing, a piece of property. But I thank God there is one spot in America upon which the slave can stand and be a man. No matter whether the claimant be a United States president, or a doctor of divinity; no matter with what solemnities some American court may have pronounced him a slave; the moment he makes his escape from under the "stars and stripes," and sets foot upon the soil of Canada, "the altar and the god sink together in the dust; his soul walks abroad in her own majesty; his body swells beyond the measure of his chains, that burst from around him; and he stands redeemed, regenerated, and disenthralled, by the irresistible genius of universal emancipation."

But slavery must and will be banished from the United States soil:

> Let tyrants scorn, while tyrants dare,
> The shrieks and writhings of despair;
> The end will come, it will not wait,
> Bonds, yokes, and scourges have their date;
> Slavery itself must pass away,
> And be a tale of yesterday.

But I will now stop, and let the slaveholders speak for themselves. I shall here present some evidences of the treatment which slaves receive from their masters; after which I will present a few of the slave laws. And it has been said, and I believe truly, that no people were ever found to be better than their laws. And, as an American slave—as one who is identified with the slaves of the South by the scars which I carry on my back—as one identified with them by the tenderest ties of nature—as one whose highest aspirations are to serve the cause of truth and freedom—I beg of the reader not to lay this book down until he or she has read every page it contains. I ask it not for my own sake, but for the sake of three millions who cannot speak for themselves.

From the Livingston County (Alabama) *Whig* of Nov. 16, 1845:

"Negro Dogs.—The undersigned having bought the entire pack of Negro dogs (of the Hays & Allen stock) he now proposes to catch runaway Negroes. His charge will be three dollars per day for hunting, and fifteen dollars for catching a runaway. He resides three-and-a-half miles north of Livingston, near the lower Jones' Bluff Road.

"William Gambrel.

"Nov. 6, 1845."

The Wilmington [North Carolina] *Advertiser* of July 13, 1838, contains the following advertisement:

"Ran away, my Negro man Richard. A reward of $25 will be paid for his apprehension, DEAD or ALIVE. Satisfactory proof will only be required of his being killed. He has with him, in all probability, his wife Eliza, who ran away from Col. Thompson, now a resident of Alabama, about the time he commenced his journey to that state.

"D. H. Rhodes."

The St. Louis *Gazette* says—

"A wealthy man here had a boy named Reuben, almost white, whom he caused to be branded in the face with the words 'A slave for life.' "

From the North Carolina *Standard*, July 28, 1838:

"Twenty dollars reward—Ran away from the subscriber, a Negro woman and two children; the woman is tall and black, and *a few days before she went off* I BURNT HER ON THE LEFT SIDE OF HER FACE: I TRIED TO MAKE THE LETTER M, *and she kept a cloth over her head and face, and a fly bonnet over her head, so as to cover the burn;* her children are both boys. The oldest is in his seventh year; he is a *mulatto* and has blue eyes; the youngest is a black, and is in his fifth year.

"Micajah Ricks, Nash County."

"One of my neighbors sold to a speculator a Negro boy, about fourteen years old. It was more than his poor mother could bear. Her reason fled, and she became a perfect *maniac,* and had to be kept in close confinement. She would occasionally get out and run off to the neighbors. On one of these occasions she came to my house. With tears rolling down her cheeks, and her frame shaking with agony, she would cry out, *'Don't you hear him—they are whipping him now, and he is calling for me!'* This neighbor of mine, who tore the boy away from his poor mother, and thus broke her heart, was a *member of the Presbyterian church.*" —*Rev. Francis Hawley, Baptist minister, Colebrook, Ct.*

A colored man in the city of St. Louis was taken by a mob, and burnt alive at the stake. A bystander gives the following account of the scene: —

"After the flames had surrounded their prey, and when his clothes were in a blaze all over him, his eyes burnt out of his head, and his mouth seemingly parched to a cinder, someone in the *crowd*, more compassionate than the rest, proposed to put an end to his misery by shooting him, when it was replied, that it would be of no use, since he was already out of his pain. 'No,' said the wretch, 'I am not, I am suffering as much as ever, —shoot me, shoot me.' 'No, no,' said one of the fiends, who was standing about the sacrifice they were roasting, 'he shall not be shot; I would sooner slacken the fire, if that would increase his misery'; and the man who said this was, we understand, an *officer of justice.*" —Alton *Telegraph.*

"We have been informed that the slave William, who murdered his master (Huskey) some weeks since, was taken by a party a few days since *from the sheriff* of Hot Spring, and *burned alive!* Yes, tied up to the limb of a tree and a fire built under him, and consumed in a slow lingering torture." —Arkansas *Gazette*, Oct. 29, 1836.

The Natchez *Free Trader*, 16th June, 1842, gives a horrible account of the execution of the Negro Joseph on the 5th of that month for murder.

"The body," says that paper, "was taken and chained to a tree immediately on the bank of the Mississippi, on what is called Union Point. The torches were lighted and placed in the pile. He watched unmoved the curling flame as it grew, until it began to entwine itself around and feed upon his body. Then he sent forth cries of agony painful to the ear, begging some one to blow his brains out, at the same time surging with almost superhuman strength, until the staple with which the chain was fastened to the tree, not being well secured, drew out, and he leaped from the burning pile. At that moment the sharp ring of several rifles was heard, and the body of the Negro fell a corpse to the ground. He was picked up by two or three, and again thrown into the fire and consumed."

"Another Negro Burned. —We learn from the clerk of the *Highlander*, that, while wooding a short distance below the mouth of Red River,[8] they were *invited to stop a short time and see another Negro burned.*" —New Orleans *Bulletin.*

"We can assure the Bostonians, one and all, who have embarked in the nefarious scheme of abolishing slavery at the South, that lashes will hereafter be spared the backs of their emissaries. Let them send out their men to Louisiana;

[8] This steamboat had stopped to take on a load of wood.

they will never return to tell their sufferings, but they shall expiate the crime of interfering in our domestic institutions by being BURNED AT THE STAKE."—New Orleans *True American.*

"The cry of the whole South should be death, instant death, to the abolitionist, wherever he is caught."—Augusta (Georgia) *Chronicle.*

"Let us declare through the public journals of our country, that the question of slavery is not and shall not be open for discussion: that the system is too deep-rooted among us, and must remain forever; that the very moment any private individual attempts to lecture us upon its evils and immorality, and the necessity of putting means in operation to secure us from them, in the same moment his tongue shall be cut out and cast upon the dunghill."—Columbia (South Carolina) *Telescope.*

From the *St. Louis Republican:*
"On Friday last the coroner held an inquest at the house of Judge Dunica, a few miles south of the city, over the body of a Negro girl, about eight years of age, belonging to Mr. Cordell. The body exhibited evidence of the most cruel whipping and beating we have ever heard of. The flesh on the back and limbs was beaten to a jelly—one shoulder-bone was laid bare—there were several cuts, apparently from a club, on the head—and around the neck was the indentation of a cord, by which it is supposed she had been confined to a tree. She had been hired by a man by the name of Tanner, residing in the neighborhood, and was sent home in this condition. After coming home, her constant request, until her death, was for bread, by which it would seem that she had been starved as well as unmercifully whipped. The jury returned a verdict that she came to her death by the blows inflicted by some persons unknown whilst she was in the employ of Mr. Tanner. Mrs. Tanner has been tried and acquitted."

A correspondent of the New York *Herald* writes from St. Louis, Oct. 19:
"I yesterday visited the cell of Cornelia, the slave charged with being the accomplice of Mrs. Ann Tanner (recently acquitted) in the murder of a little Negro girl, by whipping and starvation. She admits her participancy, but says she was compelled to take the part she did in the affair. On one occasion she says the child was tied to a tree from Monday morning till Friday night, exposed by day to the scorching rays of the sun, and by night to the stinging of myriads of mosquitoes; and that during all this time the child had nothing to eat, but was whipped daily. The child told the same story to Dr. McDowell."

From the Carroll County *Mississippian*, May 4th, 1844:
"May 15, 1844.
"Committed to jail in this place, on the 29th of April last, a runaway slave named Creesy, [who] says she belongs to William Barrow, of Carroll County,

Mississippi. Said woman is stout built, five-feet-four inches high, and appears to be about twenty years of age; she has a band of iron on each ankle, and a trace chain[9] around her neck, fastened with a common padlock.

"*J. N. Spencer, Jailer.*"

The Savannah, Georgia, *Republican* of the 13th of March, 1845, contains an advertisement, one item of which is as follows:

"Also [to be sold] at the same time and place, the following Negro slaves, to wit: Charles, Peggy, Antonnett, Davy, September, Maria, Jenny, and Isaac—levied on as the property of Henry T. Hall, to satisfy a mortgage fi. fia.[1] issued out of McIntosh Superior Court, in favor of the board of directors of the *Theological Seminary of the Synod of South Carolina and Georgia*, vs. said Henry T. Hall. Conditions, cash.

"*C. O'Neal, Deputy Sheriff, M.C.*"

In the Macon, Georgia, *Telegraph*, May 28, is the following:

"About the first of March last, the Negro man RANSOM left me, without the least provocation whatever. I will give a reward of $20 for said Negro, if taken DEAD or ALIVE—and if killed in any attempt an advance of $5 will be paid.

"*Bryant Johnson.*
"*Crawford Co., Ga.*"

From the Apalachicola *Gazette*, May 9:

"One hundred and forty dollars reward—Ran away from my plantation on the 6th inst., three Negro men, all of dark complexion.

"BILL is about five feet four inches high, aged about twenty-six, [has] *a scar on his upper lip*, also *one on his shoulder*, and has been *badly cut on his arm*; speaks quick and broken, and [has] a venomous look.

"DANIEL is about the same height, chunky and well set, [has a] broad, flat mouth, with a pleasing countenance; [is] rather inclined to show his teeth when talking. No particular marks recollected; aged about twenty-three.

"NOAH is about six-feet three- or four-inches high, twenty-eight years old, with rather a down,[2] impudent look, [is] insolent in his discourse, with a large mark on his breast, *a good many large scars* caused by the whip on his back—*has been shot in the back of his arm* with small shot. The above reward will be paid to anyone who will KILL the three, or fifty for either one, or twenty dollars apiece for them delivered to me at my plantation alive, on Chattahoochie, Early County.

"*J. McDonald.*"

[9] Heavy chain used in harnessing draft animals.
[1] A legal abbreviation indicating that an execution of a court decision, in this case regarding foreclosure of a mortgage, has been made.
[2] Downcast, averted.

From the Alabama *Beacon*, June 14, 1845:

"Ran away, on the 15th of May, from me, A Negro woman named Fanny. Said woman is twenty years old; is rather tall, can read and write, and so forge passes for herself. Carried away with her a pair of earrings, [and] a Bible with a red cover. [She] is very pious. She prays a great deal, and was, as supposed, contented and happy. She is as white as most white women, with straight light hair, and blue eyes, and can pass herself for a white woman. I will give five hundred dollars for her apprehension and delivery to me. She is very intelligent.

"*John Balch.*
"*Tuscaloosa, May, 29, 1845.*"

From the New Orleans *Commercial Bulletin*, Sept. 30:

"Ten Dollars Reward—Ran away from the subscribers, on the 15th of last month, the Negro man Charles, about 45 years of age, 5 feet 6 inches high; red complexion, has had the *upper lid of his right eye torn*, and *a scar on his forehead*; speaks English only, and stutters when spoken to; he had on when he left, *an iron collar, the prongs of which he broke off before absconding.* The above reward will be paid for the arrest of said slave.

"*W. E. & R. Murphy,*
"*132 Old Raisin.*"

From the New Orleans *Bee*, Oct. 5:

"Ran away from the residence of Messrs. F. Duncom & Co., the Negro Francois, aged from 25 to 30 years, about 5 feet 1 inch in height; the *upper front teeth are missing*; he had *chains on both of his legs*, [and was] dressed with a kind of blouse made of sackcloth. A proportionate reward will be given to whoever will bring him back to the bakery, No. 74, Bourbon Street."

From the New Orleans *Picayune* of Sunday, Dec. 17:

"Cock-Pit—*Benefit of Fire Company No. 1, Lafayette*—A cock-fight will take place on Sunday, the 17th inst., at the well-known house of the subscriber. As the entire proceeds are for the benefit of the fire company, a full attendance is respectfully solicited.

"*Adam Israng.*
"*Corner of Josephine and Tchoupitoulas streets, Lafayette.*"

From the New Orleans *Picayune*:

"Turkey Shooting—This day, Dec 17, from 10 o'clock, A. M., until 6 o'clock, P. M., and the following Sundays, at M'Donoughville, opposite the second municipality ferry."

The next is an advertisement from the New Orleans *Bee*, an equally popular paper.

"A bullfight, between a ferocious bull and a number of dogs, will take place on Sunday next, at 4:15 P. M., on the other side of the river, at Algiers, opposite Canal Street. After the bullfight, a fight will take place between a bear and some dogs. The whole to conclude by a combat between an ass and several dogs.

"Amateurs bringing dogs to participate in the fight will be admitted gratis. Admittance—Boxes, 50 cts.; Pit, 30 cts. The spectacle will be repeated every Sunday, weather permitting.

"Pepe Llulla."

The following is from the *Christian Index*, published at Penfield, Ga.:

"Executors' Sale—Will be sold at the late residence of Jesse Perkins, deceased, late of Greene County, on Wednesday, the 1st of March next, the following property, viz:

Allen, about 30 years old; Claiborn, 25; Dick, 25; Anderson, 20; Asa, 15; Israel, 14; Harrison, 13; Nathan, 13; Sirena, 14; Adaline, 12; and Wesley, 10.

"Also, stock of hogs, stock of cattle, horses, corn, fodder and oats, plantation tools, &c.

"All sold as the property of the said Jesse Perkins, deceased, under his last will, in order to make a division among the legatees of said estate. Terms on day of sale.

"Vincent Sanford,
Nicholas Perkins, } *Ex'rs.*
"Jan. 15, 1848."

Euta (Ala.) *Whig*:

"The sale of about one hundred and sixty Negroes, 44 mules and horses, 250 or 300 pork hogs, stock hogs, cattle, corn, fodder, oats, plantation tools, cooking utensils, &c., &c., will commence on Friday, the 10th of December, at the plantation of John Jones, deceased, near Warsaw, Sumter county.

"The sale will be continued on Monday, 13th of December, at the late residence of John Jones, deceased, in Greene County—say *one hundred and fourteen or fifteen Negroes,* 33 mules and horses, 7 yoke of oxen, pork hogs, stock hogs, cattle, road-wagon, ox-wagon, horse-carts, cart-wheels, cotton-gins, corn, fodder, oats, plantation tools, &c.

"The terms of sale, twelve months credit. Notes with two approved securities—interest to be added from sale. All sums under $20, cash.

"William Jones, Jr.,
John P. Evans, } *Adm'rs."*

Richmond *Whig*, 6th Jan., 1836:

"$100 Reward—Will be given for the apprehension of my Negro (!) Edmund Kenney. He has *straight* hair, and complexion so nearly WHITE, that it is believed a stranger would suppose *there was no African blood in him.* He was with my boy Dick a short time since in Norfolk, *and offered him for sale,* and was apprehended, but escaped under pretence of being a WHITE MAN.

"Anderson Bowles."

Newbern *Spectator,* 13th March, 1837:

"$50 Reward will be given for the apprehension and delivery to me of the following slaves: Samuel, and Judy his wife, with their four children, belonging to the estate of Sacker Dubberly, deceased.

"I will give ten dollars for the apprehension of William Dubberly, a slave belonging to the estate. William is about nineteen years old, QUITE WHITE, and would not readily be mistaken for a slave.

"John T. Lane."

Mobile, April 22, 1837:

"$100 Reward.—Ran away from the subscriber, a bright mulatto man slave, named Sam. *Light sandy hair, blue eyes, ruddy complexion*—is so WHITE as easily to pass for a free WHITE MAN.

"Edwin Peck."

"Oct. 12, 1838.

"$50 Reward—I will give the above reward of fifty dollars for the apprehension and securing in any jail, so that I get him again, or delivering to me in Dandridge, E. Tennessee, my mulatto boy named Preston, about twenty years old. It is supposed he will try to pass as a *free* WHITE MAN.

"John Roper."

"Ran away from the subscriber, working on the plantation of Colonel H. Tinker, a bright mulatto boy named Alfred. Alfred is about eighteen years of age, pretty well grown, has *blue eyes, light flaxen hair, skin disposed to freckle.* He will try to pass as FREE BORN.

"S. G. Stewart.
"Greene County, Alabama."

The following advertisement we cut from the *Madison Journal,* published in Richmond, La., Nov. 26, 1847:

"Notice.—The subscriber, living on Carroway Lake, on Hoe's Bayou, in Carroll Parish, sixteen miles on the road leading from Bayou Mason to Lake Providence, is ready with a pack of dogs to hunt runaway Negroes at any time. These dogs are well trained, and are known throughout the parish. Letters addressed to me at Providence will secure immediate attention.

"My terms are five dollars per day for hunting the trails, whether the Negro is caught or not. Where a twelve hours' trail is shown and the Negro not taken, no charge is made. For taking a Negro, twenty-five dollars, and no charge made for hunting.

"James W. Hall."

The following advertisement is from the Charleston, S.C., *Courier*, of Feb. 12, 1835:

"Field Negroes. By Thomas Gadsden. On Tuesday, the 17th inst., will be sold, at the north of the Exchange, at ten o'clock, A.M., a prime gang of *ten Negroes*, accustomed to the culture of cotton and provisions, belonging to the Independent Church, in Christ's Church Parish. Feb. 6th."

In 1833, the Rev. Dr. Furman, of North Carolina, addressed a lengthy communication to the governor of that state, expressing the sentiments of the Baptist church and clergy on the subject of slavery. This brief extract contains the essence of the whole:—"The right of holding slaves is clearly established in the Holy Scriptures, both by precept and example."

Not long after, Dr. Furman died. His legal representative thus advertises his property:—

"NOTICE. On the first Monday of February next, will be put up at *public auction*, before the *courthouse*, the *following property*, belonging to the estate of the late Rev. Dr. Furman, viz:—

"A plantation or tract of land, on and in the Wataree Swamp. A tract of the first quality of fine land, on the waters of Black River. A lot of land in the town of Camden. A library of a miscellaneous character, chiefly theological. Twenty-seven Negroes, some of them very prime. Two mules, one horse, and an old wagon."

12

A WOMAN ON THE
JOURNEY OF DEATH

IN THE YEARS 1846 AND 1847 — A TIME OF CRUCIAL IMPORTANCE FOR THE DIREC-
tion that the United States would take—Kentucky native Susan Shelby Magoffin (1828–1855) witnessed the push of expansionist politics out toward and across
the boundaries of Mexico. The latter country, independent only since 1821, had
lost what is now Texas in 1836 to American immigrants settled there. In 1845,
Texas was added to the Union, Mexico broke off diplomatic relations, and soon
U.S. armies under Stephen W. Kearny and Zachary Taylor were on Mexican
soil, rolling the U.S. boundary down to the Rio Grande and from there west to
the Pacific, including the future states of New Mexico, Arizona, Nevada, and
California. In the New Mexico and California Territories, there already were
sizable American settlements, composed of traders in Santa Fe and California
towns such as Monterey. These advance guards, though they often had close
personal, business, and family ties with the Mexicans, acted in general to ease
American forces and American control into the region. Not all went as
smoothly for the invaders as this summary suggests, however. Kearny had
pushed on to California after declaring Mexican authority in New Mexico null
and void, leaving in charge the Missourian Alexander W. Doniphan, who was
ordered to proceed south into Chihuahua once he was relieved in Santa Fe by
Colonel Sterling Price. Responding to a serious challenge from the Navajo,
however, Doniphan instead marched west and exacted a treaty from them.
When he finally headed south at the end of 1846, an insurgency arose in New
Mexico, resulting in the execution in Taos of several officials and Anglo-American residents, including trader Charles Bent, whom Kearny had appointed governor. The insurgents included both Taos Indians and Mexicans resistant to the
American invasion.

Susan Shelby Magoffin witnessed or heard about much of this up close
because she had left Missouri in June 1846, just after President James Polk had
declared war with Mexico and the United States was drawing up its plans for
the invasion. Her husband, Samuel Magoffin (1801–1888), was a member of a
prominent family of Santa Fe traders, that group of American and Mexican

merchants who carried on a long distance trade between Missouri and New Mexico from 1822 on. The trade was officially welcomed by Mexico, which reversed the Spanish colonial policy of essentially closed borders, but by the 1840s it was clear that the trade linking New Mexico with St. Louis and the United States had profound political and military implications. As they did on other frontiers (such as in the upper Great Lakes following the Revolution) merchants conducted their business in a quasi-military fashion, erecting fortified posts such as Bent's Fort and seeking above all else to establish a framework within which their trade would be profitable and secure. The distinction between protecting their own property and acting as a paramilitary, semi-official representative of U.S. interests was thus obscured. Samuel Magoffin's elder brother James Wiley Magoffin (1799–1868) resided in Mexican territory for twenty years prior to the war and had married into a Mexican family, but when the war came he helped assure victory to the United States.

As she passed across the plains in the summer of 1846, young Susan Magoffin—she was eighteen, married only eight months to a man twenty-seven years her senior, and would soon be pregnant—blithely espoused the cause of her country. What she saw of the Mexican population as the party arrived in Santa Fe and then moved south for the fall to the vicinity of Albuquerque did not impress her. What is remarkable about her diary of the journey south, particularly the part printed here (which details her movement across the infamous "Journey of Death" south of Albuquerque and into El Paso early in 1847) is the fact that once she began having close contact with individual Mexicans she came to express a genuine and deep appreciation for them individually and for their culture. She loved the manners of the people who, close to her husband and his family, acted as their hosts; she found their food a revelation of new flavors and ingredients, and vowed to make a recipe book of the discoveries; and, a thoroughgoing Protestant, she even at one point attended Catholic mass, uncertain of her motives and the wisdom of the act but moved by some powerful attraction to undertake it. In her prose, as a result, beyond the scatter and violence we glimpse here and there, there is the dawning of a new sense of cultural cross-fertilization.

To be sure, Magoffin also experienced serious worries in this period, doubts about the safety of her husband's brother, concerns about her own, and worse things yet. When she stopped recording her experiences on September 8, 1847, more difficulties lay ahead. Her son, born in September in Matamoras while she was suffering from yellow fever, soon died. Her own health apparently suffered a severe reversal from the long struggle of the journey; she returned by steamer to New Orleans and from there went to her home in Kentucky. In the 1850s, she settled down in Missouri with her husband, who had abandoned the Santa Fe trade for good. She was to die there in 1855, still in her twenties, following the birth of her fourth child.

SUSAN SHELBY MAGOFFIN

from *Down the Santa Fe Trail and into Mexico* (1846–47)

FEBRUARY 1847

MONDAY 1ST. BY THE GOODNESS OF GOD WE HAVE COME THIS FAR IN SAFETY. We are almost at the mouth of the *jornada* (the long journey without water);[1] have been travelling slowly, the roads being exceedingly heavy, with two or three severe hills. One we passed this morning [was] about a half mile in length, and the sand so heavy all the teams doubled and were then just able to get over with resting half a dozen times. 'Tis an ugly road—very—but they say 'twill be better after this; I hope so indeed, for the poor animals work so hard. One month of this year is gone and [it is] eight months since we started on this long journey. I wonder if I shall ever get home again? But 'tis all the same if I do or do not; I must learn to look farther ahead than to earthly things. Now that a conviction has been awakened within my dark and sinful soul, how greater is my sin if I suffer it to die away without seeking my Savior's pardon for multiplied transgressions against his infinite goodness and forbearance. I am sinful, my flesh is prone to do evil, and if I remain in this state what says the apostle is my doom—"*Indignation, wrath, tribulation and anguish* upon every soul of man that doeth evil. But glory, honor and peace to every man that worketh good."[2] The two great rewards are laid before me, with the command to choose the "evil or the good." What must I do? I am conscious of my great pollution, my unworthiness of God's mercies and shall I stop at this? No, there is certain ruin if I do. If pardon is offered the penitent, "I will arise and go unto my Father and say unto Him, Father I have sinned against heaven and in thy sight and am not worthy to be called thy child. Make me as one of thy hired servants."[3]

Tuesday 2nd. Fray Cristoval. Well, we have arrived at the last point on the river before taking the Jornaday. Fray Cristoval is a celebrated place, not from the beauty or number of its houses, but from its being a regular camping-ground never passed [unless] the traveller stops a day or two or at the least the half of a day to rest his animals for the *jornada.* One would think that as long as they have been passing towns all down the river, that this must be one too, or at least a settlement; but no, there is not even the dusky walls of an adobe house to cheer its lonely solitude. Like Valverde it is only a regular camping

---

[1] The *jornada del muerto* (literally "the day's journey of the dead man," but often loosely translated from the Spanish as "the journey of death") refers to a stretch of approximately ninety miles on the trail from Santa Fe into Chihuahua, starting roughly at Fray Cristoval in the north and so called because of a Spaniard who, seeking to find a more direct route than that which followed the Rio Grande, tried to make the waterless trek in a single day but died en route.

[2] See Romans 2:8–10.

[3] Luke 15:18–19.

place with a name. At present I can say nothing of its beauties—the bleak hillsides look lovely enough and feel cold enough. In the summer season, though, I suspect it is quite attractive: the river bottom is then green; the cotton-woods are leaved; the stream, though at all times dark and ugly, is more brisk and lively in its flow and these now unattractive sandhills serve as a variation in the scene. Withall I guess it is not so disagreeable.

Three men from El Paso passed us today; the news they bring is little and of little importance. Nothing has been heard of General Wool; they are prepar-ing at Chihuahua to receive Colonel D[oniphan], who will march to *accept of their kindness*, immediately on the arrival of the artillery at El Paso today or tomorrow.[4]

Wednesday 3rd. Three miles from Fray Cristoval tonight, ready to take the *jornada* tomorrow evening. No one has passed us today. At one time this after-noon, though, we thought to have had some news; soon after we started from F. C. we observed a wagon far off to our right, standing near a little woods, and several oxen feeding a short distance from it. *Mi alma* and Gabriel[5] immedi-ately started off, but soon returned reporting the wagon as empty and the ani-mals (which we take by the way) as broken down. They gave out, I suppose, and their owner was obliged to leave his wagon for the want of a team to pull it.

Three of the doctor's[6] men have gone on tonight as express to give Colonel Doniphan intelligence of the insurrection above. It is a dangerous journey for only three men to undertake, but I hope and pray they may be protected safely through it.

Friday 5th. A *la leguna del muerto.*[7] 2 o'clock last evening we started into the *jornada*, travelled till 5 o'clock and stopped two hours to rest the animals and get a little supper. The wind blew high all the evening and the dust [was] considerable. A short time after we stopped or when the fire was made the scene reminded me of one described by Mr. Gregg, in his prairie scenes.[8] The grass caught fire near to our baggage wagon and but for the great activity of the servants and wagoners, all of whom collected around, we should have been now without the wagon or anything in it and perhaps worse off than that, [as] the consequent explosion of two powder kegs in it might have [cost] the life of some of us. They beat it out with blankets, sticks, wagon-whips and in short everything within their reach; half a dozen of the men pushed the wagon off as

---

[4]Colonel Alexander William Doniphan (1808–1887), a lawyer by profession, led a mounted regi-ment of Missouri volunteers over the trail in the summer of 1846 and sought to link up in Chihua-hua with General John Ellis Wool (1784–1869), who was proceeding inland from Texas. Doniphan later proceeded to New Orleans and then returned into Mexico.

[5]Gabriel Valdez of Chihuahua, the brother-in-law of Samuel Magoffin's older brother James W. Magoffin (1799–1868), who had married Gabriel's sister Maria Gertrudes in 1830. *Mi alma:* "My soul" (Spanish), Magoffin's term of endearment for her husband, Samuel (1801–1888).

[6]Dr. Robert F. Richardson, surgeon of M. L. Clark's Missouri volunteer battalion.

[7]The *laguna del muerto*, or Deadman's Lake.

[8]Josiah Gregg (1806–1850), a Santa Fe trader whose *Commerce of the Prairies* (1844) was well known to Magoffin.

fast as the fire advanced towards them, till 'twas entirely extinguished. It is singular how rapidly it will spread in the dry grass—before the alarm could be given yesterday it spread several yards.

About 7 o'clock we again resumed our travel for the night. The ox teams in front, myself and train next, while the mules brought up the rear. *La luna* made her appearance about 10—and afforded us a beautiful light to travel by; the road is hard and level and we made fine progress, arriving at this place about 25 miles by 2 o'clock this morning—and here I am now to describe this place—"The dead man's lake," "*Laguna del muerto*" is some six miles from where we are camped on the road. Travellers generally stop here and send off their animals to water at this spring—quite a long distance too, but 'tis quite necessary, as we shall not find water again till we strike the river forty miles ahead. The exact circumstances of the derivation of the name of "*Laguna del muerto*" I do not recollect, but 'tis from a traveller [who] once, in attempting to find a road to the south more practicable than the river course, started through here alone, and was after found dead at the spring. How the appearance of the country is immediately about there I know not, but to judge from the appearances here, the regular camping-ground, I should fully say the name it bears is not too solitary for it. The country is quite level immediately around us, with dark hills in the distance. The grass is short and dry, the soil sandy, the little prairie dogs have spread their habitation far and wide around and the whole puts on a gloomy aspect.

Monday 8th. Neither yesterday nor the day before have I written. Friday night we travelled all night by a fine moon, till daylight, when we stopped and took a rest of a few hours. During the night we met a company of new Mexicans returning from the pass,[9] and with them an American gentleman named White[1] [to] whom *mi alma* wrote for him to come up to take some charge of his business as he is in want of such a one as he is—a persevering, hardworking and confidential man—and *mi alma* has now sent him back to buy corn and to "look out" to hear all the sly news, to endeavor to procure if possible some protection from Colonel Doniphan, as we do not like the idea of being left entirely behind and alone too. I am not an advocate though for night travelling when I have to be shut up in the carriage in a road I know nothing of, and the driver nodding all the time, and letting the reins drop from his hands to the entire will of the mules. I was kept in a *fever* the whole night, though every one complained bitterly of cold. Saturday morning early we were off again, travelled till 3 o'clock P.M., when we again stopped to rest our fatigued animals. The grass is fine, and though they are doing without water and pulling long and hard they are not suffering in this point. The grama grass is what they are fond of from its being very sweet and slightly green near the roots. It grows in bunches all over the mountains, has a jointed stem with curling blades growing out from each joint. It grows to the height of two feet, though in general not

[9] I.e., *El Paso del Norte*, or El Paso.
[1] James White, a trader who operated between Independence, Missouri, and Santa Fe.

more than six or eight inches. At all seasons the taller portion has a white and harvest-like appearance; large fields of it are like hay. Saturday evening we again started and travelled till 12, when we reached the river, camped on a high bluff about two miles from the water, and sent the stock down to it. All day Sunday we remained at this place to recruit a little, and sent Mr. White on ahead to purchase corn at Don Ana or *Don Llana*.[2] Notwithstanding the many reports of Indians stealing animals and murdering people about here, I have been bold enough to climb up and down these beautiful and rugged cliffs both yesterday and today, but I shall be more careful hereafter, as it is really dangerous. We are in the heart of the Apache range and *mi alma* thinks I am wrong to go two hundred yards from the camp, we are now putting our little *house mui cirquita de los carros*.[3]

Wednesday 10th. Don Llana. Last evening we arrived here after a long day's travel—nooned it on the river about four miles back, and came up this P.M. to the only settlement between the *jornada* and El Paso, owing to the destructive disposition of the Apaches. A few nights since they came into this town and drove off twenty yoke of oxen belonging to government. For the protection of the inhabitants against them for the future, Colonel Doniphan has left them a cannon, and, by the way, we came near getting ourselves into a fine scrape last night by the wild impudence of some of the wagoners. They went into the village, "got on a spree" and ran off with the cannon, brought it to the camp and persisted in taking it as being *unfit for Mexicans*. As 'twas done without provocation, and with seeming hostile intentions, the *alcalde*[4] told us this morning, that if *mi alma* had not then sent him an apology then—by Gabriel—that the men were drunk and he would have it returned in the morning, [the *alcalde*] intended raising a force, and immediately sending an express off to the governor in the pass informing him of the hostile move made against him. This morning the old gentleman is in a gib[5] of trouble, for the men on finding they were not allowed to retain their trophy, spiked the touch-hole so that it will not fire, and if the Indians were to come they would be without protection. *Mi alma* could only apologize, take the *alcalde's* part by agreeing with him that an express must be sent to the governor in El Paso, and at the same time [setting] down in his own private book the names of the two gentleman who committed the depredations.

Camp 10 miles from Don Llana. Mr. White came up with us this evening; has been twenty miles below El Paso to see Colonel Doniphan. The troops have all left the pass—and Col. D. has taken with him five or six of the most influential citizens as hostages for the good behavior of those remaining, to ourselves and all the traders; it is quite a proper step. Many of *mi alma's* friends

[2] Doña Ana, a settlement at the southern end of the *jornada del muerto*.
[3] That is, placing her wagon in the center of the corral formed from the others.
[4] The magistrate or mayor of Doña Ana.
[5] A term of unclear origin and meaning; Magoffin probably means "jib," perhaps in the sense of a "jibbing" animal—one that comes to a standstill or swings about to change direction.

in the pass send him word to come on without fear, that they have always been friendly to him and still are, their houses are open to receive us when we arrive. On the whole we could look for nothing better.

Friday 12th. We have come over some dark-looking ground today. This morning the whole road lay through mesquite thickets, which made me rather careful in walking out. The Indian is a wily man, and one cannot be too precautious when in his territory. Yesterday we passed over the spot where a few years since a party of the Apaches attacked General Armijo[6] as he returned from the pass with a party of troops, and killed some fourteen of his men, the graves of whom, marked by a rude cross, are now seen; he himself received a wound in his leg, from which he will always be lame. This morning we passed the spot were they attacked brother James' little party of a dozen men, this summer, and despoiled them of all their goods. And today we nooned it at *Brasito*, the battle-field long to be remembered by Colonel Doniphan and his little band of seven hundred volunteers.[7] I rode over the battleground (a perfect plain) and brought off as trophies two cartridges, one Mexican the other American.

This [afternoon] we were overtaken by an express mail from Colonel Price[8] at Santa Fé to Colonel Doniphan, and with orders for the pass only, as he has left there, and there is no one to receive it in that place. Doctor Richardson, now with us as concerned with[9] the army, has taken charge of it to send it on tomorrow; he opened it tonight, and we have all the news contained in the newspapers up to the 27th Nov. from the U.S. and to the 4th ditto from Taylor's[1] army, then just leaving Monterrey for San Luis Potosi, via [Saltillo] and Tampico. General Wool with part of his army is to join him, while the other part is sent on to Chihuahua. I hope and trust they may go and moreover be successful with Colonel Doniphan; otherwise we can have no hope of safety farther. The friends of those prisoners taken from the pass can of course have no very friendly feeling towards us, and if they once get the advantage of us what must the consequences be? I heartily wish we were back at Santa Fé in Fort Marcy,

---

[6] General Manuel Armijo (d. 1853), a native of the vicinity of Albuquerque, was a prominent trader operating between Independence and Santa Fe and a holder of many offices, and was at the moment governor of New Mexico.

[7] On December 25, 1846, Doniphan had won the battle of Brazito or Brazitos, which lay between Doña Ana and El Paso, and then went on to occupy the latter on the 28th.

[8] Colonel Sterling Price (1809–1867) had resigned his seat in the United States Congress in order to help organize the war effort in Missouri. He led the 2d regiment of Missouri mounted infantry into the war and took over command in New Mexico when Doniphan moved south into Mexico late in 1846.

[9] I.e., because of his connection with.

[1] General Zachary Taylor (1784–1850), who had previously served in the War of 1812, in the Black Hawk War under General Henry Atkinson, and in the Seminole War, had defeated the Mexicans at Palo Alto (May 8, 1846) and was named commander of the army of the Rio Grande. He moved against Monterrey and Saltillo the following fall, but his policies and actions in following months brought him considerable criticism in Washington. Following his defeat of General Santa Ana at Buena Vista (February 22–23, 1847) his popularity was considerable, as a result of which he was able to secure the presidency in the election of 1848.

and we would be soon too if our animals were in a condition to carry us. They bring me two letters from Lex[ington, Kentucky] in which I find news of the death of Aunt McDowell, and Uncle Dick Hart;[2] the marriage of several acquaintances; many wishes for my return, and sorrow that I ever left home at all. I almost wish so myself, since we have been detained so long, and if we get back at all I shall call it God's blessing.

Saturday 13th. Today we have come about ten miles. Our camp is not on the river, but five or six miles from it, in a real Indian country. The place is called *La Laguna*, simply a saltwater pond, half grown over with reeds; gloomy-looking mountains rear their heads in our rear and sides; the grass has been all *camped*[3] off, and all together it is a gloomy place. The mesquite thickets all around us look the very abodes of the savage red man, and *fear* has at length determined me to remain within my quiet little tent in place of roaming about in search of any little curiosity I might chance to find. Our stay at *Bosquesito*[4] during the fall months has prevented me from preserving many wildflower seeds as I intended; the birds and wind have well-nigh gathered all.

Sunday 14th. Three miles we are from the crossing; today the country improves a little from yesterday. *El rio* winds its way through the mountains, and if the naked cottonwood trees and willow bushes scattered along its banks were only covered with green leaves I know 'twould be pretty. I am beginning to long for a church to attend, *el camino*[5] has ceased to engage my attention as much as formerly and especially on the Sabbath, but as it is there is no preventative now; I came out on this travel regardless of the Sabbath, not bearing in mind the Lord's command, "Remember the Sabbath-day to keep it holy; in it thou shalt not do any work," etc. But God in his infinite mercy has come near unto me, when I was far off, and called me when I sought not after him. My sins and transgressions are heavy on my head, and but for the great and precious promises to the sinner penitent, everywhere to be met with in the holy scripture, I should at once and forever despair of peace and pardon in this world or hereafter. There is no excuse for me now, for "the word is very nigh unto me, in my mouth, and in my heart, that I may do it."[6] Though I am in darkness, the Lord has said "Awake thou that sleepest, and arise from the dead, and Christ shall give thee light."[7]

Monday 15th. En casa de Don Agapita.[8] Leaving the wagons this morning we crossed the river and came into town to the house of *mi alma's* old friend Don Agapita, an old Gauchupine.[9] The house is kept by the old gentleman's single daughter, Doña Josefita, a very interesting and ladylike girl of twenty-two

[2] Sarah Shelby McDowell, a paternal aunt, and Richard Hart, a maternal uncle.
[3] I.e., eaten by the animals during encampments there.
[4] South of Albuquerque, where the Magoffins had paused while awaiting word about the war to their south.
[5] The road.
[6] See Deuteronomy 30:14.
[7] Ephesians 5:14.
[8] In the house of Don Agapita.
[9] A Mexican term for a native-born Spaniard.

years; she is affable, perfectly easy in her manners, and I think if some of the foreigners who have come into this country, and judged of the whole population from what they have seen on the frontiers, would, to see her a little time, be entirely satisfied of [their] error in regard to the refinement of the people. Although I have not judged so rashly as most persons, I confess I am surprised a little—and Don Agapita is a man ever to be beloved, for his hospitable feelings extended to all classes of people. He has sympathy for those in distress or trouble and shows it by endeavoring to serve them; he is a man of learning, experience and good sound sense, and more than all he has a sincere heart. When we arrived he met us at the door with a hearty welcome to his old friend and his wife (I hope, though, he will like me for myself by and by) [and] threw open his house to us with a request for us to take it as our own. I should like to spend *muncho tiempo*[1] with them, but tomorrow we shall remove to *el señor Cura's*, as we are invited and the house has been especially prepared for us.

But a little in regard to the house of our host and hostess and its management etc., etc. *La casa* is not very large but of ordinary size; the *sala*[2] fronts the street, and is nearly the whole length of the house, the walls instead of papering[3] are painted in flowers, vases, etc., and at first had a very antique and singular [look], but now that a few hours' sight have made it accustomed to my visage,[4] I think it equally as pretty as our papering. From the *sala* opens a door into our chamber, a pretty, nice little room with one window and a snug fireplace, a bed in one corner, a lounge in an other. Outside in the patio are flowerpots, birdcages, cats playing and pigeons eating, and such a quantity of the latter I have not seen for a long time. A back door opens into a garden, where fruit trees and grape vines grow in abundance, with here and there a rosebush, a lily bed, or something of the kind; as it is wintertime now, of course there are no bright blossoms to cheer the scene, but the weather is so mild the trees are leaving, and in a little time more there will be fruit. Next comes the table in proper routine; we take coffee about 7:30, breakfast at 10, and dinner at 5—with fruit between meals. Our dishes are all Mexican, but good ones, [and] some are delightful. One great importance, they are well cooked: their meats are all boiled, the healthiest way of preparing them, and are in most instances cooked with vegetables, which are onions, cabbage, and tomatoes, with the addition of apples and grapes. The courses for dinner are four, one dish at a time; for breakfast two, ending always with beans. Brandy and wine are regularly put on at each meal, and never go off without being honored with the salutations of all the company.

Tuesday 16th. The more I see of this family the more I like them, they are so kind and attentive, so desirous to make us easy, so anxious for our welfare in the disturbances of the country. I can't help loving them. The old gentleman remarked at breakfast this morning, that he sympathized—for the experience

[1] I.e., *mucho tiempo*, much time.
[2] Hall or parlor.
[3] I.e., instead of being papered.
[4] I.e., vision.

of many years has taught him that sympathy is a soothing balm—much with me in the troubles, dangers, and difficulties I have been in, those I am now in, and those that I may be in, but with all he says I am learning a lesson that not one could have taught me but experience, the ways of the world. 'Tis true as he says; I have seen and read of Kentucky till I know it all by heart, but who could, by telling me, make me sensible of what I have seen and felt since I left home to travel. His arguments are quite philosophical, and in fine he is a man not met with every day in any part of the world.

Wednesday 17th. En casa del señor Cura.[5] Agreeable to our arrangements we moved our boarding last evening to this, the residence of the priest, who is now a prisoner in the hands of Colonel Doniphan, though I hope for no bad end. So far I find the family exceedingly kind and attentive. The affairs are in the hands of his two sisters, Doña Anna Maria, a widow lady, and Doña Rosalita; Doña Anna's daughter, Doña Josafa, with her three children compose the family. Doña Anna Maria is a second Mrs. Ross[6] in her person, age, conversation and manners. She is good and kind and seems to have rather the principal management, bears the name of a favorite in the village, she is a *mui señora*[7] in my estimation. How much I am struck with their manner of rearing children. The little daughter of Doña Josafita, only six years of age, carries with her the dignity of our girls of eighteen. It attracted my attention particularly the evening I came; with the same ease of a lady much accustomed to society, she entered the room, with a polite bow and *"Bonus tardes,"*[8] shook hands with me and seated herself. The eldest daughter of seventeen years is sick with *sarampion*.[9]

Thursday 18th. I am altogether pleased with our boarding house—the inmates are exceedingly kind and exert themselves so much to make me enjoy myself, 'twould be cruel if I did not attend to their solicitations. We have chocolate every morning on rising, breakfast about 10 o'clock, dinner at two, chocolate again at dark, and supper at 9 o'clock. All are attentive, indeed we are so free and easy, 'tis almost a hotel. Meals are served in our own room, one of the ladies always being in attendance to see and know if we are properly attended to; the dishes are often changed, and well-prepared. I shall have to make me a recipe book to take home, the cooking in everything is entirely different from ours, and some, indeed all of their dishes are so fine 'twould be a shame not to let my friends have a taste of them too.

Don José Ygnacio Rouquia, his señora and three little daughters called this [afternoon]; and la señora Garcia and daughter. My book is drawing so near to a close,[1] and I have so much to write each day, I shall only take a few notes on each hereafter.

Friday 19th. We are all getting quite familiar and friendly in our dealings;

---

[5] In the house of the curate (Reverend Ramon Ortiz).
[6] Apparently a reference to a person in Kentucky.
[7] "Quite a woman."
[8] I.e., *Buenas tardas*—"Good evening."
[9] Measles.
[1] I.e., she was running out of paper in the volume.

as our acquaintance extends it is more agreeable, and to me more improving. As I am quite inquisitive, for I see so many new and strange ways of making everything, I always ask something about it, and in return I give my way. I shall make me a recipe book.

Sunday 21st. This morning I have been to mass—not led by idle curiosity, not by a blind faith, a belief in the creed there practiced, but because 'tis the house of God, and whether Christian or pagan, I can worship there within myself, as well as in a Protestant church, or my own private chamber. If I have sinned in going there in this belief, I pray for pardon for 'twas done in ignorance. I am not an advocate for the Catholic faith. It is not for me to judge, whether it be right or wrong; judgment alone belongs to God. If they are wrong we (if alone in the right way) are not to rail at them, but in brotherly love to use our little influence to guide them into the straight path. One thing among them, they are sincere in what they do. I speak of the people; of the priests and leaders I know nothing. I am told to "judge no man but to bear the burden of my brother." As for myself I must first remove the beam from mine own eye, and then shall I see clearly to pull the mote out of my brother's eye.[2] In my weakness I will endeavor to walk according to God's laws, as my own understanding points them out to me; and at all times I have a help both in the light and in darkness. . . . The Sabbath is not enough observed, it is a day for visiting; and entirely contrary to my feelings and wishes, I have been obliged today to see several ladies that called. There is far more pleasure to me in my Bible, prayerbook, and retirement, and if I could I would have it so; here we have but one room, and persons come in and out, to see me as they are in the habit of visiting other inmates of the house. . . . I wish *mi alma* would observe the Sabbath more than he does, and, though 'tis the custom of the country to do otherwise, shut his store up. It hurts me more than I can tell that he does not find six days of the week sufficient to gain the goods of this poor world, but is also constrained to devote the day that God himself has appointed us to keep holy, to the same business. And I too am to be a partaker of the gain of this day! Oh, I hope and pray that the Lord will make us better, will create within our sinful breasts feelings holy and pious, loving his laws and commands more than we do, and desiring to walk continually in the humble footsteps of him who has offered himself as a guide and a light to those who walk in darkness.

Monday 22nd—Tuesday 23rd. Both yesterday and today I have been returning my calls. Of all the houses and families I have visited that of Don Ygnacio Rouquia pleases me most, to say nothing to disparage the others. Mrs. Rouquia is a lady easy in her own house, commanding respect from her servants, and respectful affection from her children, and exerting herself to entertain her visitors agreeably. Her house is large, though as yet unfurnished, and the *placita*[3] quite pretty, for she takes pride in rearing choice fruit trees, as oranges, figs, apricots, almonds, etc., all of which are tastefully arranged, while

---

[2] See Matthew 7:5.
[3] I.e., *plazita*—little square or plaza.

in the center of the patio she has a raised bed of earth some four feet [high], for flowers; she bears the name of an industrious housewife, and to me shows far better at home than abroad.[4] Her children are studying English and French, and their parents are very anxious to have them proficient in them.

Don Ygnacio is a second George Washington in his *appearance*, and is altogether a great admirer of the man whose name is ever dear to the hearts of the American; he says the course Mr. Polk is pursuing in regard to this war, is entirely against the principles of Washington, which were to remain at home, encourage all home improvements, to defend our rights *there* against the encroachments of others, and never to invade the territory of another nation. . . . Doña Refujio, wife of señor Belumdis, now a prisoner by Colonel Doniphan, lives opposite to Don Y. She is a lady much given to talking, though perhaps means no harm by it; but to one not accustomed to such 'tis rather strange, I must confess. Along with many like questions she asked me if I was never jealous of my husband, and when I could not understand what *"zeloso"*[5] meant she was quite particular to explain to me that at that moment he might be off with his other *señorita*. Oh, how I was shocked, I could have cried my eyes out for anyone else to suppose such a thing, let alone myself! And how 'twould hurt him too if I should tell him, when my own heart tells me he is a husband as true as the world *ever* contained. I generally tell him everything that happens in my visiting, but *this*, I couldn't try his feelings so much, but you my poor journal must hear all whether good or bad, whether in praise or disparagement.

[4] I.e., she is more impressive when visited at home than when seen in public.
[5] I.e., *celoso*.

13

Remembering the Crisis

Many terms are used for the war that erupted in America when Pierre Gustave Toutant Beauregard ordered his troops to start shelling the federal garrison in Fort Sumter, South Carolina, at 4:30 on the morning of April 12th, 1861: the Civil War, the War of the Rebellion, the War between the States, the War of Secession, the War for Southern Independence. Whatever it is called, however, most people would agree that no other single event in American history, not even the Revolution itself, so turned section against section, party against party, and family against family. By the time Robert E. Lee surrendered at Appomattox Courthouse on April 9th, 1865, this bloody experiment in modern warfare without the adjunct of modern medical care had lasted slightly less than four years, had claimed more than a half million casualties, and had left many cities and villages and whole rural districts—the great majority in the South—ruinous and economically crippled.

The war originated in a long bitter struggle between North and South in the preceding decades, but the real grounds of the conflict, like its proper name, have never been completely agreed upon. Slavery was a salient point of difference between the sections, especially once the northern states (finding it morally objectionable as well as economically expendable) abolished it, in piecemeal fashion, from the time of the Revolution onward. Crucial as the question of slavery was in the light of the nation's claim to its liberal ideology, however, it largely served to focus other fundamental differences between what were, in effect, separate nations. Beyond the shared dominance of English backgrounds and the English language in both sections (large portions of the population were not of English extraction, of course), the two sections carried forward into the nineteenth century profound differences in religion, economics, social structure, and local customs. The continuance of slavery in the South was a function of such differences more than their cause, much as its discontinuance in the North, like its always more modest scope there in the past, expressed a whole array of distinctive conditions in northern society. Had the United States been an otherwise stable and compact nation, perhaps these differences would have played themselves out in a less catastrophic fashion. The nation's territorial expansion westward, however, raised the question of which institutional and legal patterns in the East were to be reproduced in the West—or, in a sense, *which* East would control the shape of the new territories and hence of the future nation. Slavery, as the single institutional difference that most complexly captured the broad contrast between the sections, served to distill this overall contest into a readily apparent form. Because a great many people felt very strongly about this question, it became the one issue in which the sections tended to see all their contrasts summarized.

The territorial conflict that was focused on the question of slavery first became critical following the War of 1812. Various temporary resolutions to the dispute, beginning with the Missouri Compromise of 1820 (allowing Missouri to join as a slave state balanced by Maine's admission as a free state), only delayed the conflict in principle between the sections. The later attempt by Stephen A. Douglas to invoke a principle of "popular sovereignty," thereby leaving the question of slavery up to the residents of new territories, precipitated years of warfare in the territories that ended only when the larger sectional conflict began. Douglas's mistaken desire to resolve what was indisputably a national issue on a merely local level showed the degree to which the nation as a unified political entity had not yet come into being.

When arrayed against Britain in the 1770s, the disparate colonies of the eastern seaboard had found a common cause with some ease, even though many individuals, groups, and local communities in fact did not support, or even actively resisted the American cause; once independence from Britain was achieved, some internal differences were inevitably exaggerated while others were critically deepened by subsequent changes. The South, which had not begun to experiment with cotton as a crop prior to 1776, found itself in a new agricultural regime once "King Cotton" became a staple, intensifying its reliance on slavery. Even though the North abolished slavery, and the importation of slaves from abroad into the United States was prohibited by national policy, the total number of slaves in the South more than doubled between the Missouri Compromise and the assault on Sumter. In the North, industrialization began at about the same time as cotton came into production in the South: indeed, the invention of the cotton gin by Eli Whitney in 1793, which allowed the rapid expansion of cotton acreage in the South by providing an efficient means of processing the crop, exactly coincided with the erection in Rhode Island that same year of Samuel Slater's famous second textile mill, which provided a model for the broad expansion of the textile industry throughout the North.

Although a large part of the South's cotton crop was exported to European mills, cotton served as the material tie between the slave fields of the South and the textile mills of the North. The different roles each section played in regard to cotton also typified the broader underlying distinctions. Cotton's effects on society were more profound in the North than the South, since as a crop cotton tended to extend and even strengthen existing social patterns in the South, whereas the textile industry in the North (like other forms of industrialization) tended to radically alter those prevalent there. The northern cities teemed with workers who had few ties with the land, where the vast majority of Americans had always lived and worked. Manhattan alone in 1860 contained more than eight hundred thousand residents, a sixfold increase over 1820 and nearly forty times the number just before the Revolution. Towns such as Lowell, Massachusetts, rising in the 1820s as tentative experiments in the concentrated production of textiles, grew with dizzying rapidity as capital and workers poured in from New England and soon the nation at large and Europe. Southern thinkers such as Jefferson had feared urban growth, urging Americans to import European manufactured goods so they could avoid breeding at home the dangerous, unpredictable "mobs of great cities," and saw the rise of the urban industrial economy of the Northeast as a sign of changes to the fabric of the nation that threatened more than just slavery. Although the southern plantation was itself a modern social system based on the treatment of labor as a commodity and the reduction of people to their mere function as workers, it is important to remember that the plantation accounted for only a relatively small portion of the slave population in the South. When southern apologists defended slavery, as they did more and more after 1830, they often thought they were defending a rural way of life of which slavery was an adjunct rather than the central feature. As with the southern agrarians of the twentieth century, such apologists saw the South as resisting the cash nexus of northern urban society even though, obviously, no more thoroughgoing example of such a nexus could be found than in slavery itself. These massive changes in nineteenth-century American society, North and South, and the worsening disagreement as to their basic terms, led to a greater divergence in values and viewpoints that contributed a great deal to the coming split in the nation. The sectional differences that existed in 1800 did not simply continue to exist as the decades passed; they deepened at the same time that they were added to by new ones. So little agreement exists as to the proper name for the war that resulted because how one names it reflects one's overall interpretation of American history both before that point in time and afterward.

The conflict has also been called "the unwritten war." Insofar as few great works of fiction or poetry concerned with the experience emerged from among the veterans — the greatest novel of the war, *The Red Badge of Courage*, was written, after all, in the 1890s by a young man born six years after Lee's surrender — the observation is accurate enough. In another sense, however, the conflict that divided the United States in the 1860s was the subject of a great deal of writing. The number of soldiers on both sides who kept diaries, wrote letters home from the field, or later penned their memoirs was exceptionally large. In part the outpouring of language was due to the enormous size of the armies, in part to the heartrending nature of the conflict and what was at stake in it. It was also due, however, to the increasing importance of writing across American culture, which was fast becoming more scribal in its reliance on written records in business, government, and many aspects of everyday life. Farmers, for instance, were much more likely to keep detailed everyday records in the nineteenth century than the eighteenth, while the rise of a complex industrial economy helped create elaborate business records, not to mention the whole profession of accountancy, as a means of keeping written track of farflung transactions. In this scribal atmosphere, those who watched the war at home—in Charleston or Baltimore, on a Virginia farm or in a Vermont village—were moved to match the soldiers' verbal output with their own, while newspapers whose parallel did not exist during the Revolution filled page after page, and whole special editions, with detailed accounts from the field. As a result of all these factors, it in fact seems fairer to call the conflict of the 1860s America's *most* written war. Perhaps we will have to alter that judgment once the many letters, memoirs, and diaries dating from the massive conflicts of the twentieth century make their way in larger numbers into public archives and public print. Until then, though, the war that split America from 1861 to 1865 might best be imagined as having left a mountain of writing on the landscape of national awareness.

Despite the fact that a highly literate soldiery kept untold records while the war raged and an army of correspondents for the press scouted the news as it was happening, the most interesting records of the war tend to be retrospective accounts dating from the decades afterward. As with the pension narratives of the Revolutionary era, a later Civil War narrative may put events into context far better than accounts penned on the spot, if only because distance usually helps people understand precisely what they saw, heard, or felt at the time. Part of the reason, too, is that the long-term consequences of an event as complex as the Civil War, with its many roots in American society, emerged only over the years—even the decades—following, during which the sections, technically reunited after 1865, continued skirmishing over unresolved issues, and race emerged in new ways as a social and political force. In the case of this particular war, the fact that the nation so recently torn asunder and forced back together celebrated the centennial of its founding a bare decade after the cataclysm made the recent conflict of critical interest for the celebrants. The centennial had added significance, too, because it came just as Reconstruction collapsed in the wake of the contested election of 1876. Because Reconstruction was, among other things, an official political interpretation of what the war had been about, and assumed an ongoing narrative of the war's meaning, the fading prospect of more radical change invited other narrative interpretations of the conflict that came in part via the passage of laws, both northern and southern, that defined race relations and economic relations in less radical ways. Interpretations of all kinds sprang from the conflict's combatants and observers, and even members of the next generation like Stephen Crane told tales about the war to probe what it meant. Because of the varied ways in which later narratives constructed and reconstructed the war, the tapestry of Civil War memories dating from this period is especially rich.

The first selection given here comes from what the critic and historian Edmund Wilson once called the greatest American autobiography, the *Personal Memoirs* of Ulysses Simpson Grant, published following Grant's death in July 1885. The end of Grant's life, like much of the rest of it, had a certain ironic poignancy. Increasingly immobilized from cancer as he sought rest in the fresh air of the Adirondack foothills, Grant pushed himself to complete a book that was motivated by a desire not only to give his memories some lasting form but also to provide modest support for his family once he was gone. Never a financial success in a world making rapid transitions from a village economy to a metropolitan one, Grant had virtually nothing else to leave them. After his two terms as president (1869–77) and a lengthy world trip (1877–80), he had invested all his free assets in a private banking firm founded in 1881 by Ferdinand Ward and his own son Ulysses, Ward's partner. During a difficult period three years later, Ward convinced the former president to help avert a looming catastrophe for the bank by securing a short-term loan of 150,000 dollars from financier William H. Vanderbilt. When Grant & Ward ceased operations two days later and Ward was nowhere to be found, his fraudulent activities were soon uncovered, and U. S. Grant was ruined. Not only could he not repay Vanderbilt (whom he gave deeds to all his real estate, plus the gifts showered on him by leaders and ordinary people during his world tour, and his swords and Civil War trophies) — he was accused, wrongly, of being Ward's accomplice in the fraud.

Thrown once more on his own resources, Grant soon agreed to supply the *Century* magazine with articles recounting his experiences in the Civil War. He finished the first of the pieces, concerning the 1862 battle of Shiloh, Tennessee, within a month, then revised it at his editor's urging so as to make it more personal than the original had been. As the work progressed, Grant began to think that a book-length memoir along similar lines might be marketable, and in February 1885 (just as the first of the *Century* pieces finally appeared in print and Grant's doctor told him that his cancer was inoperable) he reached agreement with Samuel L. Clemens to publish the work. Within three months, Clemens's publishing company had secured sixty thousand subscribers for the yet-to-be-published work, but Grant, his health rapidly failing, had to labor very hard to finish writing it before he succumbed on July 23rd, only five days after the manuscript of the second volume was delivered to his publisher.

Grant's private situation as he wrote the *Personal Memoirs* clearly affected how he recalled the public past. Had he been hale and hearty, his recollections probably would have been confined to his Civil War days, whereas the book as ultimately written began with his earliest years, progressed through his experiences at West Point, and then covered his service in the Mexican War, his frontier years in California afterward, and his storekeeping experiences in Galena, Illinois, immediately prior to the Civil War. It is from this first part of the book that the selection here is derived; it deals with the Mexican War, during which, as Grant stresses, many of the men who were to lead armies against each other two decades later were arrayed together in the field, including Grant and Robert E. Lee. It also tells of Grant's California years and gives his compact account of the origins of the Civil War, both long-term and more immediate.

While Grant was dying and writing down his memories in 1884–85, Mary Boykin Chesnut, a southern woman who was almost his exact contemporary (she was born in South Carolina in 1823, a year after Grant was born in Ohio, and she died just a year after Grant, in 1886) was also at work, as she had been for a period in the 1870s as well, on her memoirs of the war. Although published in its three posthumous versions as a "diary," in fact Chesnut's account is a complexly layered fabric of contemporary diary entries and multiple later reflections, reworkings, and adumbrations of the original. No single temporal point of view dominates the text, so that in any one entry we may be reading Chesnut's 1880s voice mimicking her more naïve 1860s perspective, with many intervening vantage points also included. Unraveling all of the original strands would destroy the charm of the final text, and because the earlier text survives only in altered later forms, if it survives at all (much of the original diary simply did not survive: part Mary Chesnut herself burned, part simply went astray or has not turned up), it is not possible to present a "clean" text of the contemporaneous record. That is all to the best in view of how important Chesnut's later sensibility was to her reshaping of the original. Although she had profound doubts about the southern cause from the outset (one of her first 1860s diary entries questions slavery with withering directness), it was her later knowledge of the defeat of that cause that gave her 1880s version its richness. Knowing the end of the conflict, she could rewrite her diary as if her foreknowledge technically did not exist, but the tonal difference in the surviving version is of crucial importance.

That sense of what William Faulkner called "doom" that pervades his own southern tales pervades hers, too, as does Faulkner's obsession with telling and retelling old tales in the hope that they will change their inevitable shape if only they can be retold in the proper way. In order to give the reader a proper sense of how Chesnut managed the complex process of revision, some passages from her 1860s diary are included in brackets (marked with a "D") within the 1880s text printed here. Selections from her narrative cover the whole period of the war, from early 1861 to the summer of 1865. They begin a few months after her husband, the secessionist and pro-slavery apologist James Chesnut (1815–1885), resigned from his recently won seat in the United States Senate and returned with his wife to the South, where he was to serve in the Confederate Congress as well as in the Confederate forces, being Beauregard's aide-de-camp from Sumter until he received his own command as a brigadier general in 1864. In these years, Mary Chesnut's base of operations was South Carolina, where her husband's family and her own possessed extensive plantations, particularly the Chesnut property called Mulberry near Camden in the state's center. Mary Chesnut wandered a good deal during the war, however, living in the original Confederate capital of Montgomery as the Confederacy shaped itself, in Charleston during the assault on Sumter, in the later Confederate capital of Richmond, and then at the very end in small towns in the Carolinas where she hoped to avoid the march of General William T. Sherman's forces from Savannah to Richmond. Because she saw a great deal, heard much more, and thought complexly about what came her way, her observations remain extraordinarily telling today. If one keeps in mind the complex structure of the book's production—that it is not what it seems, a simple record of the times as they passed, but rather a layered fabrication of the past as Chesnut at a later time wished to recall it—the *Diary from Dixie* (as it used to be called) indeed offers a priceless window into the soul of a culture facing its crisis and death.

The third part of this section consists of the memories of ex-slaves regarding their lives in various sections of the South. For the slave still on the plantations during the war, it was hard to know what was happening at any one moment or in the overall conflict. The war did not start as a slave uprising, the way Nat Turner in 1831 or John Brown in 1859 might have insured it would. As far as the slaves could see, at the outset it was a quarrel among the whites, and the uncertainty and slowness with which the status of the slaves themselves became an issue could only have confirmed that impression. Liberty came in pieces to them. On the Sea Islands of South Carolina, the slaves were freed by the invading United States army, which set about running the captured plantations for the profit that might fall to government coffers. An experiment aimed at easing them into freedom and economic self-support turned St. Helena into a buzzing enclave of northern do-gooders soon after Sherman arrived. Still, the Sea Island slaves were exceptional in being thus liberated through invasion, and their improvised liberation was the source of much misunderstanding then and in the future. A more programmatic attempt at freeing the slaves, the Emancipation Proclamation issued by Lincoln in September 1862 (to take effect the following January), also had its pragmatic side: aimed only at those areas still in open rebellion, it said nothing about slaves living in the lands already captured by the North, let alone in the border states that sided with the Union but still allowed legal slavery. Hence it embodied Lincoln's statement to abolitionist Horace Greeley in August 1862: "If I could save the Union . . . by freeing some [slaves] and leaving others alone, I would . . . do that." From the viewpoint of black Americans, the policy announced in the Emancipation Proclamation was simply an improvement over a worse option Lincoln also listed in his response to Greeley, namely: "If I could save the Union without freeing *any* slave, I would do it." Only in the aftermath of the war, as the radicals in control of Congress and the legislatures added the Thirteenth Amendment to the Constitution, thus barring any chattel slavery in the United States, did the official purpose of the war as an antislavery campaign begin to be cast anachronistically back into the war years proper. Thus did distant effect become immediate cause.

In the 1930s, staff members of the Federal Writers' Project turned their attention toward the surviving ex-slaves, whose story was conceivably quite different. Although only a few thousand of the some one hundred thousand survivors of the system were interviewed during the course of the project, the result was a stunning collective record of black experience in slavery and freedom in the years from around 1840 on. Not since the Revolutionary War pension applications had been gathered by the government a hundred years earlier had so many ordinary Americans been so systematically interviewed about their experience in so important an historical episode. In the narratives given here, three women who had lived and labored in Alabama, Arkansas, and Indian Territory (later Oklahoma) turned a skeptical eye toward what by the 1930s— the decade that saw the phenomenal success of *Gone with the Wind* as both book (1936) and movie (1939)—was firmly ensconced in some chambers of American memory as a gallant, noble world destroyed by the nastiness of men such as Sherman. As the administrator charged with oversight of the project after 1938, Benajmin A. Botkin remarked in his published selection from the ten-thousand-page archive that the slaves' own language was flavored with "the salty irony and mother wit which . . . are kept alive by the bookless." The narratives offer more, however, than folksy entertainment. They allow us to probe the way historical experience is turned into narrative, and the way narrative interprets rather than simply "tells" events. Intersecting the diary of Chesnut with the ex-slaves' recollections introduces into the complex weave of that slave-owner's account other strands of American memory. Such pairings reveal how large public events continue to exist as contested verbal traces in the words and rhythms of popular recollection.

The fourth selection adds much to this tapestry. It offers dynamics similar to those in the Chesnut diary, though with a different scope and from a very different personal perspective. Thomas B. Chaplin, also of South Carolina, was of Chesnut's and Grant's generation—born in 1822, he outlived both of the others by only a few years, dying in 1890. The son of well-off planters on coastal St. Helena Island, center of the Sea Island district that produced an especially luxuriant cotton, Chaplin lost his father when he was only six or seven. His mother Isabella married soon after Chaplin's father died, lost that husband in a short time as well, and in the 1840s was to take yet another husband, Robert Little Baker, with whom young Chaplin was often to be at odds, especially over Isabella's complex property. Thomas himself did not long wait to begin his own family, marrying at the exceptionally early age of sixteen and shortly thereafter moving with his bride, Mary McDowell (1822–1851) into the old Chaplin family house at the 376-acre Tombee Plantation on St. Helena. Even this early, Chaplin and his wife ran the operations there, directing the work of the several dozen slaves and managing the agricultural economy of the place although the plantation's income was held in trust for them until Thomas turned twenty-one in 1843. By then he and Mary had four children of their own.

In 1845, then twenty-two, Thomas Chaplin began a journal that he was to keep up until the eve of the war. Much of it concerns the destruction of his own prosperity, which the war finished but which had begun in Chaplin's conflicts with Baker, his own mismanagement (of the plantation and, it might be said, his own life), and the general decline in his land's fertility and in cotton prices in the 1840s and early 1850s. After the gruesome last days of his drug-dependent wife in 1851 (which he described with a distraught but clinical exactness), Chaplin struggled throughout the 1850s with his own dependency on alcohol and with ever-near economic disaster. Ironically, by the time he stopped keeping his journal in 1858, things were looking better for him and for the whole Sea Island district. The push for secession that had been building earlier in the decade subsided then, while Chaplin's agricultural experiments were paying modest dividends. Then with the election of Lincoln and the start of what Chaplin himself would call "that horrid war," the mood quickly altered. Anger and euphoria mixed together in the first months, but then came a quick and complete disaster: Chaplin joined the armed effort early in 1861; by that fall, with July's Confederate victory at Manassas still fresh in mind and with cotton prices rising to unbelievable heights and prosperity seemingly around the corner for the new southern nation, William T. Sherman, in his first invasion of the South, landed on the Sea Islands and the picture suddenly changed for the planters there. Although they had been determined to defend the area, the planters quickly found out that doing so against a sea-borne invasion was impossible, and as they fled the Union forces took over. Because the federal government held the Sea Islands for the duration of the war and confiscated the planters' lands there and sold them for "taxes" (Washington had assessed a tax on all the states to pay for its war against the eleven that had seceded), there was no easy return for any of the planters to their old domains once the war ended. Chaplin, who fought through the war and survived, made it back only as a tenant, working rented lands and teaching newly freed black children in a school there and serving as custodian of federal property at a nearby site where a lighthouse was being erected. At one point he managed to borrow a northerner's money and buy back part of Tombee, but lost it again through a default on the mortgage. Only at the very end of his life, after repeatedly petitioning the federal government for return of a portion of the Tombee property still in United States hands, did Chaplin manage to recover outright a significant part of what he had abandoned in 1861. And nine months later Chaplin, who had been living at his son's home in the mainland town of Walterboro, was dead. No wonder he had called the war horrid.

Chaplin stopped keeping his journal before hostilities began, but he carried the manuscript about with him from then on. He took some melancholy pleasure in rereading it, as he noted in comments penciled in the margin, and over time he began to reinterpret his life as recorded in the book. It is, in fact, his later commentary that makes the record of his antebellum days so evocative of all that happened after those days came to a halt. Chaplin came to view the past through the consciousness of all that had served to make it so irretrievably past. Like Chesnut, though in a much more modest way and without ever destroying or completely effacing the original text, in the 1870s and 1880s Chaplin kept returning to his earlier words and offering new insights into why he had done or said what was recorded in them. And he thus brought to bear on a record that was necessarily ignorant of the coming war a full awareness of what the war produced. Although his journal describes a world antecedent to that evoked in Chesnut's text, in some ways the bitterness of Chaplin's own later life—his fate was much worse than that which awaited Chesnut, who was able to return to a family property after the war—makes what he wrote a more complete representation of the stake white southerners of the planter class felt they had in the conflict. Planters, of course, were in a minority among their own race in the South, but ordinary white southerners, though they may have viewed the sectional conflict differently, fought the war that the Chesnuts and the Chaplins started, defined, and controlled, and in the end the ordinary white southerners lost as much, certainly in life and arguably in spirit, as their leaders.

ULYSSES S. GRANT

from *Personal Memoirs* (1885–86)

MY EXPERIENCE IN THE MEXICAN WAR WAS OF GREAT ADVANTAGE TO ME AFTER-wards. Besides the many practical lessons it taught, the war brought nearly all the officers of the regular army together so as to make them personally acquainted. It also brought them in contact with volunteers, many of whom served in the war of the rebellion afterwards. Then, in my particular case, I had been at West Point at about the right time to meet most of the graduates who were of a suitable age at the breaking out of the rebellion to be trusted with large commands. Graduating in 1843, I was at the military academy from one to four years with all cadets who graduated between 1840 and 1846—seven classes. These classes embraced more than fifty officers who afterwards became generals on one side or the other in the rebellion, many of them holding high commands. All the older officers, who became conspicuous in the rebellion, I had also served with and known in Mexico: Lee, J. E. Johnston, A. S. Johnston, Holmes, Hébert and a number of others on the Confederate side; McCall, Mansfield, Phil. Kearney and others on the National side.[1] The acquaintance

---

[1] Confederate generals Robert E. Lee (1807–1870), U.S. Military Academy (West Point) class of 1829; Joseph E. Johnston (1807–1891), USMA 1829; Albert S. Johnston (1803–1862), USMA 1826, killed at Shiloh; Theophilus H. Holmes (1804–1880), USMA 1829; Louis Hébert (1820–1901), USMA 1845. Union generals George A. McCall (1802–1868), USMA 1822; Joseph K. F. Mansfield (1803–1862), USMA 1822, killed at Antietam; Philip Kearney (1814–1862), killed at Chantilly.

thus formed was of immense service to me in the war of the rebellion—I mean what I learned of the characters of those to whom I was afterwards opposed. I do not pretend to say that all movements, or even many of them, were made with special reference to the characteristics of the commander against whom they were directed. But my appreciation of my enemies was certainly affected by this knowledge. The natural disposition of most people is to clothe a commander of a large army whom they do not know, with almost superhuman abilities. A large part of the National army, for instance, and most of the press of the country, clothed General Lee with just such qualities, but I had known him personally, and knew that he was mortal; and it was just as well that I felt this.[2]

The treaty of peace was at last ratified, and the evacuation of Mexico by United States troops was ordered.[3] Early in June the troops in the city of Mexico began to move out. Many of them, including the brigade to which I belonged, were assembled at Jalapa, above the vomito,[4] to await the arrival of transports at Vera Cruz: but with all this precaution my regiment and others were in camp on the sand beach in a July sun, for about a week before embarking, while the fever raged with great virulence in Vera Cruz, not two miles away. I can call to mind only one person, an officer, who died of the disease. My regiment was sent to Pascagoula, Mississippi, to spend the summer. As soon as it was settled in camp I obtained a leave of absence for four months and proceeded to St. Louis. On the 22d of August, 1848, I was married to Miss Julia Dent, the lady of whom I have before spoken.[5] We visited my parents and relations in Ohio, and, at the end of my leave, proceeded to my post at Sackett's Harbor, New York. In April following I was ordered to Detroit, Michigan, where two years were spent with but few important incidents.

The present constitution of the State of Michigan was ratified during this time. By the terms of one of its provisions, all citizens of the United States residing within the state at the time of the ratification became citizens of Michi-

[2] Grant's knowledge of Lee dated from their service together in the Mexican War, as he states, but Lee was fifteen years older and emerged from that conflict already famous for his valor, and by the 1850s was superintendent at West Point. Grant, by contrast, carried no great reputation from the Mexican War and was forced to resign from the army in 1854 because of his drinking. Grant was so conscious of the disparity in their previous experience that even at the war's end, as he negotiated via letters with Lee before meeting him at Appomattox Courthouse in 1865, he thought his Confederate counterpart, whom he so well recalled (and admired) from the Mexican War, would not remember him at all. Grant however reported that at their first face-to-face meeting at Appomattox on April 9th, Lee graciously told him, as they chatted about "old army times," that he "remembered me very well."

[3] The Treaty of Guadalupe Hidalgo was signed by U.S. and Mexican negotiators on February 2nd 1848 and was ratified by the respective governments on March 10th and May 25th.

[4] I.e., above the low-lying coastal area where the yellow fever, especially the virulent form causing the *vomito*, or black vomit, was endemic.

[5] Julia Dent (1826–1902), daughter of Missouri slaveowners, was the sister of one of Grant's classmates at West Point. They met in 1844 when he visited the Dent farm from his nearby post at Jefferson Barracks.

gan also. During my stay in Detroit there was an election for city officers. Mr. Zachariah Chandler[6] was the candidate of the Whigs for the office of mayor, and was elected, although the city was then reckoned Democratic. All the officers stationed there at the time who offered their votes were permitted to cast them. I did not offer mine, however, as I did not wish to consider myself a citizen of Michigan. This was Mr. Chandler's first entry into politics, a career he followed ever after with great success, and in which he died enjoying the friendship, esteem and love of his countrymen.

In the spring of 1851 the garrison at Detroit was transferred to Sackett's Harbor, and in the following spring the entire 4th infantry was ordered to the Pacific Coast. It was decided that Mrs. Grant should visit my parents at first for a few months, and then remain with her own family at their St. Louis home until an opportunity offered of sending for her. In the month of April the regiment was assembled at Governor's Island, New York Harbor, and on the 5th of July eight companies sailed for Aspinwall.[7] We numbered a little over seven hundred persons, including the families of officers and soldiers. Passage was secured for us on the old steamer *Ohio*, commanded at the time by Captain Schenck,[8] of the navy. It had not been determined, until a day or two before starting, that the 4th infantry should go by the *Ohio*; consequently, a complement of passengers had already been secured. The addition of over seven hundred to this list crowded the steamer most uncomfortably, especially for the tropics in July.

In eight days Aspinwall was reached. At that time the streets of the town were eight or ten inches under water, and foot passengers passed from place to place on raised footwalks. July is at the height of the wet season, on the isthmus. At intervals the rain would pour down in streams, followed in not many minutes by a blazing, tropical summer's sun. These alternate changes, from rain to sunshine, were continuous in the afternoons. I wondered how any person could live many months in Aspinwall, and wondered still more why any one tried.

In the summer of 1852 the Panama railroad was completed only to the point where it now crosses the Chagres River. From there passengers were carried by boats to Gorgona, at which place they took mules for Panama [City], some twenty-five miles further. Those who travelled over the isthmus in those days will remember that boats on the Chagres River were propelled by natives not inconveniently burdened with clothing. These boats carried thirty to forty passengers each. The crews consisted of six men to a boat, armed with long poles. There were planks wide enough for a man to walk on conveniently, running along the sides of each boat from end to end. The men would start from the bow, place one end of their poles against the river bottom, brace their shoulders against the other end, and then walk to the stern as rapidly as they

[6] Chandler (1813–1879), a New Hampshire native, served three terms as U.S. senator from Michigan (1857–75) and as secretary of the interior, 1875–77.
[7] City on the northern coast of the present nation of Panama, then part of Colombia.
[8] James Findlay Schenck (1807–1882) later served in the Union navy and was promoted to rear admiral in 1868.

could. In this way from a mile to a mile and a half an hour could be made, against the current of the river.

I, as regimental quartermaster, had charge of the public property and had also to look after the transportation. A contract had been entered into with the steamship company in New York for the transportation of the regiment to California, including the isthmus transit. A certain amount of baggage was allowed per man, and saddle animals were to be furnished to commissioned officers and to all disabled persons. The regiment, with the exception of one company left as guards to the public property—camp and garrison equipage principally—and the soldiers with families, took boats, propelled as above described, for Gorgona. From this place they marched to Panama, and were soon comfortably on the steamer anchored in the bay, some three or four miles from the town. I, with one company of troops and all the soldiers with families, all the tents, mess chests and camp kettles, was sent to Cruces, a town a few miles higher up the Chagres River than Gorgona. There I found an impecunious American who had taken the contract to furnish transportation for the regiment at a stipulated price per hundred pounds for the freight and so much for each saddle animal. But when we reached Cruces there was not a mule, either for pack or saddle, in the place. The contractor promised that the animals should be on hand in the morning. In the morning he said that they were on the way from some imaginary place, and would arrive in the course of the day. This went on until I saw that he could not procure the animals at all at the price he had promised to furnish them for. The unusual number of passengers that had come over on the steamer, and the large amount of freight to pack, had created an unprecedented demand for mules. Some of the passengers paid as high as forty dollars for the use of a mule to ride twenty-five miles, when the mule would not have sold for ten dollars in that market at other times. Meanwhile the cholera had broken out, and men were dying every hour. To diminish the food for the disease, I permitted the company detailed with me to proceed to Panama. The captain and the doctors accompanied the men, and I was left alone with the sick and the soldiers who had families. The regiment at Panama was also affected with the disease; but there were better accommodations for the well on the steamer, and a hospital, for those taken with the disease, on an old hulk anchored a mile off. There were also hospital tents on shore on the island of Flamingo, which stands in the bay.

I was about a week at Cruces before transportation began to come in. About one-third of the people with me died, either at Cruces or on the way to Panama. There was no agent of the transportation company at Cruces to consult, or to take the responsibility of procuring transportation at a price which would secure it. I therefore myself dismissed the contractor and made a new contract with a native, at more than double the original price. Thus we finally reached Panama. The steamer, however, could not proceed until the cholera abated, and the regiment was detained still longer. Altogether, on the isthmus and on the Pacific side, we were delayed six weeks. About one-seventh of those who left New York harbor with the 4th infantry on the 5th of July, now lie buried on the Isthmus of Panama or on Flamingo Island in Panama Bay.

One amusing circumstance occurred while we were lying at anchor in Panama Bay. In the regiment there was a Lieutenant Slaughter who was very liable to seasickness. It almost made him sick to see the wave of a tablecloth when the servants were spreading it. Soon after his graduation, Slaughter was ordered to California and took passage by a sailing vessel going around Cape Horn. The vessel was seven months making the voyage, and Slaughter was sick every moment of the time, never more so than while lying at anchor after reaching his place of destination. On landing in California he found orders which had come by the isthmus, notifying him of a mistake in his assignment; he should have been ordered to the northern lakes. He started back by the isthmus route and was sick all the way. But when he arrived at the East he was again ordered to California, this time definitely, and at this date was making his third trip. He was as sick as ever, and had been so for more than a month while lying at anchor in the bay. I remember him well, seated with his elbows on the table in front of him, his chin between his hands, and looking the picture of despair. At last he broke out, "I wish I had taken my father's advice; he wanted me to go into the navy; if I had done so, I should not have had to go to sea so much." Poor Slaughter! it was his last sea voyage. He was killed by Indians in Oregon.

By the last of August the cholera had so abated that it was deemed safe to start. The disease did not break out again on the way to California, and we reached San Francisco early in September.

San Francisco that day was a lively place. Gold, or placer digging as it was called, was at its height. Steamers plied daily between San Francisco and both Stockton and Sacramento. Passengers and gold from the southern mines came by the Stockton boat; from the northern mines by Sacramento. In the evening when these boats arrived, Long Wharf—there was but one wharf in San Francisco in 1852—was alive with people crowding to meet the miners as they came down to sell their "dust" and to "have a time." Of these some were runners for hotels, boardinghouses or restaurants; others belonged to a class of impecunious adventurers, of good manners and good presence, who were ever on the alert to make the acquaintance of people with some ready means, in the hope of being asked to take a meal at a restaurant. Many were young men of good family, good education and gentlemanly instincts. Their parents had been able to support them during their minority, and to give them good educations, but not to maintain them afterwards. From 1849 to 1853 there was a rush of people to the Pacific Coast, of the class described. All thought that fortunes were to be picked up, without effort, in the gold fields on the Pacific. Some realized more than their most sanguine expectations; but for one such there were hundreds disappointed, many of whom now fill unknown graves; others died wrecks of their former selves, and many, without a vicious instinct, became criminals and outcasts. Many of the real scenes in early California life exceed in strangeness and interest any of the mere products of the brain of the novelist.

Those early days in California brought out character. It was a long way off then, and the journey was expensive. The fortunate could go by Cape Horn or by the isthmus of Panama; but the mass of pioneers crossed the plains with their ox-teams. This took an entire summer. They were very lucky when they got through with a yoke of worn-out cattle. All other means were exhausted in procuring the outfit on the Missouri River. The immigrant, on arriving, found himself a stranger, in a strange land, far from friends. Time pressed, for the little means that could be realized from the sale of what was left of the outfit would not support a man long at California prices. Many became discouraged. Others would take off their coats and look for a job, no matter what it might be. These succeeded as a rule. There were many young men who had studied professions before they went to California, and who had never done a day's manual labor in their lives, who took in the situation at once and went to work to make a start at anything they could get to do. Some supplied carpenters and masons with material—carrying plank, brick, or mortar, as the case might be; others drove stages, drays,[9] or baggage wagons, until they could do better. More became discouraged early and spent their time looking up people who would "treat," or lounging about restaurants and gambling houses where free lunches were furnished daily. They were welcomed at these places because they often brought in miners who proved good customers.

My regiment spent a few weeks at Benicia barracks, and then was ordered to Fort Vancouver, on the Columbia River, then in Oregon Territory. During the winter of 1852–3 the territory was divided, all north of the Columbia River being taken from Oregon to make Washington Territory.

Prices for all kinds of supplies were so high on the Pacific Coast from 1849 until at least 1853—that it would have been impossible for officers of the army to exist upon their pay, if it had not been that authority was given them to purchase from the commissary such supplies as he kept, at New Orleans wholesale prices. A cook could not be hired for the pay of a captain. The cook could do better. At Benicia, in 1852, flour was 25 cents per pound; potatoes were 16 cents; beets, turnips and cabbage, 6 cents; onions, 37½ cents; meat and other articles in proportion. In 1853 at Vancouver vegetables were a little lower. I with three other officers concluded that we would raise a crop for ourselves, and by selling the surplus realize something handsome. I bought a pair of horses that had crossed the plains that summer and were very poor. They recuperated rapidly, however, and proved a good team to break up the ground with. I performed all the labor of breaking up the ground while the other officers planted the potatoes. Our crop was enormous. Luckily for us the Columbia River rose to a great height from the melting of the snow in the mountains in June, and overflowed and killed most of our crop. This saved digging it up, for everybody on the Pacific Coast seemed to have come to the conclusion at the same time that agriculture would be profitable. In 1853 more than three-quarters of the potatoes raised were permitted to rot in the ground, or had to be thrown away. The only potatoes we sold were to our own mess.

[9] Simple carts or skids used to carry heavy items.

While I was stationed on the Pacific Coast we were free from Indian wars. There were quite a number of remnants of tribes in the vicinity of Portland in Oregon, and of Fort Vancouver in Washington Territory. They had generally acquired some of the vices of civilization, but none of the virtues, except in individual cases. The Hudson Bay Company had held the Northwest with their trading posts for many years before the United States was represented on the Pacific Coast. They still retained posts along the Columbia River and one at Fort Vancouver, when I was there. Their treatment of the Indians had brought out the better qualities of the savages. Farming had been undertaken by the company to supply the Indians with bread and vegetables; they raised some cattle and horses; and they had now taught the Indians to do the labor of the farm and herd. They always compensated them for their labor, and always gave them goods of uniform quality and at uniform price.

Before the advent of the American, the medium of exchange between the Indian and the white man was pelts. Afterward it was silver coin. If an Indian received in the sale of a horse a fifty-dollar gold piece, not an infrequent occurrence, the first thing he did was to exchange it for American half-dollars. These he could count. He would then commence his purchases, paying for each article separately, as he got it. He would not trust any one to add up the bill and pay it all at once. At that day fifty-dollar gold pieces, not the issue of the government, were common on the Pacific Coast. They were called slugs.

The Indians along the lower Columbia as far as the Cascades and on the lower Willamette died off very fast during the year I spent in that section; for besides acquiring the vices of the white people they had acquired also their diseases. The measles and the smallpox were both amazingly fatal. In their wild state, before the appearance of the white man among them, the principal complaints they were subject to were those produced by long involuntary fasting, violent exercise in pursuit of game, and overeating. Instinct more than reason had taught them a remedy for these ills. It was the steam bath. Something like a bake oven was built, large enough to admit a man lying down. Bushes were stuck in the ground in two rows, about six feet long and some two or three feet apart; other bushes connected the rows at one end. The tops of the bushes were drawn together to interlace, and confined in that position; the whole was then plastered over with wet clay until every opening was filled. Just inside the open end of the oven the floor was scooped out so as to make a hole that would hold a bucket or two of water. These ovens were always built on the banks of a stream, a big spring, or pool of water. When a patient required a bath, a fire was built near the oven and a pile of stones put upon it. The cavity at the front was then filled with water. When the stones were sufficiently heated, the patient would draw himself into the oven; a blanket would be thrown over the open end, and hot stones put into the water until the patient could stand it no longer. He was then withdrawn from his steam bath and doused into the cold stream near by. This treatment may have answered with the early ailments of the Indians. With the measles or smallpox it would kill every time.

During my year on the Columbia River, the smallpox exterminated one small remnant of a band of Indians entirely, and reduced others materially. I do not think there was a case of recovery among them, until the doctor with the Hudson Bay Company took the matter in hand and established a hospital. Nearly every case he treated recovered. I never, myself, saw the treatment described in the preceding paragraph, but have heard it described by persons who have witnessed it. The decimation among the Indians I knew of personally, and the hospital, established for their benefit, was a Hudson Bay building not a stone's throw from my own quarters.

The death of Colonel Bliss, of the adjutant general's department, which occurred July 5th, 1853, promoted me to the captaincy of a company then stationed at Humboldt Bay, California. The notice reached me in September of the same year, and I very soon started to join my new command. There was no way of reaching Humboldt at that time except to take passage on a San Francisco sailing vessel going after lumber. Redwood, a species of cedar, which on the Pacific Coast takes the place filled by white pine in the East, then abounded on the banks of Humboldt Bay. There were extensive sawmills engaged in preparing this lumber for the San Francisco market, and sailing vessels, used in getting it to market, furnished the only means of communication between Humboldt and the balance of the world.

I was obliged to remain in San Francisco for several days before I found a vessel. This gave me a good opportunity of comparing the San Francisco of 1852 with that of 1853. As before stated, there had been but one wharf in front of the city in 1852—Long Wharf. In 1853 the town had grown out into the bay beyond what was the end of this wharf when I first saw it. Streets and houses had been built out on piles where the year before the largest vessels visiting the port lay at anchor or tied to the wharf. There was no filling under the streets or houses. San Francisco presented the same general appearance as the year before; that is, eating, drinking and gambling houses were conspicuous for their number and publicity. They were on the first floor, with doors wide open. At all hours of the day and night in walking the streets, the eye was regaled, on every block near the water front, by the sight of players at faro.[1] Often broken places were found in the street, large enough to let a man down into the water below. I have but little doubt that many of the people who went to the Pacific Coast in the early days of the gold excitement, and have never been heard from since, or who were heard from for a time and then ceased to write, found watery graves beneath the houses or streets built over San Francisco Bay.

Besides the gambling in cards there was gambling on a larger scale in city lots. These were sold "on change," much as stocks are now sold on Wall Street. Cash, at time of purchase, was always paid by the broker; but the purchaser had only to put up his margin. He was charged at the rate of two or three percent a month on the difference, besides commissions. The sand hills, some of them almost inaccessible to foot-passengers, were surveyed off and mapped

---

[1] A game in which players bet on individual cards as they are turned over.

into fifty *vara* lots—a *vara* being a Spanish yard. These were sold at first at very low prices, but were sold and resold for higher prices until they went up to many thousands of dollars. The brokers did a fine business, and so did many such purchasers as were sharp enough to quit purchasing before the final crash came. As the city grew, the sand hills back of the town furnished material for filling up the bay under the houses and streets, and still further out. The temporary houses, first built over the water in the harbor, soon gave way to more solid structures. The main business part of the city now is on solid ground, made where vessels of the largest class lay at anchor in the early days. I was in San Francisco again in 1854. Gambling houses had disappeared from public view. The city had become staid and orderly.

My family, all this while, was at the East. It consisted now of a wife and two children. I saw no chance of supporting them on the Pacific Coast out of my pay as an army officer. I concluded, therefore, to resign, and in March applied for a leave of absence until the end of the July following, tendering my resignation to take effect at the end of that time. I left the Pacific Coast very much attached to it, and with the full expectation of making it my future home. That expectation and that hope remained uppermost in my mind until the lieutenant generalcy bill was introduced into Congress in the winter of 1863–64.[2] The passage of that bill, and my promotion, blasted my last hope of ever becoming a citizen of the further West.

In the late summer of 1854 I rejoined my family, to find in it a son whom I had never seen, born while I was on the isthmus of Panama.[3] I was now to commence, at the age of thirty-two, a new struggle for our support. My wife had a farm near St. Louis, to which we went, but I had no means to stock it. A house had to be built also. I worked very hard, never losing a day because of bad weather, and accomplished the object in a moderate way. If nothing else could be done I would load a cord of wood on a wagon and take it to the city for sale. I managed to keep along very well until 1858, when I was attacked by fever and ague. I had suffered very severely and for a long time from this disease, while a boy in Ohio. It lasted now over a year, and, while it did not keep me in the house, it did interfere greatly with the amount of work I was able to perform. In the fall of 1858 I sold out my stock, crops and farming utensils at auction, and gave up farming.

In the winter I established a partnership with Harry Boggs, a cousin of Mrs. Grant, in the real estate agency business. I spent that winter at St. Louis myself, but did not take my family into town until the spring. Our business might have become prosperous if I had been able to wait for it to grow. As it was, there was no more than one person could attend to, and not enough to support two families. While a citizen of St. Louis and engaged in the real estate agency business, I was a candidate for the office of county engineer, an office

---

[2] On March 9, 1864, Grant was appointed the North's only lieutenant general, a rank especially revived for him; three days later, he was made commander in chief of the Union forces.
[3] Frederick Grant had been born in 1850; it was Ulysses (b. 1852) whom Grant had not yet seen.

of respectability and emolument which would have been very acceptable to me at that time. The incumbent was appointed by the county court, which consisted of five members. My opponent had the advantage of birth over me (he was a citizen by adoption) and carried off the prize. I now withdrew from the co-partnership with Boggs, and, in May, 1860, removed to Galena, Illinois, and took a clerkship in my father's store.

While a citizen of Missouri, my first opportunity for casting a vote at a presidential election occurred. I had been in the army from before attaining my majority and had thought but little about politics, although I was a Whig by education and a great admirer of Mr. Clay. But the Whig party had ceased to exist before I had an opportunity of exercising the privilege of casting a ballot; the Know-Nothing party had taken its place, but was on the wane; and the Republican party was in a chaotic state and had not yet received a name.[4] It had no existence in the slave states except at points on the borders next to free states. In St. Louis city and county, what afterwards became the Republican party was known as the Free-Soil Democracy, led by the Honorable Frank P. Blair.[5] Most of my neighbors had known me as an officer of the army with Whig proclivities. They had been on the same side, and, on the death of their party, many had become Know-Nothings, or members of the American party. There was a lodge near my new home, and I was invited to join it. I accepted the invitation, was initiated, attended a meeting just one week later, and never went to another afterwards.

I have no apologies to make for having been one week a member of the

[4] Grant very briefly sketches here the tumultuous political transformations of this era. The Whig party, of which Henry Clay (1777–1852) of Kentucky and Daniel Webster (1782–1852) of New Hampshire and later Massachusetts were the preeminent leaders, first began to emerge in the 1820s in opposition to Andrew Jackson but did not capture the White House until the election of William H. Harrison and John Tyler in 1840. Partly owing to Tyler's alienation of many Whigs in Congress as he finished the term of the deceased Harrison, and partly owing to the increasingly divisive questions of slavery and abolition, by the end of that decade the Whigs had been fragmented and after the disastrous campaign of 1852 (during which both Clay and Webster died) the party ceased to exist. The Democratic party of Jackson absorbed some of the former Whigs. The antislavery Republican party, newly formed in 1854, absorbed others, along with the radical "Free-Soilers," who opposed the extension of slavery into U.S. territories. Finally, a portion of the Whigs under former president Millard Fillmore found a more suitable home in the Know-Nothing camp. The latter movement, at first a loose association of various secret organizations, found its formal political voice in the American Republican party, which emerged in New York in 1843 and soon spread elsewhere as the Native American party (or later simply the American party), holding its first national convention in Philadelphia in 1845. The Know-Nothings, so-called from their refusal to discuss what took place in their early secret meetings, opposed immigrant rights and favored only native-born candidates for political office. Fillmore was the Know-Nothing candidate in the presidential election in 1856, but by then the Know-Nothing movement, like the Whig party earlier, had succumbed to a North-South split over slavery and passed out of existence. The Democratic party felt its own sectional strains in the election of 1860; when the convention in Charleston nominated Stephen A. Douglas of Illinois, the southerners withdrew and nominated their own candidate, John C. Breckinridge of Kentucky.

[5] Francis P. Blair (1821–1875), of Kentucky and later Missouri, organized the Free-Soilers in the latter state and served in the U.S. House of Representatives as a Free-Soil (1856–58) and Republican (1860–62) member before entering the Union army.

American party, for I still think native-born citizens of the United States should have as much protection, as many privileges in their native country, as those who voluntarily select it for a home. But all secret, oath-bound political parties are dangerous to any nation, no matter how pure or how patriotic the motives and principles which first bring them together. No political party can or ought to exist when one of its cornerstones is opposition to freedom of thought and to the right to worship God "according to the dictate of one's own conscience," or according to the creed of any religious denomination whatever. Nevertheless, if a sect sets up its laws as binding above the state laws, wherever the two come in conflict this claim must be resisted and suppressed at whatever cost.

Up to the Mexican War there were a few out-and-out abolitionists, men who carried their hostility to slavery into all elections, from those for a justice of the peace up to the presidency of the United States. They were noisy but not numerous. But the great majority of people at the North, where slavery did not exist, were opposed to the institution, and looked upon its existence in any part of the country as unfortunate. They did not hold the states where slavery existed responsible for it, and believed that protection should be given to the right of property in slaves until some satisfactory way could be reached to be rid of the institution. Opposition to slavery was not a creed of either political party. In some sections more antislavery men belonged to the Democratic party, and in others to the Whigs. But with the inauguration of the Mexican War, in fact with the annexation of Texas, "the inevitable conflict" commenced.

As the time for the presidential election of 1856—the first at which I had the opportunity of voting—approached, party feeling began to run high. The Republican party was regarded in the South and the border states not only as opposed to the extension of slavery, but as favoring the compulsory abolition of the institution without compensation to the owners. The most horrible visions seemed to present themselves to the minds of people who, one would suppose, ought to have known better. Many educated and, otherwise, sensible persons appeared to believe that emancipation meant social equality. Treason to the government was openly advocated and was not rebuked. It was evident to my mind that the election of a Republican president in 1856 meant the secession of all the slave states, and rebellion. Under these circumstances I preferred the success of a candidate whose election would prevent or postpone secession, to seeing the country plunged into a war the end of which no man could foretell. With a Democrat elected by the unanimous vote of the slave states, there could be no pretext for secession for four years. I very much hoped that the passions of the people would subside in that time, and the catastrophe be averted altogether; if it was not, I believed the country would be better prepared to receive the shock and to resist it. I therefore voted for James Buchanan for president. Four years later the Republican party was successful in electing its candidate to the presidency. The civilized world has learned the consequence. Four millions of human beings held as chattels have been liberated; the ballot has been given to them; the free schools of the country have been opened to their children.

The nation still lives, and the people are just as free to avoid social intimacy with the blacks as ever they were, or as they are with white people.

While living in Galena I was nominally only a clerk supporting myself and family on a stipulated salary. In reality my position was different. My father had never lived in Galena himself, but had established my two brothers there, the one next younger than myself in charge of the business, assisted by the youngest. When I went there it was my father's intention to give up all connection with the business himself, and to establish his three sons in it, but the brother who had really built up the business was sinking with consumption, and it was not thought best to make any change while he was in this condition. He lived until September, 1861, when he succumbed to that insidious disease which always flatters its victims into the belief that they are growing better up to the close of life. A more honorable man never transacted business. In September, 1861, I was engaged in an employment which required all my attention elsewhere.

During the eleven months that I lived in Galena prior to the first call for volunteers, I had been strictly attentive to my business, and had made but few acquaintances other than customers and people engaged in the same line with myself. When the election took place in November, 1860, I had not been a resident of Illinois long enough to gain citizenship and could not, therefore, vote. I was really glad of this at the time, for my pledges would have compelled me to vote for Stephen A. Douglas, who had no possible chance of election. The contest was really between Mr. Breckinridge and Mr. Lincoln; between minority rule and rule by the majority. I wanted, as between these candidates, to see Mr. Lincoln elected. Excitement ran high during the canvass, and torch-light processions enlivened the scene in the generally quiet streets of Galena many nights during the campaign. I did not parade with either party, but occasionally met with the "wide awakes"—Republicans—in their rooms, and superintended their drill. It was evident, from the time of the Chicago nomination to the close of the canvass, that the election of the Republican candidate would be the signal for some of the southern states to secede. I still had hopes that the four years which had elapsed since the first nomination of a presidential candidate by a party distinctly opposed to slavery extension, had given time for the extreme pro-slavery sentiment to cool down; for the Southerners to think well before they took the awful leap which they had so vehemently threatened. But I was mistaken.

The Republican candidate was elected, and solid substantial people of the Northwest,[6] and I presume the same order of people throughout the entire North, felt very serious, but determined, after this event. It was very much discussed whether the South would carry out its threat to secede and set up a

---

[6] Here Grant means "the Old Northwest"—that is, the region once governed by the Northwest Ordinance of 1785, essentially the Great Lakes states—as opposed to the new Pacific Northwest of which he speaks earlier.

separate government, the cornerstone of which should be protection to the "divine" institution of slavery. For there were people who believed in the "divinity" of human slavery, as there are now people who believe Mormonism and polygamy to be ordained by the Most High. We forgive them for entertaining such notions, but forbid their practice. It was generally believed that there would be a flurry; that some of the extreme southern states would go so far as to pass ordinances of secession. But the common impression was that this step was so plainly suicidal for the South, that the movement would not spread over much of the territory and would not last long.

Doubtless the founders of our government, the majority of them at least, regarded the confederation of the colonies as an experiment. Each colony considered itself a separate government; [and believed] that the confederation was for mutual protection against a foreign foe, and the prevention of strife and war among themselves. If there had been a desire on the part of any single state to withdraw from the compact at any time while the number of states was limited to the original thirteen, I do not suppose there would have been any to contest the right, no matter how much the determination might have been regretted. The problem changed on the ratification of the Constitution by all the colonies; it changed still more when amendments were added; and if the right of any one state to withdraw continued to exist at all after the ratification of the Constitution, it certainly ceased on the formation of new states, at least so far as the new states themselves were concerned. It was never possessed at all by Florida or the states west of the Mississippi, all of which were purchased by the treasury of the entire nation. Texas and the territory brought into the Union in consequence of annexation, were purchased with both blood and treasure; and Texas, with a domain greater than that of any European state except Russia, was permitted to retain as state property all the public lands within its borders. It would have been ingratitude and injustice of the most flagrant sort for this state to withdraw from the Union after all that had been spent and done to introduce her; yet, if separation had actually occurred, Texas must necessarily have gone with the South, both on account of her institutions and her geographical position. Secession was illogical as well as impracticable; it was revolution.

Now, the right of revolution is an inherent one. When people are oppressed by their government, it is a natural right they enjoy to relieve themselves of the oppression, if they are strong enough, either by withdrawal from it, or by overthrowing it and substituting a government more acceptable. But any people or part of a people who resort to this remedy, stake their lives, their property, and every claim for protection given by citizenship—on the issue. Victory, or the conditions imposed by the conqueror—must be the result.

In the case of the war between the states it would have been the exact truth if the South had said, "We do not want to live with you northern people any longer; we know our institution of slavery is obnoxious to you, and, as you are growing numerically stronger than we, it may at some time in the future be endangered. So long as you permitted us to control the government, and with the aid of a few friends at the North to enact laws constituting your section a guard against the escape of our property,[7] we were willing to live with you. You have been submissive to our rule heretofore; but it looks now as if you did not intend to continue so, and we will remain in the Union no longer." Instead of this the seceding states cried lustily, "Let us alone; you have no constitutional power to interfere with us." Newspapers and people at the North reiterated the cry. Individuals might ignore the Constitution, but the nation itself must not only obey it, but must, enforce the strictest construction of that instrument, the construction put upon it by the southerners themselves. The fact is the Constitution did not apply to any such contingency as the one existing from 1861 to 1865. Its framers never dreamed of such a contingency occurring. If they had foreseen it, the probabilities are they would have sanctioned the right of a state or states to withdraw rather than that there should be war between brothers.

The framers were wise in their generation and wanted to do the very best possible to secure their own liberty and independence, and that also of their descendants to the latest days. It is preposterous to suppose that the people of one generation can lay down the best and only rules of government for all who are to come after them, and under unforeseen contingencies. At the time of the framing of our Constitution the only physical forces that had been subdued and made to serve man and do his labor, were the currents in the streams and in the air we breathe. Rude machinery, propelled by water power, had been invented; sails to propel ships upon the waters had been set to catch the passing breeze—but the application of steam to propel vessels against both wind and current, and machinery to do all manner of work had not been thought of. The instantaneous transmission of messages around the world by means of electricity would probably at that day have been attributed to witchcraft or a league with the devil. Immaterial circumstances had changed as greatly as material ones. We could not and ought not to be rigidly bound by the rules laid down under circumstances so different for emergencies so utterly unanticipated. The fathers themselves would have been the first to declare that their prerogatives were not irrevocable. They would surely have resisted secession could they have lived to see the shape it assumed.

I travelled through the Northwest considerably during the winter of 1860–1. We had customers in all the little towns in southwest Wisconsin, southeast Minnesota and northeast Iowa. These generally knew I had been a captain in the regular army and had served through the Mexican War. Consequently wherever I stopped at night, some of the people would come to the public house where I was, and sit till a late hour discussing the probabilities of the

---

[7]The Fugitive Slave Law, part of the Compromise of 1850 that was forged by Henry Clay and Stephen A. Douglas, required northern residents to assist federal officers in the recovery of runaways and their return to their owners.

future. My own views at that time were like those officially expressed by Mr. Seward[8] at a later day, that "the war would be over in ninety days." I continued to entertain these views until after the battle of Shiloh. I believe now that there would have been no more battles at the West after the capture of Fort Donelson if all the troops in that region had been under a single commander who would have followed up that victory.[9]

There is little doubt in my mind now that the prevailing sentiment of the South would have been opposed to secession in 1860 and 1861, if there had been a fair and calm expression of opinion, unbiased by threats, and if the ballot of one legal voter had counted for as much as that of any other. But there was no calm discussion of the question. Demagogues who were too old to enter the army if there should be a war, others who entertained so high an opinion of their own ability that they did not believe they could be spared from the direction of the affairs of state in such an event, declaimed vehemently and unceasingly against the North; against its aggressions upon the South; its inter- ference with southern rights, etc., etc. They denounced the northerners as cow- ards, poltroons, Negro-worshippers; claimed that one southern man was equal to five northern men in battle; that if the South would stand up for its rights the North would back down. Mr. Jefferson Davis said in a speech, delivered at La Grange, Mississippi, before the secession of that state, that he would agree to drink all the blood spilled south of Mason and Dixon's line if there should be a war. The young men who would have the fighting to do in case of war, believed all these statements, both in regard to the aggressiveness of the North and its cowardice. They, too, cried out for a separation from such people. The great bulk of the legal voters of the South were men who owned no slaves; their homes were generally in the hills and poor country; their facilities for educating their children, even up to the point of reading and writing, were very limited; their interest in the contest was very meager—what there was, if they had been capable of seeing it, was with the North; they too needed emancipation. Under the old régime they were looked down upon by those who controlled all the affairs in the interest of slave-owners, as poor white trash who were allowed the ballot so long as they cast it according to direction.

I am aware that this last statement may be disputed and individual testi- mony perhaps adduced to show that in antebellum days the ballot was as

[8]William H. Seward (1801–1872), New York governor 1839–43, U.S. senator 1848–60, unsuccessful candidate for the Republican presidential nomination in 1856 and 1860, and secretary of state under Lincoln; he was increasingly allied with the antislavery forces of the North and predicted that conflict between the sections was "irrepressible."

[9]The tough Battle of Shiloh in April 1862 might well have convinced Grant that a long war lay ahead. He was taken by surprise by the Confederate forces and although on the second day of the battle he forced the latter to retreat, his army suffered heavier losses overall. The Union command in the region was in some confusion in this period: Grant himself was temporarily replaced by another leader in March despite his resounding victory over the Confederates at Fort Donelson, Tennessee, in February, when Union forces lost about three thousand men and the roughly equal Confederate garrison, prior to its forced surrender on the 16th, lost perhaps five times as many.

untrammelled in the South as in any section of the country, but in the face of any such contradiction I reassert the statement. The shotgun was not resorted to. Masked men did not ride over the country at night intimidating voters; but there was a firm feeling that a class existed in every state with a sort of divine right to control public affairs. If they could not get this control by one means they must by another. The end justified the means. The coercion, if mild, was complete.

There were two political parties, it is true, in all the states, both strong in numbers and respectability, but both equally loyal to the institution which stood paramount in southern eyes to all other institutions in state or nation. The slave-owners were the minority, but governed both parties. Had politics ever divided the slaveholders and the non-slaveholders, the majority would have been obliged to yield, or internecine war would have been the consequence. I do not know that the southern people were to blame for this condition of affairs. There was a time when slavery was not profitable, and the discussion of the merits of the institution was confined almost exclusively to the territory where it existed. The states of Virginia and Kentucky came near abolishing slavery by their own acts, one state defeating the measure by a tie vote and the other only lacking one. But when the institution became profitable, all talk of its abolition ceased where it existed; and naturally, as human nature is constituted, arguments were adduced in its support. The cotton gin probably had much to do with the justification of slavery.

The winter of 1860–1 will be remembered by middle-aged people of today as one of great excitement. South Carolina promptly seceded after the result of the presidential election was known.[1] Other southern states proposed to follow. In some of them the Union sentiment was so strong that it had to be suppressed by force. Maryland, Delaware, Kentucky and Missouri, all slave states, failed to pass ordinances of secession; but they were all represented in the so-called Congress of the so-called Confederate States. The governor and lieutenant-governor of Missouri, in 1861, Jackson and Reynolds, were both supporters of the rebellion and took refuge with the enemy. The governor soon died, and the lieutenant-governor assumed his office; issued proclamations as governor of the state; was recognized as such by the Confederate government, and continued his pretensions until the collapse of the rebellion. The South claimed the sovereignty of states, but claimed the right to coerce into their confederation such states as they wanted, that is, all the states where slavery existed. They did not seem to think this course inconsistent. The fact is, the southern slave-owners believed that, in some way, the ownership of slaves conferred a sort of patent of nobility—a right to govern independent of the interest or wishes of those who did not hold such property. They convinced themselves, first, of the divine origin of the institution and, next, that that particular institution was not safe in the hands of any body of legislators but themselves.

[1] South Carolina seceded December 20, 1860, followed by six other states up to February 1, 1861. The four final states did not secede until after the fall of Fort Sumter (April, 12–14), Tennessee being the last (June 8th).

Meanwhile the administration of President Buchanan looked helplessly on and proclaimed that the general government had no power to interfere; that the nation had no power to save its own life. Mr. Buchanan had in his cabinet two members at least, who were as earnest—to use a mild term—in the cause of secession as Mr. Davis or any southern statesman. One of them, Floyd,[2] the secretary of war, scattered the army so that much of it could be captured when hostilities should commence, and distributed the cannon and small arms from northern arsenals throughout the South so as to be on hand when treason wanted them. The navy was scattered in like manner. The president did not prevent his cabinet preparing for war upon their government, either by destroying its resources or storing them in the South until a de facto government was established with Jefferson Davis as its president, and Montgomery, Alabama, as the capital. The secessionists had then to leave the cabinet. In their own estimation they were aliens in the country which had given them birth. Loyal men were put into their places. Treason in the executive branch of the government was estopped. But the harm had already been done. The stable door was locked after the horse had been stolen.

During all of the trying winter of 1860–1, when the southerners were so defiant that they would not allow within their borders the expression of a sentiment hostile to their views, it was a brave man indeed who could stand up and proclaim his loyalty to the Union. On the other hand men at the North—prominent men—proclaimed that the government had no power to coerce the South into submission to the laws of the land; that if the North undertook to raise armies to go south, these armies would have to march over the dead bodies of the speakers. A portion of the press of the North was constantly proclaiming similar views. When the time arrived for the president-elect to go to the capital of the nation to be sworn into office, it was deemed unsafe for him to travel, not only as a president-elect, but as any private citizen should be allowed to do. Instead of going in a special car, receiving the good wishes of his constituents at all the stations along the road, he was obliged to stop on the way and to be smuggled into the capital. He disappeared from public view on his journey, and the next the country knew, his arrival was announced at the capital. There is little doubt that he would have been assassinated if he had attempted to travel openly throughout his journey.

MARY BOYKIN CHESNUT

from her "Memoirs" (1880s)

MARCH 18, 1861. AUGUSTA, GEORGIA. THE DAY BEFORE WE LEFT MONTGOMERY,[3] in the midst of a red-hot patriotic denunciation of a great many people South and everybody North, someone suggested "yesterday's catastrophe" and threw

---

[2] John B. Floyd (1806–1863) of Virginia held the post named, 1857–60.
[3] Chesnut left Montgomery, Alabama, by railroad on March 16th.

open the folding doors suddenly, to be sure that the next room contained no spies nor eavesdroppers.

An unexpected tableau. A girl resting in a man's arms, he kissing her lips at his leisure or pleasure.

They were on their feet in an instant. She cried: "Oh! he is my cousin. He is married. He is taking me home from school." In the might of her innocence she seemed quite cool about it. He knew better and was terribly embarrassed. He might well be ashamed of himself. . . .

A man claimed acquaintance with me because he has married an old schoolgirl friend of mine.

"At least, she is my present wife."

Whispered the Light Brigade, "Has he had them before or means he to have them hereafter?" We had no time to learn. But one parson friend gravely informed us, "If he is the man I take him to be, he has buried two."

One of our party [D: Mr. C] so far forgot his democratic position toward the public as to wish aloud, "Oh, that we had separate coaches, as they have in England. That we could get away from these whiskey-drinking, tobacco-chewing rascals and rabble." All with votes!! Worse, all armed. A truculent crowd, truly, to offend. But each supposed he was one of the gentlemen to be separated from the other thing.

The day we left Montgomery, a man was shot in the street for some trifle. Mr. Browne[4] was open-mouthed in his horror of such ruffian-like conduct. They answered him, "It is the war fever. Soldiers must be fierce. It is the right temper for the times cropping out."

There was tragedy, too, on the way here. A mad woman, taken from her husband and children. Of course she was mad — or she would not have given "her grief words" in that public place. Her keepers were along. What she said was rational enough — pathetic, at times heartrending.

Then a highly intoxicated parson was trying to save the soul of "a bereaved widow." So he addressed her always as "my bereaved friend and widow."

The devil himself could not have quoted scripture more fluently.

[D: It excited me so, I quickly took opium, and *that* I kept up. It enables me to retain every particle of mind or sense or brains I ever have and so quiets my nerves that I can calmly reason and take rational views of things otherwise maddening. . . . "The peace this world cannot give, which passeth all understanding." Today the papers say peace again. Yesterday the *Telegraph* and the *Herald* were warlike to a frightful degree. I have just read that Pugh[5] is coming down south — another woman who loved me, and I treated her so badly at first. I have written to Kate[6] that I will go to her if she wants me — dear, dear sister. I

---

[4]William Montague Browne (d. 1884) was an Irish-born immigrant who edited the administration newspaper during Buchanan's presidency; a southern sympathizer, he became Jefferson Davis's assistant secretary of state and a Confederate officer. In her diary, Chesnut wrote that Browne "expressed his English horror" at the unruliness.

[5]Senator George Ellis Pugh (1822–1876) of Ohio sympathized with the South but sought to moderate its extreme position at this juncture. Chesnut had known him and his wife in Washington.

[6]Chesnut's younger sister, Catherine Boykin Williams.

wonder if other women shed as bitter tears as I. They scald my cheeks and blister my heart. Yet Edward Boykin[7] "wondered and marveled at my elasticity—was I always so bright and happy, did ever woman possess such a disposition, life was one continued festival," etc., etc.—and Bonham[8] last winter shortly said it was a *bore* to see anyone always in a good humor. Much they know of me—or my power to hide trouble. . . .

[D: I wonder if it be a sin to think slavery a curse to any land. Sumner[9] said not one word of this hated institution which is not true. Men and women are punished when their masters and mistresses are brutes and not when they do wrong—and then we live surrounded by prostitutes. An abandoned woman is sent out of any decent house elsewhere. Who thinks any worse of a Negro or mulatto woman for being a thing we can't name?[1] God forgive us, but ours is a *monstrous* system and wrong and [an] iniquity. Perhaps the rest of the world is as bad. This *only* I see: like the patriarchs of old our men live all in one house with their wives and their concubines, and the mulattoes one sees in every family exactly resemble the white children—and every lady tells you who is the father of all the mulatto children in everybody's household, but those in her own she seems to think drop from the clouds, or pretends so to think.[2] Good women we have, *but* they talk of all *nastiness*—though they never do wrong, they talk day and night of [*erasures illegible*]. My disgust sometimes is boiling over—but they are, I believe, in conduct the purest women God ever made. Thank God for my countrywomen—alas for the men! No worse than men everywhere, but the lower their mistresses, the more degraded they must be.

[D: My mother-in-law told me when I was first married not to send my female servants in the street on errands. They were then tempted, led astray— and then she said placidly, "So they told *me* when I came here, and I was very particular, *but you see with what result.*"

[D: Mr. Harris said it was so patriarchal. So it is—flocks and herds and slaves—and wife Leah does not suffice. Rachel must be *added,* if not *married.*[3] And all the time they seem to think themselves patterns—models of husbands and fathers.

---

[7] Dr. Edward M. Boykin, Chesnut's cousin.

[8] Milledge L. Bonham (1813–1890), recently resigned from the U.S. House of Representatives; later a Confederate general and governor of South Carolina, 1862–64.

[9] Charles Sumner (1811–1874), radical Republican U.S. senator from Massachusetts, who delivered a famous attack on a colleague from South Carolina on the floor of the Senate in 1856 and was severely beaten in the Senate by a kinsman of the latter, also a Senator, two days later.

[1] Apparently Chesnut did name the "thing" at first in her diary; the last phrase here is written over an erased entry.

[2] The words between "father of all" and "or pretends so to think" cover another unrecoverable erasure.

[3] In Genesis 29 and 30, sisters Leah and Rachel are both married to Jacob, who has children by each. (Later in her diary, Chesnut writes, with regard to her father-in-law's home, "Merciful God! forgive me if I *fail.* Can I respect what is not respectable. Can I *honor* what is dishonorable. *Rachel—and her brood*—make this place a horrid nightmare to me. I believe in nothing with this before me.") Mr. Harris: unidentified.

[D: Mrs. Davis[4] told me everybody described my husband's father as an odd character—"a millionaire who did nothing for his son whatever, left him to struggle with poverty, etc." I replied—"Mr. Chesnut Senior thinks himself the best of fathers—and his son thinks likewise. I have nothing to say—but it is true, he has no money but what he makes as a lawyer," etc. Again I say, my countrywomen are as pure as angels, though surrounded by another race who are—the social evil!]

April 29, 1862 [Columbia, S.C.]. Grand smash. News from New Orleans fatal to us. Met Weston[5]—he wanted to know where he could find a place of safety for two hundred Negroes. I looked in his face to see if he were in earnest—then to see if he were sane.

There were a certain set of two hundred Negroes that had grown to be a nuisance. Apparently all the white men of the family had felt bound to stay at home to take care of them. There are people who still believe Negroes to be property. Like Noah's neighbors, who insisted that the deluge would only be a little shower, after all.[6]

These Negroes, however, were Plowden Weston's—a totally different part of speech. He gave Enfield rifles to one company and forty thousand dollars to another.[7] He is away with our army at Corinth.

So I said, "You may rely upon [it]. Mr. C will assist you to his uttermost in finding a home for these people."

Nothing belonging to that patriotic gentleman shall come to grief, if we have to take charge of them on our own place.

Mr. C did get a place for them, as I said he would.

Another acquaintance of ours wanted his wife to go back home. They live in Charleston, and while he is in the army she could protect their property.

"Would you subject me to the horror of a captured and a sacked city?"

He answered, vacantly staring at her, "What are they?"[8]

Afterward Mrs. Izard said Byron's "Siege of Ishamael"[9] ought to have been given to him to read. It might have suggested a few new ideas.

Had to go to the governor's—or they would think we had hoisted the black flag.

They said we were going to be beaten—as Cortéz did the Mexicans—by superior arms. Mexican bows and arrows made a poor showing in face of powder and shot. Our enemies have such superior weapons of war—we, hardly any

---

[4] Varina A. H. Davis (1826–1906), wife of Jefferson Davis.
[5] Probably Francis Weston, a very wealthy planter.
[6] Deluge: in this instance, the war.
[7] Plowden J. C. Weston, presumably a kinsman of Francis, owned 350 slaves and lavishly supported the Confederacy.
[8] I.e., compared to the horror of the war as he knew it.
[9] An episode in Byron's *Don Juan* (1819–24).

but what we capture from them in the fray. The Saxons and the Normans were in the same plight.

War seems a game of chess—but we have an unequal number of pawns to begin with. We had knights, kings, queens, bishops, and castles enough. But our skillful generals—whenever they cannot arrange the board to suit them exactly, they burn up everything and march away. We want them to save the *country*. They seem to think their whole duty is to destroy ships and *save the army*.

Lovell's dispatch set me crying.[1]

The citizens of New Orleans say they were deserted by the army. Oh, for an hour of brave Jackson that the British turned their backs on.[2]

The citizens sent word to the enemy to shell away—they did not mean to surrender.

Surely this must be that so-often-cited darkest hour before our daylight.

Last night Governor Pickens[3] sent twice for Colonel C. He could not be found. The governor turned.

"Has he run away?"

"No. If he has, the war is over. This council is 'an exigency of the war.' While the war lasts—in spite of all I can do or say, he seems inclined to cleave to you."

Telegram from Mr. Venable,[4] dated Camp Moore, twenty miles from New Orleans.

There is a report abroad that Jeff Davis is expected here.

Not he. He will be the last man to give up heart and hope.

Mr. Robert Barnwell[5] wrote that he had to hang his head for South Carolina. We had not furnished our quota of the new levy—five thousand men.

Today Colonel Chesnut published his statement to show that we have sent thirteen thousand instead of the mere numbers required of us. So Mr. Barnwell can hold up his head again.

[A] pity Mrs. Governor P. selected General Cooper[6] for her communication, but facts seem to prove her theory—old Union [officers] and born Yankees are awfully unlucky statesmen and commanders for the Confederacy. In high places, they are dangerous indeed. They believe in the North in a way no true southerner ever will. They see no shame in surrendering to Yankees. They are

---

[1] General Mansfield Lovell (1822–1884) had lost New Orleans to Union forces under Admiral David G. Farragut.

[2] A variation on a traditional verse quoted elsewhere by Chesnut: "Oh, for an hour of Wallace wight / And well-skilled Bruce to rule the fight."

[3] Francis Pickens (1805–1869), South Carolina governor, 1860–62.

[4] Charles S. Venable, professor of mathematics at South Carolina College, had taken part in the assault on Fort Sumter and most recently was serving in Confederate forces at New Orleans; he later wrote Chesnut that he did "not see how we could have made a worse mess of it than we did at New Orleans."

[5] Reverend Robert W. Barnwell, professor and chaplain at South Carolina College.

[6] New Jerseyan Samuel Cooper (1798–1876), USMA 1815, was appointed a full general by Virginia in May 1861.

halfhearted clear through. Stephens as vice president—Lovell—Pemberton—Ripley.[7] A general must command the faith of his soldiers. These never will, be they ever so good and true.

Today the *Courier* pitches in, too, with the native talent which we undoubtedly possess—to think of choosing Mallory and Walker for navy and army![8] Whom they first make mad—"We can but feel it in this case."

Fancy our carrying the pamphlets and papers twice to Montgomery—fire ships and war steamers. How they laughed at J. C.'s fad! They were never looked at except by himself—their collector.

The Congress was so busy constitution-making and all that rubbish—furnishing a house afire—not running for the engine and the fire company to save the building.

Cart before the horse.

Christmas Day, 1863 [Richmond, VA]. Letters from Camden. Emma Stockton[9] found dead in her bed. Emma Lee married to Barney Stuart.[1]

At Maria's wedding we spoke of poor Rose Freeland. Not one year ago she came to see us. Dr. Harrison and his beautiful bride. Now, husband, wife, child, all gone, wiped out, nothing to show they have ever lived.[2]

Yesterday dined at the Prestons', with one of my handsomest Paris dresses (from Paris before the war). Three magnificent Kentucky generals. Orr, senator from South Carolina, and Mr. Miles.[3]

---

[7] Alexander H. Stephens (1812–1883), Confederate vice president, was born in Georgia but was opposed to secession; Mansfield Lovell was a native of Washington, D.C.; Confederate general John Clifford Pemberton (1814–1881), USMA 1837, was born in Pennsylvania; Confederate general Roswell S. Ripley (1823–1887), USMA 1843, came from Ohio.

[8] Stephen R. Mallory (1813–1873) was made secretary of the navy and Leroy P. Walker (1817–1884) secretary of the army in February 1861.

[9] Emma Stockton, whose husband Edward was the kinsman of both Chesnut and her husband. In a later entry, Chesnut wrote:

> Came home and found J.C. in a bitter mood. It has all gone wrong with our world. The loss of our private fortunes—[is] the smallest part. He intimates—with so much human misery filling the air—we might stay at home and think.
> And go mad? Catch me at it! A yawning grave—piles of red earth thrown on one side. That is the only future I ever see.
> You remember Emma Stockton. She and I were as blithe as birds, that day at Mulberry. I came here the next day, and when I got here—telegram—"Emma Stockton found dead in her bed." It is awfully near—that thought of death—always. No, no. I will not stop and think.

[1] Emma Lee, daughter of a Camden, South Carolina, family, married Barnwell Stuart, an educator in nearby Columbia.

[2] Maria Freeland of Richmond was married on December 17th to John R. C. Lewis, a kinsman of James Chesnut. Her sister Rosalie married the physician Randolph Harrison early in 1863. Wounded in the field, he "came home to die of his wounds" and by Christmas was followed to the grave by his wife and their infant.

[3] Caroline Hampton Preston and her husband, General John Smith Preston (1809–1881), were old friends of the Chesnuts. James L. Orr (1822–1873), antisecessionist Speaker of the U.S. House of Representatives, 1857–59, defeated James Chesnut for a seat in the Confederate Senate in 1861; his colleague in the U.S. House, William P. Miles (1822–1899), represented the Charleston district in the Confederate Congress through the war.

General Buckner repeated a speech of Hood's to him, to show how friendly they were.[4]

"I prefer a ride with you to the company of any woman in the world." Buckner's answer: "I prefer your company to that of any man, certainly."

This was the standing joke of the dinner, it flashed up in every form. Poor Sam got out of it so badly, if he got out of it at all.

General Buckner said patronizingly: "Lame excuses, all. Hood never gets out of any scrape; that is, unless he can fight out."

A man came. I will not give his name, as, sotto voce, Maggie[5] said, "Rich, sentimental, traveled, and a fool."

General Buckner had seen a Yankee pictorial. Angels were sent down from [heaven to] bear up Stonewall's[6] soul. They could not find it, flew back, sorrowing. When they got to the Golden Gates above, found Stonewall by a rapid flank movement had already cut a way in.

As they drove up to the Preston door met a crowd of schoolboys— one cried, "Boys, here's a fellow lost his leg at Chickamauga—cheer with a will."

Somebody confessed they used half corn, half coffee as a beverage—but it was always popcorn, for while they roasted it the popcorn popped out.

Others dropped in after dinner, without arms, without legs. Von Borcke,[7] who cannot speak because of a wound in his throat.

Isabella[8] said, "We have all kinds now but a blind one." Poor fellows, they laugh at wounds and yet can show many a scar.

We had for dinner oyster soup, soup à la reine. It has so many good things in it. Besides boiled mutton, ham, boned turkey, wild ducks, partridges, plum pudding. Sauterne, Burgundy, sherry, and Madeira wine.

There is life in the old land yet!

And now for our Christmas dinner. We invited two wounded homeless men who were too ill to come. Alex Haskell,[9] however, who has lost an eye, and Hood came.

---

[4] Simon Bolivar Buckner (1823–1914), USMA 1844, and John B. "Sam" Hood (1831–1879), USMA 1853, were two of the "three magnificent Kentucky generals" at the Preston's house in September; they had served together in the Chickamauga campaign, during which Hood lost a leg.

[5] The witty Margaret Graham Howell, Jefferson Davis's sister-in-law; sotto voce: in a whisper.

[6] Confederate general Thomas J. "Stonewall" Jackson (1824–1863), USMA 1846, was mortally wounded by friendly fire at Chancellorsville in May 1863.

[7] The Prussian officer Heros Von Borcke, who had volunteered for Confederate service and became J. E. B. Stuart's chief of staff, was wounded at Middleburg, Virginia, in June 1863.

[8] Isabella Martin, daughter of a Methodist minister in Columbia, South Carolina, was an acquaintance of Chesnut's during the war, but after it became a very close friend and eventually edited Chesnut's text for its first publication in the 1880s.

[9] Alexander C. Haskell, aide-de-camp to General Maxcy Gregg, was wounded in June 1862.

That lovely little Charlotte Wickham, Rooney Lee's wife—she is dying. Her husband is in a Yankee prison.[1]

Today my dinner was comparatively a simple affair—oysters, ham, turkey, partridges, and good wine.

Last night I saw from Buck's[2] face that she was having a hard battle to fight. Nobody went to her assistance. I had described to J. C. the behavior of the Texican when he heard of the "Charge of the Light Brigade" for the first time.[3]

So he tried it on Hood. J. C. reads admirably.

Hood was excited beyond anything I ever imagined. He sat straight up. His eyes grew flaming, scintillating. And he made a gesture, which J. C. said was like the motion of a soldier receiving his orders in a battle, at the end of every line.

While Alex Haskell and J. C. sat over their wine, Sam (Hood) gave me an account of his discomfiture last night. Said he could not sleep after it. That it was the hardest battle he had ever fought in his life. "And I was routed, as it were. She told me there was 'no hope'—that ends it. You know, at Petersburg, on my way to the western army, she half-promised me to think of it. She would not say yes, but she did not say no, that is, not exactly. At any rate, I went off, saying, 'I am engaged to you,' and she said, 'I am not engaged to you.' After I was so fearfully wounded, I gave it up. But then, since I came, etc., etc., etc."

"Do you mean to say that you had proposed for her before that conversation in the carriage when you asked Brewster the symptoms? I like your audacity."

"Oh, she understood, but it is all up now. She says no. I asked her about her engagement to Ransom Calhoun.[4] She explained it all. Then I said he was a classmate of mine, and he had made me his confidant. 'Heavens,' she said; laughing in my face. 'If I had only known that, what a different story I would have told you.' I do not know what this laugh and confession had to [do] with it, but somehow, after that I did not care so much for the 'no' as I did before. Besides, she told me to say South Carolina, to rattle the r and not to pronounce it as if it had two l's and no r. And she did not like my way of asking for more of that good Burgundy wine at dinner, etc., etc., etc."

Mrs. Rooney Lee died yesterday. One of her babies died, too. She was not twenty-three. He is a prisoner still.

---

[1] Charlotte Wickham Lee's husband William, son of Robert E. Lee, was captured in 1863 at the Wickham family home in Virginia while recuperating from wounds suffered at Brandy Station, Virginia, during the Gettysburg campaign that June.

[2] Sally Buchanan Preston, the Prestons' daughter; as the following entries make clear, she had a romance with General Hood that began in the fall of 1862.

[3] Alfred Tennyson's poem was read to the unidentified Texan two days earlier; apparently he was overwhelmed by the work's portrayal of the fatal fearlessness with which a British brigade attacked the Russian defenders of Balaclava during the Crimean War in 1854.

[4] William Ransom Calhoun, "Buck's" cousin, was killed in a duel in September 1862.

July 25, 1864 [Columbia, S.C.]. So she was in a bad way when the killing blow came.[5]

Here we are, in a cottage rented from Dr. Chisolm.[6]

Hood full general. Johnston removed, superseded.

Early threatening Washington City.[7] Semmes, of whom we have been so proud—he is a fool after all—risked the *Alabama* in a sort of duel of ships! He has lowered the flag of the famous *Alabama* to the *Kearsarge.*[8] Forgive who may! I cannot.

We moved into this house on the 20th of July. J. C. was telegraphed to go to Charleston. General Jones[9] sent for him—part of his command is on the coast.

Willie Preston[1] killed—his heart literally shot away—as he was getting his battery in position. . . .

We were the saddest three. The straits the country was in, the state of things in Atlanta then, was the burden of our talk.

Suddenly Buck sprang up.

"Mrs. C, your new house is very hot. I am suffocated. It is not so oppressively hot at home, with our thick brick walls, you know."

Isabella [Martin] soon after came here. She said she saw the sisters pass her house, and as they turned the corner, there was a loud and bitter cry. It seemed to come from the Hampton house. And both of the girls began to run at full speed.

"What is the matter?" asked Mrs. Martin.

"Mother! listen—that sounded like the cry of a broken heart," said Isabella. "Something has gone terribly wrong at the Prestons."

Mrs. Martin is deaf, however, so she heard nothing and thought Isabella fanciful.

Isabella hurried over there. They had come to tell Mrs. Preston that Willie

---

[5] "She" in this cryptic comment was "Buck" Preston, fearful for Sam Hood, who was named to replace General Joseph E. Johnston as commander of the army earlier in July and was eventually to fail during the bloody Franklin and Nashville campaign (September 1864–January 1865). In a good example of how Chesnut's later rewritings altered the point of view in her "diary" of the war, this entry casts the gloom of Hood's eventual troubles back over the previous summer. In July she of course could not have known of the future difficulties.

[6] John J. Chisolm, a medical doctor, was then head of a Charleston laboratory producing medicines for the Confederate army.

[7] General Jubal A. Early (1816–1894), USMA 1837, crossed the Potomac north of Washington on 5 July and began to move toward the Union capital; owing to Union confusion and the perception that his threat was not serious, he was not forced back until the 12th.

[8] Raphael Semmes (1809–1877) assumed command of the British-built Confederate vessel *Alabama* following its launching in May 1862 and for the next two years created havoc among Union shipping. The ship was defeated and sunk off the coast of France by the USS *Kearsarge* on June 19, 1864.

[9] Samuel Jones (1820–1887), USMA 1841, had resigned from the faculty at West Point to assume a Confederate commission; at present he was in charge of Confederate forces in South Carolina.

[1] The Prestons' son.

was killed. Willie! his mother's darling! No country ever had a braver soldier—
a truer gentleman—to lay down his life in her cause. . . .

January—[1865. *Columbia, S.C.*]. Yesterday I broke down—gave way to abject
terror. The news of Sherman's advance[2]—and no news of my husband.
Today—wrapped up on the sofa—too dismal for moaning, even. There was a
loud knock. Shawls and all, rushed to the door. Telegram from my husband.

"All well—be at home on Tuesday." It was dated from Adams Run.

I felt as lighthearted as if the war were over.

Then I looked at the date—Adams Run. It ends as it began. Bulls Run—
from which their first sprightly running astounded the world.[3] Now if we run—
who are to run? They ran fullhanded. We have fought until maimed soldiers
and women and children are all that is left to run.

Today Kershaw's brigade, or what is left of it, passed through. The shouts
that greeted it and the bold shouts of thanks it returned—it was all a very
encouraging noise, absolutely comforting. Some true men left after all. . . .

Soldiers are not demoralized. Their shouts as they go by gladden my heart.
I sit at my window and watch them hastening from one train to the other.

Went to hear Mr. Palmer,[4] to have my heart lifted up and my hands
strengthened. But no—he was demonstrating *natural* history—family relations
from a physical and biblical point of view. Just on the verge, always, of frightful
moral and indecent precipices. One difficulty is that in church [when] such
unpleasant topics are broached, one does not know where to look.

"Sit and stare blankly at the parson—even if he forgets he is a man. And
you must try and forget it, too. Think of him only as a parson," cries the irrepressible. . . .

My small drawing room crammed to its utmost limit—and I so weary, full
of care—so utterly discomfited, so stupid, so dead. How can I bear it?. . .

Today they say Sherman has recrossed into Georgia and that Hood is
between Sherman and Thomas. So goes the upper, and the nethermost, mill-
stone to work.

"No, auntie. Today they said the Hood balloon went up a skyrocket, fire
rocket—was it? At any rate, they said it had come down a *stick*."[5]

"Comments are cruel."

February 16, 1865. Lincolnton, North Carolina. A change came o'er the spirit
of my dream—dear old quire of yellow, coarse, Confederate homemade paper!

[2] Ohioan William Tecumseh Sherman (1820–1891), USMA 1841, took Atlanta in September 1864,
and from November 15th to December 21st conducted his infamous March to the Sea, ending at
Savannah. At the time of Chesnut's entry, he was preparing to head due north from there to
Columbia, under orders from Grant to join in a massive attack on Lee in Virginia.

[3] At Bull Run, Virginia (July 21, 1861), the first battle of the war, Union troops initially made a
good attack but as the tide turned were forced to retreat.

[4] Reverend Benjamin H. Palmer, Presbyterian minister and educator in Columbia.

[5] Here the common expression of scorn for grand projects that fail becomes "cruel," as Chesnut's
next line puts it, because amputee Sam Hood was at present trying to walk using a wooden leg.

Here you are again—and an age of anxiety and suffering has passed over my head since I wrote and wept over your forlorn pages.

My ideas of those last days are confused.

The Martins left Columbia the Friday before I did. And their mammy, the Negro woman who had nursed them, refused to go with them. That daunted me. Then Mrs. McCord,[6] who was to send her girls with me, changed her mind. She sent them upstairs in her house—and actually took away the staircase—that was her plan.

Then I met Mr. Christopher Hampton[7] arranging to take off his sisters. They were flitting—but only as far as Yorkville. He said it was time to move on, [that] Sherman at Orangeburg was barely a day's journey from Columbia, and that he left a track as bare and blackened as a fire in the prairies.

So my time had come, too. My husband urged me to go home. He said Camden would be safe enough. They had no spite to that old town—as they have to Charleston and Columbia. Molly, weeping and wailing, came in while we were at table, wiping her red-hot face with her cook's grimy apron. She said I ought to go among our own black people on the plantation. They would take care of me better than anyone else. So I agreed to go to Mulberry or the Hermitage plantation and sent Laurence with a wagon load of my valuables.[8]

Then a Miss Patterson called—a refugee from Tennessee. She had been in a country overrun by Yankee invaders—and she described so graphically all the horrors to be endured by those subjected to fire and sword and rapine and plunder that I was fairly scared and determined to come here. This is a thoroughly out-of-all-routes place. And yet I can go to Charlotte. I am halfway to Kate[9] at Flat Rock. And there is no Federal army between me and Richmond.

As soon as my mind was finally made up, we telegraphed Laurence, who had barely got to Camden in the wagon when the telegram was handed to him. So he took the train and came back. Mr. Chesnut sent him with us to take care of the party.

We thought if the Negroes were ever so loyal to us, they could not protect me from an army bent upon sweeping us from the face of the earth. And if they tried to do so—so much the worse for the poor things with their Yankee friends. So I left them to shift for themselves, as they are accustomed to do—and I took the same liberty.

My husband does not care a fig for the property question. Never did. Perhaps if he had ever known poverty it would be different. He talked beautifully about it—as he always does about everything. I have told him often if at heaven's gates St. Peter will listen to him awhile—let him tell his own story—

[6]Louisa Cheves McCord (1810–1879), well-known apologist for the institution of slavery and author of *Caius Gracchus* (1851), a five-act verse tragedy; her "girls" were her adolescent daughters, Hannah and Rebecca.
[7]Christopher Fitzsimons Hampton was the younger brother of General Wade Hampton.
[8]Molly (Mary Chesnut's maid) and Laurence (James Chesnut's valet) were house slaves.
[9]Chesnut's sister, Katherine Williams.

he will get in, and they may give him a crown extra.

Now he says he has only one care—that I should be safe and not so harassed with dread. And then there is his blind old father! "A man can always die like a patriot and a gentleman—no fuss—take it coolly. It is hard not to envy those who are out of all this, their difficulties ended." "Who?" "Those who have met death gloriously on the battlefield. Their doubts are all solved. One can but do their best and leave the result to a higher power."

After New Orleans, those vain passionate impatient little Creoles were forever committing suicide, driven to it by despair and Beast Butler.[1] As he read these things, Mr. Davis said, "If they want to die, why not kill Beast Butler—rid the world of their foe and be saved the trouble of murdering themselves?" However, that practical way of ending their intolerable burden did not seem to occur to them.

I repeated this suggestive anecdote to our horde of generals without troops. This very distinguished party rode superb horses and rode to the lines every day. They congregated at our house—they laid their fingers on the maps spread out on the table (covering this "quire of paper") and pointed out where Sherman was going and where he could be stopped.

They argued over their plans eloquently. Every man jack of them had a safe plan to stop Sherman if—

Even Beauregard[2] and Lee were expected. But Grant had double-teamed on Lee.[3] He could not save his own. How can he come to save us? Only read the list of the dead in those last battles around Richmond and Petersburg if you want to break your heart.

I took French leave of[4] Columbia, slipped away without a word to anybody. Isaac Hayne[5] and Mr. Chesnut came down to the Charlotte depot with me. Ellen,[6] my maid, left husband and only child—but she was willing to come—very cheerful in her way of looking at it.

"Who guine trouble my William—dey don't dares to. Claiborne" (her husband) "kin take good care of William. I never traveled 'round with Missis before—and I wants to go this time." As for Laurence, he turned the same unmoved face toward our trunks and luggage. Smith[7] grinned farewell.

A woman fifty years old, at least—and uglier than she was old—sharply

---

[1] Union general Benjamin Franklin Butler (1818–1893) had occupied New Orleans after Farragut took the city, and soon became the subject of intense criticism for his handling of affairs there. In one famous incident, he had the gambler William B. Mumford hanged for pulling the American flag down from the U.S. Mint building in the city.

[2] Confederate general Pierre Gustave Toutant Beauregard (1818–1893), USMA 1838, then second-in-command to Joseph Johnston in the Carolinas.

[3] A reference to Grant's ordering of Sherman to join in a combined attack on Lee.

[4] I.e., fled.

[5] Isaac William Hayne, grandson of the executed Revolutionary spy Isaac Hayne and a prominent member of South Carolina's ruling elite.

[6] Ellen was another of the Chesnuts' house slaves.

[7] Another Chesnut slave.

rebuked my husband for standing at the car window for a few last words to me.

She said rudely, "Stand aside, sir. *I* want air." With his hat off—and his grand air—he bowed politely.

"In one moment, Madame. I have something of importance to say to my wife."

She talked aloud and introduced herself to every man, claiming his protection. She had never traveled alone before in all her life. Old age and ugliness are protective—in some cases. She was ardently patriotic for a while. Then she was joined by her friend, a man as crazy as herself to get out of this. From their talk I gleaned she had been for years in the department.[8] They were about to cross the lines. The whole idea was to get away from the trouble, to come here. They were Yankees. Were they spies?

S. H.[9] was talking loudly and violently to a deep-toned officer. It was wonderful that his low modulated voice did not give her a hint to moderate hers. But the cars rumbled and banged—and she shrieked above all.

Here I am brokenhearted—an exile.

Such a place. Bare floors. For a featherbed, a pine table, and two chairs I pay 30 dollars a day. Such sheets!—but I have some of my own.

At the door—before I was well out of the hack—the woman of the house packed Laurence back, neck and heels. She would not have him at any price. She treated him as Mr. F's aunt did Clennam in *Little Dorrit*.[1] She said his clothes were too fine for a nigger—"his airs indeed"—and poor Laurence was as humble—and silent. He said at last, "Miss Mary, send me back to Mars Jeems." I began to look for a pencil to write a note to my husband. In the flurry could not find it. "Here is one," said Laurence, producing a gold pencil case. "Go away," she shouted. "I wants no niggers here with pencils—and airs." So Laurence fled before the storm—not before he had begged me to go back. He thought, "If Mars Jeems knew how you was treated he'd never be willing for you to stay here."

The Martins had seen my well-known traveling case as the hack trotted up Main St.—and they arrived at this juncture out of breath.

We embraced and wept.

I kept my room. After dinner Ellen presented herself—blue-black with rage. She has lost the sight of one eye—so that is permanently *bluish*, opaque. The other flamed fire and fury. "Here's my dinner. A piece of meat—and a whole plateful of raw ingins.[2] I never did eat raw ingins, and I won't begin now.

---

[8] I.e., a Confederate district or region, probably in this case the coastal department comprising South Carolina, Georgia, and Florida. Chesnut's 1860s diary identifies the woman as a "Mrs. Smith, a refugee Virginian."

[9] Sophie Haskell, Alexander Haskell's sister.

[1] When Flora Finching, whom Charles Dickens's hero Arthur Clennam once loved, has him to dinner following his return from China, her deceased husband's aunt disrupts the meal with her eccentric behavior. Chesnut's 1860s diary identifies the woman as Mrs. Johnston of Johnston's Hotel, Lincolnton.

[2] I.e., onions.

Dese here niggers say dis ole lady gives 'em to 'em breakfast and dinner. It's a sin and a shame to do us so. She says I must come outen her kitchen—de niggers won't work for looking at me. I'se something to look at, surely." She [put] down her odorous plate—held her fork and made a curtsy.

"Ellen—for pity sake!"

"Lord ha' mercy. She say you bring me and Laurence here to keep us from running away to de Yankees—and I say, 'Name o' God, ole Missis! If dat's it—what she bring Laurence and me for? She's got plenty more. Laurence and me's nothing—to our white people. De ole soul fair play insulted me.' "[3]

Then came an invitation to tea at Mrs. Munro's. Ellen retired in contrition and confusion.

Isabella [Martin] told Ellen what a shame it was to add to my trouble in this way.

We wanted to rent part of Mrs. Munro's house, but Mrs. Ben Rutledge[4] was before us. Then we tried a Miss McLean. She blew hot and cold. She would—and then she would not. I was left utterly uncertain.

Mrs. Munro's husband has been killed in battle. She has one child, a boy of seven. Her husband was a son of Judge Munro of South Carolina.[5] Mrs. Munro is handsome, accomplished, and very clever. She is from Virginia. A noted thing about her in this small town is the fact that she is a Roman Catholic.

She comes from Abingdon, Virginia, the home of the Prestons, Floyds, Lewises, etc., etc., and Joe Johnston. The latter is expected here daily—so I am in the regular line of strategic retreat. Mrs. Munro is a violent abolitionist [D: in the sense I am one.] Isabella says she never saw a true woman who was not, but Mrs. Munro is a Yankee sympathizer, and that is one too much for us.

She gave us pound cake at tea—and such nice tea it was, after a week of Mrs. ———'s horrid coffee. I forgot my beautiful tea caddy on the mantelpiece at my house in Columbia. Strange to say, a French one—on it was marked in gilt letters "Thé." Said Sam Shannon[6] once: "Here is a box with only 'The' on it. 'The'—what does it mean?" Buck asked him, "Do you understand French?" "Certainly." "There is an accent on that e, but we won't translate for you, as you know the language."

And my caddy was filled with English breakfast tea! Gone forever.

The Fants[7] are refugees here, too. They are Virginians, too, and have been in exile since Second Manassas.[8] Poor things, they seem to have been everywhere and seen and suffered everything. They even tried to go back to their

[3] Ellen's last statement seems obscure.
[4] Eleanor Middleton Rutledge.
[5] Mary Dunn Munro, daughter-in-law of Robert Munro of Charleston.
[6] Samuel Davis Shannon.
[7] An otherwise unidentified Virginia family.
[8] This battle, called Manassas or Second Bull Run by the North, took place August 29–30, 1862 thirty miles west of Washington in Virginia.

own house. Of that they found one chimney alone standing, which had also been taken possession of by a Yankee in this wise. His name was written on it—and his claim by that established, the writer said.

The day I left home, I had packed a box of flour, sugar, rice, coffee, etc., etc., but my husband would not let me bring it. He said I was coming to a land of plenty. Unexplored North Carolina, where the foot of Yankee marauder was unknown—and in Columbia they would need food.

Now I have written to send me that box and many other things by Laurence, or I will starve.

The Middletons[9] have come. How joyously I sprang to my feet to greet them. Mrs. Ben Rutledge describes the hubbub in Columbia—everybody flying in every direction, like a flock of swallows. She heard the enemy's guns booming in the distance.

The train no longer runs from Charlotte to Columbia.

Miss Middleton possesses her soul in peace—cool, clever, rational, and entertaining as ever. We talked for hours.

Mrs. Read was in a state of despair. I can well understand that sinking of mind and body in the first days—as the abject misery of it all closes upon you.

I remember my suicidal tendencies when I first came here.

We were off through mud and slush to the railroad to hear the news when the train came in. At the station, saw a wounded soldier, a handsome fellow—and sympathetic. "Madame, I feel like seizing a musket and going to help South Carolina—*whether or no.*" He was a Virginian, of course—and I wept, of course. . . .

Our landlady evinces great repugnance still to Ellen—but we begin to laugh at her tantrums. For we hope to get away.

April 22, 1865 [Chester, S.C.]. This yellow Confederate quire of paper blotted by my journal has been buried three days with the silver sugar dish, teapot, milk jug, and a few spoons and forks that follow my fortunes as I wander. With these valuables was Hood's silver cup, which was partly crushed when he was wounded at Chickamauga.

It has been a wild three days. Aides galloping around with messages. Yankees hanging over us like the sword of Damocles.[1] We have been in queer straits. . . .

Colonel Cad Jones came with a dispatch, a sealed secret dispatch. It was for General Chesnut. I opened it.

[9]Mrs. Rutledge's family, including her sisters Susan Matilda ("Miss Middleton") and Mary Julia Read and their mother Susan Chisolm Middleton of the Colleton district in South Carolina.
[1]In the fourth century B.C., Damocles, who flatteringly told King Dionysius of Syracuse that the latter was the happiest of men, was invited to a banquet by the king and, so that he would learn how uncomfortable a king might be, seated under a sword dangling on a single hair.

Lincoln—old Abe Lincoln—killed—murdered—Seward wounded![2]

Why? By whom? It is simply maddening, all this.

I sent off messenger after messenger for General Chesnut. I have not the faintest idea where he is, but I know this foul murder will bring down worse miseries on us.

Mary Darby[3] says: "But they murdered him themselves. No Confederates in Washington."

"But if they see fit to accuse us of instigating it?"

"Who murdered him?"

"Who knows!"

"See if they don't take vengeance on us, now that we are ruined and cannot repel them any longer."

Met Mr. Heyward.[4] He said: "Plebiscitum[5] it is. See, our army are deserting Joe Johnston. That is the people's vote against a continuance of the war. And the death of Lincoln—I call that a warning to tyrants. He will not be the last president put to death in the capital, though he is the first."

"Joe Johnston's army that he has risked his reputation to save from the very first year of the war—*deserting*. Saving his army by retreats, and now they are deserting *him*."

"Yes, Stonewall's tactics were the best—hard knocks, blow after blow in rapid succession, quick marches, surprises, victories quand même.[6] That would have saved us. Watch, wait, retreat, ruined us. Now look out for bands of marauders, black and white, lawless disbanded soldiery from both armies."

An armistice, they say, is agreed on.

Taking stock, as the shopkeepers say. Heavy debts for the support of Negroes during the war—and before, as far as we are concerned. No home— our husbands shot or made prisoners.

"Stop, Mrs. C. At best, Camden for life—that is worse than the galleys for you."

At Mrs. Bedon's,[7] Buck never submits to be bored. They (the bores) came to tea and then sat and talked. So prosy, so wearisome was the discourse, so endless it seemed. We envied Buck, mooning in the piazza. She rarely speaks now. Serene she seems, but in deep reveries ever.

---

[2] Federal secretary of state William H. Seward was brutally attacked the same evening (April 14) as Lincoln but survived. He became a firm supporter of Andrew Johnson and of the policy of conciliation between North and South.

[3] Mary Preston Darby, another of the Preston Daughters.

[4] Otherwise unidentified.

[5] I.e., by their desertions the ordinary people were letting their feelings be known as if they were voting in a plebiscite.

[6] All the same.

[7] Chesnut elsewhere describes Mrs. Bedon as the "wife of Josiah Bedon that we knew so well . . . killed in that famous fight of the Charleston Light Dragoons . . . [that] stood still, to be shot down in their tracks."

Softly she came in from the piazza. With face unmoved and eyes devoid of all expression, she said quietly:

"Guns in the distance. Don't you hear?" Our guests were off at a bound, hardly taking time to say good night.

"Buck, did you hear anything?"

"No."

"All the same, that was a crack shot of yours. It saved our lives. I was nearly dead." She smiled in the same listless unconcerned way and went back to her post in the piazza.

Things people say. We sit in silent wonder.

"Now, if Jeff Davis had been in earnest, if he had been truly a secessionist, no halfhearted Union man, as we all know he is and was—things would have gone so differently with us."

Again, when Col. Cad Jones brought the dispatch.

"That man is a Yankee spy. Don't tell me! If he were not a spy, would he not ride for his life and give that dispatch himself to General Chesnut? He stopped here to spy out for the Yankees."

"Man alive! This was Cad Jones, Cadwalader Jones, twice promoted for gallantry in action. This is almost his home. He was born [with]in twenty miles of this place."

"I do not believe it is Colonel Jones. I am sure he should be taken up as a spy."

Are we all going mad with misery and suspicion?

May 2, 1865. Camden. From the roadside below Blackstock.

Since we left Chester—solitude. Nothing but tall blackened chimneys to show that any man has ever trod this road before us.

This is Sherman's track. It is hard not to curse him.

I wept incessantly at first. "The roses of these gardens are already hiding the ruins," said Mr. C. "Nature is a wonderful renovator." He tried to say something.

Then I shut my eyes and made a vow. If we are a crushed people, crushed by aught, I have vowed never to be a whimpering pining slave.

We heard loud explosions of gunpowder in the direction of Chester. Destroyers at it there.

Met William Walker.[8] Mr. Preston left him in charge of a carload of his valuables. Mr. Preston was hardly out of sight before poor helpless William had to stand by and see the car plundered.

"My dear Missis, they have cleared me out—nothing left," moaned William the faithful.

We have nine armed couriers with us. Can they protect us?

Bade adieu to the staff at Chester. No general ever had so remarkable a

---

[8] A Preston slave.

staff—so accomplished, so agreeable, so well-bred and, I must say, so handsome—and I can add, so brave and efficient.

May 4, 1865. Bloomsbury.[9] Home again.

From Chester to Winnsboro we did not see one living thing—man, woman, or animal—except poor William trudging home after his sad disaster.

The blooming of the gardens had a funereal effect. Nature is so luxuriant here. She soon covers the ravages—of savages. Then the last frost occurred the seventh of March. So that accounts for the wonderful advance of vegetation. It seems providential to these starving people. In this climate, so much that is edible has been grown in two months.

At Winnsboro we stayed at Mr. Robinson's.[1] There we left the wagon train. Only Mr. Brisbane, one of the general's couriers, came with us on escort duty. The Robinsons were very kind and hospitable, brimful of Yankee anecdotes. To my amazement the young people of Winnsboro had a May Day—amidst the smoking ruins. Irrepressible youth!

Fidelity of the Negroes the principal topic. There seems not a single case of a Negro who betrayed his master. And yet they showed a natural and exultant joy at being free.

After we left Winnsboro, in the fields Negroes were plowing and hoeing corn. In status quo antebellum. The fields in that respect looked quite cheerful. And we did not pass in the line of Sherman's savages, so we saw some houses standing.

The Robinsons told us that it was a Confederate explosion yesterday at Chester. They are very cheerful and hopeful—take Mr. Boyce's[2] sanguine view of Yankees.

Mrs. Robinson said: "My son was killed in the Charleston Light Dragoons. If I can forgive that—and I do—why should not they forgive anything? Indeed they ought."

"Ought counts for nothing in this calculating world," answered Cassandra.[3]

May 16, 1865 [Camden, S.C.]. We are scattered—stunned—the remnant of heart left alive with us, filled with brotherly hate.

We sit and wait until the drunken tailor[4] who rules the U.S.A. issues a proclamation and defines our anomalous position.

[9] Bloomsbury was the home of James Chestnut's sister Sally.

[1] Otherwise unidentified.

[2] William Waters Boyce, a member of the Confederate Congress, called for the resignation of Jefferson Davis in September 1864 and urged that the South attempt to negotiate a peace with the North.

[3] The prophet Cassandra, who was doomed never to be believed, was the daughter of King Priam of Troy; Chesnut occasionally used the name for herself in the text.

[4] Andrew Johnson (1808–1875), by then president of the United States, had been raised in poverty and worked early in life as a tailor.

Such a hue and cry—whose fault? Everybody blamed by somebody else. Only the dead heroes left stiff and stark on the battlefield escape.

"Blame every man who stayed at home and did not fight. I will not stop to hear excuses. Not one word against those who stood out until the bitter end and stacked muskets at Appomattox."

Yesterday John Whitaker and Dr. Charles Shannon[5] said they would be found ready enough to take up arms when the time came!

Rip Van Winkle was a light sleeper to these two—their nap has lasted four years. . . .

Black 4th of July—1865 [Camden, S.C.]. Saturday I was in bed with one of my worst headaches. Occasionally there would come a sob as I thought of my sister—insulted—and my little sweet Williamses![6] Another of my beautiful Columbia quartet had rough experiences.

Lizzie Hamilton.[7] They asked the plucky little girl for a ring which she wore.

"You shall not have it." The man put a pistol to her head. "Take it off. Hand it to me, or I will blow your brains out."

"Blow away." The man laughed and put down his pistol.

"You knew I would not shoot you."

"Of course I knew you dared not shoot me. Even Sherman would not stand that."

But my little sweet Williamses had only Captain Kirk.[8] Even he stopped it when he saw a bushwhacker strike Mary.

Then given up to headaches and tears. Suddenly downstairs I heard a rush of many footsteps, hurryings to and fro. H[9] giving orders in a shrill voice, at the top of the stairs—mad tearings in and out of the room next to mine.

"After all, are not raids a thing of the past? This sounds like one."

"Dick has come!" said the captain, putting his head in the door. "I have brought a note from him. He is at the hotel in Camden—will be here in a few minutes. *I am the harbinger of great joy.*"

Bedlam generally outside. Maids chattering, racing about, slamming doors, giggling—shh—shh. "Miss Mary's nerves, remember." They were trampling my nerves underfoot. Then a long rolling sound. They were shutting

---

[5] Whitaker was Chesnut's cousin; Shannon was a member of a Camden family well known to her.
[6] Chesnut earlier tells of hearing of a frightening attack on her sister, Kate Williams, and Kate's children by some Yankee "bushwackers": "My sister Kate they forced back against the wall. She had Katie, the baby, in her arms, and Miller, the brave boy, clung to his mother, though he could do no more. They tried to force brandy down her throat. They knocked Mary down with the butt end of a pistol, and Serena they struck with open hand, leaving the mark on her cheek for weeks."
[7] Described earlier in the text as "a perfect little beauty" with "an eye for fun."
[8] A Union officer to whom Serena Williams appealed and who drove off the bushwackers and allowed the Williamses to escape.
[9] Harriet Grant, James Chesnut's niece, about to be married to New Jersey native Richard ("Dick") Stockton, who supported the Confederacy.

those hard creaking folding doors whose rollers make as much noise as an ammunition wagon.

The lovers were penned up in that smoking hot night. The cool captain and the Reynoldses, enjoying the breezes in the piazza, the captain for their benefit performing a pantomime—solus—of what he imagined was going on behind the venetians.

Next day bride-elect arrayed herself like a May queen—crown of natural flowers on her head and wreaths of flowers and evergreen looped up her dress on every side.

Her uncle[1] like a Goth took his knife and cut off the body garlands—left the wreaths of green flowing over the skirt of her gown.

"You are not young enough for such nonsense. You will disgust the man. Dress like a Christian woman—not in masquerade."

"A Christian woman—I would like to see her in that character."

The redoubtable Dick is fair, with light hair and blue eyes. He lisps. His trousers were blue, and he wore a shell jacket of yellow nankin. In his shirt front dully gleamed a diamond breastpin.

They say he is clever. He told that Adèle Auzé[2] was arrested by the Federals for clapping her hands when she heard that Lincoln was murdered. They seized her instantly, did not give her time to get bonnet or shawl. The general only reprimanded her sharply, and she went home wholly undisturbed by this adventure. Also, Lucy Gwin[3] introduced General Sherman to a party of ladies, among them Mrs. Thomas Anderson, who is a niece of President Davis. The ladies shook hands with him. Sherman noticed that Mrs. Anderson held back and did not give him her hand as did the others.

"Madame, *you* do not seem glad to see me."

"No, I am not glad to see you."

Wedding to be next Tuesday, then they go for a week to Mary W's and from thence to New Jersey. . . .

They talked of the Negroes wherever the Yankees had been, who flocked to them and showed them where the silver and valuables were hid by the white people. Ladies' maids dressing themselves in their mistresses' gowns before their faces and walking off. Two sides to stories. Now, before this, everyone told me how kind and faithful and considerate the Negroes had been. I am sure, after hearing these tales, the fidelity of my own servants shines out brilliantly. I had taken it too much as a matter of course.

Yesterday there was a mass meeting of Negroes, thousands of them were in town, eating, drinking, dancing, speechifying. Preaching and prayer was also a popular amusement. They have no greater idea of amusement than wild prayers—unless it be getting married or going to a funeral.

[1] James Chesnut.
[2] A Camden resident.
[3] Daughter of a former California senator who moved to the South.

In the afternoon I had some business on our place, the Hermitage. John drove me down. Our people were all at home—quiet, orderly, respectful, and at their usual work. In point of fact things looked unchanged. There was nothing to show that anyone of them had even seen a Yankee or knew that there was one in existence.

"We are in for a new St. Domingo[4] all the same. The Yankees have raised the devil, and now they cannot guide him."

A Jacquerie[5]—not a French Revolution, say the soldiers. They mean this to be a white man's country. . . .

JENNY PROCTOR, KATIE ROWE, MARY GRAYSON

from **Lay My Burden Down** (1945)

JENNY PROCTOR: ALABAMA

I'S HEAR TELL OF THEM GOOD SLAVE DAYS, BUT I AIN'T NEVER SEEN NO GOOD times then. My mother's name was Lisa, and when I was a very small child I hear that driver going from cabin to cabin as early as 3 o'clock in the morning, and when he comes to our cabin he say, "Lisa, Lisa, git up from there and git that breakfast." My mother, she was cook, and I don't recollect nothing 'bout my father. If I had any brothers and sisters I didn't know it. We had old ragged huts made out of poles and some of the cracks chinked up with mud and moss and some of them wasn't. We didn't have no good beds, just scaffolds nailed up to the wall out of poles and the old ragged bedding throwed on them. That sure was hard sleeping, but even that feel good to our weary bones after them long hard days' work in the field. I tended to the children when I was a little gal and tried to clean the house just like Old Miss tells me to. Then soon as I was ten years old, Old Master, he say, "Git this here nigger to that cotton patch."

I recollects once when I was trying to clean the house like Old Miss tell me, I finds a biscuit, and I's so hungry I et it, 'cause we never see such a thing as a biscuit only sometimes on Sunday morning. We just have corn bread and syrup and sometimes fat bacon, but when I et that biscuit and she comes in and say, "Where that biscuit?" I say, "Miss, I et it 'cause I's so hungry." Then she grab that broom and start to beating me over the head with it and calling me low-down nigger, and I guess I just clean lost my head 'cause I knowed better than to fight her if I knowed anything 't all, but I start to fight her, and

---

[4] Because of the successful revolution of the slaves there at the start of the nineteenth century, the very name of Santo Domingo had become a symbol of terror among white southerners.
[5] A reference to a bloody peasants' revolt in fourteenth-century France in response to an English invasion.

the driver, he comes in and he grabs me and starts beating me with that cat-o'-nine-tails, and he beats me till I fall to the floor nearly dead. He cut my back all to pieces, then they rubs salt in the cuts for more punishment. Lord, Lord, honey! Them was awful days. When Old Master come to the house, he say, "What you beat that nigger like that for?" And the driver tells him why, and he say, "She can't work now for a week. She pay for several biscuits in that time." He sure was mad, and he tell Old Miss she start the whole mess. I still got them scars on my old back right now, just like my grandmother have when she die, and I's a-carrying mine right on to the grave just like she did.

Our master, he wouldn't 'low us to go fishing—he say that too easy on a nigger and wouldn't 'low us to hunt none either—but sometime we slips off at night and catch possums. And when Old Master smells them possums cooking 'way in the night, he wraps up in a white sheet and gits in the chimney corner and scratch on the wall, and when the man in the cabin goes to the door and say, "Who's that?" he say, "It's me, what's ye cooking in there?" and the man say, "I's cooking possum." He say, "Cook him and bring me the hindquarters and you and the wife and the children eat the rest." We never had no chance to git any rabbits 'cept when we was a-clearing and grubbing the new ground. Then we catch some rabbits, and if they looks good to the white folks they takes them and if they no good the niggers git them. We never had no gardens. Sometimes the slaves git vegetables from the white folks' garden and sometimes they didn't.

Money? Uh-uh! We never seen no money. Guess we'd-a bought something to eat with it if we ever seen any. Fact is, we wouldn't-a knowed hardly how to bought anything, 'cause we didn't know nothing 'bout going to town.

They spinned the cloth what our clothes was made of, and we had straight dresses or slips made of Lowell.[6] Sometimes they dye 'em with sumac berries or sweet-gum bark, and sometimes they didn't. On Sunday they make all the children change, and what we wears till we gits our clothes washed was gunny sacks with holes cut for our head and arms. We didn't have no shoes 'cepting some homemade moccasins, and we didn't have them till we was big children. The little children they goes naked till they was big enough to work. They was soon big enough though, 'cording to our master. We had red flannel for winter underclothes. Old Miss she say a sick nigger cost more than the flannel.

Weddings? Uh-uh! We just steps over the broom and we's married. Ha! Ha! Ha!

Old Master he had a good house. The logs was all hewed off smooth-like, and the cracks all fixed with nice chinking, plumb 'spectable-looking even to the plank floors. That was something. He didn't have no big plantation, but he keeps 'bout three hundred slaves in them little huts with dirt floors. I thinks he calls it four farms what he had.

Sometimes he would sell some of the slaves off of that big auction block to the highest bidder when he could git enough for one.

---

[6]A cheap cotton cloth produced in the Massachusetts mill town of that name.

When he go to sell a slave, he feed that one good for a few days, then when he goes to put 'em up on the auction block he takes a meat skin and greases all round that nigger's mouth and makes 'em look like they been eating plenty meat and such like and was good and strong and able to work. Sometimes he sell the babes from the breast, and then again he sell the mothers from the babes and the husbands and the wives, and so on. He wouldn't let 'em holler much when the folks be sold away. He say, "I have you whupped if you don't hush." They sure loved their six children though. They wouldn't want nobody buying them.

We might-a done very well if the old driver hadn't been so mean, but the least little thing we do he beat us for it and put big chains round our ankles and make us work with them on till the blood be cut out all around our ankles. Some of the masters have what they call stockades[7] and puts their heads and feet and arms through holes in a big board out in the hot sun, but our old driver he had a bull pen. That's only thing like a jail he had. When a slave do anything he didn't like, he takes 'em in that bull pen and chains 'em down, face up to the sun, and leaves 'em there till they nearly dies.

None of us was 'lowed to see a book or try to learn. They say we git smarter than they was if we learn anything, but we slips around and gits hold of that Webster's old blue-back speller[8] and we hides it till 'way in the night and then we lights a little pine torch,[9] and studies that spelling book. We learn it too. I can read some now and write a little too.

They wasn't no church for the slaves, but we goes to the white folks' arbor on Sunday evening, and a white man he gits up there to preach to the niggers. He say, "Now I takes my text, which is, nigger, obey your master and your mistress, 'cause what you git from them here in this world am all you ever going to git, 'cause you just like the hogs and the other animals—when you dies you ain't no more, after you been throwed in that hole." I guess we believed that for a while 'cause we didn't have no way finding out different. We didn't see no Bibles.

Sometimes a slave would run away and just live wild in the woods, but most times they catch 'em and beats 'em, then chains 'em down in the sun till they nearly die. The only way any slaves on our farm ever goes anywhere was when the boss sends him to carry some news to another plantation or when we slips off way in the night. Sometimes after all the work was done a bunch would have it made up[1] to slip out down to the creek and dance. We sure have fun when we do that, most times on Saturday night.

All the Christmas we had was Old Master would kill a hog and give us a piece of pork. We thought that was something, and the way Christmas lasted

[7] I.e., stocks.
[8] The *American Spelling Book* of Noah Webster (1758–1843), first published in 1784, was a key implement in the spread of literacy.
[9] Splinters of pine rich in oil.
[1] I.e., would have agreed.

was 'cording to the big sweet-gum backlog what the slaves would cut and put in the fireplace. When that burned out, the Christmas was over. So you know we all keeps a-looking the whole year round for the biggest sweet gum we could find. When we just couldn't find the sweet gum, we git oak, but it wouldn't last long enough, 'bout three days on average, when we didn't have to work. Old Master he sure pile on them pine knots, gitting that Christmas over so we could git back to work.

We had a few little games we play, like "Peep Squirrel Peep," "You Can't Catch Me," and such like. We didn't know nothing 'bout no New Year's Day or holidays 'cept Christmas.

We had some corn-shuckings sometimes, but the white folks gits the fun and the nigger gits the work. We didn't have no kind of cotton-pickings 'cept just pick our own cotton. I's can hear them darkies now, going to the cotton patch 'way 'fore day a-singing "Peggy, does you love me now?"

One old man he sing:

> Saturday night and Sunday too
> Young gals on my mind.
> Monday morning 'way 'fore day
> Old Master got me gwine.
> Peggy, does you love me now?

Then he whoops a sort of nigger holler, what nobody can do just like them old-time darkies, then on he goes:

> Possum up a 'simmon tree,
> Rabbit on the ground.
> Lord, Lord, possum,
> Shake them 'simmons down.
> Peggy, does you love me now?

> Rabbit up a gum stump,
> Possum up a holler.
> Git him out, little boy
> And I gives you half a dollar.
> Peggy, does you love me now?

We didn't have much looking after when we git sick. We had to take the worst stuff in the world for medicine, just so it was cheap. That old blue mass and bitter apple would keep us out all night. Sometimes he have the doctor when he thinks we going to die, 'cause he say he ain't got anyone to lose, then that calomel what that doctor would give us would pretty nigh kill us. Then they keeps all kinds of lead bullets and asafetida[2] balls round our necks, and

---

[2] A strong-smelling plant derivative thought to ward off illness.

some carried a rabbit foot with them all the time to keep off evil of any kind.

Lord, Lord, honey! It seems impossible that any of us ever lived to see that day of freedom, but thank God we did.

When Old Master comes down in the cotton patch to tell us 'bout being free, he say, "I hates to tell you, but I knows I's got to—you is free, just as free as me or anybody else what's white." We didn't hardly know what he means. We just sort of huddle round together like scared rabbits, but after we knowed what he mean, didn't many of us go, 'cause we didn't know where to of went. Old Master he say he give us the woods land and half of what we make on it, and we could clear it and work it or starve. Well, we didn't know hardly what to do 'cause he just gives us some old dull hoes and axes to work with; but we all went to work, and as we cut down the trees and the poles he tells us to build the fence round the field and we did, and when we plants the corn and the cotton we just plant all the fence corners full too, and I never seen so much stuff grow in all my born days. Several ears of corn to the stalk, and them big cotton stalks was a-laying over on the ground. Some of the old slaves they say they believe the Lord knew something 'bout niggers after all. He lets us put corn in his crib, and then we builds cribs and didn't take long 'fore we could buy some hosses and some mules and some good hogs. Them mangy hogs what our master give us the first year was plumb good hogs after we grease them and scrub them with lye soap. He just give us the ones he thought was sure to die, but we was a-gitting going now, and 'fore long we was a-building better houses and feeling kind of happy-like. After Old Master dies, we keeps hearing talk of Texas, and me and my old man—I's done been married several years then and had one little boy—well, we gits in our covered wagon with our little mules hitched to it, and we comes to Texas. We worked as sharecroppers around Buffalo, Texas, till my old man he died. My boy was nearly grown then, so he wants to come to San Angelo and work, so here we is. He done been married long time now and git six children. Some of them work at hotels and cafés and filling stations and in homes.

KATIE ROWE: ARKANSAS

I CAN SET ON THE GALLERY,[3] WHERE THE SUNLIGHT SHINE BRIGHT, AND SEW A powerful fine seam when my grandchildren wants a special pretty dress for the school doings, but I ain't worth much for nothing else, I reckon.

These same old eyes seen powerful lot of tribulations in my time, and when I shuts 'em now I can see lots of little children just like my grandchildren, toting hoes bigger than they is, and they poor little black hands and legs bleeding where they scratched by the brambledy weeds, and where they got whippings 'cause they didn't git out all the work the overseer set out for 'em.

I was one of them little slave gals my own self, and I never seen nothing but work and tribulations till I was a grownup woman, just about.

The niggers had hard traveling on the plantation where I was born and

---

[3] Porch.

raised, 'cause Old Master live in town and just had the overseer on the place, but iffen he had lived out there hisself I 'speck it been as bad, 'cause he was a hard driver his own self.

He git biling mad when the Yankees have that big battle at Pea Ridge[4] and scatter the 'Federates all down through our country all bleeding and tied up and hungry, and he just mount on his hoss and ride out to the plantation where we all hoeing corn.

He ride up and tell old man Saunders—that the overseer—to bunch us all up round the lead-row man—that my own uncle Sandy—and then he tell us the law!

"You niggers been seeing the 'Federate soldiers coming by here looking pretty raggedy and hurt and wore out," he say, "but that no sign they licked!

"Them Yankees ain't gwine git this far, but iffen they do, you all ain't gwine git free by 'em, 'cause I gwine free you before that. When they git here they gwine find you already free, 'cause I gwine line you up on the bank of Bois d'Arc Creek and free you with my shotgun! Anybody miss just one lick with the hoe, or one step in the line, or one clap of that bell, or one toot of the horn, and he gwine be free and talking to the devil long before he ever see a pair of blue britches!"

That the way he talk to us, and that the way he act with us all the time.

We live in the log quarters on the plantation, not far from Washington, Arkansas, close to Bois d'Arc Creek, in the edge of the Little River bottom.

Old Master's name was Dr. Isaac Jones, and he live in the town, where he keep four [or] five house niggers, but he have about two hundred on the plantation, big and little, and Old Man Saunders oversee 'em at the time of the war. Old Mistress' name was Betty, and she had a daughter name Betty about grown, and then they was three boys, Tom, Bryan, and Bob, but they was too young to go to the war. I never did see 'em but once or twice till after the war.

Old Master didn't got to the war, 'cause he was a doctor and the onliest one left in Washington, and pretty soon he was dead anyhow.

Next fall after he ride out and tell us that he gwine shoot us before he let us free, he come out to see how his steam gin[5] doing. The gin box was a little old thing 'bout as big as a bedstead, with a long belt running through the side of the ginhouse out to the engine and boiler in the yard. The boiler burn cordwood, and it have a little crack in it where the nigger ginner been trying to fix it.

Old Master come out, hopping mad 'cause the gin shut down, and ast the ginner, Old Brown, what the matter. Old Brown say the boiler weak and it liable to bust, but Old Master jump down offen his hoss and go round to the boiler and say, "Cuss fire to your black heart! That boiler all right! Throw on some cordwood, cuss fire to your heart!"

---

[4] A battle, fought in northwest Arkansas in March 1862, which ended in a retreat of Confederate forces under General Earl Van Dorn.
[5] A steam-powered cotton gin, which would separate the cotton fibers from the seeds.

Old Brown start to the woodpile, grumbling to hisself, and Old Master stoop down to look at the boiler again, and it blow right up and him standing right there!

Old Master was blowed all to pieces, and they just find little bitsy chunks of his clothes and parts of him to bury.

The woodpile blow down, and Old Brown land 'way off in the woods, but he wasn't killed.

Two wagons of cotton blowed over, and the mules run away, and all the niggers was scared nearly to death 'cause we knowed the overseer gwine be a lot worse, now that Old Master gone.

Before the war when Master was a young man, the slaves didn't have it so hard, my mammy tell me. Her name was Fanny and her old mammy's name was Nanny. Grandma Nanny was alive during the war yet.

How she come in the Jones family was this way: Old Mistress was just a little girl, and her older brother bought Nanny and give her to her. I think his name was Littlejohn; anyways we called him Master Littlejohn. He drawed up a paper what say that Nanny always belong to Miss Betty and all the children Nanny ever have belong to her, too, and nobody can't take 'em for a debt and things like that. When Miss Betty marry, Old Master he can't sell Nanny or any of her children neither.

That paper hold good too, and Grandmammy tell me about one time it hold good and keep my own mammy on the place.

Grandmammy say Mammy was just a little gal and was playing out in the road with three [or] four other little children when a white man and Old Master rid up. The white man had a paper about some kind of a debt, and Old Master say take his pick of the nigger children and give him back the paper.

Just as Grandmammy go to the cabin door and hear him say that, the man git off his hoss and pick up my mammy and put her up in front of him and start to ride off down the road.

Pretty soon Mr. Littlejohn come riding up and say something to Old Master, and see Grandmammy standing in the yard screaming and crying. He just job the spurs in his hoss and go kiting off down the road after that white man.

Mammy say he catch up with him just as he git to Bois d'Arc Creek and start to wade the hoss across. Mr. Littlejohn holler to him to come back with that little nigger 'cause the paper don't cover that child, 'cause she Old Mistress' own child, and when the man just ride on, Mr. Littlejohn throw his big old long hoss-pistol down on him and make him come back.

The man hopping mad, but he have to give over my mammy and take one [of] the other children on the debt paper.

Old Master always kind of touchy 'bout Old Mistress having niggers he can't trade or sell, and one day he have his whole family and some more white folks out at the plantation. He showing 'em all the quarters when we all come in from the field in the evening, and he call all the niggers up to let the folks see 'em.

He make Grandmammy and Mammy and me stand to one side and then he say to the other niggers, "These niggers belong to my wife but you belong to me, and I'm the only one you is to call Master. This is Tom, and Bryan, and Bob, and Miss Betty, and you is to call 'em that, and don't you ever call one of 'em Young Master or Young Mistress, cuss fire to your black hearts!" All the other white folks look kind of funny, and Old Mistress look 'shamed of Old Master.

My own pappy was in that bunch, too. His name was Frank, and after the war he took the name of Frank Henderson, 'cause he was born under that name, but I always went by Jones, the name I was born under.

'Long about the middle of the war, after Old Master was killed, the soldiers begin coming round the place and camping. They was southern soldiers, and they say they have to take the mules and most the corn to git along on. Just go in the barns and cribs and take anything they want, and us niggers didn't have no sweet 'taters nor Irish 'taters to eat on when they gone neither.

One bunch come and stay in the woods across the road from the overseer's house, and they was all on hosses. They lead the hosses down to Bois d'Arc Creek every morning at daylight and late every evening to git water. When we going to the field and when we coming in, we always see them leading big bunches of hosses.

They[6] bugle go just 'bout the time our old horn blow in the morning, and when we come in they eating supper, and we smell it and sure git hungry!

Before Old Master died he sold off a whole lot of hosses and cattle, and some niggers too. He had the sales on the plantation, and white men from around there come to bid, and some traders come. He had a big stump where he made the niggers stand while they was being sold, and the men and boys had to strip off to the waist to show they muscle and iffen they had any scars or hurt places, but the women and gals didn't have to strip to the waist.

The white men come up and look in the slave's mouth just like he was a mule or a hoss.

After Old Master go, the overseer hold one sale, but mostly he just trade with the traders what come by. He make the niggers git on the stump, though. The traders all had big bunches of slaves, and they have 'em all strung out in a line going down the road. Some had wagons and the children could ride, but not many. They didn't chain or tie 'em 'cause they didn't have no place they could run to anyway.

I seen children sold off and the mammy not sold, and sometimes the mammy sold and a little baby kept on the place and give to another woman to raise. Them white folks didn't care nothing 'bout how the slaves grieved when they tore up a family.

Old Man Saunders was the hardest overseer of anybody. He would git mad and give a whipping sometime, and the slave wouldn't even know what it was about.

My Uncle Sandy was the lead-row nigger, and he was a good nigger and

---

[6] I.e., their.

never would touch a drap of liquor. One night some [of] the niggers git hold of some liquor somehow, and they leave the jug half full on the step of Sandy's cabin. Next morning Old Man Saunders come out in the field so mad he was pale.

He just go to the lead-row and tell Sandy to go with him and start toward the woods along Bois d'Arc Creek, with Sandy following behind. The overseer always carry a big heavy stick, but we didn't know he was so mad, and they just went off in the woods.

Pretty soon we hear Sandy hollering, and we know old overseer pouring it on, then the overseer come back by hisself and go on up to the house.

Come late evening he come and see what we done in the day's work, and go back to the quarters with us all. When he git to Mammy's cabin, where Grandmammy live too, he say to Grandmammy, "I sent Sandy down in the woods to hunt a hoss, he gwine come in hungry pretty soon. You better make him a extra hoecake," and he kind of laugh and go on to his house.

Just soon as he gone, we all tell Grandmammy we think he got a whipping, and sure 'nough he didn't come in.

The next day some white boys finds Uncle Sandy where that overseer done killed him and throwed him in a little pond, and they never done nothing to Old Man Saunders at all!

When he go to whip a nigger he make him strip to the waist, and he take a cat-o'-nine-tails and bring the blisters, and then bust the blisters with a wide strap of leather fastened to a stick handle. I seen the blood running outen many a back, all the way from the neck to the waist!

Many the time a nigger git blistered and cut up so that we have to git a sheet and grease it with lard and wrap 'em up in it, and they have to wear a greasy cloth wrapped around they body under the shirt for three [or] four days after they git a big whipping!

Later on in the war the Yankees come in all around us and camp, and the overseer git sweet as honey in the comb! Nobody git a whipping all the time the Yankees there!

They come and took all the meat and corn and 'taters they want too, and they tell us, "Why don't you poor darkies take all the meat and molasses you want? You made it and it's yours much as anybody's!" But we know they soon be gone, and then we git a whipping iffen we do. Some niggers run off and went with the Yankees, but they had to work just as hard for them, and they didn't eat so good and often with the soldiers.

I never forget the day we was set free!

That morning we all go to the cottonfield early, and then a house nigger come out from Old Mistress on a hoss and say she want the overseer to come into town, and he leave and go in. After while the old horn blow up at the overseer's house, and we all stop and listen, 'cause it the wrong time of day for the horn.

We start chopping again, and there go the horn again.

The lead-row nigger holler, "Hold up!" And we all stop again. "We better go on in. That our horn," he holler at the head nigger, and the head nigger think so too, but he say he afraid we catch the devil from the overseer iffen we quit without him there, and the lead-row man say maybe he back from town and blowing the horn hisself, so we line up and go in.

When we git to the quarters, we see all the old ones and the children up in the overseer's yard, so we go on up there. The overseer setting on the end of the gallery with a paper in his hand, and when we all come up he say come and stand close to the gallery. Then he call off everybody's name and see we all there.

Setting on the gallery in a hide-bottom chair was a man we never see before. He had on a big broad black hat like the Yankees wore, but it didn't have no yellow string on it like most the Yankees had, and he was in store clothes that wasn't homespun or jeans, and they was black. His hair was plumb gray and so was his beard, and it come 'way down here on his chest, but he didn't look like he was very old, 'cause his face was kind of fleshy and healthy-looking. I think we all been sold off in a bunch, and I notice some kind of smiling, and I think they sure glad of it.

The man say, "You darkies know what day this is?" He talk kind, and smile.

We all don't know, of course, and we just stand there and grin. Pretty soon he ask again and the head man say, "No, we don't know."

"Well, this the fourth day of June, and this is 1865, and I want you all to 'member the date, 'cause you always gwine 'member the day. Today you is free, just like I is, and Mr. Saunders and your mistress and all us white people," the man say.

"I come to tell you," he say, "and I wants to be sure you all understand, 'cause you don't have to git up and go by the horn no more. You is your own bosses now, and you don't have to have no passes to go and come."

We never did have no passes, nohow, but we knowed lots of other niggers on other plantations got 'em.

"I wants to bless you and hope you always is happy and tell you you got all the right . . . that any white people got," the man say, and then he git on his hoss and ride off.

We all just watch him go on down the road, and then we go up to Mr. Saunders and ask him what he want us to do. He just grunt and say do like we damn please, he reckon, but git off that place to do it, lessen any of us wants to stay and make the crop for half of what we make.

None of us know where to go, so we all stay, and he split up the fields and show us which part we got to work in, and we go on like we was, and make the crop and git it in, but they ain't no more horn after that day. Some [of] the niggers lazy and don't git in the field early, and they git it took away from 'em, but they plead around and git it back and work better the rest of that year.

But we all gits fooled on that first go-out! When the crop all in, we don't git half! Old Mistress sick in town, and the overseer was still on the place, and he charge us half the crop for the quarters and the mules and tools and grub!

Then he leave, and we gits another white man, and he sets up a book, and give us half the next year, and take out for what we use up, but we all got something left over after that first go-out.

Old Mistress never git well after she lose all her niggers, and one day the white boss tell us she just drap over dead setting in her chair, and we know her heart just broke.

Next year the children sell off most the place and we scatter off, and I and Mammy go into Little Rock and do work in the town. Grandmammy done dead.

I git married to John White in Little Rock, but he died, and we didn't have no children. Then in four [or] five years I marry Billy Rowe. He was a Cherokee citizen, and he had belonged to a Cherokee name[d] Dave Rowe, and lived east of Tahlequah before the war. We married in Little Rock, but he had land in the Cherokee Nation, and we come to east of Tahlequah and lived till he died, and then I come to Tulsa to live with my youngest daughter.

Billy Rowe and me had three children—Ellie, John, and Lula. Lula married a Thomas, and it's her I lives with.

Lots of old people like me say that they was happy in slavery and that they had the worst tribulations after freedom, but I knows they didn't have no white master and overseer like we all had on our place. They both dead now, I reckon, and they no use talking 'bout the dead, but I know I been gone long ago iffen that white man Saunders didn't lose his hold on me.

It was the fourth day of June in 1865 I begins to live, and I gwine take the picture of that old man in the big black hat and long whiskers, setting on the gallery and talking kind to us, clean into my grave with me.

No, bless God, I ain't never seen no more black boys bleeding all up and down the back under a cat-o'-nine-tails, and I never go by no cabin and hear no poor nigger groaning, all wrapped up in a lardy sheet no more!

I hear my children read about General Lee, and I know he was a good man. I didn't know nothing about him then, but I know now he wasn't fighting for that kind of white folks.

Maybe they that kind still yet, but they don't show it up no more, and I got lots of white friends too. All my children and grandchildren been to school, and they git along good, and I know we living in a better world, where they ain't nobody cussing fire to my black heart!

I sure thank the good Lord I got to see it.

MARY GRAYSON: INDIAN TERRITORY

I AM WHAT WE COLORED PEOPLE CALL A "NATIVE." THAT MEANS THAT I DIDN'T come into the Indian country from somewhere in the Old South,[7] after the war, like so many Negroes did, but I was born here in the old Creek Nation, and my master was a Creek Indian. That was eighty-three years ago, so I am told.

---

[7] As was true, for instance, of Katie Rowe, who came to present-day Oklahoma when she married Billy Rowe.

My mammy belonged to white people back in Alabama when she was born—down in the southern part, I think, for she told me that after she was a sizable girl her white people moved into the eastern part of Alabama where there was a lot of Creeks. Some of them Creeks was mixed up with the whites, and some of the big men in the Creeks who come to talk to her master was almost white, it looked like. "My white folks moved around a lot when I was a little girl," she told me.

When Mammy was about ten or twelve years old, some of the Creeks begun to come out to the territory in little bunches. They wasn't the ones who was taken out here by the soldiers and contractor men—they come on ahead by themselves, and most of them had plenty of money, too.[8] A Creek come to my mammy's master and bought her to bring out here, but she heard she was being sold and run off into the woods. There was an old clay pit, dug way back into a high bank, where the slaves had been getting clay to mix with hog-hair scrapings to make chinking for the big log houses they built for the master and the cabins they made for themselves. Well, my mammy run and hid way back in that old clay pit, and it was 'way after dark before the master and the other man found her.

The Creek man that bought her was a kind sort of a man, Mammy said, and wouldn't let the master punish her. He took her away and was kind to her, but he decided she was too young to breed, and he sold her to another Creek who had several slaves already, and he brought her out to the territory.

The McIntosh men was the leaders in the bunch that come out at that time, and one of the bunch, named Jim Perryman, bought my mammy and married her to one of his "boys," but after he waited a while and she didn't have a baby he decided she was no good breeder and he sold her to Mose Perryman.

Mose Perryman was my master, and he was a cousin to Legus Perryman, who was a big man in the tribe. He was a lot younger than Mose, and laughed at Mose for buying my mammy, but he got fooled, because my mammy got married to Mose's slave boy Jacob, the way the slaves was married them days, and went ahead and had ten children for Mr. Mose.

Mose Perryman owned my pappy and his older brother, Hector, and one of the McIntosh men—Oona, I think his name was—owned my pappy's brother William. I can remember when I first heard about there was going to be a war. The older children would talk about it, but they didn't say it was a war all over the country. They would talk about a war going to be "back in Alabama," and I guess they had heard the Creeks talking about it that way.

When I was born we lived in the Choska bottoms, and Mr. Mose Perryman had a lot of land broke in all up and down the Arkansas River along there. After

[8]Creek migration to Indian Territory began after the negotiation of a new treaty with the U.S. government in 1826. Among the first to leave were prosperous members of the McIntosh faction, who established plantations on new ground in the West. The leader of the faction, William McIntosh (1775–1825), son of a Creek woman and a British agent, was among those Creeks executed for signing the initial treaty of 1825 ceding Creek lands to the government.

the war, when I had got to be a young woman, there was quite a settlement grew up at Choska right across the river east of where Haskell now is, but when I was a child before the war all the whole bottoms was marshy kind of wilderness except where farms had been cleared out. The land was very rich, and the Creeks who got to settle there were lucky. They always had big crops. All west of us was high ground, toward Gibson Station and Fort Gibson, and the land was sandy. Some of the McIntoshes lived over that way, and my Uncle William belonged to one of them.

We slaves didn't have a hard time at all before the war. I have had people who were slaves of white folks back in the old states tell me that they had to work awfully hard and their masters were cruel to them sometimes, but all the Negroes I knew who belonged to Creeks always had plenty of clothes and lots to eat, and we all lived in good log cabins we built. We worked the farm and tended to the horses and cattle and hogs, and some of the older women worked around the owner's house, but each Negro family looked after a part of the fields and worked the crops like they belonged to us.

When I first heard talk about the war, the slaves were allowed to go and see one another sometimes, and often they were sent on errands several miles with a wagon or on a horse, but pretty soon we were all kept at home, and nobody was allowed to come around and talk to us. But we heard what was going on.

The McIntosh men got nearly everybody to side with them about the war, but we Negroes got word somehow that the Cherokees over back of Fort Gibson was not going to be in the war and that there were some Union people over there who would help slaves to get away, but we children didn't know anything about what we heard our parents whispering about, and they would stop if they heard us listening. Most of the Creeks who lived in our part of the country, between the Arkansas and the Verdigris, and some even south of the Arkansas, belonged to the Lower Creeks and sided with the South, but down below us along the Canadian River they were Upper Creeks, and there was a good deal of talk about them going with the North. Some of the Negroes tried to get away and go down to them, but I don't know of any from our neighborhood that went to them.

Some Upper Creeks came up into the Choska bottoms talking around among the folks there about siding with the North. They were talking, they said, for Old Man Gouge, who was a big man among the Upper Creeks. His Indian name was Opoeth-le-ya-hola, and he got away into Kansas with a big bunch of Creeks and Seminoles during the war.[9]

---

[9] The renowned orator Opothleyohola, who had opposed McIntosh and warned him of the dire consequences of ceding Creek lands in 1825, signed the new treaty the following year and thereafter became the main leader of his people. He resisted government plans for removal in the mid-1830s but eventually acceded and relocated to Arkansas. When the Creek council at Eufaula agreed to Albert Pike's request that the nation enter into a treaty with the Confederacy, Opothleyohola resisted and led off about a third of the people, fleeing into Kansas in support of the Union. This part of the Creek nation, suffering much hardship as a result, eventually was relieved by federal aid.

Before that time, I remember one night my Uncle William brought another Negro man to our cabin and talked a long time with my pappy, but pretty soon some of the Perryman Negroes told them that Mr. Mose was coming down, and they went off into the woods to talk. But Mr. Mose didn't come down. When Pappy came back, Mammy cried quite a while, and we children could hear them arguing late at night. Then my Uncle Hector slipped over to our cabin several times and talked to Pappy, and Mammy began to fix up grub, but she didn't give us children but a little bit of it, and told us to stay around with her at the cabin and not go playing with the other children.

Then early one morning, about daylight, old Mr. Mose came down to the cabin in his buggy, waving a shotgun and hollering at the top of his voice. I never saw a man so mad in all my life, before nor since!

He yelled in at Mammy to "git them children together and git up to my house before I beat you and all of them to death!" Mammy began to cry and plead that she didn't know anything, but he acted like he was going to shoot sure enough, so we all ran to Mammy and started for Mr. Mose's house as fast as we could trot.

We had to pass all the other Negro cabins on the way, and we could see that they were all empty, and it looked like everything in them had been tore up. Straw and corn shucks all over the place, where somebody had tore up the mattresses, and all the pans and kettles gone off the outside walls where they used to hang them.

At one place we saw two Negro boys loading some iron kettles on a wagon, and a little further on was some boys catching chickens in a yard, but we could see all the Negroes had left in a big hurry.

I asked Mammy where everybody had gone and she said, "Up to Mr. Mose's house, where we are going. He's calling us all in."

"Will Pappy be up there too?" I asked her.

"No. Your pappy and your Uncle Hector and your Uncle William and a lot of other menfolks won't be here any more. They went away. That's why Mr. Mose is so mad, so if any of you young-uns say anything about any strange men coming to our place I'll break your necks!" Mammy was sure scared!

We all thought sure she was going to git a big whipping, but Mr. Mose just looked at her a minute and then told her to git back to the cabin and bring all the clothes, and bed ticks and all kinds of cloth we had and come back ready to travel.

"We're going to take all you black devils to a place where there won't no more of you run away!" he yelled after us. So we got ready to leave as quick as we could. I kept crying about my pappy, but Mammy would say, "Don't you worry about your pappy, he's free now. Better be worrying about us. No telling where we all will end up!" There was four or five Creek families and their Negroes all got together to leave, with all their stuff packed in buggies and wagons, and being toted by the Negroes or carried tied on horses, jackasses, mules, and milk cattle. I reckon it was a funny-looking sight, or it would be to a person now, the way we was all loaded down with all manner of baggage when we met at the old ford across the Arkansas that led to the Creek Agency.

The agency stood on a high hill a few miles across the river from where we lived, but we couldn't see it from our place down in the Choska bottoms. But as soon as we got up on the upland east of the bottoms we could look across and see the hill.

When we got to a grove at the foot of the hill near the agency, Mr. Mose and the other masters went up to the agency for a while. I suppose they found out up there what everybody was supposed to do and where they was supposed to go, for when we started on it wasn't long until several more families and their slaves had joined the party, and we made quite a big crowd.

The little Negro boys had to carry a little bundle apiece, but Mr. Mose didn't make the little girls carry anything and let us ride if we could find anything to ride on. My mammy had to help lead the cows part of the time, but a lot of the time she got to ride an old horse, and she would put me up behind her. It nearly scared me to death, because I had never been on a horse before, and she had to hold on to me all the time to keep me from falling off.

Of course, I was too small to know what was going on then, but I could tell that all the masters and the Negroes seemed to be mighty worried and careful all the time. Of course, I know now that the Creeks were all split up over the war, and nobody was able to tell who would be friendly to us or who would try to poison us or kill us, or at least rob us. There was a lot of bush-whacking all through that country by little groups of men who was just out to get all they could. They would appear like they was the enemy of anybody they run across, just to have an excuse to rob them or burn up their stuff. If you said you was with the South they would be with the North, and if you claimed to be with the Yankees they would be with the South, so our party was kind of upset all the time we was passing through the country along the Canadian [River]. That was where Old Gouge had been talking against the South. I've heard my folks say that he was a wonderful speaker, too.

We all had to move along mighty slow, on account of the ones on foot, and we wouldn't get very far in one day, then we Negroes had to fix up a place to camp and get wood and cook supper for everybody. Sometimes we would come to a place to camp that somebody knew about, and we would find it all tromped down by horses and the spring all filled in and ruined. I reckon Old Gouge's people would tear up things when they left, or maybe some southern bushwhackers would do it. I don't know which.

When we got down to where the North Fork runs into the Canadian, we went around the place where the Creek town was. There was lots of Creeks down there who was on the other side, so we passed around that place and forded across west of there. The ford was a bad one, and it took us a long time to get across. Everybody got wet and a lot of the stuff on the wagons got wet. Pretty soon we got down into the Chickasaw country, and everybody was friendly to us, but the Chickasaw people didn't treat their slaves like the Creeks did. They was more strict, like the people in Texas and other places. The Chickasaws seemed lighter color than the Creeks, but they talked more in Indian among themselves and to their slaves. Our masters talked English nearly all the time except when they were talking to Creeks who didn't talk good English, and we Negroes never did learn very good Creek. I could always understand it, and can yet, a little, but I never did try to talk it much. Mammy and Pappy used English to us all the time.

Mr. Mose found a place for us to stop close to Fort Washita, and got us places to stay and work. I don't know which direction we were from Fort Washita, but I know we were not very far. I don't know how many years we were down in there, but I know it was over two, for we worked on crops at two different places, I remember. Then one day Mr. Mose came and told us that the war was over and that we would have to root for ourselves after that. Then he just rode away, and I never saw him after that until after we had got back up into the Choska country. Mammy heard that the Negroes were going to get equal rights with the Creeks and that she should go to the Creek Agency to draw for us,[1] so we set out to try to get back.

We started out on foot and would go a little ways each day, and Mammy would try to get a little something to do to get us some food. Two or three times she got paid in money, so she had some money when we got back. After three or four days of walking, we came across some more Negroes who had a horse, and Mammy paid them to let us children ride and tie[2] with their children for a day or two. They had their children on the horse, so two or three little ones would get on with a larger one to guide the horse, and we would ride a while and get off and tie the horse and start walking on down the road. Then when the others caught up with the horse they would ride until they caught up with us. Pretty soon the old people got afraid to have us do that, so we just led the horse and some of the little ones rode it.

We had our hardest times when we would get to a river or big creek. If the water was swift, the horse didn't do any good, for it would shy at the water and the little ones couldn't stay on, so we would have to just wait until someone came along in a wagon and maybe have to pay them with some of our money or some of our goods we were bringing back to haul us across. Sometimes we had to wait all day before anyone would come along in a wagon.

We were coming north all this time, up through the Seminole Nation, but when we got to Weleetka we met a Creek family of freedmen who were going to the agency too, and Mammy paid them to take us along in their wagon. When we got to the agency, Mammy met a Negro who had seen Pappy and knew where he was, so we sent word to him and he came and found us. He had been through most of the war in the Union army.

When he got away into the Cherokee country, some of them called the "Pins" helped to smuggle him on up into Missouri and over into Kansas, but he soon found that he couldn't get along and stay safe unless he went with the army. He went with them until the war was over and was around Gibson quite

---

[1] I.e., to receive government payments stipulated by treaty. Slaves freed by Native Americans frequently were offered full tribal status.

[2] A way of sharing the horse, as soon explained.

a lot. When he was there he tried to find out where we had gone but said he never could find out. He was in the battle of Honey Springs, he said, but never was hurt or sick. When we got back together, we cleared a section of land a little east of the Choska bottoms, near where Clarksville now is, and farmed until I was a great big girl.

I went to school at a little school called Blackjack School. I think it was a kind of mission school and not one of the Creek Nation schools, because my first teacher was Miss Betty Weaver and she was not a Creek but a Cherokee. Then we had two white teachers, Miss King and John Kernan, and another Cherokee was in charge. His name was Ross, and he was killed one day when his horse fell off a bridge across the Verdigris, on the way from Tullahassee to Gibson Station.

When I got to be a young woman I went to Okmulgee and worked for some people near there for several years, then I married Tate Grayson. We got our freedmen's allotments[3] on Mingo Creek, east of Tulsa, and lived there until our children were grown and Tate died, then I came to live with my daughter in Tulsa.

THOMAS B. CHAPLIN

from his "Journal" (1845–86)

JULY 4TH [1845]. FRIDAY ANNIVERSARY OF THE DECLARATION OF INDEPENdence of these United States. Felt too unwell to go to Beaufort, went to the muster house.[4] An oration was delivered by Mr. C. Belcher,[5] Declaration of Independence read, or at least spoken by E. M. Capers[6]—he had all by heart—prayer by Mr. McElheran.[7] The oration was a plain, well-written speech, a very good repetition[8] of the history of the Revolution, but not oratorically delivered. We dined about half past 2 p.m., drank twelve bottles of champagne, and returned to the village at about 5 o'clock—*all sober*. Preparations were then made for fireworks, which came off about 8 o'clock p.m. I had the misfortune to get my right eye very much hurt from the bursting of one of the rockets. They went off very well. After which, the young ladies gave a picnic in Dr. Scott's[9] piazza. I did not eat any of this supper, but expect it was very good. I furnished six bottles of champagne—I know that went off very well.

---

[3] Apparently from the tribe, not the U.S. government.
[4] Where the St. Helena Mounted Riflemen met.
[5] Charles D. Belcher (1822–1857), a local teacher.
[6] Edward M. "Ned" Capers (b. 1820), son of local planters and Chaplin's best friend.
[7] Reverend David McEleran (1793–1875), Scots-Irish immigrant and pastor of the St. Helena Episcopal church.
[8] I.e., retelling.
[9] John A. P. Scott (1794–1874), physician, planter, and an in-law of Chaplin.

Fool forgot about your ten Negroes sold! Ah, Low! Low!*[1]
Date my weak eyesight from this same occurrence

July 24th. Killed beef for market. Rode down to Coffin's Point, a part of the island I have never been at in my life. On my way I met Capt. I. Fripp.[2] Rode up to his place with him for the first time I had ever been there. He is one of the most enterprising planters I know of. Has a great quantity of thrown-by machinery which he has tried and never succeeded with, such as gins, etc.

Went to Coffin's to see [Jonathan] Cockcroft his overseer to buy some corn. Succeeded in getting fifty bushels at 75 cents. He is a very obstinate fellow, appeared to be afraid I would not pay him in time for him to pay Coffin when he returned from the North. I am to give him an order on Mr. Gray for the amt. 37½ dollars, payable the 1st of October next.

Alas, how little did I think then, that now, thirty-two years after, in 1876, I would be living on the same place, Coffin's—now Whitwell's,*[3] almost as an over-seer myself and a Yankee schoolteacher, and not worth shucks, much less fifty lbs. corn. Truly the vicissitudes of life are past the comprehension of mortal man. Coffin, Cockcroft and hundreds more are dead and a great blast of ruin and destruction passed over the country.

July 26th. Saturday. The steamboat came along about 7 o'clock. She came to opposite J. L. Chaplin's[4] landing. The captain, seeing several of J. L. C.'s family on the beach waving handkerchiefs, etc., thought they wanted to get on board, but as soon as the yawl was lowered they scampered up the bluff. The captain was very much provoked, and hardly wanted to stop for me opposite D. Jenkins'[5] landing. Bristol and Sancho[6] put me on board in J. C.'s little boat. We arrived in Savannah about half past 11 o'clock a.m. I had never been there but once before, with the company on the 28th June and had no opportunity of seeing anything but a great crowd. I cannot say that I admired the place at all, it is one of the hottest and dirtiest places I ever saw in my life. Very few good-looking stores. I got so wet with perspiration that I was obliged to go into a

---

[1] Due to "my own extravagance," as Chaplin admitted in his May 4th entry, ten of his slaves had been sold just two months prior to the present entry. (As with other similar italicized passages in Chaplin's journal, this one was added later as a commentary on earlier entries; when the date for such later additions is known, it is given.)

[2] Captain Isaac Fripp, otherwise unidentified; Coffin's Point was the fourteen-hundred-acre plantation of Thomas Aston Coffin (1795–1863).

[3] Northerner Samuel W. Whitwell (1816–1890) got control of Coffin's Point while the Union occupied St. Helena Island during the war. In the 1870s, while he was teaching in a school for black children there, Chaplin was living in the plantation house; Whitwell, who had previously been his landlord and was helping him reclaim the lost land at Tombee, had invited Chaplin and his second wife, Sophy, to share the old Coffin house while they awaited the outcome of their efforts.

[4] Chaplin's second cousin and frequent companion, John L. Chaplin did not own land but worked as a farmer and overseer. Elsewhere, Chaplin remarked that J. L. Chaplin knew the land at Tombee better than anyone and gave him good advice about crops.

[5] Daniel T. Jenkins (b. 1810), Chaplin's first cousin and owner of a plantation on St. Helena.

[6] Two Chaplin slaves.

clothing establishment and get a change [of] dress even to a linen. We partook of fine ice punch and a very ordinary dinner at the Pulaski House. Drank a good deal of iced champagne and left the Georgian city at 4 o'clock.

July 27th. Rode down home and over all the crop. Cotton looks very well, but backward. March corn tolerable—young, good and very bad in spots. Potatoes very bad. Peas miserable. Three and three-quarters acres of slips planted, no rain to plant more. Had only a few drops last eve, though we had a fine rain at the village. Ground almost as dry as it was before. Cattle suffering for water. *∗∗These must have been happy days.∗∗*

Sept. 26th. Sent the boat to the main for the rest of the corn. Went home. Did nothing but shoot pistols all day. Returned early.

Instantly after I got home, went upstairs. Mrs. C.[7] complaining, had one or two pains. Knew the time had come. Stayed with her until about 8 o'clock. Sophy[8] went upstairs, and soon after Mrs. Cook[9] went up. I remained in the hall very quietly reading the newspaper, expecting to keep awake nearly all night, when about ten minutes of ten, I heard something like a young child cry. Could hardly believe it was over so soon, but Lo! it was. A little *boy* was born. Half past ten saw him for the first time. Saw Mrs. Cook wash and dress him. He soon ate some butter and sugar. The largest child I ever saw when it was just born. Saw my dear wife, about ten minutes after ten. She does well. How much women suffer for men and how badly some and many of them are treated. I do not think that any male being [who], seeing how much his wife suffers for him, can treat her ill, can have any soul or heart, except so much as will keep life in [him]. I did not go to bed until after 2 o'clock though at any other time I would have been sleepy. I did not feel so last night even when I went to bed. Left mother and child doing well.

1876∗∗Good God, the changes since then!!!! And that boy—fell a victim to a cruel war; his bones molder in an unknown grave in North Carolina. He died from war, pestilence and famine, and cruelty while prisoner in[1] the Yankee army, in 1864. Who dreamed of the end when this page was written, thirty-two years ago. Now, poverty extreme, from affluence and wealth.∗∗

Nov. 1st. Parade day of our company. Went to Beaufort. Glad to find after I got there that there was no parade; it was put off for another time. Paid

---

[7] Mary Thomson McDowell (1822–1851), who married Thomas B. Chaplin in 1839, was the grand-daughter of a well-to-do Charleston merchant; by the time her husband reached his twenty-first year, in 1843, she already had borne four children (Ernest, 1840–1872; Maria, 1841–1845; Virginia, 1842–1867; Daniel, 1843–1924). The present entry refers to the birth of Eugene, who was to die in 1864. Prior to her own death in 1851, Mary Chaplin had two more daughters (Isabella, who died in infancy in 1847; and Mary, 1849–1851).

[8] Sophia Creighton (d. 1891), Mary Chaplin's half-sister, lived with the family at Tombee and would marry Thomas Chaplin following Mary's death in 1851.

[9] Maria Cook, a midwife.

[1] I.e., of.

O'Connor[2] his judgment against me. This is the last paper of the kind out against me, and now my property is safe, and secured to my family. Wm. Fripp, Sr.[3] spoke to me and agreed, if I would pay half the cost, to drop his suit against me, which [I] agreed to. So the two cases against me for the next court are dropped, and well for me. Mother came down from the village. All of the things could not be brought in the carts and wagon.

Some rogue broke open the carriage house door yesterday but found nothing to gratify his thieving desire. Got a box of clothes from Edgerton and Richards.[4]

Note 1876 *Said box of clothes cost more than enough to supply me with clothes at this time for two or three years.*

Oct. 12th [1847]. Since I last wrote in my journal, the hand of affliction hath been very heavy upon me. The Almighty has struck forth his red right hand against me, the angel of death hath cut off the fairest and loveliest of my flock. The soft eyes of my lovely little daughter Isabel were closed in their last sleep on Sunday, the third day of October. Alas for the poor mother! The yet unopened bud plucked from its parent stem. Woe is me, my daughter, Isabel my daughter. It is the will of God! Where are my friends? In mine adversity they rejoiced and gathered themselves together; yea the very abject came together against me unawares.[5]

I am compelled to begin in the world again, not with forty, but *nine hands in the field.* And a large family to support and educate—Well, many have commenced with *much less* and made fortunes. I do not wish a fortune, but enough to live comfortably and honestly on and educate my children. I have seen enough of men to cause me to wish to have [*illegible*] dealings with them. I know they do not care to deal with me *now I am poor.* But, by God's help, I may be worth something one of these future days, when I know how I will be again sought after and counted. And I trust this great and sad lesson will be sufficient to teach me what and who they are, and to keep them at a proper distance.

I have been sold of land and Negroes, furniture, stock, possessions and everything I was worth in the world.[6] I was fortunate enough to buy or have a little bought in for me[7] and on that little I *intend* to live. My village house was sold, and I am compelled to risk the summer with my family on the plantation.

[2] Irish-born Michael O'Connor (1795–1859), a merchant in Beaufort.
[3] William Fripp (1788–1861), member of a neighboring family much tied to the Chaplins by marriage; the nature of the suit is unclear, although Chaplin recorded earlier in the year that rumors about their strained relations were circulating on the island.
[4] A Charleston clothing firm.
[5] A paraphrase of Psalm 35:8,15.
[6] Chaplin's own debts, combined with a bitter fight over his mother Isabella's property that Chaplin and his brothers carried on with her youngish husband, the bankrupt pharmacist and portrait painter Robert Little Baker, made a shambles of his economic life long before the war. It should be recalled that at this point, although he had been married for nearly a decade, Chaplin was still only twenty-five.
[7] A common practice, whereby a debtor's allies purchased his property for him.

This alone creates in me great uneasiness, for if anyone should be taken very sick, I have not the means of removing them to any healthier spot, not even if it was on the same island, for I would not intrude them on my *kind friends*. . . . But, *God's Will Be Done.*

May 9th. Sent the men to dig out the cow wells. This weather makes me think of the time I generally move to the village. This will not trouble me this year, and perhaps never again. *Edings*[8] *now owns my house*—I am sorry I ever built it. All my trouble and expense sacrificed *by the sheriff* for 820 dollars. The billiard table also gone; it once afforded me some gratification, but *never* will again. I spend this summer on the plantation, live or die. It is strange, I have not had a visitor for near a month *except Capers*. Property gone—*friends* decrease—better for me. They were the *friends of my property, not of me.* I have just heard that Robt. Brown & Son,[9] factors, have failed. He was a factor for a number of persons in this neighborhood and they have lost a good deal of money by him. Uncle Ben[1] I learn has lost 250 dollars. He had better have taken his money and helped me in my trouble than *plead poverty* before he was ever [illeg.] and still have money in his factor's hands and to lose it too. I am sorry for him, it will [come] near on to killing him.
He is dead long since, and knows not of trouble.
I never learned any wisdom from my misfortunes, just the same now as ever. But now, I am broken down in health, in spirit and in fortune. God's will etc. 1876

I am brought down through extravagance to a mere competency, from working thirty hands in the field to bare eight, all the rest little and big sold for debt, as would these [have been], had it not been for *wife's legacy*[2]—*thank God.* Everything was sold, stock, horses, furniture and plantation carts and wagons, boats and flats. I have barely saved enough to carry on the place. My corn all sold, leaving me a bare ten bushels as my right by law, except what I was fortunate enough to buy in. My best horses have been *sacrificed*—fine colts that I had taken all the trouble to raise, and were then just old enough to use, were taken, sold for a trifle, and before it could be proven what they were fit for. All, all this for *extravagance* and *imprudence*—I hope I will *remember it.*
I have lived to see much harder times, war, pestilence and famine. I never [illeg.] at the horrid state I am now in. 1876

Feb. 19th [1849]. Monday. I received a summons while at breakfast, to go over to J. H. Sandiford's[3] at 10 o'clock a.m. this day and sit on a jury of inquest on

---

[8] Joseph D. Eddings (b. 1804), a planter who owned Eddings Point on St. Helena.
[9] The Browns served as planters' agents (factors) in Charleston.
[1] Chaplin's uncle, Benjamin Chaplin (1776–1851), lived next door to Tombee.
[2] A fifteen-thousand-dollar inheritance from her grandfather.
[3] James H. Sandiford (1795–1868), a planter who eventually relocated to Georgia.

the body of Roger, a Negro man belonging to Sandiford. Accordingly I went. About 12 [noon] there were twelve of us together (the number required to form a jury). . . . We were sworn by J. D. Pope, magistrate, and proceeded to examine the body. We found it in an outhouse used as a cornhouse and meathouse (for there were both in the house). Such a shocking sight never before met my eyes. There was the poor Negro, who all his life had been a complete cripple, being hardly able to walk and used his knees more than his feet, in the most shocking situation, but *stiff dead.* He was placed in this situation by his *master,* to punish him, as he says, *for impertinence.* And what [was] this punishment—this *poor cripple* was sent by his master (as Sandiford's evidence goes) on Saturday the 17th inst.,[4] before daylight (cold and bitter weather, as everyone knows, though Sandiford says, "It was *not very* cold"), in a paddling boat down the river to get oysters, and ordering him to return before high water, and cut a bundle of marsh. The poor fellow did not return before ebb tide, but he brought seven baskets of oysters and a small bundle of marsh (more than the primest of my fellows would have done. Anthony never brought me more than three baskets of oysters and took the whole day). His master asked him why he did not return sooner and cut more marsh. He said that the wind was too high. His master said he would whip him for it, and set to work with a cowhide to do the same. The fellow hollered and when told to stop, said he would not, as long as he was being whipped, for which impertinence he received thirty cuts. He went to the kitchen and was talking to another Negro when Sandiford slipped up and overheard this confab, heard Roger, as he says, say, that if he had sound limbs, he would not take a flogging from any white man, but would shoot them down, and turn his back on them (another witness, the Negro that Roger was talking to, says that Roger did not say this, but "that he would turn his back on them if they shot him down," which I think is much the most probable of the two speeches). Sandiford then had him confined, or I should say, murdered, in the manner I will describe. Even if the fellow had made the speech that Sandiford said he did, and even worse, it by no means warranted the punishment he received. The fellow was a cripple, and could not escape from a slight confinement, besides, I don't think he was ever known to use a gun, or even know how to use one, so there was little apprehension of his putting his threat (if it can be called one) into execution. For these *crimes,* this man, this demon in human shape, this pretended Christian, member of the Baptist Church, had this poor cripple Negro placed in an open outhouse, the wind blowing through a hundred cracks, his clothes wet to the waist, without a single blanket and in freezing weather, with his back against a partition, shackles on his wrists, and chained to a bolt in the floor and a chain around *his neck,* the chain passing through the partition behind him, and fastened on the other side—in this position the poor wretch was left for the night, a position that none but the "most *bloodthirsty* tyrant" could have placed a human being. My heart chills at the

---

[4]I.e., of the present month.

idea, and my blood boils at the base tyranny. The wretch returned to his victim about daylight the next morning and found him, as anyone might expect, dead, *choked, strangled,* frozen to death, *murdered.* The verdict of the jury was, that Roger came to his death by choking by a chain put around his neck by his master—*having slipped from the position in which he was placed.* The verdict should have been that Roger came to his death by inhumane treatment to him by his master—by placing him, in very cold weather, in a cold house, with a chain about his neck and fastened to the wall, and otherways chained so that he could in no way assist himself should he slip from the position in which he was placed and must consequently choke to death without immediate assistance. Even should he escape being frozen to death, which we believe would have been the case from the fact of his clothes being wet and the severity of the weather, my *individual* verdict would be *deliberately* but *unpremeditatedly murdered* by his master James H. Sandiford.

April 28th [1850]. Summer[5] has no fever this morning, gave him quinine.

While at supper, Amy came in crying, said Summer was worse. When I got to the Negro house found him *perfectly dead.* Never was so surprised in my life. We were all under the impression that he was getting better, and was so reported to us by his mother and Old Judy, who were attending him, but since his death, they have just thought proper to tell me of several symptoms he showed that would have made it necessary to employ a doctor, and which I had no way of knowing except through the nurses. His last was rather strange. About sunset he vomited something as black as soot, and died in an hour after. I was not even informed that he had vomited, or something might have been done for him, even at that late hour. I certainly would have sent for a doctor, but he would have been too late. He was delirious a day or two ago, and though I was away from home, wife should have been informed of it, or myself when I returned at night, but these infernal stupids kept saying he was better till an hour before his death. I blame them very much, but it can't be undone now, but they ought to have a lesson for the future.

I wished to have a postmortem examination, but could not get a physician to come. Summer will be a great loss to me. He was good steady boy, about sixteen years old. He lost one of his eyes last summer, which seemed to affect him considerably. He always appeared in low spirits. Taken sick on Tuesday, died Sunday night.

July 4th. Thursday. Anniversary [of] Independence. Dinner at muster house. Oration by Dr. Wm. J. Grayson,[6] well written, badly delivered. Splendid speech from Colonel Treville.

---

[5] Like Amy and Old Judy, a Chaplin slave.
[6] William J. Grayson, a friend of Chaplin and son of a lawyer and author of the same name who served in the U.S. Congress and was port collector for Charleston. The father strongly favored states' rights, and in his most famous work, *The Hireling and the Slave* (1854), offered rosy defenses of slavery, but he also wrote against secession.

secession I suppose, and what did it all end in 1876
Toasts, champagne, etc. Picnic at night in the village.

Oct. 24th. Must confess that I wish wife back at the village, for more reasons than one. She is dissatisfied with everything and everybody, myself *in particular*, and so intolerably cross—but poor soul, she is *ailing*, and I must only hold my peace, and so *prevent* her finding fault with what *I say*, if she does with what *I do*. I must bear with what I have brought on myself, by doing that which has given her power over me, to *upbraid* me *justly*, and she knows how to take advantage of this power. But "those who live [in] glass houses should not throw stones."
Alas, alas, I am sorry more than once for what were trifles then. Poor wife, poor me, twenty-six years after, and I can only say I am sorry, but I did nothing in bad blood

Nov. 5th. Query. Can there be anything more unpleasant to a man of family than that his wife should be a victim to the following demoralizing and injurious habits? Habits which entirely destroy all social and domestic enjoyments and comforts and prevent all chances of prosperity. The wife says it rather makes her appearance (this is, when she makes it at all for the day).

Sometime between 11 a.m. and 1 p.m. [she] remains out of her chamber one or two hours more or less, *sometimes* takes her place at the dinner table, but always takes her breakfast in bed. After dinner, retires for an hour or two to *indulge* either in [*illegible*] or what is worse, to half fill her mouth with snuff, and lie in bed, when, if perchance a little of the saliva escapes down her throat, a fit of vomiting is invariably the consequence, then farewell to the small quantity of nourishment her sedentary habit allowed her to take at dinner. She leaves her chamber *generally* just about dusk, when she walks out, to take a [*illegible*] walking about the yard—frequently remaining out of [*illegible*] after dark. Sometimes remains down to tea, but should she retire before, and her tea is sent to her, [*illegible*] the servant not unfrequently finds her unable to speak, and why? Her mouth is *full of snuff*; should she remain to tea, she retires immediately after, not to bed, to sleep, oh! no, but to put *snuff in her mouth*, take a *novel* and lie on her back till 12 or 1 o'clock at night, unless, perchance, she enacts the vomiting scene over again, and thereby loses her *tea*. At a late hour she goes to bed finally in a very ill humor with her "good man," and everybody else for she is perhaps sleepy by this time, there to remain till the late hours previously mentioned, the next day, to live the same routine of life over and over again, each succeeding day, not to mention one or two *other* items. I envy not that man's conjugal blessings.[7]

---

[7] Mary Chaplin's addiction to snuff, taken as a painkiller for a stomach disorder, dated from around 1845, when her health faltered while she was pregnant with Eugene. As with Chaplin's own addiction to opium after the war, her overuse of snuff (which may have been flavored with cognac) reflects the laissez-faire approach to drugs and self-medication in the period.

∗∗Beautiful description, wants only truth *to make it quite charming.∗∗*
∗∗Alas, it was too true, but it is past and gone and forgotten, and if she is in heaven, I hope she has forgiven.∗∗
∗∗O God, what a woman was lost. What a mind—sunk in despair and grief and disappointment∗∗

Dec. 26th. Old Sam died just before day this morning. Poor old man, he is gone at last. Twas a relief for him to die. It is now nearly three years since he was taken down to his bed, perfectly helpless, horribly afflicted with paralysis, convulsions, and perfectly blind. 'Twas a blessing to take him.
∗∗There was an instance out of many—an old man had to be fed, clothed and a woman did nothing else than attend to him for three years before he died and he wanted for nothing. How [fared] his wife, who attended him then, and died herself, since made free? Why she died of smallpox, in the most wretched manner; not even her children would go near her and she regrettably [illegible] before she died, but then, she was free!∗∗[8]

March 15th [1851]. Saturday. Negroes got back from Beaufort before day. Had a pretty good load, a hundred bushels of corn, very good and clean corn, but the measure does not hold good by my measure, loses about four quarts or more on every bag of two bushels. Two barrels molasses, and six sacks salt to sell to the Negroes for corn, one barrel Irish potatoes from Savannah, besides several small boxes. Webb[9] sent me a saddle, a much better one than I expected. Did not receive a letter, so do not know the price of any of the articles.

Received a letter from Behn,[1] in Savannah, he has sold my cotton for little or nothing. . . . I can't pay my debts in Savannah, and don't know what to do. Would to God I had never gone there at all. Turner will give no more credit till he is paid so I don't know what wife will do.
∗∗She did do∗∗

March 16th. Sunday. Aunt Betsy sent us a piece of drum fish today. J. L. Chaplin took five yesterday. Sent all to town, where he gets two dollars apiece for them. Did not go to church.

---

[8] In the original 1850 entry and the later comments, the death of the slave Old Sam raises several interesting issues. According to the 1850 U.S. census, Chaplin had twenty-five slaves at Tombee, although in a journal entry that February, Chaplin himself made the total thirty, lamenting, "God knows when I will get all of my small force at work. So many mouths to feed and so few to work that it is *impossible* for me to get along. If there is not some arrangement made so as to have fewer Negroes about the yard and more in the field, I will not be able to make enough to *feed* them—to say nothing about clothing them, and yet, it appears that not one of those about the house and yard can be done without." Old Sam was listed at this point in the February entry as beyond labor: "Not counting the children and Old Sam, who can't do anything but make nine mouths more to feed." The contrast of Old Sam's death with the last days of Old Sam's wife after the war—she died *free* but had been abandoned by her family due to the nature of her disease—suggests Chaplin's attempt at a rudimentary antebellum myth.
[9] Thomas L. Webb (b. 1810), lawyer and factor.
[1] P. H. Behn (b. 1820), factor and merchant.

March 17th.[2] Dear husband, I opened your book to put a little extract in it and read your last items, one when you comment about Turner not giving credit on *my account.*[3] Don't give yourself uneasiness for *me.* I have always endeavored to spare you any trouble I could; in this case I only reap the punishment due to my own weakness. Believe me *you* are one of the best husbands. I can only hope you will not long be troubled with a wife so frail, weak and suffering. God help you, my husband. You have but one fault that may work your ruin—for the sake of *our* children check it. Think not of the poor frail wife. I will pray for you here and if it be possible, hereafter—

Was it possible, if so I know she did pray for me

March 18th. Tuesday. Busy all day fixing up the yard fence. Finished banking up the old root patch and each hand listed a half-task of cotton land.[4] I see that my dear wife has again, very contrary to my wishes, written some of her ideas in this foolish journal.[5] But Oh! My dear wife, you may write till doomsday and never *then* can you express what I feel, I am not given to *manly words* . . . but I feel more than words can express. Try not by word or action to hide from me what *you feel.* The very *attempt* but makes your situation the more apparent. I *know* what you *feel* and *suffer* and the inability to relieve is death *to me.* Try not to hide it, it but makes things worse. To *know* that *you want* what you once valued not is more than I can bear, but I will bear it or die in the attempt.

Pretty oh!

May 2nd. Hoed the nine tasks corn at Jenkins line, and three hands hoeing one task each of cotton on Cowpen Hill, first hoeing.

Had to put Helen to mind the peas, the birds are so bad after them. Jim sick and Eliza washing in the place of Judy, who has a falling of the womb;[6] her mistress says she must not stand up much, and put her to sewing.

**Old Judy lived for many years after, passed through the horrid Civil War with all its suffering and loss, and returned to Beaufort with Bill Jenkins's[7] family and

---

[2]This entry is in the handwriting of Mary Chaplin.

[3]T. M. Turner & Co., druggists in Savannah, supplied some substance for Mary whose nature Thomas Chaplin disguised in his journal; in January of that year, he thus noted receiving an order of "a can (10 gals.) oil, vinegar and 1 gallon for wife from T. M. Turner & Co.," adding later in the margin, "**Do not name it**." Presumably the substance was medicinal, perhaps addictive.

[4]"Listing" was the process of hoeing under the plant residue left in the fields by the previous cotton crop. Under the "task system" used on the sea islands for managing plantation labor, most field labor was calculated in terms of a standard "task"—which was the work required to hoe a quarter-acre of planted cotton field. Here, then, Chaplin is noting that the workers had each spent as long cleaning up the crop residue as would have been required to hoe an eighth-acre of cotton field.

[5]Chaplin had asked his wife to keep the journal during his absences in earlier years, but by this point he did not want her to have a hand in it.

[6]Prolapse of the uterus, caused by weakening of abdominal muscles as a result of childbearing or the decrease in estrogen in an older woman's system.

[7]Dr. William J. Jenkins (1818–1883), physician and planter on St. Helena, Chaplin's second cousin.

Uncle Paul[8] *and died there about 1870 or 71. I don't think she ever saw her old home after she left it [in] 1860* * *

May 15th. I know that I am a fool, but sometimes I think I am *a very great fool.* For instance, in the management of the children, particularly Ernest— sometimes wife will say, "Good man, if *you* don't do something with that child he will go to destruction, or commit murder." Then she will tell Ernest, "If you do so and so again I will positively send you to your father to be punished," or "I'll tell your father." Ernest repeats the fault, or act. Well, *perhaps* I *am* told, *but* I must first promise not to punish him, and this is done over and over. Sometimes, but rarely, I catch Ernest in the very act of committing a fault, or have every reason to believe that he has. I punish him; directly I am asked what it is for, and very often (I won't say always), after some wrangling, I am told (perhaps in the presence of the child) that I punished him unjustly. I say to myself, well, if this is to be the way (for it always vexes me to be spoken to in this way before the children), that I am not fit to judge whether or no a child deserves punishment, you can manage them yourself in future, I will say noth- ing, you be both mother and father, mistress and master. The next thing I hear, with much fuss and to-do, "Good man, you must *positively* do something with Ernest, he is so impertinent to me you would not believe." I say, "Why don't you punish him?" "I am not able, you must do it; now when he is impertinent again, I will send him to you to be punished." "Very well," I say, "*just* send him with a note to that effect," but he is never sent, and if I am told, why, I must *let him off this time,* but the next time he won't get off so well, I can tell him. Then again, "Good man, the little Negroes are ruining the children, I couldn't tell you half the badness they learn them. That little demon Jack must be sent out of the house, he *shan't* stay another day." Jack is sent out. Next thing, Jack is mounted behind Ernest on a horse and sent off together to get plums, or Ernest is put under Sam's protection, and sent one or two miles to get mulber- ries, on foot. They have one or two creeks to cross, which are nearly dry at low water, and no danger of *them,* but it happens to be high spring tide and these little creeks become deep and unfordable even for a horse, and I had forbidden Ernest to go. I speak about this, and the risk they run and the long distance they would have to walk round these creeks, and for what good? I am told that I deprive Ernest of every *privilege, don't want* to see him do anything that every little boy of his age is allowed to do, and *only* let him enjoy himself when I am out of my *senses* (with liquor). *I am done.*[9]

Oct. 27th. Monday. Hands picking cotton, but will pick peas tomorrow.
    Wife so very sick I could not go out; in fact, she has been so for more than a fortnight, but I think her worse today. Mother came over today.

[8] Paul H. Chaplin (1788–1866), planter on St. Helena and Chaplin's uncle.
[9] Chaplin added an illegible six-line note in 1876. His reference at the end of the 1851 passage to liquor may explain the "one fault" Mary mentioned in her entry earlier in the year.

Oct. 28th. Wife no better today. She eats nothing at all. 'Tis agony to witness her suffering.

Oct. 29th. Finished picking peas in the morning. Turned miserably bad, only got twenty-two sheets in all, 5½ acres. Hands went after the cotton again. Uncle Paul digging slips. Hear that they are turning out a bushel to the bed.

I do not think wife is any better today. She is so weak—takes no nourishment and talks inadheredly[1] at times, poor soul.

Oct. 30th. Thursday. Rained this morning and continued cloudy all day. Hands could not pick cotton, had them assorting. Had the men in the garden preparing a piece of ground for the purpose of setting out some strawberries when we have rain enough for the purpose. Also had them clearing round and manuring my fruit trees.

Sent Isaac to Beaufort.

I think wife a *shade better* today, *thank God.* The sun shines out just as I am writing, half past five, so tomorrow may be clear.

I feel quite drowsy and feverish this evening, having set up with wife the greater part of last night, and exposed myself somewhat this morning. Have a sore throat and feel feverish. God grant I may not have fever at this time.

Oct. 31st. All hands picking cotton. Killed a yearling steer, as much to get the feet[2] to make jelly for wife as to get something to eat. Rather warm to keep it fresh any length of time, but am in hopes it will turn cooler.

Nov. 1st. Saturday. Wife very sick all day. She cannot last much longer. At night—Oh! What a night, she appeared to be *sinking* fast. I laid down to sleep about 12 midnight, but Rinah[3] soon called me, said wife called me. I went up, and found her worse, I think dying. Daylight came (2nd) and still she was not revived. Dying, irrevocably dying.

Nov. 2nd. Sunday. The saddest day of my life. My poor, poor wife breathed her last, and was relieved of all her sufferings (many and great they were) about 12 o'clock today. Scarcely with a struggle, her pure soul departed, to realms of peace and love and joy, above, where will be no more sorrow and care, and where her troubled soul will be at rest. My poor children, *you* have lost that which never, no, never can be replaced, a *mother's love,* a *mother's care.* Your dear aunt[4] has promised to do all in her power to prevent your want of the latter, but alas! How can she replace the former. May God bless her for all she *has* and *will* do for *you,* my poor orphans.

My heart is desolate, there is a coldness there that can never be warmed,

---

[1] Incoherently.
[2] A source for gelatin.
[3] A slave owned by Chaplin's mother.
[4] Sophia Creighton.

a blank that never can be filled. May God give me strength to perform properly and faithfully that fatherly part, which I so solemnly owe to you, and which is my sacred duty. And to Sophy—Oh! What a debt of gratitude and love I owe to her, pray for me my sister, as I shall pray, that I may truly and faithfully perform the trust bequeathed to me by *one you* loved and who loved you so well.

Nov. 2nd. Sunday. Rained hard part of the day. Sent Jim and three hands to Beaufort for coffin. Sent to E. B. Busher[5] for it. Wind very high.

> The relatives, friends and acquaintances of Mr. and Mrs. Thos. B. Chaplin are invited to attend the *Funeral* of the *Latter*, at the Episcopal Church on *Tuesday*, the fourth (4th) instant, at 12 o'clock m.[6]
> The Rev. D. McElheran is *particularly* requested to attend.
> St. Helena Isld
> Nov. 3d, 1851[7]

Nov. 3rd. Jim got back sometime after night. I went over myself *for what he brought* and landed at the riverside.

Sent Jack to the village with invitation to funeral, and Mother's Ben on the same errand to those persons on their plantations.

Funeral to take place at the P.E.[8] Church at 12 m. tomorrow.

Nov. 4th. Mother and the children went with me to the funeral, Aunt Betsy[9] kindly lending her carriage.

Attendance very numerous. The last solemn rites were performed at the appointed time, and *the dear loved one* rests by the side of her three departed *babies*, and her soul now communes with theirs in heaven. God's will be done.
Dec. 21st. Sunday night. Spent the greater part of the night of this, the very day seven weeks after the lamentable occurrence recorded above, in the melancholy occupation of reading and rereading some of the correspondence of *our early love . . .*
These letters were lost, left in a desk at house.
Oh! What *pangs* and *heartaches* did I not experience while reading and recalling to memory those incidents and passages of happy, happy days, long past, *never*, oh! *never* to be recalled, those treasured and ever to be remembered expressions of *earnest*, constant and *affectionate, doting* love. Oh! Those blessed *loved epistles*, how I *now* treasure them, would to God I had read them once every week, had learnt them by heart, the dear hand that penned them *might*

---

[5] Edward B. Busher (b. 1815), a Beaufort furniture maker or joiner.
[6] Meridian, i.e., noon.
[7] A printed funeral notice inserted in Chaplin's journal.
[8] Protestant Episcopal.
[9] Elizabeth H. Jenkins Chaplin (1785–1867), wife of Uncle Ben Chaplin but a cousin of Chaplin's in her own right.

not now be cold in death, and I *had* been a kinder, better husband, and *now* a better man. On the other hand, when I read over some of my own old letters *to her, to her,* who so sacredly treasured up the worthless trash, what feelings of shame, for their *misspelled, ridiculous,* nonsensical, *unworthy* nature, to be addressed too, to *one so infinitely superior* in intellect, so divine, so heavenly. What feelings of *utter remorse* and *unselfforgiving* for the wonted neglect, to avail myself of those *years* of happiness and the thousands of opportunities to treasure up, and shield from all harm and sorrow that precious gem it was my (great) good fortune to possess . . . Oh! Fool, fool that I was to be so blind not to have valued above all *earthly*—"*ay*" *all*—*every* other gift, *that heart so pure and so good,* ever *affectionate, loving and trusting,* so *wholly my own,* but 'tis *gone,* lost to me forever and ever, and I am desolate—yes—utterly desolate and alone, for who, who *can* ever be to *me* what *she was? None, no not one living being.*

1868, *How much truth in the above time has shown, very nearly* all *I held dear has actually passed away from me. With property has gone fortune, children, the dearest of my flock, one sacrificed to his country, another to her love or perceived love for a worthless object, two left and such, not only worthless to themselves and to me but one a disgrace to his name[1]

That one has redeemed himself by taking us under his care and support. 1884
[1868] and the other forgets his father for himself,*[2] *who, I surely believe would see me suffer and is without one sympathizing feeling or assisting hand [to] be raised to help me. Nothing but a return of fortune would call him to my side. This is as true as the above. Seventeen years ago.

1876, *Eight years more have passed and I am back on old St. Helena once again, but tis so, yes, not at the old home. I live at Coffin's Point, tried and proven by experience, 1868, [in] a stranger's land and in a stranger's house. Still I am not desponding altogether, I manage to live, only dear Sophy and I, we are almost the only ones of the old inhabitants that have got a foothold here again.

But we left it again in 1884, Daniel having persuaded us to move over to the mainland near Walterboro. We had been very sick and the change was a benefit and here I suppose we will lay our bones.

The thought has often (lately) fixed itself upon my wondering imagination, *how could such a being as she was, love so dotingly, disinterestedly* love such as *I* am, 'tis past my comprehension, yet I know 'twas so, yes, positively, and without the least foundation of a doubt. And *she is gone, gone*— Oh! The golden opportunity that I have let escape me of rendering *her happy,* yes,

---

[1] Eugene Chaplin died, as an earlier entry states, while held prisoner by Union forces in 1864; Virginia died in childbirth in 1867, some months after marrying John Wilson Glover (1846–1882); Daniel, temperamental and eccentric, had long been estranged from Chaplin, but he of all the Chaplin children produced grandchildren who lived into adulthood and in 1884, as Chaplin goes on to note, Daniel and his wife Maria Louisa (who was also his first cousin) took Thomas and Sophy Chaplin into their care.
[2] Ernest, a difficult child (see the entry for May 15, 1851), died in 1872, four years after Chaplin wrote this note regarding him.

happy, not *only here*, but hereafter. What do I not deserve, what will I not have to answer for to my maker. But *'tis past,* and she is no more. Rest on, sweet one. My *heart*, that was *all your own* when living, is now with you and you alone, in death, even in the *cold, cold grave*. There is no room, no place for it in this wretched body of mine. " *'Tis earthly, but not of earth.*"[3] *Farewell fare-well*, Oh! *Remorse, remorse.* I am *thy slave, now and forever.* Years may pass and scenes may change; all I hold dear on earth may pass away. Oceans may roll between *her* sacred resting place and I, yet *thou, thou* wilt always pursue, always retain thy unrelenting grasp upon my wretched spirit, *always* and *forever*.

March 16th [1852]. Tuesday. Rain from about 8 a.m. and continued with hardly any intermission all day. Spent a very gloomy day. Don't know what I would have done to keep off a fit of blue devils, had it not been for a novel and cigars.

Commenced planting corn, but rain drove in the hands. Had all the corn shucked out. It may last me till July. Thrashed out what peas I had left and put away what I wanted for seed.

Sophy and I sat up (wonderful to tell) till 1 o'clock, as the Irishman said, "tomorrow morning," chatting about God knows what. She is a good soul, God bless her. She is, or shall be, my guardian angel. *Could* she be anything else? Oh! me.

She has been both and a most excellent wife to me and mother to my children. Everybody has faults, hers are few, and circumstances, trouble, disappointments of many kinds have somewhat soured her temper, and I should be more patient with her, but I am also a sufferer and can't always govern my temper, but, without boasting, I think I do, or try to do so, more than she does 1876*

March 17th. Item. What shall it be? There is an item, yes, and it shall be here recorded, but *not now.* I am not likely to forget it. I will only observe that Sophy and myself are getting into a very bad habit of sitting up very late at night, even to trespass on the "small hours" —

March 26th. The secret is out. Sophy, dearest Sophy will be mine. Mother has been told of our love and she is agreeable. God bless everybody, and us in particular.

(April 4th. Coldness, first want of confidence)*
Sept. 5th, 1876. Coldness, the 40,000th want of control of temper.*

Sept. 2nd. Thursday. Neither of the boys had any fever this morning, but Eugene's came on about 10 a.m. quite hot.

This is doubly unfortunate, as Sophy and myself had arranged to meet Mr. McElheran at the church today, and be married. And, altho the matter was partially, or rather in a fair way of being postponed, we nevertheless made up our minds, late this morning, that our plans had better be carried into effect

---

[3] See I Corinthians 15.

today, for reasons I shall hereafter state. Consequently I wrote and sent a note to Mr. McElheran to meet us at the church at 4:30 p.m. Sophy wrote one also to Aunt Betsy requesting her to be there and to bring Virginia. I sent to ask Uncle Paul. These are all we expect (I am writing at 12 m., the *results* will be stated after). The only thing I truly regret is that my dear mother is not able from recent illness to be present. She could not stand the ride to the church. I should feel much more happiness could she see me married to the *only woman I know* that *I believe* can contribute to my future happiness and the welfare of my children, for who can feel that love for and interest in *them* as *Sophy*, the *loved and loving* sister of their *dear mother.*

Now for our reasons, or rather *my* reasons for thus seemingly hurrying the matter. We are, or have been, all sick. The children are now sick. It is necessary that we should help and attend each other, the children in Sophy's room, and my wish to be near or have free access to them at all and anytime, which cannot be done with propriety under present circumstances; we were *engaged*, and have been so for some time, and would be married at some time. Why defer it? I can see no reason, or at least no *pressing* one, living in the same house, in constant communication, and in love, engaged—'tis better we were man and wife, and I trust God we will be before 5 o'clock this evening.

Eight o'clock p.m. Tis all over. We went to the church a little before 5 o'clock. Met Mr. McE., Aunt Betsy and Virginia and Uncle Paul. I requested Uncle Paul to act the part of a friend in the ceremony of giving away, which he did, and with much grace. The ceremony was very soon over and we were pronounced man and wife.

Received the congratulations of all and hurried off home, for we left Eugene with a hot fever on him. Poor Virginia. She cried bitterly to return with us, but that of course was not to be thought of for a moment. We took Daniel with us, but poor fellow he had fever before he got home. Sophy and I thought *surely* that our engagement was a profound secret. We had told it to no one in the world except Mother, but *there* was the source through which it got out. *She* told it to Saxby,[4] though I begged her to tell *no one*, and he least of all would *I* tell. Saxby told it to Minott,[5] and I suppose everyone else he knew. Minott gazetted[6] the village with the news; I will know hereafter how to keep my own confidence.

I never have and never will 1877

The Negroes today averaged about 37½ lbs. cotton.

Dec. 25th [1853]. Sunday. Christmas Day. The ground is covered with snow this morning but not thick, trees covered [with] icicles. Clear but bitter cold. Saxby and I rode up to Farmer's.[7] Took him up and went on to Minott's. We all returned and dined with Mother. She had a very fine dinner, too much in fact.

[4] Saxby Chaplin, Jr. (1825–1884), Chaplin's brother.
[5] John B. F. Minott (b. 1804), a planter in the Charleston district.
[6] I.e., spread the story like a newspaper.
[7] Charles B. Farmer (1823–1885) was a lawyer and magistrate.

∗as she always did in those days∗∗
(I hear that the snow or sleet and cold weather extended to the island.)
∗∗Poor Mrs. Minott is now living at my old place in a room, in my old cottonhouse, and is very bad off indeed, quite thin 1877∗∗
∗∗I hear she died in a hospital in Charleston after her husband some years ago very bad off 1885∗∗

May 17th [1855]. Thursday. We got back about 12 m. today, and met bad news at home. Nelly's child[8] died just before we got ashore. Amy says with lockjaw. I don't know the cause. It was well, or rather not sick, when we left yesterday. I am unfortunate. This is the fourth Negro child I have lost since last fall. There is something wrong, and I will find it out yet; the one that is to blame had better be in hell.
∗∗1868, no loss if all had died then and there∗∗

Jan. 1st [1856]. Tuesday. This day eleven years ago I commenced this journal, and kept it up, with a few blanks, ever since. If it is not of much account in itself, it has occasionally afforded me some satisfaction in referring to it.
∗∗and it does now at this late day afford me some pastime 1869, 1877 and still 1885∗∗

Jan. 1st, 1886. Many eventful years have now passed since the last lines were written in this journal, nearly twenty-eight years. During that time the War of Secession has been fought and lost, and with the cause, all of our worldly possessions, or very nearly all. We were driven from our home in St. Helena Island on the 7th day of November 1861, never to return to it except on a visit as strangers. On the close of the war in 1865, I mortgaged the land left me by Mother to a man from New York named Cowle,[9] for some 8000 dollars, and tried the chances at planting, but owing to the then-very-unsettled state of the country, and unjudicious management, I made little or no crops, and lost the land. Though I had a plenty of land, I rented, on account of the buildings, the Point Island place of Oliver Middleton.[1] We lived in the overseer's house very comfortably for about two years, then, having put up a log house at Fields Point, we moved there, and I may say, lived from hand to mouth for several years, until about 1871 or 2, sometimes very bad off indeed. Ernest was there with us. His health was very bad. About January 1872, having had the keeping of a public school at Coffin's Point on St. Helena offered to me, we moved over

[8]Chaplin's slave Nelly gave birth to a son, Dick, a week earlier.
[9]William H. Cowl of Brooklyn, New York, took Chaplin's mortgage on his mother's former plantations for the stated amount on February 8, 1866. Chaplin defaulted and Cowl later foreclosed, although it was not until he outwaited Chaplin's delays that he was able to have the properties auctioned in October 1871. The auction precipitated Chaplin's acceptance of the teaching job on St. Helena early in 1872.
[1]Oliver H. Middleton (1798–1892), son of former South Carolina governor Henry Middleton. Although in possession of his mother's plantations up to the 1871 auction, Chaplin rented and lived on the Middleton land in that period.

there and occupied the house that Cockcroft—Coffin's overseer—used to live in. It was a poor cousin's but it was a shelter and a home for many years. I taught to the best of my ability a large school for Negro children during the winter and early spring months for 60 dollars per month but at first could get nothing but "pay certificates," which I had to dispose of at heavy loss, but we got credit at Oliver & Ward's store for provisions, etc., on the strength of them. Coffin's Point then was owned by a Yankee named S. W. Whitwell. He and [his] wife, a confirmed cripple, lived in the *big house*, a half mile from where we lived. They had no children of their own, but had adopted a boy and girl. These people I cannot describe. They were "different from any people I had ever met with in my life." They appeared to us to turn about, to be quite clever and obliging, and then quite mean and disagreeable, but the old man was far the best of the two and often assisted us when assistance was really needed, and about 1874 or 5, in the spring, persuaded us to move up and occupy two or three rooms in their house, and when they went North, which they did every summer, we had the whole house to ourselves. We moved up therefore in June, were better sheltered, but I don't think more comfortable. I was not paid any stated sum for taking care of the premises, but I got something—what land I could plant, for one thing. Ernest also came over from the point and lived with us the few short days he had to live and we had the satisfaction and comfort of caring for and making his last days more comfortable.

In July of that year I was offered the situation of custodian of government property on Hunting Island, North Point, where a new lighthouse was being built. I accepted of course, though I would have to stay down there nearly alone, but I thought Ernest would be able to take turns with me. He was not able to do so, and so that I could come up home when I wanted to, I got Charley Fripp[2] to go down for his grub and stay with me. My pay was 50 dollars per month and found, or 75 dollars and find myself.[3] I chose the latter after the first month or two. I was also allowed a cook or servant. I held the place till December, I think, or about five months, when the hands came back to work. I continued to teach in the winter, at less pay, but better paid, till 1877, when, having been appointed a trial justice by Governor Hampton,[4] I found I could not well attend to both. I made out to live by the office and any other jobs I could pick up. Before that I was also appointed notary public by Governor Chamberlain,[5] but that paid very little. I sometimes clerked in Oliver & Ward's store, and in 1880 I got the appointment of supervisor of the census, which paid very well considering I had to hire [a] buggy and horse. Whitwell died very suddenly in Dec'r. of this year, and then the old woman let herself loose. She

[2]Charles E. Fripp (1830–1906), Chaplin's cousin.
[3]A common set of terms: if he took the lower figure, his food would be provided; otherwise he would have to "find" his own food.
[4]Wade Hampton (1818–1902), Confederate general and first post-Reconstruction governor of South Carolina, 1876–78, had gone to school with Chaplin.
[5]Massachusetts Republican David H. Chamberlain (1835–1907) immediately preceded Hampton in the governorship, 1874–76.

immediately set to build and improve. Had the old overseer's house fixed up after a fashion, and had us moved back into it. We preferred it, as Mrs. W. had many of her relations about her by this time, and we had for some time before W.'s death been living in a small but somewhat comfortable house in the yard. We lived in this house till 1884 on what I could make in my office, and one year, about '82, Mrs. W. employed me to see after her place at a salary of 25 dollars per month. In '84 we were both sick. I could not attend to any business. Daniel and Jim Chaplin[6] came over to see us, and insisted that we should move over to a farm Jim had near Walterboro[7] where his father was living and where he died in the fall of '83. There was no alternative. Daniel could help us, being near him, and we could not help ourselves. In fact, I looked for nothing but death or starvation, or both. So on the 11th of October, Jim came over in a schooner and moved us bag and baggage. We had a tedious trip, having grounded on the marsh in the mouth of Coffin's Creek, and did not get over to Chapman's Fort (near which Daniel spent most of the time attending to his work of shipping wood to the phosphate mines[8]) till daylight on the 13th. We stayed there till the 19th of October and we began to improve in health from the day we went aboard the vessel. On that day we moved up to this place, and here we hope to remain to the end. I see no chances of my making anything to live on, and can only work a garden and try to raise poultry. My son, not well off himself and having a family of four children, has to support us entirely. God help him to be able to do so.

I find a good neighbor, and quite near, in John Witsell,[9] an old-time friend. He and wife, an excellent lady, are the only persons Sophy and I visit. I have no conveyance, so I ride into the village occasionally with John, and get anything we want from there through his kindness. Daniel and his family moved down to the pine land in the winter, and we don't see much of them. Ann[1] and her family live in Daniel's house in Walterboro, which enables us to get this house and farm. If I had a few hundreds of capital, I think I could make a living on this farm, but as it is, [I] can only try to live as cheap as it is possible to do. Wood is plentiful for the cutting.

So this brings the time up to January 15th, 1886. We have been here one year and three months, less two days, and the last week has been the coldest we have had, and the coldest here I am told, since 1880. The thermometer fell to 14 above zero. Weather clear till today. Our health, thank the Lord, has been much better than the last year of 1884. But we are both feeling the effects of age and can't stand much more thumping and tumbling about, and I pray the remainder may be passed in peace and ease. So this ends.

---

[6] Chaplin's son Daniel and his nephew, Saxby's son James H. Chaplin (1848–1930).
[7] Walterboro was located some forty miles north of Beaufort.
[8] The phosphate, mined near the Coosaw River, was used as fertilizer.
[9] John W. Witsell (1818–1892) and Chaplin, old friends, were both uncles of James H. Chaplin as Witsell was the brother of James's mother.
[1] James's mother, Ann Witsell Chaplin (1827–1915).

14

IMMIGRANT TALES

WHATEVER THEIR HOMELAND, VOLUNTARY IMMIGRANTS TO THE UNITED States
seem always to have been impelled in part by tales about the new land picked
up in the old one. The pattern is ancient, predating even the voyages of Columbus: the Viking Eric the Red is said to have given Greenland its alluring name
precisely to convince others to follow him west to his stone-rich, glacier-ridden
island. John Muir (1838–1914), to be famous in America for his geological work
in the mountains of California and Alaska and for such key environmental
victories as the establishment of Yosemite National Park (1890), recalled how
his common schoolbooks in Scotland included pieces on American birds by
the ornithologists Alexander Wilson and John James Audubon. Audubon's
account of the fabulous spring flocks of passenger pigeons, to be ravaged to
extinction just as Muir himself died, filled the Scots boy with wonder and
excitement. Muir's father was moved by stories, too, those having to do with
economic opportunity and others, that led him to think all of the new country
was wild (it was the latter kind of story that convinced him to import heavy
agricultural equipment he easily could have bought anywhere in America.)
Looking back at the end of his life on his immigration as a boy, John Muir still
vividly recalled the discrepancies between what the Muirs expected and what
they found on arrival in 1849.

A trio of German immigrants writing back home in the period from the
1855 to 1886 acted out the stories of their predecessors and related stories of
their own to those still back home. The tales sent back might be sober as well
as buoyant. Martin Weitz, who left the town of Schotten in the Vogelsberg
region of Hesse in central Germany in 1854, was a thirty-year-old wool weaver
who probably had heard that immigrants with his training might find good
work in industrializing America. He quickly found that conditions in the new
land were tough at best and might be brutal, and his first instinct was to disillu-
sion any of his family who wished to join him. "It is easy to say you want to go
to America," he wrote, "but the hard things [you] never think about. . . . When
you arrive here and don't understand English, you stand there, eyes wide open,

like a calf with its throat cut." In part, this hard-nosed advice may have been a perverse sort of boasting, for such tales could raise the immigrant's stock in the minds of those left behind. In the end, it was hard for someone who actually had made such a voyage to ward off all later immigrants, especially relatives and friends whose absence might be sorely felt. Weitz himself equivocated: "If you want to come to America you just can't let that scare you off. You have to think the best, the worst comes later. I don't want to advise anyone not to come, whoever wants to come should come." And he later enthused about the opportunity for new immigrants to buy farms in Wisconsin—even though he himself, never having seen that state, was at the time working in a textile mill in Connecticut. He presented this new prospect with a significantly wider audience in mind, suggesting he was aware how such immigrant letters and the tales they bore across the ocean might be shared about the village back home: "If anyone from Schotten wants to come here, he should come. . . ."

In a rather different vein, an immigrant named Wilhelm Bürkert filled his letters home in the 1870s with outlandish and antiquated American tales he probably picked up in Germany before he ever left, or perhaps from dime novels and cheap-newspaper stories he came across in the United States. These tales about gold mining, Indian fighting, whale hunting, fur trapping, and frontier farming he offered as a kind of glamorous, but no doubt fake autobiography, perhaps to cover the fact that he wasted much time in America, apparently drunk for a good deal of it. Born in the village of Waldenburg in the state of Württemberg in 1859, the sixteen-year-old Bürkert broke away from his apprenticeship to a surveyor shortly after his father's death in 1875 and left for America. In a letter sent to relatives shortly after arriving in New York, he reported he got work there quickly as a cook and waiter, but in his next letter a year later the fabulations began. He there claimed he had gone off on a whaling cruise, was injured in a storm off the west coast of South America that almost wrecked his ship and, now back in New York and lodged in the charity hospital, Bellevue, was only slowly recuperating. Among other implausible details in the story is his claim that the French steamer that rescued his sailing ship towed it from the vicinity of Valparaiso, Chile, around Cape Horn and up the other coast all the way to Rio de Janeiro. It seems more likely that Bürkert, who may have suffered from epilepsy as well as his evident alcoholism, was in Bellevue all along, voyaging if at all in the seas of his vivid imagination.

Bürkert's next letters, written across 1877, placed him in the Johnstown, Pennsylvania, area, mining for coal but very ill ("every day I have had nosebleeds, I spit up a lot of blood") and claiming to be in need of money to pay his doctors, who come across as a singularly mercenary lot. The reports of ill health, bolstered by a notarized letter from another German immigrant, may well have reflected a serious condition, and we must hold out the possibility (however slim, on balance) that this tale of a young man lost in the land of opportunity is a poignant cry from the depths. That his relatives did not leap to his help, or even trouble themselves with answering most of his letters, might be read either as confirming the poor man's marginality or as suggesting that those who knew him best could see through his stories and answered them with the best antidote, silence. Bürkert made such a habit of writing his way around problems in his life that it is very hard to untangle the genuine from the convenient elements in his tales. As we near their end the likelihood of fraud seems ever more certain. After an interim of three years following his recovery in Pennsylvania, Bürkert's next surviving letter, written from Missouri in 1880, claims that he went to California "to make [his] fortune" some time back, but that he and his partners had no luck, headed to Oregon "and went on from there eastward, until we came to Colorado." Then come his most mendacious details regarding work as a guide for immigrant trains—wagon trains, long out of use by 1880—during which he struggled against both the Sioux (surely an echo from news accounts of Custer's defeat in 1876) and white outlaws infesting the plains. All in all, Bürkert seems to have regarded such lies as the traveler's right (according to the old principle that travelers may lie by authority since no one can check out their tales), and in some instances, as with the question of wagon trains, it is conceivable that those to whom he wrote in Germany had little way of knowing enough to gainsay him. In the end, part of Bürkert's motivation may have been the need to prove to the people left behind that he had made his way successfully in his new world, always a key point in immigrant rhetoric.

The third German, an illegitimate young woman named Wilhelmine Wiebusch who was Bürkert's exact contemporary, told more naïve and sprightly tales of the "land of milk and honey" where she arrived in 1884. Writing to a female friend in a chatty, teasing style, Wiebusch taunted her with the idea of coming over to join in the adventure of working as a servant girl in an American home. With a fine eye for new details, Wiebusch descanted on how abundant fruit seemed in America, but then undercut the little tale with a piece of ironic advice: "I also wanted to tell you if you have an old shoe or boot, don't throw it away, tie a red or blue bow on it and hang it on the wall in your room. You may think I'm crazy, but you ought to know, dear Marie, that here in America, that's what they call an antique." Delighted to find that members of the Jewish household in Brooklyn that employed her could speak German, she was delighted, too, by her own fearless assaults on English: "I. put this Letter in the Letterbax, hve you undrstand Mary? You see i speak wery well English, i belive it is enough." Her tales of Thanksgiving, of the working girls she met from other European lands, the Chinese laundrymen who taught her how to iron shirts, and the ceremonies dedicating the Statue of Liberty in 1886 all convey the excitement this young woman of very few prospects in her own land found in her new one. For her the differences between America and Germany may have been lessened due to her evident success in finding a place and her delight in occupying it. She was an almost complete contrast to Wilhelm Bürkert on these and other grounds.

The American tales reported by Chinese immigrants returning home in the same period often painted the new land as a barbaric place wholly lacking in civilization—even though immigrants sometimes returned very rich from there. While the Canton native Lee Chew, immigrating to California in 1883, found plenty to confirm these tales in the treatment he found Americans according to his fellow countrymen, he also came to see that the tales one nation tells about another inevitably distort the realities. In the United States, legislation based on American fears about Asian immigrants showed how influential such lore could be on the lives of many individuals. Although the United States had joined with several other Western nations to force the opening of China to Western trade (including the trade in opium, pushed by the British in order to balance the cost of their tea imports), it was inconsistent in meeting its mutual obligations to China, and in a series of laws restricted and in effect ended Chinese immigration in the later nineteenth century. Lee Chew's experience as a worker likewise was shaped by American prejudice and law. His stories of how hard the Chinese workers would labor if given the chance may be somewhat self-serving, but they also contribute to his sense that American workers feared competition from this immigrant group and hence enforced restrictions that left Chinese men like Lee Chew—who knew nothing of the laundry business when they arrived—few outlets for their ambition. Lee Chew's story, printed in Hamilton Holt's pioneering magazine the *Independent* in 1903 as one of several dozen similar ordinary lives collected by Holt's staff, offers unusual insights into the psychology of immigration in the period.

So does the similar story of the Italian bootblack Rocco Corresca, published in Holt's magazine in 1902. The orphan Corresca, victim of various exploiters while still in Italy, first encountered America through the tourists he learned to follow and beg from in Italy. "They were all rich," his so-called grandfather told him, adding that the boys should especially zero in on any young man escorting a young woman around Naples—he would always come across with "silver because he would be ashamed to let the young woman see him give us less." Rocco heard other things about America, too: "that it was a far-off country where everybody was rich and that Italians went there and made plenty of money, so that they could return to Italy and live in pleasure ever after." Like Lee Chew, Rocco Corresca yearned to set off for this fabulous land, but like him, too, on arriving in 1898 Rocco found himself taken advantage of by various people who seemed lying in wait for him. Even at Ellis Island, Rocco was picked up by a sharper named Bartolo who preyed on youngsters such as himself for whom no one could vouch. Eventually, Rocco was able to set himself up in a modest shoe-shining business, and when he dictated his story to the *Independent* was doing well.

In Rocco's brief personal narrative, a broader pattern emerges as well. Beset by the many tales that painted America as a land of promise *and* danger, many immigrants found themselves in a world of singular ambiguity. They spoke again and again of how wary the immigrant must be of mere stories—in this sense Rocco Corresca's "American" experience began in his Italian wanderings—but they remained blithely certain at the same time that their own story about their past was thoroughly trustworthy. What they all had to say, notwithstanding the differences in motive, character, and circumstance, thus was structured by a disregard of tales other than those they personally told. Within this skeptical narrative framework lay a perpetual sense of naïvely alluring wonder.

JOHN MUIR, SCOTLAND

"A New World," from *My Boyhood and Youth* (1913)

OUR GRAMMAR-SCHOOL READER, CALLED, I THINK, MACCOULOUGH'S COURSE *of Reading*, contained a few natural-history sketches that excited me very much and left a deep impression, especially a fine description of the fish hawk and the bald eagle by the Scotch ornithologist Wilson,[1] who had the good fortune to wander for years in the American woods while the country was yet mostly wild. I read his description over and over again, till I got the vivid picture he drew by heart—the long-winged hawk circling over the heaving waves, every motion watched by the eagle perched on the top of a crag or dead tree; the fish hawk poising for a moment to take aim at a fish and plunging under the water; the eagle with kindling eye spreading his wings ready for instant flight in case the attack should prove successful; the hawk emerging with a struggling fish in his talons, and proud flight; the eagle launching himself in pursuit; the wonderful wing-work in the sky, the fish hawk, though encumbered with his prey, circling higher, higher, striving hard to keep above the robber eagle; the eagle at length soaring above him, compelling him with a cry of despair to drop his hard-won prey; then the eagle steadying himself for a moment to take aim, descending swift as a lightning-bolt, and seizing the falling fish before it reached the sea.

Not less exciting and memorable was Audubon's wonderful story of the passenger pigeon,[2] a beautiful bird flying in vast flocks that darkened the sky like clouds, countless millions assembling to rest and sleep and rear their young in certain forests, miles in length and breadth, fifty or a hundred nests on a single tree; the overloaded branches bending low and often breaking; the farmers gathering from far and near, beating down countless thousands of the young and old birds from their nests and roosts with long poles at night, and in the morning driving their bands of hogs, some of them brought from farms a hundred miles distant, to fatten on the dead and wounded covering the ground.

[1] Alexander Wilson (1766–1813) migrated to Delaware in 1794, and, inspired by the naturalist William Bartram, published *American Ornithology* (1808–13), which was completed by George Ord after Wilson's death.
[2] John James Audubon (1785–1851) published his *Ornithological Biography* (1831–39) to accompany the plates in *The Birds of America* (1827–38). He was one of many writers to describe the passenger pigeon and the lengths to which Americans went to kill it; as Muir later laments, it went extinct in 1914.

In another of our reading lessons some of the American forests were described. The most interesting of the trees to us boys was the sugar maple, and soon after we had learned this sweet story we heard everybody talking about the discovery of gold in the same wonder-filled country.[3]

One night, when David and I were at Grandfather's fireside solemnly learning our lessons as usual, my father came in with news, the most wonderful, most glorious, that wild boys ever heard. "Bairns," he said, "you needna learn your lessons the nicht, for we're gan to America the morn!" No more grammar, but boundless woods full of mysterious good things: trees full of sugar, growing in ground full of gold; hawks, eagles, pigeons, filling the sky; millions of birds' nests, and no gamekeepers[4] to stop us in all the wild, happy land. We were utterly, blindly glorious. After Father left the room, Grandfather gave David and me a gold coin apiece for a keepsake, and looked very serious, for he was about to be deserted in his lonely old age. And when we in fullness of young joy spoke of what we were going to do, of the wonderful birds and their nests that we should find, the sugar and gold, etc., and promised to send him a big box full of that tree sugar packed in gold from the glorious paradise over the sea, poor lonely Grandfather, about to be forsaken, looked with downcast eyes on the floor and said in a low, trembling, troubled voice, "Ah, poor laddies, poor laddies, you'll find something else ower the sea forbye gold and sugar, birds' nests and freedom fra lessons and schools. You'll find plenty hard, hard work." And so we did. But nothing he could say could cloud our joy or abate the fire of youthful, hopeful, fearless adventure. Nor could we in the midst of such measureless excitement see or feel the shadows and sorrows of his darkening old age. To my schoolmates, met that night on the street, I shouted the glorious news, "I'm gan to Amaraka the morn!" None could believe it. I said, "Weel, just you see if I am at the skule the morn!"

Next morning we went by rail to Glasgow and thence joyfully sailed away from beloved Scotland, flying to our fortunes on the wings of the winds, carefree as thistle seeds. We could not then know what we were leaving, what we were to encounter in the New World, nor what our gains were likely to be. We were too young and full of hope for fear or regret, but not too young to look forward with eager enthusiasm to the wonderful schoolless, bookless American wilderness. Even the natural heart-pain of parting from Grandfather and Grandmother Gilrye, who loved us so well, and from Mother and sisters and brother was quickly quenched in young joy. Father took with him only my sister Sarah (thirteen years of age), myself (eleven), and brother David (nine), leaving my eldest sister, Margaret, and the three youngest of the family, Daniel, Mary, and Anna, with mother, to join us after a farm had been found in the wilderness and a comfortable house made to receive them.

[3] This would have been in California in 1849; Muir at that time was eleven.
[4] Muir refers to the rough distinction between British "forest laws" and American game laws. Under the former, enacted after the Norman Conquest, hunting was a privilege reserved for the king and nobles and any game animal was owned by the landowner prior to its death, whereas in America game was unowned (except ultimately by the state) until shot.

In crossing the Atlantic before the days of steamships, or even the American clippers, the voyages made in old-fashioned sailing-vessels were very long. Ours was six weeks and three days. But because we had no lessons to get, that long voyage had not a dull moment for us boys. Father and sister Sarah, with most of the old folk, stayed below in rough weather, groaning in the miseries of seasickness, many of the passengers wishing they had never ventured in "the auld rockin'creel," as they called our bluff-bowed, wave-beating ship, and, when the weather was moderately calm, singing songs in the evenings—"The youthful sailor, frank and bold," "Oh, why left I my hame, why did I cross the deep," etc. But no matter how much the old tub tossed about and battered the waves, we were on deck every day, not in the least seasick, watching the sailors at their rope-hauling and climbing work; joining in their songs, learning the names of the ropes and sails, and helping them as far as they would let us; playing games with other boys in calm weather when the deck was dry, and in stormy weather rejoicing in sympathy with the big curly-topped waves.

The captain occasionally called David and me into his cabin and asked us about our schools, handed us books to read, and seemed surprised to find that Scotch boys could read and pronounce English with perfect accent and knew so much Latin and French. In Scotch schools only pure English was taught, although not a word of English was spoken out of school. All through life, however well-educated, the Scotch spoke Scotch among their own folk, except at times when unduly excited on the only two subjects on which Scotchmen get much excited, namely, religion and politics. So long as the controversy went on with fairly level temper, only gude braid Scots was used, but if one became angry, as was likely to happen, then he immediately began speaking severely correct English, while his antagonist, drawing himself up, would say: "Weel, there's na use pursuing this subject ony further, for I see ye hae gotten to your English."

As we neared the shore of the great new land, with what eager wonder we watched the whales and dolphins and porpoises and seabirds, and made the good-natured sailors teach us their names and tell us stories about them!

There were quite a large number of emigrants aboard, many of them newly married couples, and the advantages of the different parts of the New World they expected to settle in were often discussed. My father started with the intention of going to the backwoods of Upper Canada. Before the end of the voyage, however, he was persuaded that the States offered superior advantages, especially Wisconsin and Michigan, where the land was said to be as good as in Canada and far more easily brought under cultivation, for in Canada the woods were so close and heavy that a man might wear out his life in getting a few acres cleared of trees and stumps. So he changed his mind and concluded to go to one of the western states.

On our wavering westward way a grain-dealer in Buffalo told Father that most of the wheat he handled came from Wisconsin; and this influential information finally determined my father's choice. At Milwaukee a farmer who had come in from the country near Fort Winnebago with a load of wheat agreed to haul us and our formidable load of stuff to a little town called Kingston for thirty dollars. On that hundred-mile journey, just after the spring thaw, the roads over the prairies were heavy and miry, causing no end of lamentation, for we often got stuck in the mud, and the poor farmer sadly declared that never, never again would he be tempted to try to haul such a cruel, heart-breaking, wagon-breaking, horse-killing load, no, not for a hundred dollars. In leaving Scotland, Father, like many other home-seekers, burdened himself with far too much luggage, as if all America were still a wilderness in which little or nothing could be bought. One of his big iron-bound boxes must have weighed about four hundred pounds, for it contained an old-fashioned beam-scales with a complete set of cast-iron counterweights, two of them fifty-six pounds each, a twenty-eight, and so on down to a single pound. Also a lot of iron wedges, carpenter's tools, and so forth, and at Buffalo, as if on the very edge of the wilderness, he gladly added to his burden a big cast-iron stove with pots and pans, provisions enough for a long siege, and a scythe and cumbersome cradle for cutting wheat, all of which he succeeded in landing in the primeval Wisconsin woods.

A land agent at Kingston gave Father a note to a farmer by the name of Alexander Gray, who lived on the border of the settled part of the country, knew the section lines,[5] and would probably help him to find a good place for a farm. So Father went away to spy out the land, and in the meantime left us children in Kingston in a rented room. It took us less than an hour to get acquainted with some of the boys in the village. We challenged them to wrestle, run races, climb trees, etc., and in a day or two we felt at home, carefree and happy, notwithstanding our family was so widely divided. When Father returned he told us that he had found fine land for a farm in sunny open woods on the side of a lake, and that a team of three yoke of oxen with a big wagon was coming to haul us to Mr. Gray's place.

We enjoyed the strange ten-mile ride through the woods very much, wondering how the great oxen could be so strong and wise and tame as to pull so heavy a load with no other harness than a chain and a crooked piece of wood on their necks, and how they could sway so obediently to right and left past roadside trees and stumps when the driver said *haw* and *gee*. At Mr. Gray's house, Father again left us for a few days to build a shanty on the quarter-section he had selected four or five miles to the westward. In the meanwhile we enjoyed our freedom as usual, wandering in the fields and meadows, looking at the trees and flowers, snakes and birds and squirrels. With the help of the nearest neighbors the little shanty was built in less than a day after the rough bur oak logs for the walls and the white oak boards for the floor and roof were got together.

To this charming hut, in the sunny woods, overlooking a flowery glacier meadow and a lake rimmed with white waterlilies, we were hauled by an ox-

---

[5] The federal survey had marked off the land into mile-square "sections."

team across trackless carex[6] swamps and low rolling hills sparsely dotted with round-headed oaks. Just as we arrived at the shanty, before we had time to look at it or the scenery about it, David and I jumped down in a hurry off the load of household goods, for we had discovered a blue jay's nest, and in a minute or so we were up the tree beside it, feasting our eyes on the beautiful green eggs and beautiful birds—our first memorable discovery. The handsome birds had not seen Scotch boys before and made a desperate screaming as if we were robbers like themselves, though we left the eggs untouched, feeling that we were already beginning to get rich, and wondering how many more nests we should find in the grand sunny woods. Then we ran along the brow of the hill that the shanty stood on, and down to the meadow, searching the trees and grass tufts and bushes, and soon discovered a bluebird's and a woodpecker's nest, and began an acquaintance with the frogs and snakes and turtles in the creeks and springs.

This sudden plash into pure wildness—baptism in Nature's warm heart—how utterly happy it made us! Nature streaming into us, wooingly teaching her wonderful glowing lessons, so unlike the dismal grammar ashes and cinders so long thrashed into us. Here without knowing it we still were at school, every wild lesson a love lesson, not whipped but charmed into us. Oh, that glorious Wisconsin wilderness! Everything new and pure in the very prime of the spring when Nature's pulses were beating highest and mysteriously keeping time with our own! Young hearts, young leaves, flowers, animals, the winds and the streams and the sparkling lake, all wildly, gladly rejoicing together!

Next morning, when we climbed to the precious jay nest to take another admiring look at the eggs, we found it empty. Not a shell-fragment was left, and we wondered how in the world the birds were able to carry off their thin-shelled eggs either in their bills or in their feet without breaking them, and how they could be kept warm while a new nest was being built. Well, I am still asking these questions. When I was on the Harriman Expedition I asked Robert Ridgway,[7] the eminent ornithologist, how these sudden flittings were accomplished, and he frankly confessed that he didn't know, but guessed that jays and many other birds carried their eggs in their mouths; and when I objected that a jay's mouth seemed too small to hold its eggs, he replied that birds' mouths were larger than the narrowness of their bills indicated. Then I asked him what he thought they did with the eggs while a new nest was being prepared. He didn't know; neither do I to this day. A specimen of the many puzzling problems presented to the naturalist.

We soon found many more nests belonging to birds that were not half so suspicious. The handsome and notorious blue jay plunders the nests of other birds and of course he could not trust us. Almost all the others—brown

---

[6] Sedge.

[7] Ridgway (1850–1929) accompanied Muir and others on the Harriman expedition, conducted in 1899 by the railroad magnate Edward Henry Harriman (1848–1909).

thrushes, bluebirds, song sparrows, kingbirds, hen-hawks, nighthawks, whip-poorwills, woodpeckers, etc.—simply tried to avoid being seen, to draw or drive us away, or paid no attention to us.

We used to wonder how the woodpeckers could bore holes so perfectly round, true mathematical circles. We ourselves could not have done it even with gouges and chisels. We loved to watch them feeding their young, and wondered how they could glean food enough for so many clamorous, hungry, unsatisfiable babies, and how they managed to give each one its share; for after the young grew strong, one would get his head out of the door-hole and try to hold possession of it to meet the food-laden parents. How hard they worked to support their families, especially the red-headed and speckledy woodpeckers and flickers; digging, hammering on scaly bark and decaying trunks and branches from dawn to dark, coming and going at intervals of a few minutes all the livelong day!

We discovered a hen-hawk's nest on the top of a tall oak thirty or forty rods from the shanty and approached it cautiously. One of the pair always kept watch, soaring in wide circles high above the tree, and when we attempted to climb it, the big dangerous-looking bird came swooping down at us and drove us away.

We greatly admired the plucky kingbird. In Scotland our great ambition was to be good fighters, and we admired this quality in the handsome little chattering flycatcher that whips all the other birds. He was particularly angry when plundering jays and hawks came near his home, and took pains to thrash them not only away from the nest-tree but out of the neighborhood. The nest was usually built on a bur oak near a meadow where insects were abundant, and where no undesirable visitor could approach without being discovered. When a hen-hawk hove in sight, the male immediately set off after him, and it was ridiculous to see that great, strong bird hurrying away as fast as his clumsy wings would carry him, as soon as he saw the little, waspish kingbird coming. But the kingbird easily overtook him, flew just a few feet above him, and with a lot of chattering, scolding notes kept diving and striking him on the back of the head until tired. Then he alighted to rest on the hawk's broad shoulders, still scolding and chattering as he rode along, like an angry boy pouring out vials of wrath. Then, up and at him again with his sharp bill; and after he had thus driven and ridden his big enemy a mile or so from the nest, he went home to his mate, chuckling and bragging as if trying to tell her what a wonderful fellow he was.

This first spring, while some of the birds were still building their nests and very few young ones had yet tried to fly, Father hired a Yankee to assist in clearing eight or ten acres of the best ground for a field. We found new wonders every day and often had to call on this Yankee to solve puzzling questions. We asked him one day if there was any bird in America that the kingbird couldn't whip. What about the sandhill crane? Could he whip that long-legged, long-billed fellow?

"A crane never goes near kingbirds' nests or notices so small a bird," he said, "and therefore there could be no fighting between them." So we hastily concluded that our hero could whip every bird in the country except perhaps the sandhill crane.

We never tired listening to the wonderful whippoorwill. One came every night about dusk and sat on a log about twenty or thirty feet from our cabin door and began shouting "Whip poor Will! Whip poor Will!" with loud emphatic earnestness. "What's that? What's that?" we cried when this startling visitor first announced himself. "What do you call it?"

"Why, it's telling you its name," said the Yankee. "Don't you hear it and what he wants you to do? He says his name is 'Poor Will' and he wants you to whip him, and you may if you are able to catch him." Poor Will seemed the most wonderful of all the strange creatures we had seen. What a wild, strong, bold voice he had, unlike any other we had ever heard on sea or land!

A near relative, the bull-bat, or nighthawk, seemed hardly less wonderful. Towards evening scattered flocks kept the sky lively as they circled around on their long wings a hundred feet or more above the ground, hunting moths and beetles, interrupting their rather slow but strong, regular wing-beats at short intervals with quick quivering strokes while uttering keen, squeaky cries something like *pfee, pfee,* and every now and then diving nearly to the ground with a loud ripping, bellowing sound, like bull-roaring, suggesting its name; then turning and gliding swiftly up again. These fine wild gray birds, about the size of a pigeon, lay their two eggs on bare ground without anything like a nest or even a concealing bush or grass-tuft. Nevertheless they are not easily seen, for they are colored like the ground. While sitting on their eggs, they depend so much upon not being noticed that if you are walking rapidly ahead they allow you to step within an inch or two of them without flinching. But if they see by your looks that you have discovered them, they leave their eggs or young, and, like a good many other birds, pretend that they are sorely wounded, fluttering and rolling over on the ground and gasping as if dying, to draw you away. When pursued we were surprised to find that just when we were on the point of overtaking them they were always able to flutter a few yards farther, until they had led us about a quarter of a mile from the nest; then, suddenly getting well, they quietly flew home by a roundabout way to their precious babies or eggs, o'er a' the ills of life victorious, bad boys among the worst. The Yankee took particular pleasure in encouraging us to pursue them.

Everything about us was so novel and wonderful that we could hardly believe our senses except when hungry or while Father was thrashing us. When we first saw Fountain Lake Meadow, on a sultry evening, sprinkled with millions of lightning bugs throbbing with light, the effect was so strange and beautiful that it seemed far too marvelous to be real. Looking from our shanty on the hill, I thought that the whole wonderful fairy show must be in my eyes; for only in fighting, when my eyes were struck, had I ever seen anything in the least like it. But when I asked my brother if he saw anything strange in the meadow he said, "Yes, it's all covered with shaky fire-sparks." Then I guessed that it might be something outside of us, and applied to our all-knowing Yankee to explain it. "Oh, it's nothing but lightnin' bugs," he said, and kindly led us down the hill to the edge of the fiery meadow, caught a few of the wonderful bugs, dropped them into a cup, and carried them to the shanty, where we watched them throbbing and flashing out their mysterious light at regular intervals, as if each little passionate glow were caused by the beating of a heart. Once I saw a splendid display of glow-worm light in the foothills of the Himalayas, north of Calcutta, but glorious as it appeared in pure starry radiance, it was far less impressive than the extravagant abounding, quivering, dancing fire on our Wisconsin meadow.

Partridge drumming was another great marvel. When I first heard the low, soft, solemn sound I thought it must be made by some strange disturbance in my head or stomach, but as all seemed serene within, I asked David whether he heard anything queer. "Yes," he said, "I hear something saying *boomp*, *boomp*, *boomp*, and I'm wondering at it." Then I was half satisfied that the source of the mysterious sound must be in something outside of us, coming perhaps from the ground or from some ghost or bogie or woodland fairy. Only after long watching and listening did we at last discover it in the wings of the plump brown bird.

The love song of the common jack snipe seemed not a whit less mysterious than partridge drumming. It was usually heard on cloudy evenings, a strange, unearthly, winnowing, spiritlike sound, yet easily heard at a distance of a third of a mile. Our sharp eyes soon detected the bird while making it, as it circled high in the air over the meadow with wonderfully strong and rapid wing-beats, suddenly descending and rising, again and again, in deep, wide loops; the tones being very low and smooth at the beginning of the descent, rapidly increasing to a curious little whirling storm-roar at the bottom, and gradually fading lower and lower until the top was reached. It was long, however, before we identified this mysterious wing-singer as the little brown jack snipe that we knew so well and had so often watched as he silently probed the mud around the edges of our meadow stream and spring-holes, and made short zigzag flights over the grass uttering only little short, crisp quacks and chucks.

The love songs of the frogs seemed hardly less wonderful than those of the birds, their musical notes varying from the sweet, tranquil, soothing peeping and purring of the hylas[8] to the awfully deep low-bass blunt bellowing of the bullfrogs. Some of the smaller species have wonderfully clear, sharp voices and told us their good Bible names in musical tones about as plainly as the whippoorwill. *Isaac, Isaac; Yacob, Yacob; Israel, Israel;* shouted in sharp, ringing, far-reaching tones, as if they had all been to school and severely drilled in elocution. In the still, warm evenings, big bunchy bullfrogs bellowed, *Drunk! Drunk! Drunk! Jug o' rum! Jug o' rum!* and early in the spring, countless thousands of the commonest species, up to the throat in cold water, sang in concert, making a mass of music, such as it was, loud enough to be heard at a distance of more than half a mile.

---

[8] Tree toads.

Far, far apart from this loud marsh music is that of the many species of hyla, a sort of soothing immortal melody filling the air like light.

We reveled in the glory of the sky scenery as well as that of the woods and meadows and rushy, lily-bordered lakes. The great thunderstorms in particular interested us, so unlike any seen in Scotland, exciting awful, wondering admiration. Gazing awestricken, we watched the upbuilding of the sublime cloud-mountains,—glowing, sun-beaten pearl and alabaster cumuli, glorious in beauty and majesty and looking so firm and lasting that birds, we thought, might build their nests amid their downy bosses; the black-browed storm clouds marching in awful grandeur across the landscape, trailing broad gray sheets of hail and rain like vast cataracts, and ever and anon flashing down vivid zigzag lightning followed by terrible crashing thunder. We saw several trees shattered, and one of them, a punky old oak, was set on fire, while we wondered why all the trees and everybody and everything did not share the same fate, for oftentimes the whole sky blazed. After sultry storm days, many of the nights were darkened by smooth black apparently structureless cloud-mantles which at short intervals were illumined with startling suddenness to a fiery glow by quick, quivering lightning-flashes, revealing the landscape in almost noonday brightness, to be instantly quenched in solid blackness.

But those first days and weeks of unmixed enjoyment and freedom, reveling in the wonderful wildness about us, were soon to be mingled with the hard work of making a farm. I was first put to burning brush in clearing land for the plough. Those magnificent brush fires with great white hearts and red flames, the first big, wild outdoor fires I had ever seen, were wonderful sights for young eyes. Again and again, when they were burning fiercest so that we could hardly approach near enough to throw on another branch, Father put them to awfully practical use as warning lessons, comparing their heat with that of hell, and the branches with bad boys. "Now, John," he would say, "Now, John, just think what an awful thing it would be to be thrown into that fire—and then think of hellfire, that is so many times hotter. Into that fire all bad boys, with sinners of every sort who disobey God, will be cast as we are casting branches into this brush fire, and although suffering so much, their sufferings will never never end, because neither the fire nor the sinners can die." But those terrible fire lessons quickly faded away in the blithe wilderness air, for no fire can be hotter than the heavenly fire of faith and hope that burns in every healthy boy's heart.[9]

Soon after our arrival in the woods someone added a cat and puppy to the animals Father had bought. The cat soon had kittens, and it was interesting to watch her feeding, protecting, and training them. After they were able to leave their nest and play, she went out hunting and brought in many kinds of birds and squirrels for them, mostly ground squirrels (spermophiles), called "gophers" in Wisconsin. When she got within a dozen yards or so of the shanty, she announced her approach by a peculiar call, and the sleeping kittens immediately bounced up and ran to meet her, all racing for the first bite of they knew

[9]A succinct statement of Muir's differences with the Calvinist culture of his homeland.

not what, and we too ran to see what she brought. She then lay down a few minutes to rest and enjoy the enjoyment of her feasting family, and again vanished in the grass and flowers, coming and going every half hour or so. Sometimes she brought in birds that we had never seen before, and occasionally a flying squirrel, chipmunk, or big fox squirrel. We were just old enough, David and I, to regard all these creatures as wonders, the strange inhabitants of our new world.

The pup was a common cur, though very uncommon to us, a black and white short-haired mongrel that we named "Watch." We always gave him a pan of milk in the evening just before we knelt in family worship, while daylight still lingered in the shanty. And, instead of attending to the prayers, I too often studied the small wild creatures playing around us. Field mice scampered about the cabin as though it had been built for them alone, and their performances were very amusing. About dusk, on one of the calm, sultry nights so grateful to moths and beetles, when the puppy was lapping his milk, and we were on our knees, in through the door came a heavy broad-shouldered beetle about as big as a mouse, and after it had droned and boomed round the cabin two or three times, the pan of milk, showing white in the gloaming, caught its eyes, and, taking good aim, it alighted with a slanting, glinting plash in the middle of the pan like a duck alighting in a lake. Baby Watch, having never before seen anything like that beetle, started back, gazing in dumb astonishment and fear at the black sprawling monster trying to swim. Recovering somewhat from his fright, he began to bark at the creature, and ran round and round his milkpan, wouf-woufing, gurring, growling, like an old dog barking at a wildcat or a bear. The natural astonishment and curiosity of that boy dog getting his first entomological lesson in this wonderful world was so immoderately funny that I had great difficulty in keeping from laughing out loud.

Snapping turtles were common throughout the woods, and we were delighted to find that they would snap at a stick and hang on like bulldogs; and we amused ourselves by introducing Watch to them, enjoying his curious behavior and theirs in getting acquainted with each other. One day we assisted one of the smallest of the turtles to get a good grip of poor Watch's ear. Then away he rushed, holding his head sidewise, yelping and terror-stricken, with the strange buglike reptile biting hard and clinging fast—a shameful amusement even for wild boys.

As a playmate Watch was too serious, though he learned more than any stranger would judge him capable of, was a bold, faithful watchdog, and in his prime a grand fighter, able to whip all the other dogs in the neighborhood. Comparing him with ourselves, we soon learned that although he could not read books he could read faces, was a good judge of character, always knew what was going on and what we were about to do, and liked to help us. We could run nearly as fast as he could, see about as far, and perhaps hear as well, but in sense of smell his nose was incomparably better than ours. One sharp winter morning when the ground was covered with snow, I noticed that when he was yawning and stretching himself after leaving his bed he suddenly caught the scent of something that excited him, went round the corner of the house, and looked intently to the westward across a tongue of land that we called West Bank, eagerly questioning the air with quivering nostrils, and bristling up as though he felt sure that there was something dangerous in that direction and had actually caught sight of it. Then he ran toward the bank, and I followed him, curious to see what his nose had discovered. The top of the bank commanded a view of the north end of our lake and meadow, and when we got there we saw an Indian hunter with a long spear, going from one muskrat cabin to another, approaching cautiously, careful to make no noise, and then suddenly thrusting his spear down through the house. If well-aimed, the spear went through the poor beaver rat as it lay cuddled up in the snug nest it had made for itself in the fall with so much farseeing care, and when the hunter felt the spear quivering, he dug down the mossy hut with his tomahawk and secured his prey—the flesh for food, and the skin to sell for a dime or so. This was a clear object lesson on dogs' keenness of scent. That Indian was more than half a mile away across a wooded ridge. Had the hunter been a white man, I suppose Watch would not have noticed him.

When he was about six or seven years old, he not only became cross, so that he would do only what he liked, but he fell on evil ways, and was accused by the neighbors who had settled around us of catching and devouring whole broods of chickens, some of them only a day or two out of the shell. We never imagined he would do anything so grossly undoglike. He never did at home. But several of the neighbors declared over and over again that they had caught him in the act, and insisted that he must be shot. At last, in spite of tearful protests, he was condemned and executed. Father examined the poor fellow's stomach in search of sure evidence, and discovered the heads of eight chickens that he had devoured at his last meal. So poor Watch was killed simply because his taste for chickens was too much like our own. Think of the millions of squabs that preaching, praying men and women kill and eat, with all sorts of other animals great and small, young and old, while eloquently discoursing on the coming of the blessed peaceful, bloodless millennium! Think of the passenger pigeons that fifty or sixty years ago filled the woods and sky over half the continent, now exterminated by beating down the young from the nests together with the brooding parents, before they could try their wonderful wings; by trapping them in nets, feeding them to hogs, etc. None of our fellow mortals is safe who eats what we eat, who in any way interferes with our pleasures, or who may be used for work or food, clothing or ornament, or mere cruel, sportish amusement. Fortunately many are too small to be seen, and therefore enjoy life beyond our reach. And in looking through God's great stone books made up of records reaching back millions and millions of years, it is a great comfort to learn that vast multitudes of creatures, great and small and infinite in number, lived and had a good time in God's love before man was created.

The old Scotch fashion of whipping for every act of disobedience or of simple, playful forgetfulness was still kept up in the wilderness, and of course many of those whippings fell upon me. Most of them were outrageously severe, and utterly barren of fun. But here is one that was nearly all fun.

Father was busy hauling lumber for the frame house that was to be got ready for the arrival of my mother, sisters, and brother, left behind in Scotland. One morning, when he was ready to start for another load, his ox-whip was not to be found. He asked me if I knew anything about it. I told him I didn't know where it was, but Scotch conscience compelled me to confess that when I was playing with it I had tied it to Watch's tail, and that he ran away, dragging it through the grass, and came back without it. "It must have slipped off his tail," I said, and so I didn't know where it was. This honest, straightforward little story made Father so angry that he exclaimed with heavy, foreboding emphasis: "The very deevil's in that boy!" David, who had been playing with me and was perhaps about as responsible for the loss of the whip as I was, said never a word, for he was always prudent enough to hold his tongue when the parental weather was stormy, and so escaped nearly all punishment. And, strange to say, this time I also escaped, all except a terrible scolding, though the thrashing weather seemed darker than ever. As if unwilling to let the sun see the shameful job, father took me into the cabin where the storm was to fall, and sent David to the woods for a switch. While he was out selecting the switch, Father put in the spare time sketching my play-wickedness in awful colors, and of course referred again and again to the place prepared for bad boys. In the midst of this terrible word-storm, dreading most the impending thrashing, I whimpered that I was only playing because I couldn't help it; didn't know I was doing wrong; wouldn't do it again, and so forth. After this miserable dialogue was about exhausted, Father became impatient at my brother for taking so long to find the switch; and so was I, for I wanted to have the thing over and done with. At last, in came David, a picture of openhearted innocence, solemnly dragging a young bur oak sapling, and handed the end of it to father, saying it was the best switch he could find. It was an awfully heavy one, about two-and-a-half inches thick at the butt and ten feet long, almost big enough for a fence pole. There wasn't room enough in the cabin to swing it, and the moment I saw it I burst out laughing in the midst of my fears. But Father failed to see the fun and was very angry at David, heaved the bur oak outside and passionately demanded his reason for fetching "sic a muckle rail like that instead o' a switch? Do ye ca' that a switch? I have a gude mind to thrash you insteed o' John." David, with demure, downcast eyes, looked preternaturally righteous, but as usual prudently answered never a word.

It was a hard job in those days to bring up Scotch boys in the way they should go, and poor overworked Father was determined to do it if enough of the right kind of switches could be found. But this time, as the sun was getting high, he hitched up old Tom and Jerry and made haste to the Kingston lumber-yard, leaving me unscathed and as innocently wicked as ever; for hardly had Father got fairly out of sight among the oaks and hickories, ere all our troubles, hell-threatenings, and exhortations were forgotten in the fun we had lassoing a stubborn old sow and laboriously trying to teach her to go reasonably steady in rope harness. She was the first hog that Father bought to stock the farm, and we boys regarded her as a very wonderful beast. In a few weeks she had a lot of pigs, and of all the queer, funny, animal children we had yet seen, none amused us more. They were so comic in size and shape, in their gait and gestures, their merry sham fights, and the false alarms they got up for the fun of scampering back to their mother and begging her in most persuasive little squeals to lie down and give them a drink.

After her darling short-snouted babies were about a month old, she took them out to the woods and gradually roamed farther and farther from the shanty in search of acorns and roots. One afternoon we heard a rifle shot, a very noticeable thing, as we had no near neighbors, as yet. We thought it must have been fired by an Indian on the trail that followed the right bank of the Fox River between Portage and Packwaukee Lake and passed our shanty at a distance of about three-quarters of a mile. Just a few minutes after that shot was heard, along came the poor mother rushing up to the shanty for protection, with her pigs, all out of breath and terror-stricken. One of them was missing, and we supposed of course that an Indian had shot it for food. Next day, I discovered a blood-puddle where the Indian trail crossed the outlet of our lake. One of Father's hired men told us that the Indians thought nothing of levying this sort of blackmail whenever they were hungry. The solemn awe and fear in the eyes of that old mother and those little pigs I never can forget; it was as unmistakable and deadly a fear as I ever saw expressed by any human eye, and corroborates in no uncertain way the oneness of all of us.

MARTIN WEITZ, GERMANY

Letter to his family, July 29, 1855

Rockville, July 29th, 1855

DEAR DEVOTED FATHER, BROTHER, SISTER-IN-LAW, AND CHILDREN,

Should my letter reach you in good health, I will be overjoyed. Finally I have fulfilled my longing for you by sending a small gift; I couldn't do it any earlier since I was doing very poorly. Last year from October until March 16th this year I didn't have any work; the factory in Astoria had stopped work. I had to pay [a] ten dollar training fee. Every newcomer who comes here has to pay. When I had worked it off there was no more work there. From there we went to another factory, a fur factory, [and] there we had rotten jobs where our hands got all swollen up but it didn't last long. Finally we couldn't get any money, then I also lost a lot so I made it through the winter splitting wood for a man in Astoria who wasn't able so I could earn some money. But it wasn't enough. I looked around for work in New York and the area, but all for nothing; if I had been able to speak English I could've gotten a job but I can't. I didn't have any money to move on, [so] you can imagine it was terrible. Thousands and thousands were wandering around without work, without money, without food, dying of hunger. They've set up places where they could get lunch but it isn't enough. They poured through the town in great droves demanding that work be found for them, but all for nothing. All over America it was terrible, many hundreds of *Fektori*,[1] that means *Fabricke*, had stopped work, prices went way up and still are, it should not be called America but *Malerika*.[2] It is easy to say you want to go to America but the hard things they never think about. . . . When you arrive here and don't understand English, you stand there, eyes wide open, like a calf with its throat cut. You have to be careful—they say, there's a greenhorn. How many hundred are lied to and cheated; no one can be careful enough. In New York every day there's murder, theft, suicide, lies and cheating, and in any large town in America. If you want to come to America you just can't let that scare you off. You have to think the best, the worst comes later. I don't want to advise anyone not to come, whoever wants to come should come. It's best if you have a friend here who gets you a job in a good state. Dear father and brother, thank God I now have a good job. On March 16th in the newspaper there was a call for twenty-five weavers in a wool *Fektori*[3] in Rockville in the state of Connecticut to sign up on the 17th at 6 o'clock in the evening. We went there and were accepted. On the 18th we got on the steamboat and went to Hartford, from there to Rockville, [but] first I had to sell my watch [or] otherwise I couldn't have gotten there. When we arrived there in the afternoon they said you have to work nights from 6:30 in the evening till 6:30 in the morning—then we were shocked. I said I didn't care if I only have work. The looms all work by themselves, they are all driven by water, [and] I'd never woven on such a loom. I went to a fellow who taught me during the day; then work started. It didn't go well of course in the beginning, [for] they do difficult patterns. In March and April I didn't earn much, I hardly had enough for board; in July, $19.50. Now it's getting better, if you do good work, you earn $18–20 to $24–25 dollars. Dear father, I am now very content with my situation, I'll stay here. Last winter sometimes I just wanted to jump into the water, [for] if you don't have a job in America it's a terrible thing, I can't thank God enough that I have work and am healthy. Here in the *Willischtz* [village], . . . there are almost 250 Germans who work in the *Feckteri*, there are eleven *Feckterie* here. If you don't like it in one you go to another, [and] three more are being built.

If anyone from Schotten wants to come here, he should come. Springtime is the best. If he has money he can buy land in the state of Wisconsin; it seems to be another Germany, [and] it's healthy there. Where I am in Rockville in the state of Connecticut, 180 miles from New York, it's also very healthy, the climate seems to me like over there; we had 100 degrees of heat, but of course it's not as healthy here in America as over there in Germany. The harvest here

[1] I.e., factory.
[2] While Weitz may be playing on other, more specific meanings here, he also just means that America is not what it seems to be, that the reality is a jumbled version of the expectation.
[3] Rockville, in the town of Vernon, Tolland County, Connecticut, where one of the earliest wool-carding mills in the country was opened in 1802.

in America looks good and there's hope that things will be cheaper than a while ago. There is *Temperes* [temperance] here, that means there's no alcoholic spirits allowed, no beer, no brandy, wine, etc. In many states there's been serious fighting like in the state of Ohio. In Cincinnati there was a bloodbath; the Germans won, [but] there were many dead and wounded on both sides. The *Jenkeamerikaner* [Yankees], they call themselves *Nounorthing* Yankees, they want to have control, but democracy wins. It looks like there's going to be a revolution.[4] Every Sunday you have to go to church—then the factory bosses like you; you don't learn anything bad there [whether] you understand English or not. That's fine with me. I can go there.

With the singing clubs and music there, the Germans in America are on the rise, [and] they earn a lot of respect for that. Even we in Rockville have two singing clubs. With our German singing we earn great respect. In New York there was a big song festival that drew a lot of applause from the Americans. I am here in a German *Boarding Haus*, I have to pay $9 a month, which is cheap—you may think it's a lot, but you have to remember that the dollar can't be counted as more than the guilder over there. I can't spend any money except for tobacco; I haven't drunk any brandy in three months. Every noon there's soup, vegetables and meat, every morning and evening meat, cheese and butter. Every morning we get up at 5 o'clock, at 5:30 the bells ring, [and] we go to the factory till 12 o'clock noon; at 1 o'clock we go in again until 6:30, [and] at 8 o'clock it's already night. At 4 o'clock in the morning it is already daylight. When the sun goes down it gets dark right away. The difference between you and us is when we get up in the morning it's 11 o'clock over there, it's almost six hours. Leuning and I are the only ones here from Schotten. Leuning and his family like it very much here too; we work in one *Fektori*. We hardly see each other all day long, it's so big. His son Adam works in our *Fektori*. We live a mile apart, [but] don't see each other often. What do they say over there about the war? Sebastobel[5] hasn't fallen yet; thousands of people are being killed for nothing. We believe that Germany will be the battlefield.

Dear father, brother, sister-in-law and dear children, how are you, are you getting along together? Dear brother and sister-in-law, take proper care of my father, I ask you dearly, and take care of him like it befits good children, for you see I am so far away from you I cannot be among you, but I will do my duty as far as I am able. I am sending you the first small gift, I'm sending you $10, that is 25 guilders over there. . . . Dear brother I urge you to stop working at night, you will destroy yourself so that in your old age you will be weak, because working at night doesn't help, it doesn't get you anywhere. Take my

---

[4]The Know-Nothing movement scapegoated foreigners as the root of American social ills. Weitz is probably referring here to a violent clash of April 1855 in Cincinnati's "Over the Rhine" district. When a Know-Nothing mob invaded the German district, it was repulsed by gunfire and sustained several casualties.

[5]Weitz refers to rumors and news reports about the Crimean War (1853–56). Sevastopol, a Russian port on the Black Sea, was besieged by the British and French in September 1854 and fell in November 1855, forcing an end to the conflict.

advice, for a month and a half here I worked at night and slept during the day. I was happy to have work, but in the end I did get tired. Since the beginning of June I work during the day. . . . What is the band doing, my faithful colleagues, are they all well, have they kept going or have they given up? Practice properly because there is nothing more beautiful than beautiful music and song. How are my godfather's son Georg and his Christingen, does he have a job and are they married? What is Georg Göbel doing, doesn't he feel like coming over here?. . . With the money you should buy food and clothing. If I stay healthy you'll get more before Christmas; I haven't forsaken you, believe me, no day or night has passed when you weren't before my eyes, because you are my only cause for worry. I must close. . . .

I have forgotten something else, that in every *Fecktori* there are women weavers. There are *Fektori* where only women weave, they are called *Sassinet-mühle*.[6] [Satinette has] a cotton warp and a wool weft that makes a heavy cloth [so] you can't see that there's cotton underneath. There is a mill where woolen rags are made over and spun into weft, [though] it's hard to believe that you can make good thread out of rags. In the mill where Leuning and his son and I are, the *Feckteri* is called *Neu-Englandmühle*; there they make cashmere, beautiful woollen material. I am in the mill where I have made a cross [on the engraved letterhead]; there's nothing but *Fecktori* where there are many windows. I just read in the *Neu Jorkerzeitung*[7] that last week almost 700 people, of which 150 were children, died of *Cholera*.[8] I could get married any day, but I still want to think it over. So many German fellows take up with *Ameriganer* and *Eurische*[9] [that] you can't play around very much, otherwise they go straight to the [court], that means *vor Gericht*; the fellow gets picked up by the court marshal and there they get married, [and] that's the end of the fun. Then they go to the *Fecktori* together and work together and board with other people. No, I'll take good care not to do that for now.

WILHELM BÜRKERT, GERMANY

Letters to his family (1875–80)

New York, September 29, 1875

DEAR MOTHER, GRANDPARENTS, SISTERS AND HONORABLE GUARDIAN,

Praise be to the Lord, etc., that is the first hymn that we can strike up, for you can count yourself lucky to have arrived here safely, especially when you hear that at the same time our ship left, on the same water, no less than three ships sank from running into one another in the fog.

So, let us turn our attention to the journey. In Heilbronn there was a one-

---

[6] Mills where satinette is produced.
[7] Probably a German-language American paper, though the reference is unclear.
[8] Asiatic cholera, known also in Europe, continued to be a serious health problem in the United States.
[9] Irish.

hour stop, then straight on to Heidelberg. Here there was time to see the main sights. Then on, after refreshing yourself, to Frankfurt. Here, after getting all your things at Mr. Treschof's, the emigration agent's, which cost a lot of money as well, you were taken to an inn, the Golden Eagle. Oh, to hell with that food and those beds, bedbug covers, not featherbeds, just a miserable mattress with torn sheets, and awfully expensive. . . . Only the journey was paid for from Frankfurt on, but not the food. If I hadn't had such an honest, Christian, reliable gentleman along with me, looking after me, taking care of me, I would have been, as they say here, cheated blind. But thank God, it is a piece of good luck to have someone along on a damned trip like that. In Frankfurt we left on a Sunday at 8 o'clock in the morning and arrived the next morning at 3 o'clock at a station where we had to spend the night sleeping on the benches in the waiting room, until the train left at 6 o'clock the next morning.

In Hamburg there weren't as many swindlers and pickpockets like there were in that train station where you had to spend the night. You don't dare go to sleep there. We were in Hamburg in two hours time. We were brought by coach to our inn, to the South German Guesthouse. Here we spent two nights, but better than in that miserable Frankfurt. This innkeeper had been a ship's captain for twenty years and is only interested in taking good care of emigrants.

On Wednesday the 15th of September we had to pay, but all from the twelve marks that were part of the passage contract and which didn't go far at all. On this day we got on a nice small steamship. In two hours we were out of the Elbe. But here we were met by a ship like you can't imagine, with two big smokestacks.[1] Everyone jumped for his mattress, assigned by the main agent at the inn in Hamburg, and for his tin ware. It took me an hour to find mine. When I found it, I carried it to the sleeping place I had picked out. But before I realized it, my chamber pot and water bottle had been stolen.

I reported to a steward that they'd been stolen; he said, "Then go steal some yourself." I took one for myself and locked it up in my traveling bag, which was a great help. After two hours, the ship started out. We were given lunch.

I was all the way in the front in the first group of berths. I had to eat with eleven others, and carve the meat. Every day, rice soup, potatoes and meat, and meat, potatoes and rice soup, except for the two Sundays, when we had pudding along with it. Oh, I believe that stuff was boiled in sea water, it made me so sick, I ate nothing and drank nothing. In the morning all they had was black coffee, if you can call it coffee, then nothing until lunch mentioned above and then in the evening nothing but tea, which was just as bad as the coffee.

The next morning everyone was already seasick. For on the open sea the ship rolls terribly. It goes as fast as an express train.

I and two other friends, among them Herr Ritzer,[2] did not get seasick. Everybody was on top deck. One person puked here, another over there, for in

[1] The Hamburg-based steamship *Gellert*, under Captain Darend, which left for New York September 15, 1875.
[2] J. Ritzer was described in the passenger lists kept in Hamburg as a thirty-six-year-old brewer from Würtemburg.

steerage, way down at the bottom, you couldn't stand it. I didn't have to puke. On the 17th of September we arrived in the French city of Havre. In this port there was a twenty-four-hour stop. We were allowed to get off. We looked around this really lovely, large and luxurious city. On September 18th at 10 o'clock in the morning, we departed. But then out on the Atlantic ocean the ship really started to roll and the waves went clear up to the helmsman. On the same evening, on Saturday the 18th of September, I collapsed on the deck. They took me to my berth, where I hit, bit, scratched and ripped all the clothes of the sailors who had to hold me down. They gave me chloroform to put me to sleep. The ship's doctor gave up all hope. On the following Monday they were all waiting for me to die.

Oh, how horrible it is when you don't have anyone. My heart was pounding. They put something on it [that] was like fire. The doctor said if he hadn't done that, my heart would have burst. I was told never to drink much. It was Wednesday before I was allowed to leave the hospital. During this time I had food from the first cabin, where princes and dukes travel. So it must not have been seasickness since then you have to throw up.

The last few days we had such a storm that you couldn't stand up or lie down. The trunks we had with us were tied down. The last night we had fog. On the 27th of September, or on the Monday, you couldn't see anything at all for two nights, the ship went very slowly. The steamwhistles were blown a lot. All at once at 9 o'clock they called out excitedly, "Hurray, the pilot." He was coming toward us in a small boat. He had to guide us through the reefs off shore and in through the straits. It was a chief helmsman—almost like a ship's officer. At four in the morning we heard "Land—Land." And that is a sight, oh splendid. We were in Stett-Neuland.[3] Here the anchor was cast. A doctor came out about 7 o'clock and examined each one to see if he had a contagious disease. Everyone was healthy. We were allowed to go on. We went to the town [of] Hoboken. Here we had to go on a small ship. And everyone's trunks were inspected, to see if anyone was trying to smuggle something into America. There was a man who had to pay $40—100 guilders for two silk dresses and one gold mark. At 3 o'clock in the afternoon we arrived in New York.

Here we all went into a garden where a speech was held. It was Castle Garden,[4] which is set up to take care of the emigrants. Innkeepers came to offer their services. We went to the inn "*Zur Stadt Balingen*" the innkeeper [of which] is a Württemberger from Balingen. . . .

I got my first job only today, October 2nd, as a waiter and cook. I get food and board and when the month is over, the wages will be decided. Probably $16.00—40 guilders. They won't pay more, [though] that's very little here.

May you all be in good health. You'll write to me soon, won't you? A letter costs 5¢—7½ kreuzer. What costs 1 guilder in Germany, costs $1.50 here—3 guilders 45 kreuzer. Here in New York things are very bad. Gustav shouldn't

---

[3] Staten Island.
[4] The old fortress site at the tip of Manhattan that, until replaced by Ellis Island in 1892, served as the entrance point for immigrants.

come until they're better. Write me where he is, but soon, won't you. All the best to you all. New York is five times bigger and nicer than Hamburg, and it has two million inhabitants, you can get lost easily.

Your thankful son, grandson and brother.—Greetings, too, to Gustav.

Johnstown [Pa.],[5] March 4th, 1877

Dear mother, brother, grandparents, dear sisters and all dear relatives,

You will be astounded to receive yet another letter from me. But do not be angry with me, [for] it is a matter of life and death. Up to now I've been in the coal mine, where I tried to make my living with great effort and hard work and a miserable life. But it was not an accident, a cave-in, no, my long-feared ailment came back slowly, in the coal shaft, [because of] the miserable air from six in the morning until six at night. For lunch nothing but bread and black coffee in my pot, and on top of it the trip beforehand, 400 miles before I got here from New York. I am really ill, very ill. The company I work for has to pay the doctor. He says I have sick blood, I have consumption and may well have it until the fall. I won't be taken care of for that long, only four weeks. I can do lighter work all right, but where to find it? The doctor says if I have any relatives I should go there, if they'll have me. I will probably not live to see the winter. Oh, I tremble and have to weep when I think of it. As long as I've been in America (that is, back in New York), almost three-fourths of a year, I haven't touched any strong drink. I have a card that I'm not allowed to drink and smoke any more. It's the *Temberenz Ticet*,[6] with which the working class and also big bosses (Americans) swear not to enter any saloons.

Every day I have had nosebleeds, I spit up a lot of blood. Oh, if I were only in Germany; if I could only get better, I would do any kind of work, for I've been taught how to here. I would gladly do the hardest labor. So, please don't let me perish here. Am I not allowed to see you again? Oh, if Father were still alive I would certainly not be here! But it seems as if even my only brother has deserted me. Oh—I don't want any money, no, that did hurt me, even to accept the $25 or to have to accept it. If I had only been in a position to save one cent. So I ask you please to pay for a passage ticket, so I can come back to the German shores. I will gladly repay you if I get well again. Don't send me anything, I have a good jacket and work pants. Once again, please be so good and write back right away. I'm having myself sent to the hospital in New York. To the charity hospital.[7] Please send me an answer care of the German Society of the City of New York, No. 13 Broadway, New York, to be delivered to Willy Büerkert. Please be so good and do it, won't you, I'm going under here.

Hoping, thanking, your reformed Willy

[5] Büerkert (as he instructed his family to spell his name in an 1876 letter) claimed that he was on a whaling voyage on a ship from New Bedford, Massachusetts, in 1875–76, but his confused story of the voyage may have been made up. He does not explain how he made his way from New York to this coal-mining town in west-central Pennsylvania.

[6] A "Temperance Ticket" was a pledge to abstain from intoxicating drink.

[7] Büerkert's 1876 surviving letter, in which he tells of the whaling cruise, was written from Bellevue Hospital, a charity institution opened in 1826.

[Martinsburg, Pa.,[8] *August 1, 1877]*

To the honorable office of the mayor of the town of Waldenburg.

William Bürkert, son of the late farmer Georg Bürkert from Waldenburg, Oehringen County, Kingdom of Württemberg, fell seriously ill on June 20 and his recovery was doubtful. His illness is quite unknown to the three doctors attending him.

After he had gotten somewhat better, he himself claimed that it was a family illness [and that] his father died of it. Water on the brain. The attacks which he had during his illness every ten minutes were such that three men had to be kept in attendance to hold him down.

But the doctors have treated him, although they were not at all certain they would be paid, with a degree of loyalty and persistence that has astounded everyone. They came to see him three to ten times a day, for several hours, although the farm where he worked and then fell ill is a mile away from the town.

My request directed to the town mayor's office is that the necessary money be provided from the ward's fund for the aforementioned Wilhelm Bürkert, to pay for the costs caused by his illness as well as for his journey home, which in the opinion of the doctors would be the best for him.

I am performing this duty, since Wilhelm is still too weak to write himself.

The sum which Wilhelm must request is $150 and the money should be sent to the bureau listed below of the official authorities of the town of Martinsburg.

This letter is authenticated by the signatures of the attending physicians, the local authorities and the patient himself.

Yours faithfully, Julius Glatt[9]

Martinsburg [Pa.], October 15th, 1877

Dearest mother, brother, sisters, grandparents and honored guardian,

Two months have now passed since I've been cured again, and since a friend wrote on my behalf, because I was too weak then to do it myself; but now I am here, pretty much back on my feet again and working for the man at whose house I went through my serious illness and who took care of me. But now I am in the lurch and don't know what to do. I still have about $100 of debts at the doctor's, which was in the letter sent to the town hall in Waldenburg with his signature and the court's notarization. If I don't pay him very soon I'll be out of work today. I also owe the man where I work, but I want to work that off. I have four months to go. The doctors are screaming for their money and I either have to pay or get out of the area completely. I said that I had two thousand marks and they said they wanted to treat me, so I had to swear it in front of the court and so they sent the letter to the mayor's office.

So please help me out, otherwise I will starve this winter, or freeze to

[8] A small town east of Johnstown.

[9] Farmer Julius Glatt was himself a German immigrant.

death. I left here four weeks ago, since no letter came at all, but I had to come back and calm down the people, since it is hard to find work. All over America there are strikes, that means revolution, and you can't even get a piece of bread by working for it. In New York, Boston, Baltimore, Washington, Chicago, Pittsburgh, Philadelphia, and St. Louis, there are more than 150,000 workers out of a job and many even have families.

Yes, mother, it is hard, you don't need to be angry with me, I like to work, and I don't drink, and I don't lead a lowdown life, either. If I were at home I would surely earn my own living, but here, here it's all over. I am among Americans, if I were with German-Americans I would have been chased away a long time ago, and wouldn't be allowed to show my face. Oh, I am leaving this country, even if I have to smuggle myself onto a ship. If it hadn't been for the doctors, I would already be resting in peace. I have found out what that is. Dear mother, please write back to me immediately and dear guardian please see to my best interests. Don't think I will ever be too well-off here. Dear mother, write me above all about how my brother is and give him my address so he'll write to me after all; it is hard not to hear anything from your brother for such a long time.

Give my best to my little sisters, and [tell them] they shouldn't think badly of me, teach them to love me. . . . Oh, give my dear grandparents all my love. And all my best and loving wishes to you, too. I dream of you and my dear father every night, and I must weep for hours when I awake!

Please be so good and write straight away. Loving you and all of you with all my heart,

William.

Martinsburg, December 8th, 1877

Dear grandfather and grandmother,

It has now been a long time since I sent off word that I was so dangerously ill. But no one finds it worth the trouble to send me an answer. In the entire last year I have only received one single letter.

I have sent off a letter several times, but never gotten an answer. Now I turn to you, dear grandparents: perhaps you think better of a poor orphan in America. All that I want is just to know how you, my dear ones, are. I don't even know how things are—are you still alive, or not. Oh! May these lines reach you in good health. Oh! If only I could see you once again. How are my dear good mother, my good brother and worthy sisters? Please write me about everything; oh, you have no idea what it is like when you don't hear anything from your loved ones for years on end. I am living here with good people, but without work. I haven't heard a word of German for half a year. Oh, if I had the means, I would come to you bravely. But it won't work out like this. I often think I've been deserted. Please be so good and don't make me wait long for an answer. Oh, give my best to everyone and wish them happy hearts. Farewell, may God keep you in good health. Your loving, devoted grandson, son and brother,

William Büerkert

Jamestown,[1] *Missouri, June 27th, 1880*

My dear mother,

Once again I take up my pen to call out greetings to you across the ocean. I wrote to you three times after I got your last letter, without ever getting an answer back. I wrote you then that I was planning to travel to California. I went out there, as I thought, to make my fortune. My savings then amounted to $125. I and two others bought a piece of land for $300 and started to mine. But there was very little gold to be found and also we were dogged by the rough miners and mine owners. Then we were forced to sell our land for $175 after four months of hard work. We lost about $35. We took off for Oregon and went on from there eastward, until we came to Colorado. There we worked as guides for the trains of immigrants which move from the eastern states to the West. This job was very dangerous, [as] we had to fight too much with bands of Sioux Indians and with the so-called *outlaws* (that means with white men who break the law). I stayed there about seven months. Went through the *Indian Territory,* where we earned a few talers with *trapping,* that means catching beaver, by selling the furs in Texas and from there I came back to the state of Missouri three weeks ago,[2] and since the harvest had just started I worked through it, earning from $2.00 to $2.50 a day; if I wanted to move on with the harvest I could, if I kept going north I could still do four weeks of harvest work, but first of all I want to rest up a bit and second of all, some farmers have asked me to plow their corn.[3] That's an easier job; of course only $1.25 a day; but much quieter, and when you do harvest work for three whole weeks that is as much strain as you can take. It's now 87 degrees in the shade here. It's only 10:26. *Well,* dear mother, how are all of you? It's tough when you are begrudged writing home. Are my dear grandparents still doing well, and you, dear mother, do you have a comfortable life? What are the dear little ones doing? Have them learn some English. When I buy a small place here, about a hundred acres or morgens, which I plan to do this fall, I won't be visiting you this year but will wait until next year; but I could also visit this fall and settle down when I come back from Germany. I can get good land here for $5 an acre, of course uncultivated, but after a few years the acre is then worth $50–$60. I have enough to buy a small place. I want to live and die in America. Oh mother, if you could come back with me here, I'd like to [——] the days [*rest missing*].[4]

---

[1] A small town near Columbia at the center of Missouri.

[2] The original editors of Büerkert's letters surmise that all these "western" episodes happened only in his imagination.

[3] Little would be harvested in Missouri in the middle of June; Büerkert may be fictionalizing or he may be speaking of hay-making rather than a genuine harvest.

[4] The last surviving letter from Büerkert, written from central Missouri in 1881, claimed that he had bought land and had become an American citizen.

LEE CHEW, CHINA

"The Biography of a Chinaman," *from* the *Independent* (1903)

THE VILLAGE WHERE I WAS BORN IS SITUATED IN THE PROVINCE OF CANTON, ON one of the banks of the Si-Kiang River. It is called a village, altho it is really as big as a city, for there are about five thousand men in it over eighteen years of age—women and children and even youths are not counted in our villages.

All in the village belonged to the tribe of Lee. They did not intermarry with one another, but the men went to other villages for their wives and brought them home to their fathers' houses, and men from other villages—Wus and Wings and Sings and Fongs, etc.—chose wives from among our girls.

When I was a baby I was kept in our house all the time with my mother, but when I was a boy of seven I had to sleep at nights with other boys of the village—about thirty of them in one house. The girls are separated the same way—thirty or forty of them sleeping together in one house away from their parents—and the widows have houses where they work and sleep, tho they go to their fathers' houses to eat.

My father's house is built of fine blue brick, better than the brick in the houses here in the United States. It is only one story high, roofed with red tiles and surrounded by a stone wall which also encloses the yard. There are four rooms in the house, one large living room which serves for a parlor and three private rooms, one occupied by my grandfather, who is very old and very honorable, another by my father and mother, and the third by my oldest brother and his wife and two little children. There are no windows, but the door is left open all day.

All the men of the village have farms, but they don't live on them as the farmers do here; they live in the village, but go out during the daytime and work their farms, coming home before dark. My father has a farm of about ten acres, on which he grows a great abundance of things—sweet potatoes, rice, beans, peas, yams, sugar cane, pineapples, bananas, lychee nuts and palms. The palm leaves are useful and can be sold. Men make fans of the lower part of each leaf near the stem, and waterproof coats and hats, and awnings for boats, of the parts that are left when the fans are cut out.

So many different things can be grown on one small farm, because we bring plenty of water in a canal from the mountains thirty miles away, and every farmer takes as much as he wants for his fields by means of drains. He can give each crop the right amount of water.

Our people all working together make these things, the mandarin[5] has nothing to do with it, and we pay no taxes, except a small one on the land. We have our own government, consisting of the elders of our tribe, the honorable

[5] Local official.

men. When a man gets to be sixty years of age he begins to have honor and to become a leader, and then the older he grows the more he is honored. We had some men who were nearly one hundred years, but very few of them.

In spite of the fact that any man may correct them for a fault, Chinese boys have good times and plenty of play. We played games like tag, and other games like shinny and a sort of football called yin.

We had dogs to play with—plenty of dogs and good dogs—that understand Chinese as well as American dogs understand American language. We hunted with them, and we also went fishing and had as good a time as American boys, perhaps better, as we were almost always together in our house, which was a sort of boys' clubhouse, so we had many playmates. Whatever we did we did all together, and our rivals were the boys of other clubhouses, with whom we sometimes competed in the games. But all our play outdoors was in the daylight, because there were many graveyards about and after dark, so it was said, black ghosts with flaming mouths and eyes and long claws and teeth would come from these and tear to pieces and devour anyone whom they might meet.

It was not all play for us boys, however. We had to go to school, where we learned to read and write and to recite the precepts of Kong-foo-tsze[6] and the other sages and stories about the great emperors of China, who ruled with the wisdom of gods and gave to the whole world the light of high civilization and the culture of our literature, which is the admiration of all nations.

I went to my parents' house for meals, approaching my grandfather with awe, my father and mother with veneration and my elder brother with respect. I never spoke unless spoken to, but I listened and heard much concerning the red-haired, green-eyed foreign devils with the hairy faces, who had lately come out of the sea and clustered on our shores. They were wild and fierce and wicked, and paid no regard to the moral precepts of Kong-foo-tsze and the sages; neither did they worship their ancestors, but pretended to be wiser than their fathers and grandfathers. They loved to beat people and to rob and murder. In the streets of Hong Kong many of them could be seen reeling drunk. Their speech was a savage roar, like the voice of the tiger or the buffalo, and they wanted to take the land away from the Chinese. Their men and women lived together like animals, without any marriage or faithfulness and even were shameless enough to walk the streets arm-in-arm in daylight. So the old men said.

All this was very shocking and disgusting, as our women seldom were on the street, except in the evenings, when they went with the water jars to the three wells that supplied all the people. Then if they met a man they stood still, with their faced turned to the wall, while he looked the other way when he passed them. A man who spoke to a woman in the street in a Chinese village would be beaten, perhaps killed.

My grandfather told how the English foreign devils had made wicked war

[6]I.e., Confucius (ca. 551–479 B.C.), the "philosopher king" whose sayings are recorded in the *Analects*.

on the emperor, and by means of their enchantments and spells had defeated his armies and forced him to admit their opium, so that the Chinese might smoke and become weakened and the foreign devils might rob them of their land.[7]

My grandfather said that it was well known that the Chinese were always the greatest and wisest among men. They had invented and discovered everything that was good. Therefore the things which the foreign devils had and the Chinese had not must be evil. Some of these things were very wonderful, enabling the red-haired savages to talk with one another, tho they might be thousands of miles apart. They had suns that made darkness like day, their ships carried earthquakes and volcanoes to fight for them, and thousands of demons that lived in iron and steel houses spun their cotton and silk, pushed their boats, pulled their cars, printed their newspapers and did other work for them. They were constantly showing disrespect for their ancestors by getting new things to take the place of the old.

I heard about the American foreign devils, that they were false, having made a treaty by which it was agreed that they could freely come to China, and the Chinese as freely go to their country. After this treaty was made China opened its doors to them and then they broke the treaty that they had asked for by shutting the Chinese out of their country.

When I was ten years of age I worked on my father's farm, digging, hoeing, manuring, gathering and carrying the crop. We had no horses, as nobody under the rank of an official is allowed to have a horse in China, and horses do not work on farms there, which is the reason why the roads there are so bad. The people cannot use roads as they are used here, and so they do not make them.

I worked on my father's farm till I was about sixteen years of age, when a man of our tribe came back from America and took ground as large as four city blocks and made a paradise of it. He put a large stone wall around and led some streams through and built a palace and summer house and about twenty other structures, with beautiful bridges over the streams and walks and roads. Trees and flowers, singing birds, water fowl and curious animals were within the walls.

The man had gone away from our village a poor boy. Now he returned with unlimited wealth, which he had obtained in the country of the American wizards. After many amazing adventures he had become a merchant in a city called Mott Street,[8] so it was said.

When his palace and grounds were completed he gave a dinner to all the people who assembled to be his guests. One hundred pigs roasted whole were

[7] In the Opium Wars (1839–42 and 1856–60) the British and, later, other western nations (including France, Russia, and the United States) forced China to allow freer international commercial and cultural activity. One key element concerned opium imports into China, which China had forbidden but which the British in the 1830s had undertaken as a way of balancing British imports of Chinese tea. During the wars, the western powers made broad use of modern armaments, forcing China to submit; British control of Hong Kong dated from the first of these wars.

[8] I.e., in New York City.

served on the tables, with chickens, ducks, geese and such an abundance of dainties that our villagers even now lick their fingers when they think of it. He had the best actors from Hong Kong performing, and every musician for miles around was playing and singing. At night the blaze of the lanterns could be seen for many miles.

Having made his wealth among the barbarians this man had faithfully returned to pour it out among his tribesmen, and he is living in our village now very happy, and a pillar of strength to the poor.

The wealth of this man filled my mind with the idea that I, too, would like to go to the country of the wizards and gain some of their wealth, and after a long time my father consented, and gave me his blessing, and my mother took leave of me with tears, while my grandfather laid his hand upon my head and told me to remember and live up to the admonitions of the sages, to avoid gambling, bad women and men of evil minds, and so to govern my conduct that when I died my ancestors might rejoice to welcome me as a guest on high.

My father gave me $100, and I went to Hong Kong with five other boys from our place and we got steerage passage on a steamer, paying $50 each. Everything was new to me. All my life I had been used to sleeping on a board bed with a wooden pillow, and I found the steamer's bunk very uncomfortable, because it was so soft. The food was different from that which I had been used to, and I did not like it at all. I was afraid of the stews, for the thought of what they might be made of by the wicked wizards of the ship made me ill. Of the great power of these people I saw many signs. The engines that moved the ship were wonderful monsters, strong enough to lift mountains. When I got to San Francisco, which was before the passage of the Exclusion Act,[9] I was half-starved, because I was afraid to eat the provisions of the barbarians, but a few days' living in the Chinese quarter made me happy again. A man got me work as a house servant in an American family, and my start was the same as that of almost all the Chinese in this country.

The Chinese laundryman does not learn his trade in China; there are no laundries in China. The women there do the washing in tubs and have no washboards or flat irons. All the Chinese laundrymen here were taught in the first place by American women, just as I was taught.

When I went to work for that American family I could not speak a word of English, and I did not know anything about housework. The family consisted of husband, wife and two children. They were very good to me and paid me $3.50 a week, of which I could save $3.

I did not know how to do anything, and I did not understand what the lady said to me, but she showed me how to cook, wash, iron, sweep, dust, make

[9]Chinese immigration was facilitated by the Burlingame Treaty of 1868, to which Lee refers earlier, but that treaty did not allow for naturalization of Chinese immigrants, and riots in California against Chinese immigrants in the 1870s led to a renegotiated treaty in 1880 and finally to the Chinese Exclusion Act of 1882, which banned immigration from China to the United States for ten years. Later acts of Congress, some in violation of various treaties, effectively banned further immigration from China until the Immigration Act of 1924 formally closed it.

beds, wash dishes, clean windows, paint and brass, polish the knives and forks, etc., by doing the things herself and then overseeing my efforts to imitate her. She would take my hands and show them how to do things. She and her husband and children laughed at me a great deal, but it was all good-natured. I was not confined to the house in the way servants are confined here, but when my work was done in the morning I was allowed to go out till lunchtime. People in California are more generous than they are here.

In six months I had learned how to do the work of our house quite well, and I was getting $5 a week and board, and putting away about $4.25 a week. I had also learned some English, and by going to a Sunday school I learned more English and something about Jesus, who was a great sage, and whose precepts are like those of Kong-foo-tsze.

It was twenty years ago when I came to this country, and I worked for two years as a servant, getting at the last $35 a month. I sent money home to comfort my parents, but tho I dressed well and lived well and had pleasure, going quite often to the Chinese theater and to dinner parties in Chinatown, I saved $50 in the first six months, $90 in the second, $120 in the third and $150 in the fourth. So I had $410 at the end of two years, and I was now ready to start in business.

When I first opened a laundry it was in company with a partner, who had been in the business for some years. We went to a town about 500 miles inland, where a railroad was building. We got a board shanty and worked for the men employed by the railroads. Our rent cost us $10 a month and food nearly $5 a week each, for all food was dear and we wanted the best of everything—we lived principally on rice, chickens, ducks and pork, and did our own cooking. The Chinese take naturally to cooking. It cost us about $50 for our furniture and apparatus, and we made close upon $60 a week, which we divided between us. We had to put up with many insults and some frauds, as men would come in and claim parcels that did not belong to them, saying they had lost their tickets, and would fight if they did not get what they asked for. Sometimes we were taken before magistrates and fined for losing shirts that we had never seen. On the other hand, we were making money, and even after sending home $3 a week I was able to save about $15. When the railroad construction gang moved on we went with them. The men were rough and prejudiced against us, but not more so than in the big eastern cities. It is only lately in New York that the Chinese have been able to discontinue putting wire screens in front of their windows, and at the present time the street boys are still breaking the windows of Chinese laundries all over the city, while the police seem to think it a joke.

We were three years with the railroad, and then went to the mines, where we made plenty of money in gold dust, but had a hard time, for many of the miners were wild men who carried revolvers and after drinking would come into our place to shoot and steal shirts, for which we had to pay. One of these men hit his head hard against a flat iron and all the miners came and broke up our laundry, chasing us out of town. They were going to hang us. We lost all our property and $365 in money, which members of the mob must have found.

Luckily most of our money was in the hands of Chinese bankers in San Francisco. I drew $500 and went east to Chicago, where I had a laundry for three years, during which I increased my capital to $2,500. After that I was four years in Detroit. I went home to China in 1897, but returned in 1898, and began a laundry business in Buffalo. But [the] Chinese laundry business now is not as good as it was ten years ago. American cheap labor in the steam laundries has hurt it. So I determined to become a general merchant, and with this idea I came to New York and opened a shop in the Chinese quarter, keeping silks, teas, porcelain, clothes, shoes, hats and Chinese provisions, which include sharks' fins and nuts, lily bulbs and lily flowers, lychee nuts and other Chinese dainties, but do not include rats, because it would be too expensive to import them. The rat which is eaten by the Chinese is a field animal which lives on rice, grain and sugar cane. Its flesh is delicious. Many Americans who have tasted shark's fin and bird's nest soup and tiger lily flowers and bulbs are firm friends of Chinese cookery. If they could enjoy one of our fine rats they would go to China to live, so as to get some more.

American people eat groundhogs, which are very like these Chinese rats, and they also eat many sorts of food that our people would not touch. Those that have dined with us know that we understand how to live well.

The ordinary laundry shop is generally divided into three rooms. In front is the room where the customers are received, behind that a bedroom and in the back the workshop, which is also the dining room and kitchen. The stove and cooking utensils are the same as those of the Americans.

Work in a laundry begins early on Monday morning—about seven o'clock. There are generally two men, one of whom washes while the other does the ironing. The man who irons does not start in till Tuesday, as the clothes are not ready for him to begin till that time. So he has Sundays and Mondays as holidays. The man who does the washing finishes up on Friday night, and so he has Saturday and Sunday. Each works only five days a week, but those are long days—from seven o'clock in the morning till midnight.

During his holidays the Chinaman gets a good deal of fun out of life. There's a good deal of gambling and some opium smoking, but not so much as Americans imagine. Only a few of New York's Chinamen smoke opium. The habit is very general among rich men and officials in China, but not so much among poor men. I don't think it does as much harm as the liquor that the Americans drink. There's nothing so bad as a drunken man. Opium doesn't make people crazy.

Gambling is mostly fan-tan,[1] but there is a good deal of poker, which the Chinese have learned from Americans and can play very well. They also gamble with dominoes and dice.

The fights among the Chinese and the operations of the hatchet men are all due to gambling. Newspapers often say that they are feuds between the six

[1] Either a Chinese gambling game played with small objects counted off in groups or a card game also known as "sevens."

companies,[2] but that is a mistake. The six companies are purely benevolent societies, which look after the Chinaman when he first lands here. They represent the six southern provinces of China, where most of our people are from, and they are like the German, Swedish, English, Irish and Italian societies which assist emigrants. When the Chinese keep clear of gambling and opium they are not blackmailed, and they have no trouble with hatchet men or any others.

About five hundred of New York's Chinese are Christians, the others are Buddhists, Taoists, etc., all mixed up. These haven't any Sunday of their own, but keep New Year's Day and the first and fifteenth days of each month, when they go to the temple in Mott Street.

In all New York there are only thirty-four Chinese women, and it is impossible to get a Chinese woman out here unless one goes to China and marries her there, and then he must collect affidavits to prove that she really is his wife. That is in case of a merchant. A laundryman can't bring his wife here under any circumstances, and even the women of the Chinese ambassador's family had trouble getting in lately.

Is it any wonder, therefore, or any proof of the demoralization of our people, if some of the white women in Chinatown are not of good character? What other set of men so isolated and so surrounded by alien and prejudiced people are more moral? Men, wherever they may be, need the society of women, and among the white women of Chinatown are many excellent and faithful wives and mothers.

Recently there has been organized among us the Oriental Club, composed of our most intelligent and influential men. We hope for a great improvement in social conditions by its means, as it will discuss matters that concern us, bring us in closer touch with Americans and speak for us in something like an official manner.

Some fault is found with us for sticking to our old customs here, especially in the matter of clothes, but the reason is that we find American clothes much inferior, so far as comfort and warmth go. The Chinaman's coat for the winter is very durable, very light and very warm. It is easy and not in the way. If he wants to work he slips out of it in a moment and can put it on again as quickly. Our shoes and hats also are better, we think, for our purposes, than the American clothes. Most of us have tried the American clothes, and they make us feel as if we were in the stocks.

I have found out, during my residence in this country, that much of the Chinese prejudice against Americans is unfounded, and I no longer put faith in the wild tales that were told about them in our village, tho some of the Chinese, who have been here twenty years and who are learned men, still believe that there is no marriage in this country, that the land is infested with demons and that all the people are given over to general wickedness.

[2]The "Tongs," Chinese fraternal organizations similar in function, as Lee goes on to say, to societies formed in the United States by other immigrant groups, were subject to rumors and accusations regarding their supposedly illicit purposes.

I know better. Americans are not all bad, nor are they wicked wizards. Still, they have their faults, and their treatment of us is outrageous.

The reason why so many Chinese go into the laundry business in this country is because it requires little capital and is one of the few opportunities that are open. Men of other nationalities who are jealous of the Chinese [immigrant], because he is a more faithful worker than one of their people, have raised such a great outcry about [his] cheap labor that they have shut him out of working on farms or in factories or building railroads or making streets or digging sewers. He cannot practice any trade, and his opportunities to do business are limited to his own countrymen. So he opens a laundry when he quits domestic service.

The treatment of the Chinese in this country is all wrong and mean. It is persisted in merely because China is not a fighting nation. The Americans would not dare to treat Germans, English, Italians or even Japanese as they treat the Chinese, because if they did there would be a war.

There is no reason for the prejudice against the Chinese. The "cheap labor" cry was always a falsehood. Their labor was never cheap, and is not cheap now. It has always commanded the highest market price. But the trouble is that the Chinese are such excellent and faithful workers that bosses will have no others when they can get them. If you look at men working on the street you will find an overseer for every four or five of them. That watching is not necessary for Chinese. They work as well when left to themselves as they do when someone is looking at them.

It was the jealousy of laboring men of other nationalities—especially the Irish—that raised all the outcry against the Chinese. No one would hire an Irishman, German, Englishman or Italian when he could get a Chinese, because our countrymen are so much more honest, industrious, steady, sober and painstaking. Chinese were persecuted, not for their vices, but for their virtues. There never was any honesty in the pretended fear of leprosy or in the cheap-labor scare, and the persecution continues still, because Americans make a mere practice of loving justice. They are all for money-making, and they want to be on the strongest side always. They treat you as a friend while you are prosperous, but if you have a misfortune they don't know you. There is nothing substantial in their friendship.

Wu T'ing-fang[3] talked very plainly to Americans about their ill treatment of our countrymen, but we don't see any good results. We hoped for good from Roosevelt, we thought him a brave and good man, but yet he has continued the exclusion of our countrymen, tho all other nations are allowed to pour in here—Irish, Italians, Jews, Poles, Greeks, Hungarians, etc. It would not have been so if Mr. McKinley had lived.

[The] Irish fill the almshouses and prisons and orphan asylums, Italians are among the most dangerous of men, Jews are unclean and ignorant. Yet they

---

[3]Wu T'ing-fang (1842–1922), trained in the law in England, was Chinese minister to the United States, 1897–1902 and 1908–9.

are all let in, while [the] Chinese, who are sober, or duly law-abiding, clean, educated and industrious, are shut out. There are few Chinamen in jails and none in the poor houses. There are no Chinese tramps or drunkards. Many Chinese here have become sincere Christians, in spite of the persecution which they have to endure from their heathen countrymen. More than half the Chinese in this country would become citizens if allowed to do so, and would be patriotic Americans. But how can they make this country their home as matters now are! They are not allowed to bring wives here from China, and if they marry American women there is a great outcry.

All congressmen acknowledge the injustice of the treatment of my people, yet they continue it. They have no backbone.

Under the circumstances, how can I call this my home, and how can any one blame me if I take my money and go back to my village in China?

WILHELMINE WIEBUSCH, GERMANY

Letters to Marie Kallmeyer (1884–86)

Brooklyn, September 12, 1884

MY DEAR MARIE,

A long, long time ago it was that we left Hamburg, and in this time you, dear Marie, have often been expecting a letter from me. You mustn't be angry that I am only now writing, because in a foreign country you have all sorts of things to think about at the beginning. Oh, if only we could sit together for a while, then I could tell you many a little tale of adventure. . . .

There we were in the land of milk and honey, then we stayed in a German hotel with several others we got to know on the ship, and during this time we got to see a bit of New York. The first day it rained so badly we couldn't do anything, the second day we went to find Anna's relatives, and after four hours of asking around everywhere in our elegant English we finally found the way. Dear Marie, you really ought to see New York, when you get your Sunday off, come on over for awhile. The city must be three times as big as Hamburg; the most beautiful and main street, Broadway, is more than six hours long, with about three hundred side streets to the right and left and many many more streets, so you can't go on foot much, everything's so spread out, so you simply take the car or railroad which runs in almost every street, way up high, as high as the second floor of the houses. Crossing the street is positively dangerous, one wagon after the next, so loud you can't hear yourself talk, business and money everywhere. On August 8 we had the dumb luck of both getting a job together in a very fine private house in Brooklyn. This town is only separated from New York by water, you can go across in five minutes with the ferry, and most of the quality folks who have their business in New York live here, since Brooklyn is much prettier and the air is much healthier. Anna is the scullery maid and I'm the cook, we each get $12 a month (50 marks)—what do you think, dear Marie, don't you have the slightest desire to come to Kamerika?

There's more work, of course, since the Americans live very lavishly, they eat three hot meals a day, and then we have to do all the laundry in the house, since it's so awfully expensive to send it out. We even have to iron the shirts and cuffs; here you have to understand everything. We do our best, but we can do things when we want. The *Ladys* don't pay much attention to the household, they don't do anything but dress up themselves three or four times a day and go out. The family is remarkably friendly, there are eight persons all together, Mr. and Mrs. Moses, three grown-up beautiful daughters and three good-looking boys.[4] The *Lady* herself speaks broken German, we can make ourselves understood quite well with her; the others want to learn it too, they like German a lot. You should just hear us speaking English, we just rattle off what we hear, whether it's right or not, [so that] the *Lady* says sometimes she almost dies laughing at us.

Our house consists of a ground floor and three more stories, but they don't do all that much scrubbing and cleaning here. The rooms are like a Chinese doll house, they're all covered with rugs and carpets; it's not fashionable to have white lace curtains in the windows here; the best thing is the beds, they are big and wide. Because of the heat, they're only made up of a mattress, [a] pillow and two sheets. At the moment it is very hot here, [so] the ladies all wear real thin muslin dresses. Anna and I sometimes work up quite a sweat; we only wear a shirt and a dress and would like to take that off too. I have no complaints about the Americans, they are very friendly, gallant people, but I don't like the Germans here very much, they are all a bunch of snobs, [they] act like they can't understand German anymore, act like they know nothing about their old homeland any more, but we won't forget, since even if it is nice in a foreign country, it'll never be home. . . .

There's still lots and lots to write you about, dear Marie, but another time, because for today it is (*time to go to bed. I am wery tired. it is a quarter past one*)—translate that into German, and then write back soon how you are (do you have a little bit of news about your sweetheart?) and a lot about Hamburg. I miss my wonderful *Novellen Zeitung*[5] here a lot, I would really like to have it forwarded if it weren't so much trouble. I'd send you the money if you could arrange it for me.

Now, farewell dear Marie, warmest regards from the faraway west Anni and Meini. My address is Wilhelmine Wiebusch, *care. of.* Mr Leionel Moses, 751 Union Street, Brooklyn, New York.

Please write and tell me when you get this letter. Oh blast it, I forgot to tell you what wonderful fruit there is in Kamerika, every day we eat peaches,

---

[4]The Jewish family for which Wilhelmine worked consisted of merchant Lionel Moses, 59, his wife Silvia, 46, and six children ranging in age from 14 to 26.
[5]A German newspaper.

melons and bananas. And then I also wanted to tell you if you have an old shoe or boot, don't throw it away, tie a red or blue bow on it and hang it on the wall in your room. You may think I'm crazy, but you ought to know, dear Marie, that here in America, that's what they call an antique.

I. put this Letter in the Letterbax, hve you undrstand Mary? You see i speak wery well Englisch, i belive it is anough.

I'll give you another little idea of how it is sometimes when we talk. This evening at dinner Mr. Moses said to Anna, *plase give me some breat (bitte geben Sie mir ein wenig Brot)* and Anna understood *smal plaid* [small plate] *(kleine Teller)* and came back with an empty plate, [so] of course everyone laughed, that kind of thing happens to us a lot, but they don't take it badly, it's all right. Anna pulls a lot of such silly tricks. One time she wanted to go the drug store and get some chlorine, so she goes into the first drug store that comes along and says *speak you Germain (sprechen Sie Deutsch), no (nein), na den geben Sie mir für 10 ct. Chlorkalk, i do not undrstand you (ich verstehe Sie nicht)*, well then forget it, you dummy, and so she went to four different drug stores and finally she got so lost that the police had to bring her home.

I can't find the Fritz Stellen you told me about since there's no town hall here, for we live here like wild folks here in the land of freedom—we haven't needed any papers yet, no one has asked us about our names and origin.[6]

But that's enough for now. If there's anything else you want to know about, just ask what you want to know and then I'll write and tell you what you want to know.
Now the American post office is closing.
Good night, to be continued.

New York, February 19, 1886

My dear Marie,
.... Over here on the other side of the *Ocean*, I, too, cannot complain of being sad, I am just fine. I like being here in New York, am healthy, and what more do I want? My employer's family has also just returned from Mexico (that's caused a bit more turmoil in the household) and the *Lady* has already begged me several times to go there with her next year after all, but I can't make any promises: who knows what all will happen by next winter, and I'm a bit afraid of Mexico too, because there are still too many Indians living there. I won't tell you about my big Christmas, though, since you'd laugh at me, since it wasn't anything compared to yours. But I did trim a Christmas tree for us on Christmas eve, invited various friends, and of course made sure we had a delicious drop of wine, and so we amused ourselves in quite the German manner.

I also went to another ball recently, and I've been to the theater twice, the first time to the German Talia Theater, [where] they did *The Merry Wives of Windsor*. The other time I went to the biggest opera house in New York,

---

[6]Wilhelmine refers to the stricter rules governing domestic servants in Hamburg.

[where] they put on the marvelous opera *Rienzi, the Last of the Tribunes.*[7] I had a wonderful time that evening, it was worth it just to see the American ladies in the first and second balconies. How they glittered in their red, white, blue and so on silk dresses with matching feathers in their hair, so you're almost blinded by the sight. . . . My page is full and my time is up, please forgive me for not writing more this time. Waiting for an answer soon, I remain with lots of love and kisses, your

Minnie

[November 26, 1886]

My dear Marie,

What is the matter with you! Can't you write, or is it my fault? An eternity has already passed by since we last heard anything of one another. And now once again I have be the first to write. How are you, you dear old soul, hopefully just fine; how did you spend the lovely summer, did you have a good time at the side of your loved one? I am still waiting in vain for your picture, didn't you have one made yet? Or didn't it make it over here?

So when are you going to get married? Or are you already? But then you surely would have let me know. I'm just writing off into the blue, I don't even know if your address is the same, but I hope these lines will reach you properly. As far as I am concerned, I am still doing very well in a foreign land, I am healthy, round and plump, have to work hard sometimes, but like to eat a lot. Today, for example, I almost overloaded my stomach, for today is a holiday here, the so-called Thanksgiving Day. Then both rich and poor have a big dinner, every table is resplendent with a turkey and every kind of vegetable there is, and afterward there's a big English plum pudding, and then [you] enjoy your meal, dig in all you want, and afterward we give thanks that it all tasted so good. . . .

My friend Anna was here yesterday, the two of us still stick together through good times and bad. This summer we both had a hard time, we were far apart from one another, [but] we've also made many new friends and feel just as much at home as in Hamburg. Sometimes we do have moments of longing to be back in our northern homeland, but they disappear again as fast as they appear, for the ocean lies in the way. On December 16 we are both invited to a ball, hurrah! Then we'll get to dance again and have a swig from the bottle as well; we're looking forward to it very much, since there aren't many such amusements here, because there aren't any public dance halls here. You spend your time with friends and entertain yourself as best you can. The girls have a lot more days off than over there, every other Sunday, and if there are three or four girls, two have the same day off, and then you get another day during the week when you can leave after breakfast. I am still here with two

---

[7] The "Thalia-Theater," a German-language theater in New York, emphasized operettas and musical productions. *The Merry Wives of Windsor* may have been either a German version of the Shakespeare play or the 1849 German opera; the other production probably was Richard Wagner's *Rienzi* (1842), based on the Bulwer-Lytton novel of 1835.

other girls, one is Irish and the other one comes from Wales, very nice girls. You meet people from all different countries here, there are all kinds of blacks, including some very good-looking guys. The Chinese all have laundries. The little people with their long pigtails look very funny; a Chinaman also taught me how to iron shirts, [and] we had a good time laughing then since their English is so bad it is hard to understand them. It doesn't matter to me, I already speak English as well as German.

Dear Marie, the beautiful Christmas season is almost at the door, you should be happy since the wonderful presents you get aren't like the ones over here. Here they don't give many presents at Christmas, you have to work just like on any other day. Anna and I want to put up our own tree again this year. . . .

I still have a lot of questions to ask you, dear Migge, but that would be too boring for you. I hope I'll get a sign of life from you soon and that you write me lots of news, do you hear! Yes! I'd also like to keep on chatting with you, but I don't have much more news and it is already getting late.

Some time ago we had a big parade here; all the military in the United States was gathered in New York, they dedicated the Queen of Freedom, it's this big *Statute*, a present from the French to America.[8]

This time I can also give you my proper address, since I like it very much here and hope to stay for quite a while.

But good night for now, you dearest child of mine, sleep well! All love and thousands of kisses from your friend.

ROCCO CORRESCA, ITALY

"The Biography of a Bootblack," *from* the *Independent* (1902)

WHEN I WAS A VERY SMALL BOY, I LIVED IN ITALY IN A LARGE HOUSE WITH MANY other small boys, who were all dressed alike and were taken care of by some nuns. It was a good place, situated on the side of the mountain, where grapes were growing and melons and oranges and plums.

They taught us our letters and how to pray and say the catechism, and we worked in the fields during the middle of the day. We always had enough to eat and good beds to sleep in at night, and sometimes there were feast days, when we marched about wearing flowers.

Those were good times and they lasted till I was nearly eight years of age. Then an old man came and said he was my grandfather. He showed some papers and cried over me and said that the money had come at last and now he could take me to his beautiful home. He seemed very glad to see me and

---

[8] The Statue of Liberty, a gift from the French, was dedicated about a month prior to the date of the letter.

after they looked at his papers he took me away and we went to the big city—Naples. He kept talking about his beautiful house, but when we got there it was a dark cellar that he lived in and I did not like it at all. Very rich people were on the first floor. They had carriages and servants and music and plenty of good things to eat, but we were down below in the cellar and had nothing. There were four other boys in the cellar and the old man said they were all my brothers. All were larger than I and they beat me at first till one day Francisco said that they should not beat me any more, and then Paulo, who was the largest of all, fought him till Francisco drew a knife and gave him a cut. Then Paulo, too, got a knife and said that he would kill Francisco, but the old man knocked them both down with a stick and took their knives away and gave them beatings.

Each morning we boys all went out to beg and we begged all day near the churches and at night near the theatres, running to the carriages and opening the doors and then getting in the way of the people so that they had to give us money or walk over us. The old man often watched us and at night he took all the money, except when we could hide something.

We played tricks on the people, for when we saw some coming that we thought were rich I began to cry and covered my face and stood on one foot, and the others gathered around me and said:

"Don't cry! Don't cry!"

Then the ladies would stop and ask: "What is he crying about? What is the matter, little boy?"

Francisco or Paulo would answer: "He is very sad because his mother is dead and they have laid her in the grave."

Then the ladies would give me money and the others would take most of it from me.

The old man told us to follow the Americans and the English people, as they were all rich, and if we annoyed them enough they would give us plenty of money. He taught us that if a young man was walking with a young woman he would always give us silver because he would be ashamed to let the young woman see him give us less. There was also a great church where sick people were cured by the saints, and when they came out they were so glad that they gave us money.

Begging was not bad in the summer time because we went all over the streets and there was plenty to see, and if we got much money we could spend some buying things to eat. The old man knew we did that. He used to feel us and smell us to see if we had eaten anything, and he often beat us for eating when we had not eaten.

Early in the morning we had breakfast of black bread rubbed over with garlic or with a herring to give it a flavor. The old man would eat the garlic or the herring himself, but he would rub our bread with it, which he said was as good. He told us that boys should not be greedy and that it was good to fast and that all the saints had fasted. He had a figure of a saint in one corner of the cellar and prayed night and morning that the saint would help him to get money. He made us pray, too, for he said that it was good luck to be religious.

We used to sleep on the floor, but often we could not sleep much because men came in very late at night and played cards with the old man. He sold them wine from a barrel that stood on one end of the table that was there, and if they drank much he won their money. One night he won so much that he was glad and promised the saint some candles for his altar in the church. But that was to get more money. Two nights after that the same men who had lost the money came back and said that they wanted to play again. They were very friendly and laughing, but they won all the money and the old man said they were cheating. So they beat him and went away. When he got up again he took a stick and knocked down the saint's figure and said that he would give no more candles.

I was with the old man for three years. I don't believe that he was my grandfather, tho he must have known something about me because he had those papers.

It was very hard in the winter time for we had no shoes and we shivered a great deal. The old man said that we were no good, that we were ruining him, that we did not bring in enough money. He told me that I was fat and that people would not give money to fat beggars. He beat me, too, because I didn't like to steal, as I had heard it was wrong.

"Ah!" said he, "that is what they taught you at that place, is it? To disobey your grandfather that fought with Garibaldi![9] That is a fine religion!"

The others all stole as well as begged, but I didn't like it and Francisco didn't like it either.

Then the old man said to me: "If you don't want to be a thief you can be a cripple. That is an easy life and they make a great deal of money."

I was frightened then, and that night I heard him talking to one of the men that came to see him. He asked how much he would charge to make me a good cripple like those that crawl about the church. They had a dispute, but at last they agreed and the man said that I should be made so that people would shudder and give me plenty of money.

I was much frightened, but I did not make a sound and in the morning I went out to beg with Francisco. I said to him: "I am going to run away. I don't believe 'Tony is my grandfather. I don't believe that he fought for Garibaldi, and I don't want to be a cripple, no matter how much money the people may give."

"Where will you go?" Francisco asked me.

"I don't know," I said; "somewhere."

He thought awhile and then he said: "I will go, too."

So we ran away out of the city and begged from the country people as we went along. We came to a village down by the sea and a long way from Naples and there we found some fishermen and they took us aboard their boat. We

---

[9] Giuseppe Garibaldi (1807–1882), Italian patriot, fought many battles to liberate and unify Italy. He became an American citizen after fleeing Italy in 1849, but returned home five years later.

were with them five years, and tho it was a very hard life we liked it well because there was always plenty to eat. Fish do not keep long and those that we did not sell we ate.

The chief fisherman, whose name was Ciguciano, had a daughter, Teresa, who was very beautiful, and tho she was two years younger than I, she could cook and keep house quite well. She was a kind, good girl and he was a good man. When we told him about the old man who told us he was our grandfather the fisherman said he was an old rascal who should be in prison for life. Teresa cried much when she heard that he was going to make me a cripple. Ciguciano said that all the old man had taught us was wrong—that it was bad to beg, to steal and to tell lies. He called in the priest and the priest said the same thing and was very angry at the old man in Naples, and he taught us to read and write in the evenings. He also taught us our duties to the church and said that the saints were good and would only help men to do good things, and that it was a wonder that lightning from heaven had not struck the old man dead when he knocked down the saint's figure.

We grew large and strong with the fisherman and he told us that we were getting too big for him, that he could not afford to pay us the money that we were worth. He was a fine, honest man—one in a thousand.

Now and then I had heard things about America—that it was a far-off country where everybody was rich and that Italians went there and made plenty of money, so that they could return to Italy and live in pleasure ever after. One day I met a young man who pulled out a handful of gold and told me he had made that in America in a few days.

I said I should like to go there, and he told me that if I went he would take care of me and see that I was safe. I told Francisco and he wanted to go, too. So we said goodbye to our good friends. Teresa cried and kissed us both and the priest came and shook our hands and told us to be good men, and that no matter where we went God and his saints were always near us and that if we lived well we should all meet again in heaven. We cried, too, for it was our home, that place. Ciguciano gave us money and slapped us on the back and said that we should be great. But he felt bad, too, at seeing us go away after all that time.

The young man took us to a big ship and got us work away down where the fires are. We had to carry coal to the place where it could be thrown on the fires. Francisco and I were very sick from the great heat at first and lay on the coal for a long time, but they threw water on us and made us get up. We could not stand on our feet well, for everything was going around and we had no strength. We said that we wished we had stayed in Italy no matter how much gold there was in America. We could not eat for three days and could not do much work. Then we got better and sometimes we went up above and looked about. There was no land anywhere and we were much surprised. How could the people tell where to go when there was no land to steer by?

We were so long on the water that we began to think we should never get to America or that, perhaps, there was not any such place, but at last we saw land and came up to New York.

We were glad to get over without giving money, but I have heard since that we should have been paid for our work among the coal and that the young man who had sent us got money for it. We were all landed on an island[1] and the bosses there said that Francisco and I must go back because we had not enough money, but a man named Bartolo came up and told them that we were brothers and he was our uncle and would take care of us. He brought two other men who swore that they knew us in Italy and that Bartolo was our uncle. I had never seen any of them before, but even then Bartolo might be my uncle, so I did not say anything. The bosses of the island let us go out with Bartolo after he had made the oath.

We came to Brooklyn to a wooden house in Adams Street that was full of Italians from Naples. Bartolo had a room on the third floor and there were fifteen men in the room, all boarding with Bartolo. He did the cooking on a stove in the middle of the room and there were beds all around the sides, one bed above another. It was very hot in the room, but we were soon asleep, for we were very tired.

The next morning, early, Bartolo told us to go out and pick rags and get bottles. He gave us bags and hooks and showed us the ash barrels. On the streets where the fine houses are the people are very careless and put out good things, like mattresses and umbrellas, clothes, hats and boots. We brought all these to Bartolo and he made them new again and sold them on the sidewalk; but mostly we brought rags and bones. The rags we had to wash in the backyard and then we hung them to dry on lines under the ceiling in our room. The bones we kept under the beds till Barolo could find a man to buy them.

Most of the men in our room worked at digging the sewer. Bartolo got them the work and they paid him about one quarter of their wages. Then he charged them for board and he bought the clothes for them, too. So they got little money after all.

Bartolo was always saying that the rent of the room was so high that he could not make anything, but he was really making plenty. He was what they call a padrone and is now a very rich man. The men that were living with him had just come to the country and could not speak English. They had all been sent by the young man we met in Italy. Bartolo told us all that we must work for him and that if we did not the police would come and put us in prison.

He gave us very little money, and our clothes were some of those that were found on the street. Still we had enough to eat and we had meat quite often, which we never had in Italy. Bartolo got it from the butcher—the meat that he could not sell to other people—but it was quite good meat. Bartolo cooked it in the pan while we all sat on our beds in the evening. Then he cut it into small bits and passed the pan around, saying:

[1] Ellis Island.

"See what I do for you and yet you are not glad. I am too kind a man, that is why I am so poor."

We were with Bartolo nearly a year, but some of our countrymen who had been in the place a long time said that Bartolo had no right to us and we could get work for $1.50 a day, which, when you make it *lire* (reckoned in the Italian currency) is very much. So we went away one day to Newark and got work on the street. Bartolo came after us and made a great noise, but the boss said that if he did not go away soon the police would have him. Then he went, saying that there was no justice in this country.

We paid a man $5 dollars each for getting us the work and we were with that boss for six months. He was Irish, but a good man and he gave us our money every Saturday night. We lived much better than with Bartolo, and when the work was done we each had nearly $200 saved. Plenty of the men spoke English and they taught us, and we taught them to read and write. That was at night, for we had a lamp in our room, and there were only five other men who lived in that room with us.

We got up at half-past five o'clock every morning and made coffee on the stove and had a breakfast of bread and cheese, onions, garlic and red herrings. We went to work at seven o'clock and in the middle of the day we had soup and bread in a place where we got it for 2¢ a plate. In the evenings we had a good dinner with meat of some kind and potatoes. We got from the butcher the meat that other people would not buy because they said it was old, but they don't know what is good. We paid 4 or 5¢ a pound for it and it was the best, tho I have heard of people paying 16¢ a pound.

When the Newark boss told us that there was no more work Francisco and I talked about what we would do and we went back to Brooklyn to a saloon near Hamilton Ferry,[2] where we got a job cleaning it out and slept in a little room upstairs. There was a bootblack named Michael on the corner and when I had time I helped him and learned the business. Francisco cooked the lunch in the saloon and he, too, worked for the bootblack and we were soon able to make the best polish.

Then we thought we would go into business and we got a basement on Hamilton Avenue, near the ferry, and put four chairs in it. We paid $75 for the chairs and all the other things. We had tables and looking glasses there and curtains. We took the papers that have the pictures in and made the place high-toned. Outside we had a big sign that said:

THE BEST SHINE FOR TEN CENTS

Men that did not want to pay 10¢ could get a good shine for 5¢, but it was not an oil shine. We had two boys helping us and paid each of them 50¢ a day.

---

[2] A ferry between the Battery on Manhattan and a dock at the end of Hamilton Avenue, Brooklyn (south of the dock used by the "South Ferry" or "Brooklyn Ferry," mentioned below).

The rent of the place was $20 a month, so the expenses were very great, but we made money from the beginning. We slept in the basement, but got our meals in the saloon till we could put a stove in our place, and then Francisco cooked for us all. That would not do, tho, because some of our customers said that they did not like to smell garlic and onions and red herrings. I thought that was strange, but we had to do what the customers said. So we got the woman who lived upstairs to give us our meals and paid her $1.50 a week each. She gave the boys soup in the middle of the day—5¢ for two plates.

We remembered the priest, the friend of Ciguciano, and what he had said to us about religion, and as soon as we came to the country, we began to go to the Italian church. The priest we found here was a good man, but he asked the people for money for the church. The Italians did not like to give because they said it looked like buying religion. The priest says it is different here from Italy because all the churches there are what they call endowed, while here all they have is what the people give. Of course I and Francisco understand that, but the Italians who cannot read and write shake their heads and say that it is wrong for a priest to want money.

We had said that when we saved $1,000 each we would go back to Italy and buy a farm, but now that the time is coming we are so busy and making so much money that we think we will stay. We have opened another parlor near South Ferry, in New York. We have to pay $30 a month rent, but the business is very good. The boys in the place charge 60¢ a day because there is so much work.

At first we did not know much of this country, but by and by we learned. There are here plenty of Protestants who are heretics, but they have a religion, too. Many of the finest churches are Protestant, but they have no saints and no altars, which seems strange.

These people are without a king such as ours in Italy. It is what they call a republic, as Garibaldi wanted, and every year in the fall the people vote. They wanted us to vote last fall, but we did not. A man came and said that he would get us made Americans for 50¢ and then we could get $2 for our votes. I talked to some of our people and they told me that we should have to put a paper in a box telling who we wanted to govern us.

I went with five men to the court and when they asked me how long I had been in the country I told them two years. Afterward my countrymen said I was a fool and would never learn politics. "You should have said you were five years here and then we would swear to it," was what they told me.

There are two kinds of people that vote here, Republicans and Democrats. I went to a Republican meeting and the man said that the Republicans want a republic and the Democrats are against it. He said that Democrats are for a king whose name is Bryan and who is an Irishman. There are some good Irishmen, but many of them insult Italians. They call us dagoes. So I will be a Republican.

I like this country now and I don't see why we should have a king. Garibaldi didn't want a king and he was the greatest man that ever lived.

I and Francisco are to be Americans in three years. The court gave us papers and said we must wait and we must be able to read some things and tell who the ruler of the country is.

There are plenty of rich Italians here, men who a few years ago had nothing and now have so much money that they could not count all their dollars in a week. The richest ones go away from the other Italians and live with the Americans.

We have joined a club and have much pleasure in the evenings. The club has rooms down in Sackett Street and we meet many people and are learning new things all the time. We were very ignorant when we came here, but now we have learned much.

On Sundays we get a horse and carriage from the grocer and go down to Coney Island. We go to the theatres often and other evenings we go to the houses of our friends and play cards.

I am nineteen years of age now and have $700 saved. Francisco is twenty-one and has about $900. We shall open some more parlors soon. I know an Italian who was a bootblack ten years ago and now bosses bootblacks all over the city, who has so much money that if it was turned into gold it would weigh more than himself.

Francisco and I have a room to ourselves now and some people call us "swells." Ciguciano said that we should be great men. Francisco bought a gold watch with a gold chain as thick as his thumb. He is a very handsome fellow and I think he likes a young lady that he met at a picnic out at Ridgewood.[3]

I often think of Ciguciano and Teresa. He is a good man, one in a thousand, and she was very beautiful. Maybe I shall write to them about coming to this country.

---

[3] A then-fashionable section of Brooklyn near the boundary with Queens.

15

THE CITY AT NIGHT

BORN IN RIBE, DENMARK, IN 1849, CARPENTER'S APPRENTICE JACOB RIIS arrived in New York on the steamer *Iowa* in 1870 with the usual misconceptions. So convinced was he of the violence of American life—a Danish immigrant who returned home from California had loaded him with stories on the subject—that he spent much of his remaining cash to purchase "a navy revolver of the largest size," which he strapped on the outside of his coat and wore for all to see as he "strode up Broadway." He soon discovered his particular error (a friendly policeman tapped the gun with his nightstick and advised Riis to leave it home lest someone steal it), as well as the larger lesson about his own flawed ideas: "America was America to us. We knew no distinction of West and East. By rights there ought to have been buffaloes and red Indians charging up and down Broadway." An attentive student of urban life, Riis eventually saw New York for what it was: an enormous, complex, sophisticated city, but so overpopulated that it never was able to catch up with its own growth or provide all its residents what they needed. Before coming to this insight, however, Riis himself experienced some of the same conditions firsthand as he wandered aimlessly about the countryside. A brief period of work in a mill town near Pittsburgh was interrupted by the coming of the Franco-Prussian War. Riis, infected with Denmark's dislike of its Prussian neighbor, tried his best to enlist in some company of Frenchmen going back for the fray. He wound up instead as a tramp, drifting for several years all over the Northeast in genuine poverty, an experience that was to inform his zeal for reform and deepen his sympathy for others.

In 1874, back in New York, Riis began to work for and soon purchased a small Brooklyn paper. Three years later, he was hired as a reporter for the New York *Tribune*, Horace Greeley's old reformist paper, and then for the *Evening Sun*. His ultimate beat was the activity of the city's police. From his office in a satellite press bureau located across from police headquarters on Mulberry Street, in the heart of the immigrant district he already knew well, Riis surveyed more systematically the living conditions there. His reporting on crime, and the cultural context in which it occurred, soon made him famous, and his proposals for upgrading urban conditions—through improved housing, parks, and neighborhoods—placed him in the vanguard of the "muckrakers" of a slightly later era. He attracted the attention of the man who later would name the muckrakers, Theodore Roosevelt, and during Roosevelt's term as New York police commissioner (1893–95) the two toured the slums together in search of solutions to social ills.

Roosevelt was attracted to Riis in part because of that man's important 1890 book, *How the Other Half Lives*, in which the plight of the immigrant poor in New York was graphically described and pictured. Riis himself favored a rather simplistic self-help approach to solving such social problems, partly because he had pulled himself up from the poverty he had known after first arriving in America. Still, there is no denying the power of this immigrant's accounts of the Americans who had no land or property to fall back on in hard times, and whose material desolation often begat moral degradation as well. Nor were all the lost souls in Riis's writing immigrants who had been radically displaced into this new land. He wrote, too, about the urban blacks, whose displacements were in many ways more severe yet, and about the white "tramps" who were veterans of the Civil War, men whose lives floated on the surface of social change and economic unrest in postwar America.

Riis thought many of the problems could be solved or at least assuaged by a dose of private property; for instance, he found the tenement houses of New York appalling, since they left the individual no individuality. This environmentalist view, while it avoided the old tendency to blame the poor for their poverty, was weakened by Riis's habit of caricaturing members of various ethnic or racial groups, which he always viewed as in competition for the scarce commodities all the poor needed if they were to thrive. In the selections from *How the Other Half Lives* printed here, his descriptions of cheap taverns and lodging houses play on the ethnic theme, but they also emphasize the role of material conditions in producing such distressed and distressing lives. A more complex analysis might have emerged from his observations if only he had had the persistence, and the honesty, to call it forth; his writing survives, however, precisely because what he saw and reported was never explained by his too-pat answers. His vision of urban America at the end of the nineteenth century remains one of the most powerful in its ability to capture the rich, raucous diversity of a land bursting with people and their stories. Riis's own story, *The Making of an American* (1901), hopeful and a bit naïve in its interpretation of his success, nevertheless is also notable for opening up a place in public print for immigrant narrative as a form. Whereas the great majority of well-known American autobiographies theretofore concerned native-born men and women (even the Franco-American writer Crèvecoeur, who first described America as a "melting pot" a hundred years earlier, masked his own story as an immigrant inside that of a native-born American farmer), Riis's emphasis on the process by which an American was *made* sounded an important new note in the culture as a whole.

JACOB RIIS

from **How the Other Half Lives** (1890)

MIDNIGHT ROLL CALL WAS OVER IN THE ELIZABETH STREET POLICE STATION, BUT the reserves were held under orders.[1] A raid was on foot, but whether on the Chinese fan-tan games,[2] on the opium joints of Mott and Pell Streets, or on dens of even worse character, was a matter of guesswork in the men's room. When the last patrolman had come in from his beat, all doubt was dispelled by the brief order "To the Bend!" The stale-beer dives were the object of the raid. The policemen buckled their belts tighter, and with expressive grunts of disgust took up their march toward Mulberry Street. Past the heathen temples of Mott Street—there was some fun to be gotten out of a raid *there*—they trooped, into "the Bend," sending here and there a belated tramp scurrying in fright toward healthier quarters, and halted at the mouth of one of the hidden alleys. Squads were told off[3] and sent to make a simultaneous descent on all the known tramps' burrows in the block. Led by the sergeant, ours—I went along as a kind of war correspondent—groped its way in a single file through the narrow rift between slimy walls to the tenements in the rear. Twice during our trip we stumbled over tramps, both women, asleep in the passage. They were quietly passed to the rear, receiving sundry prods and punches on the trip, and headed for the station in the grip of a policeman as a sort of advance guard of the coming army. After what seemed half a mile of groping in the dark we emerged finally into the alley proper, where light escaping through the cracks of closed shutters on both sides enabled us to make out the contour of three rickety frame tenements. Snatches of ribald songs and peals of coarse laughter reached us from now this, now that of the unseen burrows.

"School is in," said the sergeant drily as we stumbled down the worn steps of the next cellar-way. A kick of his bootheel sent the door flying into the room.

A room perhaps a dozen feet square, with walls and ceiling that might once have been clean—assuredly the floor had not in the memory of man, if indeed there was other floor than hard-trodden mud—but were now covered with a brown crust that, touched with the end of a club, came off in shuddering showers of crawling bugs, revealing the blacker filth beneath. Grouped about a beer keg that was propped on the wreck of a broken chair, a foul and ragged host of men and women, on boxes, benches, and stools. Tomato-cans filled at the keg were passed from hand to hand. In the center of the group a sallow, wrinkled hag, evidently the ruler of the feast, dealt out the hideous stuff. A pile of copper coins rattled in her apron, the very pennies received with such show-ers of blessings upon the giver that afternoon; the faces of some of the women were familiar enough from the streets as those of beggars forever whining for a

[1] I.e., were not allowed to go off duty.
[2] Played either with small groups of objects or with cards.
[3] I.e., divided.

penny, "to keep a family from starving." Their whine and boisterous hilarity were alike hushed now. In sullen, cowed submission they sat, evidently knowing what to expect. At the first glimpse of the uniform in the open door some in the group, customers with a record probably, had turned their heads away to avoid the searching glance of the officer, while a few, less used to such scenes, stared defiantly.

A single stride took the sergeant into the middle of the room, and with a swinging blow of his club he knocked the faucet out of the keg and the half-filled can from the boss hag's hand. As the contents of both splashed upon the floor, half a dozen of the group made a sudden dash, and with shoulders humped above their heads to shield their skulls against the dreaded locust[4] broke for the door. They had not counted upon the policemen outside. There was a brief struggle, two or three heavy thumps, and the runaways were brought back to where their comrades crouched in dogged silence.

"Thirteen!" called the sergeant, completing his survey. "Take them out. 'Revolvers'[5] all but one. Good for six months on the island, the whole lot." The exception was a young man not much if any over twenty, with a hard look of dissipation on his face. He seemed less unconcerned than the rest, but tried hard to make up for it by putting on the boldest air he could. "Come down early," commented the officer, shoving him along with his stick. "There is need of it. They don't last long at this. That stuff is brewed to kill at long range."

At the head of the cellar steps we encountered a similar procession from farther back in the alley, where still another was forming to take up its march to the station. Out in the street was heard the tramp of the hosts already pursuing that well-trodden path, as with a fresh complement of men we entered the next stale-beer alley. There were four dives in one cellar here. The filth and the stench were utterly unbearable; even the sergeant turned his back and fled after scattering the crowd with his club and starting them toward the door. The very dog in the alley preferred the cold flags[6] for a berth to the stifling cellar. We found it lying outside. Seventy-five tramps, male and female, were arrested in the four small rooms. In one of them, where the air seemed thick enough to cut with a knife, we found a woman, a mother with a new-born babe on a heap of dirty straw. She was asleep and was left until an ambulance could be called to take her to the hospital.

Returning to the station with this batch, we found every window in the building thrown open to the cold October wind, and the men from the sergeant down smoking the strongest cigars that could be obtained by way of disinfecting the place. Two hundred and seventy-five tramps had been jammed into the cells to be arraigned next morning in the police court on the charge of vagrancy, with the certain prospect of six months "on the Island." Of the sentence at least they were sure. As to the length of the men's stay the experienced official at the desk was skeptical, it being then within a month of an important

[4]Policeman's club, apparently because it was made from black locust, a hard, durable wood.
[5]Repeat customers—i.e., those who have spent regular periods in jail.
[6]Sidewalk flagstones.

election. If tramps have nothing else to call their own they have votes, and votes that are for sale cheap for cash. About election time this gives them a "pull," at least by proxy. The sergeant observed, as if it were the most natural thing in the world, that he had more than once seen the same tramp sent to Blackwell's Island twice in twenty-four hours for six months at a time.

As a thief never owns to his calling, however devoid of moral scruples, preferring to style himself a speculator, so this real home-product of the slums, the stale-beer dive, is known about "the Bend" by the more dignified name of the two-cent restaurant. Usually, as in this instance, it is in some cellar giving on a back alley. Doctored, unlicensed beer is its chief ware. Sometimes a cup of "coffee" and a stale roll may be had for two cents. The men pay the score. To the women—unutterable horror of the suggestion—the place is free. The beer is collected from the kegs put on the sidewalk by the saloon-keeper to await the brewer's cart, and is touched up with drugs to put a froth on it. The privilege to sit all night on a chair, or sleep on a table, or in a barrel, goes with each round of drinks. Generally an Italian, sometimes a Negro, occasionally a woman, "runs" the dive. Their customers, alike homeless and hopeless in their utter wretchedness, are the professional tramps, and these only. The meanest thief is infinitely above the stale-beer level. Once upon that plane there is no escape. To sink below it is impossible; no one ever rose from it. One night spent in a stale-beer dive is like the traditional putting on of the uniform of the caste, the discarded rags of an old tramp. That stile once crossed, the lane has no longer a turn; and contrary to the proverb,[7] it is usually not long either.

With the gravitation of the Italian tramp-landlord toward the old strong-hold of the African on the West Side,[8] a share of the stale-beer traffic has left "the Bend"; but its headquarters will always remain there, the real home of trampdom, just as Fourteenth Street is its limit. No real tramp crosses that frontier after nightfall and in the daytime only to beg. Repulsive as the business is, its profits to the Italian dive-keeper are considerable; in fact, barring a slight outlay in the ingredients that serve to give "life" to the beer-dregs, it is all profit. The "banker" who curses the Italian colony does not despise taking a hand in it, and such a thing as a stale-beer trust on a Mulberry Street scale may yet be among the possibilities. One of these bankers, who was once known to the police as the keeper of one notorious stale-beer dive and the active backer of others, is today an extensive manufacturer of macaroni, the owner of several big tenements and other real estate, and the capital, it is said, has all come out of his old business. Very likely it is true.

On hot summer nights it is no rare experience when exploring the worst of the tenements in "the Bend" to find the hallways occupied by rows of "sitters," tramps whom laziness or hard luck has prevented from earning enough

---

[7] I.e., "It's a long lane that has no turning."

[8] Elsewhere, Riis reported that New York's Italian immigrants were "overrunning the old Africa of Thompson Street [in Greenwich Village], pushing the Negro rapidly uptown, against querulous but unavailing protests, occupying his home, his church, his trade and all, with merciless impartiality."

by their day's "labor" to pay the admission fee to a stale-beer dive, and who have their reasons for declining the hospitality of the police station lodging-rooms. Huddled together in loathsome files, they squat there overnight, or until an inquisitive policeman breaks up the congregation with his club, which in Mulberry Street has always free swing. At that season the woman tramp predominates. The men, some of them at least, take to the railroad track and to camping out when the nights grow warm, returning in the fall to prey on the city and to recruit their ranks from the lazy, the shiftless, and the unfortunate. Like a foul loadstone, "the Bend" attracts and brings them back, no matter how far they have wandered. For next to idleness the tramp loves rum; next to rum stale beer, its equivalent of the gutter. And the first and last go best together.

As "sitters" they occasionally find a job in the saloons about Chatham and Pearl Streets on cold winter nights, when the hallway is not practicable, that enables them to pick up a charity drink now and then and a bite of an infrequent sandwich. The barkeeper permits them to sit about the stove and by shivering invite the sympathy of transient customers. The dodge works well, especially about Christmas and election time, and the sitters are able to keep comfortably filled up to the advantage of their host. But to look thoroughly miserable they must keep awake. A tramp placidly dozing at the fire would not be an object of sympathy. To make sure that they do keep awake, the wily bartender makes them sit constantly swinging one foot like the pendulum of a clock. When it stops the slothful "sitter" is roused with a kick and "fired out." It is said by those who profess to know that habit has come to the rescue of oversleepy tramps and that the old rounders can swing hand or foot in their sleep without betraying themselves. In some saloons "sitters" are let in at these seasons in fresh batches every hour.

On one of my visits to "the Bend" I came across a particularly ragged and disreputable tramp, who sat smoking his pipe on the rung of a ladder with such evident philosophic contentment in the busy labor of a score of rag-pickers all about him, that I bade him sit for a picture, offering him ten cents for the job. He accepted the offer with hardly a nod, and sat patiently watching me from his perch until I got ready for work. Then he took the pipe out of his mouth and put it in his pocket, calmly declaring that it was not included in the contract, and that it was worth a quarter to have it go in the picture. The pipe, by the way, was of clay, and of the two-for-a-cent kind. But I had to give in. The man, scarce ten seconds employed at honest labor, even at sitting down, at which he was an undoubted expert, had gone on strike. He knew his rights and the value of "work," and was not to be cheated out of either.

Whence these tramps, and why the tramping? are questions oftener asked than answered. Ill-applied charity and idleness answer the first query. They are the whence, and to a large extent the why also. Once started on the career of a tramp, the man keeps to it because it is the laziest. Tramps and toughs profess the same doctrine, that the world owes them a living, but from standpoints that tend in different directions. The tough does not become a tramp, save in rare instances, when old and broken down. Even then usually he is otherwise disposed of. The devil has various ways of taking care of his own. Nor is the tramps' army recruited from any certain class. All occupations and most grades of society yield to it their contingent of idleness. Occasionally, from one cause or another, a recruit of a better stamp is forced into the ranks; but the first acceptance of alms puts a brand on the able-bodied man which his moral nature rarely holds out to efface. He seldom recovers his lost caste. The evolution is gradual, keeping step with the increasing shabbiness of his clothes and corresponding loss of self-respect, until he reaches the bottom in "the Bend."

Of the tough, the tramp doctrine that the world owes him a living makes a thief; of the tramp, a coward. Numbers only make him bold unless he has to do with defenseless women. In the city the policemen keep him straight enough. The women rob an occasional clothesline when no one is looking, or steal the pail and scrubbing-brush with which they are set to clean up in the station-house lodging-rooms after their night's sleep. At the police station the roads of the tramp and the tough again converge. In midwinter, on the coldest nights, the sanitary police[9] corral the tramps here and in their lodging-houses and vaccinate them, despite their struggles and many oaths that they have recently been "scraped."[1] The station-house is the sieve that sifts out the chaff from the wheat, if there be any wheat there. A man goes from his first night's sleep on the hard slab of a police station lodging-room to a deck-hand's berth on an outgoing steamer, to the recruiting office, to any work that is honest, or he goes "to the devil or the dives, same thing," says my friend, the sergeant, who knows.

When it comes to the question of numbers with this tramps' army, another factor of serious portent has to be taken into account: the cheap lodging-houses. In the caravanseries that line Chatham Street and the Bowery, harboring nightly a population as large as that of many a thriving town, a homemade article of tramp and thief is turned out that is attracting the increasing attention of the police, and offers a field for the missionary's labors beside which most others seem of slight account. Within a year they have been stamped as nurseries of crime by the chief of the secret police,[2] the sort of crime that feeds especially on idleness and lies ready to the hand of fatal opportunity. In the same strain one of the justices on the police court bench sums up his long experience as a committing magistrate: "The ten-cent lodging-houses more than counterbalance the good done by the free reading-room, lectures, and all other agencies of reform. Such lodging-houses have caused more destitution, more beggary and crime than any other agency I know of." A very slight acquaintance with the subject is sufficient to convince the observer that neither authority overstates the fact. The two officials had reference, however, to two

[9] One of the duties of the New York police, accomplished at this time through a special division, was to help the board of health enforce the sanitary code.

[1] I.e., inoculated.

[2] The detective bureau, headed by Inspector Thomas Byrnes, an Irish immigrant. Riis referred in a footnote to an article on cheap lodging-houses published by Byrne in the *North American Review*, September 1889.

different grades of lodging-houses. The cost of a night's lodging makes the difference. There is a wider gap between the "hotel"—they are all hotels—that charges a quarter and the one that furnishes a bed for a dime than between the bridal suite and the everyday hall bedroom of the ordinary hostelry.

The metropolis is to lots of people like a lighted candle to the moth. It attracts them in swarms that come year after year with the vague idea that they can get along here if anywhere; that something is bound to turn up among so many. Nearly all are young men, unsettled in life, many—most of them, perhaps—fresh from good homes, beyond a doubt with honest hopes of getting a start in the city and making a way for themselves. Few of them have much money to waste while looking around, and the cheapness of the lodging offered is an object. Fewer still know anything about the city and its pitfalls. They have come in search of crowds, of "life," and they gravitate naturally to the Bowery, the great democratic highway of the city, where the twenty-five-cent lodging-houses take them in. In the alleged reading-rooms of these great barracks, that often have accommodations, such as they are, for two, three, and even four hundred guests, they encounter three distinct classes of associates: the great mass [of] adventurers like themselves, waiting there for something to turn up; a much smaller class of respectable clerks or mechanics,[3] who, too poor or too lonely to have a home of their own, live this way from year to year; and lastly the thief in search of recruits for his trade. The sights the young stranger sees, and the company he keeps, in the Bowery are not of a kind to strengthen any moral principle he may have brought away from home, and by the time his money is gone, with no work yet in sight, and he goes down a step, a long step, to the fifteen-cent lodging-house, he is ready for the tempter whom he finds waiting for him there, reinforced by the contingent of ex-convicts returning from the prisons after having served out their sentences for robbery or theft. Then it is that the something he has been waiting for turns up. The police returns have the record of it. "In nine cases out of ten," says Inspector Byrnes, "he turns out a thief, or a burglar, if, indeed, he does not sooner or later become a murderer." As a matter of fact, some of the most atrocious of recent murders have been the result of schemes of robbery hatched in these houses, and so frequent and bold have become the depredations of the lodging-house thieves, that the authorities have been compelled to make a public demand for more effective laws that shall make them subject at all times to police regulation.

Inspector Byrnes observes that in the last two or three years at least four hundred young men have been arrested for petty crimes that originated in the lodging-houses, and that in many cases it was their first step in crime. He adds his testimony to the notorious fact that three-fourths of the young men called on to plead to generally petty offences in the courts are under twenty years of age, poorly clad, and without means. The bearing of the remark is obvious. One of the, to the police, well-known thieves who lived, when out of jail, at the

---

[3] I.e., manual laborers.

Windsor, a well-known lodging-house in the Bowery, went to Johnstown[4] after the flood and was shot and killed there while robbing the dead.

An idea of just how this particular scheme of corruption works, with an extra touch of infamy thrown in, may be gathered from the story of David Smith, the "New York Fagin,"[5] who was convicted and sent to prison last year through the instrumentality of the Society for the Prevention of Cruelty to Children. Here is the account from the Society's last report:

"The boy, Edward Mulhearn, fourteen years old, had run away from his home in Jersey City, thinking he might find work and friends in New York. He may have been a trifle wild. He met Smith on the Bowery and recognized him as an acquaintance. When Smith offered him a supper and bed he was only too glad to accept. Smith led the boy to a vile lodging-house on the Bowery, where he introduced him to his 'pals' and swore he would make a man of him before he was a week older. Next day he took the unsuspecting Edward all over the Bowery and Grand Street, showed him the sights and drew his attention to the careless way the ladies carried their bags and purses and the easy thing it was to get them. He induced Edward to try his hand. Edward tried and won. He was richer by three dollars! It did seem easy. 'Of course it is,' said his companion. From that time Smith took the boy on a number of thieving raids, but he never seemed to become adept enough to be trusted out of range of the 'Fagin's' watchful eye. When he went out alone he generally returned empty-handed. This did not suit Smith. It was then he conceived the idea of turning this little inferior thief into a superior beggar. He took the boy into his room and burned his arms with a hot iron. The boy screamed and entreated in vain. The merciless wretch pressed the iron deep into the tender flesh, and afterward applied acid to the raw wound.

"Thus prepared, with his arm inflamed, swollen, and painful, Edward was sent out every day by this fiend, who never let him out of his sight, and threatened to burn his arm off if he did not beg money enough. He was instructed to tell people the wound had been caused by acid falling upon his arm at the works. Edward was now too much under the man's influence to resist or disobey him. He begged hard and handed Smith the pennies faithfully. He received in return bad food and worse treatment."

The reckoning came when the wretch encountered the boy's father, in search of his child, in the Bowery, and fell under suspicion of knowing more than he pretended of the lad's whereabouts. He was found in his den with a half dozen of his chums revelling on the proceeds of the boy's begging for the day.

The twenty-five-cent lodging-house keeps up the pretence of a bedroom, though the head-high partition enclosing a space just large enough to hold a cot and a chair and allow the man room to pull off his clothes is the shallowest

---

[4]On May 31, 1889, a dam on the Conemaugh River upstream of Johnstown, Pennsylvania, burst, leading to a devastating flood in the city and the deaths of some twenty-two hundred residents.
[5]Named for the leader of a band of thieves in Charles Dickens's *Oliver Twist* (1837–38).

of all pretences. The fifteen-cent bed stands boldly forth without screen in a room full of bunks with sheets as yellow and blankets as foul. At the ten-cent level the locker for the sleeper's clothes disappears. There is no longer need of it. The tramp limit is reached, and there is nothing to lock up save, on general principles, the lodger. Usually the ten- and seven-cent lodgings are different grades of the same abomination. Some sort of an apology for a bed, with mattress and blanket, represents the aristocratic purchase of the tramp who, by a lucky stroke of beggary, has exchanged the chance of an empty box or ash-barrel for shelter on the quality floor of one of these "hotels." A strip of canvas, strung between rough timbers, without covering of any kind, does for the couch of the seven-cent lodger who prefers the questionable comfort of a red-hot stove close to his elbow to the revelry of the stale-beer dive. It is not the most secure perch in the world. Uneasy sleepers roll off at intervals, but they have not far to fall to the next tier of bunks, and the commotion that ensues is speedily quieted by the boss and his club. On cold winter nights, when every bunk had its tenant, I have stood in such a lodging-room more than once, and listening to the snoring of the sleepers like the regular strokes of an engine, and the slow creaking of the beams under their restless weight, imagined myself on shipboard and experienced the very real nausea of sea-sickness. The one thing that did not favor the deception was the air; its character could not be mistaken.

The proprietor of one of these seven-cent houses was known to me as a man of reputed wealth and respectability. He "ran" three such establishments and made, it was said, $8,000 a year clear profit on his investment. He lived in a handsome house quite near to the stylish precincts of Murray Hill, where the nature of his occupation was not suspected. A notice that was posted on the wall of the lodgers' room suggested at least an effort to maintain his uptown standing in the slums. It read: "No swearing or loud talking after nine o'clock." Before nine no exceptions were taken to the natural vulgarity of the place; but that was the limit.

There are no licensed lodging-houses known to me which charge less than seven cents for even such a bed as this canvas strip, though there are unlicensed ones enough where one may sleep on the floor for five cents a spot, or squat in a sheltered hallway for three. The police station lodging-house, where the soft side of a plank is the regulation couch, is next in order. The manner in which this police bed is "made up" is interesting in its simplicity. The loose planks that make the platform are simply turned over, and the job is done, with an occasional coat of whitewash thrown in to sweeten things. I know of only one easier way, but, so far as I am informed, it has never been introduced in this country. It used to be practised, if report spoke truly, in certain old-country towns. The "bed" was represented by clotheslines stretched across the room upon which the sleepers hung by the armpits for a penny a night. In the morning the boss woke them up by simply untying the line at one end and letting it go with its load; a labor-saving device certainly, and highly successful in attaining the desired end.

According to the police figures, 4,974,025 separate lodgings were furnished last year by these dormitories, between two and three hundred in number, and, adding the 147,634 lodgings furnished by the station-houses, the total of the homeless army was 5,121,659, an average of over fourteen thousand homeless men[6] for every night in the year! The health officers, professional optimists always in matters that trench upon their official jurisdiction, insist that the number is not quite so large as here given. But, apart from any slight discrepancy in the figures, the more important fact remains that last year's record of lodgers is an all-round increase over the previous year's of over three hundred thousand, and that this has been the ratio of growth of the business during the last three years, the period of which Inspector Byrnes complains as turning out so many young criminals with the lodging-house stamp upon them. More than half of the lodging-houses are in the Bowery district, that is to say, the Fourth, Sixth, and Tenth Wards, and they harbor nearly three-fourths of their crowds. The calculation that more than nine thousand homeless young men lodge nightly along Chatham Street and the Bowery, between the City Hall and the Cooper Union, is probably not far out of the way. The City Missionary finds them there far less frequently than the thief in need of helpers. Appropriately enough, nearly one-fifth of all the pawnshops in the city and one-sixth of all the saloons are located here, while twenty-seven percent of all the arrests on the police books have been credited to the district for the last two years.

About election time, especially in presidential elections, the lodging-houses come out strong on the side of the political boss who has the biggest "barrel." The victory in political contests, in the three wards I have mentioned of all others, is distinctly to the general with the strongest battalions, and the lodging-houses are his favorite recruiting ground. The colonization of voters is an evil of the first magnitude, none the less because both parties smirch their hands with it, and for that reason next to hopeless. Honors are easy, where the two "machines," entrenched in their strongholds, outbid each other across the Bowery in open rivalry as to who shall commit the most flagrant frauds at the polls. Semi-occasionally a champion offender is caught and punished, as was, not long ago, the proprietor of one of the biggest Bowery lodging-houses. But such scenes are largely spectacular, if not prompted by some hidden motive of revenge that survives from the contest. Beyond a doubt Inspector Byrnes speaks by the card when he observes that "usually this work is done in the interest of some local political boss, who stands by the owner of the house, in case the latter gets into trouble." For "standing by," read "twisting the machinery of outraged justice so that its hand shall fall not too heavily upon the culprit, or miss him altogether." One of the houses that achieved profitable notoriety in this way in many successive elections, a notorious tramps' resort in Houston Street, was lately given up, and has most appropriately been turned into a bar-factory, thus still contributing, though in a changed form, to the success of "the cause." It must be admitted that the black tramp who herds in the West Side "hotels" is more discriminating in this matter of electioneering than his white

---

[6] "Deduct 69,111 women lodgers in the police stations" [Riis's note].

brother. He at least exhibits some real loyalty in invariably selling his vote to the Republican bidder for a dollar, while he charges the Democratic boss a dollar and a half. In view of the well-known facts, there is a good deal of force in the remark made by a friend of ballot reform during the recent struggle over that hotly contested issue, that real ballot reform will do more to knock out cheap lodging-houses than all the regulations of police and health officers together.

The experiment made by a well-known stove manufacturer a winter or two ago in the way of charity, might have thrown much desired light on the question of the number of tramps in the city, could it have been carried to a successful end. He opened a sort of breakfast shop for the idle and unemployed in the region of Washington Square, offering to all who had no money a cup of coffee and a roll for nothing. The first morning he had a dozen customers, the next about two hundred. The number kept growing until one morning, at the end of two weeks, found by actual count 2,014 shivering creatures in line waiting their turn for a seat at his tables. The shop was closed that day. It was one of the rare instances of too great a rush of custom wrecking a promising business, and the great problem remained unsolved.

16

America's Most Celebrated Tramp

Although itinerancy of the sort depicted in the narratives of John Robert Shaw or Stephen Burroughs had long been common in America, the modern tramp in the form of the hobo appeared only after the Civil War. It was the war and the railroads that combined, in fact, to produce the new species. Josiah Flynt, to whom Jack London was to dedicate his 1907 hobo book (*The Road*), wrote that the war "left a large class of men so enamored of camp life that they found it impossible to return to quiet living." As they tramped about, they took to walking the railroad rights-of-way, which in these decades increasingly penetrated the country (from 1860 to 1916, when it peaked, trackage increased almost ninefold, from thirty thousand to more than a quarter-million miles). It was a natural development for these new tramps to take to the trains proper, which they did in increasing numbers, so that by 1880 the hobo—the origin of the term is uncertain—had become almost an institution in the United States. As long as sympathy for the genuine veterans among the wanderers remained powerful, relatively little was done to end or control the movement, but by century's end many younger hoboes joined the veterans, and a widespread view emerged from an ever-more-regimented populace that these work-shirkers deserved little or no help. Railroad companies, which had been more indulgent earlier, took a harder line, and a kind of perpetual battle began between the company security agents or "bulls" and the "knights of the road." Some hoboes targeted indulgent communities, among them the utopian centers that had sprung up in such large numbers across the land in the past hundred years. Shaker families were accustomed to the yearly influx of "Winter Shakers," who arrived "with empty stomachs and empty trunks." In Ohio, the Zoarites constructed a jail to house the most difficult of such guests. In Iowa, the Inspirationists of Amana built what came to be called a "Hobo Hotel" to isolate the itinerants from the utopian community during their visits.

Jack London, who tried the life himself, had high regard for the adaptability and improvisational skills of the true hobo. "The successful hobo," he wrote, "must be an artist. He must create spontaneously and instantaneously." Everything hinged on the hobo's improvisation of believable lies that could convince others to lend support in the form of food, lodging, old clothes, cash—or at least work. London himself claimed that his own success as a story-writer sprang from the training that the road gave him. Another self-professed hobo, Leon Livingstone (known by the moniker "A-No. 1"), was so successful in parlaying his own tales into a literary career that he authored several books about the hobo's way of life and published all of them, including one issued in 1917 about his wanderings, *From Coast to Coast with Jack London*, through his own "A-No. 1 Publishing Company" in Pennsylvania. Livingstone, the son of immigrant parents, was raised in San Francisco, where he was born in 1872. No Civil War veteran, and in fact no son of poverty (his "well-to-do" parents "owned a pretty home"), Livingstone claimed he had run away in 1883 at the age of eleven after misbehaving at school. A good deal of what the author of the several "A-No. 1" books wrote is hard to document, such as his claim that by 1910 he had traveled close to half a million miles and had spent only $7.61. Surely he claimed more than he could prove, but his books sold well and the picture of the author adorning *Life and Adventures of A-No. 1* showed a man of prosperity and ease. The books sold particularly well to railroad passengers, as they were offered on platforms and in depots across the land. Perhaps because this industrial wanderer insisted that others—particularly boys—should not follow his example, he was allowed to peddle such wares near the very premises on which hoboes had committed so many depredations.

In the selection given here, "A-No. 1" tells how, just as he was about to return home and abandon the rails early in his career, he ran into an ex-con who convinced him otherwise. It was "Frenchy" from New Orleans who gave Livingstone his moniker and sent him on the long train ride that his books (with titles like *Hobo-Camp-Fire-Tales* [1911], *The Curse of Tramp Life* [1912], and *The Adventures of a Female Tramp* [1914]) aimed to describe. Passing to Florida and from there to Germany, the young tramp finally got back to his parents, but the wanderlust on which Livingstone's books played for their factory-bound and desk-bound audiences soon was to call the hero away again. His books were "moral and entertaining"—except, of course, for their subversive message that the irresponsibilites of a wanderer's life offered their own pleasant rewards.

By pursuing an age-old desire to evade responsibility through the eminently modern means of the railroad, Livingstone's narratives suggest both continuities and changes in the long run of American personal writing. If Livingstone seems to share much with historically nearer individuals such as Burroughs and Shaw, he touches back to older patterns as well. Like so many of the writers featured in *American Voices, American Lives* from Diego Méndez on, he was a figure, restless and uprooted, on the move in a changing world. Across seas or continents, from town to town, from countryside to city—but also from slavery to freedom, poverty to prosperity, and at times the reverse—a great many other Americans have found themselves on the same journey. Maybe it was all the change in their unsettled lives that led them to tell their tales with such energy and variety, as if language could bring them all together in the comforting illusion of an end, a resting point, a home.

LEON LIVINGSTONE

from *Life and Adventures of A-No. 1* (1910)

IN MY WANDERINGS I HAD ENCOUNTERED MANY TRAMPS, BUT NEVER MADE friends with any of them, and none of them paid any attention to me, as I was so very small. At Lathrop, however, I had a new experience. While waiting for a train, I met a tramp and for want of something better to do, I suppose, he visited with me. He had just come from San Francisco, and was en route to New Orleans and Florida points. I was very much interested in his stories of adventure, and he soon persuaded me to join for tunes and tramp with him to Florida—the more he told me that there were plenty of "lemonade springs" "rock-candy-mountains" and "cigarette groves" there. That afternoon we walked twenty miles towards the south, just that many miles away from my own parents and home. We had only covered a small part of the distance, when I unburdened my heart to my newfound friend, telling him the story of my past experience. He listened very attentively, then he began unfolding the story of his own life.

First of all, he told me, never to call him anything but "Frenchy," as he was of that nationality, although born in New Orleans. His age was twenty-seven years and two days previous to our meeting he had been discharged from the state penitentiary at San Quentin, California, after "doing" a five-years' term for the crime of holding up a stage, or, to be more exact, for highway robbery. He spun the tale so earnestly and so quietly that I never dreamed him to be anything but a genuine hero (according to my ideas of a hero at that time). It was twenty miles before we reached a tank where all trains would stop for water. Arriving there, we found around a campfire a short distance away, six big fellows, each resting on a big roll of blankets. They seemed to be very neat in general appearances, and were apparently laborers out of employment. When they spied Frenchy, one of them came up and asked him for a match.

"Chase yourself, you gay cat! Go and work for your matches," was the reply he received, and a look showing how disgusted Frenchy was even to talk to the man.

Frenchy took me on the other side of the tank and said: "Kid, I don't want you to mix with these 'gay cats.'"

I inquired what he meant by "gay cats," and he commenced to laugh. "You have been traveling the 'pike' for a solid year, and don't know what a 'gay cat' is? Get out, Kid, you are joshing."

I told him I did not know, and then he explained to me: "A gay cat," said he, "is a loafing laborer, who works maybe a week, gets his wages and vagabonds about, hunting for another 'pick and shovel' job. Do you want to know where they got their *moniker* (nickname) 'gay cat'? See, Kid, cats sneak about and scratch immediately after chumming with you and then get *gay* (fresh). That's why we call them 'gay cats.'"

With this he pulled a revolver, and walking over to the "outfit," kicked their can of coffee over into the fire, and ordered them to pick up their rolls and *hike* (walk). They made no resistance, but just slung their bundles over their backs, marched down the track, Indian-file, without even turning to look back.

"You see," said Frenchy, "they are cowards. They can bawl a fellow out when they are working, but are worse than dogs when you meet them on a sidetrack or tank."

After this I could have done anything for my partner, for hadn't he made six big, husky fellows walk at his command? With their disappearance Frenchy's good temper came back again, and he was soon telling me just how gay cats would turn a poor fellow "up" just to see him hang, and with an oath told me not to let him catch me talking to any one of them, if I wanted to avoid trouble.

Just then a train whistled in the distance, and crouching behind some bushes we waited until the brakemen were busy looking into box cars for hoboes and hunting hot axle boxes. Now we made a dash and quickly swinging ourselves into an open box car door we closed it quickly and crouched into the farthest corner. We were not discovered, and rode forty miles to Modesto, a small town that to Frenchy, looking through a crack, seemed to appear a good place to stop. We climbed out, and as we intended to travel on a passenger train that night, we walked up the track, and finding a shady place underneath some trees, we were soon sound asleep.

As a train was not due till 11 p. m., we slept till about 5 p. m., then Frenchy, who had a few dollars left from the sum they give at San Quentin to discharged prisoners to reach their homes with, sent me up town to buy provisions. On my return he had a campfire burning, and had collected some empty tin cans, and we cooked ourselves a generous supper. At 8 p. m. he told me to stay quietly at the camp while he went up town to *prowl* (look for something to steal). When he returned at 10 o'clock, I hardly recognized him. He had broken into a sheep herder's corral, and while the herders snored in slumber, had exchanged his clothes for theirs in the same room where they slept. He also helped himself to eighty dollars of their money and four watches, then hurried away to rejoin me.

After relating his experience and telling me of his lucky haul, Frenchy directed me to lay quiet until we should hear the passenger train in the distance. When the faraway whistle reached our ears we walked quickly towards the depot, and arrived there just as the train came to a stop. I had ridden the front end of baggage cars many times, but when Frenchy took me back to the Pullman, and told me to sit underneath on the narrow wooden brakebeam, I nearly fainted. Frenchy had no time to lose talking about it, however, but just grabbed me and made me sit down on the beam. To encourage me, he sat on the same one and warned me to hold on. A moment later the train started.

First the wheels turned slowly, then faster and faster, and after awhile the whirling noise became deafening.

People riding in coaches on rock-ballasted roads cannot imagine how it feels to be rushing through space fifty miles an hour over a loose sand-ballasted track seated upon a brake beam. Soon my eyes were filled with dust so that I could not open them. My ears were becoming deaf from the grinding and whirling noise. My mouth and throat were as dry as a parchment. And there I held on, while Frenchy kept his arm around me to keep me from falling off. The train went faster and faster over a perfectly level road, but light rails, and as the night was very dark, I felt as though I was shut up in a barrel full of sand and rocks, which someone was rolling down an endless stairway, so terrible was the jolting and jumping at every joint of the rails.

The train's next stop, ten miles away, was soon reached, and as it slowed up and I had a chance to open my eyes, I took courage again. When Frenchy praised me for my display of nerve to ride that way and told me he never saw a kid of my age and size display so much courage the first time "underneath," I forgot all my terror and almost laughed, thinking what a coward I had been. I told Frenchy how my mouth and throat were parched, and he handed me a small piece of plug tobacco, telling me to chew it, when the dust should choke me again. He then climbed on a brake beam of the rear truck, and left me alone on the front one, thus giving me more room to hang on.

Soon we were flying again and the dust became thicker and thicker. I put the tobacco in my mouth, but just then there was an extra hard jolt, caused by a real bad joint in the rails, and before I had time to think, I swallowed that piece of tobacco. It was the first chew of the weed I had ever taken in my life. Soon I was deathly sick, and I nearly lost my grip on the truck, which was all that lay between me and death. Further explanation of the situation is unnecessary. I can truthfully add, that never since that night and ride have I touched tobacco in any shape or form.

At the next stop I slid out from beneath the car and ran back to tell Frenchy how ill I felt. He crawled out too, and after shaking the dust from our clothes we went to a hotel and paid for a lodging. The landlord showed us to the room and after we entered Frenchy bolted the door.

Then the strangest, but for my own future most vital occurence happened. Picking me up and seating me upon his knee, Frenchy asked me in a kind voice: "Say, Kid, when did you say your evening prayer the last time?" Shamefaced, I confessed that I had forgotten to thank Providence for protecting me soon after leaving home. Now Frenchy, the highway robber, burglar and ex-convict had me kneel down and repeat the following words:

"I solemnly promise never to associate with anyone in whose company I would be ashamed to pass my mother's home in broad daylight. Amen."

After this strange prayer he put me to bed, and I was soon sound asleep.

Every night after this first one, no matter if we were sleeping in hotels, barns, box cars or camping out by a fire in the woods, I had to kneel and repeat this odd supplication, and after we parted company, even to this day, I repeat it every evening and am convinced that these few, strange lines have prevented my joining that army of tramps whose inevitable destination is the "Abyss."

Next morning Frenchy bought enough provisions to last us during the day, and we camped in the woods by a cool spring, just like hunters would, washing our clothes and taking things easy. That afternoon we saw the same company of gay cats that Frenchy had chased away single-handed at the tank, passing our hiding place on a freight train. We could see them in the distance leave the train and walk uptown. That evening when Frenchy went downtown he discovered the gay cats in a saloon, seated around a table drinking beer. He walked into the place, and being differently dressed they did not recognize him. When they were not watching, just for a joke, he appropriated their blanket rolls, and came to our meeting place loaded down like a wagon with the six gay cats' "feather beds." We did not take trouble to untie any of them, but just cut the cords. One contained a Bible, some had underwear and overalls, but all had good warm blankets, and we piled them up and crawling between were soon sound asleep, not even waking to make the passenger train we arrived on the night before, and that it had been our intention to ride the beams underneath again. In the early morning we set fire to our bed and soon there was nothing left. We walked down to the depot to buy some more provisions, and there we met the six big, husky gay cats, sneaking around the depot, goggling everybody and looking underneath the platform and other hiding places trying to discover their blanket rolls. The way they sized up Frenchy was a caution. No sooner did they recognize him than all started across the street where a policeman stood. We did not wait for him to interview us, but walked down the track as fast as possible, for Frenchy's favorite proverb was: "Better be sure than sorry."

After this lesson in riding brake beams under Pullmans I soon became an expert, and as Frenchy, for good reasons and remembrances didn't like California, we quickly crossed the Colorado River into Arizona at Yuma.

At Yuma is an Apache Indian Reservation, and the government's laws against selling liquor to its red wards are strictly enforced. The informer receives one-half the fine, and Frenchy came near breaking into another penitentiary. It happened thus: A big Apache approached while we were loafing about the depot, and calling us to one side said to Frenchy: "White man want to make some money?" He replied in the affirmative. "Well, here is two bits (twenty-five cents), go get Indian some liquor, bring him back, me give two bits more, then you give me liquor." Frenchy, without a second thought went into a saloon and bought the liquor. Returning where I was waiting with the thirsty redskin, he pulled the cork out of the bottle, so he could take first a good drink himself, when a man stepped up to him and whispered in his ear: "Say, stranger, don't let that greasy Indian beg you for a drink, as he is a government spy and arrests strangers who give him booze. Why, he got $50 only last week for sending a poor hobo to the penitentiary for two years."

Frenchy just let the bottle drop, and it smashed into a thousand pieces. Then that Indian commenced to cuss and wanted Frenchy to buy him some more booze for the other twenty-five cents, but Frenchy told him he wanted to make a dollar, and that if he gave him a dollar to buy more liquor he would do

so, but the Apache had nothing smaller than a ten-dollar bill in his bead purse. That, he finally handed to Frenchy and then waited patiently in front of the saloon for our return with the booze. Frenchy and myself made our exit through the rear entrance of the saloon, and we skipped across the bridge spanning the Colorado River back into California, and laid low until after dark, when we caught a train and left Yuma and a poorer but perhaps wiser redskin behind us.

We traveled across the deserts to San Antonio and Frenchy's propensity to appropriate property belonging to other people kept us well supplied. That even thieves have comical experiences may be new, but here is one I remember well, for I never saw Frenchy more disgusted on our whole trip.

At Rosenburg Junction, a few miles west of Houston, Texas, Frenchy grabbed a large steel-hooped trunk from a railroad truck. He carried it to our meeting place, and then being afraid we would be surprised, we both carried the two-hundred-pound affair for a solid three miles on a stony railroad track in a dark and rainy night to a small wooden trestle. On the way we tried to guess its contents. I thought we had found a gold mine, but Frenchy said he would be satisfied if it contained old silver plate and the like. At the trestle he tried to open the treasure box with his *jimmy* (chisel), but in vain, as the trunk was all covered up with steel bands, and a padlock as large as a good-sized mail box. Not until we had wasted nearly two hours in trying to pry it open did he manage to loosen the bottom of the trunk sufficiently to get at the contents. It contained garden and grain seed, probably the property of some Dutch immigrant who had brought them from the old country. This suprise and disappointment was what made Frenchy so disgusted.

We passed on to New Orleans where we stopped for a few days. After leaving there we had hard luck and began walking again, hoping to turn up a job by which Frenchy could make a few dollars, but luck was against us, and we were soon dead broke. Frenchy was a nervy thief, but in begging food he was a failure. Up to this time he had paid all our expenses, but now was my turn to do the right thing by him according to the unwritten "Rules of the Road." I had to go to houses and ask for food and bring it to him. As I was small, and had had a year's experience in bumming it was fun, the more so because the people treated me well and gave plenty.

After leaving Mobile, Alabama, we found the country more and more sparsely settled, and when we neared the Florida state line, houses often were miles apart. At times I found it hard even to bum enough for myself, let alone supply my partner. Then I hit on a clever plan. Whenever a kind lady gave me a pie, a piece of roast, some cold, hard biscuit or tough old cornbread, I would appropriate the pie, roast and maybe a biscuit and bring him the rest. Poor Frenchy! How often he said to me: "The last kid I had always brought me pie, roast and cake, while you never bum anything better than cornbread and old, hard biscuits." He tried to make me feel as if I ought to bring him something better. I was getting fat while Frenchy surely lost in weight by this operation, called in the tramp-argot "robbing the mail."

We arrived at Pensacola two days before Christmas, and being broke went to a sailor "boss." This man boarded, clothed and found work for unemployed sailors. Also kept them in small sums of money, which was taken out of their advance wages later with big interest. We had no intention of going to sea, but we surely felt in need of a good rest, and after all the biscuits and fat pork, a good "square" Christmas dinner. I received a nice new sailor uniform and the promise of a job as cabin boy. Frenchy was given a nice outfit, and the promise of a cook's job, as he had learned cooking in the California State Penitentiary.

Christmas morning Boss Davis (that was the agent's name) invited all to have some eggnog, and soon the other fellows were dead drunk. Only about four of the whole houseful of sailor boarders were fit to eat their Christmas dinner, cooked for at least twenty, and I can truthfully say that this was the first and last Christmas dinner where I had more roasted turkey legs than I could master. Next day the boss came to Frenchy and told him he had a job for him, to serve as a cook on a sailing vessel bound to South American ports. Frenchy was obliged to accept the offer, but as the ship was not to sail until after New Year's there were plenty of chances for him to come back to the shore and join me at some other place.

Before leaving, Frenchy came to me and gave me his final instructions. "Listen, Kid," said he, "Every tramp gives his kid a nickname, a name that will distinguish him from all other members of the craft. You have been a good lad while you have been with me, in fact been always 'A-No. 1' in everything you had to do, and, Kid, take my advice, if you have to be anything in life, even if a tramp, try to be 'A-No. 1' all the time and in everything you undertake." Here he paused a moment as if thinking, then he continued: "By the way, Kid, I believe I have a good and proper nickname for you, one never borne by any other tramp, I am going to call you 'A-No. 1,' and I want you to live up to its meaning in whatever you do and wherever you are." Then he gave me his final instructions: "Leave Pensacola tonight and catch a ride as far as the next water tank, then start walking. Walk about a mile a day and on each mile-post mark 'A-No. 1.' Mark also under your moniker the date, and below it an arrow pointing in the direction you were traveling, so I can find you quickly when I make my 'get-away.'"

Further he made me promise to repeat the prayer he taught me every night and that I would not travel with another partner for a whole year under pain of death should he meet me. He did not need to scare me for I knew how desperate he was. That evening I took French leave from "Boss" Davis, from Pensacola and from my partner "Frenchy," whom I have never met in all my travels since.

I rode to the next tank and then on every mile post I put the mark he told me—"A-No. 1," and kept putting that mark everywhere since that date, thus winning my world-famous alias—"A-No. 1."

one morning at Funiak Springs, a place in western Florida, I picked up a small piece of paper that had this printed on it: "One thousand dollars reward— Wanted by the U. S. authorities at Pensacola, Florida—Cook named Murphy, 5 feet 6 inches, blue eyes, Irish descent, speaks English with foreign accent, for

robbery. Crime committed in Pensacola harbor, on board full-rigged sailing ship *Anna Lee*, of New York, by dosing crew and captain on New Year's Eve, 1885, with knock-out drops, and robbing the captain's safe of 3,000 pesos, Mexican currency. Any information wire promptly to United States Marshall, Pensacola, Florida."

Slowly I followed the railroad toward the east. I hoped to hear from Frenchy, and of his whereabouts, but none of the newspapers contained any reference to his capture, nor did I see his sign anywhere along the road.

Reaching Jacksonville, Florida, I found a letter from home waiting for me; Father told me Mother's heart was breaking and that she wanted me to come home. He begged me to give up the roving life and warned me that the end would be a pitiful one. It was very cold, and not wanting to write for money to return home by rail, I promised to come back in the summer.

After loafing about Jacksonville and Savannah for a couple of weeks, I went to Atlanta, Georgia, and by selling newspapers paid my expenses.

While thus making a living and a little above, one day I struck up an acquaintance with a young man named Fred Philpot—who at present owns one of the largest grocery stores in Georgia. Fred wanted to join me on my trip home, as he thought he could pick up gold in California. I had only a few dollars and when he told me that if I would first go to Savannah with him, he could maybe raise fifty or one hundred dollars from his uncle, who was then the mayor of that beautiful city, and as the prospects for us to pick up a little easy money seemed bright, we tramped to Savannah. Arriving there we separated, as Fred thought he could work his uncle better single-handed. He returned after a short absence, not with cold cash or crisp currency, but with his face wreathed in smiles, and told me that his uncle had been overjoyed at the unexpected appearance of his nephew, and that he just ached to meet his nephew's partner, and had sent Fred to fetch me to his presence. I had not a tiny inkling that anything should be wrong and followed him to the city hall.

His uncle, Mr. McDonough, was the mayor of the city sure enough, and also judge of municipal court; and no sooner had I entered the building, than a large policeman grabbed me and took me up to the courtroom. His Honor, the mayor, judge and Fred's uncle all combined, was waiting especially for me, for I could see blood in his eyes. After answering several questions he asked me how much money I had. I answered: "Seven dollars and twenty cents."

"Now then," he continued, "young man, I cannot put a charge of vagrancy against you, but my nephew here says you induced him to leave a good home in Atlanta to hobo down here, and it is the sentence of this court that you pay his way back, or work thirty days breaking stone, convicted on the charge of being a dangerous and suspicious person in the city limits of Savannah."

I paid $6.80 for my partner's ticket home. Instead of us getting $50 or $100, I nearly received thirty days, for that fool fellow told his uncle that I enticed him from home. I was thirteen years old then, he was over eighteen, and nearly a foot taller than myself. I was afraid to go back by the way of Atlanta, as I did not know what other reception I would receive from Fred's people. So after I had paid his passage home seated in a comfortable passenger coach, I walked out of Savannah as quickly as I could and headed for Charleston, South Carolina.

One day soon after my arrival in Charleston, while lounging about the wharves, the steward of a German steamer accosted me and offered me a job as waiter on his vessel. I told him that I thought I would be too small for the job and further that I never waited on tables in all my life. "Ach, mein Gott," the steward assured me, "it is such a nice pleasant job; I'll see that you don't have to wait at all, but I want you to give me half of your pay when you get it in Hamburg where we are going." I thought "Dutchy," as I will call him, was looking for graft and accepted. He took me to the captain and told him that I was the new waiter. Says Dutchy, "Ya, ya, Captain, he says he is one fine waiter, and I gives him a job." The captain promised me $15 for the trip across and a pass back to the states.

In a couple of days the steamer finished loading her cargo, consisting of phosphate rock and we steamed out of the harbor. Her tonnage was about 2500, and her speed not over eight knots an hour. No sooner were we out on the rough Atlantic Ocean, [when] Dutchy ordered me to serve coffee to the officers upon the bridge. I had never served anything in the line of glassware on solid soil, and with the old tub of a steamer making monkey motions in four different directions underneath my feet at one and the same time, suddenly I let go the tray of chinaware, silver and glass in four different curves, all smashing into ten thousand different pieces.

"Mine Gott, mine Gott," lamented Dutchy, so loudly that the captain heard him and came rushing back and cussed me terribly for my awkwardness. "Ach, mine Gott, Captain," lamented Dutchy, "he told me he was a waiter of the first-class, and now he smashed everything." The finish was that I had to make a clean confession that I never waited on any table in my life, and as a consequence they put me to work as a coal passer in the hot boiler room. I had not shoveled coal for more than ten minutes before I discovered by listening to the German conversation of the firemen, that the captain tried to hire a coal passer in Charleston, but none would work on the leaky old tramp steamer, and that Dutchy, the steward, really hired me, not to work as a waiter, but to pass coal.

It took this tub of a steamer four and a half weeks to reach Hamburg, and the way I looked and the condition of my clothes can be imagined, after passing coal from the coal bins to the firemen fourteen hours a day in a dark and hot boiler room during the entire trip. Arriving in Hamburg, the captain had the cheek to hand me a ten-mark bill ($2.50) with the remark: "Mine boy, you had better make yourself thin, or I will have you arrested as a stowaway, and you may be sentenced to jail for a couple of years."

I never expected to receive even the ten marks, and as I had small desire to get the rest of that pay I made myself "thin." I met Dutchy that same afternoon and he was rather drunk. I was a small boy and he a very large man, so revenge, less than murder, was impossible, and so I made friends with him.

"Ach, mein Gott," he confessed, "that captain was a big pig, he promised me five dollars if I gets him a coal passer, and now he only gives me two dollars and fifty cents, as he says you was too small." And he laughed about his cuteness and my misfortune until the tears trickled down his face. I never forgot this lesson, and made good use of my new hard-earned knowledge later on.

I hunted for a rooming house, and after finding one to suit, handed the landlord 12½¢ cents (fifty pfennig in German money), the price he asked for a week's lodging; for a nice clean room, as well as everything else, is cheap in Europe. He took my money and asked me to show him my papers. I stared at him in amazement, and he then explained that he would be fined 10¢ every day he kept a person who was not registered at police headquarters. As I did not have any papers to show him, he promptly called a policeman, and at headquarters they wanted me to explain how I happened to land in Hamburg, and all in rags at that. My knowledge of the German language taught me at home while a little kid, came [in] handy, and I could do this in their own tongue.

After pumping and finding out all they could from me they handed me a cardboard about six by six inches, all stamped upon and spaced off, and having my description on it, my whole past and present (according to the story I told them) outlined in detail. With this card in my possession I returned to my landlord, and after glancing over my printed pedigree he seemed kindness personified. At his place I made the acquaintance of some German tramps, who told me thrilling stories about the beautiful interior.

After I had spent my last penny I struck up a partnership with one of them, and we started to walk to Berlin, first having our papers stamped. My partner had a "wander" card as it was called, just like mine, only his was all stamped up so that it could hardly be deciphered.

In Germany, a hobo, if caught, gets one year at hard labor for walking on the track, and I believe it is life for riding on trains. Hence the German tramps never ride. They all walk the pikes, which are nicely kept and are centuries old, and we met hundreds daily. Everywhere we were received kindly, especially when my partner told them I was an American. I found that nearly all had relatives in the states, and such questions as these were usually popped at me: "Do you know Henri in Minnesota, and Jacob in New York, and John in Chicago," and one old lady wanted to know if I knew her "nephew 'Herman,' in California." Of course I knew them all, and they were getting rich, so by saying this they all treated us nicely and we had plenty to eat, but very little money, as all they give are coppers, and it takes four of these to make an honest American cent. We were stopped every few miles by mounted police, who would put their mark or stamp on our cards. These cards entitled us to stay twenty-four hours in one place but no longer, unless hunting a job, and further they gave us a night's lodging in every municipal lodging-house, and what was best, allowed us to beg without molestation, "as we were supposed to be out of work."

The German tramp is about the meanest piece of humanity I ever met. They have no friendship for one another, and are so low that they will keep part of their hand-outs and sell them to others, less fortunate, for a few coppers at the lodging-places. A pipe full of tobacco, matches, cast-off rags, and even old cigar stumps have a money value. The maxim of the German tramp is to look as ragged as possible so as to show his hard luck from the outside, and thus to be pitied the more by the people. Ragged American gay cats look like dudes compared with the German brand. They walk from morning till night, and I don't blame their government for keeping trace of them, as they might become lost. There is no honor or kindness among them—everybody for himself.

After more than two weeks of tiresome walking we reached Berlin at last, but had hardly passed the city limits when we were picked up by a policeman and taken to headquarters. As we were unable to show that we had been employed anywhere recently, they gave us each forty-eight hours in jail as punishment for too much loafing. They treated us well, however. It was more like a home than a jail. We were given five meals a day, and after two days' experience along these lines they turned us loose, not forgetting to add their record to our cards by the addition of a few more pretty seals. They also gave us twenty-four hours in which to hunt for work, after which time we would have to leave the city.

As luck would have it, while passing through a park I overheard two gentlemen speaking English. They happened to be Yankees just arrived from the other side. I told them my experiences thus far in Europe, and they each handed me a five-dollar bill, forty marks in German money, four thousand of those coppers all in a bunch. If ever Providence turned up a good thing for me it happened right there. I skipped my German partner, and went down to the railroad station, exchanged my money into German currency and bought a ticket (fourth-class) to Hamburg, $1.25 for two hundred and thirty-five miles! It was cheap—a fourth-class passage needed to be. First-class had velvet; second-class, leather; third-class, wooden seats; but fourth-class had no seats at all, and no springs either, and the windows are barred to keep people from falling out or trying to escape from the rattling torture "wagons," as passenger coaches are called in Germany, very appropriately. Cheap rate, but oh, how slow! Ten hours on a rough track. Upon reaching Hamburg I applied for a room at my old place, but the landlord would not take me in again, as I had added a genuine jail stamp to my record.

I loafed about Hamburg until the middle of June, getting plenty to eat and small sums of money from crews of English, French and American steamers and sailing ships, there being hundreds in port all the time. I saved every cent possible, so as to have enough money to pay my way back to the states. I had nearly the necessary sum to start for New York as a steerage passenger, when one day a man who hired ship labor, inquired if I could wait on tables. I thought there was another chance to be buncoed, so for the fun of it I answered in the affirmative.

Next day a steward of a cattle steamer bound for Boston called at my lodging house. He looked me over and told the other man he thought I was too small. He asked me to try and find him a waiter. The pay was $5 for the trip across to Boston. I would have gone for nothing, even in the coal hole, if I could have thus landed back in the states, as the $23 I had saved would fix me up nicely with new clothes on the arrival there. I took the steward to one side and told him what a fine waiter I was, and how I could juggle a tray full of dishes, and how I had been a waiter at one time on a German tramp steamer, etc., etc. He would not listen, but when I offered him one-half of my wages for the chance, he bit.

Next morning he called again at my rooming house and made me sign a contract, only my pay was to be $7.50 cents for the trip, thus making his own one-half share worth more. I carried a canvas bag full of my belongings aboard, and that afternoon we left Hamburg and Europe, bound for Boston. I waited on the table that evening, and as long as we steamed down the Elbe for nearly a hundred miles to its mouth and had smooth riverwater underneath all went well, 'though I was a little awkward; but as we passed into the North Sea, the stormiest part of the Atlantic, I became awfully seasick, and could not stand on my feet, let alone juggle trays and had to go to bed. When I commenced to get over the sickness, I remembered a receipt[1] Frenchy used when he was in state's prison, and didn't feel like working; I dissolved a little soap in a glass of water and swallowed it. It made me sick, and I soon began to look so much like a ghost that they put me into a good nice, clean cabin, and provided me the best of food to save me from dying.

I must acknowledge I wasn't feeling very fine, for soap and water isn't intended for human diet. Still, sick as I was, I enjoyed the trip to Boston, an even twelve days. A waiting ambulance took me to a naval hospital, but before leaving the ship the purser paid me $7.50. The steward, seeing he could not filch a cent of the money, gave me a cheerless send-off, as he had to play waiter himself all the way across the Atlantic besides attending to all his other duties. I had the $23 that I had sewed into the lining of my pants besides, and after remaining in the hospital a couple of days to get over the effects of the soap-and-water diet, I took French leave. I had surely squared my account with Dutchy, and the coal-passer lesson, six months previous, turned to some good after all.

I hit the Boston & Albany, bound for home, happier than a bird, and the way I jumped on and off the cars while in motion was a caution; one brakeman thought I was turning crazy, but it was only to get myself limbered up for the overland trip. In just two weeks after leaving Boston I landed in San Francisco. My parents were overjoyed to have me back safe and alive. As I had yet a few dollars left, and had lots of stories to relate they forgave me. For two weeks I stayed at home and enjoyed myself to the limit, then the "wanderlust" made me dissatisfied and restless, and, to appease my craving to roam, I took a trip to Victoria, British Columbia.

---

[1] I.e., recipe.

Appendix of Sources

Diego Méndez de Segura: *The Four Voyages of Columbus: A History in Eight Documents, Including Five by Christopher Columbus, in the Original Spanish, with English Translations,* trans., ed. Cecil Jane, 2 vols. (London: Hakluyt Society, 1930–33).

Job Hortop: Richard Hakluyt, *Voyages,* intro. by John Masefield, 8 vols. (London: Dent; New York: Dutton, 1907).

Edward Hayes: Hakluyt, *Voyages.*

[Gabriel Archer?]: *The Jamestown Voyages Under the First Charter, 1606–1609,* ed. Philip L. Barbour, 2 vols. (Cambridge: Hakluyt Society, 1969).

John Heckewelder: *History, Manners, and Customs of the Indian Nations Who Once Inhabited Pennsylvania and the Neighbouring States* (1819), ed. William C. Reichel (Philadelphia: Historical Society of Pennsylvania, 1876).

"A Voyage Made by Ten of Our Men to the Kingdom of Nauset": *The Journal of the Pilgrims at Plymouth, in New England, in 1620,* ed. George B. Cheever (New York: Wiley, 1848).

John Easton: *Narratives of the Indian Wars, 1675–1699,* ed. Charles H. Lincoln (New York: Scribner's, 1913; rpt. New York: Barnes and Noble, 1941).

Maria van Cortlandt: *Correspondence of Maria van Rensselaer, 1669–1689,* trans., ed. A. J. F. van Laer (Albany: University of the State of New York, 1935).

Richard Chamberlain: *Narratives of the Witchcraft Cases, 1648–1706,* ed. George Lincoln Burr (New York: Scribner's, 1914; rpt. New York: Barnes and Noble, 1946).

Pierre and Jean Baptiste Talon: "The Interrogation of the Talon Brothers, 1698," trans. R. T. Huntington, *Iowa Review* 15 (1985): 99–131.

Hannah Dustan—John Pike: *Proceedings of the Massachusetts Historical Society* (1875–76); John Marshall: ibid. (1900–1901); Samuel Sewall: *The Diary of Samuel Sewall, 1674–1729,* ed. M. Halsey Thomas, 2 vols. (New York: Farrar, Straus and Giroux, 1973); Cotton Mather: *Magnalia Christi Americana,* ed. Rev. Thomas Robbins, 2 vols. (Hartford: Silas Andrus and Son, 1853); Jonathan Carver: *Jonathan Carver's Travels through America, 1766–1768: An Eighteenth-Century Explorer's Account of Uncharted America,* ed. Norman Gelb (New York: Wiley, 1993); John Greenleaf Whittier: *Legends of New England* (Hartford: Hanmer and Phelps, 1831); Nathaniel Hawthorne: *Collected Works of Nathaniel Hawthorne,* 22 vols. (Boston: Houghton, Mifflin, 1900); Henry David Thoreau: *A Week on the Concord and Merrimack Rivers* (1849), ed. Carl F. Hovde, William L. Howarth, and Elizabeth Hall Witherell (Princeton: Princeton University Press, 1980); Sarah Josepha Hale: Robert B. Caverly, *Heroism of Hannah Duston, Together with the Indian Wars of New England* (Boston: B. B. Russell, 1875).

Thomas Nairne: *Nairne's Muskhogean Journals: The 1708 Expedition to the Mississippi River*, ed. Alexander Moore (Jackson: University Press of Mississippi, 1988).

Cadwallader Colden: *The History of the Five Indian Nations of Canada, Which Are Dependent on the Province of New York*, 2 vols. (New York: Allerton, 1922).

Elizabeth Hanson: *Puritans Among the Indians: Accounts of Captivity and Redemption, 1676–1724*, ed. Alden T. Vaughan and Edward W. Clark (Cambridge, Mass.: Harvard University Press, 1981).

George Scott: Elizabeth Donnan, *Documents Illustrative of the History of the Slave Trade to America*, 4 vols. (Washington, D.C.: Carnegie Institution, 1932).

Ayuba Suleiman Diallo—Thomas Bluett: *Africa Remembered: Narratives by West Africans from the Era of the Slave Trade*, ed. Philip D. Curtin (Madison: University of Wisconsin Press, 1967); Francis Moore: ibid.

William Moraley: *The Infortunate: or The Voyage and Adventures of William Moraley*, ed. Susan E. Klepp and Billy G. Smith (University Park: Pennsylvania State University Press, 1992).

Charlotte Brown: *Colonial Captivities, Marches and Journeys*, ed. Isabel M. Calder (New York: Macmillan, 1935).

Robert Rogers: *Journals of Major Robert Rogers*, ed. Howard H. Peckham (New York: Corinth, 1961).

Jared Ingersoll: *English Historical Documents: American Colonial Documents to 1776*, ed. Merrill Jensen (London: Eyre and Spottiswoode, 1955).

Charles Woodmason: *The Carolina Backcountry on the Eve of the Revolution: The Journal and Other Writings of Charles Woodmason, Anglican Itinerant*, ed. Richard J. Hooker (Chapel Hill: University of North Carolina Press, 1953).

Boston Massacre—*Boston Gazette and Country Journal*: Jensen, ed., *English Historical Documents: American Colonial Documents to 1776*; Captain Thomas Preston: ibid; Bowdoin, Warren, and Pemberton: *Tracts of the American Revolution, 1763–1776*, ed. Merrill Jensen (Indianapolis: Bobbs-Merrill, 1967).

Loyalists—Jonathan Boucher: *Reminiscences of an American Loyalist, 1738–1789*, ed. Jonathan Boucher (Boston: Houghton Mifflin, 1925); Janet Schaw: *Journal of a Lady of Quality; Being the Narrative of a Journey from Scotland to the West Indies, North Carolina, and Portugal, in the Years 1774 to 1776*, ed. Evangeline Walker Andrews and Charles McLean Andrews (New Haven, Conn.: Yale University Press, 1922).

Pension Application Narratives: *The Revolution Remembered: Eyewitness Accounts of the War for Independence*, ed. John C. Dann (Chicago: University of Chicago Press, 1980).

Frederika Charlotte Louise von Riedesel: *Baroness von Riedesel and the American Revolution: Journal and Correspondence of a Tour of Duty, 1776–1783*, ed. Marvin L. Brown (Chapel Hill: University of North Carolina Press, 1965).

Sally Wister: *Sally Wister's Journal*, ed. Albert Cook Myers (Philadelphia: Ferris and Leach, 1902).

Boston King: *The Methodist Magazine* (1798).

Four Itinerants—Stephen Burroughs: *Memoirs of the Notorious Stephen Burroughs: Containing Many Incidents in the Life of This Wonderful Man, Never Before Published* (Boston: Charles Gaylord, 1832); Venture Smith: *A Narrative of the Life and Adventures of Venture, a Native of Africa, but Resident above Sixty Years in the United States of America* (New London, Conn.: C. Holt, 1798); John Robert Shaw: *John Robert Shaw: An Autobiography of Thirty Years, 1777–1807*, ed. Oressa M. Teagarden and Jeanne L. Crabtree (Athens: Ohio University Press, 1992); Abigail Abbot Bailey: *Religion and Domestic Violence in Early New England: Memoirs of Abigail Abbot Bailey*, ed. Ann Taves (Bloomington: Indiana University Press, 1989).

William Cooper: *A Guide in the Wilderness; or The History of the First Settlements in the Western Counties of New York, with Useful Instructions to Future Settlers* (Dublin: Gilbert and Hodges, 1810).

William Apess: *On Our Own Ground: The Complete Writings of William Apess, a Pequot*, ed. Barry O'Connell (Amherst: University of Massachusetts Press, 1992).

Auguste Levasseur: *Lafayette in America in 1824 and 1825; or, Journal of a Voyage to the United States*, trans. John D. Godman, 2 vols. (Philadelphia: Carey and Lea, 1829).

Joseph Plumb Martin: *A Narrative of Some of the Adventures, Dangers, and Sufferings of a Revolutionary Soldier* (Hallowell, Maine: printed by Glazier, Masters & Co., 1830).

Anne Newport Royall: *Letters from Alabama, 1817–1822*, ed. Lucille Griffith (University: University of Alabama Press, 1969).

Nat Turner: Herbert Aptheker, *Nat Turner's Slave Rebellion, Together with the Full Text of the So-Called "Confessions" of Nat Turner Made in Prison in 1831* (New York: Grove Press, 1968).

Black Hawk: *Black Hawk: An Autobiography*, ed. Donald Jackson (Urbana: University of Illinois Press, 1964).

Four Fourths—Rev. Nathaniel Paul: *A Documentary History of the Negro People in the United States*, ed. Herbert Aptheker, 4 vols. (New York: Citadel, 1963); George Henry Evans: *We the Other People: Alternative Declarations of Independence by Labor Groups, Farmers, Woman's Rights Advocates, Socialists, and Blacks, 1829–1975*, ed. Philip S. Foner (Urbana: University Illinois Press, 1976); Elizabeth Cady Stanton: ibid; Catherine Haun: Lillian Schlissel, *Women's Diaries of the Westward Journey* (New York: Schocken, 1982); Frederick Douglass: Aptheker; National Woman Suffrage Association: Foner; Galiot François Edmond, Baron de Mandat-Grancey: *Cowboys and Colonels: Narrative of a Journey Across the Prairie and Over the Black Hills of Dakota*, trans. William Conn, intro. by Howard R. Lamar (Philadelphia: Lippincott, 1962); Daniel De Leon: Foner.

Henry Conklin: *"Through Poverty's Vale": A Hardscrabble Boyhood in Upstate New York, 1832–1862*, ed. Wendell Tripp (Syracuse: Syracuse University Press, 1974).

Asa Sheldon: *Yankee Drover: Being the Unpretending Life of Asa Sheldon, Farmer, Trader, and Working Man, 1788–1870*, ed. John Seelye (Hanover, N.H.: University Press of New England, 1988).

Benjamin B. Bowen: *A Blind Man's Offering* (New York: the Author, 1854).

William Wells Brown: *Narrative of William Wells Brown, an American Slave* (London: Charles Gilpin, 1849).

Susan Shelby Magoffin: *Down the Santa Fe Trail and into Mexico: The Diary of Susan Shelby Magoffin, 1846–1847*, ed. Stella M. Drumm, with a foreword by Howard R. Lamar (Lincoln: University of Nebraska Press, 1962).

Remembering the Crisis—Ulysses S. Grant: *Memoirs and Selected Letters* (New York: Library of America, 1990); Mary Boykin Chesnut: *Mary Chesnut's Civil War*, ed. C. Vann Woodward (New Haven, Conn.: Yale University Press, 1981), and *The Private Mary Chesnut: The Unpublished Civil War Diaries*, ed. Woodward and Elisabeth Muhlenfeld (New York: Oxford University Press, 1984); Proctor, Rowe, and Grayson: *Lay My Burden Down: A Folk History of Slavery*, ed. B. A. Botkin (Chicago: University Chicago Press, 1945); Thomas Chaplin: Theodore Rosengarten, with assistance of Susan W. Walker, *Tombee: Portrait of a Cotton Planter, with the Journal of Thomas B. Chaplin, (1822–1890)* (New York: William Morrow, 1986).

Immigrant Tales—John Muir: *The Story of My Boyhood and Youth* (Boston: Houghton Mifflin, 1913); Martin Weitz: *News from the Land of Freedom: German Immigrants Write Home*, ed. Walter D. Kamphoefner, Wolfgang Helbich, and Ulrike Sommer, trans. Susan Carter Vogel (Ithaca: Cornell University Press, 1991); Wilhelm Bürkert: ibid; Lee Chew:

Plain Folk: The Life Stories of Undistinguished Americans, ed. David M. Katzman and William M. Tuttle, Jr. (Urbana: University of Illinois Press, 1982); Wilhelmine Wiebusch: Kamphoefner, Helbich, and Sommer; Rocco Corresca: Katzman and Tuttle.

Jacob Riis: *How the Other Half Lives: Studies among the Tenements of New York,* intro. by Donald N. Bigelow (New York: Hill and Wang, 1957).

Leon Livingstone: *Life and Adventures of A-No. 1, America's Most Celebrated Tramp* (Cambridge Springs, Pa.: A-No. 1 Publishing Co., 1910).

PERMISSIONS ACKNOWLEDGMENTS

Thomas Bluett, from *Africa Remembered: Narratives by West Africans From the Era of the Slave Trade*, edited by Philip S. Curtin, © 1967 (Madison: The University of Wisconsin Press). Reprinted by permission of The University of Wisconsin Press.

Wilhelm Bürkert, from *News from the Land of Freedom*, translated by Vogel and published by Cornell University Press © 1981. Originally published as *Briefe aus Amerika. Deutsche Ausanderer schreiben aus der Neuen Welt 1830–1930*, Herausgegben von Wolfgang Helbeich, Walter O. Kemphoefner, Ulrike Sommer. Verlag C. H. Beck. Munchen 1988. Used by permission of Verlag C. H. Beck.

Thomas B. Chaplin, from *The Journal of Thomas B. Chaplin*, published with *Tombee: The Portrait of a Cotton Planter*, edited by Theodore Rosengarten, © 1986 by Theodore Rosengarten. Reprinted by permission of William Morrow & Co., Inc. and the Wallace Literary Agency, Inc.

Mary Boykin Chestnut, from *Mary Chestnut's Civil War*, edited by C. Vann Woodward, © 1918, Yale University Press. Used by permission of Yale University Press.

Henry Conklin, from *Through Poverty's Vale*, by Henry Conklin, edited by Wendell Tripp. © 1974. Used by permission of Syracuse University Press.

Mary Grayson, from *Lay My Burden Down*, edited by B. A. Botkin, © 1945, published by The University of Chicago Press. We have made diligent efforts to contact the copyright holder to obtain permission to reprint this selection. If you have information that would help us, please write W. W. Norton & Company, 500 Fifth Avenue, NY, NY 10110.

Diego Méndez de Segura, from *Select Documents Illustrating the Four Voyages of Columbus: Including Those Contained in R. H. Major's "Select Letters of Christopher Columbus,"* translated by Cecil Jane and published by The Hakluyt Society. Used by permission of David Higham Associates.

Thomas Nairne, from *Nairne's Muskhogean Journal: The 1708 Expedition to the Mississippi River*, edited by Alexander Moore, © 1988 by the University Press of Mississippi. Used by permission of the University Press of Mississippi.

Jenny Proctor, from *Lay My Burden Down*, edited by B. A. Botkin, © 1945, published by The University of Chicago Press. We have made diligent efforts to contact the copyright holder to obtain permission to reprint this selection. If you have information that would help us, please write W. W. Norton & Company, 500 Fifth Avenue, NY, NY 10110.

Frederika Charlotte Louise von Riedesel, reprinted from *Baroness von Riedesel and the American Revolution: Journal and Correspondence of a Tour of Duty, 1776–1783*, edited by Marvin L. Brown, Jr., with the assistance of Marta Huth. Published by the Institute of

Early American History and Culture. Copyright © 1965 by the University of North Carolina Press. Used by permission of the publisher.

Katie Rowe, from *Lay My Burden Down*, edited by B. A. Botkin, © 1945, published by The University of Chicago Press. We have made diligent efforts to contact the copyright holder to obtain permission to reprint this selection. If you have information that would help us, please write W. W. Norton & Company, 500 Fifth Avenue, NY, NY 10110.

The Talon Brothers, from *Expedition to the Mississippi River by Way of the Gulf of Mexico*, translated by R. T. Huntington, first published in 1985 in Vol. XV, No. II of *The Iowa Review*. Used by permission of Roy T. Huntington.

Henry David Thoreau, from *A Week on the Concord and Merrimack*, edited by Houde, Howarth, and Witherell, © 1980 by Princeton University Press. Reprinted by permission of Princeton University Press.

Maria van Cortlandt van Rensselaer, from *Correspondence of Maria van Rensselaer*, translated and edited by A. J. F. van Laer. Courtesy, New York State Library.

Wilhelmine Wiebusch, from *News from Land of Freedom*, translated by Vogel and published by Cornell University Press © 1981. Originally published as *Briefe aus Amerika. Deutsche Ausanderer schreiben aus der Neuen Welt 1830–1930*, Herausgegben von Wolfgang Helbeich, Walter O. Kamphoefner, Ulrike Sommer. Verlag C. H. Beck, Munchen 1988. Used by permission of Verlag C. H. Beck.

Martin Weitz, from *News from the Land of Freedom*, translated by Vogel and published by Cornell University Press © 1981. Originally published as *Briefe aus Amerika. Deutsche Ausanderer schreiben aus der Neuen Welt 1830–1930*, Herausgegben von Wolfgang Helbeich, Walter O. Kamphoefner, Ulrike Sommer. Verlag C. H. Beck, Munchen 1988. Used by permission of Verlag C. H. Beck.

Index